Endorsements

Rick and his wife Carole's family and life story embody all that is good about our America, and remind of us of what is really important as we live each day. It gives us perspective on our country and its values over the past hundred years, and stirs in us a rededication to all that has made our country great…God, Family, Patriotism, and giving to help others. The Wilcox's live faithful and giving lives and I hope you'll find this book as inspiring as I have.

Hank Rush
President & CEO
Star of Hope Mission

Despite modern technological advances, life in the 21st century often feels fractured. Families increasingly become disconnected from one another because of life's demands. The Wilcox's tell the story of a slower time through the experiences of two generations of their family. It was not an easier time, but it was a time when families and communities stayed connected and helped one another. It is an enjoyable and inspiring read.

Bob Johnson, Pastor
Chapelwood United Methodist Church

Two Generations is not just the story of the Wilcox family, father and son. It is also a study of life in America for more than 100 years as seen through the lives of one family, ranging from basic pre-electricity and plumbing small-town life in the early 1900s to modern life in a large city, with all its conveniences, far from the family's original home town. This is a fascinating book of both personal and historical scope, showing how America has changed, anchored throughout with the core values that made the United States a great country; growth and success through hard work and caring.

Jim Seitz
Audiobook narrator

A story for remembering when traveling overseas was a big adventure, a personal trans-Atlantic phone call was a big deal, and the price of gas was a lot less than a dollar! Rick shares in this book his experiences in growing up, and along with Carole, dating, marriage, family, living in Germany, and friendships-a good story that is not only true, but brings back many memories of days gone by. I hope you enjoy this book as much as I did.

Candace Hester
Home maker

The Wilcox's Two Generation is a vivid illustration of a poor rural setting and an affluent city life. The poor life in a small town setting can be simple yet full of wonderful memories of hard working people whose contribution to the society at large is commendable. The affluent life setting depicts Rick and Carole's story of courtship, dating, romance, engagement, travel, and marriage life together. They have set an example of love and respect for each other that builds a lasting relationship.

Wennie Tejada
Retired Halliburton Accounting Manager

It has been said that life can best be appreciated as if we were rowing a boat, facing not forward, but behind us to where we have been. What a gentle story unfolds when a son looks back, not only at the eddies of his own life but also upon the gentle ripples of his father wake. How pleasant to step into the boat and be drawn along, as if grasping an oar and leaning into the next stroke with them!

Dr. Kenn Munn, Pastor
Kingwood United Methodist Church

Two Generations is the sweet and very American story of one family – very American in that it reflects the values of hard work, faith, individualism and the freedom to pursue those values. The book traces the Wilcox family through the many difficulties and struggles that life can bring, and yet facing all with a constant undercurrent of hope and joy. Two Generations will so draw you in that it will remind you, this is not just their story, it is all our stories.

Ellen Kent, Pastor
Kingwood United Methodist Church

Two Generations reminds us how hard our parents worked to achieve many things we take for granted. It reflects solid values and what can be accomplished with determination. It's also a pleasant trip down memory lane for those born in the mid 1900's. A great read on a quiet rainy day.

Susan English
CPA and business owner
Oaks of Righteousness Treasurer

This book reminds us all of the importance of sharing our family's history, life lessons, traditions, and values with the next generation. This is a compelling true story of a father and son who have endured many challenges and changes throughout the course of their lives and not only persevered but had much to celebrate. As you take this journey with them, you will discover the joys and sorrows of one American family and you just may realize that your life parallels one of these "characters."

Karen Dancey
Author and speaker

This is a story of two men, molded by Christian values, historical societal challenges and the love of family. Rick has documented two generations spanning over a century of living to show how hard work, family values, serving others and exploring life outside of the United States has molded our family. I am blessed to be the result of these strong men and know you will enjoy page after page of this book.

Stephanie G. Wilcox
Career Specialist

Rick passionately takes great pride in sharing the Wilcox family history. More than learning about the trials and tribulations of a family, *Two Generations* is a glimpse of Americana when times and life were tough but simple. The tales of Rick, Carole and his family are intriguing and a significant part of America's past.

Bruce Ray
Former Project Manager
KBR (Kellogg Brown & Root)

It has been said that life can best be appreciated as if we were rowing a boat, facing not forward, but behind us to where we have been. What a gentle story unfolds when a son looks back, not only at the eddies of his own life but also upon the gentle ripples of his father wake. How pleasant to step into the boat and be drawn along, as if grasping an oar and leaning into the next stroke with them!

Dr. Kenn Munn, Pastor
Kingwood United Methodist Church

Two Generations, is about a growing family pursuing the American Dream, to provide a better life for each generation of children. The family's experiences provide an insight into how America became the country it is today. Share in one of the many adventures of Rick's family, including his father Harold as he began in 1940's one of the early Adult Education programs which resulted in an enrollment of 5,000 students in 1965. Experience this fascinating journey through the 20th Century with Rick, Carole and his family living their lives for God, family, and country.

Kerry Hamilton
Educator

Two Generations

Visions of Life

Rick Wilcox

Copyright © 2016 Rick Wilcox.

All rights reserved. No part of this book may be used or reproduced by any means, graphic, electronic, or mechanical, including photocopying, recording, taping or by any information storage retrieval system without the written permission of the author except in the case of brief quotations embodied in critical articles and reviews.

This book is a work of non-fiction. Unless otherwise noted, the author and the publisher make no explicit guarantees as to the accuracy of the information contained in this book and in some cases, names of people and places have been altered to protect their privacy.

Scripture taken from the Holy Bible, NEW INTERNATIONAL VERSION®. Copyright © 1973, 1978, 1984 by Biblica, Inc. All rights reserved worldwide. Used by permission. NEW INTERNATIONAL VERSION® and NIV® are registered trademarks of Biblica, Inc. Use of either trademark for the offering of goods or services requires the prior written consent of Biblica US, Inc.

WestBow Press books may be ordered through booksellers or by contacting:

WestBow Press
A Division of Thomas Nelson & Zondervan
1663 Liberty Drive
Bloomington, IN 47403
www.westbowpress.com
1 (866) 928-1240

Because of the dynamic nature of the Internet, any web addresses or links contained in this book may have changed since publication and may no longer be valid. The views expressed in this work are solely those of the author and do not necessarily reflect the views of the publisher, and the publisher hereby disclaims any responsibility for them.

Any people depicted in stock imagery provided by Thinkstock are models, and such images are being used for illustrative purposes only.
Certain stock imagery © Thinkstock.

ISBN: 978-1-5127-4083-7 (sc)
ISBN: 978-1-5127-4082-0 (e)

Library of Congress Control Number: 2016907406

Print information available on the last page.

WestBow Press rev. date: 5/12/2016

This book is dedicated to my parents Harold and Millie Wilcox, who supported me in all of my decisions and was always there when I needed them. This book is also dedicated to Heinrich and Louise Stein and their children Babs, Hans, and Babs's fiancé Claus Lahman, all of whom enriched our experience while living in Germany, and also to Jesus Christ, our Lord and Savior.

Contents

Comments on Harold Wilcox and his Parents x

PART 1
Father: The Life of Harold B. Wilcox 1

Preface 3
1. Growing up in Gobles, Michigan (1899-1918) 5
2. Kalamazoo College (1918-1922) 16
3. Boston University School of Theology (B.U.S.T.) (1922-1923) 64
4. Ferndale, Michigan: A Teacher and A Coach 68
5. Europe—Summer of 1924 73
6. Teaching and Coaching (1924-1934) 81
7. Ferndale's Elected Commissioner (1935-1943) and High School Teacher 107
8. Continuation as a High School Teacher and Additional Jobs 118
9. Ferndale's Adult Education Director (1944-1965) 122
10. Retirement Years—Europe, Summer 1965 144
11. Retirement Years—Ferndale 152
12. Retirement Years—Back to Europe, 1968 167
13. Retirement Years Continued—Ferndale 173
14. Retirement Years—Back to Europe, 1970 178
15. Home From Europe and Moving to Daytona Beach, Florida 185

PART 2
Son: The life of Rick A. Wilcox 191

16. Gobleville, Where our Known Family Started 192
17. My Grandparents 195
18. My Parents 229
19. My Early Years Growing Up in Ferndale, Michigan 232
20. Adrian College Years 241
21. My U.S. Army Era—Stateside 255
22. My U.S. Army Era—Germany 276
23. Carole's Arrival in London, England 298
24. My U.S. Army Era—Our First Home in Germany 307
25. Our June 1965 European Tour 371
26. Kalamazoo, Michigan 381
27. Houston, Texas 390
28. Vacations, Including our Alaska Cruise 403
29. Kingwood, Texas 423
30. My Faith Journey and Other Writings 426

31. Our Fiftieth Anniversary 442
32. George N. Brown's 1849 Exposition to the Gold Fields of California. 447
33. Son James' Story 455

Acknowledgements 459

One day in May 1976 I was working in my office on the eighth floor. I happened to turn around and saw a beautiful large, puffy, white cloud. There were other clouds, but the sun shining on this particular one lifted my soul for a few seconds. I was then inspired with the below words, and immediately grabbed a blank sheet of paper and started writing what was flowing through my mind. I knew these rushing thoughts would be lost if I didn't react immediately. This is what came to mind during that short moment.

Wisdom of a Cloud
Rick Wilcox
May 1976

In all its splendid glory,
A large, white, puffy cloud,
Floating as on a planned charter flight.
Is there a message, O cloud?
Are there stories to tell,
From places you have been?
What have you seen and
What is your belief?

I closed my eyes,
Trying to imagine as to what
It had seen,
In its splendid world of blue skies,
Surrounded by sun rays.

This cloud has existence,
Thus it must have stories to tell,
A philosophy to tell.
O how I wondered, its message to be.

But when my eyes focus
On that part of the sky;
As to where this cloud was,
It is gone!
O so fast was its journey!

Is life like this?
Are there stories to tell,
But lost forever,
As an unwritten book?
Is a journey of a cloud,
Like a journey of a father?
The father on his journey forms
The son's beginning journey,
And waits for that special time,
The right time, of stories to tell.

He teaches, he plays, he shows,
And waits for that moment.
The father's first baseball pitch

to his son, his way of life,
The little philosophies
Wait to be passed on.

And then the sunrays reach out,
His journey of manhood has started
The son has seen,
He can comprehend.
The son is looking forward.
His journey to the stars has started,
And the father's accomplishment is labeled
Finished, Well done!

But if the father's journey comes,
Immediately to an end,
Will his life to his son,
Be as a book of blank pages?
What sails will the son have
to start his journey?

Perhaps the wisdom of a cloud,
Is of truth,
Here only for a moment,
On an unknown ending journey.
But if recorded on pages,
The father's wisdom reaches out.
A record of his father's life,
A treasure to his treasured son.

Comments on Harold Wilcox and his Parents

Harold B. Wilcox was born at home during August 1899 in the village of Gobleville, Michigan, known today as Gobles. No one in the family was aware that they were a poor family since most of Gobleville's families were in this same economic category during this time. Harold's parents had eight children in a house with no plumbing; the only heat was from the wood-burning stove in the kitchen and the potbelly stove in the living room. The house had only two bedrooms for two adults and eight children. The six boys slept in the attic (no heat or air conditioning) and the two girls in the bedroom off the parlor. When the small house was expanded in the back, enlarging the kitchen, a water pump was installed next to the sink in the kitchen. This was a great improvement in the mother's life. Harold's mother had to prepare the meals "from scratch," all the bread products and desserts, to feed a family of ten. Then there was the laundry and cleaning. Harold's dad worked long hours six days a week at his barbershop. His shop today can be identified from the words "A. M. Wilcox, 1910" engraved on the top stone of his shop on Gobles's State Street.

Toys were limited in this family, which forced the children to be creative in entertaining themselves. Each child also had a limited amount of clothing. There was no money for bikes; if a child wanted a bike or whatever else was desired they had to find a paying job for their purchases. As a child, Harold took on every outside opportunity for generating income, including delivering newspapers and working in his dad's barbershop. .

Harold's Dad taught barbering to Harold and three of his brothers. This was the greatest gift they received from their father since this trade was used to support themselves through college. This financial situation molded Harold's character with determination, confidence, leadership ability, and the readiness of hard work to complete his objective. The real success of a person's life is measured by the lives they touch, the assistance given to others, and their generosity. I believe that the life of Harold B. Wilcox met these criteria.

Dad's story was never published prior to this publication, There were about fifteen copies made of his book for Wilcox family members and one for Kalamazoo College. These copies had misspelled words, which have been corrected in this edition. It should be noted that my nickname "Dick" was changed during the 1980s to "Rick." In part II, the name "Rick" was substituted for "Dick."

Dad and Mom very much enjoyed living in Daytona Beach Shores, Florida, south of Daytona Beach. The book refers to their residence as "Daytona Beach." Dad (Harold) developed the terrible Alzheimer's disease during the late 1970's and died in January 1983. He accomplished so much during his lifetime and was a wonderful and loving father. I have been blessed to have had him as my father, as I was with my mother.

Rick A. Wilcox
2016

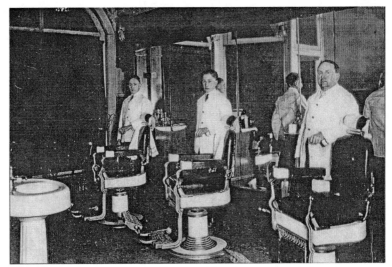

Center is Harold Wilcox and brother Monroe left and
their father Allen Monroe Wilcox right.
1916

PART 1

The Life of Harold B. Wilcox

Harold Wilcox 4th from left on front roll.
Coach Ralph H. Young back row.
1922

We are now in the second half of the year 1975 and celebrating the bicentennial of a great nation. Greatness always leaves a mark that is remembered, and that is why the United States is in a class by itself. It has touched many lives and allowed those who had the initiative and ability to reach their potential.

I feel that this same kind of greatness relates to my father, Harold B. Wilcox. He has left many positive marks on many lives, which will have a lasting effect. Harold never backed away from responsibility, but strived to reach success by doing his best and only his best and what he felt was right, no matter what the outcome might be. He went beyond the average man and strove for new challenges, leaving a trail of victories behind him. He was not afraid of life, and he took on life's challenges and mastered them.

Here in Houston I'm preparing his manuscript. I believe these words also reflect the feelings of my brother Philip in Michigan. We are proud of our father, and our memories of him will always be a part of us.

Rick A. Wilcox, Houston, Texas
August 1975

Preface

I imagine every preface is written after the book has been completed. Now that I have finished this volume, I will describe several difficulties and pleasures I experienced in writing it. Many times during the writing of these reminiscences I have thought that perhaps there was too great of a lapse of time between the writing of some sections of the book since most of it was done during the span of four winters that we spent at a motel overlooking the Atlantic Ocean.

It has been hard at times to determine which incidents and experiences should be selected for the preservation of the life history of the writer, since one realizes that many personal experiences and activities are too insignificant to dwell on.

If the reader should inquire why such a book was undertaken in the first place, there are reasons that stand out in my mind. My son Rick initiated and encouraged it because no one in the several generations of the Wilcox family had ever attempted to do a memoir that would help preserve the family history. I found it interesting and enjoyable to write my memoirs. To reread and study family pictures, scrapbooks, newspaper articles, etc. that I had preserved over the years relating to my life and the Wilcox family made the writing very exciting.

If the book appears to lack the chronological order that most readers expect, this is mostly due to the fact that I tried to organize my thoughts within the framework of certain lines of activity.

Harold Brown Wilcox

THE WILCOX FAMILY OF GOBLES, MICHIGAN

Great-Grandparents:
Seth Wilcox,   August 4, 1814-August 7, 1903
Abigail Wilcox,   October 8, 1811-April 26, 1896
Married: July 4, 1835

Grandparents:
Romaine Wilcox,   July 8, 1839-September 22, 1918
Sabrina Wilcox,   December 13, 1843-September 10, 1922
Married: December 13, 1863

Parents:
Father Allen Monroe Wilcox,   July 4, 1871-April 23, 1947
Mother Susan Belle Wilcox,   February 13, 1871-December 30, 1948
Married: May 6, 1896

Their children:
Monroe James Wilcox,   *   February 28, 1898-October 11, 1992
Harold Brown Wilcox,   *   August 21, 1899-January 15, 1983
Leland Dale Wilcox,   February 4, 1901-March 12, 1972
Allen R. Wilcox,   June 26, 1902-October 6, 1972
Whyle Standish Wilcox,   ** October 22, 1903-March 3, 2002
Paul V. H. Wilcox,   ** May 2, 1906-July 16, 1988
Abbie Irene Wilcox,   August 1, 1907-January 15, 1957
Donita Wilcox,   June 20, 1913-May 7, 2004

*   College Graduate, Kalamazoo College
** College Graduate, Albion College

Chapter 1

Growing up in Gobles, Michigan (1899-1918)

Located halfway between the two county seats of Allegan and Paw Paw on Highway number 40 lies Gobles, Michigan. When I was young it was called Gobleville. It was in this community of Gobleville that I was born on August 21, 1899. At that time it was a village of about six hundred and fifty people. In the early 1900s people decided the name was too long, so the name of the post office was changed to Gobles on April 10, 1922. As with so many American cities and villages, it got its name from a local family; the Gobles family owned a large farm in that area.

Dad was born in Gobleville, as it was called, and mother was born about one and a half miles northeast of town on a farm. Her dad, George Nelson Brown, taught in the one-room country school that was named after him. It was called the Brown School until it was torn down in the 1930's. My mother, Susie Belle Brown, lost her mother when she was around thirteen years old, as I remember it. Some time after her mother's death she went to work for a distant relative near Albion, New York. She and this family lived on a farm through which the Erie Canal was dug. After a year with this family, she returned to Gobles and kept house for her father there until he died in 1891.

There was a basket factory in Gobleville that later burned down in which my dad worked as a young man. Also there was a flour mill and a sawmill, both of which burned before I was out of high school.

Dad was a remarkable man in many ways. Although he never went to high school, he accomplished a great deal in the seventy-six years he made Gobles his home. Born a natural musician, he learned to play the violin, piano, trumpet, and drums without a single musical lesson. When spring circus time arrived, Dad, a young teenager, took the train to Baraboo, Wisconsin, to play the trumpet in the Wixom Brothers Circus Band. The circus traveled on railroad cars, and Dad had many a circus tale to tell his eight children. Mother and Dad had met at Gobles Methodist church, the church of their immediate family. We have love letters that he sent her while traveling with the circus, and they sound just like the letters you and I wrote to our sweethearts. The time came when Dad realized that if they were to marry "I had to find a new job, for circus life was no life for a young married trumpet player."

Apparently Dad thought Gobleville needed another barbershop, so he bought a set of tools, a chair, and the other necessary equipment and opened up for business. I never did hear him say how, when or where he learned the trade, but I am of the opinion he learned it as he did his music, and everything else he did—it just seemed to come naturally. Without a doubt Dad was a superior craftsman when it came to shaving and cutting hair. Men who lived in faraway cities such as Kalamazoo (twenty miles), and Chicago (one hundred miles) would wait for haircuts from him when they were going through Gobleville. Dad was my favorite barber during the forty-seven years that I had the privilege of having him cut my hair.

Our house in Gobleville was on the east side of town (410 E. Exchange St.). My dad's grandfather, Seth Wilcox, owned and lived in the house before Mother and Dad did. They moved into the house with the understanding that they would take care of his grandfather, who died on August 7, 1903, as long as he lived (Seth's wife, Abigail Wilcox, died on April 26, 1896, and my parents were married on May 6, 1896). Then the house would revert to them. I can remember my great grandfather when I was real young – his long whiskers, tall and thin stature, and being a great walker made him stand out in my mind. Many times this granddad would start walking to some other village or city because he didn't want to wait for the train.

After my great grandfather had passed away, the house, needing many repairs, became a building with several additions. First they finished off two rooms upstairs, which as the years passed by became the boys' rooms because there were six boys in our family. Then we had an expansion on the back of the house that became our kitchen. I can remember the old cook stove in which we burned wood and soft coal. This type of stove served many purposes –to cook on; to bake bread, cakes, and pies; and with the large basin tank on the side filled with water to wash neck and ears in warm weather or on cold chilly days. When my sisters Abbie and Donita came, which completed the family of eight children, they slept downstairs in the west bedroom off the parlor. Dad and Mother occupied the east downstairs bedroom off the living room.

We were a happy family. Mother worked tirelessly to keep us in clean clothes and food on the table. Dad spent long hours at the barbershop cutting hair for thirty five cents and shaving for fifteen cents. You realize that in the early 1900's barbering in a small farming village called for the shop to be opened at 7:00 a.m. and generally during the weekdays not closing until 8:30 p.m. or 9:00 p.m. Then Saturday was that long day when we opened at 7:00 a.m. and worked until 11:00 p.m. or 12:00 p.m. or until the last customer was served, who generally was Frank Friedman, the owner of the Friedman Department Store. After many years of barbering in the same community, Dad knew his customers and the day and about the time when they would be at the shop. There were the "once-a-weekers," mostly farmers who came into town on Saturdays to shop, get shaved, and possibly a haircut about every other month. They didn't mind sitting in the shop with many others, waiting their turn. Exchanging views, discussions of local and national issues, and passing the time of day were relaxation to them. Then Dad had some "twice-a-weekers," generally on Wednesdays and Saturdays. These men were mostly from the local business group. The "every-other-day" clientele were few in number. I can recall the two doctors and two or three businessmen who were in that category.

I can still remember my first day in school. There was no kindergarten. You entered school in the first grade. My brother Monroe, a year and half older than I, was held back for a year so he and I could start school together. I never did understand why Mother thought that would be best for us. The school girl living across the street from us was several years our senior and she told Mother she would take us to school and show us where the first grade room was located. I still have a vivid picture of that room as we entered the open doorway for the first time and were greeted by the teacher. The first three grades must have been in one room because I can recall the teacher would have one grade on the recitation benches while the rest of us were in our seats. The Gobleville public schools were about one-half mile from our house, which allowed us to go home for lunch. After the other boys, Leland, Allen, Whyle, and Paul, became old enough to be in school, it was a hustle and bustle at the noon hour to eat and get back to school on time.

I had been in school about one year when I came down with what the village doctor labeled typhoid fever. I was in bed for a long time, and I can still see the water glass of medicine with a spoon lying across the top near my bed. Because of my illness, Dad had put up a bed in the parlor for me. Monroe continued in school, and when I was able to return he was in the third grade and I was in the second.

In our family, like most large families of those days, every member had a job to do. In the front room we had a large hard coal stove that had to be attended to during the cold weather, and with it the kitchen cook stove. It was Monroe's job to keep the cook stove's ashes emptied and to maintain a full coal pail, and it became my job to do the same for the hard coal stove in the living room. There were a few times when we would forget to empty the ashes, and when he came home from work Dad would call upstairs, "Monroe, Harold – get down here and take care of these stoves!" To have to dress and empty the ashes out in front in the dirt street with snow on the ground was a good reminder not to forget too often.

As I have noted, most large families in those days had to be industrious and ours was no exception. While Dad made good wages from the barbershop there were always things that had to be bought, so I became conscious early in life of having to provide for many of my own needs. When I was about twelve years old I made chocolate fudge candy and went from house to house selling it for one penny per large square. I presume the men and women of the community bought some just to encourage me to become a worker.

When Monroe and I were in the seventh and eighth grades, Dad got us a South Haven Laundry Company route. We canvassed the village for customers. We would pick up the soiled laundry, which consisted mostly of men's shirts and collars, on Wednesday after school. Then we got up early Thursday morning to get the laundry basket to the depot for the 8:30 a.m. train, which went to South Haven. Saturday morning the train would bring our basket back from South Haven (twenty miles) with packages of clean laundry. These had to be delivered to the houses and collections made. As in most businesses, collections were sometimes slow and there were some Wednesdays we were hardly able to pay for the previous week's laundry bill. But people were honest in those days, as most people are today, and we eventually got our money. Living in a farm community made work opportunities possible that cities did not offer.

Memorial Day (May 30) was always a landmark in my memory. The band, under Dad's leadership, would lead the march to the cemetery after a brief concert in front of the barbershop that was located on the only business main street. I would decorate my bicycle with red, white, and blue bunting and would ride the one mile to and from the cemetery, located south of town. Then in the afternoon there were school activities in the old opera house, which terminated the school year. Following these activities, the highlight of the Memorial Day celebration, at least for me, was a baseball game between our local boys and some out-of-town team. It might have been a Kalamazoo team or a team representing some village such as Paw Paw, Lawton, Bloomingdale, or Bangor. Memorial Day also marked the beginning of strawberry season. Dad would buy enough strawberries for one good big shortcake with the promise, "Just as soon as they get to ten cents a quart you may have all you can eat!"

Ways to make money during the summer were numerous. First, it was picking strawberries at ten cents per sixteen-quart case. A fast picker could earn as much as one dollar in an eight-hour day, but we youngsters were quite elated to do half that well. Then came the cherry-picking season: an opportunity to make extra money for the July 4th celebration. Jobs of a different nature were plentiful during July and August. One August Monroe and I worked for a farmer who had two sons who were about three years older than we were. Our job was to take a row each in the cornfield and pull the weeds. The farmer would pick us up at seven o'clock in the morning and bring us home for lunch, then back again from 1:00 p.m. to 6:00 p.m. I would get so tired I could hardly pull another weed. At the close of three days we had the cornfield weeded and Monroe and I were each three dollars wealthier.

A *Chicago Daily News* agent came to Gobles one summer day hoping to introduce that newspaper to the citizens of our community. The barbershop seemed to be the place for information. First, he wanted a boy to peddle the papers and go with him on this house-to-house canvass. I was in the seventh grade and had my eyes on the *MLive Kalamazoo Gazette* route, which an older boy had. When Dad told the agent that his son Harold was looking for a paper route, he immediately made me his paperboy. I can recall going with him from house to house on that hot summer day. His sales talk was, "Try the paper for one month!" At the close of the day, we had about twenty-one subscribers on a one-month trial basis. Now it wasn't that the *Chicago Daily News* was such a poor newspaper, but that Chicago was so far away and the *MLive Kalamazoo Gazette* had become the established paper in our village. At the end of the month, my paper route dropped from the twenty-one subscribers to only three! It wasn't long after that the *Gazette* boy gave us his route and for many years the Wilcox boys were the paperboys in Gobles.

By 1909 Dad had become the only barber in the village. His sister Mildred had learned the trade from Dad and handled a chair with him in the little old shop, which was housed in a small building located where the Gobles City Hall and Fire Station are today. Business had been good for several years and it afforded the financial opportunity of a larger and new barbershop as well as an addition to our house. The new barbershop building was constructed in about the middle of the block at 205 S. State Street, on the east side. In spring 1910 I helped Dad and Monroe uncrate the new chairs and equipment in the rear room. Although Monroe and I were both young, we labeled a chair as "our chair" with the view of being future barbers—which we were. Dad taught the barber trade to four of his sons. The day Monroe started high school, he gave his paper route to Leland, and became what one might call the "prepare and finish" man in the shop. The greater percentage of the trade in those days was shaving. As I did a year later in my training, Monroe would lather the customer's face, Dad would come over to that chair and shave him, while Monroe would step to the other chair where a man had just been shaved, wash his face, put on some lotion and then powder, shave his neck, comb his hair, and collect the money, and then prepare the next customer for Dad to shave. Saturday was always the big day in a small town, and it was true in barbering. To stand at the chair from 7:00 a.m. until 11:00 p.m. or 12:00 midnight, or until all customers had been served, was an accepted duty.

When Monroe had become proficient enough to work his own chair after a couple of years, I stepped in on the third chair and Dad started training me to be a barber. There were times during my high school life that I had to work for Dad on Saturdays and had to give up the opportunity to make the high school baseball team, which I had lived for. It was a great sacrifice. As years passed, I could see that the trade Dad had taught me had proven to be far more useful than a few Saturday ball games. After my Dad felt we had become proficient in shaving and cutting hair, which took a year or two of working under him, we went to Kalamazoo and worked before the state barber's board to get our license. The license gave us the right to work in any shop in the state of Michigan. Monroe and I barbered our way through college. Monroe barbered his way through Boston University School of Theology, which was a three-year postgraduate course for the ministry. I barbered during the summers in Flint, Kalamazoo, Owasso, South Haven, Marshall, and Boston. One summer after I started teaching in Ferndale, I barbered in Royal Oak.

My Mother was a devout Christian and we all became members; you could say we grew up in the Gobles Methodist Church. In those days, I think more than it is today; community life centered in and around the church activities. Christmas Eve was a great occasion at the church. The large Christmas tree was well decorated with strings of popcorn, colored paper, and a few candles. People would bring some of their gifts to church and your Sunday schoolteacher made sure each boy and girl received at least one gift. I can remember there were a few adults who would put on a show in the presentation of presents. One such occasion I recall was when an organ was moved into the church by a parent and given to the daughter. Santa was always on hand to pass out the gifts. In one program I was to recite a three-verse poem. I knew all three verses, but because of excitement I left out verse number two. On Sunday evenings Monroe and I could always be found at the youth fellowship group, and then called the Epworth League. All these activities helped me to develop a greater self-confidence, and stimulated Monroe to the extent that by the time he had reached the seventh grade he had already made up his mind to become a Methodist minister, a vocation that he followed all his life. He spent forty-seven years in the Montana Conference of The Methodist Church as a very active clergyman.

The early 1900's were rather easy-going, relaxed days. Our country had not as yet reached a state of war and militarism, which was the pattern of governments in Europe. Business was good, taxes were low; the horse and buggy was still the chief means of local transportation; railroad passenger traffic was heavy; and people took time to relax, live and let live, and enjoy life. What did it matter if a customer had to wait fifteen minutes for a shave so that Dad could finish pitching his game of horseshoes, which was played in the rear of the barbershop, or if John Reigle put his son and daughter in charge of Reigle's Grocery Store to go fishing; or if when in Myers Department Store a farmer took a couple of crackers out of the cracker barrel and cut himself a slice of cheese to sample before buying; or if the businesses closed at 3:00 p.m. on Thursdays to help support the local baseball game! There were no robberies, no killings, and people didn't bother to lock their doors—only on such occasions as when the telephone operator got a call from a nearby town that the gypsies were headed for Gobles! As our old family friend Bert Travis, who for many years edited the weekly paper the *Gobles News*, said to me after Dad's death in 1947, "Harold, before World War I things were so different. We used to take time to play – but since World War I, it's business first and if you have a little time left to play, you are lucky. Harold, take time to play!" Over the years that statement has become more and more significant in my life. Wars, militarism, big business, heavy taxation, and so on have all contributed to a speeded-up life, which has at times caused at least some to sing (which will always be popular in group singing), "Is the struggle and strife we find in this life really worthwhile after all?"

Dad bought a cart for Monroe and me, one with roller-bearing wheels and a wooden box. We carried the groceries in it and used it to do errands. One night Monroe and I went to the barbershop with the wagon to give Dad a ride home. The sidewalk had been made of wood in our block, but the village had torn up the wooden walk and installed cement. It was a nice smooth strip about a block long. As we came to it, Monroe and I with Dad in the wagon, really cut loose with our speed. We were about eleven and ten years old, and to race down the sidewalk with Dad as our passenger was fun. We gave him several more fast rides during our youth and got the name of "Dad's span of bays."

When I was about eleven years old I learned to ride a friend's bicycle. My number-one financial project was to save enough money to buy one. We were earning money through our laundry and paper routes, but we had to buy our clothes plus our everyday needs, and we didn't save as quickly as we had hoped to do. While sitting around the supper table talking, Monroe and I took inventory of our savings. We found I had more money than he had, but between the two of us we had enough to buy one bicycle. We agreed that he would loan me his money and I would allow him to ride my bicycle until we had saved enough money for his. It was a great day in my young boyhood life when I saw the trainman at the depot taking my shiny new bicycle crated in wood out of the boxcar, for I had ordered the bicycle from a Chicago firm. I asked the deliveryman if he would take it to the barbershop, and he did without charge. There in the back room I uncrated it and put it together. I was a proud boy riding it home for the first time. I kept it in the front room until Mother said I should leave it on the front porch. That bicycle and the one I bought three years later with a three-speed coaster brake provided my transportation until I left for college.

I never did like winter. One thing that I believe caused me to not like winter as a youth was that I didn't have the necessary winter clothes to keep me warm and dry. Nevertheless, a heavy sweater, a cap, rubbers, and mittens made it possible for me to withstand the cold and snow, and that was about all the clothes any of us wore. Sliding down the hill in back of our house, ice skating, and riding on the runners of the bobsleds as the farmers came to and from town on Saturdays constituted the major part of our winter activities.

In the spring, summer, and fall it was outdoor life for all of us. There are many lakes within walking and bicycle-riding distance from Gobles, and the water is clear and pure. Swimming was a sport you learned early in life.

The Sunday school picnic was held at Mill Lake every summer. A couple of farmers would hitch their horses to their wagons with the hayracks bolted on. Parents and children of all ages with baskets of food of all descriptions would climb on the wagon and off we would go to the Sunday school picnic. The good Lord must have protected all of us on that day because I never remember a rainy day or a single accident. There were horseshoes for the men and baseball games for the younger groups. Many brought their bathing suits and went swimming. Of course, the big event of the day was when the food from the many baskets was placed on long tables and someone beat on the tin pan and called out "come and get it!" By four o'clock the wagons were loaded and the horses started on the one-and-a-half-mile ride home.

If I could have had my love, joy, and desire in a vocation, I would have become a major league baseball player. From the time I was a kid I was able to catch and throw a baseball; that was my greatest interest. I had fun playing catch, batting, and running from sunup to sundown. When I was in the seventh grade I played on the seventh- and eighth-grade team organized by us kids. We did not have a coach or manager; we just did everything for ourselves. We played South Haven, Bloomingdale, and Coloma as well as games with local groups. I would ride my bicycle for miles just to see a high school or independent team game. But apparently the good Lord never intended me to be a great ball player because I had a very poor throwing arm; as much as I tried to improve it each spring my arm would get sore and lame.

Basketball has always been my second favorite sport. As a seventh grader I organized our team, and we played several games with other school teams. The old Opera House was the only place in Gobles for community affairs. It housed the dances, the sports, the plays, the high school commencement activities, and what have you. It was such a busy place that we kids had a hard time scheduling it for basketball. Of course, the owner expected his fee to be paid, which came from our own contributions. My senior year in high school, the year 1917-1918, was a war year. It seemed that everything was greatly affected by the war, and my sport activities were no exception. The school superintendent, Hub Wood, told us he was busy with community war projects and had no time for basketball or baseball. Being such a sports enthusiast, I took it upon myself to organize a high school basketball team. I set up our schedule of games, got the referees, rented the Opera House for the games and practice, sold the tickets and did anything else that was necessary to make a basketball game possible. We played Van Buren County teams and did real well. Paw Paw played at Gobles in the Opera House for the county championship and beat us 18-16 in the last quarter. It was a great disappointment to me since we led most of the game and had packed the little hall with spectators pulling for us. The winter of 1917 and 1918 was a long and hard one, and considered one of Michigan's worst. Gobles is in the Lake Michigan snowbelt and we had so much snow that the railroad trains didn't run for three days; schools were closed for a week, and business in general was very slow. The barber business was no exception. Monroe was in Kalamazoo College and Dad was helping to finance his first college year. With a large family to feed, there was little money to pay me for helping in the barbershop.

The railroad company needed men and boys to shovel snow off the tracks at one dollar and twenty-five cents a day. Since school was closed because of the weather, Dad's business was poor, and I needed some spending money, I reported at the depot with a shovel to go to work. The first day was bitter cold and many of the workers didn't come back the second day. Fortunately for me, Dad's cousin, Elmer Howard, was working for the railroad, and he gave me an old pair of four-inch-high buckle overshoes, a heavy coat, and gloves, which kept me warm. I worked two full weeks and made enough money, with careful planning, to last me the rest of the winter.

Spring was with us and it was my senior year in high school. Dad's business had picked up a little and he could now afford to pay me seventy-five cents a week. Dad knew that I would probably not be with him next year, so he started training Allen to work in the shop. Leland, the brother next to me, had quit high school and had gone to Jackson, Michigan, to work on the railroad. Although he was only sixteen he looked older than his age, and besides it was a World War I year during which there were plenty of jobs.

It was baseball season again and my heart and soul were centered on playing high school baseball. Other high schools were playing baseball in the County League, so in spite of our superintendent's warning that he would not have time to coach since he served as the coach, teacher, and handyman at the school, I took it upon myself to organize a team. Darwin Brown, who was in the senior class, was the catcher, and I played first base. Bob Miller, who lived in a house next to the high school and was two years younger, played shortstop. I don't remember the other members of our team. We played several games before Superintendent Hub Wood called me into his office for a talk. He stressed the importance of my studies and with my barber work, and thought I should give up managing the baseball team. Of course, I followed his advice and that was the end of my baseball career.

The spring of 1915 our Sunday school superintendent announced that Albion College, one of our state's Methodist Church-affiliated schools, was sponsoring Camp Howell for boys of high school age. College seniors were to be camp leaders, and besides good food there would be plenty of swimming, sports, and fresh air activities. After talking it over with Mother and Dad, I set my mind on Camp Howell as my summer project. The morning of departure came and with two suitcases, one with my blankets and the other with my personal belongings, I boarded the train for Kalamazoo. To get to Howell, Michigan, one had to take a New York Central train from Kalamazoo to Ann Arbor, then change to an Ann Arbor R.R. train to Howell. That was quite an adventure for a fifteen-year-old boy who had never been farther from home than about twenty miles.

I arrived at Howell about 6:00 p.m. and there was no one to meet me, which was not part of the plan. I asked the station agent for directions and the location of Camp Howell. "Walk about one-half mile down the railroad tracks until you come to the road that will lead you to the lake and the camp," he said, so with a suitcase in each hand, off I went down the tracks. As I came to that road, here came a car loaded with boys. "Are you Harold Wilcox?" the driver asked. "Yes," I said. "Sorry we're late meeting you, the old car wouldn't start. Hop on and to the camp we'll go."

The camp was located on the fairgrounds bordering the lake. We had one of the fairground buildings for a mess hall. Since it had screens on the windows and doors to keep out the flies and bugs, I enjoyed all the meals. We slept in tents, three boys to a tent. Two boys had to sleep on the ground and one on the cot in each tent. You just know who grabbed the cot, for I never did enjoy sleeping on the ground. There were about twenty boys between the ages of fifteen and nineteen in camp. As we gathered around the campfire with darkness settling upon us, I will have to confess that a feeling of loneliness came over me and my thoughts wandered back to my home in Gobles.

Carrying a paper route, riding a bicycle, and playing games and all kinds of sports had made me run and walk a great deal. This helped to prepare me for the sport in which I was to be the most successful at camp. During the course of the ten days, we ran races on the fairground track. We started with dashes and jumps the first day and finished on the third day with the half-mile run, which was once around the racetrack. After the three days of events were over I was awarded blue ribbons for having won every single race. One of the customs of the camp was to award a boy an Indian name at the last night campfire for an outstanding achievement during the ten days. Little did I realize I had earned the honor of the Indian name "Kabato" (Indian Runner). To my great surprise and delight, the camp leader called Harold Wilcox to the front of the group and, with ceremonies, was given the name Kabato, which was to be my name at all future camps. Unfortunately, the European war was having its effects on American life, and when May 1916 rolled around the announcement came from Albion College through our church that there would be no camp that year.

That camp experience proved to be the beginning of my love for running and my track career. During the spring, summer, and fall months after the barbershop closed for the day, I would often jog down to the big oak tree and back, east of town on the gravel road, about a two-and-a-half-mile run. It was pitch dark most of the time, and it was uncommon for me to meet or pass someone with horse and buggy while I was running. This training really paid off and helped to build my physical strength for my future participation in track sports.

My next reward came at the annual Van Buren County Track and Field Meet which was held in Hartford in spring 1918. At this time it was rare for a small high school to have a track coach. A few weeks before the county meet Hub Wood would call a meeting of the older boys to ask who wanted to participate in the meet and which events each boy would enter. I had entered and won a second and third place in the dashes in my junior year, 1917. Having been running distances, I entered the quarter and the half mile, which were the longest races of the meet. The big day arrived; up early, we drove in a car to Hartford, about twenty miles away. The quarter mile was my first event. It started on the back stretch of the half-mile horse racing track and ended in front of the crowd of people in the grandstand. I got away to a good start and was leading until about the last fifty yards; a competitor came up alongside me to make a run for the finish. The track was just grass in the final yards and I slipped, fell flat on my face, and needless to say I didn't even place in the race. About an hour later they announced the longest run of the meet, the half mile. I was confident I could win. I trailed the front boys for the first quarter mile, then, feeling the pace was too slow, cut loose and outdistanced them and won going away. That gold medal was my first and a very highly prized one. It wasn't to be my last.

While a few of the financially better-off people had Model Ts and a very few more had more expensive cars, the old horse and wagon was still the best and most used means of transportation back in the early 1900s. It was very common for villagers to have a horse or two in the barn on the back of their property. Although I don't know the circumstances by which he acquired it, Dad had what we called "Old Doll Horse." The horse was stabled in a little barn on the rear of his father's (Romaine Wilcox) property. Dad's father took care of the horse and Dad used it when he needed it, which wasn't too often. My grandparents Romaine and Sabrina Wilcox lived on another street north of us, and we used to cut between the houses to go by their house on our way to and from school. Granddad was blind in both eyes. He had received great damage to his eyes while working in a saw mill. Wood splinters had hit him in the face and eyes resulting in his blindness. But Granddad could walk all over town with his cane as his guide. He would come to our house almost every morning about breakfast time, which was just before we went off to school. I asked him how he knew when to turn off the sidewalk across from our house and come across the dirt street. He said there were three big maple trees opposite our house and when his cane hit the third one he knew it was time to cross the street. He had landmarks all over town that enabled him to get around and live a normal life.

Dad's bachelor brother, William, lived with my grandparents. He worked on the railroad as a section hand. When they replaced the old ties with new ones, William would hitch "Old Doll Horse" to the wagon and haul them home. Then Granddad would saw them up into stove lengths. There was always a huge pile of neatly stacked wood for heating and cooking fuel for the house year round.

For several years each fall mother and we boys would hitch "Old Doll Horse" up to the wagon and drive about one and a half miles south of town on number 40 where there were big walnut trees lining the road. We would pick up and fill the wagon box full of walnuts, take them home, and bore holes in a large board just big enough to take the shucks off when we pounded the nut through. A basket under the board would catch the nuts. We would then put the nuts by the bushel up in the attic to dry out. During those long winter nights, cracking a pan of walnuts along with a pan of popcorn made the evening complete. I guess that is the reason that black walnut meat is my favorite.

Monday was always washday in most homes. A washday meant a completely different schedule. It was up early, eat breakfast, get the dishes done, and get the tubs, wringer, and boiler out. The cook stove was loaded with pans full of water to heat. Beans was the order for the noonday meal since putting on a batch of beans to cook was the easiest way to feed hungry kids as well as adults. Many times on the way home from school at noon, I would stop at Grandma's house and get a bean sandwich to tide me over until I walked the rest of the way home. Sometimes she would have apple or pumpkin pie, and that was even better. Granddad (Romaine) passed away at the ripe old age of seventy-nine. I was in high school at the time. A few years later when I was in college, Grandmother Sabrina, also at the age of seventy-nine, followed him to the eternal resting place. They were both buried in the cemetery one mile south of Gobles.

In spite of Dad's long hours at the barbershop, he always took some time to play. In my early youth dad had acquired a boat, which was docked on Lake Mill about 1 one and a half miles from Gobles. It was a nice boat, about twenty-five feet long with a canopy top. Dad put a canvas around the top so that by rolling down the canvas you could enclose it. This kept out the rain, snow, and wind. Dad was a great "steam" man. He built a steam boiler to connect the steam engine he had, and the boat became "The Cupid" owned by Tink Wilcox, called "Tink" because he was always tinkering with something. On Sundays during the late spring, summer, and early fall you could always find Dad and sometimes our whole family at Lake Mill riding around the lake in "The Cupid." "Old Doll Horse" provided the transportation, and the fried chicken, and pumpkin custard, and apple pies that mother sat up half the night preparing tasted mighty good.

I don't remember the exact date that Dad bought the first of the two old Stanley Steamers he owned. I was about a seventh grader at the time. He liked to talk about the advantages of the steam automobile over the gas engine, which helped make interesting conversation while shaving or cutting hair in the shop. To take a ten-mile drive on Sunday was some trip. Dad's interest in "Cupid" waned after he got the first of his two Stanley Steamers, and the last I remember of the "Cupid" it had disintegrated into kindling wood over a period of years. After World War I, the steam automobile found competition too great and the gasoline engine car became more popular. The Dodge automobile advertised, "No new models, just a constant change for the better!" This was during the early 1920's when Henry Ford advertised the Model T, a car of any color just so long as it was black. The Dodge took Dad's eye, and he bought a secondhand one. He then lost interest in steam, and the old Stanley Steamer stood for years beside the garage; in the end it suffered the same fate as the steamboat "Cupid."

Automobiles were not yet very numerous. The headlights were not powerful enough to encourage people to drive at night. However, the parents of one of my chums, Darwin Brown, had a Model T Ford. He was allowed to drive the car once in a while, and on several occasions during our high school days Monroe, Steve Martin, Darwin, and I would take what we called an all-night ride. After the barbershop was closed about 9:00 p.m., we four would start off for Benton Harbor, about forty miles away. Most of the roads were graveled, and to drive fifteen to twenty miles an hour was a fast pace. After dinner at a restaurant in Benton Harbor at about 11:00 p.m., we would head back through Paw Paw to Kalamazoo, where we would have breakfast. Then it was home, arriving about 5 a.m. tired but having accomplished an adventure.

All during these years mother was busy raising a family of eight children. Although I am sure she would have enjoyed more outings and companionship with Dad, she did not complain because she was devoted to raising her family.

The barber and musician "Tink" Wilcox became known all over the county in and around Kalamazoo. For years Dad organized and directed the only community band Gobles ever had. It played Thursday night band concerts that drew people from many miles around Gobles, thus stimulating business and putting the "go" in Gobles, as J. Bert Travis, editor of the *Gobles Weekly News,* said. The band also traveled to South Haven on July 4th, and to many other communities for pay. Dad also organized the Wilcox Orchestra, which played for community dances in the old opera house, commencement exercises, and on many other occasions. The result of his community spirit caused a group to draft Dad to be a candidate for the school board, a position to which he was elected and served for a number of terms. My high school diploma had Dad's signature on it as a board member. barbershop Many a night after a basketball game you could find Monroe, Steve Martin, Darwin, and I at the barbershop eating a late lunch, talking, planning, and so on. It was just clean fun when on New Year's Eve after such a lunch we would station ourselves one at each of the two churches and two at the high school. At 12:00 midnight sharp, the bells started to ring and the people would say, "Those two Wilcox boys with Steve Martin and Fatty Brown are at it again." But there was no vandalism or harm to anyone or anything, just clean fun. It's just too bad that young people today can't have the good times we had without cost or damage to anyone.

In 1917 the United States joined our allies in World War I, and this opened up a lot of good-paying jobs in the war industry. This situation stimulated a number of our high school boys to quit school and go to work. Some went to Camp Custer near Battle Creek, Michigan, to get jobs as assistant carpenters. All they had to do was keep the carpenters supplied with lumber, nails, and other materials in the building of the camp and they got big pay, some as much as fifty dollars a week. When our June 1918 high school commencement exercises took place, our class had been reduced to twelve members, six boys and six girls who made it very nice for our class skip-day. I had been elected president of the class and voted the role of salutatorian. Our class motto was one of the war-minded clichés – "Over the Top." I prepared the opening speech of the commencement exercises, drawing a verbal picture of four years of mountain climbing, after which we had gone over the top. Rehearsals were numerous and fun. I had learned my speech well, and being the opening speaker I was sort of relieved when I sat down to really enjoy the rest of the program.

High school days were over. What next? I was broke, having bought a new suit from Frank Friedman for graduation that had to be paid for, so now to find a job. Monroe was home from college and was to work for Dad in the barbershop during the summer months. Allen was still in high school and was helping Dad at the shop; Whyle had become the *MLive Kalamazoo Gazette* paperboy; and my friend Steve Martin had gone to Kalamazoo a few days before commencement (he was a year behind me in school) and had found a job in the ice cream factory. That certainly appealed to me, so off I went to Kalamazoo to look for work. Steve had a room on Cedar Court just off South Burdick Street. He and I decided to share a room and cut expenses. It so happened that the ice cream factory did not need another young man of my stature, for I was only 5 ft. 7 in., weighing one hundred and eighteen pounds. I set out to canvass the city. There was a big demand for men in construction, loading and unloading, manual labor jobs, but when the employer would look at my one hundred and eighteen pound frame he would shake his head and say, "Sorry, buddy, but you are just too light."

About 4:00 p.m. that first Monday after commencement, I ended up at the railroad station after applying for several jobs advertised in the newspaper. I was ready to go to our room and meet Steve and have dinner when I got the idea of going across the street where men were unloading boxcars, and wheeling merchandise into the warehouse with a two-wheel hand truck. I went over to where they were working and, to my great delight, saw a man who had lived in Gobles. I told him of my mission to Kalamazoo. He took me to the boss, and I was hired. I went to our room and with a happy heart told Steve I had a job and was to report for work at 7:00 a.m. the next morning. By sharing a room, Steve Martin and I paid only one dollar and fifty cents a week each. By eating at cheap restaurants where you could get pretty good meals for thirty cents, we kept our expenses low and I was able to save enough money to not only pay Frank Friedman for my graduation suit, but also to have a bank account of about sixty dollars by the middle of September.

Railroad trains had always fascinated me. I used to go upstairs at our house and watch the trains go by from the south window, since the track was only about one mile from our house with an open field between. To work on the railroad was very appealing. The men with whom I worked were very considerate of my one hundred and eighteen pounds. They would give me the lighter merchandise to truck, and when we came to a heavy piece like a stove or heavy furniture one of the stronger men would truck it. After working three days the boss called me in. "Harold," he said, "the men have been favoring you, but after a few weeks they might not continue to do so. They need a yard clerk down at the yards and that would be a good job for you. What do you think?"

The next morning found me down at Boxford's Yard Office with the yardmaster and clerks. This was an entirely new experience for me. You would think that a new eighteen-year-old boy coming on the job would have been given some training and general instructions. Not so with this yardmaster. We were at war, and the railroads were being pushed to their limits to transport soldiers and war materials to their destinations. It was a high-pressure job to be a yardmaster, and Hank Carney let everyone know that he was the boss and under pressure. He had a vocabulary all his own. Most of the words he used for communication were not in the dictionary and had never heard such use of four - letter words and profanity before or since. However, the other clerk, a man of about thirty years, told me to treat his talk and tongue-lashing like water off a duck's back.

I didn't take me long to find out that every freight car had to have a ticket to travel. The empties traveled on an empty ticket and the loaded cars had tickets that listed or described the contents of the car. A freight train would pull into the yard with about 100 cars, and the conductor would hand the tickets for his train to either me or the other clerk. It was then our job to write a number on a 4 x 4 inch card corresponding to the city the car was to be transported to. For example, if twenty was the number for Chicago, every car that was to make up a train for Chicago had to be tagged with a number twenty card. After getting our cards made out, I would go from one end of the train to the other, tacking the numbered card on the side of the car so that the switchman would know which track he was to switch that car to make up a new train. Switchmen always worked the right hand side of the train; something I found out after I tagged two trains on tracks next to each other at the same time. The switchman reported his train had not been tagged. Did that bring the wrath from the yardmaster! I was the recipient of all the profane and four-letter words he could think of.

I recall another time Hank called the Yard Office and gave me a list of car numbers with instructions to get the tickets together, stating some were empties. Not being well versed on the procedure, I made out empty tickets for all of them and took them to the Penn. Railroad office where the switchman was to take the cars. Several hours later a call came from the Penn. Office to the yardmaster about the "loads" he had just received. Where were the tickets? Boy, did I get another tongue lashing; I had forgotten to look in the "load" box and sort out the tickets of the cars going to the Penn. tracks.

We were on the job from 6:00 a.m. to 6:00 p.m. seven days a week with one Sunday off a month. I got twenty one dollars a week. We were not busy the full twelve hours since there were times when there would be two or three hours with no work, and we would just sit around waiting for another freight to come rolling in. The yard tracks were about eight hundred yards long and I got plenty of exercise running up and down those tracks looking for cars that had to be tagged.

Several weeks later I was sitting in the office and the yardmaster said, "Wilcox, you've been around here long enough to have learned the duties of a clerk. They need a clerk uptown at the depot. I am transferring you to the depot office." To me that was a very welcome assignment because the yardmaster uptown, Bill Lovett, was a rather easygoing, soft-spoken, but efficient man whom I enjoyed working with. Years later he told my brother Leland, who had been transferred from the Jackson to the Kalamazoo baggage room, that his brother Harold was the best yard clerk he had ever had. Lee, the nickname we all called Leland, spent the rest of his working life in the Kalamazoo baggage room and saw passenger traffic dissolve from a very flourishing business to just a trickle over a period of forty years. Today the railroad business isn't what it used to be with those powerful steam engines bellowing that black smoke. That made it romantic.

The work of a yard clerk afforded many amusing opportunities besides being out of doors with lots of leg exercise. There were passenger trains, troop trains, freight trains, and switch engine trains that were almost constantly moving by the depot office out of which I worked. The switch engines would haul long trains of freight cars up from Boxford yards to be switched to one of the other railroad lines running through Kalamazoo. Many times when I had a little or nothing to do I would ride the train to be switched, and would help relay signals from on top of the box cars as the train was making curves in the tracks.

One day during fall 1918 I had the opportunity to go to a movie at a Kalamazoo theatre titled "Crashing Through Berlin." During the movie I noticed scenes that were very familiar to me, and as the story progressed I saw pictures of the Kalamazoo railroad yards and station with the Lee and Cady warehouse, which at that time was located just north of the depot. My interest grew, and behold, here was a scene of a switch train with Harold B. Wilcox on top of a boxcar relaying signals by waving his arms. Of course, I went to see the film "Crashing Through Berlin" several times after that. During my many years of teaching, my students heard about the moving picture career of their beloved teacher!

This was my first experience being away from home for a long period of time, and needless to say there were many lonesome evenings. Having my friend Steve Martin to chum around with made it easier to enjoy my work during those three summer months. However, when I saw the Saturday night train (5:45 p.m.) that passed through Gobles ready to leave for South Haven, and saw some of my high school friends who were now working in Kalamazoo boarding it to go home for the weekend, I was very tempted to be a passenger also. I could have been back on the job by 9:00 a.m. the next morning. Besides, the "uptown" yardmaster didn't work on Sundays, and as long as I would have turned in the car check on Monday that I had to make each day, he probably wouldn't have known the difference. However, I was dedicated to my job, for I had learned from my parents that your job comes first and must be done right. I must admit that this theory didn't hold true in my academic work in school since I was never a very good student in high school or in my undergraduate work in college.

As the summer wore on, U.S. involvement in the war increased. The whole American economy was being geared for war. We had meatless days, sugarless weeks, and conservation of fuel supplies, as well as many other deprivations. There was newspaper talk, and Monroe was getting literature from Kalamazoo College, on the government's plan to organize each college and university into a "Student Army Training Corps" for the men, known as the SATC. It seemed that there was a great need for more officers to command the troops. You could draft boys into the service, give them six weeks' training in squads right and squads left, how to fire a gun, etc. and they were ready to be shipped overseas, but to train men to be officers was a much-longer and more-difficult process.

Chapter 2

Kalamazoo College (1918-1922)

The SATC (Student Army Training Corps), which by September 1918 had become a reality, enabled Monroe and me to enroll in Kalamazoo College at no expense since the federal government paid for our tuition and room for the full college year. By September 15 Monroe and I were a part of Uncle Sam's army with uniforms and wooden guns. The government couldn't get military guns fast enough from manufacturers to meet the demand, so, as in our case, many SATC programs were never supplied with regular army rifles. We were housed on the campus of Kalamazoo College. The gym was tuned into barracks. Monroe and I each had an army cot as did about seventy-five other boys. We were up at 6:00 a.m., marched out to the athletic field for reveille, and by 7:00 a.m. our beds were made and we were ready for mess, which was served in a wooden building hurriedly erected on the campus and known as the "Mess Hall." From 7:45 to 8:30 a.m. was free time, then classes started and continued until 12:20 p.m. After each class we had to line up in formation and the sergeant would call out, "Those having math this hour step two paces forward." Sergeant John Doe would then march them into class. This would be repeated until all had marched into their class for that hour. The mess formation was at 12:30 p.m.. At 2:30 p.m. we were marched to the athletic field for a two-and-a-half-hour drill, after which we had a 5:30 p.m. mess. Then again at 7:00 p.m. there was study formation at which time every one was marched into the Mess Hall for two and a half hours of study. Of course, these were rather difficult circumstances for a good academic program, but so far as I could determine the professors were understanding and didn't make too great a demand on the men students in the classroom since there were women students in many classes such as French and English.

The flu epidemic hit people in the United States pretty hard. Probably because everything was credited to the Germans, it was called the German Flu. I became a victim of it during the month of October. It was reported that men were toppling over in ranks, and there were many people both in the army and civilian life who were dying from it. I could readily understand that it could be true that many men toppled over in ranks because I was almost a victim of that situation. Feeling very bad and weak, I had a fainting spell come over me while standing at attention. I asked the sergeant if I could be excused, that I was sick and about ready to collapse. He said I would have to get the commanding officer's permission to be excused. I didn't want to go through that red tape so I decided that if at all possible I would stick it out. That night I went to bed immediately after study hall session, but was awakened about 12:00 midnight by lights in the gym being turned on and the commanding officer shouting "All right, if you don't want to sleep, I'll make you so tired you will want to. Get up and get dressed and line up on the outside of the gym. I'll run you around the athletic field until you drop!" He did. It seemed that a few boys got to fooling around in the darkness after taps and had made so much disturbances that the officer upstairs had been awakened, and the whole barracks personnel had to pay for it. The sergeant came in to check the beds to make sure every man was dressed. He came to me and ordered me out of bed. The men took my part by telling him I was ill and had not been a party to the disturbance so he left me alone with the order that I was to be transferred to the "sick bay" the next morning. The top floor of the men's dormitory had been transformed into a sick bay with a male nurse in charge of the floor. I was in a room with two other boys, and for about a week I was a sick man. Flu being a new disease, the doctors of medicine didn't have very many answers for how to treat the patient. After about a week in sick bay, Dr. Stetson, president of the college, assured Mother and Dad over the phone that everything was being done that could be done, and that I was improving. It was two weeks before I was able to rejoin my unit for daily military duty. Needless to say, I had fallen behind in my classroom work and never did catch up.

At 3:00 a.m. on November 11, as I lay on my cot in the gym with dozens of other boys and with Monroe's cot next to mine, the Kalamazoo fire whistle began a series of short blasts. The newspapers were carrying the word that the war was nearing an end because the German armies were in retreat and French soil was again free. At first I thought, "Oh, it's just another fire in Kalamazoo," but as the blasts of the whistle continued until it had reached about ten blasts, I, with several others, realized that it was announcing the end of the war. I spoke to Monroe and the whole unit seemed to jump out of bed in unison and start dressing. Then we realized we couldn't do anything until the officer came in and turned the lights on, giving us permission to get up and leave. It was only minutes before the officer appeared with the word that we were off duty until 7:30 a.m. mess. The history of that great day of November 11, 1918, has been written many, many times. When the excitement was over, knowing that we would never see "Gay Paree," we felt a great letdown. Of course, we were still in Uncle Sam's army and had to drill, attend classes, study, etc., but it was just different.

During the latter part of November everyone realized that the end of the SATC was nearing, and we began to wonder, "What next?" That was the position for Monroe and me. By the first of December 1918, we all were told that we would receive our honorable discharge and sixty dollars bonus (we had been paid thirty dollars a month, which was buck private pay) on December 15. In the meantime Dr. Stetson called a meeting of the men of the SATC to get information on our plans for the second college semester. The college had geared up for the one SATC year, and to lose a large portion of its men students at Christmas vacation time would result in a completely new plan of organization. We were told that the federal government would pay our room rent and tuition provided we remained in college. Monroe and I talked it over, and decided that we were going to stay in college even if we had to go hungry part of the time. Also, we now realized that our ability in the barber trade would play a big part in our college future. On that December 15 we left behind our army experiences. At home for the Christmas holidays, we started to direct our thinking along an entirely new concept of college life. It was the beginning of "four great years" of hard work, anxiety, and personal discipline. The holidays over, January 2 found Monroe and me packing our bags. We didn't have too much to pack in readying ourselves to return to Kalamazoo College. We actually did not know where the next meals were coming from.

I have often asked myself, "Just why did I go to college?" and "What was the motivating force or inspiration that made me think I should go to college?" Mother and Dad had never graduated from high school; in those early 1900's graduating from the eighth grade was about all the education one needed. A boy who had graduated from high school could take a six-week' summer school course at Kalamazoo Normal College (now Western Michigan University) and is qualified to teach grades one through eight in a country one-room school. A two-year teachers' course was all that was necessary to make one a qualified high school teacher.

After considerable thought, I have determined that the motivating inspiration may have come from several sources. Monroe had made up his mind to become a Methodist clergyman as early as the seventh grade, and that decision demanded that he go to college to fulfill his future dreams. Second, the church had an influence as one of the educational and recreational centers of our lives. Our school superintendent, Hub Wood, went to the Baptist church on the west side of town. He had received his A.B. Degree from Kalamazoo College and talked education to all of us, which resulted, so to speak, in lighting a candle in our hearts in the quest for more education, more than just high school. My mother's father (George Nelson Brown, 1817-1891) had taught the one-room Brown School; although she had never gone beyond the eighth grade Mother's great desire to see her sons grow physically, mentally, and spiritually proved to be an influence that motivated all of us. One thing we were taught to always remember was that "the ultimate attainment in education is to fit you to be better men and women. To gain this objective you must learn to be ladies and gentlemen. The possession of manners has never done anyone any harm."

I still can remember sitting around the supper table, as evening meals were called in our village in those days, talking about our college plans. Where the money was to come from was never an important question in our minds. As we boarded the 12:45 p.m. train for Kalamazoo we were mentally set that with faith and hard work the Lord would provide, and He did. Being one year ahead of me, Monroe knew the ropes and I relied on him a great deal. We agreed that for the time being we would sign up for meals at Ladies Hall (girls' dormitory) dining room where many of the fellows who lived in the men's dormitory ate.

Kalamazoo College, then as now, is Baptist affiliated and is located on a hill in the western part of the city. There were four main buildings on the campus: Ladies Hall, Men's Dorm, Bowen Hall, which was the classroom building, and the Gym. The mess hall, which was a wooden structure erected by the federal government to satisfy the needs of the SATC was soon torn down. In 1919 it had a student body of about three hundred and fifty, about half girls and half boys. We used to call it the "match factory" in those days because the student body was small enough for everyone to get acquainted with everyone else, and from such acquaintances there were bound to be some matches that would end in marriage. Today it's hard to imagine a college with only three or four hundred students, but in 1919 Michigan Agricultural College, now Michigan State University had only eight hundred and eleven students and other college and universities had comparable numbers. The great thirst for education did not get underway until after World War II when scientific inventions made it a great necessity.

I was as green as grass on that winter morning as we found our way up the winding walk that led from the men's dormitory to Ladies Hall. I was nervous since it was our first meal and I was to sit at a table with nine other boys and girls. During the SATC days we had gotten acquainted with two or three girls and I had hopes of sitting at a table with some I knew. I asked Monroe such questions as, "How do I act? When do you start eating? What piece of silverware do I use on each occasion?" Monroe told me that at the head of each table was a senior girl who was the hostess, and after the blessing I should watch her and follow along. Boy, did I have my eyes glued on her for those first few meals, but it was not too many days before I felt at ease in their presence.

The first few days were hectic in that we had to make out our class schedule, get our textbooks, locate a dormitory room, sign up for meals at the dining room and at the same time wonder where the money was to come from. We had received an honorable discharge and were given the sixty dollars bonus that all U.S. military men received, so we had a little money to get us started. Clothes were not a problem since practically every boy wore his military clothes. Besides, I had my graduation suit that I had purchased the previous June.

Monroe had roomed in the dorm the year before and was pretty well acquainted with the building. Room 46 on the third floor right above the front entrance had a study room besides the bedroom, and that was the one we got. Lucky! It was our room until both of us graduated. Many a bag of water was thrown out of those windows only to splash on the sidewalk in front of or behind a friend on whom we wanted to play a trick. Of course, after the splash it was too late to look up to see which window it came from because we stayed out of sight. Monroe and I owe a great debt of gratitude to Kalamazoo College, for never during our four years on the campus were we ever asked to pay tuition or room rent. The two summers of my second and third years I roomed in the dorm with several other fellows without any rent being charged. However, I did have campus jobs that were supposed to be done for room and tuition, but those jobs never did compensate for what the college did for me.

I didn't have enough money to continue to eat at Ladies Hall, so the first thing I had to do by way of a job was to find a restaurant or boarding house that needed a college student to work for his meals. It wasn't too long before I was referred to a boarding house at 211 S. Westnedge. A large, fat lady, the owner, told me I could have a job with two young men from the Normal College to wash dishes for about one hour after each meal. In those days the electric dishwasher was unheard of, so we had to roll up our sleeves and go to work. At least we always had clean hands. My two co-workers were congenial companions, both having been in the SATC at the Normal College and both as broke as I. We got along fine together. It wasn't too many months before I was elevated to a table-waiting job, which I liked very much. It got my hands out of the greasy dishwater!

One of the truly great men in my life was the president of the college, Dr. Herbert L. Stetson, after whom the present college chapel was named. He was an elderly, dignified gentleman during my college years, but always had a kind face and a sparkle in his eyes that made him beloved by all. Many times he was called upon at a "pep" meeting to lead a pep talk and with his whole heart in it, he would end his talk with "Fight em, Fight em, Fight em." He always brought the house down!

During the fall term Kalamazoo College had a football team. A few of the other state institutions of higher learning were playing football, so our military officers on campus decreed that Kalamazoo should also have a team and a time was allocated for practice sessions. Paul Staake, an upperclassman, was given the coaching assignment. Along with such stalwarts as Harold Andrews, Joe Mischica, Northrup Read, and a squad of new men, some of whom had never played football before, a team was formed to represent Kalamazoo College. As the 1919 *The K-Zoo* reported, "Hillsdale was the initial game and it was very evident that the old Kalamazoo spirit was still in College. Staake and 'Walk' battered the center of the Hillsdale line to pieces ... others grabbed a few passes to make a good day of it. What the lineman lacked in experience they made up for in fight, and the final score was Kalamazoo 7, Hillsdale 0." A week later "K" met Hope College on a dark and rainy day and came out second-best, 13-14. The third and final game of the season was played at Albion College, which had a more experienced team. Our commander wanted a band organized and called for anyone and everyone who could play an instrument, even to a degree.

During my high school days Dad had gotten me a secondhand clarinet that I had learned to play by ear. I volunteered for the band, which had about twenty-five members. The college chartered interurban cars to make the round trip to Albion. The interurban line ran alongside the narrow highway, uphill and down, and, I presume, at a thirty-five-mile-per-hour clip, which was really speeding. A couple hundred people made the trip, and with the band leading, we marched from downtown to the football field. We were keenly disappointed at the close of the day when Albion sang, "When the sun goes down and the moon comes up, Albion will shine," for they did. However, we did have a good, fun day, which was my first experience of real college life. It was thought that a football dinner was the proper way to honor the team, so December 6 was set as the date. It was held in Bowen Hall; I took my first college date, a very nice young lady by the name of Enid Campbell. It was an enjoyable occasion honoring the team as well as the Kalamazoo college boys who had died in the war. The banquet ended with the singing of "All Hail to Kalamazoo," a song that has become dearer to me as years have gone by.

My great interest in sports and other activities resulted in my involvement in many things. Back in my years at Kalamazoo the college landmark was Mirror Lake. It was a good-sized puddle of water between the gym and the railroad tracks that separated the campus from the athletic field. It was about four feet deep in the middle, and is described in the November 21, 1918, *Kalamazoo College Index* (weekly paper) as follows: "College poets have eulogized it and scores of Prof. Praegers' biological specimens inhabit it. For years Prof. Smith's trained robins have flown all the way from Florida each springtime to sing on its banks. Many freshmen have been led out to contemplate the beauty of its waters in the moonlight. A few, fresher than the rest, have bathed in it. ... Mirror Lake is the first thing the student sees when he comes to college, and the last as he leaves. Without it, college wouldn't be college. The mud of its shores never hardens and its waters never run away." A few years later during the college expansion program, the old landmark, which became stagnant during late summer, was drained, filled in, and fine tennis courts were built that helped to make Kalamazoo College the tennis center of the United States. Years later, the Allen Stowe Tennis Stadium was built and it has housed the Senior and Junior Boys Tennis Championship of the United States for many years.

One of the first happy announcements for all athletes at the college was that Coach Ralph H. Young, who was in the Auto Mechanics School of the SATC at the University of Michigan, was coming back and in January 1919 would continue in the position of athletic director and coach at the college. "Prospects for basketball looked good," announced the *Index*, and "Nort Reed, the veteran from last year's team, is coaching until coach Young returns." I had always liked basketball as well as all other sports, and having played two years in high school, decided I would try out for the team. Team personnel were different in the early 1900's. A man was judged by his speed, ability to dribble, to shoot baskets, etc. Size and height didn't play the part that it does in this second half century. I had been to just a few of the first practices when I broke my ring finger on my left hand, and that was the end of my college basketball career. However, my interest was maintained and many practice sessions found me sitting in the bleachers observing the fundamentals as Coach Young put the men through their daily workouts. This proved very beneficial to me since when I started my teaching and coaching career at Ferndale Lincoln High School one of my duties was to coach basketball.

We had no more settled in for the second semester academically when the call came for all who wanted to try out for the College Glee Club to report to Bowen Hall. Now, I have always liked to sing, even in the shower! At home it was not unusual for us to gather around the piano, with my sister Abbie playing, and sing old songs, some of which were church music and others more popular. Some of our favorites were "The Old Rugged Cross," "I'm Forever Blowing Bubbles," "All Alone By The Telephone," "When You Feel Another's Arm About You," and others. Then, too, our friends Steve Martin, Skinny Brown, Freeman Brown (no relation), Monroe, and I would have a late snack in the barbershop and do a little harmonizing, or we might take a drive for a few miles to Benton Harbor, Kalamazoo, Paw Paw, or Allegan and sing in the moonlight. Monroe who had a very good tenor voice, had been in the Glee Club the year before and done very well, so I decided to try out. From the time of the first tryout, it seemed to me and others that I had made the club of eighteen members. I think that if the facts were known, it was assumed that since Monroe had the good tenor voice that he had, I must also be able to sing pretty well too. Anyway, when the *MLive Kalamazoo Gazette* listed Harold B. Wilcox in the article "College Glee Club Members Named," I was really pleased. Rehearsals were frequent and interesting.

It was planned that a few weekend concerts would be given at nearby towns and cities before the club went on its spring tour. One such concert was at Paw Paw, and I was pleased that Mother and Dad could drive over and enjoy the concert. When March arrive the club management had booked an eleven-day tour in northern Michigan. In the meantime, for personal reasons, Monroe and one other member had dropped out of the club, leaving a traveling group of sixteen. We opened the tour in Grand Rapids, and I can still feel the emotional spirit I had that first morning. We had all been in the service and it was decided we would wear our military uniforms for travel and the first act of the show. Then we would change to "tails" and white bow ties (evening dress) for the second half of the concert.

Always enjoying an early start when I go places, I arose, dressed in my uniform and, with suitcase, took the streetcar downtown to eat breakfast. At a restaurant I got coffee (self-served). As I sat down I accidentally spilled coffee all over my pants. Now, what to do? I thought there is one hope. Monroe and I wear the same size uniform and if I take a streetcar back to College Hill and run to the dorm, I could change to Monroe's pants, provided he did not have them on. My heart was beating rapidly as I rushed into Room 46. Luck was with me for I saw Monroe's uniform hanging in the closet. I hastily wrote him a note explaining the circumstances, then ran down College Hill to the car tracks, boarded the streetcar for downtown, picked up my suitcase from the restaurant, and got to the Interurban station in time to join my fifteen companions.

We took the Interurban car to Grand Rapids. Because Kalamazoo College was Baptist affiliated, most of our concerts were arranged by the personnel of whatever church in the community in which the concert took place. The general procedure was to have the club at the local high school in the late morning or early afternoon, then the evening concert at the church. This plan was to advertise the college in the community and in the high school. The local arrangement committee made the necessary contacts to house the club members at various persons' homes. We paired off, and generally two of us would receive our room and meals with the family to which we were assigned. It was always interesting especially as in many cases it happened that the family included a daughter of high school age! After the evening concert the patrons always had a reception for the club members. Many times after eating, etc., we didn't get to bed very early, and getting up the next morning to catch an early train to the next city was a groggy task. One of the most humanitarian experiences I learned on this trip was that some of the fellows left Kalamazoo real buddies, but returned lukewarm toward each other. It has made me appreciate the necessity for great patience. Managers of professional athletic teams must have this in order to supervise and maintain goodwill among their athletes who travel together a great deal.

The flu epidemic was still in many communities. It was a very serious disease that was interrupting normal life, and our glee club manager experienced some disturbing situations. We had to cancel two planned concerts with only twenty-four hours' notice. It was necessary to then go to other cities where we had to stay in local hotels, make arrangements with the local theater for the evening, get fliers printed at the local print shop, and canvass the community to publicize a quickie concert! One such arrangement took place at Bellaire! The flier read, "Clean-classy, opera house tonight, Kalamazoo College Glee Club, auspices of H. S. Junior Class. Singing, reading, Scotch specialties, trombone and piano solos consisting sixteen jolly college men; admission twenty-five and thirty-five cents, comic-clever." Needless to say, we were tired that night and ready to turn in after the concert and affairs were taken care of.

On March 30, 1919, the *MLive Kalamazoo College Gazette* had the following article: "Kalamazoo College Glee Club Finished Trip. The Kalamazoo College Glee Club returned from their Spring Trip of eleven days which took them into northern Michigan. The organization, consisting of 16 men, left Kalamazoo March 20, giving their first concert in Grand Rapids at Central High School auditorium under the auspices of the Senior Class of that school. ... The club gave their program at Pellston, Central Lake, Petosky, Harbor Springs, Traverse City, Bellaire, East Jordon and Sparta. The trip was the longest one that the College Glees have attempted. Two concerts were cancelled with only a day's notice due to the influenza, and the club was forced to enter other cities without previous announcement and secure a hall, sell the tickets and distribute bills."

The *Kalamazoo College Index* had the following story on page one: "Glee Club In Concert Twice Last Week. On Tuesday evening the Glee Club gave a concert at Marshall. They sang at the high school in the afternoon and then put on a game of basketball with the high school team. Staake, Milroy, Ring, Wilcox and Carr were the mighty warriors and they went down to a glorious defeat by a score of about 50 to 8. Staake played great basketball, taking great pleasure in carrying two or three Marshall players up or down the floor with seeming ease. ... On Friday evening, the concert was given in Martin. This was likely the best program given up to this time."

After several weekend tours, we wound up the Glee Club's thirteenth annual tour with a home concert at Bowen Hall, April 25 at 8:00 p.m. Admission was twenty-five cents and thirty-five cents. Little did I realize at the time that this was to be my first and last time as a member of the club. It was an experience that I never forgot.

At Kalamazoo they have no fraternities; instead, the men as well as the women had Rhetorical Societies that met once a week, usually in their own club room. The members conducted all the affairs of the society. The men had three organizations: the Sherwoods, the Century Forum, and the Philolexian. I received an invitation to become a member from all three and attended the "open house" of each. Monroe was a Philo, and I was seriously thinking of accepting the invitation to be one of them. I guess from what I was told that almost everyone took it for granted that I would. However, after attending the open house of each and learning the type of men at the helm of each, I was convinced I would be most happy being a Sherwood, so I accepted their invitation. Of course, Monroe was greatly disappointed and surprised that I did not follow him into the Philos. When Mother heard about it she wrote that she was keenly disappointed that for the first time Monroe and I were separated in spirit and pleaded with me to change my mind and become a Philo. This upset me to no end. Never before had my mother made me feel that I had, to a degree at least, committed a sin, that I had forsaken the family. However, I enjoyed my association and companionship with the men of Sherwood very much. During my Kalamazoo College life I became an officer and had many valuable and educational experiences. Sherwood Hall was an upstairs room in the gym. Before the gym was rebuilt, years after

I had graduated, I would visit the campus at homecoming time, including Sherwood Hall. There I renewed the pleasant memories of my undergraduate days.

"'K' Club comes to life again," announced the January 9, 1919, *Index*. "The first formal meeting of this organization once one of the most influential clubs on campus, but dormant since the beginning of the war, was held last Thursday evening. ... Northrup Reed (president of the Sherwoods) was elected President." Ever since I was a youngster in grade school I remember how I greatly admired the athlete who wore the college or university letter on his sweater, and it immediately aroused within me a great determination to win the "K." As a great lover and enthusiast of all sports, I don't believe I ever missed one single home game or meet in any sport during my college days unless I myself was participating in a track or cross-country meet at some other college. When the basketball season opened with a game in our gym with Camp Custer's "Fighting Fourteenth," I was there supporting the team. We won in overtime to start a thirteen-game schedule. On March 20, 1919, the *Index* cried in headlines, "Kalamazoo Champ of the M.I.A.A. Alma College went down to defeat at the hands of Adrian and Hillsdale, leaving Kalamazoo a clean title to the M.I.A.A basketball championship for 1919. This is the 6th consecutive year that Kalamazoo has romped away with basketball honors." It's interesting to note that the championship team did not have more than three men on the squad who were six feet in height. Today in the 1970's, a six-foot boy is almost too short to be considered unless he has speed and a keen eye for the basket. In naming its All-M.I.A.A team, the *Detroit Free Press* placed three Kalamazoo boys, one Adrian, and one Alma boy on its squad.

Jobs to earn a little spare cash and to compensate for room and tuition were a part of my college life. The dean of men had assigned me to a chapel monitor position, a job I had all four years in college. Chapel was compulsory five days a week, and it was my duty to report absentees in three rows of six chairs each, a total of eighteen men. The men sat on one side of the auditorium and the women on the other. There were always absentees. I don't know of any penalty that was dealt out to them. I enjoyed chapel myself. I arrived in the Bowen Hall auditorium at 10:30 a.m., and the service lasted about twenty minutes. Chapel always opened with a hymn, then Scripture, followed by a brief talk of about five minutes, generally by someone from the faculty, then a couple verses of a closing hymn. It broke up the morning class schedule and proved to be refreshing and inspirational to me.

Our professional barber training also began to serve us in good stead. Monroe and I borrowed one of those high stools from the chemistry lab and stored it in our Room 46, where it remained until we graduated. With our tools we cut hair for twenty-five cents, which was about half the price charged in the barbershops. We did a good business on weekends, and especially before important college functions. This enabled me to buy a new suit of clothes, giving me two suits, which made me feel rich. Spring came, and the campus had to have work done on it. One of my jobs was to cut weeds off the cinder track by using a metal hand cutter. During this time of the year one could always see college men raking and burning leaves and preparing the wooded campus for the brightness of spring.

Periodically a Kalamazoo hotel that was serving a convention banquet would call the college asking for men to wait tables. I always had my name on the job-wanted list! They paid fifty cents an hour and dinner, which generally was a pretty good meal. It was a rather easy way to pick up a buck and a half.

I never was a ball of fire when it came to the classroom; I just had too many other things to do and think about to make grades a very important part of my college life. The result was I didn't have good study habits and, with my many outside activities, I didn't do justice to my studies. The flu while in SATC had set me back two weeks, and I never did catch up. However, when spring came I felt that a 2.0 average was fairly satisfactory for a fellow whose parents had never gone to high school and had never stressed the importance of getting good grades in academic achievement.

The announcement that there was to be a freshman declamation contest on May 16, 1919, gave me a desire to enter. Viewing some of the scholarly freshmen who I knew would also enter took away the slightest idea that I could win—and I didn't, but I had the fun and the experience of competing. I have always been a great competitor in activities, whether in sports or academic areas I am interested in. There were sixteen contestants, and I was number thirteen on the list. I spoke on "Americanism."

Dormitory life was both illuminating and intriguing. For the first time in my life I was living in a community of men, some who smoked, some who took a drink now and then of Prohibition liquor, and others who were great believers of the Christian principles set forth by our Christ and didn't indulge in such things as smoking, drinking, gambling with cards, or even dancing. My mother was a devout Christian, read the Bible, and accepted the Methodist doctrine in total. There were many in our church in Gobles who were just as devoted and sincere, but extremely narrow. For example, when they heard that the two Wilcox boys were going to the Baptist Kalamazoo College, one elderly couple in our church in Gobles were heard to say, "Those Wilcox boys have gone to Hades!" While I owe a great deal to my parents who always understood, patient, and interested, nevertheless the narrow interpretation of the Christian way of life to which I was subjected made me a very cynical person. My mother looked at cards as those dirty, nasty Jacks, Kings, and Queens, and they were never found in our house as long as I could remember, Dad and his orchestra had always played for public dances in Gobles. He said he didn't think a public dancehall was the place for his sons and daughters although he earned money there, so when I got to college I had never attended a dance. When the student body voted three to one to have college dances on the campus, it frightened me because I was an outcast. I wanted to go to the dance with my girlfriend who enjoyed dancing, yet I had a guilty conscience. The reason was that I had been taught to associate dancing, card playing (except for Flinch), and smoking as something evil in which I wasn't supposed to indulge. Such a state of mind gave me a great lack of social security, and I wasn't able to overcome this until several years later when I had developed the ability to think for myself and be the judge of my own activities and character.

"Athletes Show Great Promise," read the headlines in the April 3 *Index*. "Baseball and track prospects best in years …with a squad of twenty-nine candidates it certainly looks like a big track year for Kalamazoo." Then there were listed the names of prospects, with Monroe slated for the 220- and 440-yard dashes and Harold for the 880 and mile run. The spring track schedule called for participation in the state meet at M.A.C. (Michigan Agricultural College), now Michigan State University; the M.I.A.A. (Michigan Intercollegiate Athletic Association) Track and Field Meet at Albion College; and four dual meets. Our first meet was easily won with "K" getting 53 points to our two opponents' 32 and 31. Monroe won the 440-yard dash in 57.2, and I won the 880 in 2.12. The *Index* read, "Wilcox won the 880 in 2.12 which is fast time for the condition of the track. He looks better every meet and has a long, easy stride which brings a smile to the coach's face." The fourth Annual Interscholastic Track and Field meet took place Saturday, May 3, 1919. Coach Ralph Young had invited about twenty-five high schools to participate in the meet. The twenty high schools that did participate were represented by approximately two hundred athletes. The meet started at 10:00 a.m. with the preliminaries in the dashes and field events. Each Kalamazoo College track man had several athletes for whom he was responsible. He was to rub them down if they wanted it, make sure they were informed of the time of their competition, see that they were supplied with a luncheon ticket and towels for a shower, and sell them on Kalamazoo College being a good place for them after high school. Kalamazoo Central won the meet in an all-day rain.

The two big track meets that held our great interest and desire were the State Inter-Collegiate Meet at East Lansing (M.A.C.) and the M.I.A.A. at Albion. The Saturday for the East Lansing trek dawned with sunshine and warm air. We took the train to Jackson, changed, and within one half hour were on the train for East Lansing. It was my first real big test with keen competition and I was nervous, but not to the point that it affected my physical condition. Monroe was worse in this respect, for many times he would give me his two soft-boiled eggs for breakfast for fear he would lose them before the meet began! Monroe and I both did well, as good or better than the coach expected of us and also perhaps a little surprising to ourselves. The May 29 *Index* said this about our success: "Monroe Wilcox, running faster than our school record in the quarter, took third in this event which was unusually fast. He also garnered a point in the 'half-mile,' taking fourth. ... Harold Wilcox copped third in a record breaking half mile. He also ran the mile in 4:45, much better than our college record, and took fourth in this. He also finished ahead of all his M.I.A.A. competitors." Of course, Monroe and I were both elated over our first success in a big state meet because we had won our "K." The final results of the meet show

M.A.C. varsity with 57 points and Kalamazoo College second with 30 points. Now we were looking forward to the most important meet of the year, the M.I.A.A. at Albion.

"Track prospects good," said the *Index*. "If Kalamazoo doesn't take first place at the M.I.A.A. meet in Albion June 6 and 7, 1919; the squad of Kalamazoo athletes ... will have to suffer a big slump. The Wilcox brothers, both from Gobleville, that produced the famous "Runt Walker," are born runners and show it in every stride." The June 5 *Index* had a pep talk in headlines: "Will you do your part in making up field day delegation?" This was the biggest athletic event of the school year. Not only was the track team in competition, but also the tennis and baseball teams were fighting it out for All-M.I.A.A. honors. The war being over, everyone seemed to be enthusiastic about getting back to what Warren G. Harding termed "normalcy," so a big delegation wound its way to Albion by train and Interurban and private cars. The baseball and tennis teams both had a good winning season and it was expected that Kalamazoo would make a grand slam of the championship events.

The big day came, and we boarded the train for Albion. We were housed in that old hotel next to the railroad tracks. The number of passenger and freight trains that went shrieking through made a quiet, peaceful sleep a thing to be desired. However, our youthfulness and excitement made amends for any lack of sleep, and we were fit for the test. When the June 12, 1919, *Index* came out, the headlines with pictures of both the track and baseball teams read, "Kalamazoo College Track and Baseball teams win highest honors in M.I.A.A." Kalamazoo won the track championship with 57 ½ points, with Albion a distant second with 41 points. Monroe and I ran true to form – Monroe taking first in the 440-yard run and second in the 880. I took first in the 880 and second in the mile. I led off, and Monroe pulled me in as second runner on the relay team. One incident that I'll never forget took place in the 880-yard run, which is two laps around the track. Monroe stepped out and took the lead. He led until the last turn coming into the final stretch. I had been on his heels most of the race, and coming into the final stretch he gave it all he had and was greatly relieved when he saw that it was I who went by him. Monroe could beat me in any race shorter than the 880, and I could take him in 880 yards or farther. In giving his editorial recap of the field day activities, the editor of the *Index* wrote: "The running of the Wilcox brothers for Kalamazoo, which was a big factor in winning the meet for the Orange and Black, was one of the big features. They showed lots of fight as well as real running ability. With these two men in college, Kalamazoo can count itself well represented on the cinder path." Then, under "Sport Notes" among the various items of sports interest was: "Wilcox means speed."

It was the "thing" to give everyone in athletics a nickname. Monroe had received the title "Pars" for his ministerial intentions, and he became known as "Pars" Wilcox. While out on the track one afternoon, Glen "Frog" (because he could leap like a frog) Thompson said to me, "You have got to have a nickname and I am going to give you one. From now on you are 'Cocky' Wilcox," and he was right. The name became attached to me to the extent that during my junior and senior years many people on campus didn't know what my first name was. Even some of the less-dignified professors would call me "Cocky" in the classroom.

In the meantime, the college baseball team was winning games. Says the *Index*, "'K' wins twice; beating M.A.C. 6-3 and Adrian 18-6, scoring 8 runs in the 9th inning. Judging from general results, the Orange and Black has the edge on its M.I.A.A. opponents this spring in the national pastime."

The *Index* chapel notes stated that "Dean Williams was in charge of the chapel services last Thursday morning. He emphasized the everlasting permanency and inevitability of divine law." In regard to education, he said, "Civilization is and must be continuous. The present must grow out of the past, for it must grow." If the dear beloved dean could realize how 1970 grew out of the past I feel sure he would turn over in his grave!

On the other hand, the following rhyme expressed the feeling of some students toward some faculty members: "Here's To The Faculty" (*Index*, May 22, 1919) "Here's to the faculty with learning galore. Dished out at white heat in long lectures that bore. Here's to the faculty, their power they betray, by bossing us about in a high handed way. Here's to the faculty, so may their tribe decease, till they are thin and few, and we all find release." It is my feeling that some of my professors delighted in glamorizing their own academic achievements rather than the progress of their students. I can remember one of my professors who continually impressed on us students that he was a Harvard man. In the first quarter of the century the big three, Harvard, Princeton, and Yale, were tops in academics as well as in sports. Very few All-American football players came out of the west. Some Easterners still thought that we Michigan people were fighting Indians and carrying guns to church for protection.

The *Index* announced: "The Annual College Picnic. The junior and freshman classes will be at home to the other two classes and faculty at Gull Lake June 4th. Busses and cars will leave Bowen Hall at 11:30." Well, it was a great day for all who attended. We saw Prof. Smith take off his coat and, in his shirtsleeves, wade into the hot dogs, coffee, doughnuts, etc. While I never had Prof. Smith because he was the chemistry teacher, I always thought well of him and respected him for his down-to-earth teaching. He really did have an interest in his students.

This picnic was just one of the many occasions that made Kalamazoo College just one big happy family. I have always been a small college man and, later as a schoolteacher, always tried to sell my students on considering the small college of their choice. I am happy to say that through my influence several fine students and athletes from Ferndale Lincoln High chose Kalamazoo. One, Charles Cameron, has made a name for himself in the field of education by starting at Chelsea, Michigan as a football coach and classroom teacher and advancing first to the principalship of the high school and then to the superintendent's office, which he still holds after these many years. Another of my pride and joys was Gordon Rodwan. Gordon was a big, 6' 5", 180-pound boy in high school who played center on Ferndale's league championship basketball team. He went to Kalamazoo College and proved exceedingly valuable in bringing to Kalamazoo the M.I.A.A. championship in basketball. He was an All-M.I.A.A. center in his junior and senior years.

With the athletic year being over, first there were the final exams to think about, and second, what to do this summer to make money for the future. Then too, next year's jobs had to be given consideration. One of the waiters at the Ladies Hall dining room was graduating, so I made it a point to see the matron about taking his place next year. She told me that so far as she was concerned I could have the job as waiter. Meals were served at eight o'clock, twelve noon, and six o'clock. Everyone ate at the same time as one big family. Waiters had to get to the dining room about twenty minutes before the hour of the meal in order to get the tables set with bread, butter, water, etc. The meals took about one-half hour, then the waiters ate, so in about one hour the meal was entirely over. Waiters got their meals for the service. I was glad to give up the boarding house work in order to give table service right on campus. Besides, it allowed me to get to know better many more of the student body.

Exams went well, and I had gained confidence that I was capable of doing college work. Another mental encouragement came when I saw my picture in the college yearbook under "Book Worms" with this comment – "The youngest [me] may be unworthy of this classification here, but he had shown great mental precocity." Then I became curious to know exactly what "precocity" meant, so I found that Webster defined it as a state of premature mental development. While I regarded it as one man's opinion like being rated an All American, nevertheless I accepted it as something to strive for.

Mother and Dad wrote often, and once or twice Dad visited the campus either in the evening after he had closed the shop early or on Sunday. It was only twenty miles between Gobleville (now Gobles) and Kalamazoo, but Monroe and I were so busy with all our activities that we were not able to get home very often. When we did go home it was generally on the 5:15 p.m. train to stay overnight and be back again on the 7:45 a.m., which got in to Kalamazoo at 8:30 a.m. in time for classes.

At home, Dad had Allen and Whyle breaking in and learning the barber trade. They started by lathering the face since most customers got shaves. Gradually over a couple of years, by working nights after school and Saturdays they learned to shave and cut hair as Monroe and I had learned. In due time we all appeared before the Michigan Barber Board, took examinations, and received a barber license, which had to be renewed each year. Long before the class of 1919 had graduated, Monroe and I were both thinking about summer jobs. I found out that Alcock's Barbershop on West Main Street (now West Michigan) needed a summer barber, so I went down to talk with Mr. Alcock. I told him I didn't have my license yet, but would apply right away for the opportunity to take the examination.

In 1919 that consisted of bringing your own customer to the place of the examinations, in this case a hotel room, and give him a haircut and shave while the examiner stood and watched you do it. I had no trouble at all and was granted the license, which enabled me to barber almost any place in the United States. Now, a summer barber job in Kalamazoo didn't pay big money. In most shops you got a guarantee of thirty-five dollars a week and half over fifty dollars that you took in. Some weeks I made forty dollars to fifty dollars, but not many.

Monroe decided he wanted to try to get a job that would pay more money, although it would demand harder work. He and a couple of other college men got jobs in construction. Monroe worked only a few weeks before he caught his finger on his left hand between two bricks and bruised it so badly he had to quit the job and spend some time at home. During the month of August when Mr. Alcock wanted to take two weeks' vacation, Monroe came into the shop and worked. The sore finger had healed enough to allow him to use his left hand, which wasn't a handicap since the right hand is the one of action in barbering.

Before the summer had gone on too far a group of us organized a baseball team and joined the city recreation league. I played third base. We had one native Kalamazoo man on our team who had been an All-American halfback at the University of Pennsylvania the previous fall of 1918. He had played football for two years at Kalamazoo Normal College and then transferred to the University of Pennsylvania and played three more years there. Eligibility rules governing the status of athletes were few and far between in the early 1900's. There were what became known as "tramp athletes" who would enter a college in the fall, play football, and then leave at Christmastime, and by the next fall they were enrolled at some other college, likely in another state. This enabled some to be pretty good at the sport after several years in various colleges.

One of the financial advantages of working in Kalamazoo was that I could room in old 46 all summer without paying any room rent. There were a number of us, including a Japanese boy, who took advantage of this privilege. Why this generosity, I do not know! I only know that no one came around asking for money. It also saved us the job of moving out of our room at the risk of someone else getting it in the fall.

Being on campus, during the evening I would go down to the cinder path and run ten to fifteen laps three or four times a week. I wanted to keep my legs and wind in good shape for cross-country in the fall. Long-distance running is a difficult sport to maintain self-interest. One has to train oneself to sort of play a game. I designed a cross-country course of about four miles. I started out by running around the cinder path once or twice, and then I took off on the east side of the railroad tracks back of what was then Kalamazoo Normal College. Then I would run through the wooded area and continue across the fields that lay between the State Hospital and the railroad tracks until I came to Oakwood Lake. Oakwood Lake had an amusement park with a roller skating rink. We had many roller skating parties here. Then I would run back along Oakland Street until I got to the old college athletic field. Turning in through the gates, I would do about half a dozen laps around the track before finishing for the day. I would have imaginary opponents and would try to outrace them, forcing myself to put on the speed going past certain points in my course. In that way it relieved the monotony of running long distances all by myself. This self-designed cross-country course became the accepted course for college runners for years after I had graduated. Years later when the college traded with the city years old college athletic field for the portion of the city-owned golf course west of the college campus, which is now Angel Field, a new cross-country course was laid out.

In 1919 cross-country wasn't an accepted major sport among colleges. Few had a cross-country team of five men; only at universities did one find such acceptance. Because of this sport situation, I was the first cross-country runner Kalamazoo College ever had. This was the result of the interest of Coach Ralph Young, who wanted to see a well-rounded athletic program at Kalamazoo College. Coach Young had done his undergraduate work at the University of Chicago and had been an all-around athlete during his college career. In the early 1900's the University of Chicago was a member of the Big Ten. Under the famous coach Alonzo Stagg, who was known as "the old man of football," Chicago teams won their share of Big Ten championships. Coach Stagg was a fine Christian gentleman who was dedicated to coaching young men. He had high ideals and always maintained that tobacco and alcohol did not mix with sports. This theory was nationally accepted in advertising until Prohibition went out the window, and the liquor and tobacco industries gradually began to associate their products with sports in their advertising. I can remember a large billboard on Woodward Avenue in Detroit near the State Fairgrounds that during the late 1930's carried a large ad associating beer with major league baseball. It so incensed the public that public opinion caused the industry to discontinue such advertising. It wasn't until World War II that tobacco and alcohol were finally accepted by the public masses as legitimate products to be associated with sports.

Coach Stagg was the type of man everyone wanted to meet. It was my privilege to be associated with him during the first National Intercollegiate Track and Field Meet held at the University of Chicago in 1921. I ran the two mile in the meet and ran seventh, just out of the sixth-place position. After being retired by the University of Chicago, Coach Stagg became associate coach with his son at the College of the Pacific. This enabled him to remain in close contact with sports until he was around ninety years old. This "Grand Old Man of Football" will always be associated with the sport in everyone's history.

As the summer months passed I was looking forward to Labor Day, which would terminate my summer barbering job at Alcocks. I went home for a few days before returning to the campus for the fall term. Since our family was large, there was always something to keep me busy at home. Dad seldom took a real vacation nor did mother, so we would give Dad some relief at the barbershop during the few days we were home. Then on Saturday if the shop got crowded with customers, I would step up to a chair and call, "Next." With three chairs working, it wasn't long before we had them caught up, so to speak.

Monroe and I had already become sports figures in Gobles. Men would come to the shop and want to talk about our track success. Dad was proud of us. He was a sports fan himself, and could carry on conversation, sometimes a little exaggerated, about the track work of his two sons' first track year in college.

Mother always had all she could do in maintaining her children's clothing, so I learned early to provide for myself. To sew on buttons, darn socks, clean and press my trousers was a part of my home education. While we were "one-bath-a-week" people, which was standard custom in those days, I did keep clean, wore fresh and clean shirts, kept my trousers well pressed, and tried at all times to present myself as a Christian man.

Getting back on the campus at the beginning of a new college year was always an interesting experience. Old friends met again after a summer of diversified work. It was "Hello, Joe – did you have a good summer?" and the first evening was generally spent collectively in some dormitory room discussing what was done during the summer. Of course, there were the usual first day's activities such as building my class schedule, being assigned my chapel monitor duty, getting reacquainted with waiting tables at the Ladies Hall dining room, reporting to Coach Young and relating my summer training program, etc. It was always exciting, but at the same time it made me realize that it was going to be demanding.

The front page of the *College Index* of September 25, 1919, had such headlines as "You'd hardly know the college grounds. ... Campus had haircut and ears washed to greet record enrollment." The article goes on to say that the college boasted a larger enrollment of students that fall than any preceding year: "One hundred fourteen people have entered the college ... seventy-four men and forty women." Good thing that the Normal College across the tracks had an abundance of women students! By the way, we college men always compared the two institutions of learning in this respect! If you can't make a go of your educational opportunity on the first hill, you go to the second hill (Normal College)! And if you can't make it on the second hill you then can move to the third hill (State Hospital)!

One of the first thoughts of competitive sports would be of football. The *Index* headline read: "Football Team Best in Years; Many Veterans Back and New Material is Good." With such fine men as Mike Casteel at quarterback and Dutch Strome, Henry Clay, Jack Thompson, and Joe Mishica—all previously picked for All-M.I.A.A. teams—Coach Ralph Young had the right to feel very optimistic. Casteel was not a real big man, but he could have made any collegiate football team in the country. Joe Mishica from the Upper Peninsula of Michigan had played high school football against the great George Gipp of Notre Dame fame and didn't have to take a back seat to any tackler in the game.

There were several new professors at the college serving their first year. The two who received my favor were Milton Simpson, who came to Kalamazoo from Whitman College, Walla Walla, Washington; and Bobbie Cornell, who was previously at Cornell College, Mt. Vernon, Iowa. Professor Simpson is the only man who taught literature in such a way that made a literature class enjoyable to me. I had several courses from him and enjoyed every one. Bobbie Cornell was the athletes' instructor. He was not too demanding, and his classes were very informal. It was Mike, Frog, Cocky, Hooke, etc. As Bobbie said at the first of the semester, "What we do in here and how I conduct my class doesn't have to become the business of the college faculty!"

My most favorite professor was Dr. E. A. Balch, head of the history department. I think there were probably several reasons for him being my number one. First, history was and always has been my favorite subject. I got my M.A. degree from the University of Michigan with a major in history and a minor in political science. I taught history and government for about thirty years in high school and enjoyed it, so that probably played a big part in my choice. But there were other elements entering into it. Dr. Balch's son Marston, who was one year behind me at Kalamazoo, became one of my close friends. On a number of occasions I was invited to the Balchs' home, which enabled me to become much better acquainted with Dr. Balch than any other professor. Perhaps this is the reason I felt my history professor took a greater interest in me than any other person on the faculty. However, this relationship did not reflect any advantage in classroom work, for in his classes I was just another student as far as grades were concerned.

I remember one occasion that made me very discouraged and angry. It was a course I enjoyed very much. One of my friends, Ruth Vercoe, and I were in friendly competition over a mark in the course and I really studied hard to maintain that competition. However, Dr. Balch announced at the very beginning of the course that we would use no textbook. He gave us a course outline, and with the aid of library materials and references plus his lectures we would be expected to prepare for the weekly tests from which our final grade would be determined. This was a completely new course of study for me, and the first week I felt lost. I was relieved of the panicked feeling when he made it clear that, this being a new method of study, some of us would probably take a week or two to get adjusted. Well, he was correct, and when we had our first test I was not prepared. I didn't even attempt to write on it, not realizing that the test would prove to be such an important factor in my final grade. I didn't go to him nor try to make it up, feeling he would take the first week into consideration. It wasn't too many weeks before my test grades were in the A and B rank, so by the end of the term I had dismissed the tragedy of that first week from my mind. When my final grade came out I had a D in the course. You can just bet I was in no calm frame of mind when I went to his office to plead my case. He looked at my record, stating he had had a senior student making out the grades and that he could raise the mark to a C without any undue procedure. I was still belligerent and in no uncertain terms told him what I thought of his grade system, that after his announcement of the new method of no textbook I thought he would take the first week into consideration. I got nowhere. He merely said, "You should have come to me about it and made up the test." My C in the course stood as the final grade mark.

We had a professor in psychology who was a queer grader. Dr. Stetson, president of the college, was the instructor whom I am referring to. He had you labeled for a certain grade and that was the one you got. Taking this course with me was my co-worker at the Ladies Hall dining room, Harold Dressel. He and I served the ladies and gentlemen their meals. At the close of the first semester, Harold got a C in the course and I got a B. It made Dressel angry, so he told me, "I'm taking the second semester of the course, and if I do not rate better than a C at the semester break I am dropping it." The college had a policy that a mid-semester grade in a course was turned in at the office so that one could determine how one was doing. At mid-term Dressel went to the office with me. He had his C, and I had my B. He said, "That's it. I am dropping the course," and he did. He didn't attend another class, didn't take any tests, nor crack a book. When the final grades came out in June at the close of the college year, Dressel had his C, and I had my B! In spite of his classroom deficiencies, Dr. Stetson was "the grand old man" of the campus to everyone.

Another article in the first *Index* of the new college year ran as follows: "College Y.M.C.A. is ready for a good year. Last June, Robert Seward and Monroe J. Wilcox attended the college Y.M.C.A. Conference at Lake Geneva, Wisconsin. They received not only a great inspiration, but also new ideas as to the proper program for the college. Monroe was the "Y" president for the new year."

My new job at the Ladies Hall dining room was a pleasant experience that I held for my three remaining years at Kalamazoo College. The student body was small in number, and this enabled nearly everyone to get acquainted. Serving tables and eating in the dining hall made it possible for me to become a more intimate part of college life. This in itself was enjoyable. Aside from one mortifying experience, my duties were always pleasurable. It so happened that one spring we were serving stewed tomatoes for dinner. In the process of taking the dishes of tomatoes off my tray, the last dish slipped to the edge of the tray. Before I could catch it, it went right on top of a senior girl's head—Ruth Hudson's. Ruth was the charming daughter of one of Michigan's congressmen, Grant Hudson of Lansing. While Ruth undoubtedly was humiliated, she was the perfect lady. She arose from the table without a word, went upstairs to her room and I suppose took a shower and washed her hair. Thank goodness I didn't have to sweat through such an ordeal again, for I think it hurt me as much as it did Ruth!

On numerous occasions after dinner some of the boys and girls would gather in the reception room and, with one of the girls at the piano pounding out a familiar song, would exercise our vocal organs. I cannot say that we out sung the Glee or Gaynor Clubs, but we did make a bit of noise and had a good time doing it. All this added to a more enjoyable college life.

The increased numbers in student enrollment found several on campus who were from Gobles or nearby vicinity. There was a handsome young man with winning ways, Carl Markillie, who lived on a farm about a mile out of Gobles. Then there was my high school chum Beatrice Waber, who had spent a disappointing year at Michigan Agricultural College (now M.S.U.) at East Lansing and had transferred to Kalamazoo. Also a "fireball" with lots of ideas was Coleman Cheney of Gobles, who could think of more deviltry than anyone on the campus. Freeman Brown, my cousin and a member of the Gobles High School Class of 1918, was also on campus. With the two Wilcox boys, these made up what became known as the Goblite Company. We had several parties so designed that our girlfriends never knew what to expect, for that was the policy of the Goblites. One theater party ended up with midnight lunch by flashlights in the chemistry lab. How did we get into Bowen Hall, which housed the chemistry lab? There were always one or two openings; one was the fire escape door and the other was the coal shoot. It was Cheney's job to arrange the entrance we were to use during the early evening or late afternoon, and he never backed out of his assignment. Of course, such antics could not be tolerated in the late 1900's, but in the 1920's no one paid too much attention because there was no vandalism. All in the spirit of fun!

Another one of our Goblite parties was a roller skating affair at Oakwood Park. Cheney would arrange for an afternoon date with the management, then invitations were issued to our college friends. The streetcar hauled the gang to and from Oakwood. It made for a cheap but very entertaining afternoon. So that our friends would better understand the true spirit of the Goblite Company, a picnic was arranged at Lake Mill, which was about a mile from Gobles. Markillie and Brown had the job of auto transportation. The girls, our guests, supplied the lunch. After touring the town, the lake provided the spot for the afternoon. Things went off in good style and all were back on campus for study hour, a rule the girls had to adhere to during weekdays. I guess the dean assumed that if the girls were in on time, the boys would be also.

The fall term found the Sherwood inviting freshmen to the 68th Annual Open Meeting, Wednesday evening, October 15, 1919, at 7:30 p.m. at Sherwood Hall. All members were asked to be present with their best appearance, since many freshmen would choose a society by the type of men who were members. It was a very successful evening. Members were assigned to be a participant in at least one weekly program during the year. On November 19, 1919, program chairman Harold E. Hawley sent me the following notice: "You are hereby requested to appear on the program November 19th as a city commissioner to speak on the affirmative side of the proposition of submitting the question of raising streetcar fare to popular vote." I always liked such opportunities because it was a good educational experience.

Cross-country is a fall track sport, generally associated with football. To run cross-country one must train by just running, running, and running. The 1920's found few good distance runners in the United States. This resulted in few cross-country meets. There was no such thing as the M.I.A.A. meet when I was in college. In fact, I ran only two races while in college, and both of them were in my sophomore year. We had no more than settled into the fall term when Coach Young asked me about the past summer. I told him I had continued my training all summer and would enjoy cross-country if there were meets to run in. He gave me a sheet of paper with "cross-country axioms," and said he thought there would be opportunities to enter meets. There were twelve axioms, which included the following: Running on country roads is better on your feet. The stride is shorter than the mile run stride. The run is usually six miles. By the end of six weeks, by gradually increasing the distance and pace, one should be able to cover the distance at a good pace.

It wasn't until the last of October that Coach got a letter from the director of athletics at M.A.C. (now M.S.U.) dated October 29, 1919, regarding the State Collegiate Cross-Country Meet. The letter read as follows: "Dear Mr. Young: Arrangements have been completed for our annual Intercollegiate Cross Country Run, and we trust you will be represented with a team or at least an entry … we feel sure that the competition will be of the highest order. Our plans are now to start the race during the second quarter of the football game, about 2:50 p.m., which will make the finish take place during the intermission between halves of the game. The course will be third and one half miles long. Men with flags will be stationed at every turn. The race will start and finish on the track in front of the stands on the athletic field. We believe holding it at this time will add greatly to the interest of the run." Signed: C. L. Brewer, Director. It is interesting to note that the letter of invitation gave no date for the run; however, the run did take place on Saturday, November 8, 1919. Coach gave me a transportation schedule for the trip to East Lansing. Since I was going alone into a new running adventure, it really was an exciting experience.

I left Kalamazoo on Friday, November 7 at 2:10 p.m. on the New York Central train, arrived in Battle Creek at 3:20 p.m., and arrived in Lansing at 5:15 p.m. A streetcar took me out to East Lansing, and I arrived at the M.A.C. gym just at dusk when the football team was sitting down at the training table for dinner. I asked for Coach Brewer as I was instructed to do, and gave him my letter that explained that I was the Kalamazoo College cross-country runner for the meet the following day. He asked me if I had had supper, and I said, "No." "Sit down at the table and eat with the football players," he said, "and I'll find you a place to stay tonight." After eating ham and eggs plus the usual other ingredients that make up a meal, the football members were about to leave. Then Coach Brewer introduced me to them and asked if any of them had an extra bed in a fraternity house that this man could occupy tonight. One man immediately spoke up and said he had an extra bed at the Tic House and that he would take care of me. So with my bag, my new friend and I walked across the campus, up the hill east of Michigan Avenue to the fraternity house. I was made to feel at home, introduced to the members as the Kalamazoo College runner in the meet, and was told to make myself comfortable. About 9:30 p.m., I told my friend that I thought I would retire and get a good night's rest. He took me up to the dormitory and gave me a bed, one of about twenty-five in the room. I never slept sounder in my life, and never awakened until 7:30 a.m. At breakfast my friend apologized for the disturbance made in the dormitory after I had gone to bed. I asked, "What disturbance?" "Didn't you hear all the commotion that went on when the men were moving beds around with the lights on about midnight?" he asked. I didn't hear a thing, and I slept soundly all night long, and awoke very rested, I informed him.

After breakfast I strolled around the campus and, among other things, saw in the showcase in the gym the six medals that were to be presented after the meet to the first six place winners. I thought to myself, "I hope I can carry one of them back to Kalamazoo!" and I did. It was a cool cloudy day.

It had rained a couple days previously, and there were puddles of water in low spots on the ground, so I knew we probably would be encountering mud puddles in our cross country run. After watching the first few minutes of the football game, I walked over to the gym and dressed for the run. I wore a tracksuit with a paper pinned on the inside of my shirt to protect my chest from the cold air. Instead of wearing a regular spiked track shoe as some did, I wore light tennis shoes with socks. I felt we would have wet feet before the race was over.

After all the contestants were dressed, we had the course and the turns explained to us. In 1920 the athletic field at M.A.C. was located across the Red Cedar River, which has become the baseball field and playground. The run was to start, we were told, on the cinder path in front of the stands before the end of the first half of the game. We were to run one and a half laps around the track, go out the gate, and follow the trail across what is now the new football field, at that time a golf course. From there men with flags would coach us on the turns that would take us through some wooded area and out to Grand River, the main street. Then the run would come down across the campus, by the gym, across the bridge over the Red Cedar, to the track, and around to the finish line in front of the grandstand. There were thirty-five runners. University of Michigan and M.A.C. each had teams of five men. The other runners were from several colleges in Michigan.

Before we left the gym the attendant handed me a telegram that read, "Go it, we're all behind you. The gang." That made me all the more anxious to do well in the meet, and I was determined that number 29 (my number) was going to be up there! Never having run in a cross-country meet before and not knowing the course, I decided to stay well up in the pack, but sort of follow the leaders until we reached the campus that took us down by the gym. In other words, I was going to let the other fellows make the mistakes if there were some to be made and then try to profit by them. As we left the cinder path and started across the golf course, I kept well up in front with four or five men ahead of me. It didn't seem to be too fast a pace, but my plan was to be a follower. As we came down by the gym, there were seven of us all pretty well bunched in the lead. One boy with spikes on stepped on the cement approach to the river bridge, slipped and fell. Then I said to myself, "I have one of those six medals in my grasp!" As we came through the gate, I sprinted to the front, led the pack around the last curve of the cinder path, finished about three yards in front of the nearest competitor, and was the winner. The applause that came from the crowded stands was music to my ears. The football player who had taken me to his fraternity house overnight came to me, shook my hand, and said, "Last night we felt sorry for you coming over here all alone, but we don't feel that way now. Nice run and good luck to you!" Surprisingly, I did not feel at all tired. I could have run a much-faster race. When the gold medal was handed to me in front of the stands, my excitement was so great that I did not even feel the cold weather. The football game went into the second half, and I went to the gym to shower and dress.

My thoughts now were on how to get back to Kalamazoo the fastest way possible. I went to the interurban station and found that I could take a car to Battle Creek, change after an hour's wait to a Kalamazoo car, arriving in Kalamazoo about 1:00 a.m. Coach Young had asked me to let him know how I came out, so before finding a restaurant I sent a telegram stating that I had won. When I arrived back at number 46 in our dorm, Monroe and a few others were still up waiting to hear about the big win. I was told that Kalamazoo had defeated Albion in the big game for the M.I.A.A. championship, and that students had had a big celebration in the Regent Theater. The showing of the picture was interrupted, the lights went on, and the cheerleaders took over from the stage. The movie screen announced my successful run as well as the football victory. All in all, it was one of the great days in the history of Kalamazoo College athletics!

The *MLive Kalamazoo Gazette* for Sunday, November 9, 1919, had the following article on the sports page: "Wilcox wins long run for Kalamazoo College." The article went on to say, "Harold Wilcox, entered alone from Kalamazoo in the M.A.C. Cross Country Run at East Lansing, defeated the strong teams from the Aggies, Michigan Varsity, Hope, Albion and other state schools. The U. of M. placed second and Hope third. The first four men to finish were: Wilcox, Kalamazoo College, first; Thurston, M.A.C., second; Adolph, M.A.C., third; Burkholder, U. of M., fourth. Wilcox's time was

19:46. The victory ties the Michigan Aggies and the U. of M., both teams now having won two legs on the state trophy. It should be kept in mind that the winning team, M.A.C., had five men running, as did the U. of M., Hope and Albion."

When the *Index* of November 12, 1919, came out, it carried a full two-thirds front-page column with my picture and with headlines: "Wilcox Takes First in Cross Country Run ... Defeats Best in State at East Lansing Last Saturday." The article continued, "While our football team was so nobly upholding the honor of Kalamazoo last Saturday, another event was taking place of which most of us were not aware. In our eagerness to beat Albion, we almost forgot that we had a representative at East Lansing competing in the Annual Intercollegiate Cross Country Run. Harold Wilcox went alone to M.A.C. to uphold the honor of the Orange and Black. Without a coach, teammates or rooters to urge him on, he entered the field against thirty-five other runners from Michigan colleges, including the best from the U. of M. and M.A.C. With such competition, Wilcox proved to be the dark horse of the occasion and won the first place with a margin of three yards. During the entire race he was near the lead, but when it came to the finish he demonstrated that he had the best of the race by pulling away from all his competitors. He covered the distance of three and one-half miles in 19 minutes and 46 seconds. When one considers how Wilcox has trained all alone with very little instruction, how he went alone to M.A.C. with no backing, and how he won over the best which M.A.C. and the U. of M. had to offer, it is evident that he accomplished a very remarkable feat. Now that Kalamazoo has a start in cross country running, it is hoped that more interest will be shown in this new sport. On Thanksgiving morning, there is to be a race at Grand Rapids, and Coach Young hopes to send enough men to make a team (five) so that there will be a chance at the cup."

This was the time of year it started getting real chilly, and with Thanksgiving only eighteen days off there was a tendency to slacken off on the training. However, when "Dollar" Larson and I boarded the interurban car Thanksgiving morning I was in good physical and mental shape to compete in the run at Grand Rapids. When we arrived at Grand Rapids Y.M.C.A., we found it had snowed the night before and the streets were slippery. Since the course run was over the paved streets, it made it doubly hard to maintain a fast pace. As we dressed for the race in the "Y" from which the race was to start and finish we were given course instructions. We were told men would be at each turn, and there would be no street traffic allowed during the race. In publicizing the race, one Grand Rapids' newspaper printed a column with the following headline: "Thirty may start in YMCA Run. Wilcox, winner of M.A.C. Run, is most prominent entry." The article went on to say: "The most prominent runner who will start the race is Harold Wilcox, Captain of Kalamazoo College Team, who took first place in the recent M.A.C. cross country run. He and his teammate, Martin Larson, will represent Kalamazoo College."

As we lined up on the slippery pavement at 10:30 a.m. that Thanksgiving Day, November 27, 1919, little did I realize I was running and winning my second and last cross-country run. As in my first race, my running plan was to stay in the bunch until I got an idea who the leading contenders were and what each race plan was. After about a mile had been covered and I became used to the slippery pavement, I decided it was time to step out and set a faster pace in order to see who would be my real competitors. To my amazement, after another mile had been covered, there were no real contenders. I had the race all to myself! The last 200 yards or so of the race was around the corner and down a slight hill. I had finished the race and stood watching for the second runner by the name of Zander to come around the corner.

After all the competitors had finished we went into the "Y" to shower and dress. The Rev. Hendricks, pastor of First Methodist Church of Grand Rapids and former pastor of First Methodist Church in Kalamazoo, approached me and introduced himself. He asked me about my plans, knowing I couldn't have Thanksgiving dinner at my home. I told him I had none except to catch an interurban back to Kalamazoo. Then he invited me to have dinner at his home, stating that Milton Hinga was also coming for dinner. Milt was a football player as well as a member of the basketball and baseball teams at K.C. He lived in Kalamazoo, and while he and the daughter of Rev. Hendricks were at Kalamazoo Central High School they formed a relationship that lasted all of Milt's life, which ended in the 1960's while he was athletic director at Hope College. We had a very enjoyable dinner. After dinner Milt said to me, "Why don't you stay overnight? My friend has a girl chum and we can go to a show!" That sounded good to me, and we had a very enjoyable evening. Milt was a Dutch Lutheran and a fine Christian man. I often went with him to the young people's meetings on Sunday evenings at the Reformed Church in Kalamazoo. We had a number of double dates when he would bring his girlfriend and her chum, who were students at Albion College, to our campus functions.

When the morning Grand Rapids newspaper came out Friday, November 28, 1919, the sports page had this headline: "Wilcox Leads Cross Country Runners Home." The article continued, "Wilcox of Kalamazoo got away to a good lead in the annual Grand Rapids Y.M.C.A. Cross Country run yesterday morning and never was headed. Yandee of the 'Y' kept the Kalamazoo runner worried during two and one half miles of the jaunt. Wilcox then lengthened his lead, and Yandee finished about 200 yards behind ... the other Kalamazoo runner, Larson, finished fifth. Wilcox's time was 15 minutes and 25 ¼ seconds ... remarkable considering the slippery condition of the pavement."

When the December 4, 1919, *Index* came out, on the front was an article headlined, "Wilcox Wins Again at Grand Rapids." In the article was the following: "By the remarks which passed before the race it was evident that Wilcox was a marked man. He did not disappoint his competitors for he won the race in 15 minutes and 25 ¼ seconds which is a very remarkable time. The competition was not as keen as Wilcox encountered at M.A.C., yet with the experience of the intercollegiate meet behind him he was able to run a much better race at Grand Rapids. His winning is not so significant perhaps as the splendid time in which he completed the course. Larson also made good time."

It was an enjoyable experience to take the interurban back to Kalamazoo that Friday morning and the noon train to Goble, where Monroe and I spent the Thanksgiving recess. Of course, when I was helping Dad at the shop on Saturday the center of the customers' conversation was cross-country running, such questions as, "How many times did you stop to rest?" and "How much did you walk during the run?" When we got back on campus Sunday night there were the usual greetings of, "Have a good weekend? How was the Grand Rapids run?" Now that we had only three weeks before the Christmas recess, we had to start thinking about that.

Football has always been a very popular sport and was when I was in college. I enjoyed the games, although I never saw a game until I was at Kalamazoo. I can remember when I was in high school, I asked, "What does it mean when you hear someone say second down and five yards to go?" That was as much as I knew and understood football, but it didn't take long to learn, and by the end of the season I was a veteran. The 1919 football team was one that made history for Kalamazoo. It lost only to Notre Dame by a 14-0 score in a game in which tackle Joe Michica bottled up his old high school competitor, the great George Gipp. It wasn't until the last quarter when the Kalamazoo players were tired that Notre Dame scored its two touchdowns. This was the lowest score that Notre Dame was held to all year, and it was considered one of the strongest elevens in the west. The second loss of the season was to the University of Detroit, which in the early 1900's was a football power to be reckoned with. The 1920 *Boiling Pot*, our college yearbook, had this to say about the football season of 1919: "Kalamazoo won the 1919 football championship of the M.I.A.A. because it had easily the best team in the association." The article continued, "The two big features of the season were the splendid showing made by Kalamazoo against Notre Dame University, one of the strongest elevens in the west, and the game with Albion College here. In the former both teams made the same number of first downs and made about the same number of yards. Both went scoreless in the first three quarters, and only in the last quarter was Notre Dame able to put across two touchdowns. The contest with Albion was noteworthy for the exhibition of spirit by the student body whose members staged two grand marches through the city, introducing Albion's coffin and goat between halves. The student body attended the Regent Theatre in the evening, after an old time celebration around a bonfire on campus. More than that however, was the brand of football put up by the Kalamazoo team. Albion was unable to cross the Orange and Black goal line, making its score on a safety."

The *MLive Kalamazoo Gazette* ended its description of the Albion game with this statement: "Albion proved to be a good losing bunch and at the conclusion of hostilities paraded off the field with heads up, band playing and colors flying. The finest sporting spirit was shown throughout, and over 4000 fans, just common folks, enjoyed the enthusiasm." So ended the victorious football season for the Orange and Black!

Like everything else, football in the 1970's has undergone great changes from that of the 1920's. In 1920 one and only one football could be used throughout the whole game, and it was much more rounded with less-pointed ends, which made it much harder for the quarterback to pass. Therefore football was much more of a running game. Then too, if it was raining and the teams had to play on a muddy field, toward the end of the game the ball was waterlogged. It made it very difficult to handle and to kick. The result was lower-scoring games.

To say that everything that goes up must come down is true in some instances, but it certainly was erroneous in my case. When grades came out at the close of the first semester in January, I came down with a great bang, and it was so unnecessary as my later records show. My big trouble had been that I had allowed my devotion to sports in general and my success in cross-country running to supersede what was the true and most important value of college life, the academic. After the shock of my low grades had worn off and the *MLive Kalamazoo Gazette* had proclaimed my ineligibility for the spring track season, I began to review the previous ten-weeks attitude toward classroom activity! Doc Gallop, president of the sophomore class and a member of the Glee Club, and I had spent afternoons lying on a bed building imaginary spring Glee Club castles. I became conscious of the fact that my instructors would have been more appreciative of my efforts if I had been in the classroom. Only a few people really gave me encouragement for the future. When I asked Monroe what he thought I should do—drop out of college and transfer to the next hill, the Normal College, he said, "No. Settle down and fight it out." When Coach Young came to me about the situation I was in, he said, "You have proven by your last year's grades that you can do college work. I had to take five years to finish my undergraduate work at the University of Chicago and I made it all right, and you can do the same." He wanted me to continue my track training in the spring and felt that there might be a possibility of my running in some non-M.I.A.A. meets. He would have to talk it over with Dr. Stetson. After I had told her that I guessed I was the object of heredity since Monroe and I were the first in our family to graduate from high school, my classmate and friend Ruth Vercoe said to me, "Harold, you are just not applying yourself to your studies. You can do it if you try hard!" So I made up my mind to settle down to good hard academic work and apply myself to my duties in the classroom.

Sometimes it takes a jolt to wake a person up and a kick in the pants to get a person going! I had felt the effects of both! So when I went in to talk to Professor Praeger and listen to him state, "Mr. Wilcox, there are some people who should never go to college, and I believe you are one of them," he did not deter me from my plans to continue at Kalamazoo. May I add here, dear professor, that I did get my B.A. degree from Kalamazoo! The University of Michigan also conferred an M.A. degree in history and political science on me, and I spent forty-two years in the public schools of Ferndale, Michigan, with at least a fair degree of success!

The Goblites were still active and making campus history with a column in the *Index* now and then. The December 4, 1919, *Index* stated: "The members of the Goblite Company returned to their native city Gobles for Thanksgiving vacation. They were Carl Markillie, Monroe and Harold Wilcox, Freeman Brown and Coleman Cheney." The December 18, 1919, issue of the *Index* announced: "Goblite Company Has a Party." The features of the program were a vocal solo by Coleman Cheney (with three encores), a toe dance by Harold Wilcox (notice how he limps now), 'Spanish Influenza' by Monroe Wilcox, a lecture on 'Advice to Young Ladies' by Freeman Brown, Carl Markillie failed to appear on the program but did his share of entertaining on the davenport! Emil Howe gave an 'illustrated' lecture on 'How to be happy when the lights go on strike.' Group photos of the Goblites and their guests were on sale at the Goblite office, price one dollar." The office was Coleman Cheney's room in the dorm. My guest for the evening was Doris Adams, who was living in Kalamazoo attending college, and a very charming but petite young lady. This was just one of several good times we Goblites had while at Kalamazoo.

What songs were we singing during these clean fun events? Among the songs was "Remember," which had just been written by Irving Berlin. We were still singing "All Alone by the Telephone" which became popular a couple of years earlier than 1920. Then there was that always-popular "Margie," which never seems to lose its charm for harmonizing. "Pretty Girl Like A Melody" from one of the several Broadway musicals was just being heard in some quarters. With no radio nor TV it took much, much longer for tunes to reach the masses of public. "Let a Smile be Your Umbrella on a Rainy, Rainy Day" was one of the top songs of this period, and today in the 1970's it's still a favorite. "I'm Forever Blowing Bubbles" was another popular hit that has lived all these years. Then the song "Pretty Baby" was well known and being sung by most of the younger generation. It wasn't unusual for all singing groups to include "Blue Skies, Why Are You Blue."

In 1920 we had just finished fighting the "war to end wars." The youth of 1920 were just as much interested in making that slogan come true as the youth of 1970, but for reasons beyond the control of the average citizen, the United States is now fighting its third war since that "war to end all wars" slogan was the accepted goal of most all people. To think that the United States has been in war eighteen of the last thirty years makes us question the policies of our present government. We ask ourselves, "Where did our youthful intentions and dreams go when we reached the age of 'maturity'? Well, we college students of the 1920's were sold on the League of Nations. It was the golden peace dream of President Woodrow Wilson, but because of politics the U.S. Senate did not ratify it. In New York City (*Index*, January 8, 1920) an organization was polling college students all over the country on their feelings regarding the League of Nations. "Kalamazoo College students will discuss the question at 7:30 p.m. Friday evening in Bowen Hall, and every member of the student body should be present as the matter is one of vital importance to all," stated the *Index*. One week later the January 15, 1920, *Index* came out and announced: "Students vote on League of Nations: favor immediate ratification of the treaty by the United States Senate. Brought out by discussions at the meeting at Bowen Hall, Friday evening with Dr. Stetson presiding the consensus of opinion seems to be in favor of the immediate ratification." Students all over the country were voting on the League of Nations idea.

Although so many young people are reared to attend church and Sunday school, when it comes to the true test of the youngsters who leave home for college or work, it sometimes becomes a habit to forget about the religious aspects of one's training. That was not true in my religious life. Monroe, studying for the Methodist ministry, centered his religious activities at the Simpson Methodist Church in Kalamazoo. He taught a Sunday school class for several college years and was a very active member at Simpson. While I went to Simpson now and then during my freshman year, I did not make it my church home. I had heard of a Normal College professor's student Sunday school class at the First Methodist in Kalamazoo and thought I would visit it to determine if I would enjoy making the First Methodist my church home. Visiting the class, I found that there were about one hundred students attending, most from the Normal College. The teacher of the class was most inspiring, and he greatly impressed me. I decided that the First Methodist would be my church home while I was in Kalamazoo.

I have never forgotten some of the truisms that the Sunday schoolteacher left with us. While I cannot remember his name nor what he taught at Normal College, I'll never forget some of the things he said. It was after my feat in cross-country running that the teacher of the class said one Sunday, "We should elect a president of the class, a secretary and a treasurer." The very next Sunday someone nominated me for president. The class teacher called me to the front, introduced me to the class members, and remarked, "If you give Harold Wilcox a 300-yard head start, there isn't a man in Michigan who could catch him!" That did it. I was elected president of the class. The February 12, 1920, edition of the *Index* had the following in its Campus Column: "Harold Wilcox has been elected president of the large student class No. 20 of First Methodist Church." As I look back on this honor I now realize it helped renew my confidence, which I greatly needed after the jolt I had received at the end of the first semester. Also, I became acquainted with a large number of Normal College students whom I never would have known had I not been a member of that class. Not only did I attend and remain active in the Sunday school class, but I also became a member of the Youth Fellowship Group, then called the Epworth League.

Basketball takes the limelight as a winter sport; it did in the 1920's and still does in the 1970's. After winning the M.I.A.A. championship in 1919 the followers of old Kalamazoo were looking forward to a repeat season in 1920. Coach Ralph Young had built a strong schedule of nineteen games, including games with the University of Michigan, Michigan Agricultural College (now M.S.U.), Notre Dame, and the University of Valparaiso. A great deal was expected of our varsity, but we suffered a big letdown as game after game was played and the loss column grew bigger and bigger. As the 1920 *Boiling Pot* (yearbook) states, "The basketball season was a peculiar one for Kalamazoo. No Orange and Black quintet ever faced a harder schedule, and considering the long list of incapacities on the part of the players, no team ever put up a gamer, more characteristic Kalamazoo fight. How well the season's record testified to this! Seven losses in nine games then ten consecutive wins, including two over Valparaiso, one over Hope and a glorious victory over Hillsdale with the M.I.A.A. flag at stake." And how well I remember the Hillsdale game! They had clobbered Kalamazoo in our game with them at Hillsdale, 36–12, and came to Kalamazoo expecting to win again without too much trouble. On the day of the game the emotional tension was so great on the campus you could almost cut it with a knife. No matter where you went the conversation was the same: "Beat Hillsdale!"

Dad came down on the evening train from Gobles to see the game. As the carefree jovial man that he was, he borrowed a trumpet, joined the band, and blew the bell right off it, so to speak, as only he could do. He had a cast-iron lip, as described in musical circles. The February 16, 1920, *Index* describes the game as follows: "The much touted Hillsdale aggregation which defeated the University of Detroit last week met defeat at the hands of the fighting Kalamazoo's 18 – 17 last Monday night in a game that was full of thrills from start to finish." This game completely upset the basketball hope of the state as Hillsdale, the only team in Michigan to defeat the University of Detroit, claimed the state championship. And wow! Monday night we beat Hillsdale and won the M.I.A.A. flag! A repeated victory over Alma and Albion and the flag was ours by precedent. Kalamazoo did defeat Alma and Albion to retain the championship. After staying overnight in our dorm room, Dad took the 7:45 a.m. train back to Gobles, a happy man after having participated in college life!

One might ask the question, "How do all those low-scoring games of the 1920's compare to the high scores reached in games of the 1970's?" Well, basketball rules were different than they are today, and playing conditions are greatly different. First, the gyms were much smaller. In fact, the high school and college gyms of today were few and far between. The backboards (wood) and baskets were nailed against the two end walls of the large area that housed the basketball court. Some courts were only about forty feet long while others might be seventy feet long. In other words, the game was played in any area that would house the game regardless of size. The ball of yesteryear was much harder to handle. It was a leather casing with a rubber bladder inside. The bladder was blown up with a pump. A string was tied around the neck of the bladder to keep the air in. Then it would be tucked under the casing at the opening. The ball was laced up as tight as one could draw the leather laces. There was always a knob on the ball where it was laced of course. This made it more difficult to dribble and shoot, therefore you didn't have the accuracy in basket shooting that players have today. Guarding a man really close was allowed by the rules. You could block a shot from behind without fouling, which made it difficult to get an accurate shot away. All foul shots were generally taken by the best foul shooter on the team, and because of the irregular shape and balance of the ball it was unusual for the team to convert as many as sixty percent of foul shots. For a boy to shoot overhand or by one-hand push shot as they do today was considered showing off.

Other activities in which I participated in the spring of 1920 included interclass basketball. I played forward on the sophomore team, and it was lots of fun. The sophomore team was leading the class league, and it looked as though we had the college class championship in the palm of our hands. We defeated the freshmen by the score of 11-10 in overtime. The sophomore team made only two field goals during the game, and I made one of them. Says the *Index*, "Inability to throw free throws caused the downfall of the first year men for they made but two baskets in twenty changes while the sophomores caged even free throws in twelve changes. The play was fast throughout. Close guarding by Doyle and Leaned accounted for the low score of the sophomores, the second year men making only two field goals." We had only the juniors to beat, whom we had beaten before, to clinch the championship, but the juniors beat us by a 12-6 score. Says the *Index* of March 18, 1920, "Friday evening the juniors sprung a surprise on the sophomores by defeating them 12-6. The game was slow and was featured by the inability of the sophomores to get excited when given an easy chance to score. The game was one of the cleanest of the inter-class contests played this year. In the playoff the following Monday night the juniors again defeated the sophomores 13-11 making only three field goals to five for the juniors."

"Sherwood Hall, last Wednesday evening, was the scene of one of the most interesting and inspirational meetings held this year. The meeting, after the reading of the last minutes, was conducted by Harold Wilcox as chairman." (Index 3/18/20)

"Baseball squad looks good. Twelve vets out for track," were the headlines of the *Index* of March 25, 1920, which featured the picture and roster of the M.I.A.A. championship basketball team. It's interesting to note that in a basketball squad of sixteen men, only three were six feet tall and only one was as tall as six feet two inches. The best guard on the team, a fast dribbler and a good shot, was only five feet seven and one-half inches in height and weighed only 147 pounds. Kalamazoo shot only 86 foul goals out of 193 chances. Our opponents shot only 84 foul goals out of 163 chances. From the view of 1970 basketball, this would be considered very poor foul shooting for a league championship team.

In the spring of 1920 two sports, baseball and track, took the campus limelight. The baseball team played fifteen games and was defeated only by Notre Dame there, by a 3-2 score on a rough cold day, and on another rough cold day Valparaiso University there, by 10-1. However, Kalamazoo evened the score with the latter, beating Valparaiso 13-2 on the Kalamazoo diamond. We won eleven straight M.I.A.A. games; the team led the association with a perfect percentage. Six of the varsity had a batting average of over three hundred for the fifteen games played.

The track team of 1920 was equally successful. It finished a good second in the State Inter-Collegiate meet held at M.A.C., and it won the annual track and field meet of the M.I.A.A. held at Albion by a top-heavy score. Dual meets held with Ypsilanti, Hope, and Hillsdale resulted in the Orange and Black men being victorious by a large majority of points. Further evidence that the team was extraordinary is that many of the college records were broken. Nine of the old marks were replaced by new records by this year's team members. I broke one of these nine records in the two mile, for I was allowed to compete in the interclass meet.

As the spring days grew longer and the sun warmer, we were reminded that the college year was drawing to a close. That meant a summer job had to be located, and fortunately Mr. Allcock, as in the previous summer, needed a barber in his shop. I had my summer job and could again live in the dorm, room 46, without paying rent. Examinations over, I was pleased that I had proven to myself and to all others that by applying myself I could do college work. I knew now that I could graduate with a college degree and that my track experience could continue during my junior year.

The June 17, 1920, *Index* reported in the Campus Column: "Cheney, Markillie, two Wilcoxes and lady friends had a picnic at Gull Lake last week." This was our farewell to campus life for the 1919-1920 college year. With commencement over I went home to Gobles for a few days before returning to Kalamazoo to work during the summer. It was a warm one. Business was pretty good, and having had the barbering experience of the previous summer it was much more enjoyable. I can remember the first young lady's hair I cut. For the first time women were wearing their hair bobbed short with bangs in front. This custom, we were told, grew out of Germany when, during World War I, the women cut their hair to give to the government. It was used in the military program. Here in this country women adopted the short hair custom just for a change. Many older women frowned on the short hair, believing that it made a woman's appearance unfeminine, but it wasn't too many years before short hair became the accepted custom of young and old. I can still hear my mother strongly voice her opinion: "No sir, no daughter of mine will have her hair cut!" But it was only a couple of years before I found that mother was wearing short hair too.

I had my first young lady customer in my chair. By working slowly on my previous customer, I had tried to avoid getting her, hoping one of the other three barbers would call, "Next" before my turn came. No luck! So I started in on the redhead. It was the style to cut the length to the lower tip of the ears, and then bang the front to about half an inch above the eyes. The hardest part of her hair job was getting the back rounded to conform to the sides. I probably took twice as much time with her hair as I did with a man's haircut. After taking a little more off here and little off there, and looking over to the barber next to me for any suggestive glances— which I did not get—I showed her the back by using a hand mirror. She said it looked good and that she was satisfied. I took off the apron and breathed a sigh of relief! After working hours I asked my barber friend, who was much older and experienced than I, what he thought of my first woman's haircut. He said he thought I did a pretty good job. That made me feel good! I was now ready to tackle any future job that might present itself.

My summer evenings were spent in a more-or-less carefree way. There were several men staying in the dorm over the summer, and I did not want for companionship. A movie once or twice a week, a jog for a few miles on the track for exercise and leg-muscle building, and home on Sundays was generally my summer routine. To conserve my pocketbook, I would often eat my breakfast in my room, consisting of dry cereal and doughnuts. Then I would eat a good meal after work at one of the downtown restaurants. Our shop hours were from 8:00 a.m. to 6:00 p.m.

As the hot month of August 1920 came and passed, Labor Day found me in Gobles taking a couple weeks off before returning to the campus life. Monroe had barbered for Dad during the summer. Leland was working in the New York Central Railroad baggage room in Kalamazoo, a job he held the rest of his working life. Allen had quit high school just a few weeks before he was to have graduated and had gone to Kalamazoo to work. That left just Whyle and Paul at home to learn the barber trade while working for and with Dad. Of course the two youngest of a family of eight children, Abbie and Donita, were still at home and in school. Dad turned the shop bathroom into a "beauty parlor," and before they were through school both my sisters learned hairdressing for women. This trade undoubtedly was one that grew out of the fad of women's short hair. "Abba-Dona" was the name of the parlor.

I went back to the campus a few days early for several reasons. First, during my working life I never have been a fellow who liked to sit around doing nothing for a long period of time. Being busy doing something had always been a lifelong habit. Then too, I wanted to line up a furnace job for the year. The college is located in the western part of Kalamazoo. There were well-to-do people living within a few blocks of the college. Practically all homes had coal-burning furnaces. Some of these families would pay a college boy about two dollars and fifty cents or three dollars a week to have the furnace cared for. The job would mean that about 6:00 a.m. you would go to the home with your rear-door basement key, enter, shake down the furnace grate, shovel out the ashes, open up the draft and load it up with coal. In an hour's time the fire was hot and the house was warm for the family. If it had snowed during the night I got my morning exercise by cleaning the walks. Several fellows had at least one furnace job, and if one of us wanted a weekend off there was always someone to take over for you.

Two or three days before registration of classes the students started coming back to the campus. It was always interesting to meet them and say, "Hello, Joe, did you have a good summer?" The gang would gather in the evening in the reception hall of the dorm and talk over summer experiences. It was always characteristic of me to want to be early. If I was taking a train or flight I wanted to be at the station or port in plenty of time to analyze the situation, so at the beginning of my junior year I was on campus in old room number 46 a couple days before the initial registration began. Because of this early arrival, I had an evening with nothing to do, and that evening was the beginning of a relation that affected the next five years of my life.

Harold Dressel, my co-worker in the Ladies Dining Hall, said to me, "Harold, we have a lady-friend from South Haven, my home town, who spent one year at M.A.C. and is transferring to Kalamazoo. She doesn't know anyone on campus except my sister Evelyn and me. Why don't you take her out tonight and help her get acquainted?" So he took me to Ladies Hall dorm and introduced me to Ruth Flory, and that introduction was the beginning of a companionship that lasted for five years, at the end of which we decided we just were not meant for each other.

It wasn't too long after classes started that Coach Ralph Young approached me about running cross-country and helping him create an interest in this sport on campus. I had already made up my mind that my goal this junior year was to maintain a satisfactory academic standard and not to try to be a state champion cross-country runner. I explained my position to him. Monroe and I were cutting hair in our room, I had my furnace job to make some extra spending money, and I was carrying a little heavier classroom load to make up for the previous year's deficit, so I told the coach I would have to bypass fall sports.

The first *Index* of September 16, 1920, announced in bold type: "1920 Football Team Looks Like Champions." The article continued: "Football prospects have never been as right for Kalamazoo as they are this fall. Every regular from last year's team, with the exception of Captain Stromie, is back. ... This is Kalamazoo's best year. The schedule is the best ever. So is the desire to win!" The schedule included games with M.A.C., Notre Dame, and Washington and Jefferson University, which was a power in the east in the 1920's. All before Kalamazoo would start playing the M.I.A.A. teams! It was Coach Young's theory that if a small college could beat a big university, it gave the school a national name. During these years it was the custom and policy of universities to open their football schedules with one or two "practice games" with small colleges before tackling teams of their own class. When little Centre College of the south went down to Cambridge, Massachusetts and defeated mighty Harvard that bright Saturday afternoon in October 1920, Centre College became the talk of all sportswriters in the nation. Coach Young had that goal as his aim in fall 1920.

The season's first game was a tremendous success as the September 30 *Index* screamed in headlines: "Kalamazoo Overwhelms Aggy [Michigan Agricultural College, currently MSU] eleven with a superior attack. College triumphs by a score of 21-2 Saturday." To beat M.A.C. by such a big score was a great feat for the college, and now the game ahead with Notre Dame was on everyone's tongue. Kalamazoo had held Rockne's western champions to a 14-0 score, their lowest of the season last year, and our team's victory over M.A.C. had generated great enthusiasm on the campus. An upset victory at South Bend, Indiana, was in the making, so it appeared at the moment!

The South Bend newspaper stated: "When Gipp and Bahan, stellar members of the 1919 backfield, were declared ineligible by the university faculty a few days ago gridiron stock on the local campus sank to a moody depth." This news, although false since Gipp did play, also had the tendency to boost the stock of the Orange and Black. The *Index* continued with spots in bold type: "After we get back from Notre Dame, Centre College won't be in it," and "If you want to see the game of the season, go to Notre Dame Saturday." Well, I went to Notre Dame Saturday, my first trip out of Michigan, and came home with a long face – Notre Dame 40, Kalamazoo 0!

Before we members of the student body could collect the pieces and buoy our spirits we had another shocker that really hurt because it spelled the end of the greatest team in Kalamazoo history. It seems that a large number of football team veterans had reported to the college a week before registration. They got a few footballs from the gym and took off to Crocked Lake on a week's outing and fellowship. They exercised, threw the footballs around, and worked on condition, but without coaching or college sanction. When some outside source informed the M.I.A.A. Board about it, the board labeled it "a football training camp" and made all the participants ineligible for all M.I.A.A. games. Coach Young then started the plan of two football teams. The one minus the ineligibles would play M.I.A.A. games and the other one, including the ineligibles, would play the non-M.I.A.A. schedule. The Orange and Black got by all M.I.A.A. teams until we came to the last big one of the season, which was Albion 35 – Kalamazoo 7. Olivet, Hillsdale, Hope, and Alma were all clobbered with shutouts. The 1921 yearbook *The Boiling Pot* summed it up as follows: "The football season was a peculiar combination of disappointments and surprises. The first blow came when the M.I.A.A. Board made the majority of the first team ineligible. Despite the handicap, however, the season was very successful, losing only three games."

Of course, freshmen get a great deal of attention each fall, and at Kalamazoo there were no exceptions. The first published *Index* of the new college year had a front page headline: "Freshmen, Attention!" The article read: "Freshmen – open your ears, and then lend them to us. If present plans materialize, and it seems probable they will, the time-honored Freshmen initiation method is due for a change:" Then the article continued on with what the Student Senate had in mind. The same issue of the *Index* listed "Don'ts For Freshmen!" including "Don't be fresh for Mirror Lake has just been deepened, and baths are free at all times. Don't call the faculty by their first names to their faces. Don't buy any chapel tickets on which the war tax has not been paid, as by doing so you will be laying yourself liable to Federal prosecution. Don't wear your high school letter around; the big orange "K" is king on this campus, and all others are persona non grata. Don't forget to put a minimum of 10 minutes study on each course."

The November 11, 1920, *Index* came out with an article headed, "Men's Societies Adopt New Rushing Plan." The article set up the rules to give each organization a fair opportunity to invite new members to join their society and also to give new men the opportunity to decide for themselves which society they would join. It was signed by Harold B. Allen, President, Century; Monroe J. Wilcox, President, Philo, Maurice D. Armstrong, President, Sherwood

In fall 1920 the college had a cross-country team for the first time. While I had my mind made up to not run in the fall, Coach asked me to take over the training of the team, which was made up of all freshmen. There were the same two meets that I had won the previous year. At first Coach Young thought I would be eligible to represent the college in these fall meets, but a ruling of the faculty resulted in my ineligibility extending over two semesters. I took four freshmen to East Lansing for the meet. Says the November 18, 1920, *Index*: "With only four men on their team to compete with five other teams, Kalamazoo vowed that her fighting spirit would last to the end." University of Michigan had six runners in the race, while M.A.C., Alma, Albion, Detroit, and Hope all had five each. Kalamazoo's first runner came in fourteenth place. Says that same *Index*: "If Wilcox had not been ineligible we would have shown them all up. He will not be able to represent us at Grand Rapids Thanksgiving Day." Because of the inexperience of the freshmen team I did not take them to Grand Rapids.

The fall semester always brought many entertaining functions, including literary societies, athletic banquets, and other social groups. The fall of 1920 was not an exception. One of the first that I participated in was the Sherwood host to the men of 1924. Entertaining them with literary programs, refreshments, and an informal finale, the sixty-ninth annual opening meeting in Sherwood Hall was well attended and a great success. President Maurice Armstrong, following devotions and roll call, told the men that it was to be action and not just words that would express to them the true purpose of Sherwood. A program followed consisting of a debate between Harold Hawley and Marston Blach on "Resolved, that the President of the United States should be nominated and elected by popular vote," (it seems we have been hearing a lot about that political question in the 1970's), and a cornet solo by Harold Carlyon assisted by Clifton Perry's violin and Bradford Morse at the piano. Then Wilbur Permelts read that old blood-tingling "The Shooting of Dan McGrew." Of the class of 1924, the Sherwoods got twenty-one fine young men, three more than the Centurys, which was second in numbers.

Being president of the Sunday school class at First Methodist Church enabled me to meet a number of Western Michigan College girls and boys. One, Dorothy Crawford, was one of my lady companions during this fall term. We had enjoyable times at our Sunday school class parties and went to the theatre several times. But by the end of the football season Ruth Flory had become my girlfriend, and from then on we were seen together at the many college functions. It was the football banquet, the Messiah at the Kalamazoo Armory, the Euro and Sherwood parties (she was a Euro), Goblite activities, church functions, debates, Glee Club concerts—we were always found together. Two outstanding stage plays we saw at the Regent Theatre were *Nothing But the Truth* and *Pollyanna*.

One of the questions debated in college circles in the early 1920's was "Resolved, that Japanese Immigration into the United States Should be Prohibited."

The November 25, 1920, *Index* came out with a full-column editorial written by a student named Charles Linihan, titled "A Great Statesman Passes." "With the incoming administration the world will witness the passing of a great statesman," said the editorialist. It continued, "Woodrow Wilson, a man who has suffered many wrong, yet has shown no malice, suffered serious afflictions yet has not cried out, been given tremendous responsibility and has not shirked it, stands today as one of the greatest men this country has ever produced. When elected to the highest office in the gift of the American people eight years ago, Woodrow Wilson was a young man, spry of step and erect of carriage. He was the picture of health and happiness. Today, as he sits in his chair in the White House waiting for the call when he will be mustered out of service, our President presents a pathetic figure. The light is gone from his eyes, his face is haggard and wrinkled. We greet you, our President! The world has been made better for your having been in it. Your best years have been given to us, and may we have the grace to appreciate it!" So says a student at Kalamazoo College who was fond of the president, who died within two years after he left office. Fifty years later, history has yet to record the true value of the Wilson Administration, or has it?

Vacation, looked forward to by most students, was one of work for Monroe and me. The Sutherland Paper Mill Company in Kalamazoo was putting up a new building. A former Kalamazoo College man was foreman of the construction, and he sent a notice to the college that if there were men who wanted to work during vacation he would give them a job. Of course, Monroe and I and several others were in the group who went out to make that extra green stuff. It was a pick and shovel job. It wasn't too cold, so we were not bothered with the outside conditions. We got paid by the hour. We started working at 8:00 a.m. and threw down our shovels at twelve noon. After lunch it was back to work at 1:00 p.m. until five o'clock. We were not used to such hard manual labor, but fortunately our boss was not very demanding nor did he do much checking on us. Monroe pulled a muscle in his back shoveling and had to go to the doctor. My opinion was that the boss was just helping some Kalamazoo College men finance their education!

When I stop to analyze the number of different jobs I had during my college days, it's amazing what we can do if we set our minds to it. In referring to one's working years the remark is often made that some people are educated in the college of hard knocks! Well, I have never had anything handed to me on a silver platter, nor have I ever had anyone put a gold spoon in my mouth. However, I did learn early in life that hard work never hurts anyone, and I have had that axiom as a guide to my living.

The fall semester exams over, I anxiously waited for the student report to be ready at the dean's office. I felt that I had had a good academic fall semester and wanted to vindicate my poor showing of the previous year. I was really happy with the report, which showed I had two B's and three C's in seventeen hours of work. This included a C in French III, which was my least desired course. Now I could again walk the campus with a smile on my face, knowing that when spring came I would be out on the cinder path preparing for a good track season.

Coach Young had seventeen fine potential basketball stars on the 1920-21 squad, and they carried the high hopes for a great season. Kalamazoo opened with a game at Ann Arbor with the University of Michigan and came home on the losing end of a 44-32 score. M.A.C. won the game at East Lansing by a score of 30-18. At the close of the season, the college team had played twenty-seven games with a record of eighteen wins and nine losses. This could not be considered too bad when the type of competition is considered. The 1920-21 *Boiling Pot* had this say about the basketball season: "The Kalamazoo College Basketball team pushed its 1920 world's record for consecutive victories a notch higher when it again finished at the top of the M.I.A.A. in 1921. This makes the eighth consecutive year that the varsity has finished at the top of the Michigan Intercollegiate, the largest squad in the history of the school turned out for the court game, another fact that points to Kalamazoo's superiority is that out of five selections for the mythical all M.I.A.A. team, three Kalamazoo men were chosen by all five of the coaches making the selections." This closed the basketball season of my junior year at Kalamazoo.

One of the most stirring and inspirational talks during my junior year was given by the president of the University of Michigan, Dr. Marion M. Burton. He stated, "There are two ways of living; drifting and planning." I asked myself if I was one of the former groups, or was I living up to a plan? Dr. Burton went on to say that the United States amounts to something because of our ideals. "We plan, other countries do not." He described the plight of China with a population of 400,000,000 whose people are starving, all because China had never learned to use her resources. She had never learned to follow a plan. "We, as America's younger generation, must develop the capacity to think, must learn to solve America's problems." In 1970 I ask myself if the succeeding generations have taken the advice and philosophy of Dr. Burton and achieved the American Dream.

"Junior Frolic Monday Night," reported the February 17, 1921 *Index*: "Several star performers on class of 1922 program of June." The article continues: "Everyone knew that 'Cocky' was an athlete but he was never before seen to balance gracefully on a cushioned broomstick and remove handkerchiefs from the knobs of the chair placed in front of him with the point of the umbrella he wielded. He couldn't tell you how he managed to do it himself. Prof. Roope made a graceful imitation of said 'Cocky' and even surpassed him in the speed with which he performed the stunt." Just an example of the good clean fun programs that we enjoyed!

"Sophomores and Juniors playing off tie," announced the *Index* of March 17, 1921. "The end of the inter-class basketball series resulted in two ties: the Freshmen and the Seniors running even for the tail position. The Sophomores and Juniors tied for first. The coming Wednesday is planned to stage a post season contest to decide the college class championship. ... "The Juniors took rather a slump when they suffered a 20-13 defeat by the Seniors. Perry and Casteel played for the losers, and Cutting and Wilcox made two baskets each." The Juniors didn't win the championship!

March 1921 arrived with several weeks of fairly warm weather and the track, baseball, and tennis candidates started working out. Both Monroe and I were anxious to get started. This was Monroe's fourth season in track, and while he didn't leave college with any records after his name, he proved to be a fine athlete at Kalamazoo, as stated to me by Coach Young the following year. Monroe ran the 440-yard dash and the 880-yard run. He could always be depended on to give the college some first and second places in these events. Monroe was also a very valuable man on the college mile relay team, which won the M.I.A.A. the three years that it was held, due to the war. The track schedule for 1921 was as follows: April 30 – Ypsilanti Teachers at Kalamazoo; May 7 – Interscholastic meet at Kalamazoo; May 14 – Detroit Junior College at Detroit; May 21 – Albion at Kalamazoo; May 28 – State Meet at East Lansing; June 3 and 4 - M.I.A.A. Meet at Albion.

"Kalamazoo Track Team Overwhelms Squad From Ypsilanti," headlined the *Index* for May 5, 1921. "Although the weather conditions were somewhat unfavorable, two records were broken. 'Cocky' Wilcox lowered his last year's college record for the two mile from 10:41:1 to 10:38:3." The *MLive Kalamazoo Gazette's* article on the meet read: "Due to a strong wind and the earliness of the season no records were hung up in the short runs. In the Two Mile Run, Harold Wilcox broke the college record which he set last year. Both the Mile and Two Mile runs were finished in the same order, Harold Wilcox, Osborn and Peterson. Monroe finished second to Petschulat of Kalamazoo, and won the 880 yard run in the good early season time of 2:07:1." Monroe also ran anchor position on the winning relay team.

The following Saturday found two hundred and four track and field men from all around the state high schools participating in the annual interscholastic track and field meet. Monroe and I were officials for the meet with Captain Frog Thompson as referee and starter. The smashing of seven meet records and the tying of another marked the biggest and probably the most successful interscholastic track and field meet ever held at Kalamazoo College. The boys performed under ideal weather conditions, which is always advantageous to record breaking.

The following Saturday we boarded the New York Central train for Detroit. Our meet with the Detroit Junior College (now Wayne State University) was held to dedicate a new track and athletic field at Belle Isle, which is still in use in 1970. Says the *MLive Kalamazoo Gazette*: "The new track at Belle Isle was very soft making fast time impossible. The Kalamazoo's track team made a very poor showing in the field events but showed strength in the runs, winning first, second and third in the mile and two mile run." The record shows that I got a third in the mile run and a second in the two-mile run.

It was the policy at Kalamazoo that a man had to win a first place in a dual meet or place in the state or M.I.A.A. meets to win his "K." I wanted to see Osborn and Forman qualify for their "K," and since the mile and the two-mile runs were not very competitive, we three decided that Forman should win the mile and Osborn the two mile unless, on the last lap, it was evident that a Detroit boy was pressing. If he was then I was to do battle. When we came to the middle of the backstretch we three from Kalamazoo had our own way, so it resulted as we had planned. I don't believe that Coach Young had any inclination of what was going on during the races until we revealed the plan to him afterward. I am not sure that he appreciated it being done that way!

Monroe won the 440-yard dash handily and was second in the 880-yard run, which was won by a Kalamazoo man. The meet was close, and Kalamazoo was behind in the scoring 62 to Detroit's 64 until the last race, which put the final results of the meet in the hands of our relay team members who came through like true champions. Kalamazoo's team, with Monroe holding down the anchor position, won by twenty yards, and the meet score was 67-64.

A conversation took place near the finish line that I never forgot. A gentleman track enthusiast stood near the finish line, and as I finished the two-mile run, which was the last race of the meet except the relay, he approached me and said, "Say, Wilcox, how can you stand it to run the 440, 880, mile and two mile and relay and not be completely exhausted?" I replied, "I don't run them all. My brother is on the track team too, and I only run the mile and two mile." Monroe and I have always closely resembled each other, resulting in many people taking us for twins. The track enthusiast couldn't distinguish us as two persons.

One of the spectators who witnessed the meet was a Kalamazoo alumnus, Charles Brake. Chuck had graduated in the class of 1920 and was working in Detroit and living at the YMCA. After the meet he asked me if I would care to stay overnight with him, take in a show, etc., and go back to Kalamazoo on Sunday! Coach Young said it would be OK. So I spent my first night in Detroit, little realizing that it was only the beginning of a lifetime of visits since Ferndale is a suburban community on the north side of Detroit. Knowing I had little money, Charlie made it clear that he would foot the bills if I would stay. I greatly appreciated his hospitality. It helped to make it a very enjoyable ride on the train that Sunday afternoon as we speeded back to Kalamazoo. During my long venture in Ferndale, I had the privilege of renewing my acquaintance with Charles Brake, who lived in and around Detroit most of his life.

The college authorities and friends were talking expansion. Dr. Frank B. Bachelor was hired as business manager, and one of his duties was to initiate and lead a campaign for money raising. There was a great need for a new ladies dormitory, a library building (the library was housed in Bowen Hall), a new classroom building, a science building, and several others that were the dream of the college Board of Trustees. During the week of May 18, 1921, the *MLive Kalamazoo Gazette* had an article "Exchange Club Has Luncheon. Plans for raising a sum of money to improve and greatly enlarge Kalamazoo College were broached to the Exchange Club at a noon luncheon in Bowen Hall Monday by Frank B. Bachelor, head of the Extension Department of Kalamazoo College." The article went on to say, "The campaign to raise the funds to carry out these plans will be started in the immediate future. The opening address of welcome was given by President Stetson of the college. An excellent luncheon was served by the Eurodelphian girls of the college. Music was furnished by an orchestra under the direction of Harry Lenox and also by the sextet of the college Gaynor Club." Reading about this Exchange luncheon became of interest to me as April 1971 completed my forty-fifth year in the Ferndale Exchange Club. The Kalamazoo Club of about one hundred members has always been one of the leaders of Exchange in Michigan. I have attended many Exchange conventions, some in Kalamazoo, and have heard of the many fine accomplishments and activities of the wide-awake men of the Kalamazoo Exchange Club. Now, in 1971, the dream of the Kalamazoo College Board of Trustees has become a complete reality. It is a college of fifteen hundred students, and not a single building has been left standing that housed my college education.

Our last dual meet before the two big ones, the Intercollegiate at M.A.C. and the M.I.A.A. at Albion, was with Albion College at Kalamazoo. We had expected to find the Albion team much more competitive than what the finals in the meet showed. The Albion report of the meet was as follows: "Yesterday was a sad one for Coach Ike Field's Albion track team. The Methodist cinder men were completely out-classed and never had a chance to even make things interesting. Judging by the showing made against Albion and Ypsilanti, the Kalamazoo tracksters are due to repeat at Albion in a couple weeks when all the M.I.A.A. Schools get together and find out most exactly who is the best in every line of sports. 'Cocky' Wilcox set out after the college record in the two mile run and succeeded in his attempt, lowering the mark to 10:20:2. The doughty little distance runner simply ran away from his competitors and finished more than a hundred and fifty yards ahead of his nearest rival." The Sunday edition of the *MLive Kalamazoo Gazette* had this to say about the meet: "Kalamazoo College out pointed and out classed the much vaunted Albion track team yesterday afternoon by a score of 100 3/6 to 30 3/6 in the last local track meet of the season on the college field, Harold Wilcox's record run against time in the two mile was a feature of the afternoon. 'Cocky' took the lead from the start and led the field by from an eighth to a quarter of a lap throughout the distance. By the sixth lap all the Albion distance men had dropped out, including their much heralded equaler of Addington's record. With the final sprint Wilcox crossed the line with the watches at 10:23. The winner of the 440 yard dash, Monroe Wilcox, stumbled at the finish and took a nasty fall on the cinders but not till he had broken the tape." Monroe also ran and placed second behind a Kalamazoo man, Ray Forman, in the 880 yard run. Monroe also held down the anchor position on the winning relay team.

It was a great day for the Wilcox brothers, and we were now looking forward to the big one at East Lansing. It was beautiful sunshine weather the following week, just the kind that made running for practice on the cinders a pleasure. During a lull in our training that week Monroe and I stood chatting when he said to me, "Harold, I have two more track meets to run in, and then my athletic career is over. You have a whole year ahead of you. Enjoy it and make the best of it for once it is over it's over forever!" That bit of philosophy has been with me all these years. There have been times of unpleasantness when I would say to myself, "Enjoy yourself, for once it's over it's gone forever!"

The big Saturday came and found us at the M.A.C. at East Lansing for a meet with the cream of Michigan track and field teams. It was a warm day, but not too hot for the participants. The meet started in the a.m. with preliminaries in the dashes, hurdles, and some of the field events. During our lunch hour of soft-boiled eggs, toast, and milk, I found out that Thurston, the M.A.C. two miler, was expected to win the race. He had done around ten minutes and was expected to do that in this meet. That time was a good twenty seconds better than I had made. However, all the two-mile races I had run were in meets where I had no competition. In all the meets it was expected that I would just take the lead and hold it by setting the pace in all the meets.

With Thurston the man to beat, I made up my mind that I would hang back in the pack for the first lap, then when Thurston stepped out and took the lead I would try to keep pace with him as long as I could. As the race progressed it developed into a two-man race, Thurston setting the pace and I on his tail trying to keep up. To my and everyone else's surprise, I was hanging in there at the gun for the last lap. Every time we would pass the finish line (four laps to the mile) the crowd, largely M.A.C., would cheer Thurston on, but my teammates, with Monroe in front, were giving me words of encouragement such as, "Hang in there, Cocky! Stay with him. Don't give up!" When the gun went off for the final lap, Thurston gave a little burst of speed that carried him about five or six yards out in front. Then he seemed to continue a pace I was able to follow. On the backstretch I could see I was gaining on him, and by the time we reached the last curve I was going stride for stride. Then I cut loose with a sprint for the last seventy-five yards and went by him. He offered no opposition, and then I knew I had him. Going across the finish line, the crowd gave me a big hand. When the time of 9:57:3/5 was announced as a new Michigan Collegiate Record, there was more applause. I had visited M.A.C. twice, once in cross-country and now in the two mile, and had won both races. This was the second big moment of my track career. I had one more left, the last race of my Kalamazoo College days.

The newspaper on Sunday, May 28, 1921, came out with an article headed: "Ags Capture Meet: Kalamazoo's Runners Up." It continued, "The Aggies piled up 59 points which Kalamazoo College was second with 33 markers. Quite the feature of the meet was 'Cocky' Wilcox's win over Thurston, Aggies two miler star who was generally conceded to win in the long distant event. Wilcox trailed about five yards behind Thurston until the last fifty yards when he cut loose with a spurt which put him in the lead. The Aggie tried his best to close up the gap, but the plucky Kalamazoo runner held his advantage and breasted the tape a winner, the time of 9:57:3, breaking the state record by 23 2/5 seconds."

Says the June 3, 1921, *Index*: "The most spectacular event of the whole meet occurred when 'Cocky' Wilcox shattered the record for the two mile. For seven strenuous laps Thurston of M.A.C. led the field at a strong pace but with 'Cocky' at his heels without falter. Finally, on the straight stretch of the last lap, Wilcox called on his last bit of strength and drew up foot by foot on the big Aggie runner, and then, with a spurt that drew tremendous applause from the tense spectators, he sprinted around the bend and over the finish line. A spontaneous shout arose when the caller announced the time of 9:57:3, twenty-three and two-fifths seconds less than the old record held by Addington of Albion." That summer when I was barbering at Owosso, Michigan, my brother Leland sent me a letter addressed to "Michigan State Champion Two Mile Runner, 321 North Washington Street, Owosso, Michigan."

The following Friday, June 3, 1921, found the track team, baseball squad, and tennis team heading for Albion for the annual M.I.A.A. games. We stayed again in the old Albion hotel next to the New York Central Railroad tracks, and as usual had the screeching of the trains as they thundered through Albion on their way to destinations. But we were young and it didn't bother us too much. Besides, the same rail tracks went by the Kalamazoo College campus so we were pretty much immune to all the noise that railroad trains can make.

After eating our soft-boiled eggs, toast, and milk or coffee, we went to the athletic field. To our surprise and disgust the dressing quarters assigned to Kalamazoo athletes were terrible. It was dirty, the showers had no hot water and the toilets were out of order! It seemed to us that although there were some traces of "war conditions" left in our society, the Albion Athletic Department as the host of the M.I.A.A. field day activities should have made an effort to clean up and fix up the place. But the situation didn't dampen our spirits.

There were some surprises and disappointments in the meet, although Kalamazoo won the meet very handily by a score of 59 5/6, Hillsdale 29, Ypsilanti 16 ½, Albion 12 ½, Alma 6 1/3, Adrian 0. This was the first meet that neither Wilcox brother scored a first. Monroe got second in the 440-yard dash in very fast time with Kirk of Hillsdale winning, and he scored second to Forman of Kalamazoo in the 880-yard run in real good time. To the surprise of everyone including myself, I was beaten in the two mile by Vreeland of Alma. Says the *MLive Kalamazoo Gazette*: "The two mile run was the surprise race of the day. 'Cocky' Wilcox, who stepped the distance in less than ten minutes last week, took the lead from the start and settled into an easy pace which seemed to be plenty fast enough to bring him home comfortably in the lead. At the start of the last lap, however, Vreeland of Alma stepped out in front with a remarkable burst of speed, and, in spite of the fact that Wilcox nearly doubled his speed, he was unable to overtake the flying Vreeland who fell across the finish line exhausted, a winner by several yards. It is doubtful if the Alma runner could accomplish the feat again, for Wilcox was comparatively fresh at the finish and had he known his man, could have set a much faster space from the beginning!"

This is just another example of being great one week and falling to defeat the next. I was also beginning to analyze how I could do my best running—taking the lead or running on the tail of the front runner. Too bad that I had to wait until the last race of my college career to prove to myself that I saved energy and ran best by trailing my opponent until the last 300 yards. This was my first defeat of the year, but I had already learned that there were other two milers in the state and none of them to be taken lightly!

The Sunday *MLive Kalamazoo Gazette* printed an article: "College Has Easy Picking in All Events. Athletic teams representing Kalamazoo College made a clean sweep of all events held in connection with the Annual Field Day Ceremonies at Albion yesterday. Baseball, track and tennis titles were won by the local Collegians, while an additional trophy was captured by the Kalamazoo relay team which won from the other M.I.A.A. entrants with ease. The relay, which was run just preceding the afternoon ballgame, was won by the Kalamazoo quartet composed of the Wilcox brothers, Coleman and Forman. Monroe Wilcox gave his brother, who ran second, a nice lead, and the younger brother more than made up for his defeat in the two mile."

The *Index* of June 10, 1921, had two items of interest to me. One, "Harold Wilcox set the college two mile record at 9:57:3, which is also the State Record." Then, looking ahead to the fall, the article continued, "Captain Harold Wilcox will have Forman, Osborn, Peterson, Glass, Seward, Davis, Waters, Travis, Littell and Lundy for his Cross Country Team next fall, and we want the State Cross Country Title!"

A few days after the college athletic season was officially over, Coach Young came to me with the information on the first annual meet of the National Collegiate Athletic Association. It was to be held in Chicago at Stagg Field, University of Chicago Saturday, June 18, 1921. He said that there were two of us whom he thought could make a good showing for the college. Ray Forman had set a new college mile record and was a sophomore with good potential, and Coach wanted the two of us to enter the meet. The coach said we would have to stay on campus for a week after the semester was officially over, and since he had duties to attend to we would have to make and live up to our own training schedule. I told Coach Young I would be pleased to be a participant in this first N.C.A.A. meet.

Examinations were over, and I was elated to see my academic records when I visited the dean's office to get my semester report: I had three B's and two C's in seventeen hours of classroom work. This was my best record, and I knew I could finish college in spite of the opinion my dear Dr. Praeger had of me as a student. Commencement was over, and Monroe had the A.B. degree conferred on him. I went home for the weekend. When it was noised around the village that I was going to go to Chicago to run, it seemed the whole town became inquisitive. Of course, my dad was pleased and it gave him a subject for conversation with his customers. barbershop

In the meantime the members of the track team had held an election for next year's captain, and I was elected. This made me captain of two teams for the 1921-22 athletic year. The *MLive Kalamazoo Gazette* ran my picture and the caption: "The New Captain." The two-column article stated in headlines, "Harold Wilcox elected Captain of Championship Track Team at College." In bold type it read, "Star Athlete who holds record in Cross Country and distant events will head bunch selected by Coach Young to annex further honors." The article read as follows, "Harold Wilcox of Gobleville, star cross country and distance runner, was elected Captain of the 1922 Kalamazoo College Track Team by members of this year's varsity squad. He has just completed his second year of running at Kalamazoo College and has made an enviable record for himself and the school. He has been a big factor in many past track meets and was one who could always be counted on to come through for at least one first place. Wilcox did not commence his track work until his junior year in Gobleville High School where he ran in a number of county meets. In all his high school meets he finished first in the quarter mile and half mile runs. He has just finished two years on the Kalamazoo track squad. During his first year he ran the half mile, the mile and was a member of the relay team. At M.A.C. in the State meet, he finished 4th in the mile, 3rd in the half mile, and the relay team finished second. In the M.I.A.A. Meet at Albion that year he beat runners from six colleges in the 880 yard run for first place. In the mile he won second, and the relay team won first. In the fall of 1919 he won the state Intercollegiate Cross Country run at both M.A.C. and at Grand Rapids. The best college men from all over the state, including the University, were present. It is no small honor to be the best cross country runner in the State. This spring Wilcox set a new State record when he stepped the distance in 9:57:3 which is remarkably fast time. He beat his old record of 10:41:3 which also stood as a State record. In the Ypsilanti meet he finished first in the mile, and in the Detroit junior meet he was not able to judge the strength of the wind so only finished third. He was also a member of the winning relay team at Albion. Saturday the new Captain will go to Chicago with two other Kalamazoo track men, Praeger and Forman, to compete in the Chicago National Intercollegiate meet." The *MLive Kalamazoo Gazette* was the local daily, and it was read by a large percentage of the Gobles residents, so they pretty well knew what the sons and daughters of the village were doing when they got their names and or pictures in the paper.

It was Friday, June 17, 1921, that Ray Forman, William Praeger, and I, along with Coach Young, boarded the New York Central train for Chicago. We stayed at the Chicago Y.M.C.A. hotel, which was right next to the elevated train tracks, and the trains rumbling past did not do my sleep any good.

Besides Forman and I had not stuck too closely to our training schedule during the week, and frankly I was tired and knew it. Coach Young had always encouraged me to step out and take the lead, which was all right when I had little or no competition. I was beginning to feel that I could run behind the leaders with less expenditure of energy.

At first sight Stagg Field, named after the great and famous Coach Stagg, was rather awesome. I had never run on such a large athletic field. The University of Chicago was a member of the Big Ten and under Coach Stagg was turning out good athletic teams, so I felt that it was a real privilege to be in the first N.C.A.A. track and field meet. I was more than anxious to make a good showing. However, I was disappointed with myself because I didn't use my head. Instead of hanging back and not trying to keep pace with the three leaders, I stepped out and took the lead for the first 300 yards. I ran the first mile under five minutes, which was several seconds too fast for me. The result was I did not have enough left for the last two hundred yards when three men went by me and I got sixth place, one place out of the medals since only the first five places counted. The race was won by Romig of Penn State in the time of 9:32. While Ray Forman ran a very good race in the mile, setting a new college record of 4:28:2/5, he suffered the same fate I did. There were several Kalamazoo College students who lived in or around Chicago, and some attended the meet. They had arranged a beach roast and invited me to be their guest. I stayed overnight with one of the fellows. The next morning I took the Lake Michigan steamboat from Chicago to Petoskey, then to South Haven, and then the train to Gobles where I stayed for a few days.

Summer work was now my main concern. I felt that I wanted to get away from Kalamazoo. Monroe had graduated and was making arrangements to enter Boston University School of Theology. I had to find myself a new roommate for old 46. One of the new students on the campus was Phil Vercoe of the class of 1924. He was the son of a Baptist minister in Flint and a brother of my friend Ruth Vercoe, a member of the class of 1922. Phil had joined the Sherwood, and he and I had become real friendly. I invited him to be my roommate for the 1921-22 school year in old 46. This taken care of, I could finally concentrate on summer work. The newspaper want ads always carried barber jobs, but the question was could anyone make any money since times were rather tough financially. President Harding said, "There was unemployment due to the change-over from a war economy to a peace economy." Phil told me there were a large number of barbershops in Flint, and he felt sure I could find a job there. He asked me to come to Flint and stay at his house for a few days while looking for a job and a place to live.

After spending a few days at my home, I took the train to Kalamazoo and the interurban car to Flint. Phil met me at the station. A day or so later I found a barber job in a barbershop pool hall. I had been reared in an atmosphere that taught that pool halls are the work of the devil, a place where rough elements of society hang out. I worked Friday and Saturday, asked for my pay, and left. The Friday night Flint paper had a want ad for a barber job in Owosso, about thirty miles from Flint. During my lunch hour on Saturday I called the Owosso shop and asked if the job was still open. It was, so I told the boss I would be over Monday morning on the bus from Flint, which arrived at 9:00 a.m. He said it was all right and that he would be looking for me. I found out later while talking with one of the barbers that the boss's "all right" didn't mean anything. He would have hired the first man that came in the shop to work, and that I was lucky I got there before someone else walked through the door asking for a job. That did not enhance my confidence in the boss. However, we got along beautifully all during the summer. It was a cut-rate shop with four barbers, including the boss. I made good money for the times. The boss was pleased with my work. I proved to be the fastest man at barbering he had ever had, and he had worked in shops in Detroit before coming to Owosso.

I got a room in a private home about four blocks from the shop. It was a cheap room, which fit my pocketbook. It had rather old and makeshift furniture. The room consisted of a lounge bed, a table and chair for writing purposes, and a bureau for my clothes. Of course, living out of a couple suitcases didn't demand too many drawers.

The barber in the shop whom I liked best was a man about forty years old. He had been a conductor on the interurban line. Since autos and buses were beginning to cut in heavily on passenger traffic, he saw, as he said, the handwriting on the wall. He decided to go into barbering. He had some interesting tales to tell about being a conductor on the interurban trains, as he called them. The other barber was a younger, short man of about twenty-eight. He was the one I worked next to. I was the number-four barber and worked on the end of the line. He was what we called in the barber business a "hacker"; most good barbers are "shavers." He was rather jealous of my ability to turn out more customers than he could.

I remember one Saturday when business was good and all four of us had one customer after another, I noticed that he was trying to race customers with me. He did his best to try to maintain my speed in shaving, but his hacking method not only slowed him down but also pulled at his customers and caused some of the men in his chair to complain to him to get a sharper razor. At the end of the day he told me, "You win. I tried to keep up with you, but I couldn't." I told him he should learn to shave the whiskers off instead of hacking them off and he would be able to barber faster. He didn't change, and he remained a not-so-good barber. Although business was good, I had to save every nickel I could. It would be my senior year and, from hearsay, I knew that the senior year was always more financially demanding. I didn't spend very much on entertainment or amusement. To go to a show was a rarity.

The summer of 1921 was about the most lonesome one I ever spent. If it hadn't been for being able to take a bus to Flint on two or three Sundays, go to church, and have dinner and companionship with the Vercoes, it would have been even more lonely. The bus left Owosso about 8:00 a.m. Sunday morning, getting to Flint in time for church. After the evening service I would take the late bus and get to Owosso about 10:30 p.m. This opportunity gave me something to look forward to periodically.

I hadn't been in Owosso very long before I got a letter from Coach Young stating he was going to mail me some college athletic stationery with names and addresses of some potential Kalamazoo athletes. He was asking me to write them a letter telling them about the college and particularly about the athletic department. He wanted me to make sure and tell them that we would be pleased to have them wearing the Orange and Black! A few days later the package arrived, and to my surprise, my name was on the letterhead twice stating that I was captain of the 1921 cross-country team and captain of the 1922 track team. The coach asked me to inquire about any good athlete who had graduated or who would be a high school senior. I visited the high school office to carry out his request.

The summer was well along when I received another letter from Coach Young. He explained that he needed a person to report to the campus a week early and work with him lining up jobs for incoming athletes. Would I want the job? I would get paid for the week's work, and after classes started I could continue on as an assistant trainer. He needed someone to rub down the football players after practice and after games. I wrote back and said that it sounded good and that I would like to have the job. I felt I was set for my senior year. I would continue cutting hair in old forty-six, serve ladies and men at Ladies Hall dining room, and try to keep up with my studies.

It was a hot August. The county fair was on. Whyle wrote me stating he would like to come to Owosso and spend a few days with me. He could take in the fair during the day while I was working, and we could chum around in the evening. That suited me just fine. He came on the interurban car. It was sure good to see someone from home, especially a member of the family. It being race and county fair week, business was good, and I made extra money during the week. Whyle brought me up to date on what was happening in Gobles and all the family news. He told me that my mother's sister, Aunt Abbie Odell, and her two married daughters, Winnie and Kitty, were coming to visit us in Gobles the latter part of August. I would be through with my job the Saturday night before Labor Day, and that would enable me to be in Gobles in time to see them before they went back to Minot, North Dakota where they lived. Aunt Abbie was my favorite aunt. Early in the 1900's her husband took out a government claim on a large (about 360 acres) ranch near Minot. They moved out to settle on the land, which was a provision of the government. Aunt Abbie had some hair-raising tales to tell when she and her daughters came to visit us, which was only every four or five years, so I was pleased to be able to get home in time to see them. The summer passed without further incidents, and since time heals all loneliness that last Saturday before Labor Day found me jubilant for I was going home to Gobles the next day.

Business was slacking off, and I rather think the other two barbers were glad I was leaving. During the summer the other shop in Owosso had cut their prices, which had forced my boss to trim his prices on haircuts and shaves, and it hurt the pocketbook. With one less barber the other two would be making more money. That last Saturday night before Labor Day found me collecting my final summer's pay, shaking hands with my fellow employees, and packing my two suitcases ready to take the interurban to Kalamazoo and then the train to Gobles. Sunday morning I was up early. I went to my favorite but cheap restaurant for my last Owosso breakfast, and, as the interurban car left the business section of the city, I had the feeling, "I am glad that one is over!" Home on the 6:30 p.m. train was a great feeling. Whyle was at the depot to meet me and carry one of my suitcases. It was an enjoyable event to sit around the house visiting and hearing what everyone had been doing all summer. Monroe had gone to Boston early to find barbering and restaurant jobs and to get located in Boston University School of Theology. He was to spend three years there to complete his studies, which would qualify him for the degree of Bachelor of Theology. Also in a couple of days Aunt Abbie and her daughters, Winnie and Kittie, were on their way back to North Dakota.

While Ruth Flory and I had corresponded all during summer, we had not had the opportunity to see each other since we said goodbye in June at the end of the college year. Ruth lived near South Haven with her parents, who owned a fruit farm located just about one mile east of the city limits. She had an older sister who was teaching school, two younger sisters, and a younger brother. They were a hardworking family and during the fruit harvest there were jobs for all. Ruth invited me to come down the weekend following Labor Day, which I accepted.

In the early 1900,s South Haven was a great resort city of about five thousand native inhabitants. During the summer the people who spent their vacations in the city, which had beautiful sandy beaches on Lake Michigan, swelled the population to twice its size, so during the summer months there were lots of activities for tourists and vacationers. There were boats that sailed between Chicago and South Haven that brought visitors from Chicago and other cities. Some of these ships that thrilled me were the *City of South Haven*, the *Iroquois*, and the *Eastland*, which turned over at the Chicago pier when loading, with hundreds of people drowning.

Returning home for a few days after the long weekend with Ruth, I readied myself for my senior year at college. I got back on campus a whole week before the members of the football squad began to gather for practice. It was Coach Young's idea that if I canvassed the city's industrial and food-serving businesses, we would get the jump on Western Michigan students who might be looking for jobs. Well, I never put in such a week in all my life! Jobs were not plentiful! Employers didn't want to commit themselves when I asked if they could use one or more college athletes for a few hours a day. At the end of the week I could not see that we were any further ahead in job opportunities than we were before I started. I told the coach I had done all that I knew how to do in order to line up jobs. I still have a vivid picture of that scene, which terminated my employment responsibilities.

I was at the gym helping Coach Young get ready for the opening football practice. A couple of newcomers to whom the coach had promised financial help came in. After Mr. Young had finished talking with them he introduced them to me and said, "Take these two men out and find them jobs to earn their board." I looked at the coach and with a look of frustration on my face I am sure, I said, "Coach, I canvassed the whole city last week and found no promises of job opportunities. I just don't know where to take them to get a job for board." "All right," said Mr. Young in his very smooth and patient voice, a voice of understanding, but while coaching one with firmness that commanded respect, "There will be job opportunities opening up a little later. In the meantime, fellows, just be patient." There was never any more said to me about jobs for athletes. I had done all I could, and the coach realized I could do no more.

As students, some new and many old, started arriving on campus it was as usual: "Hello, Jim," "Hi, Bill, did you have a good summer?" Then a few of us upperclassmen would gather in someone's room and have one of those good old "bull sessions" that would last until we were all "bulled out." The Ladies Hall dining room opened, and Harold Dressel and I continued our dining-room duties. Mrs. Wheaten, the matron, got the idea that we waiters should wear white coats, so she provided them. Harold and I thought it was a very good idea, because always wearing clean shirts and ties was a little expensive.

I continued to mail my dirty clothes home for mother to wash and mail back within a few days, and she never failed. As I now look back on it, there was never a more-devoted mother than she was to her family. Dad's barber business did not provide enough to support two boys in college and finance his family at home, but we did have the encouragement that came from home. Periodically Dad would write a letter enclosing a couple of bucks, and when he came down three or four times a year he would say, "How are you fixed for cash?" It was always the same answer, "I'll get by." Then he would pull out his wallet to give me a couple of dollars. I knew he would give me more if he could, but when you have four kids at home to support and business not too good, I knew he just didn't have it to give me.

The first few days on campus of a new college year are always exciting. Besides meeting old friends and "lining up" the newcomers, there was the class schedule to make. We all tried to make our classroom program fit our most desirable instructors, and in a small college that was often difficult to do. Besides, I had to carry a heavier class load in order to qualify for the minimum number of hours for graduation. Within a week we were organized in the routine of the college year. In general, it was up at 6:45 a.m. to serve breakfast at 7:30 a.m. in Ladies Hall dining room. Then an "eight o'clock," which got me off to a good day's academic start. Four thirty found me at the gym ready to rub down the football players' sore muscles with Sloan's Liniment. How that stuff smarted my eyes! At 5:45 p.m. I washed up and reported at the dining room, ready to wait tables by 6:00 p.m. Sometimes after dinner some of us who had girlfriends living in the Hall would go into the reception room for a chat, and once in a while sing with one of the girls at the piano. Then it was back to the dorm for an evening of study.

Cross-country was out as far as I was concerned. I had very little time to run with my schedule and working hours, and I told the coach how I felt about it. He was understanding but disappointed because he figured we had made a good start in building that sport into an athletic program at Kalamazoo. However, to spend so much time training for only two meets just wasn't worth the sacrifice in my book.

Football was the talk of the campus. After last year's great disappointment and with a number of fine recruited players that helped make the largest freshman class, totaling one hundred and fifty, Kalamazoo was to have better days. Coach Young had built a nine-game schedule that included Notre Dame and the University of Indiana. There were fifty-three candidates seeking places on the varsity. This was Kalamazoo's largest football squad as of 1921. Says the September 22, 1921 Index, "With a greater number of candidates in daily work out than ever before, Kalamazoo's outlook on the football season is brighter than for some time. There has been and there will be absolutely no let-up in the practice in view of the first game of the season this Saturday when the eleven travels to the Hoosier State to meet the University of Notre Dame. Notre Dame is known as one of the strongest football schools in the country, and our showing against its powerful team will be awaited with interest." Well, it didn't take too much time when the game got underway to determine which the better team was. Our boys of Kalamazoo came home with a 55-0 clobbering. The game the following Saturday against the University of Indiana looked better on paper at least, since they only beat Kalamazoo by a 29-0 score. One of my observations of interest is that the University of Indiana football team of 1921 didn't have a man on the first-string list of players who weighed 200 pounds. There were two one 190 pounders in the line. The backfield had a 165 pounder at quarterback, two halfbacks at 165 and 160 pounds, and a 195-pound fullback, yet they were undoubtedly an average Big Ten team in 1921. Contrasting them with the today Big Ten Teams, they would be classed as lightweights! Kalamazoo finished the season with seven wins and two losses. The highlight of the whole season was Kalamazoo's defeat of Albion by a 7-0 score and the M.I.A.A. championship.

The football season of 1921 officially ended with the big football banquet at the Knights of Pythias Hall December 10, 1921. It was probably the nicest affair that I had attended during my four years of college. Ruth and I enjoyed our last athletic banquet together. The whole menu was built around a football game. Fried chicken and mashed potatoes were the highlights of the menu as far as I was concerned. There were selections by the Gaynor Club, and my friend from Ferndale, Helen Hough, sang a solo. Little did I realize I would be located in Ferndale for my life's work! Says the *Index* of December 15, 1921: "The football banquet is a memory now, but it is a memory which will endure as long as the name of Kalamazoo College endures, for it was one of the big events in the whole history of the college. And why shouldn't it be? It was given in honor of one of the greatest elevens ever possessed by any college, a team that fought and struggled and pounded and won its way to the intercollegiate championship of Michigan, not to mention such places as Valparaiso and Franklin." After reading the cleverly written program and eating the well-prepared feast, the great congregation of Kalamazoo students and friends sat back for a fine program they knew was coming, and it was some program, we'll tell the world! The big banquet closed with a fine address by Dr. Stetson. "Prexy" made a brief and glowing speech in tribute to the 1921 championship team and Coach Young, the man behind the team. That speech was a fitting climax to the most successful banquet in Kalamazoo's athletic history.

One of the most far-sighted statements of our time was made by Dr. Stetson in his address to the students at the first chapel exercises of the year. I have lived long enough to realize how true his statements were. He said, "We are not living in a paradise today. A few years ago when we were in the midst of the great war [World War I] men prophesized that when it ended the world would undergo a great change. These prophets, consciously or unconsciously, implied that all conditions would then be improved and we would then find ourselves in an area of the best possible things. But we find today that in some ways the world seems even to have gone backward and that there is a vast uncertainty everywhere as to what men and nations ought to do." I am afraid that Dr. Stetson would turn over in his grave if he could realize what seventeen years of war by the United States since 1940 has done to our great nation, which was founded on the principles set down by our master Jesus Christ! Yes, the world of people, in spite of great scientific progress, seems to have gone backward, and today there is vast uncertainty everywhere.

The Sherwoods got off to a good start. At our first meeting we laid plans for a big year both financially and socially, as well as along the regular literary lines of activity. Our president, Wilbert Bennetts, was the type who put his heart into the job. It is interesting to consider the topics for discussion at our second meeting, held the following week. Phil Vercoe, my roommate and years later the principal of Flint Central High School, spoke on "The Functions of the Sherwoods," Harold Allen discussed "Who Will Win the World Series," Bradford Morse spoke on "The College Band," even though at that time the college had none! The Sherwood open house was very successful.

The October 13, 1921, *Index* carried a letter written to the *Index* by Coleman Cheney. Coleman was a Goblite; in fact, when he and Monroe graduated in June 1921, it was the end of the Goblites on campus. One paragraph of Cheney's letter read, "But however much we are interested in Harvard football [Coleman was taking work at Harvard], we will never lose interest in the Orange and Black. Between the two of us, the style of game played by Kalamazoo is the more interesting to watch. If I had my choice I think I would prefer to see Kalamazoo 'crock Albion' November 5 than to see any one of the Harvard games, unless perhaps it is the one with Yale. Speaking of Albion, if for no other reason than for the sake of the Kalamazoo College Alumni in and around Boston, you have got to beat Albion! Monroe Wilcox, as you know, is at Boston University School of Theology, and of course I go over there frequently. There are also three Albion men over there, one of them Benish, captain of the Albion football team last year, one of the men who beat us November 6, 1920. We should never hear the last of it if they should defeat us this year. And they never will hear the last of it when we defeat them!" The same edition of the *Index* carried a picture of Prof. Praeger with his description of his summer trip to Ireland. Well, as far as I was concerned he could have stayed in Ireland! He added nothing to my pleasure on the campus.

"Gospel Teams will give Inspiration," announced the *Index* of October 20, 1921. I enjoyed the part I played in the gospel teams' work. The team I was on included Maurice Armstrong, Phil Vercoe, Vern Bunnell, and Elmer Littell. Our first assignment was at the First Baptist Church of Mason, Michigan on November 18, 19, and 20. The weekend program generally opened with a banquet for the young people. Our team members would describe interesting things about the various phases of college life, emphasizing the religious atmosphere of the Christian college.

My part was to describe our college athletic program. I would bring out some of the teachings of the famous University of Chicago coach Alfonzo Stagg. He openly condemned drinking and smoking, especially for all athletes. Saturday was visiting day, and we would call on senior and junior high school students who were considering college and talk Kalamazoo to them and their parents. Weather permitting, a Saturday afternoon hike and roast for the boys of the church was usually given with the team members in charge. Generally around a campfire, I described how athletics and Christianity go hand in hand. Sunday was the real big day since we were in charge of the whole worship service and program, which consisted of Sunday school and morning worship in the forenoon, and young people's meeting and evening worship during the evening. We divided the worship services between the four of us, two speakers at each service. The fifth team member would take the Sunday school session and the young people's evening meeting. At Mason I was one of the morning church service speakers. We were housed and fed by members of the church, and the college paid our transportation costs. Every meal was a banquet, and of course we enjoyed the home cooking as a change to food served at the Ladies Hall dining room. It was real work because there was a lot of studying to be done to prepare for these meetings; nevertheless, these gospel trips were a fine educational experience. Such gospel team work cut in to my studies. We tried to do some studying on the interurban going to and from our assignments as well as over the weekend, but it is my opinion that very little real studying took place. It was very late Sunday night or early Monday morning when we arrived at the interurban station in Kalamazoo returning from a gospel service weekend.

The Exchange Club of Kalamazoo scored again by hosting the M.I.A.A. championship grid team at their regular Monday noon luncheon. For me this was the beginning of a long series of Exchange Club luncheons for football teams since we in Ferndale Exchange have made that a part of our youth activities program for years.

"Back to Normalcy" was the slogan of President Warren G. Harding. It was popular since the American people were tired of World War I. Quite often one would pick up a newspaper and read someone's opinion on what should be done to ensure continued peace on earth and goodwill to all mankind. On December 1, 1921, the *Index* printed one such bit of philosophy from *The Antelope*, Kearney, Nebraska:

- We believe in a sweeping reduction of armaments. We believe in a world-wide association of
- Nations for World peace.
- We believe in equality of race treatment.
- We believe that Christian patriotism demands the practice of good will between nations.
- We believe that nations that are Christian have special international obligations.
- We believe that the spirit of Christian brotherhood can conquer every barrier to trade, color, creed and race.

You be the judge in these 1970's of just how much of the "I Believe" has proven to be the accepted philosophy of nations and people.

The December 8, 1921, issue of the *Index* announced a twenty-eight-game basketball schedule with Coach Young's picture. Under the photo was written, "One of the most capable mentors of the middle west." There was no doubt in people's minds of Ralph H. Young's coaching capability. What made him more outstanding was that he coached all sports at Kalamazoo College and his teams excelled in all four of them: football, baseball, basketball, and track. That he was recognized as a fine coach with high ideals was attested to when Michigan Agricultural College (now M.S.U.) hired him away from Kalamazoo in 1923 to become athletic director and football coach. Mr. Young continued at M.S.U. until he was retired. He was the driving force behind getting the state legislature to change the college's name from M.A.C. to Michigan State College because he said, and it was the truth, young men with athletic potential didn't want to go to a "Cow College." Years later he was instrumental in getting the state legislature to make "M.S.C."[Michigan State University]. There was a great deal of opposition to making Michigan State College a university. Many arguments were advanced; one that it would hurt the prestige of the University of Michigan. In the 1950's as athletic director of M.S.C. and later M.S.U., Mr. Young built the college and university into a nationally known school in athletics. The next step for Athletic Director Ralph H. Young was to make M.S.U. a member of the Big Ten. Up to this time M.S.U. was a free agent, scheduling games with other universities located in all parts of the country.

After Coach Stagg retired, the University of Chicago's athletic program gradually deteriorated to the extent that it became the doormat in Big Ten athletics. This led to its withdrawal from the Big Ten and while the association continued to be called the "Big Ten" it was really the "Big Nine." Over the course of many years it was rumored that the University of Notre Dame was to fill this vacancy, but it never proved to be a reality. In the meantime, under the direction of Ralph H. Young the athletic plan was expanded. The football stadium was enlarged from about 35,000 to about 76,000, which made it comparable to Big Ten university stadiums. Then it all happened. Coach Young's great ambitious goal was reached: M.S.U. was accepted into the Big Ten. This took place in the twilight of his athletic career, and I feel sure that when the university regents retired him he felt that he had reached the ultimate in his profession. He was outstanding in his great athletic accomplishments, which were Big Ten championships, Rose Bowl winner, and coach of the United States Olympic track and field team. In his retirement his home district elected him to a seat in the Michigan legislature. Coach Young died from a heart attack while dressing.

So it's easy to understand why Coach Young built a twenty-eight-game schedule for his 1921-22 basketball team, also why he had four games before Christmas with the University of Michigan at Ann Arbor. In addition, he had home and away games with Notre Dame, the University of Detroit, and University of Valparaiso. A game at East Lansing with M.A.C. was also included in the schedule. When we got back to the campus after the Christmas holidays we learned that the University of Michigan had cancelled the four games' practice session that had been scheduled at Ann Arbor. We built up our ego by telling each other they were just afraid of our team. Says the *Index* on December 15, 1921: "The basketballers have been going strong lately and are making steady progress under Coach Young's strenuous course in training. Come down and watch the practice some night. You'll learn a lot more about basketball than you see on the floor during a game when you are too excited to notice the fine points." I was one of the few spectators at these practice sessions. While I was learning some of the finer points of basketball I am afraid my subjects were suffering, for my academic record in my senior year was not as good as it had been my junior year. However, when I began my coaching of basketball at Ferndale High School these observations proved to be an educational benefit.

I spent most of the holidays on campus. I did a little hair cutting, took care of some furnaces for fellows who wanted a few days off, and did some studying on papers that were due after the holidays. The three weeks after the Christmas holidays were always hectic ones. Papers had to be finished and study for the finals were foremost in our minds, but they always came and went as do all things in life. When I called the dean's office for my grades I was not too satisfied, not being on the "Dean's List." I had never made the dean's list so my attitude was, so what, I have one semester to go.

We hadn't gotten too far into the basketball schedule when we began to realize that this could be Coach Young's year. He had tried to build a football team that would gain national recognition and so far had failed. This could be the year in basketball, and it proved to be true. The team split with University of Valparaiso, losing there by a 22-20 score and winning at Kalamazoo 24-23. The Kalamazoos won both games from the University of Notre Dame and the University of Detroit. They also showed M.A.C. who was the Michigan king of basketball by a 39-28 score at East Lansing. The squad suffered only two losses, one by two points and the other by one point. At the close of the season the N.C.A.A. chose the Kalamazoo team to play in the N.C.A.A. college division tournament. The Kalamazoo team beat the University of Idaho by a 38-31 score. The next night they met and beat Grove City College, PA by a score of 22-13. This brought the team to the final game and an opportunity for a national championship in the N.C.A.A. college division. We were all disappointed when we learned that Wabash University had defeated our team 43-23. When the coaches of the association named the

All-M.I.A.A. team the entire Kalamazoo College team was selected. This truly was Coach Young's year so far. With the great football team, which won seven of the nine, losing only to Notre Dame and University of Indiana, the Kalamazoo teams were off and running for their greatest season of sports.

I had already experienced some of the added pressures of the senior year of college. I had been elected vice president of the Sherwoods, which entailed more work and planning. As the *Index* described it: "The vice president of the Sherwoods, Harold B. Wilcox, had a mighty good program arranged for last week's regular meeting of the Society, but for certain physical conditions there was no meeting." This was due to the outside Eskimos or polar bear conditions with no heat in the Sherwood Hall. However, this condition didn't endure, for in the January 12, 1922, *Index* the heading read, "Sherwoods have a Snappy Program." The article continued, "The Sherwoods had a mighty snappy meeting last week when the new members entertained the old with a diverting program. The Sherwoods are getting an unusually large number out to the meetings. Vice President Wilcox is preparing a classy set of programs for the next few meetings, and not a single member can afford to miss them."

As the winter months faded away into spring, I found myself loaded with work both inside the classroom and out. I was spending more time than I should have earning the extra cash that the senior year cost. Then too, the social life on campus was drawing on my time. Ruth and I were spending just too much time together. I should have been putting more energy on the books, on the track, and more time in slumberland.

For the first time Coach Ralph Young decided that Kalamazoo College would have an indoor season in track. As the February 9, 1922, *Index* wrote: "Tuesday afternoon the 1922 track season got under way when the first practice of the year was held in the State Armory. While the Armory has no track, it is a good 150 yards around the wall, fully as large as any indoor track and the handicap of not having the corners banked will have to be endured." Well, we endured it all right, although it was rather hard on the feet and muscles of the legs. But we were young, and in my college days there was nothing like Sloan's Liniment to take away the aches and pains resulting from athletic exercise.

When February 25 rolled around the track team was headed for East Lansing to participate in Kalamazoo's first indoor track meet. The various men's societies at M.A.C. took good care of all the visiting track men during our stay in East Lansing, and the Aggies were noted for their hospitality. I had experienced that pleasure when I had competed in the state collegiate cross-country meet two years previously. There were no long-distance runs, which were my specialty. However I had always been a quick starter, so the coach entered me in the forty-yard dash. While I wasn't last in my heat, I did not qualify for the final. Kalamazoo did take the M.I.A.A. class relay, and several of our men piled up some points.

My last Washington banquet, with Ruth as my date, came and went, and each participant got his or her two dollars and twenty-give cents worth. It was truly one of the cleverest banquets I had ever attended, full of imagination and originality.

Money being a problem, I asked for and got a job on the campus for the spring recess. Four of us fellows were assigned the task of mopping the wooden floors of Bowen Hall. Now, to mop floors eight hours a day was hard enough and would toughen anyone's back muscles, but to have to carry the buckets of water from the basement floor up three flights of stairs was an added stress. Needless to say, when bedtime came we were ready. On top of that workload, I took a couple of furnace jobs for fellows who wanted to leave the campus for the spring recess. That was not too difficult since during the spring of the year a house didn't demand too much heat, and there was no snow to be shoveled from walks. I did find a few hours during the evenings to go to the public library to work on semester papers, which were coming due before final exams.

With spring recess over, the track schedule was announced as follows: we had meets with Ypsilanti Normal College (now Eastern Michigan University), then a member of the M.I.A.A.; with Detroit Junior college (now Wayne State University); the State Collegiate meet at East Lansing; the Invitational at Northwestern University; and the final and all important M.I.A.A. at Albion.

The April 14, 1922, *Index* put it this way: "With the reopening of College after Spring Vacation, the Orange and Black trackmen are getting down to business. About forty-eight men have reported so far. The squad is the largest and classiest that the college has ever had." After naming several of the outstanding men who were sure to bring honors to old Kalamazoo, the article stated, "Captain Wilcox holds the State two mile record 9:57:3, Walker holds the M.I.A.A. record for the 100 yard dash, Petschulat holds the State 220 yard record at 22:1, Casteel holds the State outdoor pole vault record at 11 feet 3 inches [the fiberglass pole was not yet heard of], Hamill holds the M.I.A.A. record in the Javelin at 153 feet, Forman holds the local College record in the mile at 4:28:2." With this array of talent the Orange and Black was sure to reap honors in all these meets, and we did.

Founder's Day has always been a great day for the senior class at Kalamazoo College since it is the debut of the seniors in their impressive cap and gown array. The *Index* of April 20, 1922, announced that day by stating, "Saturday morning the seniors will have charge of the Annual Founder's Day exercises which commemorate the 89th birthday of our Alma Mater." Those of the class selected to have a part in the Founder's Day class program were Harvard Coleman, orator; Dorothy Fitch, prophet; Marion Graybiel, historian recorder of the will; Emily Tedrow, chaplain; Emil Howe, the song composer; Ruth Vercoe, the ivy poet; Dora Anderson, and Harold Dressel, the author and director of the class yell. The class always planted an ivy, which seldom ever grew but gave us the feeling that "our class" had left something that in the years to come would remain to enhance the beauty of the campus. The big day came and went as all days do, but to us, the seniors, it marked the beginning of the end. We knew that there were about two months left for us to be Kalamazoo College students.

The months of April and May 1922 were filled with social affairs. One such occasion was the Sherwood annual banquet held April 28 in Bowen Hall. As usual, my date was Ruth Flory. It was a very enjoyable farewell to seniors. Says the *Index*: "The April 23 date was a grand and glorious celebration of a successful Sherwood year." It made me feel really good that I had been a part of this organization. I could only think back to my freshman year when mother had put all kinds of pressure on me to join the Philos. I thanked my lucky stars that I knew I had made the right choice. Then too, there were the "home concerts" of the College Glee Club and Gaynor Club that were always so entertaining.

"Senior Play Cast Has Been Selected" announced the *Index* of May 11, 1922. The cast for the senior play "The Man of the Hour" by George Broadhurst had been selected following two tryouts said the *Index*. "It is a play with a political problem of great importance, and the issue is satisfactorily solved at the close. ... Those in the play will be George Walkotten, Mictor Malcomson, John Clark, Harvard Coleman, Emil Howe, Lisle Mackay, Harold Wilcox, Lester Graybiel, Paul Schrier, Harry Bell, Harmon Everett, Louise Every, Emily Tedrow, and Ruth Vercoe." Here I was, loaded with academic work, trying hard to make enough money to pay my expenses, attending the many social functions that are a part of college life, captain of the college track team that expected so much of me, enjoying the last of my college romance with the girl I was counting on for a life partner, and then becoming a member of the senior play cast. While my part was a minor one, it nevertheless entailed some work. Our rehearsals were held in Sherwood Hall located in the gym. The play, the prize feature of the commencement program was staged in one of the local theaters on Monday evening, June 19 before a packed house. It was a thrill for me to be a part of the senior project, but I had to pay for the privilege by being overworked.

We opened the spring track season with a meet with Ypsilanti Teachers College on April 29. I had been working hard to get into condition, but so many other activities seemed to be taking their toll. When the two mile was finished it found Wilcox placing third instead of his expected first place. The May 4 *Index* had this to say about my running: "The work of Captain Wilcox in the two mile was not up to standard. He allowed two men to finish ahead of him in time that was thirty five seconds slower than his state record. He will have two weeks before the next dual meet which will be held here with Detroit Junior college May 13 and it is expected he will show decided improvement by that time."

It was the policy of Coach Ralph Young to hold an invitational Interscholastic Track and Field meet each spring, and this spring was no exception. Nearly two hundred high school athletes were to take part, and it required the services of every college track man to make it a successful day. Hospitality was the key word since we all wanted to sell Kalamazoo to these young high school athletes. Coach Young asked me if as captain of the college track team I would accept the position of referee and starter of the meet. I told him I was honored to be asked, and would be delighted to do so. It was a jam-packed day from morning to later afternoon, but the meet went off in grand style with many records broken. The next day, Sunday, the *MLive Kalamazoo Gazette* had this among many things to say about the meet: "Smashing seven records and equaling another was the remarkable record accomplished during the Interscholastic Track and Field Meet yesterday on College campus. The meet was the most successful one ever held by the college." Highland Park finished first with a total of 33 1/3 points and Grand Rapids Central was second with 21 points. May I add that we enjoyed nice warm sun all day long, which added to the comfort of all.

The following Saturday, May 13, we took on Detroit Junior College at Kalamazoo. It was another nice warm spring day, and my mother had come down to see me run. I am sorry to have to write that I let her down. Although I ran the fastest mile in my life, Zek Osborn, my company distance man, beat me in 4:34:3, and also beat me in the two mile in the good time of 10:16:3. These defeats caused me to wonder if I was really up to running both the mile and two mile in the same afternoon. I went to Coach Young and told him of my feelings. He said I should run a pace that would win but not try to run all out in order to make good time. I agreed with the coach, but argued that we were winning our meets quite easily and with a big track squad there just was no real reason for me to run two distance events in one afternoon in order to build up a high score. "Well," he said," if you prefer to run just the two mile then that is all I'll enter you in."

The following Saturday, May 20, we ran against Albion at Albion. I ran the two mile and was an easy winner. My company distance man, Zek Osborn, ran the mile, which he won in good time and finished second in the two mile behind me. Spannenberg of Albion, touted as a future great, finished third in each of the two events. Says the *Index* for May 25, 1922: "Captain Wilcox is getting back into form again with his old stride in the distance event."

The first of the two big ones was the state intercollegiate meet Saturday, May 27 at M.A.C. (now M.S.U.) M.A.C. again won the meet with Kalamazoo second, beating out Kalamazoo Western by the close score of 27 ½ to 24. It was a perfect day for record breaking and several were broken. Coleman broke the college record in the 880 yard run, a record that had stood since 1900. The relay team, winning by inches in the mile relay in record breaking time, was the most spectacular event of the meet. Zek Osborn covered himself with glory by winning the mile event from a crack field of runners in the splendid time of 4:33:4. But Wilcox just didn't have it to run the others into the ground. Coach told me in planning the race to step out and take the lead. I was a marked man, and before the race people were asking me if I thought I could break ten minutes again as I did the year before. I told them I felt good and should run a good race. As the race started the field held back for me to take the lead. After the first lap I was out in front setting the pace and stayed that way until the gun lap, when Carpenter of Ypsilanti and Vreeland of Alma went by me. I could not overtake them and I ran third, with Carpenter the winner, tying my state record. Says the *Index* about the two mile: "Another surprise of the meet was the fast time made by Carpenter of Ypsilanti (MI) in the two mile when after running a shoulder to shoulder race with Vreeland of Alma he broke the tape in the time of 9:57:3 equaling the record made by Captain Wilcox in 1921. 'Cocky' led the field for seven laps with his consistent stride that won last year, but Carpenter's strong reserve that enabled him to make his spectacular finish brought him first place in the last two hundred yards."

It was very discouraging to me that in my senior year I was not making as good a showing as I had in my junior year. However, over the many years I have followed sports I have found that in track as well as in other sports some days you have it and some days you don't. Track is an individual effort. You don't have a team of men to cover up your mistakes or failures. If you win you're great, and you have run a fine race. If you lose, you just got beat by a better man on that day.

As I prepared for my last race of my college career, the M.I.A.A. meet at Albion June 2 and 3, I analyzed myself and tried to come up with what kind of a race I should run to beat Vreeland of Alma.

Coach Young had entered some of us tracksters in the DePaul University of Chicago First Annual Track and Field Meet to be held on the Northwestern University Field, Evanston, May 30, 2:00 p.m. This was to be the warm-up for the Friday and Saturday M.I.A.A. meet June 2 and 3. As we boarded the New York Central train for Chicago, I had made up my mind that I would not go all out to win the two mile, and also I was not going to set the pace. When the gun went off for the start of the race I held back to determine who the leaders were going to be. Then I took third place and held it during the whole race, never trying to sprint down the stretch in the drive for home. On this day third was just what I had planned. When I got home to the dormitory Coach asked me about the run. When I told him of my plans he didn't appear to be much impressed.

It was an enjoyable visit to Chicago. We were well housed and entertained. We couldn't get an early train back to Kalamazoo, so we took in the play *Lightnin'*, with the star Frank Bacon playing the lead, at the Blackstone Theatre. It was one of the very best, and we all enjoyed it. We were a sleepy bunch of tracksters as our train rolled into Kalamazoo about 2:30 a.m., but we had three days to get rested up for the big one.

Friday morning, June 2, found the college track team, baseball team, and tennis team all at the railroad station waiting for the train to take us to Albion.

Again we were housed in The Hotel Albion! "Service and cuisine unexcelled" read the menu. The two mile was run on Saturday, which gave me an extra day of rest. I was in a room with three other fellows, and when we awoke Saturday morning the sun was shining and we all said what a beautiful day. This just had to be it. After breakfast, as we walked over to the athletic field, I reached down and picked up a nickel. One of the fellows said, "That means five points, which is first place." I replied, "I hope so."

In discussing the race plan with Coach, I told him I was not going to step out and set the pace. I had done that a year previous when Vreeland had beaten me, and I had done it at the state meet and was beaten again. Coach said, "Well, whatever you think is the best way for you. But Harold, this is your last college two mile run, make it your best." As is customary, each contestant drew a number out of the hat to determine the position on the starting line. I drew a high number, which put me in the second line for the start. My teammate Zek Osborn offered to give me his frontline position, but I turned it down. I was determined that I was not going to set the pace.

The first lap was rather slow, and when Vreeland saw I was not going to lead he jumped out at the beginning of the second lap and set the pace. I immediately got on his tail and stayed there all of the race. When the gun went off for the final lap he jumped out for about a ten-yard lead. I took after him, and gradually closed the gap on the backstretch. When we reached the beginning of the last turn, I was even with him. Then I pulled out and went by him. He had shot his strength and had nothing left. I sprinted to the tape a winner, setting a new M.I.A.A. record of 9:59:2. After I had rested for a few minutes, Coach came over to congratulate me and said, "When you reached the back stretch still with that long stride of yours I knew you had him."

After dressing I picked up my gold medal and started walking down the railroad tracks to the depot. I wanted to send Dad a telegram about my victory and record since I knew it being Saturday the shop would be full all evening and the general conversation would be my win and record. Also, I was exceedingly tired, and I wanted to catch an early train to spend a few minutes with Ruth and give her my medal (the second one of my medals that I gave to her).

Almost all of the men on the teams remained for the finish of the baseball game, so I was by myself as I rode the rails for the last time as a Kalamazoo College athlete. I couldn't help but be reminded of that conversation I had with Monroe the year before when he said, "Harold, this is my last year. You have one more. Enjoy it for when it's gone it's gone forever." My track experiences were now a thing of history.

The *Index* wrote: "Wilcox pursued the same tactics that won for him a year ago at M.A.C. For seven driving laps he trailed Vreeland with dogged determination. Then the Alma star, who had generally been conceded first place, looked around at the insistent rhythm of the pounding feet behind him and saw 'Cocky' steadily closing the gap. It was the final turn of the last lap, and 'Cocky' was putting all he had into that desperate effort that spells victory. Vreeland was gasping and tried to sprint, but the pace was too stiff and 'Cocky' passed him in a terrific spurt that put him thirty yards in the lead when he broke the tape, breaker of the M.I.A.A. two mile record. Captain Wilcox now holds both the M.I.A.A. record and the State intercollegiate record."

It was a great weekend for the Orange and Black. We cleaned the slate by winning all three championships; track, baseball, and tennis. The Kalamazoos ran up 55 points to second-place Ypsilanti with 26 ½ points.

The following day the *MLive Kalamazoo Gazette* announced in big headlines on the sports page: "Kalamazoo College again wins M.I.A.A. championship. The two mile mark was broken by Wilcox of Kalamazoo who trailed Vreeland of Alma until the last eighth of a mile and then sprinted home in 9:59:2." The 1922 *Boiling Pot* described the spring track season as follows: "Winning first in three dual meets, second in the State Intercollegiate, third in the mid-western meet, in addition to gaining indisputable claim to the M.I.A.A. championship, Kalamazoo College track team made an enviable record during the spring of 1922. In the fastest opening meet Kalamazoo ever entered, the Orange and Black topped the Green and White of Ypsilanti, 71-60. Ypsilanti had the strongest M.I.A.A. team Kalamazoo has ever opposed. Dual meets were won against Detroit Junior College [now Wayne State University], and against Albion who was defeated 71 ½ to 59 ½. Coach Young's men took second in the M.A.C. Intercollegiate [now M.S.U.], first honors going to the Aggies. The feature of this meet was the establishing of a new State relay record by the Kalamazoo team made up of Kern, Travis, Davis and Coleman. In the mid-west special invitation meet held on the Northwestern University track at Evanston, Illinois, Coach Young sent six men, who piled up enough points to take third place for Kalamazoo." I have to confess, as I told Coach Young on returning home, this was the first two-mile race I ever ran when I didn't do my very best. For some reason I was content to take a third place without extending myself. Of course, Coach didn't like to hear that; however, it seemed to me at the time that I should save myself for the last race of my collegiate career, the M.I.A.A. at Albion the following week. "For the fourth consecutive year," says the 1922 *Boiling Pot*: "Kalamazoo won the M.I.A.A. track and field meet and relay championship at Albion, despite the fact that the other teams were out to get Kalamazoo's scalp. Kalamazoo earned 55 points, while second honors went for 26. Captain Harold B. Wilcox, Kenneth "Zek" Osborn, and Ray Forman were outstanding men during the season."

It's hard to believe that this M.I.A.A. two-mile record held up for thirty-six years. It wasn't until Sunday, May 18, 1958, that in describing the M.I.A.A. track meet held in Kalamazoo the *MLive Kalamazoo Gazette* reported: "Five M.I.A.A. track and field records tumbled in the 66th small college meet, including the oldest one in the books the two mile run. Thirty-six years ago Harold Wilcox of 'K' College ran the two mile in 9:57:6. Jim Taup, Albion Junior, cracked that mark Saturday in the excellent time of 9:53:7 although he has done far better than that this spring." I had read in the newspapers that Jim had bettered my record and was favored to set a new two-mile record in the M.I.A.A. meet. I wrote him a letter stating it was a disgrace to the M.I.A.A. schools that they had not produced a two miler who could run it faster than I had thirty-six years ago, that I wished him luck, that he would know when he lined up to face the starter's gun I would be pulling for him. He wrote me a nice letter after the meet, expressing his appreciation for my goodwill and hoped we would meet some time. We never did, and as so often happens he did not run as well in his senior year as he did on that day of May 18, 1958.

Where am I, who am I, and what am I was questions I was asking myself. Sure, I was a senior in college, but what next? Was I capable of getting a school teaching job and coaching? Did I want to attempt such a career at this time? All these were questions that were going through my mind. Then too, there was the problem of a summer job. Applying for school teaching jobs in the 1920's was a whole lot different than in the 1970's. I asked Herman H. Severn in whose class I had sat, and my favorite professor of history Dr. Balch if they were willing to write me a recommendation for a teaching job. They both agreed to do so, as did Coach Ralph Young. On hearing of an opening I sent my application to the superintendent of Coopersville, located a few miles west of Grand Rapids. A few days later I received a call from him asking me to come up to interview with him. He needed a man to teach history and to coach basketball and track. I told him I would take the interurban to Grand Rapids, change for Coopersville, and be there about noon. I was so undecided I almost backed down on going, but in fairness to him I carried out my agreement for an interview.

It was a pleasant spring day and Coopersville with all its trees looked like a very hospitable place to be. After talking with the superintendent for a couple of hours, looking over the school building and program, he took me over to the drugstore to meet the president of the school board. By this time I knew I didn't want the job. I lacked the feeling of confidence and security that one had to have in taking any job. After talking with the president of the board who seemed very favorable toward me, the superintendent said, "All right, you stay overnight at my house and the board president will call a meeting tonight and confirm your appointment."

"Well," I said, "I need time to think this over [knowing full well I didn't want the job]. I must get back on the campus tonight for I have a lot of work to do." I also had a date with Ruth that I didn't want to pass up, so I shook hands and said goodbye. "I'll get in touch with you," I said. Back on the campus I just knew I was not ready for a school teaching job.

The following recommendation by Dean Herman Severn was carefully placed in my "valuable papers" file, feeling that sometime later I might want to use it.

4-14-22
To Those Concerned:
   This statement will certify that I have known personally Mr. Harold B. Wilcox during his course in this college. He has been under my instruction for two semesters. He is a good student, attentive to duty, painstaking in his work, and has ability to make plain to others what he himself has mastered. I have observed his teaching in the conduct of several classes and believe that he will prove to be an excellent teacher.
   In personal appearance he is pleasing and attractive, strong and forceful in personality, and in Christian character of unquestioned integrity. He is, moreover, a fine athlete and has had unusual athletic training along with his college course. In my judgment Mr. Wilcox will make an excellent coach and will undoubtedly exert the right sort of influence upon those with whom he may be associated in athletics. I can unqualifiedly recommend him as a Christian gentleman, a good scholar and teacher, and an excellent athletic director.

Sincerely yours,
Herman H. Severn

The 1922 *Boiling Pot* came out and I rushed over to Bowen Hall to pick up my copy. I was keenly disappointed in it, for the editorial staff had failed to make the class will, prophesy, and many other personable things pertaining to the class of 1922 a part of the book. I thumbed my way through the section that contained a separate picture of each member of the class accompanied by a brief sketch of their activities. Opposite my picture was the following:

Harold Brown Wilcox – Gobleville
History Sherwood
"K" Club
Secy.-Treas., Dormitory Association 1920-21
Secretary Sherwood '21
Y.M.C.A. Cabinet 1920
Captain Track Team '22
Captain Cross Country team '20:21
"K" Track '19, '21, '22
"K" Cross Country '20
Glee Club '18, '19
"Best in the long run"

Several years later when I was teaching and coaching in Ferndale, I was master of ceremonies at the football banquet. In the fall of 1923 Ralph Young left Kalamazoo College to become athletic director and football coach at M.A.C. (now M.S.U.) I wrote him to invite him to be our football banquet speaker. He accepted and did his usual fine job, speaking highly of me to the students and parents attending the banquet, which made me feel good. As we shook hands on his departure, he asked me if I remembered the axiom after my name in the *Boiling Pot*. I said, "No, I don't remember it." He replied, "Well, it said: 'Best in the long run,' goodnight," and he made his departure. Coach Young spent the rest of his working life on the campus of M.A.C. (Michigan State University).

After four years on campus and living in the same room for three years one does accumulate many things that mean something. Having saved a few dollars, I went to a luggage store and bought a small steamer trunk and a small traveling bag. At the time I did not know just how useful these two items were to become. They made the trip first to Gobles, then to Boston, back to Gobles, and then to Ferndale.

For weeks I had been pondering what to do that summer and my path for the future! Monroe was spending the first of his three years at Boston University School of Theology, located at 72 Mt. Vernon Street on Beacon Hill just a few blocks from the Commons and Public Gardens. He wrote me of the splendid opportunity to go to school in the east. The theology students were housed in the same building in which classes were held. Barber jobs and restaurant jobs were plentiful. You didn't have to pay tuition and room rent, you just signed a note or I.O.U. for them. Monroe stated that it was very easy to get along there financially. "Why don't you plan on coming out here for at least a year. That will help you to find yourself and determine what you want to do."

In the early 1900s the eastern colleges, Harvard, Dartmouth, Yale, and Princeton, were, you might say, in a class by themselves as far as academics and athletics were concerned. When the one and only "All-American" football teams were chosen by the great Walter Camp it was the official team and nearly all the boys who made All American played football for one of the eastern universities. Going to school in the east had a strong appeal to me. Maybe that was the subconscious desire that made me feel that I didn't want to sign a contract to teach and coach in Coopersville.

Another factor was that my mother had used her influence over a period of years to try to steer me into the Methodist ministry. My dear devout Christian mother would have enjoyed seeing all six of her sons in the path that her first son had chosen. I had gone on college gospel teams, worked with youth, participated in church services, etc., and rather enjoyed it, so I said to myself, "This will be a good chance to determine for myself, with no outside influence, whether or not I should become a Methodist clergyman." It was with that "escape," you might say, that I didn't force myself to make an early decision on "what next year."

A good barber job for the summer was my paramount aim and desire. My co-worker in the dining room waiting on tables, Harold Dressel, lived in South Haven on Lake Michigan just eighteen miles from Gobles. Also, my girlfriend Ruth lived on a fruit farm about a mile east of the city limits. Harold Dressel said, "Why don't you get a barber job in South Haven?" It certainly appealed to me. "But how would I go about getting a job," I asked Dressel? "There is a barbershop in the Reid Hotel," he said. "Why don't you write to them. They may need a good barber." That was all the encouragement I needed. Ruth thought it was a good idea too. It didn't take me long to get a letter off, giving Al Cock's barbershop as a reference as well as my dad who was known countywide for barbering and as a band leader. Only a few days had passed before I received a letter from the boss at Reid's barbershop saying that he did need a summer barber, and I could have the job. I would start the last week in June and work to Labor Day. I would get a guarantee of thirty-five dollars a week and half over fifty dollars. Our shop hours were from 7:00 a.m. to 6:00 p.m. and to 8:00 p.m. on Saturday.

Hearing from Dressel that I was going to work in South Haven, a college girl from South Haven who lived across the street from Dressel's asked me where I would room. Hearing that I was not yet located, she said, "I am going to be away all summer. Why don't you stay at my house, using my room? My parents would enjoy having you there since I am going to be away." So it was settled that I would be at the Harris's for the summer working in South Haven. This eased my mind, knowing where my bread and butter were coming from when college closed for the summer.

Since this semester was the final one, I knew I had to pack my trunk and move out of old 46. I could always go home, but Dad's business was not good. We were still in the Warren G. Harding back to "normalcy" period or a postwar economy, so to go home was something that never entered my mind—sure, for a few-days visit but not for long; I had to make a living.

That last week on campus was a great deal different to me than the previous summers. Instead of "So long fellows, have a good summer and I'll see you in the fall," this time it was goodbye John, Dick, Mike, etc. It sure has been great to know you and we'll be seeing you at Homecoming." Oh, it left a funny feeling to know that this was the end, but it was something we all, I do believe, looked forward to, and we were glad that the college days at Kalamazoo were over. I personally felt that Kalamazoo had done all it could for me. I now had to get out and launch my new goals in life.

My brother Leland was in the baggage room at the New York Central depot (Kalamazoo). He checked my trunk to Gobles while Ruth and I took the train to South Haven, where I spent a long weekend with her on the farm. The Sunday night beginning the last week in June found me housed in the Harris's home, ready to report for work the next morning.

Already the hotels in South Haven had begun to fill up with tourists and vacationers. The steamboats were running daily from Chicago, bringing in thousands of visitors who wanted to enjoy a few days or a few weeks of the carefree life that a resort city on Lake Michigan could give. The automobile had not yet taken over. I was told by my boss that business might be a little slow for a week or so, but after the 4th of July we would have about all we could do. There were three barbers at the beginning of summer, but it was only about three weeks before one barber got sick and was off for the rest of the summer. That really forced us to work our tails off. There were very few times when I was able to sit down with no customers waiting. It was a steady rush from 7:00 a.m. to 6:00 p.m. and on Saturdays until 8:00 p.m. Working six days a week didn't allow me to get to Gobles very often during the summer. I was fast in barbering. In fact, the boss told Dad when he was down at South Haven directing the Gobles band on the 4th of July that I was the fastest barber he had ever had. He said, "I have had barbers from Detroit, Chicago, St. Louis, and around, and none of them can turn out the haircuts, shaves, tonics, etc. that your son can."

It didn't take me long to figure out that by paying me thirty-five dollars of the first fifty dollars that I took in and half of all over fifty dollars he had a pretty good deal. I averaged seventy-five dollars a week take-home pay plus tips (no deductions in those days), so my chair was grossing around hundred and thirty dollars a week, and I did it on thirty-five cents a shave, fifty cents a haircut, fifteen cents a tonic. What I tried to do was get a dollar job from as many customers as possible. Tips ran ten cents and fifteen cents; once in a while twenty-five cents tip. I made eight dollars to ten dollars a week in tips, and with my tip money I bought a very nice tailor-made suit of clothes from a tailor right there in South Haven. The resort season standard of ethics more or less prevailed, which was get all you can from the visitors but treat the natives as you want to be treated. As the boss said, "These homeowners are the bread-and-butter customers for nine months of the year."

In my youthful memories South Haven always had a big 4th of July celebration. The committee would hire the Gobles band to play during the day. After working until midnight on the day before the 4th, after only about six hours sleep Dad would get up about 6:00 a.m., get the music set for the day, and take the 8:30 a.m. train for South Haven with the band members. Mother would say, "Allie, just how do you stand the hot sun and the walking around with the band all day long," but Dad seemed to thrive on it. It was a day away from the barbershop doing what he enjoyed doing. So it was on that July 4, 1922, as I have related, Dad and the band were in South Haven. We barbered in the a.m. until the celebration activities got started, and then the shop was closed.

One of the sports I participated in was the track events. These were staged on the paved main street where the people could line the street and watch the races. At first I thought it was for the birds and didn't consider entering, but after talking with some of the promoters they sold me on the idea of running in the events. They seemed to think that I would lend prestige to the occasion. Since there were money prizes, and I was after all the money I could make, whether running or barbering, I dressed in my "K" college tracksuit and was ready to answer the starters' gun. Well sir, do you know I won every race up until it was announced that two relay teams would race for the final prize money. One of the officials called me aside and said, "Can't we arrange this race so that some of these other fellows can earn some prize money?" I said "Yes, put the best men on the other relay team and give me their fastest man to run against, and I'll see that we come in a dead heat." The race was run by a man of each team starting at the finish line, running about 200 yards up the street, touching his teammate who then ran back to the finish line, touching his teammate, who then ran back up the street where his teammate and I were waiting to run the last distance back to the finish line. As he and I started off on the final lap of the race I told him, "Now save some for the last seventy-five yards and when I say go, give it all you have. I will stay with you, and we will run a dead heat and divide the money among the eight of us who make up the two teams." After the race one person asked me, "Didn't you let him tie you at the finish?" I didn't answer. I counted up my winnings which was between thirty and forty dollars which I considered a pretty good day's work.

Needless to say, Ruth and I spent a great deal of our time together. There were two casinos in South Haven on the lake, and during the summer "named bands" were brought in for dancing. Ruth enjoyed dancing, but I had been raised to believe that dancing was a sin so I was opposed to going to a dancehall. They had dancing at the Euro's senior party at the college. Ruth begged me to go; I did, and she enjoyed dancing while I sat it out. That, up to the summer of 1922, was as near to a dance party as I got. But as the summer wore on, Ruth wanted to teach me a few steps more and more and to go to the casino with her. So I gave in, and we went. I enjoyed it. What followed was the most humiliating thing my dear sweet mother could have done. There were some young people from Gobles who were at the casino that night, and they went home and told my brothers that they had seen Ruth and me at the dance. That upset my mother. She asked my brother Whyle to call me and ask me to come home on the 5:00 p.m. train. In getting the call I asked Whyle, "Is something wrong at home?" For me to come home I had to leave work one hour early and report to work two hours late in the morning. So I said, "Why should I come home? What is it all about?" "Mother wants to see you," was his reply. So I said, "Okay, I'll arrange to get off and be home on the 5:45 train." As I walked up the sidewalk to the house, Whyle was sitting on my trunk, which was on the front porch (no one worried in those days about thievery. People seldom locked their house doors). "Here he comes," I heard Whyle say as he ran through the door into the house, and I thought, "Now, what is up?" As I walked in the front room through the open door, it was like a morgue. No one said a word, and again I said to myself, "What has gone wrong here at home?" Then my mother spoke the first words, "You have been dancing!" Of course, I was very angry and said to her before my brothers and sisters, "And to think I am twenty-three years old, a college graduate, working hard to save money, and you called me home to tell me that I have been dancing! If Ruth and I want to dance, we'll dance and it's none of anyone's business." Since it was nearly time for the 6:30 p.m. train to South Haven, I said I would stay overnight and go back in the morning on the 8:30 a.m. train. As we were all eating supper, I am sure Mother realized her mistake, for we all became one pleasant family. Never again did my mother treat me like a teenager who couldn't make decisions for himself.

My most embarrassing moment of the summer job came one Saturday about suppertime. There were several men waiting in the shop. The boss was out to eat, and I was working alone. A gentleman came in and asked how long it would be before he could get in my chair. One of those waiting said, "I am next and this young fellow is really fast. It will be no time before he has you in his chair." So the gentleman sat down to wait his turn. I appreciated the complimentary words, and as he got in my chair I realized I had shaved him several times before and he always tipped me well. Working fast as I drew the straight-edge razor across his chin when a nerve twitched in my hand resulted to a cut on his face. It really bled, and I had to put on the powder we used to stop bleeding several times. I said to him in a low tone that I was sorry and explained what had happened. I could see he was rather upset about it, but he never said a word. I told him he didn't have to pay if he didn't want to, but when he got out of my chair he paid me with the usual tip. I really felt bad since he was a once-a-day customer. I said to myself, "I'll never see him again." To my surprise, the following Tuesday he came in and got in my chair. You can believe it, I didn't hurry as I shaved him!

As the summer wore on business remained really good. I was saving a good percentage of my earnings, and letters were coming from Monroe stating he would like to see me come to Boston in the fall. Ruth and I were enjoying the summer, for we had beach parties on the beautiful sandy shores of Lake Michigan as well as swimming. I was fulfilling a youth dream by being able to enjoy the things that resorters and vacationers paid good money to experience.

Monroe came back to Michigan in August and came to South Haven to see me. I told him I was very much sold on going to school in the east. "Good," he said, "I'll write and make application for your room." Then he said that Coleman Cheney of Gobles and John Mowrey of South Haven were also going back to Boston. Cheney was enrolled in the Harvard Business Administrative College and Mowrey was going back to B.U.S.T. (Boston University School of Theology) at 72 Mt. Vernon. Mowrey had a little money, and it was being planned that he would get a Model T Ford that we four would drive to Boston. He would sell it there, and we would all have very cheap transportation. It sounded good to me, and as my job would terminate on Labor Day it was agreed we would then have time to make all the final plans.

As Labor Day drew near I began to realize that not only a new experience was about to terminate, but Ruth and I were to be separated for the whole college year. I had done well financially and had about five hundred and fifty dollars in the bank. I had lived as cheaply as I possibly could, eating most of my meals at the restaurants in which the natives ate. The amount of money I spent on entertainment was almost nil. Labor Day was our last day to barber. The *Iroquois* arrived from Chicago at about one o'clock in the afternoon, turned around, loaded up, and by 2:20 p.m. it was on its way back. The *Petoskey*, or "Old Pet" as she was called, loaded up next with hundreds of carefree resorters, and by 5:00 p.m. she was on her way back to Chicago. The *Pier-Marquette*, a much-smaller boat that could carry just about four hundred passengers plus the baskets of fruit that would find their way to the early marketplace in Chicago, then loaded and by eight o'clock was on her way for a six-hour sailing.

Tuesday morning after Labor Day found me at the depot at seven o'clock with my bags all packed, ready to board the train to Gobles. The summer job was completed.

Ruth's oldest sister had graduated from Hillsdale College and was teaching in the Hillsdale school system. It was decided that Marjorie, Ruth's younger sister, would enter Hillsdale College as a freshman. To take the train to Hillsdale required several changes, so it was agreed that Ruth and I would drive Marjorie in the family Model T Ford. There were very few paved roads in 1922, and road maps as we know them today were nonexistent. Gasoline was purchased in the city. I took the 6:30 o'clock train to South Haven the evening before we were to drive to Hillsdale. When six o'clock the next morning came, we were on our way. We had a book of directions describing how one could get from one city or village to another. It read something like this: "Go five miles south out of the village, and when you come to a four corners with the church on the right-hand side you turn left. Go about eight miles on that road, and when you come to a corner that has a big red farmhouse and a cemetery turn right." So it went, and if we thought we were lost we stopped at a farmhouse for directions to Hillsdale. We got to Hillsdale and back to South Haven in fifteen hours and three flat tires. Of course, we were young and enjoyed the drive.

Chapter 3

Boston University School of Theology (B.U.S.T.) (1922-1923)

The plans for Boston were completed, and when I got home to Gobles I found out just what they were. John (Jack) Mowrey was to buy a Model T Ford, in which Jack, Coleman Cheney, Monroe, and I would drive to Boston, sell the car there for a higher price than it had cost in Michigan, divide the total expense by four, and arrive at the cost of transportation for each of us. The night before we were to leave Gobles, Jack gave me the car to drive to South Haven to say "Fare thee well" to Ruth. It was about the middle of September that we said goodbye to our parents, brothers, and sisters. On a day with clear skies, off to Boston in "three days of driving" was our goal.

Now, the old Model T couldn't go over thirty-five miles an hour and with the roads as they were, still in the horse and buggy stage, that was fast enough. I was driving when we went through Detroit up Gratiot to Port Huron and across the river on a ferry to Sarnia, Ontario, Canada. It was midnight before we found some cheap hotel rooms in which to catch a few winks of sleep, then on to Niagara Falls. It was our first view of the falls, and to Monroe it was disappointing. He said, "Is this the great Niagara Falls?"

After an hour stop we crossed the bridge into New York heading toward Albany. Again about midnight, we found two rooms in which to go to bed for a few hours. It was up early, since now we were on our third day and we had to drive until we got there. Out of Albany we took the old Mohawk Trail with its hairpin turns and up mountains, wondering why the Model T wouldn't run in high. It was a beautiful trip for us because these were the first mountains we had ever been in and to have to look straight up in order to see the stars was exciting to us. Did it get cold! The Model T had no heater, and we were not dressed for September mountain air. I thought my feet would freeze. It was a welcome sight when we drove down through Lexington and Concord. Monroe said, "We are almost there." It was midnight when we drove across the Charles River Bridge, up Mt. Vernon Street to "old 72," and I said, "So this is Boston." We got up a little late the next morning and walked across the Commons to a restaurant to eat breakfast. I had enough money so that I didn't have to worry about my next meal. However, I wanted to save as much of it as possible for I didn't know what the future would hold.

After we had taken Cheney over to Cambridge where he would enroll for his second year at Harvard, we three, Monroe, Jack, and I, went to the dean's office to sign up for the year. There was a student a few years older than I who was coming from Montana. I was asked if I would care to room with him. I had no objections, so it was arranged.

About the first thing on the agenda was to get a restaurant job to earn our meals. One of the most popular places to work was the famous old restaurant "Durgin Parks." It was located right in the heart of the marketplace opposite old Faneuil Hall, about a ten-minute walk from old "72" near old Sculley Square. The first time I ate in Durgin Parks, I walked up those old narrow stairs that took one above the market. It opened up into the center dining room. There were also dining rooms to the right and the left. The old furniture, the colored checked tablecloths made you wonder what kind of a place you were getting into, I said to myself, "What kind of a dump is this?" But for over two hundred years now Durgin Parks has been noted for its food and hospitality. Many years ago when it was founded the boss had one slogan: "keep plenty of good food on the table and you'll have plenty of customers." The boss liked to hire men students from the theological school since one of the students he had hired later became his minister. He engaged eight men, but because I was only a first-year man and there were eight who wanted a job including Monroe, I didn't count in his initial plans. So I got a job over the river in Cambridge. The only trouble with that job was that I had to walk a good mile to and from work, plus walk over in the morning and also in the evening for my breakfast and supper. I worked at noon from 12:00 to 2:30 p.m. and my job was to bus dishes. However, one of the fellows working at Durgin Parks quit his job after about three weeks, so the boss hired me and for the rest of the year I worked at Durgin Parks. My hours were 12:00 to 2:00 p.m. six days a week. We got all our meals, and since Durgin Parks wasn't open on Sunday the boss gave us two dollars a week for Sunday meals.

Down on Charles Street at the foot of Mt. Vernon was a barbershop in which Monroe had worked the previous year. The boss allowed us the privilege of working the chair so that neither of us would be tied down Friday p.m. and Saturday, provided the other was free to work.

Coming to Boston as a student in the University School of Theology, I made up my mind to accomplish two purposes. I was going to study hard and apply myself in order to prove to myself that I could be a fairly good student. My senior year at Kalamazoo had left something to be desired. Then too, I was going to settle within my own self whether or not God was calling me into the ministry.

I enjoyed the life of the college. Classes were made up of men only, and everyone seemed to have a purpose. The professors were very democratic. They didn't even bother to take roll in the class. Monroe and I both sat in Dr. Cell's class in the "History of Methodism," and when it came to the final grade he didn't even know there were two Wilcoxes in his class. I was the one who was nonexistent.

I did apply myself and got good grades. The year at Boston was my most fruitful college year.

In the fall of the year I went to Harvard football games. I saw the great little Centre College play great big Harvard to a standstill; also saw Harvard upset mighty Princeton.

During the winter months we did not lack for entertainment. There were always many church activities to take our attention. We were given tickets to the B.A.A. track and field meet, to hockey games, and when the big league baseball season opened, the Red Sox and the Braves opened their gates free to us. Nor did we have to eat Thanksgiving and Christmas dinners alone. Families would call the dean's office to invite students to their homes for the holiday meal, knowing that there were some of us who couldn't get home. Both Monroe and I were entertained on these two holidays.

During the fall months I became very homesick. Ruth and I had agreed to correspond, but I knew I was stuck in a completely new environment for the whole year whether I liked it or not. The city of Boston with its winding streets made it very difficult for me to get around without sometimes getting lost. For example, one street was called Winter Street north of Washington Street and Summer Street south of Washington. By the holidays I had learned to ride the subways, take the streetcars, and walk the streets of downtown Boston with confidence.

We were also meeting new friends, who in turn broadened our companionship. There were the Fuller twins who were students at the College of Secretarial Science. They lived in Taunton, Massachusetts, about thirty miles out of Boston. They invited Monroe and me with two other couples to a weekend house party at their cottage on the bay. Their mother and father were very good hosts, and we had a very enjoyable time. Bertha and I became very good friends and we corresponded for several years until we each got married.

Jack Mowrey and I would take the train to Wellesley, the home of Wellesley College, about eleven miles out of Boston. He had met a girl who lived in Brockton, Massachusetts, about thirty miles out of Boston who was going to Wellesley. She had to come into Boston to transfer to the train going to Brockton. Jack would go to the depot to keep her company between trains. This friendship grew until they were married about a year later.

As the winter months passed and spring was in the air, I was enjoying my work at the College of Theology more and more and learning to like the city of beans very much.

I had the privilege of teaching a Sunday school class and getting paid for it. I had served as a part-time monitor with pay at Sussex (evening) Law School, which prided itself on turning out better and more-prominent lawyers than did Harvard Law College. All these odd jobs kept the pocket lined with that green stuff which is so necessary to have.

As we were approaching the week of spring vacation an opportunity presented itself that proved to be a deciding factor in my life. One of the fellows at the college filled a church pulpit in Raymond, New Hampshire. He would take the Friday afternoon train out of Boston that got him in Raymond early in the evening. One of the church families would house and board him for the weekend. He would have all day Saturday to prepare his sermon. He preached both Sunday morning and evening services, as in most churches in the 1920's. He would then return to Boston Monday a.m. in time for the classes. The church paid him a liberal amount, which financed his expenses and made possible his attending B.U.S.T. (Boston University School of Theology). John wanted to leave town for the spring vacation, and asked me if I would be interested in filling the pulpit the two Sundays he was gone. I said I would because I needed the experience and the money. Little did I realize what I was getting into. To prepare a brief talk for a Sunday school lesson was one thing, but to prepare two sermons of about twenty minutes in length was another thing. I immediately got copies of sermons I had heard while in Boston. Some churches printed the sermon so that those who desired could take home a copy. As I started to write, I found that perhaps this was not a good way to do it since these experienced clergymen were way above my ability to deliver on the subject chosen. I had to get down to some of my own experiences.

When the Friday p.m. train time arrived for me to go to Raymond, I was not too confident. Raymond was a small city with two shoe factories that employed a few hundred men. One of the plant managers was a member of the Methodist Church and he offered to show me around, but I felt I needed all the time I had to study my sermons. As I knocked on the door of the home of my host and hostess, total strangers, I had a feeling of despair coming over me, but when the door opened with the words, "We're expecting you," I took heart. They first showed me to my room. Then we ate supper, after which I excused myself to study in my room. All day Saturday I read and reread the Scripture and text of my sermon, studied and rehearsed it so that I felt that I was prepared. Then I took a walk around town, went to bed early, and slept well.

The morning service didn't go as well as I had hoped. The type of sermon I preached or tried to preach had too many ideas from the other sermons I had heard so at the close of the service I went to the pulpit anteroom and stayed until nearly all the congregation had filed out. While eating dinner my host said, "There were young ladies who wanted to meet you. Why didn't you come down to shake hands with the people like the other minister does?" That did it. I made up my mind that whether or not I felt I had done a good job, I would be at the door shaking hands with a smile on my lips.

The next morning as I rode the train back to Boston, knowing I had one more Sunday ahead of me, I began to realize that God did not call me for the ministry. It being a week of vacation, I had no classes to study for, so I spent a lot of time preparing my next Sunday's sermons. The church day went off much better, and as I bid my host and hostess goodbye, thanking them for their hospitality, he said, "We believe you have the makings of a good minister."

It was a peaceful and relaxing ride on the train to Boston that Monday morning. I had proven to myself that by hard work I could get good grades; that I had learned how to study. I had peace of mind for I knew without a doubt that I would never be a clergyman. I also realized I did not want to return to B.U.S.T. next year. I would get a school teaching job some place in Michigan. I told Monroe of my decision and wrote home explaining what I intended to do.

I wrote an Ypsilanti Teachers Agency that had job referrals. They started mailing me the names and addresses of schools that had job opportunities. My Kalamazoo College dining room co-worker, Harold Dressel, who was teaching history in the upper peninsula of Michigan at Crystal Falls, wrote me that he was not going back next year. He had told the superintendent about me, and if I wanted the job I could write or wire him to that effect. I wrote him that I would accept the assignment. He wired back that he would put a contract in the mail.

In the meantime the Ypsilanti Teachers Agency had given me the name and address of Ferndale, Michigan (a suburb of Detroit), which was requesting teachers. I wrote Ferndale, giving my qualifications, etc. A letter came back stating they were interested in my application. They wanted a man to teach history and to coach basketball and track. On my way back from Boston to Gobles I would go right through Detroit on the train. "Why don't you stop over, take the interurban out to Ferndale for an interview," wrote the superintendent. That seemed very feasible, and I wrote them the day and time (about noon) I would arrive at Ferndale. Ferndale had an appeal for me. It was located north of Detroit. Detroit had a baseball team, riverboats, good theaters, libraries, and good railroad service. For me it was an ideal spot to start my teaching, so I held off from the Crystal Falls position until I had a chance to interview with the superintendent at Ferndale.

Final examinations at B.U.S.T. were somewhat different than I had experienced at Kalamazoo. The professors accepted the fact that the men were there to learn all they could within the time they had, taking into consideration that most of the students were out earning a living as well as going to school. It gave one confidence in himself.

It was at that time when we say "Monday we leave" that I was asked to preach the Sunday evening sermon at a small church in Boston. Dorothy Fuller attended the service with me. They said the collection would go to the preacher, so I picked up a few dollars my last night in Boston.

Coleman Cheney, who had been at Harvard during the year, was ready to go back to Gobles, his school year being over. Monroe was going to stay on in Boston with the idea of filling a pulpit the coming year, and also to bring back from the west his bride, who graduated from Kalamazoo College that June. Cheney and I had decided to take a little sightseeing trip on the way home. There was a night boat from Fall River, Massachusetts to New York City. We decided to take the train to Fall River, about fifty miles from Boston, and board the boat, which got us into New York Harbor about 8:00 o'clock in the morning. My brother Leland, who worked in the New York Central baggage room in Kalamazoo, sent me the checking tags to send my trunk to Kalamazoo and then to Gobles. So it was farewell to Boston. I had had a very profitable and enjoyable experience, but I felt Boston had done all that it could for me. It was my first trip on a boat and as we sailed into the New York Harbor the next morning, past the Statue of Liberty, I got a real thrill. Cheney and I did the town all day long. We walked from the Battery up to 42nd Street and from one side of Manhattan to the other. Tired but happy, we found a room to rest our weary bodies.

Chapter 4

Ferndale, Michigan: A Teacher and A Coach.

School Year (1923-1924)

My train left for Kalamazoo with a Detroit stopover around noon. Cheney decided to stay in New York to see some friends. We pulled into Detroit about 11:30 a.m., and immediately I found the interurban car that ran out through Ferndale. Ferndale was four corners at 9 Mile Road and Woodward. The streets were sandy and the sidewalks few. I inquired at the four corners about the location of Lincoln High School and was told to just follow 9 Mile west about a quarter of a mile and I would come to it. As I walked in the front 9 Mile entrance, I was asked if I needed information. I said, "Yes, I would like to see Superintendent Harris." "He is not in his office," was the reply, "but Maurice Cole, the high school principal is here. Would you care to see him?" "Yes," I said, so for the first time I met Mr. Maurice Cole.

Maurice and I held an interview. He wanted a man to coach basketball and track and teaches history. I was confident I could do the job and told him so. During my visit with Mr. Cole, I learned that his sister was Laura Wancheck, who lived in Gobles with her husband, Albert, and taught the elementary grades in the Gobles schools. I also learned that the Mrs. Cole living in Gobles was Maurice and Laura's mother.

Before too long Superintendent Harris arrived, and after a brief conversation the Superintendent told me that he and Mr. Cole would recommend me to the board, that the board seldom if ever turned down their teacher recommendations, and that I could feel certain that a contract would follow. I was to receive seventeen hundred dollars for a ten-month school year. They were allowing my study at Boston to count as one year's experience. The starting salary was fifteen hundred dollars. I immediately wired the superintendent at Crystal Falls of my decision, which he didn't like. As I took the interurban car back downtown to Detroit I thought to myself, they had me pretty well scouted before I even got to Ferndale.

My train arrived in Kalamazoo just as it was getting dark. As I got off, it felt good to be back. I walked up to the college with my one suitcase, entered "old 46," and said to Phil Vercoe, my senior year roommate, "Do you think there is an empty bed in the dorm?" It was sort of an accepted custom for alumni to come back and pile into an empty bed for the night, and if the owner of the bed came in he merely looked for another one. I stayed on the campus a couple of days and then went home to Gobles for a several-days visit.

After the senior exams were over, I returned to the college campus to see Ruth graduate. In the meantime, my teaching contract had come in the mail. Ruth had signed up to teach in Bloomingdale, a village five miles west of Gobles. After the commencement exercises Ruth's parents loaded her belongings in their Model T and prepared to leave for their home in South Haven. They expected me to go with them and were rather surprised when I told them I was taking the train to Marshall where I would be barbering during the summer. Before leaving Boston I had contacted a barber in Marshall, Michigan, located about twelve miles east of Battle Creek on the New York Central line. Monroe had worked in the barbershop the previous summer, and the boss said as long as Monroe wasn't coming back I could have the job. I would have liked to have gone back to South Haven to barber, but I found out by writing letters that the shops had already hired all the barbers needed.

It was just another one of those summers. Marshall was then and still is a city of about six thousand people, with one main business street, two theaters, and a nice residential section of good citizens. We barbered six days a week from 8:00 a.m. to 6:00 p.m. I got the thirty-five dollars a week plus half over fifty dollars, which seemed to be the accepted wage scale for barbers. Of course, my take was a lot less than it had been the previous summer for Marshall was no summer resort. It was a job, provided me with enough money to live on, and financially prepared me for my teaching job in Ferndale. I roomed in a large house right on the main street, which ran east and west. Ruth came down to Marshall by way of train to Kalamazoo and a bus. She stayed two days and three nights, rooming with a family who had a room to rent. That was the only contact I had with the western side of the state all summer.

I'll never forget the August of 1923 in Marshall. I was awakened one early morning an hour before the sun was up with a paperboy crying on the street, "President Warren G. Harding is dead."

I left my job the last week in August because I had to report to Ferndale for a teachers meeting on Labor Day at 2:00 p.m. After spending that last week in August between Gobles and South Haven, I packed my suitcase and Sunday I took the 5:45 p.m. train to Kalamazoo, got a train for Detroit, found a hotel room, up early Labor Day morning, ate breakfast, and took the interurban car out to Ferndale, where I spent forty-two years in the public school system.

Ferndale, at the corner of Woodward Avenue and 9 Mile, a village of about 8,000 with its sandy dirt streets, was as unattractive in 1923 as could be imagined. Then why did I choose Ferndale to start my teaching career? Well, for one thing and probably the most important factor, it was a suburban community on the north boundary of Detroit. Where Detroit left off at 8 Mile Road, Ferndale began. I have always been a city man. I like the bright lights, the crowds of people, and the opportunities that city life provides. There are the Detroit Tigers, the river with all its boat traffic in 1923, the colleges and libraries, the movie theaters with their fine stage productions of the 1920's, and the playhouses that staged the most beautiful musical comedies. I have ridden the Bob-Lo boats, the *Put in Bay*, the *City of Buffalo*, and the *City of Cleveland*, and many of the other boats that used to ply the waters of the Great Lakes. Baseball at its best was at my fingertips, and there was nothing I would rather play or see than a game of baseball. I have seen them all: Babe Ruth and Ty Cobb, in the 1920's to all the greats in the 1970's, the World Series of 1934, 1935, 1945, 1968, the All Star games played in Tiger Stadium. All these desirables were great attractions to me. You could take a bus or interurban car and be in downtown Detroit in about twenty minutes.

So when I got off the interurban at the corner of 9 Mile and Woodward that Labor Day morning 1923, with a suitcase in each hand, and walked up the sandy 9 Mile Road west to Lincoln High School, I started a completely new venture that didn't terminate until forty-two years later when I stood before a large group of people at my retirement reception in 1965.

Our instructions from Superintendent Harris were to report to a general teachers' meeting at 2:00 p.m. on Labor Day and to be ready to start the classroom work the following day. As I walked into the entrance of Lincoln High School the halls were deserted. As I put down my suitcase, I heard voices coming from a room on my left. I walked into the room and introduced myself to three men and a woman whose names were Chet Nelson, science teacher, Al Wiitanen, math instructor, Gerry Gaskill, shop teacher, and a very charming young lady whose name was Florence Crissman, English teacher. After a brief chat at which time I learned that Florence Crissman had gone to Kalamazoo College for a short time before transferring to the University of Michigan, that Gerry Gaskill was married, and Chet Nelson and Al Wiitanen were in the same boat as I was in, no place to sleep that night. Chet and Al invited me to go room hunting with them after the general teachers' meeting. I was more than pleased to immediately find fine companionship in a completely strange community. I was informed they had some names and addresses of families who had rooms to rent to schoolteachers, so I went into the two o'clock faculty meeting with confidence that I wasn't alone in searching for a place to sleep that night.

The superintendent introduced the new teachers, and there were many of us since the high school was built in 1920 and we were a very young faculty. Then he gave a welcome talk before we divided up into groups according to the building in which we taught. Of course, I was very attentive. With notebook and pencil, I took down the main points of the opening day meeting. Afterward one of the older teachers (three or four years' experience was considered an older teacher in Ferndale in 1923) said to me, "You can always tell those who are teaching their first year, they take notes." A few years later I could easily understand her thinking.

When the meetings were over, Chet, Al, and I set out room hunting. "If we find a house that can house all three of us, would you want to room with us?" asked Al. "Sure," I said, so we concentrated on addresses that might house all three of us. After looking at a couple of places we found ourselves on Beaufield Street at the home of Mr. and Mrs. Clayton Burns. Clayton was a Ford man and Dora, his wife, a housekeeper. They had two rooms for rent upstairs, and Beaufield Street was only about a block and a half from Lincoln High. Not one of us had a car since Chet and Al were only beginning their second year of teaching, so car parking was not a problem. We asked her if she could fix one room into a den with a lounge in which one could sleep and then two would sleep in the other room. Dora said, "I never thought that I would get men teachers requesting rooms, but I can arrange it that way for the three of you." Chet and Al, both University of Michigan graduates, had roomed together the previous year, so they said I could occupy the den's lounge and they would sleep in the other bedroom. We contracted for room and board by the month, eating our lunches at Ray Croton's delicatessen shop across the street from the high school on 9 Mile Road. We three celebrated that evening by going to a show in downtown Detroit.

Up at 7:00 a.m. for breakfast and at school by 7:45 a.m., I was to experience my very first classroom situation. Now, the difference between a new teacher today and in the 1920's is training. In my Kalamazoo College course of study I took a class from Dean Severns called "Pedagogy," defined in the dictionary as "the art, practice, or profession of teaching." We had a textbook, and once during the term we were given a topic to prepare and on a given day stand before the class as the teacher of that subject. Then we were required to visit three classes at Kalamazoo Central High School to view their methods. That constituted the training I had to start my teaching career. My schedule called for two classes in American history, a twelfth-grade subject, a class in European history, an eleventh-grade subject, a class in ancient history, a tenth-grade subject, and a class in ninth-grade physiology. Four preparations and study hall for a beginning teacher who was to coach basketball and track was a real challenge.

I had observed just enough of the teaching profession to allow me to come to definite conclusions as to the type of a teacher image I wanted to portray. In high school I had had a history teacher who had a daily outline on a paper that she held in her class book. She walked around the room always with her nose in her class book and we knew and felt that she didn't know her subject well enough to present it. That was not the type of teacher image I wished to create. Then too, I had sat in high school classes when the instructor did not have good discipline, and I couldn't understand how one could have a learning situation in the classroom under those conditions. Therefore the classroom image I wanted to develop was one where the teacher at least appeared to have a firm grasp of the subject being taught, and had the respect of the members of the class to warrant good discipline and a learning situation. At the same time, I did not try to impress my students with the idea that I was a walking encyclopedia. If I didn't know something I was going to tell them and we would look it up. So with this preclass room philosophy, I entered my first class that Tuesday morning with some nervousness but yet a feeling of confidence. The subject was American history, and I had about twenty senior students. They were very cooperative, probably knowing that I was just fresh out of college. These students as well as those in my other classes proved very interesting and friendly as days passed. That first day we had short twenty-minute periods, which allowed enough time to get acquainted, get the names of the students, say something about the text to be used, and make the next day's assignment.

If I had studied as hard while I was in college as I studied those first two years teaching, I would have undoubtedly been on the dean's list. I would get up at 5:30 a.m. to review what I had prepared and learned the night before in order to go into the classroom with confidence. After making the next day's assignment, I would throw the text on my desk and by sitting on the desk, walking around the room, writing on the blackboard in a very informal way, we would discuss the subject of the day. While I tried to be tolerant with students who would crack a joke now and then to produce a good laugh, no one was allowed to make my class a joke. Over a period of years My name "H. B. Wilcox" developed into "Hard-Boiled Wilcox."

It was customary at that time for the P.T.A. to give a reception in the gym for new as well as old teachers. It was held in the evening when parents could find time to attend. Refreshments were served and Superintendent Harris introduced the new personnel in the district. While I enjoyed meeting the adult members of the community, nevertheless it gave me a feeling that they were looking me over. Due to being a Kalamazoo College graduate and the fact that the college is a Baptist affiliate, many people reasoned that my religion was that of my college and invited me to become a member of the Baptist church. I did attend a few Sundays, but I learned that there was a Methodist congregation meeting in the "Odd Fellows" Hall located on Woodward about three blocks south of 9 Mile Road. Al Wiitanen had accepted the superintendent of the Sunday school and asked me to teach a class of high school boys and girls. I readily accepted, and for twenty-five years I was a Sunday schoolteacher in the Ferndale First Methodist Church. The following year, 1924, ground was broken to start the building of the present church on the corner of Woodward Avenue and Leroy. I was a member for forty-five years before we transferred our church membership to the Royal Oak First United Methodist. During those many years I organized the first youth fellowship, coached the church basketball team, participated in the many church functions, held several official positions and greatly benefited from all my church activities.

The fall weeks, crammed full of activities and hard work, passed in no time, and as I took the train home to Gobles to spend Thanksgiving with my parents, brothers, and sisters. I became fully aware that the basketball season was upon us, and that meant more hard work and long hours. While in Kalamazoo I called a Kalamazoo College friend who had been one of the stars on the college basketball team. He said, "Come over to the house and we'll talk it over." He gave me a small book on basketball that discussed the defense and offense, with diagrams showing the position of the men on the court. Having a profound interest in the game while in college, I felt very confident that I could handle the coaching job, and with this book on basketball I built my offense and defense. The coach whom I succeeded had not had a winning season, but he did leave me with some boys who had previous experience.

Now, high school athletics in the 1920's was considerably different than they are in the 1970's. There was no other coach of basketball in the school system than myself. The call went out for all who were interested in making the team to report to the gym at 7:00 p.m. because we held our practice sessions in the evening. About fifteen boys reported, and they made the Ferndale Lincoln High School basketball squad for the year 1923-24. From this group of boys I had to mold the varsity and reserve teams. We started each day's practice with the fundamentals, which many of the team members didn't like. The big interest was just shooting baskets. We played such schools as Royal Oak, Birmingham, Rochester, and Imlay City. We had a sixteen-game schedule, and after the last game was played with Birmingham on the Ferndale floor, Ferndale stood fourteen wins and two losses. The only team to beat us was the Birmingham squad, which won two hard-fought games, the last one by two points.

Coaching at Ferndale in 1923 was a lot different than it is in 1970. As a basketball coach in addition to my academic duties, I had to build the schedule, buy the equipment, contract for the referee, supervise the ticket sales, and hundred and one different duties that today are all the responsibility of the director of athletics. So when my landlady, Mrs. Burns, said to me, "Mr. Wilcox, why don't you move your bed over to the high school that will save you walking back and forth" she was merely reminding me that for six days a week I was practically living in the building. We did most of our traveling by interurban car. For example, when we played Rochester we boarded the interurban about 5:40 p.m., walked to the high school, dressed for the reserve game, and were ready to play at 7:00 p.m.

It was the rule that anyone playing in the reserve game could not participate in the varsity game, so I held out my seven best players for the varsity.

The varsity game got under way about 8:30 p.m. It was 10:30 p.m. before the boys were dressed and ready to leave the school. Then we had to eat, which meant it was nearly 12:30 o'clock before we got off the interurban at Woodward and 9 Mile. By the time I got to my room on Beaufield and in bed it was after one o'clock. If it had been a rather close game I would lay in bed unable to sleep as a result of replaying it. This wouldn't have been too bad if all these situations were on Friday nights, enabling me to sleep in on Saturday morning, but when the game was played on Tuesday night and I had to be in the classroom by 8:00 a.m. Wednesday, it was pretty tough on my physical self. When that last season game was played, I breathed a sigh of relief for I was glad it was over. My stomach had begun to bother me as a result of the nervous tension.

Coaching track was not as hard a task since there was little or no audience participation. Ferndale didn't get an athletic field until a year later, so our track meets were all on foreign fields. Because the school system was growing by leaps and bounds, a man by the name of Cal Knox had been hired to teach in the science department the second semester. Cal was a University of Michigan man and had done the broad jump on the track team. He volunteered to come out and work with the boys in the field events while I handled the running events. The property across the street from the high school on 9 Mile Road was vacant so we used it for the field events while I used the dirt road of 9 Mile for the running. This only lasted to the spring of 1924 because you could see houses going up all around the school building. Things were moving so fast that the new addition to Lincoln High was to be finished by September.

The spring months have always been my favorite time of year. In the school business it was and still is contract time. While I felt I had done a very acceptable job in both athletics and academics, I was pleased when Maurice Cole, our principal, came in the room where I had a desk, sat down and began to chat. "Have you enjoyed your first year of teaching?" he asked. "You have done a good job, and we want you to return next year." My answer was, "I would like to return provided the salary is right." "Well," he said, "you would get the maximum raise of two hundred dollars." "That sounds reasonable," I said, "and you can count on me being here next year." While I had worked to no end, coaching, etc. without the additional pay coaches receive today, I was pleased that my services were appreciated.

Little did we realize what lay ahead of us next year, because Principal Cole was retiring from the school profession. He had been studying law at the Detroit College of Law night school and had made up his mind to take the bar examinations and if he passed, which he did, he would set up a law office in Ferndale. Maurice and I have been friends all these forty-nine years that I have been in Ferndale. He graduated from Alma College, a member of the M.I.A.A., and has since served on its board of trustees. He has been very active in Ferndale social and civic affairs. He is a charter member of the Ferndale Exchange Club organized in May 1924, a club of which I have been a member since April 1926.

Chapter 5

Europe—Summer of 1924

Chet Nelson had left the Burns home at Christmastime and was going to be married. Al Wiitanen and I remained the rest of the year, but Al was also to be married during summer 1924. What about the summer, I was asking myself! One day Cal Knox and I got to talking while he was up in my room. There were only about three choices: go summer school, which I didn't want to do, get a barber job, which didn't appeal to me, or do something exciting and different. So I said to Cal, "Let's go to Europe." "Okay," he said, "When shall we leave?"

My Boston friend Jack Mowery was going to be married in June 1924. He had met the young lady at Wellesley College for girls when he and I would go out for parties, etc. She was the daughter of the Episcopal rector at Brockton, Massachusetts. Jack wrote early in the spring, telling me of their plans and asking if I could arrange to be his best man. They would set the wedding date to suit my convenience. Our school term wasn't over until the middle of June. If we were going to Europe our plans could easily fit into the wedding plans, so I told Jack that a wedding date any time during the last week of June would be convenient for us, and that my friend Cal Knox would be coming to Boston on our way to New York. I knew Cal and I could stay up at old 72 Mt. Vernon during the time we were in Boston with little extra expense to ourselves. The wedding date was set for June 30, 1924.

After spring vacation Cal and I started to make our plans. First, we had to set down on paper a rough schedule showing where we intended to travel and about how long we could stay in each place. I went to a steamship agency, the Cunard Line, in downtown Detroit and noted the sailing time of the various ships. In 1924 all travel to and from Europe had to be made by ships, and there were a number of ships going from and coming to New York every day. The sailing of the *Lancastria*, about a twenty-five thousand-ton ship, on July 3 from New York City seemed to fit our plans. This would give us plenty of time for the wedding party and getting to New York.

Our sailing date was July 3, 12:00 noon. We planned to be in Europe and England about thirty days, so by scheduling our return trip on the *Acquitania* out of Southampton, England we would be back in the United States about August 21, 1924. We purchased our round-trip steamship tickets to make sure we were going to get home all right. Then there was the expense of the passport, which was ten dollars and the visas, which were ten dollars for each country to be visited. Our schedule called for visas to travel to England, France, Switzerland, Holland, and Germany, so we had sixty dollars invested besides our passage before we even left Ferndale, a total of about two hundred and ninety dollars.

During the last month of school we got serious about our trip. We visited people who had gone abroad, getting information on the customs of the several countries to be visited, the money system, etc. In the 1920's we didn't have the wash-and-dry, no-wrinkle clothing we have today in the 1970's, so we each took a suitcase and a small bag called a grip or valise since we were informed that each train passenger had to be responsible for his own luggage. This European custom of travel has never changed.

When Memorial Day arrived, I had a big letdown. The track season was over and we were within two weeks of the end of my first year's teaching experience. I had my contract for the year 1924-25 at nineteen hundred dollars. We had a big summer planned ahead of us. My nervous stomach couldn't help but feel better. After spending a few days in Gobles with my family and visiting Ruth in South Haven, I went back to Ferndale to pack my suitcase, say goodbye to Al Wiitanen and his bachelor days, and prepare for our big venture.

I had been able to save about three hundred dollars during the year but needed two hundred dollars more to make the trip, so I went to the Ferndale American State Bank and was told my credit was good for the two hundred dollars loan. Europe had not yet recovered from World War I. Everything was dirt cheap for Americans. At the bank in Paris one could buy thirty-three to forty francs for one U.S. dollar. The same money situation existed in all the other countries except Switzerland, which had not been harmed as much by the war. When I left New York on the *Lancastria* I had about one hundred and twenty dollars to take me though Europe.

To go abroad, as people in the 1920's called it, was really something. Being a history teacher, I planned on making this trip a very educational one. Today people fly to Europe for the weekend, and high school senior classes make Rome or some other European city their senior trip. Cal and I decided we would take the night boat, *City of Buffalo*, out of Detroit to Buffalo, leaving at 5;00 p.m. That would get us into Buffalo at about 8:00 a.m. in time to catch a train to Boston, arriving early in the evening. It was a pleasant trip across Lake Erie. The boat wasn't crowded, our cabin was satisfactory for an overnight trip, and the food was good.

Arriving in Bean Town (Boston), we took the subway to the Commons, then walked up Beacon Hill to "old 72." The term for the School of Theology was over, and there were plenty of vacant rooms. Since I had been a student there, the only cost to us was for the sheets and towels we used. It really felt good to be back in "72," to walk across the Commons," to eat at Durgin Parks, and to relive some of the atmosphere and environment that made my Boston year one of the best in my life.

After several days of preparation such as renting an evening dress suit, receptions, and wedding rehearsals, the day of the wedding dawned. We took an early afternoon train to Brockton, and Jack took us over to the rector's house where we ate and dressed for the big event. It was a delightful one, but I am sorry to have to report that the last time I saw Jack was during World War II days. He had divorced and was married to another woman.

We spent July 2 making plans to leave for New York. There was a night boat leaving at 5:00 p.m., which would get us into the city in plenty of time to board the *Lancastria*. It was a pleasant and uneventful overnight trip. As we sailed by the Statue of Liberty I began to feel a little flutter in the stomach; a feeling of do we want to make this trip into the unknown after all? I said to Cal, "How do you feel now about going to Europe?" He also expressed a similar anxiety, but it didn't stop us from walking up the gangplank to board the ship. As 12:00 noon drew near, the whistle blew three long blasts announcing the ship's readiness to sail. As the tugs pushed her into the river and we sailed down past the Statue of Liberty, again we realized we were about to experience one of the great adventures of our lives; we were off to Europe.

It wasn't too long before we encountered our first unpleasant situation. It was mealtime, and when we walked into the poorly equipped dining room we found tin plates and cups on the table. The food was brought in on tin dishes, which killed our appetite for most of us. We later learned that the *Lancastria* was the first Cunard Line ship to introduce the tourist class, making it a two-class ship. However, the tourist-class passengers were being treated as immigrants and that was very distasteful to all of us. The tourist class section of the ship had doctors, lawyers, schoolteachers, and other professional people. We were not used to eating off tin plates or drinking out of tin cups. You should have heard the rattle of the tin announcing our protest; you would have thought that the inmates of a prison had gone on strike. It wasn't long before the ship's steward and a committee representing the tourists had resolved the obnoxious situation and our mealtime became a pleasurable one. With apologies, the steward explained that this was the first tourist class for the ship and the employees had not yet adjusted to it.

The first day out was calm. We got up the first morning onboard in bright sunshine, a calm sea, and very little wind. In the afternoon the seamen began to decorate the rear deck in honor of July 4th, and the menu at dinner portrayed a American 4th of July firecracker. We had the Princeton University dance band on board, which played almost exclusively for the tourist-class people, leaving the English ship band for the first-class passengers. Everything was in readiness for a big 4th of July celebration and dance. Dance partners were plentiful since everyone on the ship was out for a good time, and we were just one big happy family of about five hundred tourist-class passengers. But there is always an end to every good thing, and so it was on the *Lancastria* that 4th of July evening. About eight o'clock it clouded up, the wind started to blow, and the rain came down. The decorations and all that went with it were gone with the wind; the ocean began to roll. The ship started a rocking chair motion that lasted for days. Stabilizers were unheard of on ships in the 1920's. You either had to be a seaman or suffer, and there were a lot of people on board who suffered. I'll admit I fed the fishes a few times, but after a few days had passed most of us got used to the ship's motion.

The *Lancastria* was an eight-day ship, but she was taking ten days and ten nights for the crossing. We were told that the *Olympia* was a ship chartered by a delegation for a worldwide convention meeting in London. The *Lancastria* took the convention delegation overflow. Since the *Olympia* didn't leave New York until several days after we did and they wanted to get the convention delegates to London about the same time, our ship slowed down to meet the schedule. It was a welcome sensation to no longer feel the throb of the engines as we anchored in Southampton at the end of the ten days and ten nights on board.

One morning after about five days, a seaman said to me, "Did you see the *Leviathan* pass us early this morning?" I said, "No, I didn't. I am sorry I missed her." The *Leviathan* was the fastest ship on the ocean and one of the largest if not the largest afloat. The Germans had built her several years before World War I started, and when the United States declared war against Germany in 1917 the ship was in the New York Harbor. The U.S. officials seized and remodeled it to carry twelve thousands troops across on each sailing. Our government kept it running at high speed continually for the two years of the war. After the war was over and there was no longer a military need for the ship, it was converted to passenger traffic between New York and Europe. The ship needed new engines and a good overhaul. It was continually breaking down on the high seas and was proving to be expensive to run. It happened again. The last morning out as we began to see land, we passed the *Leviathan*. One of her engines had given out. The next morning we awoke, docked in Southampton, ate breakfast, and then went out on deck to see the *Leviathan* being pulled by tugs as she came into the harbor. It took a few hours for the passengers going to England to disembark. At the same time, there were tons and tons of mail, etc. to be hauled out of the "ship's hole," so it was around noon before the tugs pushed the *Lancastria* away from the dock and headed across the channel to Cherbourg, France where our first ocean voyage came to an end.

The harbor of Cherbourg had been destroyed by the Germans during the war and had not yet been completely rebuilt. This made it necessary for our ship to anchor outside of the old harbor and a tender came alongside to take us off. I can never forget those first sights of French life as we saw it in Cherbourg. There were all kinds of hucksters trying to peddle their wares to the newly arrived American tourists. Before we left the United States we had been warned about prices. "Never pay their price, offer them about half and then turn to walk away." The huckster would follow, and when the final deal was completed one would get the article for about half of the amount that the peddler first quoted. This was standard procedure while we were in Europe.

Our boat train for Paris was supposed to leave about seven o'clock in the evening. For some unknown reason it was about ten o'clock before the train pulled out. The war had taken a heavy toll on France. The rolling equipment was in bad shape. The coal-burning locomotives were very old, and some looked like toys compared to the monsters we had in the United States. About 1:00 a.m. our train stopped for apparently no reason at all, and it was an hour before we started again for Paris. It was just the break of day when we pulled into the Paris depot. We had been with many of these people only ten days, yet it seemed we had known some of them for weeks. We had had so much fun together. It was "goodbye," and then, "Have a nice stay in Europe."

Cal Knox and I hailed a taxi, and with my meager French and the driver's few words of English, which he had learned from the English and Americans during the war, we conveyed that we wanted to find a cheap hotel and would he drive until we found one. We stopped at one small hotel—there were many all over Europe, rang the night bell, and asked in French as the door opened, "Do you have a room?" "No," he said in English, "but I'll let you use the phone to call if you can converse in French." "I'll try," I said. Sure enough, the man on the other end of the line understood me and said, "yes, we have a room." The taxi driver got the address and off we went. We had heard how cheap taxis were in Paris, so we were nearly shocked to tears when the driver told us we owed him one hundred and seventy-five francs, or about five dollars. We put up a good argument but to no avail. He informed us that between certain morning hours, which I don't remember, they could charge almost any amount they wanted to. Boy, five dollars for a taxi to find a room sure put a cramp in our financial schedule. It was a real small hotel. The room was rather dirty, but not having had any sleep for the past twenty-five hours, we didn't hesitate to hit the bed.

We spent a week in Paris. The hotel room cost us seventy-five cents each, and by eating at the restaurants where the natives ate, one could buy a good meal for ten to fifteen cents. It was our aim to see as much as possible of Paris and its environs for as little money as possible. As a teacher of history I wanted to make the most of it for its educational value. We took one sightseeing bus trip to view the war ruins, which resulted when the Germans fought their way toward Paris, never reaching it. One city of about one hundred thousand people, the city of Reims, was almost totally destroyed. Only the cathedral was left standing, but it was badly damaged.

Another side trip we took was out to Versailles. We got out there by train, but when we were ready to return to Paris the station agent said there was no trains running back to Paris. After trying to find out from him how we could return, a young lady spoke up in English and said she was going back to Paris and if we wished we could go with her because it was necessary to make several streetcar changes. In talking with her we discovered that she was English, had been living in Paris for a number of months, and had learned French. We sure did appreciate having her escort us back to the city.

We enjoyed our week in Paris. Our next destination was Switzerland. In order to cut expenses and save money we decided to take a night train to Luzern. We found an empty compartment on the third-class car, tied a handkerchief on the door handle to keep people from coming in, stretched out on the seats and slept part of the time we were aboard. Our schedule called for an arrival in Luzern about ten a.m., but we rode until twelve noon before our train pulled into an Alsatian city in Alsace, France. We sat on the train for some time, expecting it to start, only to be told by a trainman, "All out, it's the end of the line." We got off the car, found a couple who had a daughter of about eighteen years of age who said in English that we should have made a train change several hours back, that they were going to that city and would be glad to have us accompany them so that we wouldn't get lost again. We greatly appreciated the opportunity, so after eating lunch with them at the station dining room we boarded a train back to the terminal, where we changed for Luzern. Since we didn't leave the railroad station our mistake didn't cost us any money since in France you didn't surrender your ticket until you left the depot.

It was a very pleasant ride as we slowly snaked our way through the Alps. While standing in the aisle, our ears caught English being spoken in another compartment. We introduced ourselves and learned these two ladies were from England and were getting off the train in Bern, Switzerland, which would also be our destination since this train didn't go any farther. "Have you your hotel reservation?" one of them asked. Our answer of course was no. "We are staying at the Bahnhof just across the street from the depot," said one. "If you wish you could accompany us to the hotel and perhaps get a room." We had been on the train nearly twenty-four hours and were tired, so we agreed to accept their hospitality. Our room was luxurious and cost us only one dollar and seventy-five cents for the night, which, however, was a little more than we were used to paying.

Our first impression after transferring at the French-Swiss border was the cleanliness of the Swiss trains. Switzerland had not been touched by the war, and there was a very noticeable difference between the two countries. It was a short train ride from Bern to Luzern, so after a beautiful sleep in Bern, the capital of Switzerland, we spent the forenoon seeing the sights. Bern has always been noted for its fine zoo, and we visited it. Our train arrived at Luzern in the late afternoon. We immediately found a cheap hotel room. We didn't have to be concerned about is cleanliness because the Swiss have always been accorded that distinction. After a couple of days in Luzern we took the train to Interlaken, a city I have since visited three times and have fallen in love with its always-quaint appearance. One side trip we took was up the Jung-Frau, which is 13,668 feet high, enabling it to always have snow for tourists.

Leaving the very pleasant country of Switzerland, our next stop was Strasbourg, a city of about one hundred thousand people. It was here in our hotel room, located just across the court from the depot that we had to make a decision. While in Paris we had bought a book of railroad third-class tickets that included Berlin on our itinerary. Going over our finances, we determined that if we held to our schedule that took us to Berlin for a few days, it would really force us to watch our pennies. The other alternative was to skip Berlin and get a few days earlier sailing out of Southampton. We slept on it for twenty-four hours and decided to cancel Berlin from our trip. We went to the hotel clerk and asked for information. He said we would have to wire the Cunard Office in Paris and ask for an earlier sailing. The wire came back that we could sail on the *Mauretania* leaving Southampton August 9 and arriving in New York about August 14. If we wanted the *Mauretania*, we should mail our tickets to the Paris office and they would wire our new accommodations.

We really gave Strasbourg the going over. Compared to other cities we had visited in Europe, it had little to offer. We played tennis at the municipal tennis courts, took in theater shows, went to a nightclub that had the finest vaudeville entertainment I had ever seen, and did things just to kill time waiting for the wire from Paris giving us our new ship reservations. After extending our stay in Strasbourg from three to five days, we came to our hotel room after taking in a show to find the long-awaited telegram under our door. It was a welcome sight.

We got out our suitcases and began to pack. We wanted to get an early train to Mainz on the Rhine River, where we were to take the day riverboat to Koln, Germany. Arriving in Mainz late in the afternoon, we found an acceptable hotel room, had dinner, and went to a nightclub, where we saw how distasteful it was for Germans to have foreign soldiers, French and English, inhabiting their city.

Boarding the Rhine steamer about 8:00 a.m. we heard a voice say, "Hello, *Lancastria*." Looking up we saw two American schoolteachers whom we had met onboard. They too were going down the Rhine. "A small world," we said. We docked at Koln about six o'clock after a very interesting river trip. We found a nice small hotel to fit our pocketbook. Koln had been hard hit by World War I, and all around one could see some destruction. German money was cheap, although the government had just initiated a new currency to stabilize the money exchange. When we went to the hotel desk to pay our bill upon leaving, we found that it was more than what we had expected. Our first thoughts were—another European trick. The clerk couldn't talk English, and we couldn't talk German, so our arguing didn't get us anywhere. A moment later a German gentleman, upon hearing our discussion and realizing that neither of us could understand what the other was saying, stepped up and said, "Pardon me, fellows, but I can speak German and maybe I can help you." We told him about our hotel bill. In a very diplomatic way he explained to us that the government had levied a tax on hotel bills and that was the reason for our differences. He did such a nice job of selling that we left Koln and Germany feeling that after all, they were pretty nice people.

We had always heard so much about Holland and the Dutch that when we arrived in Amsterdam we were thrilled. Everything was so different from other places in Europe. The canals, the clothes, the food, the customs all made us feel welcome. We took a canal boat trip to the island of Marken, where we saw a small community of a few hundred people living as the Dutch had always lived. We went out to the Hague where the Hague conferences were housed, to the seashore where we went swimming in the sea, dined in restaurants with music by a Dutch street band, went to the theater, and heard a good Dutch orchestra that could really play music the American way. Yes, we really enjoyed Holland, but when the train pulled out of the Amsterdam Bohnhof for Ostend [Belgium] where we took the night boat to England, we were ready for the departure. Another hotel bill was saved. It was a cold night crossing the Channel. We were told the boat was delayed in sailing because there were important government officials from Europe going to London for a conference and the boat awaited their arrival.

Anyway dawn was breaking when we boarded our train for London. We found a hotel room that fit our pocketbook, got a few hours' sleep, had breakfast of the good English-American food, ham and eggs, then set out to see London. During the course of the several days we were there we took some side trips that were historically enjoyable. A day at Plymouth viewing the spot, marked by a plaque, where our first Pilgrims boarded the small sailboats that took them to Plymouth Rock, Massachusetts was another story I could relate to my American history classes. Besides visiting the many government buildings, the London Tower, viewing the changing of the guard, etc., we spent several hours out at Wembly where the British Empire Boy Scout Jubilee was being held in the British Empire Stadium.

We had about reached the saturation point and had begun to look forward to that long ship ride back to the good old United States. Before leaving home I had given Ruth and my parents our itinerary. That enabled them to write a letter, general delivery, at several designated cities. Upon arriving at these cities we would head for the post office to inquire about mail. We would generally have some. One letter I received in London was from Ruth. She said that before her school year had terminated, she had made up her mind to have her nose rebuilt. She had had it done before she enrolled at Kalamazoo College and I thought it looked good, but her image of a good-looking nose on her face was one thing, and the ability of a doctor to give her that look was another. This was the first I had known about her anxiety over her nose.

We inquired at a travel agency about a train to Southampton on Friday, August 8 for the *Mauretania* sailing Saturday, August 9. The agent said, "Why don't you take the boat train leaving Saturday morning?" Well, at that time we just didn't know what a boat train was, and we didn't want to risk missing the ship's sailing. So we took an afternoon train for Southampton so as to be early for the embarkation. At that time we did not realize that a boat train was a special nonstop loaded with passengers for the ship's sailing, and that the ship wouldn't leave until the boat train had arrived with its hundreds of people safely on board.

We boarded our train at the Waterloo station and in about two hours were in Southampton. Our first concern was to get a place to sleep. An English bobby was at the station and our first inclination was to get directions, where was the business section, the boat docks, restaurants, etc. He was very friendly and helpful. When I asked him if he could refer us to a place where we could get a bed for the night, he said, "Well, you know the *Mauretania* is sailing tomorrow and the hotels are pretty well filled. However," he continued, "there is a lady who runs a restaurant in the business section of the city. She has good food, it's clean, and she has a few rooms upstairs that she rents. You probably can get accommodations there." We Americans have never had as much respect for and confidence in our policemen as the Englishmen have in theirs. This caused me to ask in a questionable voice, "Do you think that her rooms are really safe for tourists?" He answered with a hint of sarcasm in his voice, "I beg your pardon, the thing for you to do is to find your own room." I recovered immediately, realizing I was dealing with an English police officer and apologized for questioning his information. Then I asked how to locate this restaurant. He gave us good directions, and we picked up our suitcases and were on our way.

Finding the restaurant and inquiring about a room, the lady said she had one left. However, it was located at the head of the stairs, and for the man and his wife to get to their room they would have to go through our room. Of course, that didn't sound very inviting to us. Although we were living in the 1920's when people went to bed at night without bothering to lock the door, we were not used to the idea of having other people walk past our bed in the middle of the night. But what were we to do? So we said, "We'll take your last room." She said, "If you don't go to bed too early the other roomers will probably be in bed and won't disturb you."

We left our suitcases in our room and took off to see the city. Southampton had been hit pretty hard during the war since the Germans tried to knock out all shipping and industrial centers. Being young, we were in good condition to walk miles a day without tiring us a great deal. One most interesting place we wanted to walk to was the ship docks. There we saw the beautiful tour funnel, a quadruple-screw turbine ship that was to take us back to New York in world-record time.

It was getting dark as we found our way back to the restaurant and our room. We ate a good English dinner, then sat for what seemed hours before going to bed. It was eleven o'clock, and the couple who were to occupy the room beyond ours had not yet returned to the restaurant, so we told the clerk that we were going to bed. It wasn't too long before we heard the next-room occupants coming. They passed our bed very quietly and closed their door. I said to Cal, "Do you think it is safe now to go to sleep?" "Yes," he said and off we went to slumberland.

Awakened at about 6:30 a.m., we hurriedly dressed because we didn't want the other occupants to come through and find us in our birthday clothes. Going downstairs with our baggage, we were one of the first customers for breakfast. The foremost thing on our mind was, "Today we sail." Walking over to the docks, we found we were early arrivals. There was a tent on the passenger deck where foreigners coming to America were examined for diseases, etc. since steamship companies were responsible then and today for allowing illegal people to be transported on their ships to the United States. If there were illegal passengers onboard when the ship arrived in New York, the steamship company would have to transport them back to Europe. The only thing we had to do was to roll up our sleeve to show our vaccination scar. Regardless, I don't know what the officers could have done with us any way. We were American citizens with passports.

It was just as much of a thrill to walk up the gangplank to board the *Mauretania* as it had been to board the *Lancastria*. We were ready to go home. The *Mauretania* was a much-larger ship than the *Lancastria*. Our cabin was nicer, and there was no trouble with the dining room facilities. About 11:30 a.m. the whistle blew three long blasts, announcing to the natives as well as to the hundreds of passengers that we were nearing the twelve o'clock hour, the time the ship was to sail. As the tug pushed her into the Channel we bid farewell to dear old England and to the big tour funnel ship *Olympia*, which was to sail a couple of days later, docked across from us. The ship headed across the Channel to Cherbourg to pick up passengers. We left Cherbourg at 5:45 p.m. G.M.T., and the ship headed into its course with full speed ahead. During the course of the trip we learned the ship's engines had been overhauled, and the captain, A. H. Rostron, was trying for a new record crossing that we had a good chance of making if the weather held.

In our dining room an attorney and his wife approached us stating that several had arranged for a table and would we care to join them. "We sure would," was our reply. All during the voyage I ate meals in the company of the attorney and his wife, two young businessmen, a member of the U.S. Olympic team, two or three others, and my partner Cal Knox. We had a very enjoyable trip. Probably, because I was a track man and had seen the tail end of the Olympic Games while in Paris, an Olympic team member by the name of Coultier of Iowa University and I became companions for the five days and six nights we were abroad. Also onboard and one of our "table gang" was a June West Point graduate. He had spent the summer in Europe before going into military service for the duration of his enlistment

As our ship passed the Ambrose Channel Light Vessel 3,157 miles from Cherbourg, it was 5:05 p.m., New York time. It was announced that the ship had set a new world record passage of five days, three hours, and twenty minutes. The ship's printing press went to work, and before docking about nine o'clock every passenger got a card with the record statistics and a picture of the *Mauretania* on the other side. The next morning the New York newspaper carried an article reporting the steamship Mauretania had established a new trans-Atlantic record between Cherbourg, France and New York City. The time of the Mauretania's crossing was five days, three hours and twenty minutes. The route was 3,157 miles, averaging 25.60 knots per hour. The previous record was held by the Leviathan, four hours longer than the Mauretania.

There was a rule that if the ship docked after eight o'clock in the evening passengers could stay on board overnight if they wished. It was about a twenty-four hour train ride between New York and Kalamazoo, so I wanted to get a train out of New York around late morning in order to get the train from Kalamazoo to Gobles at 5:45 p.m. With the opportunity to stay onboard overnight, I could adhere to my schedule without paying for a room. Cal had gotten off the ship the previous night, having plans that didn't coincide with mine, but there were dozens of people who took advantage of this rule. One of our table crowd, the West Point graduate, and I spent the evening talking about our experiences abroad. We agreed we would get off the ship together. He had had some military officer's uniforms tailor made in France and was anxious to bring them in duty free. So about 7:30 a.m. Friday, August 15, 1924, he and I walked down the gangplank together. He was dressed in one of his best new uniforms. Out of habit, the customs official asked, "Are you American citizens?" "I beg your pardon," said the young lieutenant. Realizing his mistake, the officer said, "I am sorry. Have you anything to declare?" "No," was our answer. "OK" he said, and wrote an "OK" on our baggage with chalk.

    I took a taxi to Grand Central Station. There was a train leaving around noon, which got me into Kalamazoo about 11:30 a.m. the next day. I purchased a ticket, got some breakfast, walked over to Times Square, and whiled away a few hours until train time. I was to occupy the upper berth of a seat and an elderly lady was to have the lower. After our conversation had made us better acquainted, she asked, "Are you Harold Lloyd, the famous movie star?" No, I said. "Well I noticed by your baggage you just came in from Europe and with your bone-rim glasses you do look like him."

    It was raining at 11:30 a.m. when our train pulled into Kalamazoo. I ran to the waiting room, deposited my baggage in the baggage room where my brother Leland worked, and found a phone to call Ruth to let her know I was home. To my surprise her mother told me that she was in Grand Rapids having her nose reshaped and wouldn't I go up there to visit her? "Yes," I said, "in a day or two, I'll do it." The 5:45 p.m. train to Gobles brought me in on time. I was delighted to see my sweet little sister Donita at the station to meet me. It was sort of getting acquainted again. In a small town most people are aware of what other people are doing. Like my college track days, the natives kept up with the activities of the Wilcox brothers. So as then, "What was your trip like?" "Did you enjoy Europe?" etc. The pastor of the Methodist Church asked me if I would take over the Sunday evening service by describing my experiences in Europe. I said I would, and prepared about a forty-minute talk. It got noised around that Harold Wilcox was talking on "Europe" and the church was packed. After about forty minutes relating my travel, I didn't want to bore them so I said, "I hope I have not talked too long." Their reaction was that they wanted to hear more, so I gave them another twenty minutes and then sat down. I can still see my Dad in the front row urging me to continue. Mother and Dad, it seemed, were so occupied that I had had very little time to really sit down and talk with them. Of course, their family was still young—Whyle, Paul, Abbie, and Donita were still all at home and in school.

    After a couple of days at home I took the train to Kalamazoo and the interurban to Grand Rapids. I found Ruth staying in a hotel with her nose all bandaged. She had seen the job done on it and was very disappointed. In her opinion the surgeon had left it too long. I spent several hours with her, then took the interurban car back to Kalamazoo and the evening train to Gobles. Ruth got home to the farm in South Haven a few days before I had to leave for Ferndale because we had the opening teachers' meeting on Labor Day. I spent a couple days with her on the farm before saying farewell for a few weeks. She was a most unhappy schoolteacher as she headed back to Bloomingdale for her second year. Her intentions were to have a "repeat job" done on her nose during Christmas vacation.

Chapter 6

Teaching and Coaching (1924-1934)

School Year 1924-25

Labor Day 1924 arrived, and it found me back at the Burns residence on Beaufield. Wiitanen was married, so I asked a new teacher, Edward Ferguson, a graduate of Western State College at Kalamazoo, to occupy the other room. Mrs. Burns didn't want to serve us our meals so we made the Realto Restaurant our headquarters for breakfast and dinner, eating our lunches across the street from the high school at Crotons Delicatessen Store.

Maurice Cole had resigned the high school principal position, having gone into legal work. The school board had hired Leon Plumb to succeed him. Leon was a fine, honest, sincere, and dedicated man, but he wasn't an administrator. Leon lived with his wife in Ferndale and had been teaching math in the Detroit Public School system for years. He was a member of the Ferndale board of education and had resigned so that the board could appoint him principal. He was not the choice of Superintendent Harris, who himself was treading on thin ice as far as his job was concerned. It was evident from the first day that we were in trouble. There was no schedule of classes, no preorganization, and we all felt that we were wasting a lot of time getting started. After two weeks had passed, the principal stated at the teachers' meeting, "We have been two weeks getting organized but some other schools take that long so we didn't do too badly."

Unfortunately the superintendent's office was in the high school building right next to the principal's office. It didn't take long before there was dissension in the ranks and the faculty began to divide into two groups, those on the side of the superintendent and those for the principal. While I didn't feel the school had good leadership, I felt that I should be loyal to my boss, the principal. That did not endear me to the superintendent. However, I did manage to "keep my nose clean" as they say, and did not get too involved in the controversy. By the time Christmas vacation had arrived Principal Plumb had given the board his resignation, and we all went on our vacation knowing that when we returned there would be some changes. The superintendent appointed a woman who had come into the high school just the previous September as acting principal. At the first teachers' meeting we were told that the superintendent would run the school, working through the acting principal.

The fall weeks slipped by, and before we realized it the Kalamazoo College homecoming game, dinner, and dance were history. Ruth and I had spent the weekend on campus, and I took a late train on Sunday night, getting into Ferndale real early in the morning without too much sleep. I then put in a good day in the classroom.

Thanksgiving found me across the state eating my dinner in Gobles, then a couple of days in South Haven before returning by train to Detroit and Ferndale.

First call for basketball, I announced, and we had about the usual number turning out. We had graduated a couple of our better players in the June graduating class, and I didn't have a good group coming out to compensate for the loss. The result was Ferndale had only a fifty percent winning season. This upset Superintendent Harris to no degree. His job was in jeopardy, and he wanted to see that team win more games. He had brought in a new football coach from the University of Michigan, Fred Wall. Fred was a very likeable fellow. Harris wanted Fred to take over the team to try to win more games, but Fred told the superintendent Wilcox is doing the best that can be done with the material he has. So Harris didn't say any more about my coaching. In 1924-25 the basketball season was, as it is today in the 1970's, a long season. Teaching a full load and coaching a sport was difficult enough, but the added tension resulting from the lack of administrative leadership resulted in my old stomach giving me fits. While home for Christmas our family doctor, Wescott, gave me a box of stomach powder to be taken after meals in water. It sure did the trick. One thing I had learned in these first two years of teaching was that I was fed up with coaching varsity basketball. I planned to make my desire known to the new principal when he was hired.

Spring arrived as usual, track season one of doubt and uncertainty. The school board had finally purchased an area of land, about a half mile from the high school, to convert into an athletic field, so we used it to the best of our advantage. Also, Fred Wall was made athletic director, and that took a load of responsibility off my shoulders.

The question I always asked of myself during the spring of the year was what am I going to do this summer? I made up my mind to go to summer school at the University of Michigan. I wrote to Kalamazoo College and Boston University to mail a transcript of my credits to the university, which they did. Our school year extended into the middle of June. The eight-week summer session started the Monday after our school year terminated on Friday, so Saturday found me with a packed suitcase riding the train to Ann Arbor. I got a room and spent the weekend looking over the campus and familiarizing myself with the different buildings I probably would be working in. Monday morning was registration, and in talking to the dean about my college record he remarked that it wasn't too impressive, and he asked me what I had been doing the past two years! Teaching history in high school was my answer. "Well," he said, "if you want to try graduate work here at the university it's all right with us." It was a long, hot eight weeks, and when my last final examination was over I took the train back to Detroit and Ferndale.

Ed Ferguson, my roommate on Beaufield Street, had purchased a Chevrolet coupe during the spring and had asked me to take a trip east with him in the last two weeks in August. Believe you me, going from a hard school year right into an eight-week summer term at the university was no play. I had had it, and was delighted when we packed his car with a tent, sleeping bags, etc. and left Ferndale for the east. Fergie, as everyone knew him, had a relative living in Pittsburg and that was to be our first destination. There were no freeways in the 1920's and it was a good two days drive to Pittsburgh. On our arrival it didn't take long to realize that his relative was a great sports fan. He insisted on taking us to a Pittsburgh Pirates baseball game, which we greatly enjoyed. Leaving Pittsburgh, we headed for Washington, D.C., where we spent several days touring the city. I was greatly interested in the political and historical phase of D.C. life because it coincided with my educational pursuits. We pitched our tent in the tourist camp and didn't think anything about going away for the whole day, leaving some of our belongings in it. Oh, if we could go back to those days of honesty! Leaving D.C., we headed for Atlantic City. It was permissible to pitch a tent on the sandy beach and again we enjoyed the free but safe life that characterized the 1920's. Fergie also had relatives living in a suburban community outside of New York City. We took the commuter train into the city and enjoyed walking from the Battery up to Times Square, observing city life as only New York City has. After spending a day at Niagara Falls we found ourselves back in Ferndale, with the long Labor Day weekend ahead of us. Our expense account showed the trip had proven to be an economical one.

Taking the train home to Gobles and spending a couple of days in South Haven brought my summer vacation to an end.

School Year 1925-26

When we opened the school year with a teachers' meeting on Labor Day, we were facing a new superintendent, Edgar F. Down, who had been an administrator in the Highland Park Public Schools.

Also new to the system was Cleve Bradshaw, principal of the high school. Cleve had come from the Saginaw Public Schools. It didn't take long to realize that the turmoil from the previous year was a thing of the past. During his long tenure in Ferndale, Ed Down was just like a father to everyone. His characteristic understanding and appreciation made him "the grand old man" of Ferndale. Cleve was the kind of principal who gave his teachers wide latitude of understanding. He believed a teacher could do the best job if he or she could find his or her best methods of teaching. Student leadership was his key philosophy. The teacher should be in the background with the students setting the educational atmosphere. This was a direct contrast to what I had experienced during my first two years of teaching, but it wasn't long before I had moved my desk to the rear corner of the room, making the student leader of the day a more pronounced figure in the classroom.

Cleve was ready to listen to all problems, and it wasn't hard for me to convince him that I should no longer be varsity basketball coach. He reappointed me head of the history department, a position that had been taken away from me the previous year by Harris, and asked if I would settle for the assistant basketball coach and head track coach. "Sure would" said I. Then he told me that Fred Wall would handle both basketball and football, and I could coach the reserve squad. Although I continued to have some of those Tuesday night games, the pressure was off and the winning or losing did not bother me.

Over the two years that we had been teaching Ruth and I had seen less and less of each other as months went by. So it happened that she and I each had different dates to the fall homecoming at Kalamazoo and it was "the parting of the ways" for us.

As the school year wore on without undue incident, teaching became more pleasurable to me, and I began to think of it as a career job. Our faculty became one with the spirit of "one for all." Being a young faculty, there were after-school dances, Christmas parties, faculty dinners, etc. that created within us a feeling of teamwork.

By the spring of 1926 I had been able to pay off all my college debts. I had never owned a car and it now seemed time to go in debt again to buy one. There was a Chevrolet agency in Royal Oak, so one bright spring Saturday morning I took the interurban car to Royal Oak to drive back my first owned automobile, a 1926 Chevrolet coupe. Spring vacation came in April, and I was a little proud driving my new Chevrolet coupe home to Gobles only to find the roads around there well-padded with that white stuff, snow. It wasn't uncommon for me to leave Detroit in the fall, winter, and spring with little or no snow around, but find a heavy snowstorm in Gobles. Gobles was on the fringe of that snowbelt that runs from Chicago north along Lake Michigan up to the straits. In spite of the cold spring weather, our little family reunion at the homestead was restful. Whenever I found myself loaded down with work, worry, tension, etc., spending a weekend in Gobles, sitting around the barbershop, and talking with the customers was very relaxing. I would get back to Ferndale with new vigor and a healthier spirit.

Needless to say, the Chevrolet of 1926 didn't compare with that of later years. Driving thirty miles an hour was a fast pace. Thirty-seven miles an hour was about top speed unless you were going downhill. The roads were mostly gravel. The only paved road between Kalamazoo and Detroit in the 1920's was a strip of a few miles east of Battle Creek, so it was a long drive of six to seven hours whenever I went home, compared to about two and a half hours today. The distance covered was about a one hundred and sixty miles. I used to rather enjoy driving through the towns of Parma, Chelsea, Albion, Marshall, and Ann Arbor. Each one designated a point nearer my destination.

Our Ferndale Methodist Church had built the first section of its present edifice, and now we were housed in our own building. The philosophy in those days was to build a gymnasium where the young people as well as the old could play during the week. It could be used on Sunday for the regular services. It was in our church gym that I organized and coached our church basketball team. Soon after, we older young people organized a team on which I played forward, the minister's son, an Ohio Wesleyan graduate was our center, and we had one guard who was a dentist but was an All-M.I.A.A. guard during his college days at Albion. We played a schedule of games with other churches and recreation teams in and around Detroit. It was fun to win as well as disappointing to lose.

When I finished my track work at Kalamazoo College, Coach Ralph Young told me to continue hard athletic work and not allow myself to get pudgy or fat. He said your heart is a muscle, you have developed the heart muscles through your long-distance running and it's necessary to continue to exercise it. I have always tried to heed his warning and to exercise strenuously. In my younger days basketball proved to be a good sport to keep me in good condition during the winter months. The following year, and for several years after, I played on our Ferndale faculty team. We had some good men on the team, three of whom were six feet or over. We played a schedule of mostly faculty teams around the state. Being undefeated one season, we issued a challenge to any state faculty team to play for the state championship. Our next game ended in a close defeat, and that ended any claims we might have had for a state championship. Another sport that I was able to play during the winter months was called "paddle tennis." It was a game played on the gym floor. Our tennis coach and I used to do battle about twice a week. When we had finished three games we both knew we had had our exercise. It was great sport.

Then in the summer it was tennis and golf. The Ferndale schools had no tennis courts. There were courts in Highland Park that we could make reservations to use. There was also a family living on Crooks Road in Royal Oak who had a cement tennis court. One daughter was a teacher in the Royal Oak School, and we had a standing invitation to use the court whenever it was vacant. While I never had any instruction in playing golf in my life, I have always enjoyed the game although being just a dub at it.

During the 1930's and 1940's the Ferndale Recreation Department sponsored a Ferndale badminton club. We played among ourselves one night each week throughout the winter in the Lincoln High gym. The better players of our club, of which I was one, would engage in contests with other badminton clubs around the state. Most were held on Saturday, which made it very convenient. I continued to play this very fast and exciting sport until I realized that after each strenuous contest I was tired the following day. I knew then that the sport was too fast for a forty-plus-year-old man, so I gave it up for something less strenuous.

Softball was a great game all during the 1920's, '30's, and '40's. I played on several teams over a period of fifteen years. The first, the Ferndale Exchange, had a team in the Ferndale Recreation Department league. We won the city championship in our class, namely men twenty-five to thirty years of age. One year I played left field and greatly enjoyed snagging long flies that some expected to go for home runs. In the 1940's the city installed lights on the ball diamonds. After playing a few games under the lights I sensed my eyes did not focus on the speed of the ball as quickly as in daytime, and it was time for me to lay my glove on the shelf.

One of the great events of my life happened to me in April 1926. Being a young and rapidly growing community, Ferndale had two luncheon clubs, Exchange being one of them. Our high school principal belonged to Exchange. Our superintendent Ed Down belonged to the Rotary. The president of Exchange, Guy Stark, approached me, requesting the privilege of submitting my name for membership. Guy was village president, an attorney, and a member of the Ferndale Methodist Church. While I didn't know him well, I did respect him highly. Before I gave my answer to his request, he said something that has stuck with me all my life and proven to be very true: "Harold, if you become a member of the Ferndale Exchange Club, it probably will never make you one penny richer, but it will give you fellowship with a fine group of business and professional men, some of whom you will never have another opportunity to become acquainted with." It was the philosophy of our school administration for teachers to be involved in community life. When I told Cleve Bradshaw, our principal, he encouraged me to accept the invitation, stating he could arrange my class schedule to allow me to have from 12 noon to one thirty off to attend the weekly luncheons. The third Tuesday in April 1926 found me with two others, one a dentist and one an optometrist, standing before the club members, getting the "low down" on what the club expected from its members and what membership meant. It was forty-five years later that, as a retiree, I wrote my letter of resignation. During those forty-five years I had been exceedingly active, holding every office in the club except treasurer. I was club secretary for a total of about twenty-five years.

Fergie had surprised us by getting married over the Memorial Day weekend. It was rather an unusual surprise, almost a shock, since only on Monday night after the long Memorial Day weekend did I learn what had taken place. I came home from school, and as I looked in his room he was packing his clothes. I said, "For goodness sakes, where are you going with only two weeks of school left?" "I got married over the weekend," he replied. So we had a vacant room for the coming school year. Dora (Burns), as she now was to me, said, "If you know of another man teacher who would want to live here, invite him and I'll give you a week's room rent." Ed Mosher, our new and very personable music teacher from Centerville, Michigan and a University of Michigan graduate, was finishing his first year at Ferndale. He and I had become very friendly, so I asked him to room at the Burns' residence the coming year. He accepted. I had my third companion for my fourth year in Ferndale.

As the end of the school year approached it was again the same old question; "What am I going to do this summer of 1926?" A trip was out because I didn't have the money. I had gone into debt in buying my Chevrolet coupe and monthly payments had to be made. We were getting paid once a month in ten installments, and it was hard to put a little aside for the summer months. I knew I didn't want to go to summer school. I had decided that summer school every other year was about all I could take since to leave day school on a Friday the middle of June and start studying at the University of Michigan the following Monday for an eight-week grind was no small task for me. There was only one solution to the problem and that was to get a barber job which was always quite plentiful. Long hair was not in style in the 1920's. There was a barbershop in Royal Oak located on Center Street that needed a summer barber. I drove over to talk with the boss. He asked, "When can you start?" "On the Monday following the close of school," I stated. "OK," he said, "the job is yours."

School wound up with the usual activities. The junior-senior prom and the senior banquet were always highlights. By now I had learned to dance satisfactorily, and the high school girls were always anxious to dance with their teachers. We men had plenty of dance partners, including the ladies on the faculty. Attending school functions was accepted as a part of our responsibility as a schoolteacher.

Friday morning of that last day of school found most of us with all our work done, waiting for twelve noon when all reports, keys, etc. were turned into the office and our final paycheck of the year was handed to us. Then it was "So long" until September and "Have a good summer." I jumped in my Chevrolet coupe and headed for Gobles, carefree, relaxed, with money in my pocket and a contract for the 1926-27 year.

The summer was uneventful; in fact, it was dull and dragged. The barber job was far from the one I had had in South Haven. However, it was a six-days-a-week job that was making me a living, and I was able to put a few dollars aside for a vacation in August. Coleman Cheney, who had been teaching at Skidmore College for girls in New York, wrote me that he would finish summer school at Harvard the middle of August. "Why don't you drive out here to Boston and spend a couple of weeks? I have a room for which we don't have to pay rent; we can eat cheap and have a good time," was his appeal. It sounded good to me and I wrote back, "It's a deal." I started making my plans, both calendar and financial. August came and a letter from Cheney told me he was going to be near Buffalo, New York over the weekend of the middle of August, that I could leave Ferndale early on Sunday morning of that weekend and meet him at the Y.M.C.A. Then we would drive on to Boston. It must have been my lucky day, for the next to the last Saturday I was working. With the barbershop full of people I glanced down at the floor and saw some greenbacks. Reaching down and picking them up, I put them in my pocket. No one seemed to have noticed my action and nothing was said. At first I thought I should ask right then if anyone had lost the money. Then again I said to myself, anyone could claim it. If I turned it over to the boss I'd never see it again, so I reasoned that I would keep still about it and if anyone came to the shop to inquire about the money I would give it to them. I got home about ten o'clock since our shop was open until nine o'clock on Saturday nights, I looked at the bills and there were two twenties. Now, forty dollars was quite a sum of money in the 1920's, so I really did expect someone to call at the shop the following week to inquire about the lost money. No one did. I bid my barber companion's goodbye the following Saturday night with money for my trip to Boston. I really was sorry for the person who lost it and sincerely hoped it didn't prove to be a financial hardship.

However, I felt that if I had been the one who had lost the money, I would have back tracked my steps that Saturday evening, inquiring at each place I had been.

Before going to bed I set my alarm for 5:00 a.m. since it was quite a drive in a Chevrolet coupe to Buffalo. I had washed and polished my car, packed my bag, and was ready to take off. When I got around Cleveland it was raining, which slowed me down. There were no superhighways, freeways, city bypasses, etc. in the 1920's and the pace was rather slow compared to later years. Cheney was at the arranged place of meeting. In order to conserve time I had not had lunch, so that was the first order of the day. Cheney explained that Marion Vosburgh, a Boston University girl who lived at Canajoharie, New York had given us a standing invitation to stop over anytime at the farm on the outskirts of the city.

By the time we pulled into the city it was midnight. We didn't want to get people out of bed at that time of night. I had a couple of blankets in the car so we tried rolling up in them on the ground beside the car, but the mosquitos were so bad we couldn't stand it. They just seemed to find a crack in the blanket to get at us. Then we retreated to the car and slept sitting up with the windows up. Daylight awakened us. Driving into town, we had breakfast. By that time we felt it safe to continue to the farm and put in our appearance. Marion and her parents were very hospitable and scolded us for not driving in at midnight. We remained all day and accepted the invitation to stay overnight. In the meantime, we prevailed on Marion to go into Boston with us the next day. It was fun to again drive the Mohawk trail, which took us through Lexington and Concord and into Boston. After a few days I drove Marion back to her home, stayed overnight, and returned to Boston. It was great fun to just play and relax with no real responsibilities.

My brother Whyle, fifth of the six boys in our family, is four years younger than I. As it so often happens in a large family of children, two will have the same interests and dislikes, which make them more compatible, and that was our relationship. I wrote Whyle that he would enjoy a few days in Bean Town: "Why don't you hitchhike out here and ride home with me?" A letter a few days later said he would be glad to visit Boston, giving the day he would leave. In the 1920's it was a common and accepted custom to hitchhike all over the country, something that today is not allowed and is very dangerous to the one hitchhiking as well as to the one picking up the passenger. We just can't help but wish for the "good old days" when we recall the peace and tranquility that was ours, when the streets were safe day and night to meander as we pleased. Are those days gone forever? Cheney and I were just ready to go out for a bit of breakfast when a telegram came from Whyle stating he was having good luck and would be in Boston that day. I had not more than read the message and remarked to Cheney that he could be along almost any time when I looked out of the window and saw Whyle walking toward the house. It was a gay reunion; we three ate breakfast together. Whyle said he was lucky in that he was picked up by a man and woman the day before in Western, New York; they were driving right into Boston, and were glad to have him as a passenger. We left Boston in my Chevrolet coupe a few mornings later and headed for our first overnight stop at Marion's in Canajoharie, New York. She had given me an invitation to stop on our way back to Michigan. We reached Gobles without undue trouble, refreshed and ready for another school year.

The new west addition to our high school building made it possible for me to be centered in what we called the social studies section of the building. Room 318 was more or less my room because it was where my desk was located. While still five classes, my teaching load was now confined to modern European history and American history. My travel in Europe had given me firsthand experience, and with the pictures I had taken I could present a more vivid picture of the subject we were studying.

School Year 1926-27

The opening day of school held the same routine that all opening days hold. There were the usual instructions at the general teachers' meeting with Superintendent Ed Downs presiding, the introductions of the new instructors, and the preparation for the opening of classes the following day. Of course, it was "Hello John, hello Mary, did you have a good summer?" That to me was an important part of the first day. During my forty-two years in the school business I always enjoyed meeting the returnees, many of whom I had gotten to know very well over a period of several years.

Now that I owned a car I could more easily visit the Tigers ballpark. Since most final games of the season in Detroit were scheduled on Sunday, sometimes a double-header, I would manage to get to the ballpark to say "Farewell until the opener." The football season has always been one of great interest to me. Seldom have I missed a high school game on each weekend of the fall season. I would also often drive to one of our Michigan College or University games on Saturdays.

Ed Mosher proved to be an enjoyable companion, and now that I was a single man as he was also, we took in many entertainments together. Being a music teacher, Ed's chief interests were along that line. I have always enjoyed good music. My one regret has been not learning to play the piano.

The many interesting opportunities offered to a dedicated schoolteacher keeps one feeling young and useful and give you the feeling that you are in a profession that is highly respected by all segments of society. At least, that was the consensus during my tenure in the field of public education. The school year passed rapidly. There was peace and harmony in the ranks, which made teaching a pleasure. Our faculty was a team "one for all and all for one." If we could help a fellow worker, whether it was discipline or something personal, we were pleased to do so. Our principal Cleve Bradshaw gave each teacher free rein of his classroom as long as it fit with good classroom procedure. Teachers make mistakes as everyone does, but you could always rely on the backing of the administration to help correct the mistake. You could go to the office with a problem, asking for help from the principal, and you always came out with a "Yes" or "No," never leaving you on the fence.

My coaching job was enjoyable since as I have mentioned, I always have been a sports fanatic. I turned out some really good reserve teams, and although there was no pressure to win a game it was always a pleasure and a bit of satisfaction to come out on top. We did win most of our reserve games.

Our faculty basketball team was a lot of fun. We would play our game after the high school varsity. The crowd rarely left before the faculty game was over. I guess the kids as well as most adults enjoyed seeing their "dear teachers" play. Even if I do say so, we had a pretty good team that played good ball and won a large percentage of our games.

It was about this time I got itchy feet to do a little refereeing. I saw other coaches and athletic directors going out on Fridays and Saturdays making an extra nickel, and I saw no reason why I shouldn't do the same. It all looked so easy. I got a football rule book and started studying up on the regulations. Coaching basketball had kept me acquainted with all the rules, but there is a lot more to refereeing than just knowing what the guidebook says. There is always that element of judgment, and that is where a referee either does a good job or a poor one. As all sports fans know, a poor judgment call by the referee brings the audible displeasure of both coaches and audience. Every referee misses one now and then, but you can't miss many plays and get by. While my refereeing was acceptable, I wouldn't say it was of the highest quality. I didn't see that I had a future as an official in the sports field. However, I did satisfactorily umpire some football games in cooperation with a referee, since in the 1920's most of the decisions were the responsibility of the referee, he being the head official. But in basketball it was a different story. One man handled the whole game alone. He was also expected to referee the reserve game, and one evening at Rochester, Michigan I refereed three games in one night: the reserve, the varsity, and the faculty game, all for five dollars. After paying interurban fare, I had about four dollars left and was a tired man. I knew one Detroit schoolteacher who was very good and in great demand as an official. He punished himself in officiating games to the extent that during his last game he lay down on the bench and died.

I'll never forget the last game of basketball I refereed. It was at Roseville. They were playing their nearest competitor. It was a tough game to handle due to the closeness of the score and the rivalry. About every decision I called was unsatisfactory to one side or the other. Every time I called a foul on the home team, the crowd would yell while the visitor was making a foul shot. It got so bad that I stopped the game to announce to the audience that thereafter if the home crowd didn't show good sportsmanship by keeping quiet while the visiting teammate was making the foul shot, I would let him shoot until he made the basket. A voice from the home team followers, cried out, "If you do, we'll throw you out." I later learned after the game that "my friend" was the president of the school board. I stuck to my guns. The very next foul on the home team was a test. Would I carry out my ruling? I did. The boy took three shots before he put it in the basket. The crowd knew that I meant what I had said. However, I said to myself after the game, "I have had it. There must be an easier way to earn five dollars." I threw away my whistle. That was the end of Harold B. Wilcox the sports official.

A very inspirational incident happened to me during fall 1926 when the principal and I were talking in a nonprofessional way. I might add here that it was one of the pleasures of working with the administration. Both Ed Downs and Cleve Bradshaw were men you could talk to without fear of them holding something against you. If they had something to say to you, a word of advice or criticism, both men said it in no uncertain terms and then forgot it. I'll never forget one day when Principal Bradshaw didn't like something I had done. He called me into his office, told me about it, and then said, "Now I have given it to you, so get out of here and forget about it." That was the last that was ever said regarding it. During one of our friendly talks, Cleve said to me, "Harold, you are highly respected around here by both students and faculty, but many students don't get to know you and to like you. What you should now do is to try to cultivate a more friendly and likeable personality." Well I had become known as H. (Hard) B. (Boiled) Wilcox. I believed that there could be only one boss in the classroom, and I was getting paid to be it. You could have called me a strict disciplinarian. Of course, some students didn't like a classroom with that philosophy.

It was the policy of the administration to allow the sophomore classes to choose one man and one woman to be their advisors for the last three years of their high school education. It was only a couple of weeks after my conversation with Bradshaw that the sophomore class chose me their male advisor. That caused me to analyze which was more preferable, to be well liked or well respected. After seeing many people who tried to make themselves well liked, I came to the conclusion that to be highly respected was more desirable. May I add here that those three years with the class of 1929 were three of the most satisfying years I enjoyed during my forty-two years of tenure in the Ferndale school system.

In the 1920's it was the tradition that the senior class would go to Washington, D.C. for their senior trip. That required several thousand dollars. I spent days, evenings, and hours working with this fine group of boys and girls. We had newspaper collections, and on a given Saturday I would supervise the loading and selling of these old newspapers by the truckload. Many other money-raising activities were used. It was gratifying to see young people who had the goal to work hard to accomplish their aims. It certainly gives older people a great deal of confidence and respect for youth. This was one of the several rewards of my teaching career.

I presume most everyone has a calendar of time. I always thought of the school year as being divided into four parts, as four laps to a mile run. The first one was from Labor Day to Thanksgiving, the second one would take us to the Christmas holidays, and then we had the third lap, the longest of the four, stretching to Easter vacation, which took in those long winter months. The fourth, during the spring months, was always the most enjoyable to me.

I had been corresponding with Bertha Fuller, who lived in Brockton, Massachusetts. I had met her during my year at Boston University School of Theology. Now that I was single and was beginning what my many friends and acquaintances termed my "bachelor days," I thought it would be enjoyable to accept an invitation to come to Brockton for the Easter vacation. That Friday evening in spring 1927 I boarded a Pullman train for Boston. When I arrived at the station, Bertha and her twin sister were there to meet me. We took the train to Brockton, about an hour's ride from Boston. Her mother and stepfather were very hospitable, and it appeared we were in for a very enjoyable week. Along about Monday I began to feel bad, and by Tuesday I was in bed with the flu. The doctor came and gave the usual instructions, stay in bed, drink plenty of liquids, and take these pills. Well, I was in bed until Friday and what was to be a delightful week in the east turned out to be otherwise. However, I could not have had a better nurse than Bertha. We did enjoy Saturday because I decided not to go back until Sunday, which brought me into Detroit Monday afternoon.

Now our principal prided himself on having teachers who had "student-run classrooms." He would remark, "Miss so and so" was gone all p.m. and her classes went along in just as orderly a fashion as if she had been there. My classes were student run, and I thought they could run without me for the day. I failed to take into consideration that Monday was the first day after a vacation and that might make a difference. I had that called to my attention after I got back. I didn't wire the high school office that I would be a day late in returning. As I passed the high school on my way from the Detroit depot, Bradshaw saw me and called out, "Wait a minute. I want to talk with you." The gist of our conversation was that I should have wired the office that I would not be in the classroom that Monday. Also, he would recommend to the superintendent that I be docked one day's pay. I told Cleve I didn't like it and would see Mr. Downs, although I realized my mistake in not notifying him. After talking with the superintendent he said, "If you will get me a letter from your Brockton doctor that you had the flu and were unable to travel I will not dock you." So I wrote Bertha, and a letter from the doctor arrived that saved me a day's pay. Needless to say, I had learned a lesson in professional ethics.

My room companion Ed Mosher had decided to go to England for the summer. It was summer school at Michigan for me. The school year came to a close during the middle of June with all the excitement that takes place during commencement week. The Tigers were playing baseball, and on that Saturday I took in a game before heading for Ann Arbor. It was a long hot eight weeks; the book work was so demanding that there was little time for social life. It was get up in the morning, go to the union for breakfast, read the newspaper, then a day of classes and study. It was so hot (air conditioning was little known in the 1920's) that one of my professors got sick with the heat and couldn't meet his classes. Taking a couple of hours off in the afternoon, I would go down to the field house, put on my tracksuit, and do about eight laps on the track. This would relieve the monotony of a study day and tend to keep me in good physical condition. There was generally a Saturday night dance at the union. There were thousands of young ladies who were glad to be a companion. Sunday it was church and more long hours of study. I had never been too much of a scholar, but I had now convinced myself that by hard work I could attain what in my Kalamazoo College days appeared to be an educational mountain too steep for me to attempt.

When the middle of August came, with final examinations over, I got in my 1926 Chevrolet coupe and headed for Gobles. For the first time in years things were decidedly different. No longer would I wind my way through Bloomingdale and Grand Junction to the fruit farm near South Haven. Those days were history. As I guided my Chevrolet back to Ferndale that Sunday afternoon before Labor Day 1927, there was an empty feeling in my heart. You can't go with a girl for five years, enjoying college life for two years together and then cut it off with no fond memories, although I knew without a degree of doubt that it had to be. I pulled the car to a stop in the Burns' drive on Beaufield for my fifth year rooming at their home.

School Year 1927-28

Our faculty was a young one. The large majority of the female part of the faculty was unmarried, so we had a lot in common. Generally speaking, married women were not considered good risks. The professional spirit called for dedicated teachers, and it was thought that a married woman would be serving two interests. In many school systems when a young lady signed a contract to teach, the fine print read that if the person married the contract was void. I knew some women teachers, especially during the Depression that got married and lived secretively. They just didn't want to lose their job for financial reasons.

As the school year progressed, the excitement made the long hours sitting up grading papers, working out class study programs that we hoped would sustain student interest, and all the other tedious jobs connected with the teaching profession seem worthwhile and enjoyable. Any person who doesn't enjoy working with young people should never impose on those young people by trying to teach school.

The holiday seasons found me driving home to Gobles. I still had two brothers and two sisters at home, and it made for a very enjoyable and relaxing visit.

Coaching the reserve basketball team kept my hand in the sports program. Then too, our faculty team was still playing a full schedule of games.

Spring came in all its glory. The Tigers opened the league schedule of baseball. The Great Lakes and riverboats carrying their shipments of iron ore, cement, and other products plowed through the water past Detroit on their way to their final destination. On some Saturdays or Sunday afternoons I would drive down to Bell Island. There I would sit and see one boat after another pass through Detroit. They were either going into Lake Erie or on their way to Lake Huron and Lake Superior and to Duluth and other points on the Great Lakes.

One of the occasions that I enjoyed each spring was the Detroit section of the Kalamazoo College Alumni Association dinner. Most often some popular professor from the college would come to Detroit as the dinner speaker. It so happened that Professor Smith, one of the most popular faculty members of long tenure was our banquet speaker in spring 1928. He gave us a bit of philosophy that evening that has stuck with me all my life. "Money isn't everything," he said. "I have attained during my life at Kalamazoo College all that as a kid I ever dreamed of having. I have the respect of the people I know and work with. I have a fine family, a nice car, a home in which to live, a job that pays enough to carry on the standard of living I always as a kid dreamed of. Now, just what more could I ask for or want? You, the alumni and friends of Kalamazoo College will, when you are my age, have attained all that as a kid you dreamed of having." It was one of the most thought-provoking, down-to-earth talks I have ever heard. As I sit here in the 1970's on the shores of the Atlantic Ocean, I too say "Amen" to what Professor Smith had experienced.

The school population was growing by leaps and bounds, and after the new addition was opened up the high school building seemed about as crowded as it had ever been. New teachers were hired for the second semester due to the increased enrollment. One of these male teachers was Allen Haslitt. He had lived in the Upper Peninsula and graduated from Northern State College, now the University of Marquette. When Al, whom we nicknamed "Duke," reached the high school principal's office, one of the first questions Bradshaw asked him was, "Where are you rooming?" "I don't know yet," said Duke. So Bradshaw told him to go up to see Wilcox. "He probably can help you find a room." I took him to the Burns' residence where he occupied the room left vacant by Ed Mosher, who was remaining in England for the year. "Duke" was a very likeable and congenial fellow who spent his whole teaching life in Ferndale. He married one of the high school secretaries, reared a family of four fine boys, became known as the mathematician of Ferndale, was many years a member of the Ferndale Kiwanis Club, and a good church man. He is another man who I believe attained the success in life that he dreamed of as a kid.

I had put quite a lot of mileage on my 1926 Chevrolet coupe, about 18,000 miles, which was high for cars of the 1920's. I decided to trade it in on a new 1928. The Chevrolet of the 1920's was certainly a different car than ones of later dates. It couldn't run faster than thirty-seven miles per hour. You had to change the oil every five hundred miles. If you wanted top performance you ground the valves every 5,000 miles. The engines were rather simple, and with the use of a few tools borrowed from a friend I would grind my own valves, which saved a garage bill. Breaking in a new car right was very important. You never drove it faster than twenty miles per hour for the first five hundred miles, so it was somewhat tedious breaking them in.

As the school year of 1927-28 was coming to an end, it found me with a new 1928 car that, of course, was not paid for. I didn't want to go back to summer school. Every other summer was enough for me. Our new administrator decided to run a six-week summer school program in the high school and asked faculty members to apply for the jobs. I asked for and got the position teaching history and government. It was a warm summer, but the six weeks passed quite rapidly. One big difference I found was that those kids who enrolled in summer school were there to study and learn.

With summer school over about the first of August, I went home to Gobles for a few days of rest and relaxation. Then I decided it would be interesting to drive east. Staying overnight in Syracuse,

New York became a forced necessity. The afternoon that I was driving just on the outskirts of the city my Chevrolet must have been going forty-five miles per hour since it was a downhill drive. All of a sudden my engine had the worst knock and rattles imaginable. I turned the car around and drove back to the city's Chevrolet garage. The mechanic said I had burned out a connecting rod; I would have to leave the car overnight to be repaired the first thing in the morning. I got a room at the Y.M.C.A. The next morning after a breakfast at a restaurant, I was at the Chevrolet garage waiting for my car. It didn't take too long to put in a new connecting rod, they just dropped the oil pan and worked from underneath.

In two hours I was on my way again, but not for long. I was just on the outskirts of the city, not going too fast, and away went the connecting rod. I drove back to the garage, and believe you me I was pretty warm under the collar. The head mechanic said he didn't know what could have happened; that they would do the labor free and I would have to pay for the part. "OK," I said. What could I say, being several hundred miles from home? By noon he had the car in shape for me to take off. He told me to hold my speed down to about thirty miles per hour until it had gotten well broken in, which I did. I had no more car trouble that summer.

School Year 1928-29

As fall approached I was back in Ferndale for my sixth year. I now began to feel like a veteran teacher. Before we had left school in June, Bud Brown, our football coach, and Carl Forsythe, a social studies teacher and debate coach, approached me about the three of us rooming at the Fred Wall home right near the high school on Withington. I had roomed at the Burns' for five years. While I had enjoyed rooming there, having had several different schoolteacher companions, I felt it was time for me to change to a new environment. So when the fall term of 1928 opened it found Bud, Carl, and me occupying rooms at the Wall residence.

We had to eat all our meals down at the corner of 9 Mile Road and Woodward Avenue. The Realto was our spot each morning and about six o'clock each evening. There were others, one a doctor of medicine and another doctor of dentistry, who generally joined us for these meals. We were all young and single, and having companions at mealtime helped make it an enjoyable occasion.

As usual, I attended football games at University of Michigan as well as our high school games. One Saturday morning on my way to Ann Arbor by the way of Michigan Avenue, [which was the main highway in those days] I was driving along at a steady pace when. yes, it happened again, out went the connecting rod. Needless to say, I didn't see the football game, but ended up in a garage in Ypsilanti. I had had it; I resolved to get rid of that 1928 Chevrolet. But that wasn't the last of it.

A few weeks later I was on my way home to Gobles. It was Friday night, a teacher's delight. Just to be on my way to relax at the homestead for a weekend was an inspiration. I was enjoying my ride and was thinking about getting something to eat in the small village of Parma, located a few miles west of Jackson when yes, it happened again. That connecting rod went out for the fourth time in less than a year. Luckily Parma had a garage that was open. I told the mechanic of the trouble I was having and while he was working on my car I went to the village restaurant for dinner. When I returned he had the job about done. I stood there and watched him "burn it in." They did that by starting the engine with no oil pan. Just the second the rod started to smoke he shut off the engine and put on the oil pan, and I was ready to take off. He said he had surveyed the situation and believed my trouble was due to a warped engine block. In other words, I had gotten a lemon. I knew right then that Harold was going to be driving a 1929 car just as soon as they came on the market the first of the new year. When spring came I drove to Royal Oak one bright sunny day, and made a salesman happy by telling him I wanted to trade my 1928 for a new 1929. This 1929 Chevrolet was the first six-cylinder Chevrolet that had been produced, and when I drove my four-door green sedan into Ferndale I breathed a sigh of relief. I had gotten rid of my lemon.

The yearly model changed at the beginning of the new year back in the 1920's. It was considered a good policy to give factory employees a Christmas vacation during the changeover. As the Depression lengthened and years went by, one after another industry concluded that Christmastime was no time to have men unemployed, so the new models were brought out in the fall of the previous year. This was supposed to help stimulate new car sales. By the 1970's it had been pretty much accepted that September and early October are the months they pull the wraps off the next year's models.

There were many class activities that I had to participate in as an advisor of the class of 1929. It was the custom and school policy for the seniors to have a trip to Washington, D.C. in the spring of their year. I had worked hard with them in all their money-raising functions and felt I had earned my trip with them. When the time came to announce the names of the teachers who would make the trip as chaperones, my name was not on the list. I was really disturbed and immediately made fast steps to the principal's office. "What is the reason for my name not being on the list to go to D.C.?" I asked. Before Bradshaw had time to answer, I related to him of all the work I had done over the three years I had been an advisor and told him I was not going to stay home without a fight. I was going to take it to the superintendent if necessary. His given reason was that I had not had previous experience on senior trips and that I wasn't used to traveling. "What an excuse," I said. "I have done more traveling than any one of those you have appointed as chaperons." "OK," he said, "You win. You will go with the seniors to D.C." Arrangements were made for the trip by an agent in Highland Park, a neighboring city within Detroit. There were meetings to discuss such things as clothing, behavior, etc.

I might add at this point that no one ever had the privilege of chaperoning a nicer group of high school kids anywhere than we had that May 1929. About 120 of Ferndale's finest students boarded the six-car Pullman special train on the Baltimore and Ohio Railroad that late afternoon, May 18. Leaving the old Union Station at the foot of Third Avenue, Detroit at about 3:00 p.m. put everyone in a joyous mood. For most of our youth this was their first overnight train ride. The menu in the dining car advertised a one dollar and twenty five cents dinner of the following: a dish of chilled celery, green olives, chicken rice soup, baked lake white fish, minced chicken cutlets, roast young lamb, creamed new potatoes, fresh buttered beets, fruit salad, dessert and beverage. Don't you think that these 120 plus kids didn't devour the food. They ate as all teenagers can. Then too, they were buying snacks whenever the train stopped at a station long enough for the vendor to sell his wares. The arrangement was for the girls to occupy the rear two Pullman and the boys the front two with the diner in between. My berth was the one next to the diner. It was the men's job to see to it that the boys were in their own Pullman cars by 10:30 p.m. Wouldn't such an arrangement get a big laugh in this day when girls and boys are occupying the same college dormitories with little or no restrictions? Need I tell you that when our train pulled into Harper's Ferry the next morning, we were a rather tired group of tourists. Little sleeping was the order of the night. A good old Southern breakfast was had at one of the restaurants, which started us off on a sight-seeing trip at Harper's Ferry.

Arriving in D. C. that afternoon, we were bussed to our hotel. Again, great care was taken to make sure that the girls and boys didn't see too much of each other. The girls occupied rooms on the upper floors and the boys on the lower. Three full days of delightful sightseeing on busses was the order of the stay in Washington. When our special pulled into the Union Station there were tired but happy youths greeting their parents with smiles and cheers as they walked toward the waiting cars for their ride home. It was a great experience for these graduating kids, and I personally enjoyed it.

I had taken the summer off the year before and felt rested enough to stand another eight weeks of summer school at the university. As the middle of June was becoming a reality, I began to look forward to another summer on campus. I said to myself, this is sort of a queer philosophy for a fellow like me. I had never been a scholar. My grades in high school and in college were not something to be desired. So I said to myself, "Why am I seeking a master's degree when there had been no pressure on me to return to college to work for one?" I concluded that studying was a habit one had to acquire, and in high school and college I had never had the time to make the classroom my number one objective. It was always earn my bread and butter first, and what time I had left was devoted to studying. Now, with enough money in my pocket for room, board, and the necessities of life, I could relax and make academics my number-one job. When I arrived at Ann Arbor I sought a rooming house that was close to the campus but not crowded. I didn't want to be bothered with other people who intended to spend less time on the courses than I intended to do. I knew from previous experience that I would have to continue to work hard. In graduate school a grade of less than B was a failure, and I didn't want any such grades.

School Year 1929-30

October 1929 is a month long to be remembered in American history. It was the month of the "Stock Market Crash," the beginning of what has become known as the "Great Depression." Business had been getting noticeably poor, but the public had been assured time and time again that there was nothing to worry about. We were in just a slight recession that would fade away. Prices were high, and the laboring man's paycheck was correspondingly high. My salary during these seven years had increased two hundred dollars a year. My seventh contract paid me twenty-nine hundred dollars, which we felt wasn't too bad pay for a schoolteacher. In those days there were no deductions.

Notwithstanding, my realtor friend Phil Watson came to me one day in the mid-1920's with a check in his hand for about fifteen hundred dollars. In a friendly way, he showed it to me and said, "Why are you fooling around in the school business when you could be out here in real estate making as much in two months as you are making in a year." I remember a few years later he was one of the first to complain about high school taxes after the bottom had dropped out of the market.

Before Bud, Carl, and I had departed in June we concluded we didn't want to go back to the Wall residence. We had been eating for several years at the Realto Restaurant. While the food was good as restaurant food goes, we were tired of a steady diet of it. Bud was a good cook, and Carl and I could do more than just boil water. So he said, "Why not rent an apartment and do our own cooking? This will be a new experience and we can save money." So we rented a one-bedroom apartment for about ninety dollars a month right on the south side of 9 Mile Road in the heart of the small Ferndale business district. Bud and I slept in the bedroom, and Carl occupied the pull-out bed in our living room. We had a small kitchen and a bath. We found it very comfortable and much cheaper. I was chosen to be the male faculty advisor by the class of 1933, with Mary Humphrey the women's advisor. Mary and I had the pleasure of working together six years with two of the finest groups of boys and girls ever graduated from any high school. I do believe that these six years were the high-water mark of enjoyment during my teaching career.

We were a small high school of about twelve hundred students, and over a period of four years a student was able to learn the faculty, and the faculty members could really get acquainted with the students. As years went by and the student body became much larger the personal touch between students and teacher became less and less possible. It got to the point where each new semester I would get an entirely new group of about thirty-five students in each of my five classes. It took almost the whole semester to learn their names, let alone their personalities. The result was that student interest was much harder to maintain; because of a lack of understanding between student and teacher there were also more discipline problems, although I was never bothered with too many.

From the beginning of my Exchange Club membership I had taken a great interest in the activities of the club. One of the national projects of Exchange was service to aviation. I spent one whole Saturday up on the roof of the Ferndale Lumber Company building, painting "Ferndale" in big letters to help aviators flying over determine their position. After the stock market crash the Exchange secretary ran off with the Exchange bank account which totaled several hundreds of dollars. He was never heard of again. He had appeared to be a very fine businessman and was well liked. The club needed a new secretary and wanted me to take the position. The job paid fifty dollars a year plus the yearly dues. It was a great experience for me. I got out the club's first weekly bulletin listing both local and state Exchange events. In order to liven it up, I brought in the names of the members as often as possible, since who doesn't like to see their name in print, regardless of where it is?

When spring came the talk in Exchange was the state convention to be held on the Great Lakes steamship *Tionesta*. The ship was to sail from the Detroit docks at the foot of Woodward Avenue at about 4:00 p.m. Friday, June 14, and return Monday a.m., June 17. As secretary of the club and single, I was anxious to go even though I had to pay my own expenses. I asked Bradshaw what the possibilities were to come in late Monday a.m., which was the beginning of the last week of school. He said he could arrange it and to go ahead and make my plans. I was on the *Tionesta* when pulled away from the dock that Friday afternoon. We had a fine trip. I felt I had learned more about Exchange, which would enable me to do a better job as secretary of the club.

While the stock market crash the previous October was being felt by businesses, its impact had not yet reached public education finances. That allowed Ferndale to run another summer school. I again applied for and was given the job of teaching history and government.

After the six weeks were over I drove home to Gobles to relax and rest. I helped Dad on Saturdays at the barbershop, visited with the customers, and forgot about my work in Ferndale. On Sundays I would drive with Mother and Dad to various places they wanted to see. One Sunday morning we drove to Benton Harbor for breakfast, then we took the boat from Benton Harbor to South Haven and back for a ride on the *Great Lakes*.

My cousin Al Brown (mother's brother's son), who lived in Gobles during our youth, was in show business as a stage manager. He would take a "public state show" out of New York around the circuit, playing the major cities in the United States. His shows came to the Michigan Theater in Detroit. He would call me by phone to arrange for a visit and for me to see his show. It was interesting to go backstage while the show was in progress to watch and hear the actions and comments of the young singers and dancers. I learned wherever and whenever you have groups of people closely associated in work there is bound to be some discord. It was Al's responsibility to keep the young men and women working in harmony.

One Sunday while I was in Gobles Dad, I, and a couple of other people planned to go to Chicago to a Cubs ball game. Al had a show in Chicago, and he wrote that he and his wife would be pleased to have me stay over a week with them. I wrote that I would see them after the ball game. I sure learned a lot about the show business after spending a week there. One could easily see that it wasn't as glamorous a job as the audience would presume. I rode back on "Old Pet" from Chicago to South Haven. This was my last boat ride on Lake Michigan. The Depression, the automobile, and the truck were its death blow.

Monroe was pastor of the Methodist Church in Hobson, Montana. My mother's sister (Abbie Irene Odell) and her married daughter Kittie and husband Philip Ellihorpe lived in Minot, North Dakota. It had been several years since we had seen any of them, so I said to Mother and Dad, "If Whyle will run the barbershop for three weeks, I'll drive you two with my young sister west to see our Minot and Hobson folks." It sounded good to mother and dad, but for Donita it was, "I don' want to go." My mother said, "Donita, you are going. We are not going to leave you home with nothing to do." So with some hesitancy she consented to go. In order to cut down on expenses I arranged to borrow an umbrella tent and set of springs that rolled up. Dad and I planned to sleep in the tent on the springs covered with blankets, and mother and Donita would stay overnight in a tourist room.

We had a family friend who used to live in Gobles. He was in the automobile business in Paw Paw, a city ten miles south of Gobles. I decided to drive by Paw Paw on my way home and have him service my 1929 Chevrolet. I got to Paw Paw about 2:00 p.m. When my friend listened to my engine he said, "Harold, your car has a piston slap. They put cast iron pistons in these new cars, and they don't hold up." "What shall I do?" I asked, "We're ready to leave for the west this afternoon!" "I'll put new pistons in your car this afternoon, and it won't cost you a cent. Then we will know your car is in good shape for the trip," he stated. So it was about 5:00 p.m. when I wheeled into the drive of the homestead in Gobles. It had started to rain. To load the car in the rain with all the luggage we were taking, and to get going at that time of night was not feasible, so we all agreed that it was better to get a good night's sleep, rise early in the morning, pack the car, and take off.

This was mother and dad's first trip of any magnitude and they were anxious about it. Dad told me later that it was so much of a dream comes true he didn't dare think about it too much for fear something would happen that would prevent us from going. Up at 5:30 a.m. was the schedule. We had the car pretty well packed before we went to bed, so there remained only the suitcases and personal things. I had a luggage carrier on the driver's side of the car that allowed us to carry the suitcases on the outside, wrapped in a canvas that protected them from the rain and dust. Car trunks had not yet become a part of the automobile; instead, the cars had "running boards," a sort of step on each side of the car body that could be used as a carrier. We were really packed in. Because of our baggage carrier on the driver's side, we had to enter and leave on the right hand side.

When the morning dawned it was evident that the rain was over. We bid goodbye to Whyle and the homestead at about 6:30 a.m. with the understanding that we would eat breakfast in Benton Harbor, about fifty miles from Gobles. Mother had bought three quarts of huckleberries to take to her sister Abbie living in Minot (North Dakota), and she cradled those berries for the better part of four days before she handed them to her sister. I did all the driving. We were in route from about seven o'clock in the morning until about six in the evening. Of course, we took time off to eat some meals. Sometimes mother would issue a few words of warning such as, "Harold, it's way past lunchtime and we haven't eaten yet." So I would say, "All right, Mother, the next restaurant we come to will be lunchtime."

When we got up into the northern part of Wisconsin and Minnesota the cities and villages were quite far between. When you reached North Dakota you were really out in the open, with miles upon miles of wheat fields and few villages. And the roads! They sure were something. Only in the larger cities did we have any kind of a paved stretch of highway. We would drive all day without one bit of hard road other than gravel. At best it was a rather dusty trip, but Mother and Dad in the rear seat and Donita in front with me didn't mind the atmosphere. We were going to places and to see people we enjoyed.

When we got to Fargo, North Dakota it was a great experience on Highway 10. We drove along the Northern Pacific railroad, and in 1930 there were trains with their large super-steam coal-burning locomotives pulling a mile-long train. We got to Bismarck late in the afternoon of our fourth day. Mother and Donita got a room in a hotel right on the main street. Hotels were generally higher priced than tourist rooms, but we had a reason. Dad and I had not had a bath since we left home, and it was agreed that Mother and Donita would get up early enough so that Dad and I could take a shower if they had one or a bath if they didn't.

I inquired about a campground and was told that there was a space used for camping down near the bridge over the Missouri River. So we bid mother and Donita good night and drove to the river, which separates Bismarck from Mandan, North Dakota. I unloaded the tent, put it up, made our spring bed, and by dark Dad and I were on our way to dreamland.

Up early the next morning, I took down and packed the tent and bed on the car. Dad was no help. He enjoyed standing around talking and joking with the natives or other fellow travelers. I didn't mind doing all the work; I just wanted my parents to enjoy themselves.

In Gobles, living on our east side when I was a boy was a neighbor whom I always remembered as Aunt Martin. She was now living with relatives in Mandan, and had asked that we stop and say hello, which we did. Mr. Young, her son-in-law, was an engineer on the railroad and drove the passenger train that ran north one hundred and twenty miles to Minot. He would leave about twelve noon for work and would probably pass us on the highway that ran pretty much along the railroad tracks. After a hearty lunch we bid them all goodbye and retraced our drive over the Missouri River to Bismarck. Minot is located one hundred and twenty miles directly north of the capital city of Bismarck, and because there was a lot of travel between the two cities the gravel road was a pretty good one, considering what we had been on. It was late afternoon that we arrived at Leon and Kittie Ellithorpe's residence, where my Aunt Abbie also lived. Needless to say, we had a great three days with them.

Then it was on to Hobson, Montana, and what a drive. There were miles and miles where the road, the main highway if you please, was nothing more than a cow path. At one point the road came to a dead end at the railroad track. "Now what do we do?" I said in great discouragement? There was a sign that gave directions. It read, "Near the tracks is a telephone. Give it a ring and wait for an answer." So I did. At the other end of the line about a mile away came a voice, "Hello, what do you want?" "I want to get on the road going west," I answered. "OK," he said. "The tracks are clear, and there will be no train to interrupt you driving down the tracks. Report to me when you have reached this station." Driving down railroad tracks was a new experience for me, but we made it okay.

It was a long trek to Hobson. Those gumbo soil roads were sometimes a cloud of dust, and we had to drive part of the time with windows open, and it was hot. When we got to Hobson I told Monroe, "I have had it, you couldn't get me out here again to what you call God's country under any circumstances." Of course, the road building of the Depression days and since has changed all of that. Millie and I drove to Montana the summer of 1934, and in the late 1950's and 1960's we spent eight consecutive months of August in Montana and enjoyed it very much.

After several days in Hobson, during which time Monroe and I helped to save the town from burning down, Dad, Donita, and I packed the car and headed for home. It had been decided that Mother would stay on about a week with the Monroe's, then take the train to Minot to spend a few days with her sister. While I had to pretty much keep to a schedule, having to be back in Ferndale on Labor Day ready to start the new school year, this did allow us to drive south to Yellowstone and spend one day and one night there. Dad and I pitched our tent without any visitation by bears. Driving those mountain roads was very exhausting. I certainly breathed a sigh of relief when we reached the cornfields of Iowa. To me the trees, flowers, etc. are "God's country." We pulled into Gobles on the Friday afternoon before Labor Day. It had been a great trip, but now it was back to Ferndale and work.

School Year 1930-31

By fall 1930 the general public could begin to feel the effects of the stock market crash. There were no pay raises for Ferndale teachers, and it was the talk that we would all have to start tightening our belts. Bud, Carl, and I found an apartment that was only half as expensive right on 9 Mile Road, a few doors west of where we had lived. To have our rent cut in two was a real financial lift. I had been elected president of the Ferndale Education Association, and this, with teaching a Sunday school class of high school boys, kept me busy. But it was all enjoyable work. I always figured it made me a more valuable schoolteacher.

A couple of years previous I had had my tonsils out by one of our local doctors, a friend of mine. Now I found that one side of my nose was almost closed due to a crooked bone. I therefore arranged to have my nose operated on to remove the bone that was causing my trouble. The depression had already hit some doctors because my nose doctor said, "My fee is seventy-five dollars. However, if you give me fifty dollars cash, I'll do it for you." He got his fifty dollars and I got my nose fixed.

My 1929 Chevrolet was showing signs of the need for repairs. I could not see the point of spending money on it and still have an old car, so I went to the Chevrolet dealer and traded for a new 1931 four-door sedan.

Christmas found me in Gobles. Dad's business was showing the effects of the Depression. Men were letting their hair grow longer and shaving less often, or getting safety razors to do the job. We began to think in terms of economizing.

Eager to do a good job with the Teachers Association, our officers planned a big dinner dance at Northwood Inn on Woodward Avenue just about a mile and half north of Ferndale. We set the date of Thursday evening, February 12, 1931. It was a gay affair, a nice dinner, some paid entertainment that shocked some of the "old maids" of the faculty, and dancing. We had collected the cost per individual before the event, and the money had been deposited in the Ferndale American State Bank. During the course of the festivities I paid all the costs by check. We all went home with a full stomach in fine spirits, knowing that tomorrow was Friday night and teacher's delight. However, when we were in the middle of the forenoon, word got around school that the Ferndale American State Bank on this Friday, February 13, 1931 had a sign on its doors reading "Closed." Fortunately I personally had only about one hundred and fifty dollars in the bank, having had installments to meet each month. I gave the one hundred and fifty dollars certificate to the Ferndale Methodist Church to help pay off its mortgage held by the bank. But what about our checks issued the night before? Well, I had to go to each individual teacher and request that they pay again to cover the defunct bank checks. I'll confess, it didn't make me any very popular with my co-workers.

Mother was at the house alone from early morning until late in the evening while Dad was still putting in long hours at the shop but not making too much money. Whyle and Paul were in Albion College, having a hard time keeping body and soul together. Abbie was still single, and it was more or less expected that she and I would sort of look after Mother and Dad.

When Mother returned from the west she was not feeling well. She had a hernia that the doctor said ought to be fixed, but Dad's business just didn't allow for all such health expenses. Those were the days in which everyone was responsible for his or her own health care costs. I took the responsibility for her operation, making the contacts with the doctor and Bronson Hospital in Kalamazoo. On the appointed day I drove Mother to the Kalamazoo Hospital. They didn't have the methods then as they do today to diagnose one's trouble, so they didn't find her gall bladder trouble until they had operated for the hernia. After a few days of recovery the doctor informed us that mother should have her gall bladder out. "OK," said Mother, "I am ready," and the operation was performed with great success. I had contracted with the doctor to pay him by the month. The total cost including the hospital came to over five hundred dollars, which today is a small fee, but hospital costs and doctor's fees were not on the same financial plateau as of today. I paid the doctor monthly installments until things got really bad financially, then I wrote him a letter explaining my position, namely that I was paying off a debt with high priced money that had been contracted for in times of cheap money. He must have agreed with me for I never heard another word from him.

When it was noised around, and it didn't take long, that the Woodward Bank had closed, the people started lining up on 9 Mile at Woodward to get their money out of the 9 Mile bank. Of course, no bank could stand such a run on it and in two or three days it also closed. For the first time in many years Ferndale was without a bank.

Living in an apartment, cooking our own meals, etc. reduced the cost of living for all of us, so I was able to put aside enough money for my third summer at Ann Arbor studying at the university. After two summer schools and eight years of successful teaching behind me, I now had confidence that I was able to continue working for the Master's degree. My two fields of study, history and political science, were not considered easy ones. Some of my fellow co-workers were getting their Master's in the field of education, which most graduate students the least demanding of graduate fields. However, being a history teacher, I felt that my number-one requisite was to gain a thorough understanding of the subject that I was teaching.

School Year 1931-32

When school opened in fall 1931 we all were aware that we were in financial trouble. The administration stressed the great need for economy and conservation. No new teachers had been hired. That necessitated larger classes; history and government classes had forty to fifty students packed in a room built to comfortably house about twenty-eight students. Of course, there were no salary raises. We were told that the financial picture called for either salary cuts or larger classes. We chose the latter even though it meant a heavier load of classroom work.

Carl Forsythe was going to Detroit College of Law night school. He felt he could do his night school work much more efficiently if he roomed at a law fraternity house so he moved out of our apartment, leaving Bud and me to room alone. Our rent had now been reduced to thirty dollars a month. The apartment building had numerous vacancies, which again emphasized the financial characteristics of the times. Many high school sports were curbed in order to save money as well as the cost of fuel to heat the gym.

I had become known as "the bachelor." People would ask me, "When are you going to get married?" My pat answer was always, "When I find a girl I would enjoy marrying and one who will have me." One of my friendly high school students said to me, "Mr. Wilcox, why don't you pick out one of our good-looking senior girls and marry her" as if there was no more to getting married than that. Since many of my friends and acquaintances had become convinced I was doomed to bachelorhood, I was beginning to believe it myself. Then it suddenly happened. I had religiously gone to the Ferndale Methodist Church ever since my first year of teaching; had taught the high school age boys' and girls' Sunday school class; attended the various meetings and functions of the church, and was well known by almost everyone. It was the fall of my ninth year of teaching, 1931, that I saw a very-attractive young lady singing in the church choir. After several weeks I learned she lived in Highland Park and was coming to our church because she was the girlfriend of Gladys, the daughter of the choir director. It happened that Gladys was dating a fellow who was a good friend of mine, so one Sunday after church I got Paul to introduce me to the young lady, Mildred Burrows. At first I was just one of several dates, but by the summer of 1932 Millie and I had confessed our love for each other, and I knew she was mine.

During winter 1931 we received another shock. One afternoon Principal Bradshaw came around to our teachers' room on the third floor and announced that beginning today everyone must be out of the building by four o'clock. "Heat and lights will be turned off, and the building will be locked up," he said. Of course, this was to cut down expenses. I replied, "But I can't get my work done." "Well, we'll all have to do the best we can and let the rest of the work go," he replied. For almost ten years I had just about lived in the building. Many times I would return after dinner and on Saturday to grade papers, think, and plan. Now I was told to go home at four o'clock and let the work go. "What is this Depression doing to all of us?" I asked myself. It would be doubly hard on the student body. This meant there would be no clubs and organization meetings, no athletics and no place to go for those who had made the school building their social meeting place. When there was a great need for school buildings to be open day and night we were closing them up, and there was nothing the local taxpayer could do about it. After spring vacation the faculty was told that because of the lack of money schools would have to be closed two weeks earlier than the schedule called for unless teachers were willing to teach for nothing those last two weeks with the hopes that someday the board could get the money to pay the full-year contract. The teachers agreed to finish the school year.

By summer 1932 times were really tough. Looking for a job was like looking for a needle in a haystack. There was widespread unemployment all over the United States, and in 1932 there was no government-backed guaranteed insurance, no welfare department, and no unemployment insurance. It was a case of everyone scrambling for himself in hopes that friends, neighbors, or relatives would provide enough to keep body and soul together. President Herbert Hoover was trying to convey to the general public what the federal government was doing to maintain big business and the employer. The whole idea was if the government poured money into big business it was bound to trickle down to the employee. However, President Hoover and his Wall Street advisors failed to recognize that very little ever reached the poor unemployed worker.

In spring 1932 a man, looked up to by the masses as the hope of America, started preaching over the radio in his silver-tongued voice that the government policy was all wrong. Franklin D. Roosevelt presented the poor man's version of an economic philosophy, which made him famous. He said, "Pour money into the poor unemployed man's pocket. He will spend it for the necessary goods. This will start the wheels of industry rolling, and eventually we'll be out of the Depression." The fall election for president of the United States was bound to be a hard tough one, with President Hoover being backed by the Wall Street interests versus the Democrat Franklin D. Roosevelt.

After nine years of teaching in Ferndale it had become pretty much my home. I had no desire to go to Gobles for the summer, leaving Millie in Highland Park. The Wiitanens, both schoolteachers, had a home on West Cambourne in Ferndale, and they asked me if I would care to live at their house for about six weeks of the summer while they visited their relatives in the Upper Peninsula. They said all I would have to do was keep up the nice yard and eat and sleep there. I jumped at the opportunity since it would allow me to be with Millie over the summer months. At the same time, I could spend a few days now and then at Gobles. I also had a two-week barber job in a Ferndale shop, which made me an extra nickel.

When I visited the homestead in August I could easily see that financial times were not good with Dad. Farmers (no farm support in those days) were having a hard time selling their crops at almost any price, and many were plowing under their crops rather than trying to market them. Dad's barber business was mostly farm trade, and when they didn't have money for a shave or haircut they just didn't get one. at home I also found that Donita and "Bub" had moved in with Mother and Dad since there was no work in Plainwell where they had lived. Donita married Lawrence "Bub" Filkins in May 1931 while Donita was a senior at Gobles High School. They eloped and married in Angola, Indiana one hundred miles from Gobles. They didn't tell anyone until Thanksgiving of that year. Donita lived at home, and Bud continued to live at his residence. On Thanksgiving they started living together. Dad was never one to complain or relate to any of us his bad financial straits. It wasn't until that fall that I learned of his true financial position.

School Year 1932-33

School opened in September 1932 for my tenth year of teaching, and the talk was that we would all undoubtedly get a pay cut during the year. There would probably have to be another notch taken in the belt, so as to speak. It was the consensus that if anyone had a job and a paycheck coming in, they were well to do. This was becoming the image of the schoolteacher held by the general public. Industry was making an effort to keep employees on the payroll by dividing the work among its employees, some working only two days a week. Banks and businesses all over the United States were going bankrupt. There were rumors that the unemployed were going to organize and take over food markets, retail stores, etc. to keep from starving and freezing to death.

As the Thanksgiving holiday approached, Franklin Delano Roosevelt had been elected President of the United States. There was already a feeling in the air that economic times were due for a change. I drove my Chevrolet home to Gobles that Wednesday evening before Thanksgiving, looking forward to a visit and relaxation. When I walked into the house it was cold. I said, "Mother, why doesn't someone go down in the basement and put some coal on the fire?" Mother looked at me and said, "We have no coal. We are using the kitchen stove to give us heat." "Why doesn't Dad order some?" I asked. "Why wait until you're out before putting in an order?" I can still see the look on her face. "We don't have any credit. We haven't got last year's bill paid yet." I was dumbfounded. Here was a man, Bill, the coal dealer who had been friends of our family for many years, and he had cut Mother and Dad off, leaving them there to freeze. "I'll go right now and talk with Bill," I said. "We have got to have coal." I found Bill at the mill office. He owned the gristmill and also the coal yard. "Bill," I said, "We need coal at our house, what's the trouble?" "Harold," he said, "No one hated to do this to your dad more than I did. But Harold," he said, "I have so much credit on my books that I just had to close credit on last winter's bills or go out of business." I pulled out my checkbook and asked, "How much does Dad owe you?" "About one hundred dollars," he said. I wrote a check for $100.00, stating, "Apply fifty dollars on his account and I'll pay you the balance next month." Bill said, "Harold, I hate to see you have to do this for I have been a good friend of the Wilcoxes here in Gobles for a great number of years. But you know that we all sometimes have to pitch in and help out dear old Dad." The next morning we had coal in the bin and a fire in the furnace. For the first time, I began to realize what the Depression was doing.

There was a noticeable difference in the attitude of students in the classroom. It seemed we were having fewer cases of discipline, but yet a mental lethargy, a "What's the use?" attitude. For many boys and girls, having a warm, comfortable place to spend several hours a day with friends and companions was greatly appreciated.

I learned one lesson that I'll never forget. I was trying to maintain a high standard of learning in my classroom. One sweet young lady of about seventeen years of age was slumping in her work. In front of the whole class, I remarked that I didn't think she was trying. She began to cry, and said, "You wouldn't feel like studying either if you had to come to school without eating any breakfast." After class I called her up to my desk and apologized for making an embarrassing moment. After talking with her, I learned that her dad had been out of work and the family was destitute. Then I realized that she must have plenty of company in the same financial situation. I never again prodded a student for not doing their work without knowing more about their home situation.

The expected came. It had been rumored that some kind of salary cut was in the offering. The public was very conscious of the high school taxes and what were now teachers' high salaries. Milk was six cents a quart, beef steak was sixteen cents a pound, bread was six cents a loaf, and other prices were correspondingly low. When it came to the salary cut, I argued that it should be on a percentage basis. That would cut administration in proportion to classroom teachers. My position on salary cuts was acceptable to both administration and teachers alike, but when it came to cancelling out all sick leave benefits for classroom teachers without touching the administrators, I voiced a loud protest. Superintendent Downs reasoned this way, "A principal of a building can be absent and the classes continue uninterrupted. However, if a classroom teacher is absent we have to hire a substitute." I then came back with this argument. "If a classroom teacher doesn't leave anything in the classroom from day to day, why not hire substitutes all the time and do away with contracted teachers." Of course, I was popular with the instructors but I immediately sensed that battling the administration was a hopeless cause. After the general meeting Principal Bradshaw said to me, "You sure put yourself in a position where you will never get a promotion in this school system."

One of my closest friends in our first years in the Ferndale school system was made a principal before the Depression hit us. He became a staunch administration conservative and never forgot the argument I presented at that general teachers' meeting. Until his death he was anti-Wilcox. Even after Bradshaw and Downs were gone and I was elevated to an administrative position, I had to personally go to the school board members to gain a salary commensurate to my position. Yes, I had to pay for what I knew was fair and right. At least I became recognized as a person who was not afraid to say what he thinks. This characteristic gained me the respect of a great many people, although it made me some enemies. Salary cuts were made, and my salary went down from twenty-nine hundred to nineteen hundred plus dollars. However, we did have a job and a paycheck with a reasonable amount of job security, and that was more than thousands of others had.

Depressions are a good thing financially for those who have money. Stock prices were way down, commodities of all kinds were very cheap, houses and all kinds of property were crying for buyers. If you had money you could make money. I had a friend who had a little money and made thousands with ease. He would find a person in Ferndale who was losing his house because he couldn't make the payments. My friend Phil would give him fifty dollars for his equity, take over the mortgage on the house, rent it, and as prices started going up sell the property. At one time he owned fifty houses in Ferndale, all purchased from the owner for a ridiculously low payment for the equity. This is just one example of what we had going on all over the United States. The rich were getting richer and poor were getting poorer.

I have never in my life spent money on liquor, tobacco, or gambled it away. Instead I enjoyed wearing nice clothes, traveling, high-class entertainment, church, and other organizations for the betterment of society. No wonder then I was greatly astonished when one nice young lady student of mine came to me and said, "Mr. Wilcox, you dress too well." "I do?" was my answer. "Yes, you do for the times we're living in." she said. It just never occurred to me that as a schoolteacher I was presenting the picture of a well-to-do person. I replied, "You know, Betty, I don't spend my money for commodities that so many people spend for. I enjoy being clean and wearing nice clothes." That was the end of that conversation, and I continued to enjoy my way.

A college friend of mine edited the *Ferndale Gazette*, a weekly paper. He and his wife were both Kalamazoo College graduates. I played golf with him on numerous occasions. He was a quiet mannered, jovial, well-liked man about town. His wife worked on the *Gazette,* and many times when we were scheduled to play golf her response was, "When are we going to get the copy for the week's issue out?" Times were tough for all newspapers, and the *Ferndale Gazette* was no exception. In order to get ads you must have circulation, and to get and keep circulation a newspaper must be interesting to read. So my friend Harvey got an idea to stimulate circulation. He would get various people to write the history of the Ferndale organization to which they belonged for publication. This would fill his paper with articles about clubs, churches, etc. and things people enjoyed reading about. He asked me to write the history of the Ferndale public school system and the Ferndale Exchange Club, which I did. These two histories that I wrote are in the *Ferndale Gazette* archives, stacked away in the Ferndale Public Library for posterity.

The Exchange Club membership roster listed the names and addresses of business and professional men of various walks of life. When business began to taper off, whether it was the dentist, the doctor of medicine, the realtor, or what have you, men found that the fifteen dollars per quarter fee could help pay expenses, so they resigned from the Exchange Club. When I joined the club we had seventy members; by 1933 we were down to about twenty-five. Our president, a dentist, was not at all optimistic about the future of the club. As secretary, I had already sacrificed the fifty dollars a year secretarial fee and was more than willing to pay my dues in order to keep the club in existence, but when I called on the president he said, "Oh, let's forget about Exchange and close it up." My answer was that Exchange was needed more now than at any other time. All people needed a lift, and I for one was going to do all I could to give them that lift by keeping Exchange an active club. So they made me president of the club. With the help of two other school men and Maurice Cole, an attorney, and Bill Vignetto, a dentist, we held the group together with a very energetic program. A few years later while I was in his dentist office one day the former president said, "Harold, if it had not been for you our Exchange Club would have folded up."

I did have a job and a paycheck coming in. I needed one more eight-week summer school at the university to finish requirements for a master's degree in history and political science. After I had talked with Mr. Downs, Millie and I had decided to be married that summer of 1933. When I asked my boss if he thought it was feasible to get married, his reply was, "Why not, the rest of us married school men are living and eating." Perhaps my anxiety was due to being a bachelor for all these years.

I'll never forget the moment I purchased that car. The business street 9 Mile was deserted at six o'clock to the extent you could shoot a shotgun down toward Woodward Avenue and not hit a thing. We parked our cars on 9 Mile in front of the apartment. I was coming from school about 4:00 p.m. I parked the car just as a young gentleman of about thirty-five was passing on the sidewalk. He said to me, "You ought to buy a new 1933 Chevrolet. I can give you a good deal." I said, "I have been thinking about it, and why not do it today?" "Come on in and we'll write up the deal." When the salesman left our apartment with the signed contract in his pocket I thought to myself, "I have sent one salesman home happy at least for today." I bought a new 1933 maroon four-door sedan Chevrolet and made plans for summer school at the university.

Before I left for Ann Arbor Millie and I had to make plans for our wedding. When Monroe heard of our decision, he said he and his family were planning on driving to Michigan in August and to try and delay the wedding until he got here to marry us. As the summer months passed, it was evident to us that Monroe would not get here by August 27, our wedding date, so I made plans for us to be married in Stetson Chapel on the campus of Kalamazoo College. Rev. Hahn from the Gobles Methodist Church would marry us. My brother Whyle would be my best man, and Millie's sister Dorothy would be her maid of honor. It was to be a very simple affair. My sister Abbie played the piano. The time of the ceremony was set at 4:00 p.m. In order to have money for the first month of school and the wedding, I had to borrow one hundred dollars from a finance company. We didn't get paid until October 1. In our circle of friends as well as with both our parents, money was a scarce commodity. Therefore there was no reception, and only about three carloads of friends and relatives from Detroit drove down. My parents and a few friends from Gobles were also present.

Since Monroe's family from Montana was scheduled to arrive the following Wednesday and we were going to drive to Chicago with Monroe and Heloise for a few days at the Chicago World's Fair, our honeymoon was a short one. We drove down to Indiana for two days and three nights, arriving back in Gobles Wednesday noon to greet Monroe and his family upon their arrival. I knew Dad was not in a financial position to feed all of us, so I noised it around to Lee's and Allen's families that I thought whenever we came to eat at the homestead we all should make our contribution in either food or money. Previously when mother would give one of us a list of needed groceries it was, "Stop at the barbershop to get the money." I took it upon myself to make sure the barbershop was bypassed on such future occasions. When we were ready to start back to Ferndale, Dad said to me, "Harold, I was really worried about you and Monroe coming home. I didn't know what I could do to finance it, but I didn't need to worry because it all worked out fine with no financial hardship." We had a great time with Monroe and his first wife Heloise. (She died a few years later.) We were housed at a minister's home, which really made for a cheap trip. One thing about a Methodist minister, they generally have a bedroom at the parsonage wherever they go. It sure is a fine arrangement among the "members of the cloth."

The World's Fair was interesting, as all fairs are. I had one experience that I'll never forget. We sat in a large hall and watched a woman's face projected on a screen located about twenty-five yards from the camera, the first television. The lecturer continued to tell us of the great possibilities of this invention, sometime in the near future we would sit in our homes and watch on a screen what was going on miles away. It all seemed as improbable as it later did when scientists told us that by 1970 we would have a man on the moon. Today in 1972 nothing seems improbable.

Leaving Gobles on Monday for Ferndale, we bid Monroe and his family goodbye, not knowing just how many years it would be before we would see them again. However, Monroe did assure me that when we drove to Montana again we would find far better highways than those we drove on in 1930. The federal government was financing a big road-building program that was making such attractions as Yellowstone and Glacier National Park accessible.

The Wiitanens invited us to stay at their house for the week or until we got our apartment furnished. Before our wedding we had made a survey of the available apartment buildings and had chosen the Withington right off Woodward Avenue. We got a really nice unfurnished, one-bedroom front apartment for thirty dollars a month. All utilities were paid, so we spent the last week before school started looking for and buying furniture. Sears was our choice of a bedroom suite as well as davenport, lamps, and chairs. Our dinette set was purchased from another furniture store. The furniture was, of course, on a charge account. Schoolteachers had a job for at least a year on contract and were not considered risks, so we had no trouble with our credit. Our furniture was delivered on the following Friday, which enabled us to spend our first weekend in our own home.

One would think the hundred dollars I borrowed to tide us over to October 1 payday wouldn't go very far, but when I tell you that our budget allowed two dollars and forty cents a week for groceries and we ate well, and other costs were correspondingly cheap, it is understandable. Millie was then and still is a good cook as well as a fine seamstress. She made many of her own clothes, including her wedding dress and hat. We got a big kick out of the fact that when we were driving from Ferndale to Gobles the Saturday before the wedding she was still sewing her wedding dress, but it was completed on time.

Among the many best wishes we received was one from Millie's Uncle Walter, who lived in Toronto, Canada. His telegram read: "Regret cannot be with you Sunday. Best wishes for your happiness." A few years later Walter visited us in Ferndale. He certainly was an extremely likeable man. Of course, the newspapers had to give some ink to this bachelor schoolteacher who had finally "up and done it." The *Ferndale Gazette* had our pictures with the caption in bold type: "Harold Wilcox and his bride." The article mentioned that I was one of Lincoln High School (the name of the Ferndale High School) popular instructors. The *MLive Kalamazoo Gazette* had an article with the caption: "H. B. Wilcox and Detroit girl wed. Kalamazoo College graduate takes Mildred Burrows as bride." The article then went on to tell about the ceremony and terminated with, "Mr. Wilcox is a graduate of

Kalamazoo College, and is now head of the History Department of Lincoln High School, Ferndale." The *Gobles News* carried an article with a caption "Wilcox-Burrows Nuptials." The article had several incorrect statements, which didn't bother us in the least.

Having gone to my last summer school, gotten married, visited the Chicago World's Fair, and elected president of the Ferndale Exchange Club, I was ready for my eleventh year of teaching in the Ferndale public schools.

School Year 1933-34

It was about this time that it was very evident that a different arrangement would have to be made in Gobles for Mother and Dad. Business was so bad that the barbershop could not support two places during the long hard winter months in Gobles.

During the spring of the year we made a trip to Gobles. After talking it over with Mother and Dad, it was agreed that we could all pitch in and make the back room of the barbershop a living quarters for the winter months. The shop bathroom, which in the 1910's and 1920's allowed us to advertise "baths for twenty-five cents" with a good run, especially on Saturday nights, was turned into a kitchen. This provided them with a comfortable apartment during the winter months from January into spring. It was quite a job to move all the canned goods and things that could freeze from the house to the barbershop. We always figured that waiting any longer than the first week in January could mean trouble since Gobles is in the snowbelt along Lake Michigan. A few times after a mild fall that extended into the holiday season Dad would put off moving that first week and get caught in a blizzard. This arrangement continued until the winter of 1946 and 1947 when Dad became ill and could no longer go to the shop.

The new school year opened with the same fanfare as always, but for me it was really different. I received congratulations on getting married, "I hope all your troubles will be little ones," etc.

The local newspaper ran an article, which helped to describe my position that fall of 1933. The article mentioned that the Ferndale Exchange Club, which had been inactive for two months, met at the Ferndale Methodist Church. I being the President presided, but during this session Andrew S. McGeachy conducted, a shower for my marriage in August. The paper mentioned that I received useful and necessary gifts.

The usefulness of these gifts was questionable. At least the club members had a little fun at my expense. The one thing I'll always remember, and to me the most regrettable and disappointing was that after the fun was over, I looked for but did not receive a small gift or token of their best wishes for our happiness. I realized that money was tight, but I reasoned, and justifiably so, that each member could have donated a few nickels toward a small fund of three or four dollars that would have purchased a small gift for my bride. To a small degree at least, this reflects the spirit and thinking of the times. The Exchange Club was made up of small business and professional men. I, a schoolteacher, was probably netting as big a salary as they were or even more. The average person was just not philanthropic minded. Because I sensed this situation, I immediately dismissed from my mind the lack of thoughtfulness of the club members. When I got home after school and told Millie of the shower, we both accepted the occasion without any lingering feelings.

It wasn't too long before most school districts in and around Detroit saw the financial handwriting on the wall. In order to stretch the cash into ten paydays, one each month, the board of education got permission to print what became known as "scrip." It was a small piece of paper about the size of U.S. paper money used as evidence that the holder was entitled to receive good U.S. currency just as soon as the school board could find the cash. Money got so tight in 1933 that the board paid us with one-half cash and one-half scrip. It didn't work too much of a hardship on any of us; some of the single teachers just stored it up as an investment. I personally found a Detroit schoolteacher living in Ferndale who was willing to trade some scrip with me. That enabled him to use Ferndale scrip and me to use Detroit scrip to pay some of our bills, since most of the larger businesses took it in trade.

Since the school building was closed at 4:00 p.m. each day, we had more time to do things we enjoyed. We learned to entertain ourselves without too much expense. Many of our friends made through the church came to visit us for a game of cards. Also the Fergusons were our frequent companions to dances as well as cards. Our first New Year's Eve in our apartment was a memorable one. We invited our friends, about six couples, to an all-night party or as long as they cared to stay. Of course, we were all young and what did it matter if we lost a few hours of sleep. We served a buffet dinner at eight o'clock. From about nine o'clock to twelve we played cards or games for amusement. After midnight we celebrated the New Year by dancing to radio music, then a lunch. By that time some decided to go to an early morning show. Millie and I got a little shuteye with the understanding that breakfast would be served at five o'clock. We were a tired host and hostess when they all said "Happy New Year" about six in the morning.

Franklin D. Roosevelt was inaugurated president of the United States on March 4, 1933. Almost immediately there was an air of confidence among almost all people. One of the first things he did, which didn't affect Ferndale, was to declare a bank holiday, a period of a long weekend during which time all banks in the United States were closed. Then he gave one of his famous "fireside chats" over the radio, assuring that all financially sound banks would be allowed to open and those that were not financially sound would remain closed.

Ever since I had my first attack of flu in 1918 when I was in the service, it seemed I was due for a return engagement with the flu each winter. The winter of 1934 was no different than past years. I was down in bed for several days.

I had a boy in my class named Mickey. He was not very big but had a strong competitive spirit. He loved to play basketball, and under my friend Bud Brown the recreation department had a recreation basketball league. Mickey wanted to enter a team in the league, had all his boys lined up, and wanted me to coach or be manager of his team. He came to me while I was sick with the flu on that Friday afternoon. He explained that he didn't expect me to spend a lot of time with them. If I would attend all the games and manage the team, such as give the starting lineup, etc., that would take all responsibility off his shoulders. Not being connected with high school sports any longer, I consented to his request. It was a very enjoyable relation, and when we reached the playoff game it was my coaching that evening that enabled Mickey's team to beat a team with superior talent and win the city championship. I had made a lifelong friend.

A summer recreation program was being set up with the financial aid of government funds. A former Ferndale Lincoln High School man was given the directorship, and when he asked for applicants for playground directors I put in my application. I was assigned to the Jefferson Elementary School playground, which also housed the high school athletic field. Equipment was rather scarce; there was little money for it. We had a few bats and balls, etc. I was able to use the track for meets, which I believe gave my playground an advantage over some of the others. It may seem easy to run a playground, but it wasn't as soft a job as one might think. A good director constantly had to invent new programs to attract the kids to the grounds. You could keep them interested for a short time, but the recreation grounds were open from 11:00 a.m. to 5:00 p.m. and six hours made a long day for me.

By the middle of July I began to think of giving up my job and doing some relaxing. Monroe had written often and invited us to drive west. He pictured a great time up at Glacier National Park. Then he said he also had access to a cabin on Flat Head Lake where Millie could fish to her heart's content. This, of course, was an attractive invitation. Millie and I began to plan for the venture by first informing the director that I wanted to be relieved of my playground assignment by August 1. This did not prove to be a hardship for him since there were others who would be glad to fill in for the rest of the playground season. The money I earned by being a playground director was used for the trip. We purchased an umbrella tent and two army cots from an army outlet store. We also bought a small gasoline camping stove. We wrote Monroe to start making his plans for the Glacier Park trip and that we would be on our way by at least August 1. That would give us a good five weeks for the trip.

Millie wrote in our scrapbook, "1934 went to Montana during the latter part of July and August for our vacation. Monroe and Heloise went camping with us in Glacier National Park for two weeks."

We planned to sleep in the tent. While I put up the tent and made the beds, Millie would cook dinner. In the morning Millie would make breakfast while I took down and packed the tent, cots, and blankets in the car. We would park overnight at tourist grounds with picnic tables. We left Ferndale on a bright sunny Friday morning with plans to stop at Gobles for the weekend.

The first of the week found us on the highway routed for Chicago and up into Wisconsin for our first night. We had written Aunt Abbie (Abbie Odell, my mother's sister) and Kittie and Leon Ellithorpe, Abbie's daughter and son-in-law that we would arrive in Minot, North Dakota that first weekend. We had good weather, nice campgrounds, and an enjoyable trip to Minot. My 1933 Chevrolet could run a steady pace of about forty-five miles an hour, and the roads were much better than we had found during the 1930 trip. When we arrived at Minot, North Dakota, we were received with open arms. On the Sunday we were there Leon and Kittie arranged a picnic dinner in a park following church services. Many of their friends and relatives were present. Kittie told me after we returned to their house that some asked when they saw Millie and me, "Are they brother and sister?" "No," said Kittie, "They are husband and wife."

It took us two full days to trek across western North Dakota and eastern Montana. We drove long hours since there wasn't too much to do otherwise. When it got dark we were in bed with only flashlights to use for illumination. Generally speaking, we were up early and on our way by seven o'clock. In 1934 there was little for a tourist to see and do while traveling this part of the country. We arrived at Fort Benton, located on the Missouri River, late in the afternoon of the second day. Reaching Fort Benton was exciting. We drove by the church parsonage looking for it, so I had to pull off the dirt road and swing into some long grass to turn around. In doing so I didn't see a piece of sewer pipe covered up in the long grass and my front wheel hit it and cut the tire open to the extent I was only able to get into their drive before it was flat. "A nice way to greet your brother," I said to Monroe. Although we treated it as a joke and laughed it off, having to purchase a new tire was not a joke, but what could one do?

It sure seemed good to sleep in a bed again since while in Minot, due to crowded conditions in the house, we pitched our tent in the backyard and slept in it. Monroe and Heloise and their two children, Nan and Jim, were already making plans before our arrival. They had borrowed a large tent with cots, and we were to load our cars and camp out two weeks in Glacier National Park. After three days resting up from our long drive we took, off making Great Falls our first stop for lunch, then into Glacier.

The first place we camped was at Two Medicine Lake at the foot of Mt. Rockwell. Putting up our tents, making the beds, building a campfire, etc. was our first tasks, then a good meal and in bed shortly after dark. It had not been too cold during the day, but Millie and I both awakened from the cold during the early morning hours. When we got up after daylight we found our water supply out of the stream was iced over. We knew then we would have to rearrange our sleeping conditions. We spent several days at Two Medicine taking hikes up the mountains, playing in the snow, and sticking our bare feet into "Iceberg Lake' where there is ice year round. It was a fine experience, but I am a warm-climate man and when Monroe announced we were breaking camp to move west of the Divide where we would find it much warmer, I said, "Good, I am all for it; no more Two Medicine for me."

Across the Divide we settled in a camping site where we had the company of other tourists. It was warm and balmy, my kind of climate, no more awakening in early morning hours cold in spite of wearing everything I had to put on to bed. There were picnic tables, campfires, etc. In order to preserve our food, Monroe had brought along a big tin can. After filling it with bacon, bread, butter, etc. we let it dangle from the limb of a tree high enough, we thought, to keep the bears that visited the camp during the sleeping hours from getting it. However, we found out that bears can really jump when they smell bacon. We were awakened by Monroe telling us to get our flashlights and arm ourselves with stones, kettles, and anything of the noise making variety because we had bears. We turned our lights on them. With one gigantic leap, the bear got that tin and away went our bacon, etc. We threw stones at them, and the whole camp was armed with noisemakers trying to drive them away. They left, but the taste of our food didn't satisfy them. We hadn't been in our beds too long before Millie said, "Harold, I hear them coming back." Up we got to use the same noise-making, rock-throwing procedure as before. We stayed there in that camp for several days, and each night we had bear visitors. Monroe and I prided ourselves for getting in some solid rock hits.

One of the most interesting experiences I had came when I was sitting at a picnic table eating popcorn. It was early afternoon, warm and delightful. All of a sudden I looked up, and half startled I saw within five yards a most beautiful deer. Without making too much of a move since I didn't want to drive him away, I held out to him my sack of popcorn. Step by step he edged a little closer until I had him eating out of my hand. He remained with me until other campers noticed him, and their attention resulted in his departure.

At the end of our two-week camping trip in Glacier we headed back to Fort Benton. After resting up, as Monroe called it, for a couple of days, it was time for us to hit the trail back to what we called civilization. We had been sleeping in a tent for the better part of nearly four weeks, and to be frank with you I just never was and never have been a camper. I told Monroe if we didn't have these five days of driving in front of us before we reached Gobles it would be nice. Bidding them all goodbye and thanking them for a great experience, although some of it not greatly appreciated, we headed our Chevrolet east for a five-day jaunt. The excitement of cooking meals on a camp stove, setting up tent and beds, etc., was diminishing. Several times we cheated on our budget and ate at restaurants. When we got into Wisconsin the weather turned into a cool rain so the last night out before reaching Gobles was spent in a tourist room.

Arriving in Gobles for the weekend, we were just in time to enjoy a good old-fashioned Methodist Church dinner. We stopped at the barbershop to say hello to Dad. He said, "Your mother is at the church helping to prepare the dinner." We stopped at the church to greet Mother, and then drove the block to the house. When we opened the door I thought I smelled something hot. Walking to the basement door off the dining room I found the cause of the odor. Mother had been ironing, had set the flatiron on the floor, and had forgotten to pull the electric cord out of the socket. The flatiron was red hot. It sure was a good thing we arrived as soon as we did, no telling what the results might have been.

We returned to Ferndale and our Withington apartment on Sunday the day before Labor Day. It was good to get home again and to relax in the comfort of our own abode.

Chapter 7

Ferndale's Elected Commissioner (1935-1943) and High School Teacher

We were no longer called to report on Labor Day (1934) for meetings of teachers; the new school year was scheduled to start the Tuesday after Labor Day. It was also the date of our first fall meeting of the Ferndale Exchange Club. Little did I realize on that September day 1934 what the year had in store for us. We were never to be the same.

The Ferndale political situation was at low ebb. In 1931 when the banks closed, which was a city election year, the tide of resentment swept into office questionably qualified commissioners, one of whom could hardly read and write! Ferndale has a city-manager type of government, with an elected mayor with a two-year term and four commissioners with four-year terms. Jay Gibbs, the city manager, kept a pretty tight rein on things. He could pinch a nickel and make it go farther than any public official I have ever known. However, there were influential people who could see the handwriting on the wall when it came to visualizing the future of Ferndale. A city manager could keep such men on a commission in line just about so long before they started to stray from the main purpose of their commission.

According to the city charter, it was the mayor and commissioner's business to make policy, which the city manager was to carry out.

In November 1934 I was talking with my principal, Cleve Bradshaw. He said he had talked with influential people in the community about the spring city election. It was the consensus of these people that there should be new faces on the city commission. These people said, "We ought to have a schoolteacher running for office," and I was the one they thought should do it. "Give it some thought and consideration." Cleve said. I went home that evening and told Millie about our conversation. I tried to analyze the pros and cons of the idea.

Then I went to my boss and superintendent Ed Downs and presented the idea to him. Ed had been mayor of Highland Park, where he had been an elementary school principal prior to his coming to Ferndale, so he knew the ins and outs of city politics. Ed said, "Sure, why don't you run for the commission. I'll stand behind you if we should have some repercussion from some Ferndale citizens."

I had never run for an office before. To a degree, I had always thought that the office should seek the person, but I got over that conception immediately after talking with men who were in a position to know. After visiting with numerous people, I threw my hat into the ring and became a candidate.

When I was seeking advice on how to campaign my friend Guy Stark, a former village president (before Ferndale became a city in 1927), said to me, "Harold, do you really want to be elected?" "Sure I do, or I wouldn't be running," I replied. "Then I'll tell you how you should do it. Go out and talk to the women, they will do more for you than any other type of campaigning." The pattern for seeking office was set.

In the meantime, Millie and I became involved in another episode that was to greatly affect our living. It was around Thanksgiving while talking to our friends the Fergusons that we got the bug for house hunting. Ed said he and Myrtle had just purchased a house on West Woodland. "You ought to give some consideration to doing the same," said Ed. "But what are we going to use for money?" I asked. "You don't need too much," he said. "We bought our house on a shoestring."

I went to my friend and realtor Philip J. Watson, and discussed it with him. He told me that all we had to do was drive up and down streets to see the "For Sale" signs. Then he asked, "Do you have life insurance?" "Yes, I have some," I answered. "Well," he said, "You can borrow on it for a down payment. You are already paying rent, and to pay on a house wouldn't run your monthly payments too much higher." I wrote to the two insurance companies requesting the amount that could be borrowed. Then Millie and I started to look at houses. We drove up and down streets. When we found something we thought we might like we got Phil to show it to us. Many of them were unoccupied. This procedure went on until about the middle of January, and we began to think we wanted something that didn't exist. Millie has always had a keen sense of artistic beauty and finding a house that we would enjoy living in was not too easy.

One day after school in the middle of January, we drove up and down West Maplehurst. Our eyes fell on a white frame house, one and one-half stories with large columns in front. "That is the house I would like," said Millie. "Well, take down the number 250 and we'll go ask Phil if it's listed for sale." I said. "No," said Phil, "I don't have it listed, but I'll tell you what I can do. I'll make them a visit, and ask if the house is for sale; that I have a party interested in it and get their response." The next day Phil told me he had talked with them and their attitude was, "While we haven't put the house up for sale we might consider it, provided you have someone who has some money and a steady job." "My client," said Phil, "is a schoolteacher here at Lincoln High School. They would like to look at the house." A couple of days later we visited the residence and fell in love with it.

Then we had to consider the price and the amount of our down payment. I found I could raise enough money for the down payment but not enough to pay Phil his realtor fee. "Well," said Phil, "I'll take mine whenever you get it so we won't worry about that." Phil was very generous. He had some daughters in school. His older daughter was going to Albion College. He asked me to tutor her over the summer. In this way I worked off the realtor fee. The contract was signed with the understanding we could move in March 1, 1935. A few days later we delivered to Phil our down payment. That evening we entertained the Fergusons, announcing we had bought a house on the street just south of their residence. We thanked Ed for getting us interested in making such a deal.

This house at 250 Maplehurst, Ferndale, has been our home ever since that memorable March 1, 1935. It was a beautiful warm day that Saturday when we moved our furniture from the Withington Apartment Building to "our home." We had no heat in the house over the weekend. It had a coal-burning, steam-heat furnace, and the former owners took every lump of coal with them. Remember, these were Depression times and everything that cost money was valuable.

I launched my campaign for Ferndale City Commissioner in February 1935. One newspaper reported that I was a candidate for the city commissioner seat and the primary election would be held on March 4th. It stated that I was the first schoolteacher candidate to run for a Ferndale commissioner seat. The article continued that I was a Ferndale high school history and government teacher during my twelve years of residence in Ferndale. The article mentioned also that I was a graduate from Kalamazoo College, spent one year at the Boston University School of Theology, and completed the requirements for my Master of Arts Degree at the University of Michigan. The article added that I am running for the office of commissioner because I believe I am capable, qualified, and desirous of serving the people of Ferndale. My platform is good, clean, dignified, honest and progressive government. The article also mentioned that I am an active and social worker at church and hold the offices of secretary and president with the Ferndale Exchange Club.

I spent almost every evening ringing doorbells, visiting organization and club meetings, and just meeting people. There were twenty-one candidates for the two vacancies on the commission. The office paid ten dollars a meeting up to five hundred dollars a year, and to some this was their living. I was already being accused by some of taking the bread and butter right out of their mouth. I had several conferences with Ed Down on my campaign if elected to the office. I told him of some of the remarks I had already heard. He listened, then said, "Harold, if you are elected you had got to expect and accept the whiplashing that goes with politics. You will find that there are some people that are cracking the whip on your back almost continuously. If you can't take it, you have no business running for office." I thanked Ed for his "voice of experience" and told him I could take it.

One of the most interesting things about my campaigning was the attitude of the student body at the high school. Many of them asked me for campaign literature and at one basketball game in the latter part of February the cheerleaders led a cheer for Wilcox. All these things helped to offset some of the adverse criticism I received.

The primaries on March 4 gave me first place with 941 votes. Second-highest and an incumbent had 761 votes. I sweep every precinct but two. I was advised by my political friends not to let up on campaigning. I took their advice, and when the election results were released on April 1st I led the ticket with 1,834 votes compared to Tilden's second place finish with 1,654 votes. The first meeting in April starting at 7:30 p.m. had its usual best wishes and floral pieces. In addition there was a large audience that taxed the commission room to the very limit.

Our life seemed to be undergoing great changes. Almost everyone knew who Harold B. Wilcox was, and his wife Millie was being ushered into a new realm of social living. Millie became a member of the Ferndale Women's Club and was appointed by the President to serve on a committee. She also was asked to model a wedding gown at a wedding gown pageant held at the Ferndale Presbyterian Church and sponsored by the Women's Club.

Seldom had a week gone by without my name being headlines in the local newspapers. I was being called upon to speak before clubs and organizations. All this took time and energy, but the Good Lord gave me twenty-four hours in a day, seven days a week and he blessed me with good health and energy, so I held up and was in good condition. Opportunities to speak were becoming numerous. Now, I was never was a politician. A good politician keeps his mouth shut and his nose clean. Well, I could and did, but when it came to keeping my mouth shut and running a "shut-eye" government, that I couldn't go for. My first two years in office were hectic ones. It seemed everyone had their eyes glued on everything the city was doing, and regardless of what was done some toes were stepped on. "Ticket fixing" was one of the first situations that had to be cleaned up. The noise made by the young people at the Beerless Garden on West 9 Mile was a city problem. The firing of the Police Chief for being drunk on duty and incompetency was nerve-wracking because everyone has friends. Making "a political football" of the appointment of a new chief was another issue. These were just a few of the many problems confronting the commission.

When the local newspaper came out with the names and pictures of the "Leading and Prominent Citizens of South Oakland County," my picture was on the second row with the following information: "Commissioner of the City of Ferndale, Member and past president of the Ferndale Exchange Club." May I add that other than Edgar F. Down, my boss, I was the only schoolteacher and commissioner to be honored.

In February 1936 the sports editor of the *Royal Oak Daily Tribune* asked me to pick an "all-time" Lincoln High School basketball team. I consented to do it, and a few weeks later in March the *Royal Oak DailyTribune* gave my "all-Lincoln High team" a big two-column spread on its sports page with my picture. The headline read: "Wilcox Picks All Time Cage Quintet at Lincoln High. Commissioner Holds Track Record at Kalamazoo and It Remains Unbroken. Selects Old-Timers on A-1 Team." The article listed my college athletic exploits, then it inked the record of sixteen wins and two losses by the 1923-24 team I coached. Following that was the all-time team that I had picked, with a story about each player.

In April 1936 Millie took part in the Women's Club "Pageant for Neighbor Club." A musical picture pageant titled "Songs and Scenes of Motherhood" was presented to several different clubs around south Oakland County.

In August 1936 the *Detroit Free Press* printed an article regarding the Consumers Power company rates that stated: "Commissioner Harold B. Wilcox, leader in the fight to oust the power company, declared that protests against rates and treatment of patrons by the company had so increased that action by authorities is imperative." I answered the *Detroit Free Press* with this statement: "This erroneous impression leads me to state that I am not and never have been the leader to oust the public utilities from Ferndale, although I am for low rates. If the present existing Public Utilities companies give the citizens of Ferndale and vicinity fair and just rates I see no reason for a change in service, but if they do not then I believe the citizens of Ferndale should look to other sources for these services." May I add that during the Depression years those who had money were fighting to keep and improve their financial position. The public utilities were no exception. My efforts were rewarded with lower rates.

In October 1936 the Ferndale city employees wanted to be put under civil service, and I was one hundred percent for it. Commissioner Harvey Horn enjoyed the political patronage system and was elated when he felt he had put a friend on the city payroll through his political influence. The question before the commission that fall day was whether to allow the people to vote on this issue in the November 1936 election by placing it on the ballot. The commission voted four to one for its passage, and the civil service issue was accepted by the people. The newspaper announced that I was given credit in the newspaper for the passage of this issue and Harvey Horn's opposition to it was also mentioned in the paper. In September 1936 I was asked to be the Ferndale Chairman for the Community fund and Edgar F. Down was the Township Chairman.

In December 1936 the faculty of the high school had their usual after-school Christmas party. An unknown giver gave me a gift with the following rhyme: "H. B. Wilcox, H. B. is a man of versatility; agent with a rare personality; he can teach, he can preach, and at politics he is a peach; but, gentle folk, lend me your ear, next spring he will be papa we hear, Merry Christmas, Harold." Yes, Millie and I were looking forward to March 1937 when we expected Philip Harold to be born.

Also in 1937, Kalamazoo College was beginning what was ultimately was a transformation of the entire college campus. "The 90 year old Hall at Kalamazoo must go," stated the *MLive Kalamazoo Gazette* on January 2, "Grads Start Rush for Bricks from Doomed Landmark." Well, I didn't get a brick, but I still have my key to old room 46 in which I lived for three and one-half years while I was on campus.

February 1937 saw one of Ferndale's finest improvements. The new Radio City Theatre was opened, and at the opening ceremonies the city commission was invited to be the guests of the theater management. The entertainment was the movie *Pennies from Heaven* with Bing Crosby.

February and March were the months for baby showers for Millie. Financial times were greatly improved, and it didn't prove to be a hardship for people to return to some of the friendly and neighborhood American customs. We had gone back to full paychecks, and a raise in pay was in the offing.

The day came as all days do, and I took Millie to the Highland Park General Hospital where her doctor sent his patients. It wasn't long before the doctor came into the waiting room and said, "Congratulations, you're the father of a fine baby boy." After visiting Millie, I rushed to the telephone to call Millie's mother and to send a telegram to my parents. Philip Harold was born on Tuesday evening, March 23, 1937 at Highland Park General Hospital.

Under "Briefs Concerning Alumni" the *Kalamazoo College Index* had: "Congratulations to – 1922 – Mr. and Mrs. Harold B. Wilcox on the birth of a baby boy, Philip Harold, born March 23." Of course, there were dozens of other well wishes that came in the mail from our relatives, friends, and acquaintances. One of my political friends who never had children said to me as I gave him a cigar, "Congratulations, Harold, but you're starting rather late in life, aren't you, to rear a family?" My answer was, "Better late than never." My mother and father both mailed us nice letters regarding Philip. Dad said, "We got your telegram this morning. Hurrah-Hurrah for our side. I took the telegram right over to Bert Travis [editor of the *Gobles News*], and he went right to work setting it up for this week's paper." Would you believe it, our hospital bill for Philip Harold's birth was exactly sixty-one dollars, and our doctor charged us seventy-five dollars for total nine-month care. What a difference from the 1970's.

Being a good cook, Millie answered the request of the *Highland Parker* newspaper by mailing them a recipe for a good dish. A letter arrived dated April 23, 1937, from the newspaper that read:

"It is with pleasure that we inform you that your recipes were considered among the best submitted in the last week's contest. Enclosed are four complimentary passes to the R.K.O. Uptown Theatre." This was in the day when movies were worth going to see.

"Whiskey by the glass" probably constituted the biggest issue of my eight years on the commission, and in all probability helped in my defeat for a third term. Newspapers saw a lucrative advertising program from the liquor interests and, while the local papers didn't come right out for "whiskey by the glass," they sure kept the issue hot with lots of publicity. During September 1937 the issue was spearheaded by some three hundred-odd persons who petitioned the commission for that privilege. The commission went on record opposing liquor by the glass by a three to two vote. Opposing it were Roy Tilden, Arthur Bartlett, and me (Harold B. Wilcox). The mayor and Jules Bols favored it. I felt that if the people want it, let them vote it in. I personally was one of the many who kept liquor by the glass out of Ferndale for about twenty-five years. After several votes by the people, it was accepted by the citizens of Ferndale in a close vote in the 1960's.

My 1933 Chevrolet was in pretty poor shape, and I needed a new car. During fall 1936 business conditions had improved to the extent that the automobile industry was selling more cars. Then in the winter and spring of 1937 we had what economists called a little recession. Men who had bought new cars in the fall were unemployed, and the finance companies were ready to grab them. I put an ad in the *Royal Oak Daily Tribune* announcing that I had a 1933 Chevrolet sedan to trade for the equity of a late-model car. Well sir, when I went home from school at 4:30 o'clock there were six cars parked in front of my house, all people wanting to trade. After questioning each about the miles on the car, his payments, etc., I chose a 1937 Plymouth that had only about 2,000 miles on it. It proved to me again in a small way that those who have money can make money during a depression.

All during the fall of 1937, Millie continued to mail recipes to the *Highland Parker* and to be rewarded with money prizes or theatre tickets.

An issue arose in reference to having a city ambulance. I favored organizing a committee to look into this issue before making up my mind. This controversy was the result of an aged woman being hit and killed by a car on a street in Ferndale. Because of the lack of a city ambulance, she was carried to the hospital in a police car. With two local weeklies trying to gain the inside track to city publicity, it created a tense and cautious attitude within me. I never knew which one would take a crack at me; after all, I was a schoolteacher by profession.

When I was first campaigning for office one of the men (a so-called big shot) on our high school faculty remarked to a teacher friend of mine, "Does Wilcox really expects to get elected to office? If he should happen to get in, those politicians down on the corner will make a jackass out of him." Well, I had been in office three years and so far no one had made a jackass of me, although I'll have to confess there were times when I thought someone was trying to.

Every organization, including our Ferndale Methodist Church, was trying to raise money. A lady representative sold the church committee on buying "The Womanless Wedding." The main idea was to get all the prominent people of the community into the cast. This made it a fun night that proved to be a drawing card for ticket sellers. I remember the "child" in the baby carriage was a small man well known in the vicinity, a doctor of medicine. He was dressed as a small child. The bride was a huge man dressed in a woman's attire, and the groom was a really slight, short man in evening dress. I played the part of a bridesmaid, dressed as a young lady. We had several rehearsals with only the narrator doing the talking, the cast doing the acting. A good crowd turned out for the "wedding." The church made a little money; the lady representative and director made her keep. It was still Depression times, and everyone had a good time.

The Cowells, Larry and Faye, had moved into a house across the street from us on West Maplehurst. Millie had practically grown up with them when the three of them lived in the same Detroit neighborhood, so they were welcome neighbors. We had a great deal in common. As city commissioner I was tied to Ferndale, you might say, the year round. However, we did spend a long weekend in Gobles now and then, and found time to spend a week or two at a cottage. One of our vacations was at a cottage at East Tawas, Michigan. In order for Larry and I to play a game of golf and

Millie and Faye to relax free from Phil's care, we took my niece Pat Wilcox, who lived in Kalamazoo, to be a babysitter. Although Phil was only a year and five months old, the arrangement provided all of us with some free time. This marked the beginning of many vacation trips with the Cowells.

One of the saddest moments of our family life was in winter 1939 when my brother Paul had to go to the state hospital in Ypsilanti. Paul was a graduate of Albion College, married with one child. He just couldn't take the Depression. When Paul was about two years old he was very badly burned. Our mother was at the outside toilet when Paul's shirtsleeve caught on fire from the kitchen stove. It left him with bad and ugly scars on his back, right arm and neck, and Paul could never forget his marked body. I do believe this played a part in giving him a personality that with the pressure of being jobless during the Depression caused him to mentally crack.

January, February, and March 1939 found me putting in my spare time punching doorbells, giving speeches, and campaigning for reelection. When the ballots were all counted, it was announced that I, Harold B. Wilcox was reelected to a second four-year term. There were many problems during the four years of my second term, 1939-1943. One headlined that I still wanted to know about those pinball games! It was a Monday night Ferndale City Commission meeting, and when all the issues had been addressed I asked some questions relating to pinball machines in Ferndale. The members also had questions, and there were different opinions on this issue. Nothing was settled and there was no effect for the current pinball machine operators. I was a little proud of the fact that before my second term ended Ferndale was rid of the pinball machines. I was also proud that during my eight years on the commission, through my influence, the city of Ferndale replaced the old paper ballots with voting machines.

The year 1939 was significant in our lives, with so many pleasant memories. One thing to be thankful for was the easing of the Depression. President Roosevelt was in his second term of office, and the people of the United States had great faith in his ability to establish a better-balanced economy.

There was the New York City World's Fair. Millie and I wanted to go, so we arranged with Millie's sister Dorothy in Kalamazoo to care for Phil for a week while we drove first to Boston and then down to New York. We spent two days and three nights at the fair. When we returned home we packed our things and, with the Cowells and Charlotte Jaeger, our babysitter, hit the trail across the state to Silver Lake, just off Lake Michigan, for a week at a cottage.

Things were not the same at the high school when we opened for the fall semester in 1939. We had weathered the depression under Principal Cleve Bradshaw, who was a fine man to work for. The public seemed to be restless, and at the end of the school year in 1935 Cleve was let go. Now in 1939 we had a principal by the name of Ralph Van Huesen. He was beginning his fifth year. Ralph had earned his Doctor of Philosophy degree at the University of Michigan. He had a distinctly different philosophy of education than did Bradshaw. Ralph was a man who seemed very undecided about issues pertaining to school matters. One could seldom get a yes or no out of him. As a result of his administration policy, classroom teachers were rather uncomfortable, with a feeling of insecurity. I remember one English instructor he let go because he didn't feel she was doing a good job. She applied to another school system. The superintendent came to visit her classes and hired her for the coming year.

Ralph told me as the head of the history department that he felt social studies teachers were doing the poorest teaching job of any of the departments. I said, "What are you doing to correct it? Our history classes are loaded with 40-45 students. The math classes have only 20-25. You go to the university and talk to the professors in the history and political science departments, and they will laugh at you people in the education school." He replied, "I know it." I never heard another word from him about the inferior history teachers.

The school year was full of activity, but we reduced our socializing to a degree because we knew the stork was to again visit 250 Maplehurst in the spring. If it was a boy his name would be Richard Allen; if it was a girl, we thought we would name her Gail. On Sunday, April 14, 1940 Richard Allen arrived. I had just gotten home from church when Millie told me she felt she should get ready for the hospital. It was about four o'clock when we left for the hospital. By seven o'clock, Richard Allen was a reality. His weight was six pounds and was born at the Highland Park Hospital. Our hospital bill was only fifty-nine dollars and twenty-five cents.

The school year of 1939-40 was a good year for us. Monroe had come home for a short visit in March, and we had all congregated at the homestead for a big weekend. Everyone seemed to be a little more prosperous and all in good health. We had a lot to thank God for.

Now that we had another mouth to feed I was asking myself, "What can I do this summer to make an extra nickel?" Many people looked at the city commission office as a good-paying job, but the five hundred dollars a year was not all profit. It cost money to get elected. Each of the local newspapers expected a candidate for office to do so much advertising. Then there was postage, handbills, cards, etc. that had to be paid for whether or not one got elected. It was somewhat of a gamble. Every fund raising agency that started a money drive always visited the commission meeting, first to gain permission to make the drive for money, and second to take a five-dollar bill away from each of us. That didn't happen just once or twice a year. There were times when I thought I couldn't afford to be a commissioner. Everyone, it seemed, wanted some bit of that check. The city charter established the fee paid to the mayor and commissioners. Back in 1927 when the village of Ferndale became a city the new city charter stipulated that the mayor should receive seven hundred and fifty dollars a year and a commissioner would receive ten dollars a meeting and up to five hundred dollars a year. In the 1950's I started a movement to have the salaries of the mayor and commissioners raised to a respectable amount. However, when putting the idea before some civic groups they thought that the economic times would discourage people from voting for it. The issue was dropped, and no one has since raised the issue.

Higgins Pontiac was located just a block from our house on Woodward Avenue. Mr. Higgins, George to most of us, had a soft spot in his heart for schoolteachers and education in general. While he was in the state legislature, first as a representative and then as a senator, education always had a friend in George Higgins. I had had the Higgins children in class at the high school, and being in city politics I became very well acquainted with George. In the middle of May George asked, "What are you doing this summer with your spare time?" I replied, "I am looking for a job at which I can make my bread and butter." "I'll give you a summer job selling cars. How much do you expect to make per week this summer?" he asked. "Well, George, if I could make twenty-five dollars a week for the ten summer weeks of vacation time I would be satisfied," I replied. "Well," said Mr. Higgins, "You would have to sell only one car a week to do that, and I'll guarantee you the twenty-five dollars a week plus twenty-five dollars for all cars you sell in addition to the first one. You can also come over to the salesroom and work Saturdays and evenings if you desire." "Fine," I said. "I need a new car. My Plymouth has seen its best days – maybe I can make enough to get into a new Pontiac." "I am sure," he said, "we can work you into the Pontiac class." It wasn't long before George called the head man at the Pontiac division asking for an official's car with about 4,000 miles on it for one of his salesmen. Before the summer was over I was driving a 1941 Pontiac, the high water of my automobile career, I thought.

In May 1939 the *MLive Kalamazoo Gazette* published an article concerning the M.I.A.A. Track and Field Meet to be held at Olivet College. It mentioned, "The oldest mark is the 9:59:4 made by Wilcox of Kalamazoo in the two mile in 1922." The May 21, 1942, issue of the *MLive Kalamazoo Gazette* listing the M.I.A.A. Track and Field Meet records the article was headlined: 'Wilcox Two Mile Time in 1922 Not Touched." The article continued, "The 9:59:4 mark in the two mile run by the Hornets Harold Wilcox has stood up for twenty years. Wilcox at present is a Social Science teacher and City Commissioner in Ferndale, Michigan." I might add here that my record stood for another sixteen years before an Albion runner broke it in 1958.

While we were very busy with our social, political, and economic affairs, Millie and I did have time for our household and family duties. I was still teaching a Sunday school class of high school-age young people at the church. Millie was very active in and around our home. There were flowers to be planted and cared for, lawns to be cut and weeded, rooms to be painted, and the upkeep of the exterior of the house. While I received the credit for it, I am sure Millie should have when the Ferndale local weekly stated in their "Of Reader Interest" column, "Delphiniums grew seven and one half feet tall for Harold B. Wilcox of Ferndale."

One of my first lessons in salesmanship came when the city of Ferndale was to buy a new fire truck. Up to this stage in the city's life, all of the city's firefighting equipment had been purchased from the LaFrance Company located in Elmira, New York. The chief of the fire department recommended that we continue to do business with the LaFrance Company since they built their own equipment. Others wanted to employ the Columbia Company in Ohio. This company assembled its machines by using parts from other factories. The two agents representing the two companies wanted to take the commissioners to the factories to show the equipment in action. During August I became available to go to Elmira to observe firsthand the LaFrance fire engines. From the moment we left the Ferndale City Hall to the time we returned five days later, we were the guests of the LaFrance representative, and there was nothing that was mentioned that he did not respond to. We stayed at a hotel in Elmira. We were dined and entertained. The representative was the last to bed and the first to be seen in the hotel lobby in the morning. Orph Homes, our city attorney, and I wanted to see the minor league Elmira team play baseball, and one night we saw the game from box seats, having being driven to the ballpark in a taxi. For the first time in my life I had firsthand understanding of what it took to produce big and expensive equipment. I am sorry to say the mayor and two commissioners voted to give the purchase to the Ohio Company in spite of the recommendations of both the city manager and the city fire chief.

The summer of 1941 was a pleasurable one in many other ways. Monroe and his children came to Michigan, and we enjoyed very much the picnics, the trips to the sandy shores of Lake Michigan at South Haven, the ball games at the Detroit Tigers ballpark, and many other fellowship occasions. Heloise had died, leaving Monroe with the three children. She had become infected with a streptococcus bacteria that could not be cured. It was a few years later that the sulfa drug was discovered which is used with great success in treating streptococcus infection. Monroe and Ruth were married on September 4, 1939. Ruth gave up school teaching to become a pastor's wife, a homemaker, and the stepmother of three children. What a terrific job she has done all these years. I am sure the good Lord guided her to Monroe's parsonage.

In fall 1941 the *Detroit Free Press* was running a Sunday series on "Seeing Michigan." On Sunday, December 21, 1941, the paper featured Ferndale. The caption read, "Camera Caravan Visits Ferndale," under which was the picture of the Ferndale city commissioners around the table in an actual session. The article continued: "Ferndale, a fast growing Oakland county city which is Detroit's next door neighbor on North Woodward, is doing its part to help the United States win the war." The article went on to tell that from the time of World War I in 1918 to World War II in 1941, the city had grown from twenty-five hundred people to twenty-five thousand and was still growing.

During the early days of the Franklin D. Roosevelt administration the "President's Birthday Ball" was inaugurated to raise money for a fund to fight infantile paralysis. While I had been active in all the previous fundraising ventures, this one in January 1942 found me serving as the general chairman. The newspaper wrote that I was the general chairman of this year's celebration of the President's Birthday Ball which was held in Lincoln High School gym during Saturday night. The City Commissioner worked out an elaborate program of dancing novelties to the accompaniment of Dave Diamond's big orchestra and entertainers. All our committees were made up of leading Ferndale citizens, business and professional people. Each one of them did a tremendous job. The ball was a great success and, while tickets cost only one dollar, there was a large sum for the Foundation.

What happened on that day of days, December 7, 1941, when the newspapers screamed: "Hawaii and Manila Bombed" is history. The war completely changed the whole social, political and economic structure of American life. No longer was our attention centered on local politics and issues; it was now "Win the war," and everything done was done to the credit of the war, at least supposedly. The school teaching profession was seriously affected, as were all jobs. The younger teachers, both men and women, left the school building to go where there was money being made or to join the military service. Teachers who had been asked to leave the system by our principal Ralph were now being pressured to stay on as a war duty. Almost overnight we found big ads crying, "Men and women wanted." There was no such thing as unemployment, which we had so dreadfully experienced the past decade.

One of the tasks for our new mayor, my old friend and roommate in bachelor days Carl Forsythe, was to appoint a city salvage chairman. Carl asked me to take the chairmanship. He caught me in a weak moment, and I said yes. When I reached home and told Millie of my new war job, she broke down and cried. I had been so involved already that my family had begun to wonder if they had a husband and father.

Having worked at Higgins Pontiac during summer 1941 with a fair degree of financial success, I continued on Saturdays and some evenings. Whyle was working out of Detroit. He was doing a lot of driving and needed a good used car. He proposed the idea of me selling my 1941 Pontiac to him and buying a new 1942 Pontiac. Always wanting to help my brother, it seemed that this would be a good deal for both of us. It turned out to be just that! In October 1941 I asked Mr. Higgins to put in an order for a 1942 four-door hardtop Pontiac, and I sold my car to Whyle. I was able to drive a used car from off the lot until my car arrived. It generally took about a month. I did not yet have my new car when it was announced on December 8, 1941 that the United States and Japan were at war. Immediately we began to hear of the Industrial Revolution that would gear the American peace industry into a war industry. Soon after the declaration of war it was announced to the public that there would be no more automobile production for the public. I didn't think too much of this; my car had been ordered for over a month.

One evening as we were getting ready to close the salesroom I asked George where all of the new cars parked in front of the building had come from. George said that they had just been driven down from Pontiac (Michigan). "We've got to put them in the garage; you drive this green four-door in for me." I jumped into the car and drove it into the garage. "This is just like the one I ordered." George responded, "That is the one you ordered. That is your car!" I was elated. I went home and told Millie that our car finally had arrived. For the duration of the war we drove the latest model car on the highways.

During the early years of World War II, with my responsibilities continuing as Ferndale Commissioner and high school teacher I accepted the position of Salvage Chairman. One of my very early salvage collections of 6,253 pounds of wastepaper was turned in by thirty-one persons. These persons received pay in the form of defense stamps [these stamps could be used to buy war bonds]. I reported in the newspaper that if all residents did as these thirty-one persons did each week wastepaper of sixteen hundred tons would be turned over to the city, thereby eliminating a fire hazard, aiding national defense and boosting the sale of defense stamps in Ferndale to over seven thousand dollars each week. I also mentioned that Ferndale (Lincoln) High School alone salvaged one hundred and seventy-five pounds of wastepaper daily.

In another issue released during March 1942 I reported that seventy-five thousand, and seven hundred pounds of salvage was collected for February 1942. This consisted of twenty thousand, two hundred pounds of paper and fifty-five thousand, five hundred of tin. Eventually almost every person in Ferndale was conscience of the need for paper, tin and even surplus grease. These same people would display in their windows some sign of their patriotism. It would be a patriotism sticker, a service flag or some other sign of participation. It seemed like every homeowner started flattening out their tin cans and gathering surplus grease for the next weekly citywide drive. They all were helping the boys at the front. As the war continued and reports of the tremendous waste by our military of such things as meat, fruit, and wastepaper came drifting in from eyewitnesses, my enthusiasm for the salvage drive dimmed.

Higgins Pontiac had sold all its used cars. The garage used for repairing cars was sectioned into a machine shop. George was made local chairman of the gasoline ration stamps. Because of my position in a government capacity, he decided I rated special consideration. This enabled me to do more driving than the average citizen. Driving was limited to thirty-five miles an hour to get the most mileage from your gasoline.

As it always has been and always will be, I presume, I became cognizant of the fact that those who wave the flag, talk big, and have money are not always the most law-abiding and loyal citizens. Many were able to get gasoline for their cars, fuel oil for their furnaces, and butter from the farmer and sugar on their table without ration stamps. There were times I said to myself, "Why am I working my head off for the war effort when there are many in the business and industrial world who are making huge profits and deep down in their hearts are wishing the war to continue until they have made theirs and can live for the rest of their lives on easy street." War is made to make profits for mankind; God has nothing to do with its winning or losing.

My sister Abbie, named after my mother's sister, had been going with a Kalamazoo young man and they decided it was time they were married. Abbie was working in Kalamazoo managing a confectionary shop. Her boyfriend, Donald Iles, had been unemployed, but the war had now opened up good employment opportunities for everyone. Don came to Ferndale, lived at our house for a few weeks, and found employment as a tool and die maker at the N.W. Woodworth Company. May was the month set for the wedding. Because of Don's employment in Ferndale, they decided that they would marry in our home. We were delighted, and I helped to arrange the wedding plans. Our Ferndale Methodist minister, Rev. William Moulton, conducted the wedding ceremony. Don's brother stood up with him, and Abbie chose Donita to be her bridesmaid. Mother, Dad, Whyle, Audrey, Hilda and Lee, Danita's husband Bub and daughters were also present, along with Don's parents from Kalamazoo. We enjoyed having all of them at our house. The Sunday afternoon weather was ideal for outdoor visiting, so we did not feel crowded with all our guests present.

Another city election occurred in 1943. I had to decide whether I should run for a third term. As of this election date, no person except Commissioner Arthur Bartlett had ever been elected to three terms of four years each. I decided early in the fall I would try for my third term. Conditions seemed favorable for my re-election. The war effort had taken most of the limelight off local affairs, and I had become very influential in the local war programs. It seemed that most people just assumed I would be re-elected.

In November 1942 one of the local newspapers came out with a two-column article. It was reported that I entrenched myself in the Ferndale community. The article mentioned my wife Millie and two sons, and that I was elected commissioner for both 4-years terms starting 1935 and 1939, that I was a member of the Ordinance Committee and was appointed coordinator of all Ferndale Savage Committees. It continued that I was a past president of the Ferndale Exchange Club, past president of the Ferndale-Pleasant Ridge Teachers Club, a member of the Ferndale Methodist Church, and a Sunday school teacher for 19 years. This article also mentioned that my wife Millie was a "superb cook" and had won many prizes for her recipes and that she was a member of the Ferndale Woman's club.

Between the months of November and April 1943 there must have been situations that made it possible for the *Detroit Free Press* to announce to its readers on Tuesday, April 6, 1943, "Mayor of Ferndale wins – Wilcox is Defeated in Election Upset." As late as February 2, 1943, I seemed to be in good favor with the newspapers and city leaders. On February 2, 1943 the *Royal Oak Daily Tribune* front page had this to say: "Wilcox Plan is Adopted on Price Ceiling." The article continued, "Commissioner Harold B. Wilcox succeeded on his third attempt Monday night in getting the Ferndale City Commission to adopt his plan for enforcement of price ceilings in Ferndale. By a vote of 4-0, the commission ordered the city sealer to check posted price ceilings against true lists on file either in stores or with the O.P.A. and report suspected violations to that agency. Wilcox's theory is that the sealer is in a better position than the average housewife to determine whether posted prices are the actual ceiling prices registered last March. Enforcement of price ceiling of meats particularly he argued will help keep 'black market' meat out of the city."

There may have been several incidents that could have played an important part in voters turning against me. A very noticeable one occurred when I fell into disfavor with Sam, the owner and editor of the *Ferndale Gazette.* He was constantly on me to vote for and promote his ideas to the Ferndale city government. One day I very undiplomatically told him that I would not be his spokesman and asked,

"Why don't you run for the commission and voice your own opinion around the table?" That didn't sit well with Sam, the Hearst newspaperman, and he replied, "I'll go out and get my own candidate" and he did. Who did he choose to try to elect? His selection was a very popular woman from my church. She also had been a fine leader in the Ferndale P.T.A, and a well-known and well-liked person. Sam was out to split my vote, and to a degree at least he did, although his candidate ran a poor last.

Another incident that took place in March about three weeks before election was at the high school. The son of the president of the school board got to torment a black boy by throwing his hat in the basement corridor. A group of blacks surrounded the white boy and someone who was never identified sunk a knife into his back that perforated one of his kidneys. It didn't prove to be fatal, but immediately it was whites against blacks. There were state police in the corridors of the high school for weeks. Although there were no more clashes between the blacks and whites, the public didn't forget that I was a schoolteacher. Right after the entrance of the police into the building, a student standing beside me said, "Mr. Wilcox, there goes your re-election." He was right.

I'll have to admit I took my defeat pretty hard. I had enjoyed working in city politics for eight years. It had opened the door to many opportunities that gave me a better understanding of government and politics, a subject I taught in high school and had minored in getting my master's degree at the University of Michigan. But every dog has its day, and for eight years I had mine. After several days to analyze my position, I decided to look for a new avocation that would enhance our financial picture.

Chapter 8

Continuation as a High School Teacher and Additional Jobs

A woman who lived on Beaufield Street, Ferndale, and who had worked for my reelection was employed by the "Woman's Home Companion Readers Club." She worked out of the Detroit office located in the Industrial Bank Building on Washington Boulevard. Salesmen would canvass Detroit, which was divided into "selling districts," to sell combinations of magazines. The most popular group was the *Woman's Home Companion*, *Colliers*, and *American*, all out of existence at this writing. These magazine groups were paid for with monthly payments of about seventy-five cents to one dollar over a period of two and one half years. The collections were made by agents, each of whom had a district to cover each month. The agent would receive twenty-two percent of his collections. The agent was also encouraged to write renewals, which netted about three dollars each. To me this sounded like a profitable sideline to pick up some extra money, so I went to talk with the manager. Of course, this took a car, and the car had to have gasoline. Gasoline ration stamps were given to people, who depended on a car for business, provided it was deemed an essential one during wartime. I had been given ration stamps for city business, etc. and the stamp commissioner had not withdrawn the supply, so I did have gasoline for the work. I told the manager I could manage my car driving to meet the requirements, so he gave me a territory which had about eight hundred collections a month.

I worked to get people to pay double payments each month, selling them on the idea that the fewer times I had to call the more gasoline I would save. About everyone who was employable had a job, so it wasn't difficult to sell my collection plan. By working Saturdays and some evenings I covered my district and made good money. One Saturday I made over fifty dollars, which was the most anyone in the office had ever made.

Although it was hard work, especially in the winter when it was cold with ice and snow, I got good outdoor exercise, and this kept me in the pink of condition. I would park my car at the head of a street that had anywhere from three to ten collections. It was trying to go upstairs to the second floor of two family flats, stand at the door waiting for someone to open it, and in some cases have to go back in the evening two or three times to find someone at home who had the money. Then there were people who questioned the legitimacy of a bright shiny 1942 Pontiac being used on such a questionable occupation during the war. When the war was a thing of the past, jobs were scarce and hard to find. Many husbands strenuously objected to their wives taking a group of magazines that were not read in some instances. Therefore the job proved to have its liabilities as well as its assets.

What did we do for recreation during the war years? Well, we did things that didn't demand too much the use of a car. The Ferndale Dance Club was organized with that in mind. It was made up of thirty-six couples who enjoyed the fellowship of a congenial group for an evening of social dancing one Saturday night a month at the Ferndale Women's Club. Our program started at 9 o'clock and we danced until twelve by the music of a four-piece orchestra. Dance programs were in vogue and no one was supposed to dance with his wife more than twice. Then we adjourned to the basement dining room, where our president conducted a business meeting after we had enjoyed sandwiches, dessert, and coffee. Like so many of these wartime activities, the Ferndale Dance Club folded in the late 1940's because of lack of interest.

The movie houses did good business during the war. People had money to spend and were having a hard time finding places to spend it because of so much rationing. The candy counters were well filled with cookies, nuts, and wafers that took very little sugar. Popcorn was plentiful, although there was no butter used to make it tasty.

Summer 1943 found me at the N. A. Woodruff Aeroplane parts factories in Ferndale working as a guard. I was in uniform and carried a gun. Looking back on it today (1970's), it seems so unreal. I worked until Labor Day without a vacation before going back to school. The following summer I was again at the same plant but this time as a stockman. This I didn't enjoy, and by the middle of August I told my boss I had had enough, I needed a vacation. Some said they hated to see me go because I was the best stockman they had had. I did try to do a good job, but I never was and never have been a machine parts man. However, the extra cash came in handy for paying our bills.

During the month of August 1944 after I had said goodbye to N. A. Woodruff, we spent two weeks at Colchester on Lake Erie in Canada. It was just one hour's drive from Ferndale by way of the bridge. By filling my gas tank and a few containers with gasoline before leaving Canada I had enough to make a drive down to Gobles. There were always some ways to get a little extra gas, and I knew some of the so-called flag wavers that were using "black market gas." Our city treasurer had rented a cottage for the season at Colchester, and he in turn sub rented for a few weeks to some of his friends. That made it a good deal for all of us and enabled us to have it for the two weeks. The Smith family from Ferndale was also at one of the cottages. They had three daughters, all of school age. The family made fine company with swimming, cards at night, etc. Summer 1945 found us again at Colchester, this time for two whole months.

Millie had been having a little heart trouble. Dick was never a strong healthy baby, and his mother had given him lots of attention. I sometimes presume this made Phil, who was three years older than Dick, feel he was being neglected. I had been spending a great deal of my "free from school time" on magazine collections. This left the heavy burden of the house and family on Millie's shoulders. On New Year's Eve 1944 the strain of work, excitement, etc. took its toll. The members of the dance club were dancing the old year out and the New Year in when Millie began to have a hard time breathing. We took her to a little anteroom in the Women's Club, and with the help of our friends the Widmans, Bests, Thompsons, and others we tried to make her comfortable, both mentally and physically, without drawing it to the attention of the other members of the club. I tried to get a doctor, but the only one I could get on the phone asked me to describe her condition and remarked, "She won't die tonight, I can't come." After the dance ended and the members had adjourned to the basement for lunch and the business meeting, I backed my car up to the side door and with his strong arms Paul Best picked her up and carried her to my car.

When we arrived home there were the Widmans to help me take her in the house and put her to bed. Then I got my chiropractor on the phone. He came and administered treatments, which I do believe saved Millie from having a damaged heart. I had become acquainted with Dr. Travis in 1939. I had been working too hard and had become run down under the pressure that any elected office produces. I went to my doctor and he found I had extremely low blood pressure. In fact, it was so low that when I got up in the morning I was dizzy until I had built up a better circulation of blood to my head. For one whole year I doctored with my physician. He gave me every test in the book. I took all kinds of pills, rested a great deal, and played a little golf in the summer of 1939, but took no outside job. When September came I started school really rested I thought, but in three weeks I was right back where I was the previous year. "So," I said, "I am going to try a chiropractor." In six weeks I was much better. At the end of the school year my blood pressure was up to normal. I have never had really low blood pressure since. That is the reason I felt sure Millie could be helped by such treatments. The next day we called Dr. Howard Schuneman, M.D., and he has been our medical doctor ever since. It must be remembered that in 1944 and 1945 we were still at war. Doctors were extremely busy and hospitals were overcrowded. Therefore we had to keep Millie in bed at home for two weeks before Dr. Schuneman finally got her admitted to the Highland Park General Hospital.

In the meantime I had the burden of all the household activity. Every day while I was at school I had to have someone come to the house to care for our boys as well as to be with Millie. We were very fortunate to have Millie's mother and younger sister, who were living in Highland Park. They spent many days at our house during this time that she was in bed.

Weekends I did the cooking, the washing and ironing, the shopping, and all other household chores. When Millie did get to the hospital, we were fortunate to have our good neighbors next door, the Goodspeeds, to care for Dick, and Faye and Larry Cowells across the street (271 W. Maplehurst) who helped with Phil. For the two weeks Millie was in the hospital I had to keep assuring Phil and Dick that their mother was coming home soon. As days passed, and they began to wonder if she was ever to come home again, I took them to the hospital and placed them on the sidewalk where they could see her room. Then I went up to her room, moved her bed over to the window and had her wave to the boys. "Yes," said Dick, "Mother will come home for we saw her wave at us." Children were not allowed in the hospital in 1945. It was two weeks to the day after her admittance that I drove her home. Dick and Phil were at the Goodspeeds when we drove into the drive. I can still see them looking out the window to see their mother come home. The doctor stated that while there was no damage to her heart, she had to take it easy for some time.

I was still working hard on my magazine collections and would sometimes take the boys with me for a few hours. One cold day the latter part of February, Phil rode with me all day Saturday. There was snow and ice on the ground and it was blustery. I would park the car at the head of the block, leaving Phil while I would walk the street and make collections. When it came one o'clock, we stopped at a Saunder's store to get sandwiches, ice cream, and what have you. I was sure proud of Phil. He rode with me all day and never once let out a whimper. It was dusk when we arrived home since it got dark early and it was hard to read the numbers on the houses.

In the summer the doctor said that a change of environment would do Millie good, so we drove over to Colchester, Canada, on Lake Erie to look for a rental. We found an upstairs apartment right on Lake Erie for a rent that would fit our pocketbook. The Smith family and the Lakings, both of Ferndale, had rented the two single-family cottages and they proved good company for the two months that we were there. While at Colchester we had many enjoyable occasions. My mother and dad took the train into Detroit, where I met them and drove them to our cottage for a long weekend. Millie's relatives and our friends the Thompsons also paid us a weekend visit.

We had heard all about racetrack people; they were supposed to be a rather rough crowd. However, we rented our house to a racetrack trainer and he and his wife proved to be the ideal couple. They took excellent care of our house from June 15 to September 1, 1945, and they paid the rent in advance. We were thankful to have such nice Canadian people in our home.

During the summer I spent time collecting on my magazine route, driving over to Ferndale the morning of the first of two days and staying overnight at the house of our friends and neighbors Paul and Louise Shaw. Also, for the only time in the thirty-seven years we lived at 250 West Maplehurst, I hired a schoolteacher friend to paint the outside of the house. All other paint jobs I did myself.

When May 9, 1945 arrived, the war in Europe had come to a close. Now it was the goal to put the finish on the Japanese and all our military might was focused on the Eastern Theater of the war.

We left Colchester, Canada on August 15, 1945 and drove to Gobles, Michigan to visit my parents for two weeks. When Labor Day rolled around we were back home in Ferndale, having had a very rewarding summer.

Dick had never been very robust, and during the summer at Colchester he evidenced several unusual physical ailments. He would complain of his toes hurting, chest pains, slight colds, etc. We took him to a doctor in Harrow about five miles from Colchester. After an examination and a shot the doctor thought he would be all right, so we more or less dismissed from our minds any seriousness that might come from his ailments. Being five years old, Dick started in the Roosevelt School the day after Labor Day. After two weeks it was very evident that he was not physically up to par, so we took him to our family doctor, Howard Schuneman. After tests, etc., Dr. Schuneman diagnosed his ailment as rheumatic fever, a noninfectious but acute disease characterized by inflammation and pain around the joints. For two years Dick was kept in bed or in a chair with little or no exercise. The visiting teacher from the Ferndale Public School came three times a week to tutor him in reading, writing, and arithmetic. His mother gave him the utmost care, and at the end of the two years his fever had subsided and the doctor found no heart damage, which is so much a characteristic of rheumatic fever patients. In September 1947 the doctor pronounced Dick physically able to continue his schoolwork at Roosevelt. At this writing Dick has lived a healthy and vigorous life with no evidence of any physical handicaps, for which we are very thankful.

Chapter 9

Ferndale's Adult Education Director (1944-1965)

The fall of 1944 found me with a new educational interest. I had enjoyed classroom teaching very much and had been awarded my Masters of Arts degree at the University of Michigan in history and political science. However, I had begun to cast a longing eye on an administrative position. I talked to my superintendent, Ed Downs, and he advised that if I wanted to get out of the classroom I should get out of Ferndale into another school district. To pull up my ties and leave Ferndale was a thing I didn't give too much thought to at that time. After all, we owned or were buying our home, had made a host of friends, and really enjoyed living in Ferndale.

It was about this time, 1943-44, that the state legislature was considering a pilot program in adult education. This resulted in an appropriation by the state legislature of the sum of three hundred thousand dollars. Ferndale was chosen as one of the several school districts in Michigan to offer a pilot program in adult education and was awarded a grant of six thousand dollars for the year 1944-45. The assistant superintendent, Paul Best, was given the responsibility of inaugurating a series of adult education classes that were started in fall 1944. The enrollment for the initial fall term was about 400 students.

The program demanded that an administrator be in the building three nights a week. Paul Best approached me with the idea of taking over the evening work. He explained that it would obligate me three nights a week. I replied that I was used to night work and would be glad to work in the adult education pilot program. It was a great success, and when the state department announced that there would be a three-year grant Mr. Best asked me if I would want to serve as its administrator. I replied, "It would be a stab at an administration job, and I would be glad to get the opportunity." That spring of 1945 the school board, on the recommendation of Mr. Best and Superintendent Downs, appointed me the adult education director of the Ferndale public schools. I served in this capacity until 1965 when I retired. The Ferndale Gazette reviewed the adult education program during 1971. It was recognized that I had one of the best adult programs within the state. It was not too many years before Royal Oak, Berkley, Oak Park and Hazel Part were meeting the demands of their adult community by inaugurating similar adult education programs. By the 1970's adult night school had become a vital part of the total public school education program in most communities in Michigan.

In April 1946 an immense occasion took place in Gobles. It was Mother and Dad's fiftieth wedding anniversary. We children sent out invitations to their old friends, and on Sunday afternoon we had open house at the homestead. It was an enjoyable affair and one of the very last, for Dad passed away the following year on April 23, 1947.

The summer of 1946 Monroe and his family drove from Montana for a visit. With Mother and Dad, they came to Ferndale on an August weekend. After a dinner at our house, Monroe and Dad went to the Detroit Tigers ball game while I drove Phil up to Port Huron for his first Methodist Camp. I never saw a happier lad welcoming his dad to take him home. It was a great experience for Phil.

The last two weeks in August found us in Colchester at a cottage on Lake Erie. We were beginning to see the last of the old sidewheelers, the *City of Cleveland* and *City of Buffalo,* as they plied their way on Lake Erie between Detroit, Buffalo, and Cleveland.

The summer of 1947 was one of great memories. The old homestead in Gobles was disintegrating. The barbershop was closed, and Mother couldn't come to a decision on what to do with it. Over Labor Day weekend we all went home for the last time. We slept on cots, floor, etc. Mother enjoyed having all of us home before she flew to Montana to spend the winter with Monroe and his family. My mother arrived back in Michigan in the spring of 1948. She had had one of her greatest desires come true as she lived in the Methodist parsonage with her son Monroe, who was pastor of the Glendive Methodist Church.

The school year found me working hard on building a good adult education program. At the same time I was working Saturdays and some dinner hours on the collections for the *Woman's Home Companion* Reader's Club, which netted us good yearly moonlighting revenue.

My adult education job took me to several conferences during the year. To direct a good adult program in the state was the desire of everyone connected with this new phase of public school education. Michigan State College, later to become a university, and the University of Michigan were offering workshops, conferences, and study sessions to better acquaint educators with the philosophy of adult education. These sessions proved very valuable in generating new programs in adult education throughout the state.

One out-of-state conference I had the privilege of attending was the United Nations Conference in New York during March 1948. The *Royal Oak Daily Tribune* ran my picture in the March 11 issue with the headline, "Returns from U.N. Session." The article continued: "Ferndale's adult education director, Harold Wilcox, is home after spending three days at Lake Success, New York as a delegate to the UNESCO Conference. He also attended several UN Security Council Sessions. Wilcox also teaches American History and Government at Lincoln. He is a former city commissioner and former president of Ferndale Exchange Club. He is married and lives at 250 West Maplehurst. His sons, Dick and Philip are students at Roosevelt School." This was the first of many trips I had the privilege of making to conferences held in all parts of the United States. Some of the cities holding such conferences were San Diego, Los Angeles, San Francisco, Denver, St. Louis, Chicago, Buffalo, Cleveland, Cincinnati, Columbus, Washington, D.C., New York City, Atlantic City, and Miami. It gave me a broad philosophy of adult education. While these conferences meant hard work, at the same time I was brought into association with men from all over the United States. I enjoyed the work so much that I became recognized as a willing worker for the cause of adult education.

One of the most pleasing compliments a mother can get comes from her own sons and daughters on Mother's Day. Millie was rewarded when she received the following class composition from Phil, who was in the fifth grade at Roosevelt Elementary School. Phil wrote: "I like Mother's Day because you give a present or two to your Mother. Mother's Day is the best day in May. Mother's Day is a nice day because you get a big dinner. When my Mother cooks a dinner, it is really good. Mother's Day is a fine day for me."

The summer of 1948 was a busy one. There were always walls to wash, as well as paint and fix up, and a yard to care for. Millie and I both tried to keep our home attractive. On Sunday nights it was a fire in the fireplace with the boys and us toasting hot dogs and marshmallows and popcorn.

We belonged to three dinner groups, each meeting once a month so generally speaking we had every Saturday night taken. Some of these friends became lifelong friends with whom we enjoyed many, many years of our working life.

Labor Day found all of us at Gobles for our last one with my mother. When my mother returned from Montana in the spring it was still furnace-heat weather, but she insisted that she wanted to go home to Gobles although she had to live alone. When we got to the homestead for Labor Day, it was easy to see my mother had been doing too much trying to make the house ready for us. Whyle's family was home too, and we all went to South Haven on the Sunday before Labor Day to swim in Lake Michigan and play on the sandy beach. While my mother sat on a blanket, the damp beach got to her and she awakened that Monday morning with a sore throat. As the time drew near for us to leave for Ferndale my mother said, "I'll guess I'll go with you and visit Abbie." Abbie was living in the west side of Detroit. On the way back to Ferndale I stopped and purchased some cough drops and throat aids for my mother since I could see she was not felling at all well. When we reached Abbie's house, I told Abbie to be cognizant of her condition and if she didn't get any better to call me. About three days later, Abbie called that my mother was in pretty bad shape and she wanted me to come right over to see what could be done. I drove over after school and found my mother in a semi-conscious state. I called our family doctor Howard Schuneman and told him of her condition. He said to get her to the Highland Park General Hospital right away and he would take care of her. I contacted an ambulance service and in a short time she was in a hospital bed in an oxygen tent. It was touch and go for several days, but finally she responded to the treatment and in ten days she was at our house at 250 West Maplelhurst. As she regained some strength she decided she wanted to go back to Abbie's, so we again contacted the ambulance service that took her there. It was her last ride in a car. Mother passed away on December 30, 1948.

True, the old homestead in Gobles was now just an empty house, but Mother and Dad left their marks on their family and the community that could not be erased by the stroke of death. One of the strings that has bound us Wilcoxes has been the "Round Robin Letter." As the letters come to each of us, we take out our old one and write the new one then send it along to the next member of our family. This "Round Robin" letter writing has been in existence for about thirty-five years. It generally gets around about once a month.

As spring showed its first signs Millie and I had a job to do. Someone had to take charge of disposing of Mother's property and getting it ready for sale. It doesn't take too broad an imagination to realize that after living in a house for over fifty years there is a huge accumulation of almost everything that Mother took a fancy to. Millie and I spent a weekend in Kalamazoo and Gobles getting the house ready for sale. (Brother) Allen and (his wife) Recil worked with us. In the attic there were bushel baskets filled with old letters that Mother and Dad had received from their children. It was interesting for me to read some of my letters sent to them years earlier in life.

As the school year drew to a close I realized that what we all know must come to pass was a reality. For me Gobles was different; no longer could we drive down for the weekend, lounge around the barbershop chatting with old acquaintances, and enjoy the leisure time that had always been so refreshing to me.

An interesting occasion in June 1949 was the 1929 Lincoln High class reunion. Here I saw my students of 1929 grown into manhood and womanhood, some naturally disappointing and others surprisingly matured. It was a very pleasant evening. I was closer to and had a better understanding of this group of high school seniors than any other group I had contact with.

In August 1949 I was privileged to spend three weeks on the campus of Michigan State College. A national foundation had set up a series of economic workshops in various parts of the United States. This one at M.S.C. had school men from almost every state in the union attending it. We had our board and room paid. My only expense was for the bus as I traveled to East Lansing on Monday morning and came home Friday night. Millie and the boys met me at Eight Mile and Grand River as I got off the late afternoon bus. My roommate at the conference was a man in adult education work by the name of Leon Carey from Joliet, Illinois.

One of our field trips was into Detroit to visit the assembly lines of the Ford Motor Company and to discuss the economics of car building with some of the Ford executives. We were bussed back to Detroit Business Center by the Ford Motor Company late in the afternoon. It was hot, and we had a couple of hours to kill before our bus took us back to the campus of M.S.C., now M.S.U., so I said to my roommate, "Do you want a nice cold drink of the most delicious ginger ale you ever tasted?" His reply was, "I sure would like it." So we walked down to the foot of Woodward near the Detroit River to the Vernor ginger ale plant. We drank their product until we could hold no more. Leon said it was the best he had ever tasted.

At the close of the workshop Millie and the boys met me with a loaded car, and we drove over to a cottage on a lake near Brighton for a week. It was good to relax and get refreshed for a new school year. The new school year of 1949-50 passed without any undue incident.

The adult education program was now becoming nationwide. We in Michigan had already organized the Michigan Public School Adult Education Association, and there were lots of talks and conferences that would snowball into a National Association of Public School Adult Educators.

In June 1950 Millie and I were chosen by the members of the Ferndale Exchange Club to represent the club as a voting delegate at the state convention, which was held on a Great Lakes cruise ship, the *City of Cleveland*. While the old sidewheeler was not too reliable in getting us to our stopover destinations on time, nevertheless no one was in a hurry and we all were having fun aboard. The cruise was to start at 5:00 p.m. Friday afternoon and the ship was to dock at 8:00 a.m. Monday morning. It was 10:00 p.m. before we pulled away from the dock that Friday night, and it was 7:00 p.m. Monday eve before our ship crawled on one engine into the Detroit dock. I called Mother Burrows, who stayed with the boys when we were on trips, that we would make it and not to worry.

Flora, Millie's youngest sister, was being married to Ted Uhlig on July 1, 1950, at a church in Highland Park. They asked if we would host the reception at our house! We said yes, if they would do the work, so the evening of July 1 found our basement clean and decorated for the many youths and adults invited to partake of refreshments.

It had been several years since we had taken a good vacation trip. Now the boys were old enough to travel with at least some degree of enjoyment. We started planning a trip west that would take us into Colorado, Las Vegas, Utah, California, and up the coast to Oregon and Montana, where we expected to spend a week or ten days with Monroe and family. George Higgins had gotten me a 1948 Pontiac but it seemed to be on the "lemon" side. I had trouble with the engine, having to have the valves ground and the body tightened up.

The latter part of July found us with a packed car heading for Chicago and the West. We stayed in motels and ate our meals at restaurants. This was to be a real holiday trip for us. As we wound our way through the mountains and into California we were seeing sights we had never before seen. In California we visited Millie's cousins in Arcadia, the Zolas, for three days. Then we went over to my cousins, the Welches, and spent several days with Kitty and Leon Ellithorpe and my mother's sister, Abbie, who was in her eighties. We headed north on 101 and spent two days with friends just outside of San Francisco. We visited Stanford University campus, had dinner in Chinatown, and walked around on the Fisherman's Wharf. Then we got on highway 101 again, which goes along the coast and drove north. It was beautiful to see the redwood forests, the seals on the oceanside rocks, etc., but the highway was so winding that to go faster than thirty miles per hour was dangerous. Before we got to Newport, Oregon I had it. I had asked Millie to take over while I rested in the rear seat.

At Newport it was raining so I said, "Let's find a motel, have dinner, and get up early so as to get going," since we still had a good two days drive to Missoula, Montana. When we awakened in the morning we still had a little drizzle, and as we were eating breakfast the waitress remarked that while they needed the rain it was hard on us tourists. I didn't sense the importance of that remark since I was used to driving in rain in Michigan. As we drove down a small hill about three miles out of Newport we came to a very sharp turn, about like turning off one street onto another. Here is where I learned what the waitress meant by her remarks. As I put on my brakes it was just like hitting a sheet of ice, and over the bank we went. Millie's head was pushed down hard on the dashboard as the result of the boys in the rear seat coming over on top of her. It cut her head open, and she had a slight fracture of the skull. The people right behind us stopped, helped us out of the car, and drove us to Toledo, Oregon, where Millie was in the hospital for seven days. I called Millie's cousins at Dallas, Oregon whom we were to visit that evening, and they came over and got Phil and Dick for the week. I found a room in Toledo. Besides my family responsibilities, I had to sell the car for what I could get out of it and pack and ship home all of the things we wanted but couldn't carry.

I called Monroe in Missoula, telling him about our accident and that at that moment I just didn't know when we could continue the trip by train. I had what was first thought to be broken ribs, but x-rays revealed them to be just badly bruised; still, they were painful. A couple of days later after talking with the boys and assuring them that their mother was all right, I called Monroe and told him that perhaps under the circumstances we should take the train from Portland, Oregon, and go home without stopping at Missoula. That really brought Monroe to his feet, as we say. "What are you going to do," said Monroe, "go home with your tail between your legs like a whipped dog or stop here to see us and go home with your chin up?" That settled it. We would stay a week with Monroe and Ruth in Missoula. That was what I needed to make the decision.

On the eighth day in Toledo, Oregon, I picked Millie up at the hospital and we took the short walk to the bus station. I had called Dallas, Oregon, and Millie's cousin said she would have Phil and Dick at the bus stop. We were happily united again as our bus pulled out of Dallas for Portland, Oregon. We got to Portland by noon and found at the railroad station that our train to Missoula didn't leave until 8:30 p.m. We took a long time eating lunch, went to a movie in the p.m., and lounged around the station until train time.

The next morning our train had about a two-hour stopover at Spokane, Washington, so we went up town and had breakfast. When the Seattle, Washington section pulled in about 8:30 a.m. and united the two trains we were on our way, arriving in Missoula about 6:00 p.m. Monroe and Ruth welcomed us with wide-open arms. We spent a long weekend at Missoula, and the rest was a welcome one since all of us had been through a lot during the previous week.

Monroe, Ruth, and Sue had committed themselves to attending the youth church conference at a camp near Livingston, Montana. Not having completely recovered from her head bump, Millie decided to stay at the Methodist parsonage with Jim and Nan Wilcox, Monroe's two oldest. Monday a.m. we loaded Monroe's car with our baggage and his camping equipment and arrived at the campsite in the middle of the afternoon. It was cool and damp, and the sleeping quarters were far from appealing to easterners who were used to sleeping in comfortable beds. Added to that, the young folks of the previous institute camp had not left the building in good clean order. This caused me to remark to Monroe, "We don't have to stay in these quarters, do we? We'll freeze here." We had not come on this trip with the warm clothes that are needed in the mountains of Montana, regardless of the time of year one camps. Monroe said, "There are a couple of cottages here for the administrators, and I'll see if I can get one for all of us." That saved the day, for we had one with a wood-burning stove and with good beds. Phil, Dick, and I, with Monroe's family of three, enjoyed the five days we were there.

We had agreed before we left Missoula that we would take the Union Pacific evening train on Friday, which would get into Chicago Sunday morning in time for us to get a forenoon train to Detroit. Millie was to get on the train at Missoula, and we were to board the train at Livingston several hours later. It was just dusk when Monroe, Ruth, Sue, and we three left the Institute campsite for the half-hour drive to the depot. As the train pulled into the depot there were three pairs of anxious eyes piercing the car windows to locate mother. She wasn't hard to find since she sat next to the window with her eyes glued on the railway station, searching for the first glimpse of her family. As the train rolled out of the station with the waving of a fond farewell, it was a good feeling for all of us to be together and on our way home again.

Jim and Nan had helped Millie with all the baggage that we had left at the parsonage. We took inventory and determined who was to be responsible for what luggage. By the time we got off the train, first at Chicago and then at Detroit, we could imagine ourselves looking like a family of immigrants just off the ship from Europe. We sure were loaded down with suitcases, fishing equipment, coats, shoes, etc. I had written Howard and Ruth Thompson, close friends of ours living in Ferndale, of our unfortunate experience and suggested that if it was convenient we sure would appreciate their meeting us at the depot. When we came up the long tunnel leading to the depot waiting room, our spirits rose when we saw Howard waiting for us. Howard said we would first stop at their house on Livernois where Ruth was preparing a lovely "welcome home" dinner. Then he would drive us over to our home on West Maplehurst. The Thompsons have always been very generous and genuine friends, and this time when we were sort of down in the mouth we found them coming to our aid.

Howard was superintendent of one of the Chevrolet automobile plants in Detroit. He got at least one new car every year and sold his old one to a friend or acquaintance. Howard was an excellent mechanic, knew cars from A-Z, and always kept his in A-1 shape. In my letter to him I explained my carless situation, and with school opening in the very near future it was imperative that I get a car, which was very essential to my job. On the way out of the depot Howard said that the Chevrolet we were riding in was a good car and if I wanted it I could have it immediately. Boy was that welcome news. After a very enjoyable dinner Howard drove us to our home. After we had unloaded I drove him back to his house in "our Chevrolet." It is said that it sometimes takes an unfortunate circumstance to test the mettle of a person or a family. While there had never been any doubt in any of our minds regarding the intestinal fortitude of us as a family, this proved conclusively to all of us that we were a family of one for all and all for one.

School opened the day after Labor Day 1950 with all the fanfare that characterizes such an occasion. I had now become an established adult education director, and I wanted to make the 1950-51 program an outstanding one. Our State Association of Adult Educators was a firm reality, and we members were working as an association to influence the state legislature to incorporate money for adult education in the state education finance bill. We were selling the philosophy that it is just as necessary for society to have educated adults over nineteen years of age as it is to have educated youth. After fifteen years (1965), I am pleased to say that the legislature struck out the age limit from the education finance bill. This made it possible to collect state aid for any person taking night school academic classes who did not have a high school diploma. This was another step in the right direction of total education regardless of age.

There had been a lot of talk in adult education circles about the need for a national organization for all people working in that field. We in Michigan had had numerous conferences on the problems confronting adult educators, and we had discussed the question of a national association. In spring 1950 it was announced that there would be a conference in Los Angeles in November to adopt a constitution that would initiate an adult education association of the United States. College and university professors interested in adult education were the backbone of this new interest, but all adult educators were urged to join and help promote the idea. Michigan was allowed five voting delegates, and it was suggested that I, being vice president of our Michigan Association of Public School Adult Educators, be a delegate from Michigan. At first I dismissed it from my mind, stating that the Ferndale Board of Education wouldn't pay my expenses to a conference in Los Angeles. My boss, Superintendent Roy E. Robinson, said, "Don't be too sure that the board won't send you. Let's sound them out." I said, "Roy, do you mind if I approach a couple of the board members whom I know are friends of adult education in Ferndale?" "Go ahead," said Robinson, "and let me know what you find out." So I called up two of my friends on the board and asked them if I could set a time for a call at their house to talk over a proposition that I had encountered. After explaining to each of them my position of being a Michigan voting delegate, I got their hearty support. At the next meeting the board voted their approval. So November 1950 found me again in Los Angeles, at which time I visited Millie's sister and husband, Flo and Ted, as well as my relatives. I took the train out and flew home. It was an experience that was to be repeated many times during the next fifteen years as a director of adult education.

The year 1950 was a big year in the lives of the Wilcox family in that we burned the mortgage on our house. "It's ours," we said as the family gathered around the table to eat a celebration dinner. It was a happy occasion. This marked the end of my work with the *Women's Home Companion* Reading Club, which had been an extra source of income. Now that we had no more monthly house payments, I felt I could slow down a little and spend more evenings at home.

However, my good intentions didn't hold up for very long for it wasn't long before I had become engaged in more adult education activity. At the annual spring state adult education conference held at St. Mary's Kellogg Camp near Battle Creek, Michigan, I was elected vice president of our state association. This made me the program chairman for our next conference, which was to be held in Traverse City, Michigan, the following spring of 1952. At this conference I was elected president for the year 1952-53.

The adult education programs (called night school in most districts around the state) were directed by men, except for two women directors, one in Highland Park and the other in Flint. This afforded me the privilege of congenial companionship in all our professional undertakings, which were many since we all considered ourselves pioneers in the new public education field. The philosophy of too many educators was that when a person got to be twenty years of age they had had their educational opportunity, and if they had not completed high school or couldn't read nor write it was their hard luck. After years of hard work by the adult educators, day-school-minded people gradually expanded their educational horizons to include a philosophy that an uneducated person, regardless of age, is not conducive to a healthy society.

When June 1951 rolled around I was asking myself, "What am I going to do this summer to make the extra vacation money that would enable the Wilcox family to go to Caseville, Michigan on Saginaw Bay for a couple of weeks of rest and relaxation?" Most educators were acquainted with *The World Book* and *Compton's Pictured Encyclopedia*. Since one schoolteacher was already selling *World Book* in our school district, I chose to sell the *Compton's*. I studied the sales talk for two weeks before going out to try to make a sale. It was really hard work, but as the summer wore on and I gained experience I began to write orders. It was interesting work, and I knew I would never have any repercussions since every family who values education enjoys having good books in their home. For three consecutive summers I sold *Compton's* and realized a nice summer income from the work.

I had reached the stage in life when one's interests narrow. Mine now centered on the church, the Exchange Club, and my job of adult education. Exchange had done a lot for me. One of National Exchange's most outstanding projects was and still is "The Freedom Shrine," a collection of documents handed down by our forefathers that expresses the spirit of freedom. The Ferndale club presented the "Freedom Shrine" to the Ferndale Public Library on February 13, 1955, to be hung from the wall in a conspicuous place to remind all people of the freedoms that serve as the basis of democracy in the United States. I was asked by the committee to make the presentation speech. One of the main thoughts I expressed in my speech was, "Freedom wasn't something awaiting them on this side of the ocean. Freedom wasn't then and isn't now something to be purchased with money. Freedom is a philosophy of thinking and living. Freedom is acceptance, acceptance of your right to think, to say, and to print what your convictions dictate."

When 1956 rolled around our family was reaching maturity and along with that goes individualism. Millie's mother had moved to California to live near her youngest daughter and family, Flo and Ted. So when January 1, 1957, arrived it found Millie and Dick in Los Angeles visiting and viewing the Parade of Roses. Phil and I were at home, doing our best to keep from starving since Dad's cooking was far from the quality that had been on our table over the years. Dick flew in ahead of his mother since he had to go back to high school. I can still see Dick walking from his flight into the airport with the confidence of a seasoned air traveler, although this was his first flight of a long distance. Phil being a senior in high school and Dick an eighth grader, I was becoming conscious of the fact that all our good times as a young family were nearing an end. It wouldn't be too long before we would be seeing them pack their suitcases and off to college and after that, who knows. Of course we wouldn't have wanted it any differently.

Jobs were a little hard to get. Through acquaintances, Phil was employed one summer at the State Packing Market packing groceries. Dick took over Phil's *Royal Oak Daily Tribune* paper route. This afforded him an opportunity that has proven to be a financial reward. He became interested in coin collecting as did his mother, a hobby they have retained for many years.

June 1955 found us all at the high school gym where the commencement exercises were being held with Phil a participant.

Phil had always wanted a car, as do most boys his age. He had saved his money and did buy from his mother's aunt an old but good Mercury. He used it for transportation to and from Adrian College in the fall.

All eight brothers and sisters in our family had gone year after year with no signs of physical trouble. It was between Christmas and New Year 1954 that my sister Abbie Iles came to our house with an air of alarm. I asked her what the trouble was. She replied, "I have discovered a lump in my right breast and I am scared to death." Unfortunately Abbie was the sole support for herself and two young daughters, named Donna Gayle and Sharon Lee. Dr. William Jasman, a member of our

Ferndale board of education, was a practicing physician at the Henry Ford Hospital. I said to Abbie, "Go call him and tell him you are my sister and want him to examine you. I am sure he will give you immediate attention." In three days Abbie was on the operating table, and it proved to be the worst. Abbie was in and out of the Ford Hospital for over a year. Cancer had settled in her liver. On January 15, 1957 we Wilcoxes suffered our first break in the family of eight children.

In the spring of 1957 the chairman of the committee for the Gobles High School alumni banquet called to invite me to be the toastmaster. The gala affair was to be held on the evening of June 8, 1957. My calendar was free, so I accepted the invitation. The banquet was housed in the high school auditorium that was also used for the gymnasium. It was well attended, including Donita and Bub from Flint, and Allen and Leland with wives from Kalamazoo. "In Memorian" was the names of Abbie Wilcox Isles, 1926, Phillip Miller, 1912, and Grace Stanton Adriance, 1944. Millie and I both had an enjoyable time, and at the close of the banquet I felt that the others had also.

Fall 1957 found Millie and me on the city of Los Angeles train out of Chicago, headed for San Diego, California, to the national public school adult education conference. I was chairman of the conference news committee. It was my duty to get a committee member in attendance at each session and meeting of the four-day conference. I then took their reports and compiled them into a conference newspaper, giving all in attendance as well as those in the various parts of the United States who could not attend the conference a complete summary of what went on at the conference. I was exceedingly busy during the four days. However, Millie and I did take time to say hello to her sister Flo and family, and to my cousins Kittie and Winnie who lived in or around Los Angeles. We flew back to Ferndale on a Sunday night, ready to start work on Monday morning.

After each conference I attended there was always a huge pile of mail, notes from my secretary Mrs. Dorothy Barte, and telephone calls to be answered. It meant long hours for several days before I could catch up with my work, but it was worth it. To meet and mingle with other directors of adult education from all over the United States was a morale builder as well as educational.

The year 1958 was unusual for one big reason—I broke my right heel. Son Dick and I were on our garage roof putting up an antenna for his new radio that would enable him to tune in stations from all over the world. As I stepped on the ladder to come off the roof, it slid out from under me and my right heel hit right on the edge of the fallen ladder. Off to the Ardmore Hospital I went, with Dick driving the car. After three days in the hospital, my first stay as a patient, the doctor put my leg and foot in a cast and with crutches I walked out to the car where Dick was waiting to drive me home.

We had planned to go to Caseville for two weeks, but my accident delayed our arrival at Caseville by a couple of days. Phil was working now, so it was just the three of us who headed for Caseville, with Dick and Millie doing the driving. Our neighbors and close friends Larry and Faye Cowell also came to Caseville, and in spite of me not being able to play in the water, etc. it was a restful two weeks.

Going back to work on crutches and walking those long corridors in the new high school building (Ferndale High opened in fall 1958) was really a task, but I did it as anyone else would have done.

One of our keen disappointments came on August 27, 1958, which was our twenty-fifth wedding anniversary. We had planned to make it a big day in our lives, but my being on crutches put a damper on that. However, we did go out to dinner, inviting Faye and Larry Cowell to join us. By the first of October the cast was off my foot. To my amazement and disappointment I still had to use a crutch because my leg and foot had little strength. It was then that I realized it was going to take time to get back to normal. It was two years before I could completely forget about that foot.

The National Conference of Adult Education Directors was held in November 1958 in Cincinnati, Ohio. Millie and I left early and drove to the Ohio city. I was still using one crutch to walk, and many of my friends and acquaintances asked, "What on earth happened to you?" Then I would go into detail of what happened and would wind up the conversation by saying, "It's just going to take time." By this time I had become accustomed to driving with my left foot, so we got to and from Cincinnati without trouble.

When 1959 rolled around, little did I realize I was in for another big year. Our adult education program in Ferndale as well as in the state was growing by leaps and bounds. Through my work on national committees and sessions, I had become nationally known in the adult education circle. Some of my associates in Michigan wanted to run me as a candidate for the National Board of Directors. I thought the idea a good one since it would give me an opportunity to help mold the future of adult education in the United States as well as in Michigan. I was elected for a two-year term and went to Washington, D.C. in the spring to attend our board meeting. The board consisted of a president, vice president elect, five board members, and a secretary, all elected by a national ballot of adult education directors.

Another big event that is always a great one for proud parents was Dick's graduating from the new Ferndale High School. Now both our sons were maturing into manhood. The previous year Dick and I had driven to Adrian to look over the college. It so happen that it was commencement weekend and exercises were being held in the gym, so Dick and I made ourselves at home and took a backseat. A boy from Pennsylvania whom Phil had brought home for a weekend was a graduating senior. As he passed through the line and was handed his diploma, Dick said, "I sure wish I could have that privilege." I said, "You can if you want to pay for it in hard work."

As the summer arrived Dick continued to work at the A and P grocery store on 9 Mile. Phil was working at an electrical plant on Hamilton in Detroit, turning out telephones. Millie and I started to make plans to spend the month of August in Montana. Monroe and Ruth had urged us to come, fish, and eat fish, since there was no fish like the Montana mountain-stream trout. I encouraged Dick to take a brush-up English course being given at Cranbrook School just north of Ferndale. Like all young men who had just graduated from high school, Dick was rather reluctant to do summer school studying. His remark was, "I just got out of school, and I don't want to start right in again." I reasoned, "Your English grammar needs some brushing up and taking the course will help you when you get to Adrian College this fall." "Well, if you think I should, Dad, I will." So the following week Dick started at the Cranbrook Summer School.

The adult education programs now included high school completion courses for adults who were without a high school diploma. In Ferndale we had several adults who were receiving the diploma. Some of them graduated with the senior class, and those who didn't aspire to that routine called at the adult education office for their diploma. For the first time Highland Park had a commencement for the graduating class of adults. My friend and adult education director William Valade asked me to give the commencement address, which I did.

Our first of eight trips to Montana was very invigorating and delightful for both of us. Monroe and Ruth had friends who had cabins in the mountains just south of Red Lodge, Montana. When we arrived the welcome mat was out at "Happy House," owned by Florence and Burr Conrad who lived in Billings. The other cabin, which Millie and I occupied, was owned by the Wilsons, who also lived in Billings, Montana. We spent two full weeks with them. Several times Millie, Burr, and Monroe went up "on top" for an all-day fishing trip. They always came back with their fishing baskets full of beautiful mountain trout. While I never did get any real enjoyment out of fishing, I sure do like to eat fish. I made up eating what Burr didn't, since he doesn't like fish although he enjoys catching them. During the eight consecutive Augusts that we spent in the west we made a host of friends and were always treated as one of the western family.

Another of our prime pleasures was the "Festival of Nations" held every year at Red Lodge, Montana, and just a few miles from our mountain cabins. The Festival was highlighted with evening performances. The Red Lodge citizenry was made up of many different nationalities, and at one time coal mining was its chief occupation. As the mining opportunities decreased, discord among these nationalities began to develop in the city of a few thousand, which resulted in a divided community. As I understand it, a schoolteacher in Red Lodge became aware of this situation and decided to try to do something about it. This resulted in the "Festival of Nations." Each evening for a week in August, one nationality would put on a program in the high school gym that centered on their folklore. This could not be organized in a short time; it took months of preparation and rehearsing before the night of the performance. We always enjoyed taking in one or two of these evening shows. They were always free to the public, and it was surprising and gratifying to Red Lodge people to learn of the number of states represented in the audience of several hundred each night.

As we turned our car to the east for the long five-day trek back to Ferndale, we were rested and refreshed. We ate our meals at restaurants and stayed in motels at night. It was good to get home.

Dick was preparing to leave for Adrian College. This stimulated a desire in Phil to want to go back to the campus, so the middle of September found Mother and Dad with a loaded car and two college youths heading for Adrian. These were four delightful years for both Millie and me. I have always had fond memories of campus life in spite of all the hard work and hardship we had to endure, since my brothers and I were not what some would call "blessed" with parents who had the money to send their children to college. However, we learned to work and to meet and fight the many difficulties that confronted us, and after all that is a part of the very best education one can get. That is life.

Two letters that Dick sent to us from college have always been very gratifying to me, which caused me to preserve them over these years. He wrote one of them on May 13, 1960, two weeks before the end of his first college year. "Well, Dad, I guess by the time this letter arrives, you will be back from Lansing [where I had participated in a conference program]. You probably did a good job as you always do. I still like it up here and have been enjoying myself. If I didn't benefit from the courses I took, I can say I have benefitted in other areas of education. I believe I have accomplished a greater faith in myself, especially during this semester. Next year I will take American Literature, Principles of Accounting, Principles and Problems of Economics, United States History to 1865, Philosophy and Physical Education. It's going to be rough, but if I can get through this semester then I will know that I can graduate from college. I think there is a good chance for my success."

Three years later on May 21, 1963, Dick wrote: "Well, Mom and Dad, your youngest son has just completed his education at Adrian College. I stopped writing my last exam for this school at 12:00. No more studying and exams. It is still hard to believe that the best four years of my life are all over with. There were times I thought I never would see this week, but here it is. These years went by fast, but they have been sweet and a lot of good times. In many ways I am looking forward to being an alumnus and again I hate to leave Adrian."

With his dry wit Dick always had a pleasant way of talking about finances. He wrote: "You probably hate to hear this, but don't be shocked when you ask me how are my finances and the reply is broke-penniless. Guess I'll see you folks real soon. Thanks again for making graduation possible. Your six thousand investment, Dick." We had great pride and joy when we watched Dick walk across the platform and receive his diploma from President Dawson the May day, 1963.

It didn't cause anxiety in Mother and I when Phil decided Adrian was not for him. He had spent three years on the campus and received a great benefit from it. I had been in public education long enough to realize that a liberal arts college is not for every boy and girl. In my years of teaching experience I have seen hundreds of young people who had never had set foot on a college campus but by study and hard work had risen to some of the highest pinnacles of financial life. At this writing 1972 I can say we are proud of our two sons and their families. No parents could be blessed with two finer daughters-in-law. We love them just as much as if they were of our own blood.

In February 1960 I was elected to the national board of directors of the Adult Education Association. The winter meeting of the board was in Atlantic City. One of the rewards of hard work was having one's expenses paid to conferences, so I was looking forward to walking the boardwalk with men from all over the United States who were on the board. Millie had developed a tumor in the breast, which our family doctor didn't appear to be worried about. Before I had made my travel arrangements I asked him if he thought it would be safe for me to go out of town for a few days on business. He replied that her condition was nothing to worry about; that it would clear up in a few days, so I bought my flight tickets to Atlantic City and started to pack my bags. The day before my leaving Millie went to the doctor for an examination. He immediately changed his diagnosis and said for precautionary measures he wanted to operate on her just as soon as the hospital could give her a room, which should be in a day or two. Our anxiety about her condition increased, and I turned in my tickets and wired the Washington, D.C. office that I would not be able to attend the Board meeting. The national president wired back their regrets and the wish that my wife was not seriously ill. Then, to my disgust, we waited for a whole week for the hospital room. We were very thankful that the operation proved to be a simple one and that the doctor's initial diagnosis proved to be correct.

Summer 1960 found all of us at home. Dick had a job driving a pickup truck for Hodges Auto Sales. Phil had a job in Adrian and was staying on campus doing some extra coursework in summer school, after which he came home. As July waned, Millie and I were packing for another trip to Montana. Mother Hulda Burrows (Millie's mother) would stay at our house and do the cooking so that the boys wouldn't be alone.

It was always a delightful pleasure to hit the trail for a five week vacation in the West. One year we took a route around Chicago, through Wisconsin and Minnesota to Fargo, North Dakota, where it seemed to us the West really began. Then the return trip guided us through Duluth, across the Upper Peninsula of Michigan, and down I-75 to Ferndale. Over the eight-year period during which we spent every August in Montana, we fell in love with certain cities, motels, etc. in which we stayed overnight. We were generally on the road by six thirty in the morning, and after about an hour's drive we would stop to eat breakfast. One of those places was Jamestown, North Dakota. The small Jamestown College campus was always one of my favorite driving spots. The restaurant located north of the railroad tracks was the place we always ate our meals when in Jamestown.

Another of our favorite cities for the night stopover was Miles City, Montana. Several times when we were going through this city the American Legion state baseball tournament was in progress. It was here in Miles City that we first saw a seventeen-year-old youth pitching for Billings, Montana, who we saw pitching for the Baltimore Orioles years later. His name, Dave McNally, will undoubtedly be a candidate for the baseball Hall of Fame sometime in the future.

The number 10 highway would take us to Billings, where we met and became friends with Florence and Burr Conrad, the owners of the "Happy House" cabin. After a couple of weeks at the mountain cabins south of Red Lodge with Monroe and Ruth and the Conrads, we would eat our last breakfast of the year at the Red Lodge restaurant and head for Bozeman, Montana, where Monroe was pastor of the First Methodist Church.

Bozeman is a fine college town, the home of Montana State University; small in comparison to the large cities and universities of the East but large for the state of Montana. We enjoyed our visit at Monroe and Ruth's in Bozeman. After a week or ten days, we bid goodbye to Bozeman and friends and headed our car east on number 10 highway for the five days and four nights that we took to get home.

The boys would welcome us with outstretched arms and were doubly glad to get some of their mother's fine cooking again. Their chief complaint about their grandmother's meals was that she never threw anything away. It went back in the icebox, and they had to eat it for the next meal. Well, I guess a little economizing is good for all of us.

During the years around 1960, Monroe was a district superintendent in the Montana State Methodist Conference. His position called for him to do a lot of traveling, attending conferences, interviewing potential candidates for the Methodist clergy, etc. Many of his trips east, which took him to New York City, Boston, and Durham, North Carolina, the home of Duke University, enabled him to stopover in Chicago, from where he would take the passenger train to Kalamazoo, Michigan. One such occasion was in March 1960. Over the weekend Millie and I drove to Kalamazoo for a family get-together at the homes of our brothers Al and Lee. Whyle and Audrey drove in from the east. Hilda, Lee's wife, generally gave us one of her famous dinners of buttermilk pancakes with good sausage and coffee. It was always refreshing for all of us brothers to get together for a weekend of companionship.

Labor Day 1960 found me back in the adult education office with my secretary, Mrs. Dorothy Barte, preparing the fall-term adult education schedule of evening-school classes. Dick and Phil both were resting up from a summer of profitable activity. Both were readying themselves for another year at Adrian College. When the Sunday arrived for their departure, we loaded the car and they bid goodbye to 250 Maplehurst for another college year.

The fall of the year passed rapidly it seemed. It was a high school football game each Friday night, and during the winter months several of us made it a practice to follow the basketball team wherever they played. Then too there were college games on Saturday, which I sometimes attended. "K" College homecoming was an attraction for me, and at times Millie and I sat in the stands watching football and basketball games.

For several months Millie had been having gall bladder trouble. There were times when she would have an attack, and she would have to have a shot to ease the pain. On one such occasion I got Dr. Dwayne Plankell, our neighbor across the street, to come over at eleven o'clock at night to give her a shot. As the winter of 1960-61 continued, it was becoming more evident that surgery was going to be necessary to correct her trouble. In the middle of May 1961 Millie entered the Highland Park General Hospital for a gall bladder operation. Dr. Howard Schuneman took out her appendix at the same time, which might have given her some trouble at a later date.

Our Methodist Church pastor, Rev. John W. Parrish, took a great interest in youth. At times he remarked that the Ferndale Methodist Church had never had one boy who had made the Methodist clergy his life's work. He introduced a Bible study in which all four of us enrolled. We met once a month for four years. He would give out monthly lesson sheets. On the last Sunday night of the month, we would turn in our sheets after a two-hour discussion. During the course we read the Bible from cover to cover, and we were real proud of Dick because he was the youngest person in the group of about one hundred who completed the Bible study course. Dick completed it during his freshman year at Adrian College.

Phil has always been interested in other people. He has a winning personality that makes it easy for him to be a leader. On June 18, 1961 Millie, Dick, and I sat in our church pew listening to Phil occupying the pulpit. He did such a remarkable job that Rev. Parrish, as well as many others, told us we were going to have a boy who would follow in the footsteps of his Uncle Monroe. This proved to be a tonic for Millie and me, and his mother forgot all about her "operation" of one month past.

In fall 1961 Millie and I went to Denver to attend the national adult education conference. We flew both ways. It was our first visit to Denver, and we made a restful and interesting trip out of it. Shortly after I was elected for my second term to the National Board of Directors of the Adult Education Association in spring 1962 we decided we needed a new car. I went to my friend George Higgins, the Pontiac dealer in Ferndale, and asked him if he could get me an official's car with low mileage. "Sure, Harold," he said, "what kind of a car do you have in mind?" My reply was, "Any model that you can get at the right price. I would prefer a four door, but I won't be choosy." A month went by, but knowing George I wasn't concerned. If George said he would do something for me I knew he would, just give him time. That is the kind of a man George Higgins was and is. He was a state representative for several terms and then was elected to the state Senate. I had gone to Lansing a number of times about education legislature. He was always a good listener and was very dependable. He was the schoolteacher's friend, had a Higgins scholarship fund that made it possible for over 150 boys and girls to get a college education, and was the type of public-spirited citizen who was highly respected by his hometown people. I knew I would have a new car for the summer trip to Montana; "Just have patience," he would say to me, "I'll get you a car." It was about the first of June that Mr. Higgins called to tell me he wanted to talk with me. It was my lunch hour, so I went down to his office. He said Lucy Miller had her 1962 Pontiac for sale and it had very low mileage. "Why don't we go over to see her, which is a block away, and take a look at it." "Sure," I said, "there is no harm in looking." Lucy was a retired Ferndale High School dean of women. She came to Ferndale High School in 1922, the year before I arrived. She had poor health and retired early. A few months previous to our visit she had a stroke and was paralyzed on one side. Being confined to a wheelchair made her mentally upset because of her inability to do the things she had planned to do in retirement. I took her 1962 two-door Pontiac hardtop out of the garage, where it had been since winter. It was a lovely car, just nicely broken in. Without asking the price, I told George and Lucy that I would take it. I knew that George would be fair to both of us. I gave Lucy a check for the amount, went to the Higgins Pontiac office for a bill of sale and transfer of title certificate, and then went over to get the car.

I never saw Lucy again. She died a few months later.

When we packed the new Pontiac the last of July, readying it for our trip west, I was at ease because I knew I had good transportation for the trip. Our visit to Montana, "Happy House," Bozeman, and Red Lodge were all pleasant memories. We loaded the Pontiac in September to take Dick back to Adrian for his senior year. Phil had decided to find a job and work so he wasn't a back-to-college passenger.

Little did I realize that this school year of 1962-63 was to give me the two greatest thrills of my life. We greatly enjoyed the fall football season, as we always did. To me sports events are some of the rewards of being in the public school business because I love all sports. Being at the age that makes it impossible to participate, the next best thing is to watch others in the contest.

When the basketball season opened in December 1962 we all knew Ferndale had a good basketball team. For years Roy Burkhart had been turning out really good teams, but we never seemed to be able to get that last basket that would send us to Lansing for the finals in the state Class A tournament. Back about 1947 Burkhart's team had made the Lansing trip to the semi-finals, but Kalamazoo Central, which won the state championship three consecutive years, beat us, and that was the closest we ever came. Would this 1962-63 season team be any different than the previous ones? That was the question! Well, when "March Madness" in Michigan rolled around, there was Ferndale undefeated in sixteen season games. When the last whistle had blown the end of the game with Adrian High, Ferndale was state champion, having won twenty-two consecutive games, several by coming from behind in the closing seconds to snatch victory out of an inevitable defeat. It was one of the biggest thrills I could ever have. For years I had been going to the state semi-finals in Lansing at M.S.U. field house, watching other high school teams play and win championships. Now it was our night, and as I walked up to Roy Burkhart to congratulate him my old spine tingled. At the championship banquet held at the high school, I asked the father of our basketball center who sat opposite me, "Do you think Ferndale will ever win another championship in basketball?" "Sure," he said. Little did any of us realize that three years later in 1966 Ferndale High would again be state basketball champion.

The four years of Dick's college life at Adrian passed all too soon, for it was one of my pleasures to be able to drive to "college town," walk around the campus, eat lunch or dinner in the college dining hall, and relive college life to a degree. When we got the commencement invitation announcing the exercises of the Adrian College class of 1963 on Sunday, May 26, at three o'clock, we realized that Mother and Dad had arrived at a new plateau in life. Dick, of course, kept us posted on time, events, etc. His question was, "When will you arrive?" He suggested we come Saturday, stay overnight at a motel, and enjoy ourselves. That we did do.

Dick and Carole Taylor had met during the beginning of Dick's sophomore year during a dance in the gym in the first week, and they had been almost inseparable ever since. So Carole became a part of our family plans. While we were eating breakfast at a small restaurant just off the main street leading into Adrian, Larry and Faye Cowell saw our car and joined us. Phil also arrived in time to eat with us. It was church, lunch, and then the big event. As Dick walked across the platform and received his B.A. degree, we beamed with joy and pride like all proud parents. After the recessional we all walked over to the "Mound" to hear the "Cane Ceremony." While it didn't mean much to the Adrian students, the alumni had learned to appreciate its meaning and significance. Commencement exercises over, we went to Dick's fraternity, which had open house, and packed his belongings for the last time. As we drove back to Ferndale I felt as though I was in a mental vacuum. I was happy that Dick was able to finish college, but it left me with a feeling that one of the big jobs of a parent to rear a family was terminated.

Phil was a working man and was still very much interested in church work. He was working with the youth in our Ferndale Methodist Church and doing an excellent job. Everyone in a position to know would commend Phil for his excellent leadership. He has an outstanding personality and gets along well with people, and was a leader among youth. He had a slight speech handicap that made people who didn't know him a little wary about his ability to go into the ministry. However, he could stand in the Methodist Church pulpit in Ferndale and conduct and preach a sermon with high commendations. Our pastor, Rev. John Parrish, had great expectations for him, and urged Phil to get his lay local preacher's license, which he did. Dr. Parrish and I were in hopes that the district superintendent of the Methodist Church could give him a small church near Adrian, which would aid Phil both in his studies and financially. However, it did not occur, so Phil continued in his job into the spring of 1964.

The East Grand Boulevard Methodist Church was integrated and had a black pastor by the name of Woodie White. He wanted a youth director, and many of the church membership felt that a white assistant would be preferable, so spring 1964 found Phil the director of youth in a church that had mostly black teenagers. That year was a great experience for Phil. He was doing a highly commendable piece of work. He was well liked by both young and old. One evening in spring 1965 he was supervising a youth fellowship party at the church. A drunken black teenager tried to crash the party, so the boys at the door, who had instructions to allow only church members to be admitted, called for Phil to come to their aid. While Phil was trying to talk to the lad and was completely off his guard for any kind of violence, the drunken lad landed a hard blow to Phil's mouth, breaking off a tooth. The police were called, and the boy was taken to police headquarters. To me this seemed to be a turning point in Phil's religious life in that it appeared to me he was losing interest in becoming a Methodist clergyman. My feelings were later proven to be right.

Phil hadn't been affiliated with the East Grand Boulevard Methodist very long before he was asked by its pastor to preach the sermon. I remember one sermon very distinctly that he preached on June 21, 1964. His subject was "From Here to Eternity." He did a masterful job in his organization, speech, and depth of thought. Of course Mother and I with Bonnie drove to the church to hear him, and people made it a point to come to us in praise of his work.

Bonnie Phillippi was a "hometown girl." She lived with her parents, Ken and Mary Phillippi, in Oak Park, which is a city bordering Ferndale on the west side. She graduated from Ferndale High School, being several years Phil's junior. Then she studied four years on the campus of Central Michigan University located in Mt. Pleasant, Michigan. She was a member of the Ferndale Methodist Church when she and Phil started to keep company. Their admiration for each other continued during the four years of Bonnie's college life and led to marriage. No parent could want a sweeter daughter-in-law. After Phil finished the church year at the East Boulevard Church he found another job and moved back to 250 West Maplehurst to keep Mother and Dad company.

Feeling that the draft law would catch up with him, Dick lightly considered enlisting in a branch of the military so as to put in his two years. During Dick's army physical he was told that his history of rheumatic fever would likely cause him to be rejected into military service, so he felt that it was safe for him to apply for an accounting job at Adrian. This allowed him to continue his campus and fraternity life and be near Carole, who had one more year on the Adrian College campus. Mother and I were pleased in that I personally have little faith in the military's ability to train young men and women for democratic living. The military is a profession that trains boys to be human killing machines, and while I realize the United States must maintain a system of security to allow our government to develop an industrial military complex, it is detrimental to our whole democratic principle of life created and handed down by our forefathers.

Businessmen hesitated to take on young men before they had put in their two years of government service, but Dick was confident he could go to the employer with assurance that his employment would not be of short duration. He was hired at an accounting firm in Adrian and was very happy about his setup. It was the middle part of July that Millie and I was packing our bags getting ready to hit the trail to Montana that the postman delivered a letter that made me very curious. It was addressed to Dick. I did something I never had done before nor have I done since—I opened it, and my heart went into my mouth. It was such a shock to me. It was a government military notice for Dick to report for military duty some time about the first part of August. We debated what to do. Dick was just nicely getting acquainted with his work, and to go to the office and tell them he was liable to be drafted would probably cost him his job. Then too, we had planned to leave for Montana about three days ahead of the time he was to report to the military. Should we cancel or cut short our trip? I decided to hold the notice from Dick as long as I felt it was feasible. I didn't want him to be concerned until it was necessary for him to be concerned.

About two weeks before the date for him to appear for a physical/draft, Dick came home Friday night. I knew this was the time I had to give him his notice. However, I was not going to do it until Saturday morning. I wanted a nice enjoyable evening for the four of us at home. Saturday morning we got up, had breakfast, and started to visit about plans for the coming year. I knew this was the time to let Dick know what his future two years might be like. I gave him his notice telling him why I withheld it and what I had done. He took it very calmly, stating, "Well, I guess I may have to change my plans for next year." I gave him two letters, one from our eye doctor stating the conditions of his eyes and one from our family doctor giving the history of his rheumatic fever. I told Dick to take them with him for his final physical. Dick went back to Adrian Sunday night with a different perspective of what the next two years might be like. As I understood it, Dick told his employer of his circumstances and asked him if he wanted him to leave the job. His employer said, "No, stay on until you report and if you are turned down for physical reasons come back to work."

The day Dick reported for induction was the day we left for Montana, knowing that he would be immediately transferred to Fort Knox. Saying goodbye at 250 West Maplehurst was hard, for the future was in doubt. Phil drove Dick down to the Fort Wayne induction center with the understanding we would call that evening to get the news of Dick's status. As Phil's voice came on the phone stating Dick was in the army now, we felt that we had done everything we could to save him from two years of learning how to kill. Now we could only hope for the best. We had our usual good trip to Montana. It was interesting to again rub elbows with our western companions and enjoy the fresh clean air of the mountain region.

We got home the week before Labor Day, and I immediately turned my whole attention to the organizing and promotion of adult education for the fall term. I knew that I had two years left in the Ferndale public school system since the board policy was to retire the personnel at the age of sixty-five. Since my sixty-fifth birthday came after July 1, 1964, I was allowed to complete the school year 1964-65 at the age of sixty-six. I was in very good health, and made up my mind that I would give these last two years my very best with no let-up or coasting.

Football was the big sports attraction in the fall, and my interest took me to a Ferndale High game each Friday night and a college game almost every Saturday. I belonged to the Michigan Athletic Coaches Association. This afforded me the privilege of going to almost all games in the state of Michigan just by showing my membership card. This card also allowed me to attend many of the Detroit Tigers baseball games, which I was greatly interested in and enjoyed.

We were kept posted on Dick's situation by his weekly letters to us, and his communication with Carole. It was early fall when Dick wrote that his "boot training" was drawing to a close, that he was going to be sent to Fort Polk, Louisiana, that it was a possibility he might be shipped out after his training at Fort Polk to almost any place they wanted to send him. "So why don't you and Mother pick up Carole at Adrian and drive down to Fort Knox the following weekend?" I called Carole at Adrian College and asked her if she wanted to drive down with us. Her reply was, "I sure do." I wrote Dick to expect us Saturday noon. Mother and I left Ferndale about two o'clock to find Carole waiting for us, and off we went headed for Fort Knox. We drove until we got south of Cincinnati, stopping at the roadside to eat sandwiches Millie had made. We put up in a motel about 9:30 p.m. and as we said goodnight to Carole next door to us I said, "We'll get an early start in the morning."

We were up at six o'clock. Traffic was fairly heavy and the single-lane roads going into Louisville were pretty crowded, so we didn't reach Fort Knox until about 12:30 p.m. Saturday. We stopped at the gate for information on how to find Dick. The attendant gave us a map of Fort Knox and pinpointed Dick's location. Fortunately we asked a soldier if he could tell us the location we were looking for, and he was kind enough to guide us to Dick's quarters. I went into the office to ask for Private Dick A. Wilcox, and the officer said he would notify him that we were there. In about five minutes Dick came running over to the car to greet us. He was dressed and ready to leave just as soon as the officer in charge of his company got around to inspecting his gun, which he had laying in parts on a canvas. When the officer saw that I was his dad and waiting for him, he got busy and immediately passed inspection of Dick's gun. We drove into Elizabethtown where we got two adjoining motel rooms. Our room had two large beds, which Dick and we occupied; Carole had the adjoining room. It was late to bed and early to rise since we had just twenty-four hours together. It was a rather sad occasion that Sunday afternoon bidding Dick goodbye, for how long we did not know. We left Carole at Adrian and arrived home at midnight, tired but happy that we had had a weekend reunion with Dick.

Mother and I were still worried about Dick's health, and in a letter to our Senator Philip Hart I asked him to review the case, which he did with good results.

October 22, 1963
Senator Philip Hart
United States Senate Building
Washington, D.C.

Dear Honorable Phil:
Re: Private Dick A. Wilcox
R. A. W. U. S. 55768610
C. O. E., 4th TNG REGT (CST)
Fort Polk, Louisiana 71446

Thanks to you, on Tuesday, October 8, 1963, my son Dick was called to the hospital at Fort Knox and given a thorough heart examination by the army doctors.

Dick reports to us that the doctors told him that his heart is good but he has a slight murmur but nothing serious. Also the doctors told him that rheumatic fever is a little easier to pick up in the army and army life could be the agent for a recurrence of the fever. He gave him a bottle of penicillin tablets and told him to take two a day.

Now, Senator, it is a common known fact that doctors do not like to prescribe daily dosages of penicillin because a patient will gradually get immune from its effects. So Senator, let's look at the facts, Dick is a rheumatic fever patient who was in bed as a child for two and half years whose health has been guarded by both his doctor and his parents. Then, to the surprise of his doctor, friends and his parents, he is drafted and inducted into the army at Fort Knox. After ten weeks training he develops a heart murmur which the army doctors say is not serious but to guard against recurrence of rheumatic fever gives him a bottle of penicillin tablets to take two a day.

Senator Phil, if we were at war and the army was in great need for every man available, then it would be justified, but for my son in peace times to be subjected to army life at the risk of his whole future health just isn't justice. Of course as an attorney friend of mine said, "He could get a government pension the rest of his life. But my son would not want that in preference to health.

I am asking you, Senator, to use your influence to get Dick A. Wilcox a medical discharge. If you are not in a position to do this then maybe you can advise me to whom I can see to get Dick's case reviewed.

Mrs. Wilcox and I both appreciate greatly your interest in Dick's case.

Most Sincerely Yours,

While sitting in a classroom at Fort Polk, Dick relates that he was notified to immediately report to the hospital for a physical examination. The doctors reported to Senator Hart, and he in turn reported to us, that Dick's physical condition was good and that military life would not prove to be injurious to his health. Mother and I felt much better.

My second term on the National Board of the Adult Education Association was coming to an end. A friend and fellow director informed me that California was putting my name on their state ballot for reelection and they hoped I would swing Michigan to their candidate. I was now in the next-to-last year in the field of public school adult education, and I didn't think it would be fair to the association to run for reelection. I told my friends how I felt. However, they did put me on the ballot, and I was nominated for reelection.

Our national conference was held in November 1963 at the fabulous new Deauville Hotel, Miami Beach, Florida. November is off season and our association was able to get almost unbelievably cheap rates. Millie and I planned to go, and made our reservation for an oceanfront room. Since breakfast and dinner were included in the room rate, we could eat a late breakfast and an early dinner and cut expenses. Our flight left on a Friday at about twelve midnight.

I attended the Ferndale Hazel Park football game and left a little early so that I could be home at 10:30 p.m. Phil drove us to the airport. We had a nice flight and arrived in Miami about 2:30 a.m. It was warm and balmy. This was my first trip to Florida. We enjoyed the week and mixed work with pleasure. I informed my California friends that I had withdrawn my name for reelection to the board, but I would use my influence to swing Michigan to their candidate. For two years I had served as chairman of the Constitution and By-laws Committee. It was the opinion of most informed members of our association that we needed changes. After two years of conferences, letter writing, etc., I had my report ready to submit at the business session. I was very pleased that my report on changes in the constitution and bylaws was accepted. I left Deauville for home, feeling that my work in the National Association had been completed. When it was announced that next year's conference would be held in San Francisco in November, I said to Millie, "Start packing, we're going. This will be my last session with my fellow Adult Education co-workers."

We hadn't been home very many days before we got a letter from Dick that it looked as if he was to be shipped to Germany but that he would be able to spend the Christmas holidays at home before sailing. A few days later we were surprised to be informed in a letter from Dick that he and Carole were going to be married during his leave, and he asked if we would help them in their arrangements. He had pretty definite information that as soon as Carole graduated on May 31, 1964, she would fly to Europe and be with him until he was shipped home. Knowing Dick as we do, we were positive that he and Carole had given this a lot of thought and consideration. We wrote him that we would do everything we could to make their plans a reality. The wedding date was set for Saturday, December 21, 1963, at the First Methodist Church in Niles, Michigan, Carole's home. Dick's plans were to take a train from the south to St. Louis, which according to the railroad timetable would get him into St. Louis in time to catch the Wabash Cannon Ball to Detroit. But train service was already deteriorating to the degree that time schedules meant nothing. It was in the forenoon that our house telephone rang and a very discouraged voice on the other end said, "This is Dick. We were too late arriving at St. Louis to make our Detroit train. I am flying home. Can you meet me?" Of course we could meet him. It was dark when we saw Dick get off the plane, happy to be home. We drove to Adrian to pick up Carole and again our family was together.

We had two cars, the Pontiac and the Plymouth. I made the Plymouth at Dick and Carole's disposal. We began to make plans for the big day at Niles. Millie and I drove over to Niles on Saturday and got a hotel room that Mr. Taylor had reserved for us. Phil and Bonnie drove also, but did not stay overnight. It was cold and there was plenty of snow on the ground, but the weather didn't dampen the spirits of the wedding party. The ceremony was scheduled for 4:00 p.m., after which there was a reception in the church. Then our families adjourned to a nice restaurant that Mr. Taylor had reserved for me and we had the wedding dinner.

Sunday morning Millie and I drove home. A few days later Dick and Carole joined us and remained until we had to say goodbye to Dick as he took the plane for the East Coast, from where he was to be shipped to Germany, and to Carole as she began her final months of college life at Adrian as a married woman.

February 1964 found me attending my last national board of directors meeting in Washington, D.C. When we adjourned the session on Saturday noon I called Whyle, who lived in Silver Springs, Maryland, that I was now free and would he pick me up to visit with them overnight. Sunday night I took the B and O passenger train, which got me in Detroit at about 8:00 a.m. After breakfast and a little nap I went to my office to again wade through all the letters, phone calls, etc. that Mrs. Barte had for me.

As spring wore on we were kept posted on Carole and Dick's plans. Dick was to get two weeks leave June 1, 1964, and he would meet Carole in London, England, at the airport. They were to make their headquarters at the Strand Palace Hotel in the heart of London. Dick wrote that he needed a car, a VW, that would cost about fifteen hundred dollars and would I make the necessary arrangements to get him the money. I wrote him that I would and that the money would be waiting for him when he and Carole returned from England. The money was there.

Sunday, May 31, 1964, found all of us at Adrian College to see our daughter-in-law awarded the B.A. degree cum laude. The Taylor family (Bryce and Louise Taylor and their daughters Kay, Connie, and Candace) from Niles was there of course. After the exercises and a good dinner at the college dining hall we all drove to Ferndale for an overnight goodbye to Carole, who on Monday, June 1, 1964, was flying to London to join him "until death do us part."

Significant to me also was that I signed my forty-second Ferndale board of education contract which was my last. I knew that the board policy said that I must retire from the school system at the end of the 1964-65 year since I would be sixty-six years old.

Phil was working and living in Royal Oak. Bonnie was still going to Central Michigan University, and would start her senior year in the fall. She and Phil seemed to have mutual interests and respect for each other, for which we were pleased.

As August drew near Millie and I again packed our bags for our August in Montana. We had the usual good time. The Wilsons, Conrads, Richardsons, and Wilcoxs all held out the hand of Montana hospitality when we arrived. For two weeks we relaxed, ate those mountain cold-water trout, went to the Red Lodge Festival, and breathed the fresh clean air out of the clear blue sky. It was certainly a great inspiration to have such opportunities each August. Then the last week there we celebrated my birthday with Burr Conrad's. His was just seven days later than mine, which comes every August 21 whether I like it or not. By the 23rd of August we were again pounding the pavement on our way home.

The first week in September 1964 found Millie and me working on the opening fall term of our public school adult education. For about twenty years Millie had been teaching classes in silversmithing and enameling. Over the period of these many years she had studied and worked until she was known nationally in the field of art. Her classes were always filled before the first night of official enrollment. There were some adult students who paid their enrollment fee months in advance in order to hold their place. These extra earnings made it possible for Millie to attend the National Adult Education Conference with me.

As November approached Millie and I planned our last National Conference of Adult Education to be held in San Francisco. We flew both ways. We stayed at the Palace Hotel convention headquarters. Knowing that the delegates would write "finished" after my name when I made it known at the business sessions that I was retiring at the end of the year, I sat back to enjoy myself.

It was just about the time we returned from San Francisco that Dick suggested in a letter that we come to Europe in the spring. Our high school principal, John McGregor, was a reserve in the United States Air Force. Each summer for a month he would fly, and many times it took him to German cities. One day as I was discussing Dick's location in Germany with him he remarked, "You and your wife ought to go to Europe while your son is stationed there. It is so much cheaper when a military man has connections and opportunities that the average civilian doesn't have." That got us thinking; why not celebrate my retirement in June 1965 with a trip to Europe? I wrote Dick our thoughts on the trip, and he wrote back that he was making a request to have the month of June for travel since he was due to be shipped back to the States in July 1965. We four would travel together in their VW.

So we went to the Holland American Steamship Company in downtown Detroit right after Christmas to inquire about sailing dates. Dick's letter said, "Be here by June 1st." Millie said, "In order to get there by June 1st we will have to fly." Having had two crossings of the ocean back in 1924, I had always dreamed the time might come when I again stepped onto one of the ocean liners for another crossing. So I said to Millie, "I am going by ship and if you want to fly, I'll meet you over there." Well, it didn't take too much discussion to agree that we would go by ship. As we sat around the table in the office of the steamship company with the date of June 1st in mind, the gentleman in charge explained to us that we should allow eight days and nights for the crossing.

The Holland American ships all had stabilizers that allowed the ships to ride smoothly, which was so different from the ships of the 1920's when I first traveled to Europe. He offered us Room 202 on the main deck, which he called an "alternating room," that is, one that was used for first class when needed or for tourist class. That gave us an incentive to want 202 since we were really in first class yet only paying for a tourist room. He said he would wire the New York office to hold the room for two weeks until we had made our decision. We left the Holland American office in a jubilant spirit.

The next thing to do was to talk with Superintendent John Houghton about leaving early since my school year wasn't up until June 30, 1965. John and I had known each other ever since he sat in my history and government classes back in the 1920's. John graduated from Ferndale Lincoln High in 1929. He went on our class of 1929 trip to Washington, D.C., entered and graduated from college, and became a teacher at the Roosevelt Elementary School. He became principal of Roosevelt School when Paul Best was made assistant superintendent. When the high school principalship became vacant, he was transferred to Ferndale High School. Several years later he was made the superintendent of the Ferndale public schools. When I approached John about sailing on the Nieuw Amsterdam on Thursday, May 21, 1965, I got a very cool reception. After explaining this once-in a-lifetime opportunity, that I had 120 sick-leave days stored up and that I could be sick the rest of the year and still draw my salary, he began to see that my case of leaving early was not setting a precedent. After all, I stated, "I am retiring." "I'll have to talk to the board members about it," he said. "Do you mind if I present my plan to the board?" I asked. Knowing some of the board members personally, I didn't have any doubt that the board would grant my request. His attitude was that he could handle it.

Within the time limit we were given by the Holland American Company to decide on Room 202 and sailing on May 21, 1965, the board gave me permission to leave May 19 in order to get to New York in time to board the ship. Needless to say, our spring months had one main thing in mind, retirement and Europe.

Another factor that made this trip abroad a very relaxing one was that Dick and Carole were making all the plans and taking all the responsibility. All we had to do was to get to Stuttgart, Germany, since Dick would do the driving in the VW and Carole would be the navigator. Millie and I planned to go to England after our June trip around Europe was finished on June 30, so I wrote the Strand Palace Hotel in London for a week's reservations. We had such details as tickets, passport, etc. to consider, but by May 1 all was in shape for our sailing.

We got the spring term adult program underway by March 30, and as our registrations closed with a really good spring term enrollment I sighed, thinking to myself, this is the end of adult education for me. Forty-two years in the Ferndale Public School system is coming to an end.

As the weeks passed the superintendent considered it wise to name my successor before I left town, so he sent out a notice stating that applications for the director of adult education would be taken. Each applicant was referred to me for an interview, then I would call the superintendent to relay my impressions and recommendation.

The most surprising applicant was a woman in the high school who was teaching commercial studies. She had taught in the night school program, was a member of the Ferndale Methodist Church, which my family had attended for forty-two year, had a nice jovial personality, a family, and showed a great deal of desire and enthusiasm. When I interviewed her, perhaps showing some surprise, I asked, "Do you realize, Dorothy, that this job means working four nights a week until ten and eleven o'clock?" She replied, "I do, and my family is so organized that it would not be a family burden."

It was evident to me that the superintendent was impressed with Dorothy, so I recommended Mrs. Dorothy Kosovac to be my successor and the board made the appointment. The several years of my retirement have proven that Dorothy has met and surpassed all expectations in her work.

The Board's appointment of Dorothy Kosovac made people and my fellow co-workers very conscious that my days in the school system were numbered. The *Royal Oak Daily Tribune* published an article that covered my forty-two years tenure in the Ferndale school system. With the headlines: "Pioneer of Adult Education to Step Down After 22 Years." The paper printed a picture of me "turning over the reins" to Dorothy Kosovac. The one-column article read: "The Daniel Boone of Adult Education in South Oakland, Harold B. Wilcox, is being turned out to pasture. Wilcox who sired night school from a simple Mom-Dad program in the war time years to Ferndale's high 5,000 students, something for everyone, in the family operation, is reluctantly retiring. Ferndale School District has a mandatory retirement age of 65, and the silver-topped Wilcox wouldn't mind staying around a little longer, but it's the law. And besides, he wants to take Mildred (his wife) to Europe this summer." The article continued on to my life history, starting with "The Gobles (Michigan) native finished college in Kalamazoo before moving to sparse, suburban, Ferndale in 1923 to teach social studies at old Lincoln High School." The article covered some of my experiences and life as an employee of the Ferndale School District. "Public demand now calls the shots, Wilcox said it's like clothing and automobile styles. The demands change and you've got to meet them. A good director has to keep his eyes, nose and ears glued to the ground to sense what the public wants. … Wilcox has served on State and National Adult Educator's governing boards and eight years on the Ferndale City Commission between 1935-43."

The announcement of my retirement seemed to spread to other sources of communication. The Ferndale Methodist Church had my picture in the May 9, 1965, Sunday bulletin with a brief article that started, "At the end of this school year, Mr. Harold B. Wilcox will retire after 22 years as Director of Adult Education in the Ferndale School system." It continued with brief notes on my work and our family. "Mr. Wilcox started with the schools here in 1923 as a teacher of social sciences at the old Lincoln High School and so concludes 42 years of service to our city."

The month of May was a very exciting and busy one for me. I was working long hours in order to wind up the 1964-65 year of adult education. Reports to both the state and to the Ferndale board had to be completed. Since some classes did not terminate until the first week in June, my faithful Dorothy Barte had to be instructed on the closing of the program. Because she had been my team worker for nearly thirteen years, she was well acquainted with the procedures.

Millie and I had to get our wardrobe together since Dick had informed us of the amount of luggage it was feasible to bring. After all, four people traveling for a month in a VW, one had to be very choosy about what to pack and what not to pack. We carefully weighed the value of each article. Such things as shirts, socks, handkerchiefs, ties, etc. were few in my bag since I could buy those things as I needed them. We each had one suitcase and a tote bag in which we carried our extra pair of shoes, etc. It was decreed that I was to carry and be responsible for the suitcases and Millie was to be the custodian of the tote bags.

As we turned the calendar to May I became all the more conscious of the end when the mailman started to leave me "best wishes on your retirement" cards, letters, and messages. Friends, former students, faculty members were wishing me happiness on retirement and Millie and me a bon voyage. One such card came from Elinor K. Rose, who wrote "Out Woodward Way" in the *Royal Oak Daily Tribune*. I had known Elinor for a number of years. She had assisted in the adult education program and could be called a friend of adult education. Believe you me, we in the new education field needed all the friends we could get. Some of our worst enemies were public school personnel. Elinor's 4/29/65 card read: "Dear HBW, 65? Impossible! Not with all that energy and enthusiasm. Somebody's looking at the wrong calendar. I have a friend who is now teaching in your program. She's taught in a number and says yours is the best, bar none. Congratulations on all the lives you have touched. How many people must feel taller because of you. Sincerely, Elinor K. Rose." What a compliment coming from such a prominent and gracious lady. It made me feel that all the sweat, worry, etc. I had put into my forty-two years of work in Ferndale had really been worthwhile.

Our ship, the *Nieuw Amsterdam* of the Holland-American Lines, was to sail Friday noon, May 21, 1965, out of New York City. We had decided to drive our car to New York and park it in the company's warehouse for the duration of the trip. It would then be waiting for us when we got off the ship on our return voyage. Whyle had written from their home in Silver Springs, Maryland, that he, Audrey, and

Debbie wanted to see us off as the ship sailed. They would meet us the afternoon of May 20 at a motel on the New Jersey turnpike that was about an hour's drive from the Holland-American loading site. We would have dinner, spend the evening together, and drive into New York the following morning in time to board the ship shortly after 9:00 a.m. I wrote Whyle that the arrangement sounded good to us and to go ahead with the motel reservations and let us know the name and location of the motel.

It was the second week in May that my secretary, Dorothy, asked me the date of our leaving. I told her of our plans and that we would be leaving the afternoon of Wednesday, May 19 and would take our time getting to the motel where we would meet my brother and family on Thursday, May 20. Dorothy then informed me that she and Bess Tweksberry were heading a planning committee for a farewell retirement reception for me the night before I was leaving, which would be Tuesday, May 18, 1965, at 8:00 p.m. in the high school cafeteria. Bess Tewksberry was as well known a person in South Oakland County as existed. She had taught with great success, oil painting in the adult education program since its very beginning. Her three and sometimes four classes a week were always filled to the turning-away point. Bess had been and still was a pillar in the P.T.A, the woman's club, her church, the Ferndale Library board and numerous other civic organizations. Several years prior she had been awarded the "Book of Golden Deeds" by the Ferndale Exchange Club for her outstanding and philanthropic deeds over many years of service in Ferndale. Dorothy told me that the reception would be from eight to ten o'clock, that Superintendent John Houghton was program chairman, and that refreshments donated by faculty and students of the night school classes would be served.

The May 13, 1965, *Ferndale Gazette* announced that all "Wilcox Friends" were invited to an open house from 8:00-10:00 p.m., May 18, 1965 for honoring me as the "retiring director of Adult Education," at the Ferndale High School cafeteria. The Superintendent of Ferndale Schools, John J. Houghton was the master of ceremonies. It was announced that Millie and me would be leaving the following week for a tour of Europe with our son Dick and his wife Carole.

The big night of May 18, 1965, came as all nights do. It found us with our bags packed, our tickets and travelers' checks in our pockets, and our passports safely tucked away in my inner coat pocket. The reception far exceeded my greatest of expectations. There were napkins with "Harold B. Wilcox, Retirement Tea, May 18, 1965" printed on them. The *Royal Oak Daily Tribune* photographer was present, and the following day the *Royal Oak Daily Tribune* carried a picture of me flanked with Millie and Mrs. Robert Maher, one of my hard-working instructors, on one side and Mrs. Dorothy Barte and Bess Tewksberry on the other. The article read, "Sand Path to Success. Adult Education Chief Retires. It was September, 1923 when Harold B. Wilcox, a suitcase in each hand, got off the interurban car at 9 Mile and Woodward and walked the sand path up 9 Mile to Lincoln High School. This was the beginning of a forty-two year tenure in the Ferndale public schools. In 1944 the Board of Education appointed him director of Adult Education, a position he held until retirement this week. An open house was held Tuesday evening in the Ferndale High cafeteria. Numerous students and friends wished Wilcox, 'Bon Voyage.' Yesterday he left for Europe with his wife Mildred. During the month of June, he enthused; 'We will tour Western Europe in a car with our son Dick and his wife Carole.' Dick is in the U.S. Army Administration in Stuttgart, Germany. Wilcox has another son Philip. After that he plans to 'keep busy,' but not so busy he can't enjoy his retirement."

The article goes on to tell of my church and civic affairs as well as in the State and National Adult Education Association: "He was a Ferndale City Commissioner from 1935-43. He taught a senior high Sunday School class at the Ferndale Methodist Church for 25 years. He is past President of the Ferndale Education Association, the State Association of Public School Adult Education and the Ferndale Exchange Club. He has served two elected terms on the National Board of Directors of the Public School Adult Education Association. Wilcox says he likes all sports. 'My hobby is following sports, and my greatest sports thrill was when Ferndale High won the State Basketball Championship.' He was born in Gobles, received a Bachelor of Arts Degree from Kalamazoo College in 1922, attended Boston University graduate school for one year and received a Master of Arts Degree from the University of Michigan."

John Houghton called me May 17, 1965, to tell me that while it is a mandatory retirement policy of the board, it was also customary for the retiree to send a "resignation into retirement" letter to the superintendent, to be presented by him to the Board of Education. He stated that I could make it reflect any kind of opinion I desire, and that he would like me to follow what had become the custom of the school district. So I wrote the following letter dated May 17, 1965:

"Mr. John J. Houghton, Superintendent.

Forty-two years in the same school district is a long time.

This resignation into retirement carries my very best wishes for the continued success of all who are connected with the Ferndale School district.

I came to Ferndale in 1923 when it was a sand-lot community. Today I leave a school system which has matured and which the Board, the employees, and the citizens of the community can be proud.

Ferndale is my home. I will look for opportunities so I can continue to be of some service to the community. Signed Harold B. Wilcox."

Apparently this pleased John, for when he as master of ceremonies introduced the speakers of the evening he included the reading of my retiree statement with the remark that it represented "the spirit of Harold all during his 42 years of service." For the program John had representatives from many walks of life. The mayor, Bruce Carbutt, a representative of the school board, the pastor of my church, the president of the Exchange Club, and several others spoke in praise of my forty-two years of work. Also a great surprise to me was the presence of the members of the State Board of Adult Education Association. The state president had sent the following telegram, which John read: "The Michigan Association of Public School Adult Educators joins in wishing Bon Voyage to Harold Wilcox as he retires. He has served Adult Education long and faithfully on the local, state and national levels. His leadership will be sorely missed-but his influence will linger on. Thank you and best wishes to 'Mr. Adult Education of Michigan.' William J. Valade, Pres. MAPSAE." Having read the telegram, Mr. Houghton called on William Valade, who said he sent the telegram in case he and the board members might not be able to be present. This whole program was taped and it was good that it was since it wasn't until I had returned from Europe that by playing the tape I could appreciate the very kind and generous remarks that had been made on my behalf.

While I greatly appreciated all the best wishes received from many, many people, it's impossible to recognize all of them here. One telegram that meant a lot to me was from Art Elliott, class of 1933, of which I was one of the advisors. Art had been president of his 1933 class, had become Governor George Romney's campaign manager, and was a well-known man around the state. His telegram read as follows: "Your enthusiasm for Ferndale through 42 years of service has helped the city to be a better place to live and recognized by all. I remember your guidance when I was in school and I wish I could be with you and your many friends as they honor you tonight. As a member of the class of 1933, may I send for the entire class our best wishes and congratulations. Art Elliott." This reception meant more to me than all the money and presents I received because I knew that those who took part in the planning, speech making, etc., did it because they wanted to.

I owe a deep debt of gratitude to my wife Millie, who during my last few years as director lived the program with me, to all my instructors who made the program an outstanding one, and to Mrs. Dorothy Barte, my secretary, who was a tireless and loyal worker in adult education.

I knew that I was going to miss the excitement, the associations, etc. that made the job an enjoyable one, but I also knew that time marches on and that there is no indispensable man.

Chapter 10

Retirement Years—Europe, Summer 1965

My work in the field of education was finished. At 1:30 p.m., May 19, 1965, Millie and I loaded our baggage in the Pontiac car, bid goodbye to Phil who was going to be caretaker of the house while we were gone, and headed down Southfield toward Toledo, the Ohio Turnpike, and east. We reached the Pennsylvania Turnpike before dark and found a nice motel at the first exit. We had a nice dinner, read the newspaper, watched TV, and retired early. Arising about 8:00 a.m., dressing, etc., we were on the turnpike by 8:30 a.m.. When traveling by car we always enjoyed driving for about an hour before stopping for breakfast, and this morning proved to be no exception. We knew we had plenty of time to get to the motel that Whyle had reserved for us on the New Jersey turnpike. Four o'clock was the agreed time to meet, so we drove at a leisurely pace and really enjoyed ourselves. We arrived at the motel a little early, but had hardly got our bags in the motel when the car from Maryland pulled in. After a good dinner together we visited, walked around the motel vicinity for exercise, and turned in for the night.

We were about an easy one-hour drive from the Holland Tunnel, and allowing another fifteen minutes to arrive at Pier 40 made it necessary to leave the motel at about 7:00 a.m. We wanted to get aboard as soon after nine o'clock as possible, which was loading time. That would enable all of us to get acquainted with the ship and allow Whyle, Audrey, and Debbie, their daughter, to enjoy looking around. We unloaded our baggage, which was immediately taken care of by the dockhands. I had to call at the office to get instructions on where to leave my car for the duration of the trip, then I got in line to have our tickets stamped and our passports "okayed." In the meantime Whyle, Audrey, and Debbie had gotten a visitor pass and were ready to go aboard.

It was a big thrill to be walking the gangplank onto the ship. Of course, the ship's photographer was right there to snap our pictures in hopes that we would want to buy some copies. Our room, 202 on A deck, had two beds, a bath and shower, and two portholes. It was located in the very forward of the ship on A deck, which was a very favorable location. We called the room steward to order sandwiches and coffee, then for two hours we made a ship survey. At 11:30 a.m. the ship's whistles blared three long and two short blasts, loudly proclaiming that it was time for all visitors to leave the ship that the twelve o'clock sailing time was nearing. We bid goodbye to Whyle, Audrey, and Debbie and they took their place on the upper tier of the dock opposite the rear deck of the ship. The tugboats were in place, and as the dock men with their high cranes lifted the gangplanks clear of the ship the tugboats started to push her away from the dock and out into the river channel. Waving a fond farewell to Whyle's family, I said to myself, "My dream of another trip to Europe has come true after forty-one years." As our ship sailed past the Statue of Liberty, passing other ships coming into the New York Harbor with their three-whistle salute, I stood on the rear deck thinking back to the time I was on the lower end of New York called the Battery, watching the *United States* sail down the river, under the bridge, and into the ocean, and wishing I was on her.

It took about one hour from the time we pulled away from the dock to the time we hit the open water of the ocean. Millie had gone down to the dining room for lunch, but I didn't eat lunch until we glided into ocean water. It was a lovely dining room. Millie and I had asked for a separate table for the first setting and our request was honored. Breakfast was at 8:00 a.m. If you didn't want to go to breakfast the room steward would serve you in your room. We did enjoy that privilege a few times, but generally we were up, dressed, and ready for breakfast by 8:00 a.m. Every meal was a banquet. The menu was yours; order anything to your heart's content. There was always fruit at the dining room entrance for one to help themselves for room snacks.

We had a beautiful trip across the ocean. The weather was mild and the ocean calm. There was always something to do on the ship. Reading in the library, playing bridge in the card lounge, sitting on deck with the deck steward ready to throw a blanket over you the moment you reclined in your chair were some of the time-consuming activities in the morning and afternoon. Then after a lovely dinner at 6:00 p.m., the first sitting, we would indulge in the evening activities of dancing, horse racing (ship's game) bingo, moving pictures, and almost anything else you wanted to do could be arranged. Millie and I had more than ordinary luck in playing the horses. She would bet on number three and won more times than she lost. One night she won the full card coverage in bingo prize money of thirty-six dollars. Spending eight days and eight nights on a floating hotel was pure luxury to us, and we enjoyed every minute of it.

The morning of May 26 we saw land and were told we were approaching Ireland. We would put into the Bay of Cobh to let off passengers, mail, and express, and take on passengers who were going to the continent. We were in the Bay of Cobh for about four hours. The ship's tender steamed alongside to transport the passengers to and from the shallow port of Cobh. The native Irish women brought their wares to sell aboard our ship. There were bedspreads, tablecloths, sweaters, shawls, and what have you, all beautifully made. We were told by fellow passengers to not buy until about the time the vendors had to pack up to get off the ship, then the prices were greatly reduced for last-minute sales. It was getting dark (10:30 p.m.) as we entered the English Channel. As I stood on deck I gave England a salute and said to myself, "I never expected to see you again." Little did I realize at the time that Millie and I would be passengers on this same ship, the *Nieuw Amsterdam*, in 1968 and again in 1970.

We were to dock at Southampton early the next morning, so my full night's sleep was cut short when I climbed out of bed at five thirty and out on deck to see our ship wend its way down the channel into its berth at the Southampton docks. It took about five hours to discharge passengers, unload freight, cars, baggage, etc. We ate a hurried breakfast in order to not miss a thing. At twelve noon we were speeding across the English Channel to Le Harve, France, where we again went through the same procedure. It was evening when we set sail for our last night aboard. Many passengers had left the ship and things were rather quiet, but it being our last night we didn't mind.

I wanted to be up early to see Holland as our ship slowly plowed its way down the river to Rotterdam. After we had docked we went to the dining room to eat our last breakfast, which terminated a glorious eight days and nights aboard. We were told it would be about two hours from the time we docked until we could leave the ship. All the baggage had to be unloaded so that passengers could claim it just as soon as they disembarked.

Now our thoughts turned to Dick and Carole at Cooke Barracks about thirty miles from Stuttgart. The ship's purser had ordered our train tickets to Stuttgart. We purchased them they were brought aboard at Southampton, so we felt we had everything under control. We began to think about what we would do from the time we left the ship until 7:30 p.m. when we boarded the train. Of course, there were passports to be examined and the routine checks before leaving the ship. As we walked down the gangplank we wondered what kind of a social climate we would find ourselves in!

It didn't take long to find out, for it seemed everyone spoke English and were very hospitable. I couldn't help but ask myself, do we Americans give foreigners the same "glad hand" that we received as we looked for our baggage and asked questions about the day's activity?

After our baggage had gone through customs, which in Holland was just answering a few questions, we walked out to the taxi stand, me with a bag in each hand and Millie with our two tote bags. We climbed into a taxi, a black Mercedes. The driver loaded the two bags in the trunk of the car and, unnoticed by me, he put my tote bag in the trunk also. Millie got in the rear seat with her tote bag and I, interested in sightseeing, rode in the front seat with the driver. This position in the car allowed me to become familiar with both the car and driver since it was about a fifteen-minute drive to the depot. Upon arriving at the station I paid the taxi, Millie got out, and the driver took our two suitcases out of the trunk. Thinking that we both were aware of our assignment, I picked up the two suitcases and we walked into the railroad station.

My first impression was that there were no seats or benches on which we could sit down or place our tote bags. Then I noticed that Millie did not have my tote bag. I asked, "Where is my tote bag?" "I don't know," she said, "Didn't you get it out of the car trunk?" "No, I didn't." I rushed out to where the taxi let us off, hoping he had not yet gone, but he had. Expecting everyone to understand English, I asked, "Where did the black Mercedes go with the heavyset driver that just brought us from the steamship docks?" "Oh, that driver just drove to the station parking lot to wait in the lineup," he said in perfect English. I rushed to the "line up" side of the depot and asked, "Did you see a heavyset man with a black Mercedes just drive in?" "Yes," he said, "He's just parking over there," as he pointed to a parked black car. I rushed over there and asked the driver, "Are you the one who just taxied us over here from the steamship docks?" "Yes," he replied. "Where is my other tote bag that you put in the trunk of your car?" I asked. The driver opened the trunk, and sure enough it was there. Boy, was I relieved. Some of the other drivers started to chide him. I didn't understand all they said since some of it was in Dutch. I don't really believe he was in any way dishonest; in my opinion it was just an oversight on his part as well as ours. As I walked in the depot with a smile on my face, Millie knew right away that our luck was holding out.

We checked our luggage at the depot baggage room, confirmed our 7:30 p.m. departure time, inquired about getting over to the "Needle" that overlooked the river and steamship docks as well as the city, and asked where people went to sit and rest while waiting for a train. We were told that we could take streetcar number three, which would take us within a block of the "Needle," and the same car number would return us to the station. It was interesting paying our small fare to the streetcar conductor. We had purchased some Dutch money onboard the ship, enough. we thought to last the day. The elevator at the top of the "Needle" opened up into a dining room. We found an unoccupied booth and ordered lunch. Having time on our hands, we were in no hurry to leave. We looked out from all sides, which gave us a good picture of Rotterdam. It was interesting to see our ship, the *Nieuw Amsterdam*, docked and already preparing for the next day's sailing to New York to pick up another thousand American tourists.

By early afternoon we found ourselves back at the railroad depot with time on our hands, so we walked up the city streets where we found a park bench to sit on and just watched traffic. What a difference between Rotterdam and U.S. cities. Yes, they had traffic lights, but bicycles and motorbikes far outnumbered the automobiles, and when the light turned green there were so many two-wheel carriers that one wondered how they kept out of each other's way.

At about 4:00 p.m. we walked back to the train station, still with three hours to kill and no place in the depot waiting room to sit. There were a few people sitting on the curb, but that was no place to park yourself for three hours. I asked a station agent, "What do people do while waiting for a train with no place to sit and rest?" He said, "Go outside on the track platform and you'll find a stairway that leads to a restaurant. Order some food with tea or coffee and no one will say anything to you about when you are supposed to leave." During the time we were in the dining room we noticed that there were others who had time on their hands. They were reading papers, magazines, etc. while taking an hour to sip a pot of tea or coffee. We sat there until about 6:30 p.m. when we left a tip on the table, paid our bill, and went to the baggage room, where we retrieved our two suitcases and two tote bags.

Walking up the stairs to the train platform, we spotted an empty bench and parked our baggage and ourselves on it. I said to Millie, "You sit here while I find someone who speaks English who will tell us on which track and which direction our train is going."

Most European trains are pulled by an electric engine. They are quiet and speedy. In Western Europe as well as in England railroads are owned by the government and passenger trains are run for the benefit of the people. This seems to be directly opposite to the American railroads. The private owned railroads are operated for profit and the public is ignored.

We didn't have to be too concerned about the time element since when it got to be about 7:25 p.m. our train would arrive. You could be sure that when the platform clock, which had a second hand with a red ball on it, pointed to 7:30 p.m. the train would pull out. Most trains were several cars long. Some had ten to twelve coaches, so we wanted to be in a middle position on the platform since our tickets called for seats in a numbered coach. As the coaches passed by us while we were standing on the platform, we could tell whether to move up toward the front or the rear end of the train.

It was a good thing our tickets called for the numbered car and the two numbered seats in the compartment since when we got on our car and opened the compartment door we found all seats taken. We showed the two occupants our tickets, which called for the seats they were sitting in. They were a little reluctant in giving up the two seats but did, and moved their baggage out of the compartment. The train was crowded, and later as we moved up and down the aisle of the car we saw people sitting on their baggage in the rear of the coach.

It got dark about ten o'clock and then it was just a long ride, passing through cities at breakneck speed and making few stops. We were due to arrive in Stuttgart, Germany at 4:11 a.m. I didn't want to run the risk of falling asleep and going past our city so I told Millie, "You go to sleep if you can and I'll assume the responsibility of being awake." We had a time schedule and by the dim light in our compartment I could tell about how far along we were whenever the train stopped. It was about three thirty that I said to Millie, "The next stop must be Stuttgart." It was just breaking the light of day at 4:05 a.m. I said to Millie, "Get the tote bags, and I'll get the suitcases from the baggage rack." We put them in the aisle outside of the compartment. As the train started slowing down I looked at my watch and said to Millie, "This is it."

There were a good number of passengers that got off the train. Millie and I didn't know just how to get to the waiting room, so we hung back to sort of follow the crowd. By the time we got to the gates that opened up into the waiting room we were the last to get there. As Dick and Carole spotted us I heard Dick say, "Here they come." It was a happy reunion early that morning of May 30. We hadn't seen Dick for a year and a half and Carole for a year and it sure was good to be with them again. Dick grabbed our two suitcases and we walked out of the station to the VW that was to drive us on our European tour.

After a brief drive around the city of Stuttgart Dick headed the VW toward Goppingen where Cooke Barracks is located. We drove up in front of the house that contained their apartment, if you could call it that. It was the top floor of a nice house, but it had no running water. The toilet across the hall had a wash basin that provided some warm water if you had patience to wait for it to heat. They were guaranteed one bath a week in the owner's bathroom on the first floor, provided the owner was at home when they wanted the bath. Of course, Dick had access to the showers at the barracks.

Since we had arrived at Stuttgart on May 30 and our tour didn't start until the early morning of June 2, 1965, we had some time to get acclimated. Dick had arranged for us to sleep downstairs in the spare room of the house's owner.

While Dick reported for a few hours of duty at the Cooke Barracks, Carole, Millie, and I drove around to see the German city with its winding streets, etc. Not having slept for twenty-four hours while we were in Rotterdam and on the train, I found myself pretty weary after we had had some breakfast. I went into Dick and Carole's bedroom, covered up because it was chilly, and got a few hours of shuteye while Millie, Carole, and Dick visited in the other room, which was the kitchen, living room, etc.

Dick and Carole had become acquainted with the Stein family who lived at Waldenbuch south of Stuttgart. They had a daughter, Babs Stein, who was an exchange student for the school year of 1959-1960 at Ferndale High School. Earlier Hans was an exchange student at an Ann Arbor high school. Mr. and Mrs. Dave Wilson, friends of ours, took in Babs while she was attending her school year at Ferndale High. The Wilson's daughter Davi got acquainted with Babs when she was home from college. Both Davi and Dick graduated from Ferndale High during June 1959. Sometime after

Babs returned to Germany, Davi visited her and met Babs's brother Hans. I had written Dick about Babs, and the Wilsons wrote Babs and Hans about Dick being in Cooke Barracks, Goppingen. So one Sunday, as Dick told it, here came Hans, Babs, and her fiancé (Claus Lahmann) to locate him. That was the beginning of a friendship that has endured ever since. Hans later came to Ferndale to study and complete his course in medicine, and at this writing Hans is on the medical staff at the Wm. Beaumont Hospital in Royal Oak, Michigan. Hans and Davi were married on December 18, 1965, and Dick was honored to be included in their wedding. Hans and Davi now live in Royal Oak, and have three nice children.

Dick and Carole had told the Steins of our arriving that Sunday morning, and they invited all of us to their home in Waldenbuch for a Sunday evening supper. Since Hans and Babs both spoke good English and Mr. and Mrs. Stein some, we got along nicely in our conversation. They lived in a very lovely house, and we had a very appetizing meal. One thing I noticed about the German houses that differs from those built in America was that the doors to all rooms fit tightly so as to preserve the heat. Also, when one room was vacated, the lights were turned off and the door was tightly closed.

June 2, 1965, found the four of us up early with a suitcase for each family, a five-gallon tank of gasoline in reserve, and a tote bag for Millie and I all packed in the VW. We each took a top (rain) coat since we probably would encounter some cool and perhaps rainy weather. Dick and Carole had planned the trip. Dick was the driver and Carole with her maps, guides, etc. sat in the front seat as copilot. Millie and I rode in the rear seat, and to our great surprise the VW was really a nice-riding car.

It was just a great trip, and we all enjoyed it immensely. The little VW never gave us a moment of trouble, and we went over all kinds of roads and mountains. Of course, sometimes we made fun of it when it appeared the little VW would slow down to a walk on a long climb, but we always made it. While Millie and I made two more trips to Europe, one in 1968 and the other in 1970, neither could compare to the enjoyment we got from traveling with Dick and Carole in the little VW. It was just one of those great moments of a lifetime.

We pulled into Goppingen early in the forenoon of June 30. We became aware there were a number of things we had to do, since Millie and I were leaving the next day, July 1, 1965, for London, England. First we had to get a hotel room for the night. After Dick and I tried a couple of small hotels without success, we did find one that had a room for us. It became noticeable to Dick and me that the innkeeper was a little suspicious when two men asked for a room, so we took Carole in with us on the third attempt, and while the lady at the desk could understand little or no English Carole could speak enough German to convince the clerk that we wanted a room for one night and that "Mother and Dad" were leaving for London early in the morning.

As we walked up the stairs to our room number all talking about our experience we were met by two young ladies who came running down the corridor saying, "You are Americans and so are we." After a visit with them we found out they were two college girls from the eastern United States who were working at the hotel for expense money while they were in Europe. We asked the girls to make it clear to the lady at the desk that our plans didn't call for all of us to sleep in the one room. They did, and since Dick and Carole had to drive us to Stuttgart to catch a 2:30 a.m. train for the Channel crossing she gave them a front-door key with which they could leave and return to the hotel in the middle of the night.

Then we drove over to Cooke Barracks where Dick purchased our train tickets for us. Carole, Millie, and I had lunch at the snack bar while Dick was arranging his affairs. He was to be shipped back to the United States in about two weeks, and he made arrangements to get Carole up to Frankfurt for her flight home as well as getting his VW shipped to the United States.

On our way back to the hotel we stopped at Dick and Carole's apartment, which had already been rented to another GI, to pick up the baggage we had left behind while traveling Europe. As we carried it all to our hotel room I wondered what the clerk thought was really going on since we sure had plenty of baggage given that Carole and Dick had all of their things to ship back home. Dick said, "Dump all of your things on the bed, then pack your suitcases with what you want to take with you. We'll get boxes for what you have left and pack it with ours to be shipped home." Of course, you don't travel Europe without accumulating a lot of knickknacks, and Millie and Carole had every available space in the VW packed with them. We had more things to send home than we could carry. I said to myself, "Boy, what a job packing all of that which was left on the bed," but Dick and Carole did it in good style. Everything got to our house without anything broken.

It was about eleven o'clock when we cleared the bed of our luggage, ready for the train. We set the alarm clock for 1:30 a.m. and got a little shuteye before it was time to go to the railroad station in Stuttgart. It was about a thirty-minute drive. It was chilly, but we didn't mind it in our emotional state. When our train backed into the Stuttgart station, Dick, Carole, and we grabbed our luggage and went searching for a car that had an empty compartment. The train was a long one, and we were in the third car from the rear.

It was rather sad leaving Dick and Carole after spending over a month with them with no travel responsibilities. However, we knew that Carole would be home before we were and that Dick's "ship," which would be carrying him to the United States, would be following our ship, the *Rotterdam*, by a few days since Dick was to sail from Bremerhaven.

As we neared Cologne, Germany, in the forenoon we began to notice that the rear cars of our train seemed rather deserted and quiet but didn't think anything of it since at each station along the Rhine River people were getting on and off. But when a trainman came through the car and said something in German and pointed to the front of the train we wondered what he was talking about. After he had viewed the vacant cars to our rear and on his return still found us sitting in our compartment, he again said "terminate" and in German said words we didn't understand. I showed him our tickets, thinking he might have thought we had missed our station, but that didn't satisfy him. It was lucky it didn't, because he finally made us understand that we had to move forward in the train since these rear coaches were being taken off the train at Koln. I took the two suitcases off the rack and Millie picked up the two tote bags, and he led us to one of the front cars that would carry us right to the Channel. We arrived about 2:30 p.m. and found our channel boat within a stone's throw, ready to be loaded with passengers from the train. We had one hour before the boat sailed so we got a lunch. At 3:30 p.m. we were on our way. The Channel was rather calm and the bright sun made it a very pleasant crossing.

There was no custom inspection upon our arrival in England. Our train to London stood on the track, waiting for its passengers. We occupied a compartment with an elderly English lady who had experienced the German bombing in World War II, a German lady who spoke good English, and two other Americans. One had worked in General Motors and knew our friends Howard and Ruth Thompson. It was a pleasant train ride. As we entered the outskirts of London, the English woman started to tell us Americans what the Nazis had done to the section of England that we were passing through. Of course, we asked questions about this and that. The discussion about the war ended by her saying, "Before it was over we gave the Germans just as much and more than they gave us." I would not have been surprised if the German lady had retaliated to some degree at least, but she kept quiet.

We arrived in London at the Victoria Station at about 7:30 p.m. and it was raining. We got a taxi. "Strand Palace Hotel, please," I said, and it wasn't more than fifteen minutes before we pulled up in front of the hotel, tired and hungry but in high spirits. We had our reservations and were given a nice room on the second floor, which made it unnecessary for us to take the lift (elevator). That we enjoyed. By the time we got settled in our room it was about 8:30 p.m. The famous Simpsons Restaurant, right across the street from the Strand Palace, closed at nine o'clock. We had heard about this famous place to dine, and we wanted to have dinner there. It is noted for being English, and where men are given the same service that women receive in the United States. So across the busy Strand we ran.

During our travels with Dick and Carole our dress had not been an issue of too much consideration; we seldom ever wore a tie and most of the time no coat. So before I left our hotel room I grabbed my coat without giving a thought to a tie. I had on a sports shirt. As we walked in the front entrance of the Simpson, the doorman asked if we had a reservation. "No," I said, "We just got here this evening." "Well, you go upstairs and they will give you a table, but you must wear a tie." "Oh," I said, "I'll have to run across the street to our hotel room and put one on. We just arrived from the continent." "No, don't do that," he said, "Right at the head of the stairs you can ask the lady at the desk for a tie." "Okay," I said, and after putting on the tie we were ushered into the dining room where the head waiter pulled out my chair and seated me, and took the very large cloth napkin and laid it across my lap while Millie had to serve herself with her chair and napkin. We were hungry, tired, and relaxed. We enjoyed our dinner very much. The men waiters with their white shirts, black bow ties, tailcoats, and large and long white aprons gave us excellent service in English style. The rain had stopped, so we walked up and down the Strand for a few blocks before retiring to our room and bed, and how we did sleep.

While in London we visited the place that all tourists and sightseers go. At the Changing of the Guard we were fortunate to be standing beside a native-born retired Londoner who explained the meaning of each routine to us. That made it much more interesting, but to think that they go through that routine every day, seven days a week and year after year seems rather useless to some of us Americans.

Dick had told me that clothing, especially shoes, were much cheaper in London than they were in the United States, so early the second morning we made our way to Regent Street where we were told we would find the very best men's clothing. After window-shopping we went into Austin Reed, where I bought a new suit and a topcoat with a take-out lining. Then I went to a shoe store to buy a nice pair of shoes at about half the price they would have cost in Detroit. Austin Reed mailed my old suit to Ferndale so that I wouldn't encounter any trouble getting through the U.S. customs.

The week in London went all too fast, but as we packed our bags in our hotel room on the day of sailing we were nevertheless glad we were going home. We did some last-minute shopping such as ties and socks, got my hair cut at half the price I would have had to pay in Ferndale, and sat around the hotel lobby until about 3:00 p.m. We then took a taxi to the Waterloo Station where there was plenty of train activity. England was still using some of the old steam engines. On the many tracks trains were coming in and leaving continually.

The *Queen Elizabeth I*, now a ship of history, was sailing at high tide early the next morning. It had two "boat trains," one leaving at 4:00 a.m. and one at 5:00 a.m. The steamship *Rotterdam* boat train was leaving at 5:30 a.m. All these trains were going to Southampton where the ships were docked, awaiting the arrival of the passengers. As our boat train pulled out of the Waterloo Station I said to myself, "Another era of my life history has ended."

It took about an hour and a half to get to Southampton. Our train circled right around onto the steamship docks, at which time we left our luggage on the curb as we got off the train. We were told the dockworkers would carry our bags on the ship right to our room, and they did. We had Room number 258 on the lower promenade deck. On the way down to Southampton the ship officials who were on the train examined our tickets, passports, etc. so that we were not detained for long after we reached the docks. The *Rotterdam* was a rather new ship built in the early fifties. It is the largest of the Holland American Line fleet and in my opinion the nicest. We again had an "alternating room," which allowed us to use first class as much as we liked except, we were assigned to eat in the tourist dining room. The two dining rooms appeared to be identical; I was told the difference was in the menu and service.

We had a beautiful crossing. There was a great variety of entertainment so there was always something to do. As it is on most ships, the food was out of this world. The 11:00 p.m. snack "horseshoe" table was so beautiful that some took pictures of it. As our ship passed Ambrose Lighthouse, marking the end of the ocean voyage, and sailed under the bridge into the Hudson River I stood on the front deck saying, "Hello, America." Some passengers who had never before been to the United States stood on deck asking, "Where is the Statue of Liberty?" I explained to them it would be a good half hour before we passed her and another half hour before we were docked. After the tugs had tucked her into the ship's slip and the crew had her safely tied, we went down to our dining room and ate our last meal aboard.

By 1:00 p.m. the baggage was off the ship and in the warehouse, and it was announced that passengers could leave the ship. Millie and I went with our tote bags down the gangplank, located the letter "W" hanging from the ceiling under which we would find our baggage, went through customs without questions, carried and loaded our baggage into our car, and by three o'clock we were going through the Holland Tunnel. As we left the tunnel on the New Jersey side that led into the New Jersey turnpike, I looked over to my left and thought as I last saw the Statue of Liberty that Dick, you're on your way home. Have a great trip. As the sun sank in the west we were on the Pennsylvania Turnpike, taking the next exit to get a motel. After eating we called Phil and told him we would be home the next night, Saturday, July 17, 1965.

It was enjoyable to turn into our drive at 250 West Maplehurst, Ferndale after having been gone eight weeks. Phil and Grandmother Burrows were there to greet us, as was Bonnie, our daughter-in-law to be. After dinner out we all gathered and relaxed and described some of our experiences. We also heard of Phil and Bonnie's plans for their wedding, set for July 30, 1965. Then there was a two-month accumulation of mail, newspapers, etc. that took hours of time to review.

Chapter 11

Retirement Years—Ferndale

There were more retirement best wishes. The Ferndale board of education agenda stated: "RESIGNATION-RETIREMENT—HAROLD B. WILCOX. Harold B. Wilcox, Director of Adult Education, will retire at the end of the current school year. His services in this school district began in September 1923 when he was employed to teach social studies at Lincoln High School. Mr. Wilcox had completed requirements for the Bachelor's Degree at Kalamazoo College and a year of graduate study at Boston University. Later he completed requirements for the master's degree at the University of Michigan.

The Adult Education Department's comprehensive program came into being under the direction and leadership of Mr. Wilcox. The appeal of its diversified program is reflected in an enrollment of approximately 5,000 persons. The program began twenty-two years ago when the Board of Education authorized arrangements for a 12 week adult education program—an experimental program. The experiment was and is most successful. Prior to his appointment to the directorship of the adult education program Mr. Wilcox had been the Department Chairman for Social Studies at Lincoln High School.

The widespread appeal of this district's adult education program is no accident but a reflection of the constant activity of Mr. Wilcox in search of ways to improve the program. He is well-known in local, state, and national adult education groups as a strong proponent for improved and expanded adult education programs."

Along with the letter from Superintendent John Houghton and a copy of the agenda, a resolution was passed by the Ferndale Board of Education:

RESOLUTION

Moved by Mr. Stevenson, supported by Mr. Morris, that the resignation-retirement of Harold B. Wilcox, Director of Adult Education, be approved and that the following resolution be adopted:

WHEREAS, Harold B. Wilcox, Director of Adult Education, will retire at the conclusion of the 1964-1965 school year; and

WHEREAS, Mr. Wilcox has served this school district with distinction since September 1923 when he was first employed; and

WHEREAS, Mr. Wilcox has rendered outstanding services to this school district as a classroom teacher, as a department chairman for social studies at Lincoln High School (now Ferndale High School); and

WHEREAS, the teaching performance of Mr. Wilcox, his participation in community activities, and other fine qualifications resulted in his appointment to the directorship of adult education, a fledgling program at the time of his appointment; and

WHEREAS, under his dynamic leadership, personal involvement in the adult education movement at all levels (local, state, and national, in the capacity of either rank and file member or officer), constant attention to the development of a program designed to meet all kinds of public interest, constant re-evaluation of the program, continuous search for improvement in program, dedication to an ever increasing outreach of the program, the original experiment in adult education has become an established program of pleasing dimensions retaining, nevertheless, its original interest in experimental programs designed to meet the needs of adults; and

WHEREAS, this district is well pleased with the many fine contributions of Harold B. Wilcox, to this district as a classroom teacher, community leader, and director of adult education throughout these many years;

NOW THEREFORE BE IT RESOLVED, that in the retirement of Harold B. Wilcox, the Board of Education herewith officially states the above in recognition of his fine services, and wishes him many, many pleasant years of retirement; and

BE IT FURTHER RESOLVED, that this resolution be recorded in the minutes of the Board of Education, and a copy be sent to Harold B. Wilcox.

Yeas: All. Nays: None. Motion carried.
Dated: May 19, 1965
By_____
President   Secretary

After we had re acclimated ourselves to American living at 250 West Maplehurst, my first big job was to go to my office at the high school and prepare to vacate my desk, etc. I spent hours going through my files, making decisions on what the new director could use and what to discard. Much of my personal activity had been centered in my office, and the files contained such things as letters, programs, clippings, etc. covering forty-two years of education, religion, and civic life in Ferndale. I just took my time, informing Dorothy Kosovac by phone that I would be ready to turn over the desk and office to her in a few days.

The big event of Phil's and Bonnie's wedding was only days off. While the major activity of a church wedding was the responsibility of the bride's parents, nevertheless Millie and I had to arrange for some procedures that are always the groom's parents' obligations. The wedding was to be on July 30, 1965 at the Ferndale Methodist Church with Rev. John Parrish, our minister, performing the ceremony. The rehearsal dinner was scheduled for Devens Gables, a very nice restaurant about ten miles northwest of Ferndale. Millie had to shop for a new dress and all the trimmings that go with it, and Dad decided he had better break down and buy a new suit.

One of the most pleasant knocks on our door came on the morning of July 20, 1965. It was just 8:00 a.m. and Millie and I were ready to climb out of bed when the doorbell rang and there was what seemed to us a "hurry-up" knock on the screen door. I said to Millie, "Now, who on earth can that be so early in the morning?" I opened the hall door so as to see who it might be through the front-door French window, and lo and behold I saw a young man wearing a military uniform. I said to Millie, "It's Dick!" and ran to the door. Were we glad to see him! We had not expected him for two or three days, but Dick explained to us that his "super-duper, luxury ocean tub" got across okay and that he was lucky in that the ship that carried his VW across the ocean had unloaded it that late afternoon. He was just about ready to give up and be reconciled to the fact he would have to find a bed to sleep in some place around New York when up came the red VW. It didn't take him long to get the car clearance, and before dark he was on the New Jersey Turnpike headed for Michigan. He was determined to reach Ferndale as soon as possible. His high spirits and anxiety were greater than his desire for sleep, so he drove all night. After getting a good night's rest, Dick continued on across the state to Niles where Carole was waiting with outstretched arms. Dick's military life was a thing of history.

As most all weddings are, Phil and Bonnie's wedding was a beautiful one. There was a reception at the church and then a few close friends along with Bonnie's parents and family gathered at our house for refreshments and a fond farewell to the newlyweds, with best wishes for a happy and prosperous future. When Phil and Bonnie returned from their honeymoon they had a furnished house that they had rented. The owner was going to be away for several months and was pleased that they would live in their home while they were away.

When the end of Dick's military service was near and he was soon to be shipped back to the States in July 1965, the first question on his mind was, "Where are Carole and I going to settle?" In the spring I wrote Dick and Carole that Kalamazoo, which I was probably partial to as a Kalamazoo College graduate, would be a good city to consider. It had fine industries, including paper mills that even during the Great Depression didn't suffer financially as much as most industrial companies. It is a city of culture with two higher education institutions—Western Michigan University and Kalamazoo College. Thus they decided that Kalamazoo would be their home.

After a few days Millie and I met Dick and Carole in Kalamazoo, and by appointment we visited Harold B. Allen, a college friend of mine who was secretary to the Upjohn Pharmaceutical Company. He gave them some good pointers regarding to employment conditions in the field of accounting, which is Dick's working interest. While in Germany Carole had also applied for a teaching job in the Kalamazoo public schools and had received a verbal agreement that when she got back from Germany she would be interviewed and under normal circumstances would be given a contract. So it was settled in their minds that Kalamazoo, Michigan, was to become their new home. They found an upstairs apartment on a residential street a short walk from Carole's school. Dick accepted an offer for a job in the accounting department of one of the paper mills in Kalamazoo.

With no job responsibilities myself, Dick and Carole located in Kalamazoo, Phil and Bonnie nicely housed near her school teaching job, there was nothing more for Millie and me to do but to take off for the golden state of Montana, a trip we had been taking each August for several years. Before we left for Europe I had assured Superintendent John Houghton that I would make myself available to Dorothy Kosavac, the new director, during the launching of the fall term of the adult education program, but that did not make it necessary for me to be back in Ferndale the week before Labor Day as I previously had to do. This allowed Millie and me to take a more leisurely trip.

We had our usual great trip and visit to Montana. I presume some of our friends got tired of hearing us relate some of our European experiences, but they were patient and seemed to enjoy the tales of Europe. In Wisconsin we got off the main highway and paid a visit to the city of Baraboo, a city that used to be the winter quarters of several circuses. It is today the circus museum city.

On our return home I went to the adult education office and turned over the keys to the new director, which opened all rooms in the building and operated the elevator. Dorothy Barte, my secretary for nearly thirteen years, was very well acquainted with the procedures involving the opening of a term of adult classes. The whole adult evening school was as different from day school as night is from day. The director of the adult program was literally a one-man show. He or she had to build the schedule of courses that he or she thought the public would be interested in. The fees were largely determined by the amount of money needed to run the program since it had to be pretty much self-supporting. This was especially true until the state legislature changed the law to enable all people, regardless of age, who didn't have a high school diploma to be counted in the total school enrollment of the school district. The old slogan "It pays to advertise" also had to be a part of the philosophy of any adult director. Brochures listing the schedule of courses were printed and mailed to all residences of the school district, as well as to former students who didn't live in the Ferndale district.

Instructors had to be found from all walks of life, and they were only under a verbal contract for the term. It was a real job launching a term of adult classes. I would spend many hours in the afternoon and evening working in the adult education office during the last weeks in August and September before the opening of classes. The Ferndale Public Library employees were always cooperative during registration, taking registrations all during the enrollment period.

The last Thursday evening in September 1965 found me in the adult education office for the last time. People would remark, "I thought you had retired." My reply was, "I am just helping out this first week of classes." I realized, "This is it." As I left the school building about 10:00 p.m. I had a feeling of loneliness. It really hit me that I was an unemployed man for the first time in my life. I had no job. My life's work was finished. I had plenty of time to prepare for retirement since I knew what the school board policy was and still is, but I was in good health, energetic, and just not ready to divorce myself from the working man's life.

I think one reason that women live longer than men do is that they never retire. As the family matures, the responsibilities diminish; the workload becomes lighter, and women just naturally slow down to a pace that fits their physical self. A man is supposed to work at a full-time job that knows no age differences until the clock and calendar says you are finished; go home and sit in a rocking chair and watch TV or find something to amuse yourself. I said, "I'm going to become a member of two bowling leagues, follow high school and college sports, and enjoy myself." But that just wasn't what I would be content doing, and I knew it. I had told Dorothy Barte that I was going to find another job that had little or no tension with shorter hours.

It was the first week in October 1965 that my phone rang one morning with the voice of George Higgins of Higgins Pontiac on the other end, "Harold," he said, "I want to give you a job. You'll live longer if you have something to do." "Thanks, George," I said, "But I am just retired, and I would like a few weeks to see what it is like." "OK," George said, "But when you get ready come over to see me." The Higgins Pontiac salesroom was located on Woodward Avenue in Ferndale, just one block from our house, and would be very convenient. So I took life easy around the house, helped Millie get her materials ready for the jewelry and enameling classes that she taught Monday and Wednesday nights, bowled Monday and Wednesday mornings in two retiree leagues, and just rested.

Our house was a one-and-a-half-story frame that we had lived in since 1935. I kept it painted inside and out, but as the years went by I realized the time would come when I would no longer be physically able to climb the ladders and brush paint. In the back of my mind I began to understand that the upkeep of our house would someday be a problem. I had watched my parents' house in Gobles, in which they lived fifty years and where I was born, deteriorate year by year. I had gone home weekends and fixed this and that. One summer I painted three sides in one long weekend, hoping that Lee and Al in Kalamazoo could finish the job.

I had become discontent with my retired life. One of my retired Ferndale teacher friends who was a few years older than I told me, "Harold, the first year of retirement nearly drives you crazy, then you sort of fall into a pattern of idleness and it's not so bad." I had gone to Kalamazoo College homecoming that fall. I met one of my old college friends who were a couple of years ahead of me. He had just retired from the position of secretary of the Upjohn Corporation. I asked, "How do you like retirement?" "Well, I'll tell you, Harold, old age and retirement are all right, but I'll take youth any time." That expressed my feelings. I couldn't help but remember the many, many times when things on the job were not going well. There was tension, I couldn't sleep nights, and I would start counting the years before I would be retired. Now that I had reached that stage in life, I saw the many horizons we all picture in life; that the grass is not always greener on the other side, that life goes on and there is no turning back. If one lives long enough he retires in some form or other. That had to be my philosophy of life.

For the past several weeks I had been thinking about what kind of employment I would enjoy. The high school secretary to the principal told me before I left, "Harold, we need substitute teachers, so if and when you feel like working give me a call, we can use you." I didn't feel that I wanted to go into the classroom again as a substitute; I felt that I would be more content if I had a change of job atmosphere.

It was about the second week in November 1965 that I called George Higgins and said, "I want to talk with you." As I walked over to George Higgins's office I was wondering what kind of a job he had in mind for me and just how much he would expect of me in regard to clock hours and work week, etc. After the usual greeting I said, "Well, George, I guess I would enjoy some work. What do you have in mind for me to do?" "Well," he said, "I need a 'write-up' man that would be too long hours for you and would give you some pressure, which you don't want, so that one is out. How about working in the parts department? You can answer the phone, sell parts, let people pay you for the work done on their cars and sit at the desk when there aren't things for you to do. You can go to work at 9:00 a.m. and stay until 5:00 p.m. with an hour off for lunch."

This sounded pretty good to me because I knew I could get a lot of free work done on my Pontiac, but at the same time I questioned the fact that I would be pretty much tied down five days a week. That wouldn't be too bad in winter, so I said to myself, "We'll play it day by day." I was taken down to the service department by the service manager Gary Duncan and introduced to "Skip," the parts manager. Gary told him I was going to be a helper. I had been around Higgins Pontiac enough during the past number of years to get to know most of the mechanics and other long-time employees, so I wasn't in strange territory. But it didn't take me long to realize that what George Higgins had in mind for me didn't coincide with the parts manager, who was a young, energetic man. One day when Gary Duncan came into the parts department, I was sitting on a high stool. After he left Skip said to me, "That man who was in here is in charge of service, and don't let him see you sitting around. Look busy doing something." I said, "I know him well, and Higgins doesn't expect me to be on my feet all the time, and furthermore I couldn't stand it physically standing on my feet all day." "Why not?" he asked? It was very evident that being a young man he just couldn't understand what old age was like. I didn't argue with him, I just kept sitting, but after a couple of weeks I knew that working in parts just wasn't up my alley.

Michigan State University had a great football team in fall 1965, and as the season progressed it became more evident that they would be the Big Ten champions and would go to the Rose Bowl. I had always dreamed of going to California for the Tournament of Roses parade and seeing the Rose Bowl football game, and it appeared now that my dream could come true with a Michigan team playing against the Pacific Coast champions U.C.L.A. I told Millie, "This is our year." I began to inquire around how I could get two tickets for the game. I was told by M.S.U. ticket office that their allotment of tickets had already been sold to alumni, students, and friends. I wrote to John and Kathleen Zola, Millie's cousins, who live in Arcadia, California, asking if they could get me tickets. Her reply was that the tickets were all in the hands of transportation companies. She gave me the name of a contact. I wrote and found I could get a package deal that included hotel pickup, lunch, grand stand seats for the Tournament of Roses parade, bus to the Rose Bowl with a ticket, and bus back to the hotel, all for forty-three dollars. I sent them a check for eighty-six dollars and told them the hotel at which they were to pick us up, since Kathleen finally found us a hotel room, for which we were very grateful.

After about two weeks in the parts department, I told Mr. Higgins, "This is no job for me. The fellows expect me to learn enough to sell all the parts of an automobile. I am not a mechanic, never have been, and never could be because I am just not interested. I can dole out the spark plugs, points, and a few simple parts like that, but that is as far as I can go. Also, I am going to California right after Christmas for a few weeks, so that is it." "Well," said George. "It's only three weeks until Christmas. Stick it out, and then when you get back from California we'll find something else for you to do." "OK," I said, and for the next three weeks I just put in my time doing the jobs I could do and paying no attention to the other two men in the department. The Higgins Pontiac Company always gave every employee a turkey for Christmas. When the station wagon came into the service garage, the call came out. "Come and get your turkey." I asked Gary Duncan, "Do I get one?" "Sure," he said, "Help yourself." I put the turkey in my car and drove home, glad that I was finished with the service department.

Christmas was a great day for all of us. We had both our sons and daughters-in-law home. Mother Burrows would stay in our house while we were in California to look after things.

The day after Christmas found us packing, taking down decorations, and preparing for four weeks in California. On December 27, 1965, Millie and I were aboard the 11:30 a.m. train that left Detroit for Chicago. I had told my brother Lee, who worked the baggage department in Kalamazoo that we would be on the train and for him to look for us. He did, and as the train was pulling out, we exchanged hello and goodbye. Arriving in Chicago about 4:00 p.m, we had two hours before we got aboard the City of Los Angeles. We got a taxi to the Union Pacific Station where we ate our dinner and waited for train time.

When the call over the PA system announced, "The City of Los Angeles is loading," we wheeled our baggage down the track to our train and looked for our car number. It was the longest train in the world. Being a Rose Bowl special, the train had twenty-five sleepers and five engines. The day coach section followed our train and carried hundreds of passengers, most of whom were Rose Bowl bound. It was a delightful train ride, taking about forty hours. During the daylight hours we mainly sat in the dome car nearest to our part of the train for there were three Dome cars. It was very interesting to see the scenery and watch those five engines snake that long train through the mountains.

When we arrived on the afternoon of the third day, our train was so long that they had to split it and run it into the station on two tracks. My sister Donita and her family Bub, Sharon, and Vaughn were all waiting for us. Donita said, "What took you so long to get into the station?" We told them about our long train and the reason we were about twenty minutes late. It was a delightful, warm, sunny day, quite a contrast to the weather we left behind in Michigan. Donita and Bub gave us that good California hospitality. Sharon gave us her room, and Vaughn kept us in good music with the hundreds of records given to him for his radio show. The afternoon of December 31, 1965, was spent sightseeing, with Bub doing the driving. We ended up at our hotel room where we were to stay overnight and were to be picked up in the morning at 6:30 a.m. It was about eleven when we turned out the lights, with our alarm set for 5:15 a.m.

There was an open-all-night restaurant about two blocks from our hotel room, and at 5:30 a.m. we were eating our breakfast, preparing for that day of dreams. Our grandstand seats were located right at the starting line of the parade, and when the eight o'clock starting time arrived we were in our seats. It was a beautiful thrill. The parade lasted about two hours, after which we wandered over to the place where the driver had told us we would find our bus.

When the bus was about loaded, he proceeded to hand out the box lunches that our forty-three dollars included. What a lunch: two skinny pieces of fried chicken, a stale cupcake, and an apple with a bottle of pop to wash it down. The bus took us to the Rose Bowl. The driver asked, "Where can I park in the lot for buses so that you can identify my bus?" To me that was the sixty-four-dollar question since buses were buses to me. "Well," he said, "I'll be standing out in front of the line of buses in which ours is located. Take a good look at me." We did, but??? The bowl game was a great disappointment for all of us Michigan people. Michigan State University, undefeated and one tied game with undefeated Notre Dame, was doped to be a rather easy winner. But as the game wore on and U.C.L.A. had a 14-0 lead at the half, it was evident that our Michigan team had better settle down and play football. Well, Coach Duffy didn't get the team moving and waited until the fourth quarter before he began to use his bench. State scored two touchdowns and went for two points after each touchdown and failed twice. The game ended: U.C.L.A. 14, Michigan State 12. It was the upset of the year and to me, being a great sports fan, it was a disaster.

Millie and I finally got over to the bus parking lot and walked up and down the front lines of parked buses. Some lines had as many as a dozen buses lined up bumper to bumper. It was getting dark. There were crowds of people looking for their buses. After we had walked rather slowly from one end of the line of buses to the other, I was about to say to Millie, "I give up," when a hand grabbed my shoulder and a voice said, "Our bus is the sixth one down this line." It was dark and an hour later before enough of the dozens of buses had pulled out so ours was able to take us back to our hotel loading point.

Bub and Donita were to pick us up at about 7:30 p.m. at our hotel. We waited and waited, and it was after eight o'clock when they arrived. Vaughn had been able to get two tickets for the game through the radio station. Their car was tied up in heavy traffic, and they were late in getting to our hotel. It was after nine o'clock that evening when we sat down to a nice dinner that Donita had prepared before going to the game. We were all tired, but it was a great day. Another dream of mine had come true.

After staying a few days longer at the Filkins, Millie's sister Flora and her husband Ted Uhlig, we loaded our baggage into their car. We spent a very pleasant week with them and their family.

The time always arrives when it's time to go home. Ted and Flo drove us to the depot, where we met Donita. We all had a good lunch together at the station before getting aboard the City of Los Angeles bound for Chicago. It was a very pleasant trip home.

We had written Dick and Carole that we would be coming through Kalamazoo on an afternoon train. When we arrived at Kalamazoo we were all ready to step down from the car, and sure enough, Dick and Carole were there to say hello. It was cold, quite a contrast to sunny California.

Phil and Bonnie met us at the depot in Detroit. We had a good dinner together. Were we glad to get back to 250 West Maplehurst, Ferndale, Michigan! I'll say so!

After a couple of days of acclimation, I began to consider my work status. I certainly didn't want a full-time job. I knew positively that I didn't want any more automobile service work. The Social Security law didn't allow a retiree to earn more than one hundred and twenty-five dollars a month without losing a percentage of the Social Security payment, so I reasoned, "Why should I work for the government?"

One afternoon I drove to Pontiac to visit Judge Art Moore, probate judge in Oakland County. I had known Judge Moore for a number of years, and when he saw me enter his court during a trial it wasn't too long before he recessed the trial and came down off the bench to shake hands. "Come into my office," Art said. We had a brief visit, and I told him I was looking for a part-time job. Would the probate court have anything that I could help with? He referred me to the judge in Royal Oak and said he would talk to him about my desire. Several days later I got a phone call from the Royal Oak judge. After a brief conversation I could see that what he had in mind for me just wouldn't be to my liking.

For several days I analyzed the situation. I didn't really have to have a job, financially speaking, yet I needed something to do. I really felt that George Higgins was right when he said to me, "If you have a job you'll live longer." Taking a job as a part-time salesman didn't appeal to me because I knew that full-time salesmen were out to make all the money they could and I would get little consideration as a part-time employee.

After a week of consideration I had made up my mind I should be fair to Mr. Higgins. I would go to his office and lay the cards on the table that I just wasn't cut out for the automobile business and that we should both forget about the whole thing, and that I greatly appreciated what he was trying to do for me. So early afternoon a couple of days later I got on the phone and called Higgins Pontiac, asking for Mr. Higgins. Almost immediately George was on the phone. Before I could say too much he said, "Come on over to my office, I want to talk with you." It was only a good block from our house to his office. On the way over I slowly walked and thought, "Just how will I say what I want to say and do it with a voice of appreciation and confidence?"

Being the aggressive businessman that he is, George didn't give me a chance to get in the first word. He began to tell me of his immediate plans to expand his used-car sales office and lot. He said answering the phone, keeping the records of the used cars on hand, etc. was the job that he had for me. He also had two good fellows over there to work with, Nix and Mel. I told him I didn't want any pressure nor set hours of work. He said there would not be any. I could set my own hours, come and go as I pleased. He had purchased the gas station on the corner of Woodward opposite the used-car lot and he was going to build a new used-car lot and a new office. It was going to be a very pleasant setup for all of us. "Let me take you over and introduce you to Nix, the manager of the used cars," he said. Well, with no alternative and the proposition of nice surroundings, I could only say, "OK. It sounds good to me." We climbed in his car and in three minutes we were at the used-car lot. It was on Woodward Avenue only about four blocks from the new-car salesroom, so it was very handy for me. We walked into the old, small office for used cars that only had room for three small desks. George said, "Nix, this is Harold Wilcox, who is to be the third party in this office. He will be part time only and will come and go as he pleases." I shook hands with Nix and Mel Mulcaster, whom I had known for years. I had had his wife in my classes in the late 1920's and his two daughters in the late 1940's. Mel Mulcaster had been with the Higgins Pontiac for a good thirty years, and was the one man in a thousand who would do a job on a used-car lot as though he owned it. Nix was an easygoing man, easy to get along with, who had also spent the greater part of his working life in the used-car business.

As I walked home, it being agreed I would start February 1, 1966, I said to myself, "I have a job that I do believe fits what I am looking for." I walked into our house and said, "Millie, I am a used-car salesman." Then I explained the setup to her and I said, "I do believe it will work to our advantage. I could continue bowling in the teachers' league at 4:00 p.m. on Thursdays, could retain my membership in the Service Club golf league, would be able to attend all functions such as the Retired Teachers Association Luncheon and program, the Exchange Club luncheon on each Tuesday noon, etc. Then too there would be certain fringe benefits that would be available to me." I was really satisfied with the deal.

We got some really cold weather in February and one needed a heavy coat and gloves to show cars, for I did want to do some selling. I'll always remember the first sale I made on the used-car lot. I had shown a 1964 convertible to a young man just discharged from government military service. He was working in the automobile parts business right on the corner of Woodward and West Maplehurst. One cold day about the middle of February he came on the lot, walked into the office, and said to me, "Do you want to sell that 1964 convertible you showed me?" I said in half amazement, "Sure." We walked out on the lot, started the engine, then came back into the office and Nix helped me write up my first deal.

As the 1965-66 basketball seasons wore on, it was very evident that Roy Burkhart had turned out another great basketball team. When the state tournament games started the first week in March the only team to have beaten Ferndale was East Detroit, which was undefeated for the season and was ranked the number-one team in the state. They had a tall boy about 6' 10" who jumped center, and an All-State guard who was an accurate basket shooter, making about 50 percent of his shots. Ferndale had two guards, one black and one white, whom Burkhart said he wouldn't trade for any two guards in the state. They were both fast, over six feet tall, and good ball handlers and accurate shooters. As the tournament games continued it became more and more evident that Ferndale and East Detroit could meet each other in the semi-finals being played in the M.S.U. field house. The Ferndale team had a sincere and dedicated group of boys. There were two religious leaders, one black and the center, a white boy, who had asked the coach if they could hold a little prayer meeting in the dressing room by themselves before and after each game. Burkhart said he had no objections.

Time after time during the season it would look like these boys were doomed to inevitable defeat, but they never gave up and their superb physical condition gave them an advantage in the fourth quarter of play. So we were at East Lansing on that Friday night of the semi-finals. East Detroit led nearly the whole game by as much as ten points, but during the third quarter Ferndale began to close the gap. When the horn sounded the end of the game, Ferndale had pulled off the biggest upset of the basketball season, winning by one point in the last seconds of play. The next evening, Ferndale beat Ann Arbor High School in overtime for its second state championship in four years.

I had been going to the state basketball tournaments semi-final and finals for a number of years. After the boys were old enough to leave home, Millie and I made the tournament games our "spring tonic." Each November I would reserve a motel in East Lansing for the Friday and Saturday nights of the tournament, which occurred on the last weekend in March. We would leave Ferndale about 2:30 p.m. on Friday, take a leisurely drive to East Lansing of about one-and-a-half hours, get our motel, go to the Michigan State Union Cafeteria for a nice dinner, and be in our seats for the first of two Class A semi-final games starting at seven o'clock. After a nice breakfast in the Kellogg Center dining room Saturday morning, we would take in all four games for the state championship. The Class B games started at 11:30 a.m. Class C and D followed in the afternoon. At eight o'clock the twelve thousand fans would be in their seats for the final Class A Championship game. Sunday morning we would again have a nice breakfast in the Kellogg Center dining room, then head the car for home, arriving around 1:00 p.m. To me it was always the climax to a great season of football and basketball, and was the signal that the final ten weeks of the school year was about here. Now it was the spring of 1966, and Ferndale High was state champion for the second time in four years.

I was in retirement working for Higgins Pontiac. I was still bowling and golfing, but I could see that my sports skills were not as keen as they were a few years previously. I said to myself, "What's next, or is this the end of the exciting part of life?" One day in May 1966 my phone rang. It was my old friend Bess Tewskbury on the line. She had taught oil painting in the adult education program since its beginning. For years she had also been the president of the Ferndale Public Library board. "Harold," she said, "We have a vacancy on the board and I would like your consent to submit your name to Mayor Bruce Garbutt as a candidate to fill the vacancy." The library board is one of authority by city ordinance. The board appoints the librarian and the working personnel as well as making out and submitting the yearly budget to the city commission. I said, "OK, Bess, I will serve if appointed." It wasn't too long before I got a letter from the mayor stating that he had appointed me to the library board and that I should call at the city clerk's office to be sworn in and get my identification card. I did just that.

As we got into May I was learning more and more about used-car sales. I had also asked George Higgins if he would be able to get me an official's car before July 15 because we were planning on going to Montana again for about five weeks. "Sure, I'll get you a car," he said, "and it won't have more than four thousand miles on it. What kind of car do you have in mind? What color do you want?" One of the new car salesmen had just gotten an official's car. It was dark red, a four-door Catalina sedan with air conditioning, etc., so I said to Mr. Higgins, "If you could get me a car just like the one that salesman has I would be very happy." "Okay," he said, "I'll get you a car." Now, when George Higgins said he would do something for you, you could rest assured it would be done if at all possible.

At our May library board meeting we began to talk about the National Conference of Librarians and Trustees to be held in New York City in July. It was noted that the library budget allowed the expense account for each trustee who could attend, and I was encouraged to go. I talked it over with Millie, and we decided we could afford her expense account and that we would drive our car to save travel expenses. The conference was held in one of the nicer hotels in New York City, and we had a very pleasant time. I learned a great deal about public libraries as well. Our last day in New York the All Star game was being played. Of course, I was glued to the TV in our hotel room until it was finally won in extra innings—National League beat American League 2-1 in ten innings. I had also read in the New York newspaper that the *Rotterdam* was due into New York at four o'clock and an hour later the *Queen Elizabeth* would follow her up the Hudson River. Just as soon as the ball game was over Millie and I took a taxi to Pier 40 where the *Rotterdam* was docking. As I stood on the upper deck of Pier 40 I could not help but say to myself, "A year ago, Millie and I were on her, getting ready to disembark." As we looked over toward the Statue of Liberty we saw the *Queen Elizabeth* slowly making its way up the Hudson River to its berth, which was located about a mile up the river from Pier 40. I have always enjoyed boating, large and small, and to again see these big ships come into New York was a thrill. At the time I didn't realize that the *Queen Elizabeth* was making one of its last season's runs and that the beautiful *Rotterdam* would soon be transferred to a cruise ship and no longer be on the North Trans-Atlantic run. The old era of steamship travel between the United States and Europe was on its way out because the airplane was taking over as the means of getting to and from Europe. As of this writing (1973) there are only two steamships that provide crossing to Europe, and for only nine months of the year: the *France* and the *Queen Elizabeth II*.

George Higgins told me to go ahead and sell my car and drive one off the lot until he got mine from the factory. As the date approached our leaving for Montana and I didn't have a car, Mr. Higgins assured me that he would have a car for me to drive to Montana. Two days before our scheduled departure George called me at the used-car office and said, "I have a car for you to drive to Montana. Come and get it. The keys are in Gary Duncan's office." I walked over from the used-car office and Gary took me across the street, where a 1966 white, four-door Catalina stood. He handed me the keys and said, "This is the car George told me to give you. It had five thousand miles on it." I said later to Mr. Higgins, "Do you realize that before I get back there will be close to another five thousand miles on the car?" "That's all right. I want you to drive a 1966 and this is the one for you." Boy, was I elated.

Leaving Ferndale rather early, having breakfast in route, we stopped at Dick and Carole's in Kalamazoo to say hello and goodbye. We had a grand trip and enjoyed the five weeks that we were away from Ferndale.

In fall 1966 came the football season, which as always was an enjoyable one and centered my attention. Leaves fell and had to be raked, and we knew that winter was not too far off.

My new car, exactly what I had asked for, was delivered to me in September, and I was pleased to be able to drive a new car with about four thousand miles on it and call it ours.

The slow season in the used-car business is December, January, and February, so I told Mr. Higgins I thought it a good time to spend a few weeks in Florida. "OK," he said, "Let me know when you're leaving and about when you expect to be back."

We were again pleased to have all of our family of six together for Christmas. Between Christmas and New Year's we started packing and getting the house readied to leave for a few weeks. Aside from our convention in Miami, this would be our first stay in Florida. Millie had had a lady in her jewelry class who owned a very nice winter home in Marathon on the Keys. She had passed away a few weeks previously, and her husband said, "Go down and live in the house at Marathon for a couple of weeks." So that was to be our first location to head for. The day after the big football bowl games, January 1, 1967, we left Ferndale and headed for Florida. After two weeks at Marathon, during which time we visited Key West and other points of interest, we headed for Daytona Beach where our friends Howard and Ruth Thompson had their winter home. Their house is at 111 Van Avenue running west off South Atlantic Avenue on the peninsula. We stayed two weeks at the Caribbean Motel located about one-half mile north of Van Avenue, right on the ocean. We fell in love with the "world's most famous beach," and decided that the following winter would find us on South Atlantic not too far from Van Avenue. There was a new motel, the Nomad, being built at 3101 South Atlantic, right at the head of Van Avenue, and before we left for home we inquired as to its availability for 1968. We were told that it would be ready for occupancy.

We got to Ferndale in February right after a big snowstorm. Our driveway at 250 West Maplehurst was impassable. I called Phil's house and he came over to help me shovel it out so that we could drive the car into garage. Returning to Ferndale in such cold and snowy weather made us realize that next winter we should stay in Florida for a much-longer period of time.

I continued my work at the used-car office, bowled in the teachers' league, and attended basketball games. The last of March found us again in a motel at East Lansing that I had reserved in November to watch the state basketball tournament games.

As the weeks went by I had housework to keep me busy in my spare time. I also went to see some of the Detroit Tigers baseball games, being the avid sports fan that I am.

Then too I read in the newspaper that what inevitably would happen someday had after forty-six years became a reality.

"A John Wismer of Kalamazoo College had set a new school record of 9:37:4 in the two-mile run. The former record had been 9:57:3 held by Harold B. Wilcox set in 1921 at the State Collegiate meet held at M.A.C. (now M.S.U.)"

I wrote John a letter of congratulations and expressed to that I felt it was a disgrace for Kalamazoo College to have a record on the books for forty-six years; that I was pleased he had set a new record.

John wrote me a really nice letter stating, "I was extremely surprised and gratified to receive your letter of congratulations. Now, like in the days when you ran for "K" College, I imagine that track, cross-country, and distance running is an expression of one's self through the nothingness of encouragement, congratulations and appreciation. For this reason, that running hardly even attracts any attention, I am especially pleased to hear your congratulations. It is a voice in the wilderness, but a warm friendly voice that will long be remembered and appreciated...

Once again, thank you very much for your letter, and I hope that I can bring that athletic honor to Kalamazoo College as you did in your college days as well as becoming such a successful and wonderful person. Thank you. Sincerely, John Wismer."

May I add that John was running for "K" College when its track fortunes were at its very lowest ebb.

During my four years at "K" College (1918-1922), our track team won the M.I.A.A. track and field meets during each of my four years. We never lost a dual meet during those four years. Kalamazoo was rated third place in the state behind the University of Michigan and Michigan Aggie College (now M.S.U.) Kalamazoo was rated third place in the state. How much greater pleasure and satisfaction we had during those four years than did John during his track experience. But I couldn't help but be reminded that if we had had the tracks to run on that the 1960's provided, we would have made much better times than we did back in the 1920's.

It was early in May 1967 at the library board meeting that one of the items discussed was the National Library Conference in San Francisco in June. The library budget included conference expenses for all directors who could attend the conference. Chet Nelson and I decided we could make the trip. The other man on the board, Larry Mead, an attorney, said he wouldn't be able to go, so it was decided that the three women, including the librarian Enid DeTar, Bess Tewksbury, and Janet Grow, would also attend the conference. Enid asked, "What hotel shall we house in and how many reservations shall I make?" When Enid read off the list of conference hotels available, I spotted the Palace, in which we had held the adult education conference a year and a half previously, so I recommended it to the members of the board, who approved the Palace.

We flew from Detroit and arrived in San Francisco about three o'clock, took a taxi to the hotel, and settled in a room on the same floor that Millie and I had occupied less than two years previously. It was a very worthwhile conference, and mixed in with the library duties we enjoyed the sights of San Francisco. Of course, we had to ride the famous trolley car again, take a boat trip around the bay and observe the famous island for the convicted criminals, Alcatraz prison, and other recommended tours.

After conference duties were terminated, Millie and I took the train down to Los Angeles where we spent several days visiting both Millie's and my relatives. Then we boarded the train for a nice thirty-six hour ride to Chicago and then on to Detroit. Little did we realize at the time that this was our last long train ride in the United States because passenger travel was being discontinued at a rapid pace. At Kalamazoo Dick and Carole were at the station to say hello. Phil and Bonnie met us at the depot in Detroit. As usual, it was good to be home again.

Another very interesting event took place the week of July 30-August 5, 1967, when my hometown of Gobles had its centennial celebration for 1867-1967. The ninety pages of the centennial booklet gave a history of Gobles and pictured many of the leading citizens who had put the "go" in Gobles. While I had thought a great deal about the part my parents had played in the centennial history since they were born, reared, lived and died there, I was never conscious of what others thought of my parents until I read page forty-five of this centennial booklet, which was dedicated to my dad's and mother's place in the life of Gobles. At the top of the page was "A. M. Wilcox" in bold type, then in fine print, "Oh for the good old days when a shave and a haircut were two bits." The upper right-hand corner had the picture of "This token sold at 3/25 cents. They were good for one shave each at Tink's Shop." My dad was known to everyone as "Tink" because from the time he was a little boy he was always tinkering with something. While waiting for customers he would sit at his little workbench in the rear of the barbershop and repair watches, clocks, etc. that people would bring in.

In the upper half of page forty-five was a picture of Dad and his sister Mildred, each shaving a customer. The caption read, "In this brother and sister team, Tink and Mildred Holland barbered side by side." As of this date March 26, 1973, Mildred Holland is still living in her nineties (life span:1879-1983). Following was a six hundred word story of the civic and business contributions of Tink and Susan Wilcox:

One of our fair villages' most fun loving characters was Allen M. Wilcox, better known as "Tink". He and his wife Susan were both born and raised in Gobleville. Susan was a daughter of the Browns after whom the Brown school was named. Both attended the early day Gobleville School and the Methodist Church.

Tink grew tired of his employment in the old basket factory located just east of the old gristmill. He was a bachelor, footloose and fancy-free at the time. He was keen on circus life and so he went to Baraboo, Wisconsin, the winter quarters of several circuses. His idea was to make his cast-iron lip earn him a living on the trumpet. He realized his dream and spent several years enjoying it. Probably Sousa's band was the greatest one with which he played.

Eventually Susan won the day. Tink returned to become a married man. They settled down in the house (410 E. Exchange St.) that was to be their home for the following fifty years.

One must work for a living and Tink made barbering his life trade. He made his first shop in the old peaked roof grandstand. It stood somewhere near the old town hall. This was early in the 1900's. His old shop building was later moved to his residence to be used as a garage. It may still be recognized there by its odd shaped roof. Mrs. Rose Stech now owns that property. In 1910 Tink had built the shop which still bears "A.M. Wilcox 1910" above part of the front. It stands across the street from the pharmacy and is now a dress shop.

The Gobles music program and Tink were synonymous. He organized the band and directed it for weekly night concerts, during the summer for ball games, for Memorial Day marches to the cemetery and for the July 4th celebrations at South Haven.

The Wilcox Band obtained new uniforms in 1907.

Tink not only managed the band but an orchestra which furnished the music for shows, dances, and commencement exercises held in the 1902 Opera House. These events revive memories of such Gobles leaders as the Reddings, the Reigles, Bert Travis, the Albert Waucheks, Bill and Phil Miller, Herb Wood, Bill Davis, the Myers brothers, Orley Graham, Frank Freedman, and many, many more.

Tink did his share in public office as township treasurer and a member of the school board.

Allen Monroe's Stanley Steamer was his pride. Another of his interests was steam boating on Lake Mill. His first launch the Monroe burned. Undaunted he invested in a second steam boat called the Cupid. It was one of the villagers' most enjoyable outings to take a trip on it around Lake Mill for a paltry sum. Later the Cupid sank when the ice went out of Lake Mill. It may still be seen in company with many virgin logs from the old Holmes saw mill in the clear waters.

The Wilcox's raised eight children, namely Monroe, Harold, Leland, Allen, Whyle, Paul, Abbie, and Donita. All survive except Abbie. This group was graduates of Gobles High School (except Leland and Allen). Also Monroe and Harold are graduates of Kalamazoo College and Whyle and Paul graduates of Albion College.

Would that everyone enjoyed life to the full as "Tink" did.

During the centennial week Millie and I drove to Kalamazoo, stayed with my brother Al and Recil, and spent a day in Gobles visiting with old-timers of our generation. We also met a few who would say, "Your dad cut my hair all his barbering life." There were exhibits housed in various buildings, one depicting Dad's old barbershop, and others that served as reminders of some of the more prominent citizens of the past. There were other attractions that proved very interesting. Of course, there had to be a parade led by the Gobles High School band, with my old school chums and high school classmates Darwin and Open Graves Brown clowning all during the parade. The day we were there it was estimated that there were ten thousand people in town, Goble's largest gathering in its history. A pageant was presented each night in the high school athletic field that depicted in a series of scenes the growth of Gobles over the past one hundred years. This pageant was then followed with a fine fireworks display, which was the climax of the day's activity.

The centennial booklet was filled with pictures of individuals and other scenes that played a large part in Gobles growth. Page 37 included a picture of Dad and his marching band going up the dirt main street. On page 39 one saw Dad's two steamboats, the *Monroe* and the *Cupid*, riding passengers around Lake Mill located one and a half miles northwest of town. Page 44 was given to J. Bert Travis, editor of the *Gobles Weekly News* from 1905-1947. Bert Travis was Dad's closest friend. They were within a few months of the same age, and Bert died about three months following Dad's departure. Bert told me he was the last man Dad shaved. Page 63 of the booklet pictured the 1924 Gobles High basketball team with my brothers Whyle and Paul Wilcox among the seven players. Goble's Class D state champion basketball team of 1954 was pictured on page 67. The centennial booklet had a "Do You Remember When…" page. Some of the items were: "Gobles had six passenger trains daily. Harold Wilcox won the Cross country run at Michigan State University in 1919. In 1925 you could buy a new Ford for about two hundred sixty dollars."

I had been spending a lot of time on the used-car lot from the time we returned from Florida. August was now upon us, and we were packing the 1966 Pontiac four-door sedan for our eighth and what proved to be our last trip to Montana. It was always a treat that we greatly enjoyed, and now that I had no business ties to force me to set my date of our return we could make it a leisurely venture. I told Monroe by letter the time we were leaving. He wrote that they and the Conrads would be at the Conrad "Happy House" cabin located five miles south of Red Lodge in the mountains. After so many trips I could just about map our time of departure and arrival for each day's drive. I told Monroe we should arrive at "Happy House" at four o'clock on Sunday, and to tell Florence and Burr Conrad to have the trout fried and ready for dinner. Millie and I had a real pleasant trip visiting our favorite Jamestown, North Dakota, motel and restaurant and reaching Billings, Montana, about two o'clock that Sunday.

As I remembered it, the time I set to reach the cabin was four-thirty and since we had, I thought, about two and one-half hours to drive about seventy miles we got coffee in Laurel, ten miles west of Billings, and leisurely drove south. At Red Lodge we did a little window-shopping until 4:10 p.m. in order to kill time so as to make our arrival at 4:30 p.m.. We then drove south up into the mountains always with an eye on my watch. It was just 4:25 p.m. when we left the main highway and circled back down about a half a mile to the cabins. As we came into the clearing with the "Happy House" in front of us, I blew my horn and looked at my watch. It was exactly four-thirty. Monroe came running out of the cabin looking at his watch and yelling, "You're a half hour late, where have you been these last five days?" I said, "Oh no, we're right on time." "No, you are not," Monroe said, and ran into the cabin to get my letter that stated a four o'clock arrival. Then we had a laugh over the lateness. We explained to them the effort we had made to arrive exactly at 4:30, the time I had in mind. However, the fish were fried and the Wilsons, whose cabin Millie and I occupied, were also there for an enjoyable, restful, and exciting time.

Monroe, Burr, and Millie were the fishermen. They went up the top of Bear Tooth Pass several times and fished the mountain streams and lakes. They always came back to the cabin with plenty of beautiful trout. Florence had been frying fish for nearly all her life since she and Burr were native Montanans, and she knew how to cook to get the best out of every ingredient. She and Ruth loved to curry the roadside for wild berries, and we had many a pie as a result of their pickings. What did I do while the others were doing their thing? I just loafed, read, drove five miles into Red Lodge to window shop and get a cup of coffee, or took a long walk up the lightly traveled highway into the mountains.

Before their marriages to Burr and Monroe both Florence and Ruth were schoolteachers. Florence directed the church choir while Monroe was pastor of the Laurel Methodist Church, and he had married Florence and Burr at the "Happy House" cabin.

When we made our first of eight trips to Montana, Monroe was pastor of the Bozeman, Montana Methodist Church. Bozeman is a really nice western city of about ten thousand people, right on number 10 highway, and is the home of Montana State University. Millie and I always enjoyed our stay in Bozeman after spending several days in the mountains. When Monroe became a senior citizen nearing seventy years old, in spite of his ruggedness, good health, and youthful features, he decided to ask the bishop for an assignment that required less physical and mental effort. The bishop assigned him to the Stevensville Methodist Church. Now that Monroe was at Stevensville, a small city of about one hundred people located about twenty-five miles south of Missoula, the home of the University of Montana, we had another half-day's drive west to visit him and Ruth at their home. After several days at Stevensville we headed our 1966 Pontiac east for the long five-day trek home. Little did we realize that we were saying goodbye to Montana for the last time.

It was just a day's drive to Billings, and Burr and Florence invited us to stay overnight with them. The next morning we got an early start with Bismarck, North Dakota, as our destination for the day. It was our intention to stay at the Holiday Inn located on number10 highway just after crossing the Missouri River going into Bismarck. A funny thing happened when we were about ten miles from Bismarck. We were driving behind a truck, the road had just been refinished with gravel, and this truck was throwing it. Millie was driving and I said, "Hurry up and pass this truck!" because its speed wasn't fast enough for us. As we drew up behind it to pass our car was just peppered with small pebbles. I said to Millie after we had passed, "I hope the stones didn't break out any of our headlights." We pulled up in front of the Holiday Inn motel at which I had made a reservation while in Billings. As we shut off the motor steam was rolling out from under the hood. I said, "Must be we got low on water in the radiator." Fortunately there was a gas station right next to the motel. I drove over and asked the attendant to check the radiator. He said, "You have four holes in it and that is why you are low on water." That truck had thrown pebbles so hard that they had gone right through the grill, the bug screen I had on, and had punctured the radiator in four places. The attendant said that he could have it repaired by morning so we were not delayed getting an early start.

After settling in our room and eating dinner we walked over to the Bismarck minor league ballpark where they were playing the last game of the season before the league playoff series started. The next morning, our car repaired, we got an early start and covered the fifty miles to Jamestown, North Dakota, where we ate breakfast at our favorite restaurant. We reached Ferndale without any further mishaps, and as always we were glad to get home.

I continued my work at the used-car lot, selling a car now and then. It was very evident that the automobile business was slowing down. I didn't know just how long I would be working for Higgins Pontiac. I did know that it wouldn't continue for very many more years because I was approaching my late sixties and began to consider complete retirement. I asked George Higgins if he could get me an official car (1967) after the 1968s came out. He said he had one in mind for me that was owned by a retired Pontiac executive living right in our community. Within a week I had sold my 1966 Pontiac and was driving a 1967 four-door hardtop.

I was still making the weekly Tuesday noon meetings of the Ferndale Exchange Club, but had given up the secretary job after four terms of several years each.

Larry and Faye Cowell, who had been our neighbors and close friends for many years, had sold their house and moved to Royal Oak, where they transferred their church membership to the Royal Oak Methodist Church. He was bowling in the Methodist men's bowling league and invited me to fill in on his team when he lost a team member. This was the beginning of several years of bowling with the Royal Oak Methodist men. Phil and Bonnie had transferred their membership to the Royal Oak Methodist Church, and we followed soon after. I bowled with the church league until we moved to Florida. I was first asked to be chairman of the league banquet committee, then was made vice president, which led to becoming president my last year of bowling in the league. I had never been associated with a finer group of men. It was one of my great pleasures in bowling.

The football season came and went as I saw the Friday night high school games and generally a college game on Saturday. We generally made it a point to go back to Kalamazoo College homecoming each fall. We not only saw a few of the old-timers of my college days, but at the same time we had an overnight visit with Lee and Al's family. Then Sunday after dinner we headed for home, arriving in time to visit with Bonnie and Phil, who had purchased a house on Maywood in Pleasant Ridge just a ten-minute walk from our house.

One day while Millie and I were discussing future plans and travel the subject of going to Europe again came up. We had already made reservations at the Nomad in Daytona Beach for the winter and were planning to leave Ferndale the day after "the day of football," which was January 2, 1968. We had enjoyed our first trip to Europe in 1965 so much that we decided there was no time like the present to travel, so why not! I made a call on the Royal Oak Travel Service and talked to a lady named Dorothy. I found she was in my classes when she was a student in Ferndale Lincoln High School. After our initial conversation she informed me that she would get steamship reservations and hotel accommodations for us. All I would have to do would be to give her the dates of our itinerary and the prices we had in mind. I asked for the same room 202 on the *Nieuw Amsterdam* that we had been given on our previous trip, which was to sail the latter part of May. The Holland American Line in New York wrote that 202 was taken, but we could have 201 on the opposite side of the ship that was also an alternate room. We set the date of the steamship sailing in July for a return trip and got very favorable accommodations. Knowing then the number of days we were to be in Europe, I would sit at my desk in the used-car office and map our trip around Europe. By the time Christmas approached I had given Dorothy in the travel service a complete schedule of our trip. We were to visit some of the cities we had visited in 1965, and I had added some since on this trip we would be traveling by train.

Now that Dick and Phil had in-laws, the holidays had to be divided between two parents. No parents could have had two more loyal sons and daughters-in-law since Millie and I have never had to spend a holiday alone. Phil and Dick have always made certain that one of them would be home on such occasions.

I always enjoyed our drive to Florida. Once we got into Ohio the highways were clear and one had good driving conditions all the way to Daytona Beach. Young people make the trip of about 1,250 miles in two long days of driving, but we always made it a two-and-a-half-day trip. The first night we stayed in Kentucky then arrived in central Georgia for the second night. That would get us to the Nomad, 3101 South Atlantic, right on the ocean, where we spent five winters in unit 108. When we reached the Florida state line, we would yell, "Hello, Florida." Then we would stop at the reception center and get our free orange juice. Our unit 108 in the Nomad Motel looked right out on the ocean. We enjoyed eating breakfast while viewing those ocean waves. Most winters the ocean was warm enough for a dip. The winter of 1972, a very warm one, I never missed one week without going in the ocean, with water temperatures between 65 and 70. During our five winters at the Nomad we made many friends because, like us, many of the occupants were coming back year after year. March 15, 1968, was "We hate to leave Florida," but necessary for arriving home in time for the state basketball tournament that was my chief pleasure.

One of the first things I did was to visit the travel service and check with Dorothy on hotel reservations, etc. Everything seemed to be in good order with a down payment at each hotel since we thought that one of the worst things that could happen would be to get to a city with no hotel reservations. We ran across many young people, mostly students, who never let that bother them, and when I first went to Europe in 1924 we never thought of reservations. I guess that is just a characteristic of old age. When the month of May arrived we had our passports, tickets, reservations all in order, so there was not a thing to worry about.

I went to our family doctor to have my prostate gland checked. He found nothing wrong with it but gave me a prescription and said, "Take them now and then. Take some with you." I started taking this very strong drug now and then.

Chapter 12

Retirement Years—Back to Europe, 1968

Whyle, Audrey, and Debbie said they wanted to see us sail, so Whyle made motel reservations off the Pennsylvania Turnpike about a four-hour drive from the Holland Tunnel since our ship didn't sail until 4:00 p.m. Saturday, May 25, 1968. We left Ferndale early in the afternoon of Thursday, May 23, and stayed at a motel at the first exit on the Pennsylvania Turnpike. Whyle said he would meet us about one o'clock on May 24 at Hershey, Pennsylvania, and we could all go through the Hershey Chocolate Candy Plant. Leaving our motel after breakfast, we had a leisurely drive to Hershey. After spending a couple of hours sampling their candy, we started our drive to our motel about three hours east. Arriving at the Pennsylvania Turnpike exit it started to rain. I thought, "Will we make it before the storm?" Whyle and I went to the office and got rooms right next to each other.

Leaving the office Whyle said, "You go ahead to your room. I forgot to tell the manager something." I wasn't the least bit suspicious about what was to happen. About five o'clock while viewing the nice restaurant across the parkway I said, "We had better go over and eat hadn't we?" Whyle said, "Let's wait a while. I ate too much Hershey," so we did. About 6:30 we drove one car over to the restaurant where we had a very good dinner at a reasonable price. When we finished eating I went out and stood on the front veranda. It was still raining. The others of our party had gone downstairs to the gift shop. As I stood there watching it rain a person grabbed my arm from behind. I turned around and said, "Bonnie! Where did you come from?" "Hi, Dad," she said. "Phil's parking the car." We all went back into the restaurant and chatted while Phil and Bonnie ate their dinner. Whyle explained that he had made three reservations at the motel but began to wonder if Phil and Bonnie would make it. They drove all the way from Ferndale after an early-morning start in their VW. Phil had worked in the computer department at the Wayne Oakland Bank in Royal Oak, but had transferred his work to AAA office in Detroit where he was then working. Bonnie was still teaching school, and they both took Friday off in order to drive to New York to see us off.

By 10:30 p.m. we were all in bed because we wanted a fairly early start so as to be at Pier 40, ready to board the *Nieuw Amsterdam* at 1:00 p.m. Our room 201 was identical to 202 that we had in 1965 on our first voyage on this ship. We all did the ship from top to bottom and bow to stern. At 3:30 p.m. the ship's whistles gave three long and two short blasts, announcing we would sail in half an hour and for all visitors to disembark. Whyle, Audrey, and Debbie with Phil and Bonnie stationed themselves on the top deck of Pier 40, and as we started moving away from the dock there were many goodbyes and "happy voyage." I'll never forget seeing Bonnie with her red dress jumping up and down to get the last glimpse of us as the tugs pushed the ship out into the river channel. The five of them spent the night in New York before heading for home. It was another grand send-off, and Millie and I greatly appreciated the effort and money it cost them to say goodbye to us.

We were again off for Europe. I stayed on deck during the time it took to pass the Statue of Liberty, Coney Island, and under the bridge, which was the gateway to the ocean. It was 5:00 p.m. We had reserved a table for two at the first seating. Dinner was served at 6:00 p.m. It had been a hard day and

I felt tired, so I told Millie that it being the first night aboard and there wouldn't be too much evening activity, I was going to turn in early.

We had a nice trip with bingo, horse racing, cards, dancing and lots of good food keeping us all in good spirits. However, I just didn't seem to have the pep I normally had, and it began to worry me. Little did I realize that the drug my doctor had given me was slowly poisoning my system. On May 30 it was warm, calm, with sunshine, but I didn't get up until 11:00 a.m., having the room steward serving me my breakfast in bed.

The following day, May 31, the ship entered the English Channel at 9:30 p.m. and since it didn't get dark until 10:30 p.m. I stood on deck and again thanked God for the privilege of being able to salute England. It was really a thrill.

June 1st we docked at Southampton at about 9:00 a.m., and twenty-four hours later we were docking in Rotterdam, Holland. We had a reservation at a hotel in Amsterdam so I asked the taxi driver to drive us to the railroad station so that we could get a train. He spoke good English and sold us on the idea of paying him twenty dollars to drive us to Amsterdam. He said this would save us two taxi fares, a crowded train ride and would give us a sightseeing trip all in one. I wasn't feeling too peppy so I said to Millie, "Let's let him drive us." She said, "OK." We arrived at our hotel in Amsterdam about one o'clock. We ate a lunch in the hotel dining room, then the clerk told us our room was ready. After the disposal of our baggage in our room, we walked down the street about three blocks where sightseeing canal boats were harbored. In 1965 we boarded one of these boats with Dick and Carole at this same location. The trip took us around the city, and we recognized many familiar landmarks that we remembered from our 1965 canal ride. Not feeling too well, we turned in early for a good night's rest.

Monday, June 3, 1968, was a nice warm day and we set out on foot to see some of the things we had missed three years prior. One of the most interesting was the Anne Frank's hideout, which we were allowed to inspect.

After dinner at the hotel I told Millie, "I am exhausted and just have to go to bed for a nap." Now generally after one rests in bed for about three hours one gets up feeling better, but it was 10:00 p.m. and I felt no better. I told Millie she would have to go to the hotel desk clerk and ask for a doctor. It wasn't long before the doctor arrived from the hospital. He checked me over and said he found nothing radically wrong. He would give us a prescription and that he thought if I took it easy the next two days I would regain my strength. His fee was only six dollars and eighty-five cents in U.S. currency. Millie went to the clerk to get information as to where there would be an open pharmacy. He said he knew of one that served night calls and he would drive her since it was across the canal and very hard to find. Millie returned about 11:30 p.m. with the medicine and we went to bed.

Wednesday, June 5, at 7:27 a.m. we boarded a train for Copenhagen, Denmark. It was a very interesting ride. Our train was put on a car ferry in order to reach Copenhagen. We arrived at 8:51 p.m., and as we approached the desk clerk of the Webber Hotel the first words he said to us was, "Do you know they shot Bobby Kennedy today?" We said no, we had not heard the terrible news. He remarked, "It could only happen in the United States." I thought to myself, "What a bad impression of the United States these foreign people must have."

It didn't get dark until eleven o'clock so Millie and I walked the streets. One thing I noticed as we walked past a theater was the many, many bicycles and motorbikes of all types and descriptions parked on the sidewalk and curb, with no locks and chains for protection against stealing. I said to Millie, "Just how long would these bikes be here if this was a United States city?" We both had the same answer in our minds.

Our train for Stockholm, Sweden, on Friday, June 7 left at 9:50 a.m. and we didn't' arrive at our new destination until 7:30 p.m. We were housed at the Hotel Gillet, a nice, comfortable place to stay. We took the usual sightseeing trips and enjoyed the ventures. However, this was a city of hippies. We had never seen so many congregated in one city.

Sweden is a highly socialistic state and it seemed there were new improvements going on everywhere. We were told by a U.S. engineer who had been staying at the hotel each summer for a number of years that this one would be his last since the government was destroying all the buildings around there to develop a new beautiful center that would have parks, businesses, and apartment buildings, etc.

While I had been taking the drug that the Amsterdam doctor gave me, I had laid off the little black pills that were poisoning me. Therefore I was feeling much better and gaining strength. When we boarded the 7:13 a.m. train for Oslo, Norway, on Monday, June 10 I felt that my illness was a thing of the past and that now I could begin to really enjoy the trip. However, it took just twenty-four hours to convince me differently.

We arrived at Oslo at 1:50 p.m. after a short train ride. Oslo is a beautiful small city where in June the sun never sets. Twilight occurred about 1:00 a.m., and by three o'clock it was daylight again. We got to our hotel room in the Hotel Stefan with shower and bath for only twelve dollars a day, then we walked the streets until we located a restaurant that we had heard about that served American food cafeteria style. We had a very enjoyable and cheap meal.

Before I went to bed I must have taken one of those black pills that I later found out was doing me so much physical harm, for early in the morning of June 11 I woke up with a fever and cough, feeling like a wet towel. Millie went to the hotel desk and asked them to get us a doctor. It was about one hour before the doctor arrived. He examined me and said he thought I had a mild case of pneumonia and that I should stay in bed the three days we were to be in Oslo. He gave Millie a prescription, and the American drug was cheaper than we could have purchased it in the United States. His fee was five dollars and sixty cents in U.S. currency. I didn't see much of Oslo. Millie, as much as she felt she could, did do some sightseeing a few hours a day.

Because of the East German Corridor we were told it was advisable to fly from Oslo to West Berlin, so we had made our plane reservations before leaving the United States. Our flight left Oslo at 8:55 a.m. on June 14, 1968, with a change at Hamburg, Germany, that made our arrival at Tempelhof Airport in West Berlin at 2:05 p.m. Franz and Beth Weeren, who had lived in Pleasant Ridge, were now living in West Berlin. For several terms Beth had been in Millie's jewelry class and through this interest the Weerens and the Wilcoxes became well acquainted. When we made our plans to be in West Berlin, Millie wrote Beth of our schedule and had given her our plane flight and time of arrival. Sure enough as we came into the waiting room from the plane there was Beth to say, "Welcome to West Berlin." Millie told her of my physical condition and she remarked that their doctor's office was right across the street from the Hotel Am Zoo where we were staying. She would make me an appointment with the doctor.

Saturday Beth drove us around the city and with Franz and their two fine boys of about ten and twelve years of age took us to the American Officer's Club for dinner. Franz had been in the German army under Hitler, was wounded, captured by the Americans, and sent to the United States for the duration of the war. When he was released from the army he wanted to remain in the States and become a U.S. citizen, which he did. His father owned and operated a small factory in West Berlin. When his father retired it was either go to Germany and supervised the plant or give it up since they could not take German wealth out of Germany, so they moved from Pleasant Ridge, Michigan, to West Berlin rather than lose everything.

Sunday morning they called the hotel and invited us to their home for dinner. They drove to the hotel to pick us up. It was about 3:00 p.m. that I asked if I could take a nap. I was very weak. "Sure," Franz said, "why don't you let me call our doctor. It's a weekend holiday, but he might be in town." Millie and I were very discouraged, and I had told her I just didn't see how I was going to be able to continue on; we might have to fly home from Berlin. When we explained to Beth and Franz what we had in mind, Franz got on the phone and contacted his doctor, who said he would be over to the house about five o'clock. Franz and the doctor talked in German, and after he had listened to my symptoms and examined me he told Franz that if I would stay in West Berlin for a week and take treatments he felt sure he would have me in an improved condition that would allow me to enjoy the rest of our trip.

Millie and I agreed that it would be worth a try so we started thinking about hotel reservations, etc. Franz phoned the Am Zoo explaining we wanted to stay until Saturday, June 22. He also called the Hotel Marktplatz in Garmisch and arranged for a change of schedule. I wanted longer stays in the cities to be visited. Then I sat down and rearranged our travel dates by cutting off Florence, Italy, and Luzern, Switzerland. I wrote letters to the hotels explaining the reason for the cancellation.

We were getting a lot of newspaper publicity about the railway strike in England. Pictures showing huge crowds of people at the London depots discouraged us. Feeling as I did, there was a question in our minds as to whether we wanted to complete our scheduled trip to England and Scotland. We decided to cut off that part of our trip and make our stay in England a shorter one, provided there was a Holland American line ship leaving earlier than the *Rotterdam* on which we had a ticket reservation.

Early in the week while we were in West Berlin, Beth took us to the Holland American office, which was located in a building about four blocks from our hotel. The agent said the *Statendam*, a twenty-five thousand-ton ship, was scheduled out of Rotterdam a week earlier than the steamship *Rotterdam*. He could call the home office in Rotterdam for a reservation that would be equivalent to or better than the *Rotterdam* cabin. We told him to make the arrangements and to give me a call at the Am Zoo hotel. After a couple of days without a message, I walked down to the Holland American office building. I took the elevator up to the floor on which the office was located and found the door locked.

Saturday morning arrived, the day we were to fly out of West Berlin to Munich and from there take a train to Garmisch. I visited the doctor's office, got a shot and medicine, paid my bill, which came to only thirty-five dollars, and went back to the hotel to pack. I was feeling much better. I asked the hotel clerk if there was a message for Harold Wilcox and he said no. I was rather disturbed, so I decided to walk down again to the Holland American Office building. I took the lift to the office floor and again I found the door locked. On the way back to the hotel I passed an American Express office. It gave me an idea. I went in and just as soon as an agent was free I talked to him about my problem. He said, "I'll call the steamship office and question them on why you haven't been notified at your hotel." I said, "I just returned from there and the door is locked." "That's funny," he said, and then he made the call. The Holland American agent was in and said he had tried several times to get a message to me but I had not responded. When the question of the locked door was mentioned he said you have to ring the doorbell. I said to myself on my walk back to the steamship office, "What a funny business setup, to have to ring a door bell to get in." When I got off the elevator I could hear him on the phone, so I rang the doorbell and waited.

He said, "I have a really nice room for you on the *Statendam*, and if you want me to transfer your crossing to it I will." I said, "OK, make it the *Statendam* sailing from Southampton Saturday, July 6 and arriving in New York on Saturday, July 13." He said we would have outside room 181 on the main deck. As I walked back to the hotel I felt much better. I was feeling that to get home a week to ten days earlier would be to my liking. However, I realized it was hard on Millie since we had planned that this summer's trip would be the most delightful and was also rather costly. When I got back to the hotel I said to Millie, "We sail on the *Statendam*." Then I told her of my experience that morning.

We had intended to take a taxi to the airport, which was not a great distance, but about eleven o'clock. Franz called and said he wouldn't hear of it. He would pick us up at 12:30 p.m., which would get us to the airport in plenty of time. At twelve noon I paid our hotel bill and with our baggage we parked ourselves out in front of the main entrance in the warm sunshine.

Our eight days in West Berlin had not been a total loss. We had taken a bus trip to East Berlin, visited numerous shops of all kinds, and bought a beautiful old clock for thirty-five dollars, which was well wrapped and enabled us to carry it like a suitcase. We had also had an enjoyable time with the Weerens, and owed them a great debt of gratitude and thanks.

It didn't take long to fly to Munich. We took a taxi to the railway Bahnhof. What a railroad terminal! There were about thirty-five tracks with trains coming and going constantly. A man with a sign reading "Information" on his cap circulated among the crowded station, and he told us the number of the track and time of departure of our train to Garmisch. It was our first visit to Garmisch, a southern German Bavarian city of about thirty thousand people and a great winter resort. We fell in love with it. The U.S. military had a "retreat" in Garmisch for men and families who were on leave. The food was cheap and because we were Americans we were allowed to eat in the dining room.

Garmisch has beautiful shops, a lovely park with well-kept gardens of flowers, and a free band concert each morning and evening for hotel guests. It was relaxing to go to the park and listen to the concerts.

We took an all-day bus trip to Oberammergau, the home of the Passion Play produced every ten years. We visited King Ludwig's old but beautiful castle, and had dinner at the ice-skating evening show that was famous for its food as well as its show. Our hotel was such a homey place with everyone so cheerful that in 1970 we returned to it for our stay in Garmisch.

Our next stop was my favorite city in Europe, Interlaken, Switzerland. Getting there from Garmisch was an all-day trip with train changes. We arrived Friday, June 28 late in the afternoon and were housed in the Hotel Krebs for five nights since we had also cancelled out our night in Mainz, Germany where we were to ride the steamer down the Rhine River to Koln. My diary of Interlaken, my third visit there, reads, "A very nice hotel with room and bath in the rear, quiet and looking into the mountains, just a half block from the Bahnhof. Good food, good service, a nice restful stay. We attended several concerts at the Casino and Millie trying her luck in the 'game room' came out six francs ahead. We bought gifts and enjoyed the four full days and five nights here."

On Wednesday, July 3 we took a 9:49 a.m. train out of Interlaken for Basil, Switzerland, where we changed to a train that took us to Koln, Germany, on the Rhine. It was a beautiful all-day train ride on the smoothest track I have ever experienced. We ate lunch and dinner in the dining car with comfort. For an hour and a half we rode along the Rhine River. It was so picturesque that I stood looking out the window on the Rhine River side of the train for the last two hours before arriving at Koln.

Our hotel was within a half block of the Bahnhof but not being very strong, although I was feeling much better, we took a taxi to the hotel. At night in the quiet of it all we could hear the P.A. system calling the arrival of the trains.

A beautiful, sunny day dawned on July 4, 1968. After having such poor food and service at the hotel dining room the night before, we decided we would bypass it and eat at some other place. Then we visited the old and famous Koln Cathedral. It was under repairs since during World War II it had been damaged badly.

We took a boat ride on the Rhine River and a bus tour of the city including the 4711 Koln factories where cologne lotions of all kinds are made. Then we walked the several-blocks-long mall where not a vehicle is allowed. We visited the beautiful shops, ate lunch and dinner at Wimpy's on the mall that served American food and is patterned after Big Boy restaurants in the States. They served hot dogs, good burgers, French fries, ice cream, etc. It was a revelation to see the new city that the war had made necessary. The cities in the United States are getting worse living and shopping conditions each year, yet we helped destroy German's large cities and financed their rebuilding with American taxpayers' money.

In the meantime we had read more about the railway strike in England, so we reasoned, "Why go to London for only a couple of days and risk the mental distress that such a situation might bring on?" I had written the Holland American office in Rotterdam to change our tickets to board the *Statendam* in Rotterdam on Friday, July 5 instead of at Southampton on Saturday, July 6. As we went to bed early at 9:30 p.m., we were conscious that this was our last night in Europe.

We got up at 5:30 a.m. on July 5, 1968, and I said to Millie, "Today we sail." We went down to the dining room at 6:00 a.m., all packed and ready to leave, and had the usual Continental breakfast. Our train to Rotterdam left at 7:12 a.m. so I asked the desk clerk if one of his porters would carry our bags the short block to the Bahnhof. "Certainly," he replied and the porter picked up the two bags and away we went to the station. The train and track schedules were well posted at each entrance to the stairways that led up to the platform so there was no difficulty in finding the right track on which our train would arrive. I tipped the hotel porter and thanked him since he could speak English. Then I located a Bahnhof porter and asked him to put us and our baggage on the train leaving for Rotterdam at 7:12 p.m. We were sitting on a platform bench as our train pulled in about 7:05 a.m. Our porter picked up our bags and said, "Follow me." He asked what part of the train was going to Rotterdam and was motioned to the front by the trainman. We shared a compartment with a middle-aged couple who we later found out lived in Rotterdam. He could converse in English very well, but she wasn't so good. We told them we liked their small country and that we were sailing at 5:00 p.m. on the *Statendam*.

We arrived in Rotterdam at 9:34 a.m. I got a porter to carry our bags to the taxi stand. I was feeling much better. The West Berlin doctor had done what he said he thought he could do, that is, put me in physical shape so that I would enjoy the trip, yet I did not feel strong. I had taken the medicine he had given me and not taken any of the little black pills. The taxi took us over to the old section of Rotterdam where the ships docked. There was the *Statendam* being readied for a 5:00 p.m. departure. We checked our baggage for room 181, ate lunch right at the dock's snack bar, and sat around until the one o'clock embarkation time. When I got up to the window "W," the clerk said she did not have our reservation. I told her that our reservation called for boarding in Southampton, but because of the railroad situation I had written the London office to transfer our embarkation to Rotterdam. After about one-half hour she came back to the window with everything straightened out. I was to pay her the additional fare to Southampton, which to me was an exceedingly low fee. I went back to where Millie was sitting and said, "OK, we're ready to go aboard."

We had a real nice outside room with private bath on the main deck front. Our baggage was in our room, and after a little unpacking I went out to survey the ship. We sailed promptly at 5:00 p.m. after which Millie and I went to the dining room for the first dinner seating.

We awakened in the morning Saturday, July 6, 1968, in the English Channel on our way to Southampton, where our ship docked and took on passengers. After several hours at Southampton our ship set sail for a stop in Ireland, where we took on passengers and baggage. We were late getting to Ireland because one engine was impaired. It was not until early morning hours that we left Ireland with all engines working.

The activities aboard were very enjoyable. Millie won thirty three dollars at bingo and her number-three horse in the evening horse race gave her the usual luck. I rested a great deal, going to bed rather early and two mornings had the room steward bring me my breakfast in our room. We had a home talent show on Wednesday night and the crew show was on Thursday night.

Thursday afternoon I must have taken a little black pill before going out on deck to sit and watch the ocean. At about 4:00 p.m., I began to feel very weak. I went to the room and went to bed. At 6:00 p.m. we went to dinner, but even with the delicious steak dinner I ate very little. By 8:00 p.m. I was in bed with a chill, then a temperature and a cough. Millie called the ship nurse and she in turn called the ship doctor. He gave me some tablets that knocked the fever and cough out of me and by Friday afternoon I was feeling much, better although I was still in bed. I was pretty worried, for I had visions of them having to take me off the ship in a wheelchair and that Millie would have to drive us all the way home. However, Millie had kept Phil and Dick posted, and Phil said he would fly to New York and drive us home if "Dad wasn't feeling well." When Saturday, July 13, 1968, dawned I was feeling good enough to know I could drive home. The ship nurse and doctor came in about 9:00 a.m. and after an examination said, "Take a shower, get dressed, and go out on deck, you are OK." I thanked him for what he had done for me and asked, "How much do we owe you?" "Not a cent," he said and left our room.

We went under the bridge into the Hudson River at twelve noon and passed the Statue of Liberty at 12:30 p.m. By the time we were docked and the ship crew had all luggages in the warehouse ready for passengers to claim it was about 2:30 p.m. We were off the ship by 2:40 p.m., claimed our baggage, went through customs, loaded it into our car, and by 3:30 p.m. we had bid goodbye to the Statue of Liberty and were driving along the New Jersey Turnpike. We stayed overnight at the Wiltshire Motel at the Breezewood exit. We called Phil and told him that we would be home the next day. We arrived home Sunday afternoon at about 4:00 p.m., and I thanked God I was home safely.

Chapter 13

Retirement Years Continued—Ferndale

When Phil read in his mother's letters that I was having trouble he called our doctor and made an appointment for me. I told him of the experiences I had overseas. He was disturbed and said, "Harold, how long has it been since you have had a good physical?" I said, "A long time." "Well, then, I would like to put you in the hospital and have you checked from head to toe." "OK," I said, "When the William Beaumont Hospital calls that there is a room for me I'll be ready." I stopped over at Higgins Pontiac to tell George of my trouble, that I was going to the hospital to get a physical, and that when I got out I would return to the used-car office. That following Thursday I got the call, so Millie drove me to the hospital. I was hospitalized for eight days—x-rayed from head to foot—and they found nothing wrong with me. All during that time I had been taking no medicine.

While in Europe I had written Monroe and Ruth that we would not be making the trip west in August so Monroe and Ruth had made plans to come to Michigan. They were in Kalamazoo for several days. Whyle and Audrey had driven to Kalamazoo and Monroe and Ruth were driving back east with to visit the New England states and Boston. They stopped in Ferndale overnight and came to the hospital in the evening to visit with me for about an hour. Then they went to the Detroit Tigers' ballgame. It was rainy, cool, and a very poor game to watch and they said it was a wasted evening. The eighth day my doctor called at the hospital and said I could go home.

The following Monday I went to the used-car office. Nix said Mr. Higgins had not told him of my being hospitalized and he didn't know where I was. He thought I had gone off on another trip.

A couple of weeks later I got to analyzing in my mind the type of medicine I had taken and when I had taken it. As I remembered it, my trouble really started before we sailed for Europe, and that was the time I began taking the little black pills. I got up one morning and said to myself, "I am going to experiment. I am going to take the black pill and see the reaction, if any, it has on me." So before going to the used-car office I took the pill. About 11:30 a.m. I began to get the reaction that I had had so many times before. I went home for lunch and didn't go back to the used-car office because I had a chill, then a sweat, a cough, and was weak! I told Millie to get rid of those black pills. It's done all the dirty work on my physical self it's going to do. I haven't taken another one of those pills, and I have never had a reaction such as it gave me.

The doctor who had prescribed the pills made this comment, "I take one once in a while myself, but it is just too bad that the little black pill should destroy the pleasure of such a fine and expensive trip." I replied in a discouraged tone, "Some people are allergic to one drug and other people get adverse reactions to certain other drugs. I guess that's just a part of our life experience." At least I was very thankful that my illness did not destroy the total enjoyment of our European travel.

Back on the used-car lot I mixed business with pleasure. I generally went to the office about 9:30 a.m., took an hour off for lunch and said goodnight to Nix and Mel about 5:30 p.m. I occasionally worked on evenings and Saturdays, just to help out when one of the other two wanted to be off. During the four and one-half years on the Higgins Pontiac payroll we had just one very saddening situation. Mel Lancaster, who had worked for Higgins ever since the late 1920's and was one of those types of employees who is hard to replace, got up one morning with a dizzy spell. While shaving he fell in the bathroom unconscious. They rushed him to the hospital, but he never regained consciousness. After a few days he was dead. A few weeks later Evan Swanson became the third member of our used-car office force.

For me fall 1968 was a great one, since not only did we have high school and college football games to go to, we also had the Detroit Tigers fighting for the American League Pennant. It was the Tigers against the St. Louis Cardinals when the World Series opened in October at Detroit. Detroit split the home two-game series, with our thirty-one-game winner Denny McLain getting beat in the opener, and a great pitcher, Mickey Lolich, who all season pitched in the shadow of McLain, winning the second game. They moved to St. Louis where the Cardinals won both games, making the series one game won by Detroit and three won by St. Louis. Too many people thought the world championship was in the bag for St. Louis since very few teams had ever won three out of four games and ending up losing the World Series championship. However, the Tigers had been coming from behind in game after game all season long, winning games in the seventh, eighth, and ninth innings when they seemed to be hopelessly beaten. Detroit won the last three games of this World Series to win the championship.

World Series tickets were as hard to get as hen's teeth. There were hundreds of thousands of applications for about forty thousand seats. Of course, the season ticket holders and big brass had the first chance at tickets. However, I was lucky. After mailing in three applications, one in my friend Howard Thompson's name, and putting the three in mailboxes in three separate sections of the city, I got results. Although I got my money back from two applications, Howard called me and said, "I have just received two tickets to the World Series fifth game by mail." The tickets called for center-field upper-deck seats. My thinking was any place in the ballpark was fine. We drove our car down to the state fairgrounds on Woodward, where we transferred to a stadium bus.

The first half inning was heart breaking. With Lolich pitching, St. Louis got two men on base, followed by a home run, making the score 3-0. I said to Millie, "The game's over and St. Louis is world champion before we even get a turn at bat." But when the ninth inning arrived it was 5-3 in Detroit's favor, and Mickey Lolich had won his second World Series game.

The teams went back to St. Louis, and two games later Detroit was the world champion. McLain had pitched Detroit to its third victory in a Detroit slugfest, and after only two days rest Lolich shut out the Cardinals for eight innings, giving up a home run in the ninth and winning his third World Series game 4-1. The people in the city of Detroit and suburbs went wild. Thirty thousand people jammed the metro airport where the Tigers were supposed to land. Such a mob of people made it necessary to close the airport, and the Tigers' special flight had to land at Willow Run airport. Although our European trip had not been one of great pleasure, it proved to be a great season of baseball for us. I attended a number of games, and Millie and I had seen Denny McLain win his twenty-eighth and thirtieth games It should be noted that Denny McLain is the last pitcher to win thirty or more games during a season.

Many people felt the Tigers had helped quiet the emotional feelings that had resulted in the 12th Street burning, a riot within an African-American area during July 1967. A total of 1,400 building were burned, 43 people killed, and 342 people injured. In the fall season I spent many hours on the used-car lot, did the usual tasks around the house and yard, saw football games on Fridays and Saturdays, and again was feeling my old self.

The approaching holiday season made us conscious that January 2, 1969, would find Millie and me on Highway 175, heading for the Nomad Motel, Daytona Beach, Florida. We began to look forward to meeting the "old gang," who like us had been coming back each year. There were the owners, Frank and Arlene Ritchie, whom everyone liked and appreciated since they treated you as though you were one of a big family. Then there were John and Theresa Lenney from Montreal, who were always everybody's friends, and their Montreal companions Frank and Marg Shields, who were well liked by everyone. The Thompsons left Michigan for their Daytona Beach home in November. They lived at 111 Van Avenue, just a half block down the hill from the Nomad. We also became friends with Paul and Viola Rhodes, who had moved to Daytona Beach several years prior and had a beautiful home on Peninsula Drive South.

These with a host of other people made life during the winter season one of constant activity. It was dancing, cards, and shuffle at the Peabody Shuffle Club, Tourists' Travel Lodge each Tuesday night at Peabody Auditorium, golf at the city golf and country club, swimming in the ocean and pool, and other activities that kept us busy every day of the week. Sundays found us in church at the Community Methodist just off Peninsula Avenue South.

Mainland Methodist Church had an adult Bible class taught by a Bible scholar, Betsy Hall that proved to be a real religious inspiration to me. It was at the church and Bible class that we became friends with Doris and Bill Ruland, who are two of the few natives of Florida that we met.

Then there is my number-one golf companion Alex Roy, who lived at the Nomad and who had only about one-third of a stomach. Alex and I played golf together all during the winter months. Alex is truly a good golfer with fine form in spite of his physical handicap. He and his wife Susan come to Daytona Beach in November and leave for their Montreal home April 1. He and I enjoyed Mondays, Wednesdays, and Fridays together, they being our golf days.

As we became acquainted with more people and institutions we began to enjoy Daytona Beach more and more. Each March 15 and later April 1 when we were packing to leave the Nomad, it got to be a little harder to say goodbye until the next winter, but as of 1968 we had not yet had any great desire to leave Ferndale. After all, we had friends and acquaintances in Ferndale, and after living there since 1923 it was home for both Millie and me. Then too, Phil and family were living within a half mile of our house and we greatly enjoyed visiting several times a week back and forth. Dick and Carole were in Kalamazoo, and every few weeks we would either drive to Kalamazoo, which would give me an opportunity to say hello to Lee and Al and families, or they would drive to Ferndale. So Ferndale had a lot to hold us at 250 West Maplehurst.

In fall 1968 when the new cars came on the market, a friend who had been in Millie's adult classes for several years bought a new 1969 Cadillac. She was going to turn in her 1965 Cadillac with only fourteen thousand miles on it for a new one. She told Millie that it was a shame none of her friends wanted it. Well, after Millie and Phil had sold me on this offer I sold my 1967 Pontiac at the used-car lot and now we were driving a 1965 two-door Cadillac.

In June 1969 the National Library Conference was held in Atlantic City. Millie and I decided we would attend the conference, as did three other members of the library board. We took two days to drive to Atlantic City. It was my third visit to the Great Seashore Convention City and Millie's first. We stayed at the Howard Johnson where many of the conference sessions were held, and enjoyed it. We strolled down the famous boardwalk, which is about five miles long, and I marveled at the city's great job in keeping it in such a fine state of repairs. After the convention was terminated we headed the Cadillac toward Boston. I had not been to Boston for about twelve years, and I wanted to walk the Commons and Public Gardens once more, stroll up Beacon Hill, and again look at old 72 Mount Vernon Street where Monroe and I lived and went to school, me for one year and Monroe for three years. Yes, Boston was changing as all cities were changing, but I did enjoy reliving for a few hours some of the most pleasant and worthwhile experiences of my life since it was at the School of Theology that I really found myself. It was there that I made up my mind I wanted to teach school.

Driving out of Boston, we took the old Mohawk Trail over which I had driven a number of times. In my younger days it was "Lovers Lane" to most of us since it was such a beautiful drive. We stayed overnight about fifty miles east of Niagara Falls in a nice motel. Leaving rather early and eating breakfast at the Falls, we again relived some of the pleasant experiences that we had enjoyed previously in our several visits. Driving down through Canada, we were home by 4:00 p.m. Grandmother Burrows, who stayed at our house while we were away, was glad to see us get home. We called Phil and Bonnie, and we all went out to dinner together.

As the summer wore on into fall Millie and I started talking about another trip to Europe "next summer" in 1970. We figured we were not getting any younger, and if we ever were to go again the summer of 1970 was the time to do it.

Car business was not good, and when new cars don't sell old cars don't sell either. There were beginning to be days when we didn't have a "looker" on the lot. Mr. Higgins began talking about a reorganization of his business. To me at least this meant that anything could happen to the employees. Some of his best mechanics had already left for other employment. Also, after teaching adult night school for over twenty years Millie was beginning to feel that she had had it. So we sort of made an agreement to ourselves that when we left for Florida in January 1971 we would both be fully retired.

The late summer and fall of 1969 was as usual. I went to the used-car office about 9:30 a.m. and left about 5:00 p.m. Business was very slow. Now and then I would work Saturdays in order to give Evans or Nix a long weekend, but not often because I valued my evenings and Saturdays for our own pleasures. It was a Tigers baseball game now and then and football as usual on Friday nights and Saturdays. Millie and I went to "K" College's homecoming, said hello to Lee's and Al's, and spent the weekend with Dick and Carole, who now lived in a really nice house in Portage. In the meantime, Bonnie and Phil had given us our first grandchild, Stephanie, who was born on August 4, 1969.

It was about this time that Dick began talking to me in terms of moving to Houston, Texas. It had been pretty well established that the Channing Company, Inc. was going to move out of Michigan to the home office in Houston. They wanted Dick to stay with the company and moved to Houston at the company's expense. Dick was to manage the accounting department when the company was in Houston sometime during the summer of 1970. Dick and Carole also informed us that we were going to be grandparents again, which of course we were delighted to hear. The expected Jimmy was to be born in September.

Thanksgiving was a happy occasion because it marked the last time that the whole family was together at 250 West Maplehurst for a holiday. As late fall 1969 approached, Dick and Carole extended an invitation to both sides of the family to have Christmas at their home in Portage (outside of Kalamazoo) since it would be their last opportunity to have all of us together for the holiday season. On December 24, 1969, Millie and I drove to Kalamazoo, and a little later in the day Phil, Bonnie, and Stephanie followed. It was a joyful Christmas Eve with all of us Wilcoxes together. Christmas morning Carole's parents with her sisters, an aunt, and grandparents drove from Niles, Michigan, where they had lived all their lives. The Christmas tree was loaded and there were boxes, boxes, and boxes all over the corner of the large living room, which had a nice fireplace. It was hours before all the presents had been distributed and opened. It was great fun and a very enjoyable Christmas. Late in the afternoon after a delicious Christmas dinner the Taylors drove back to Niles. After an enjoyable weekend at Dick's, Phil and we drove back to Ferndale and Pleasant Ridge where Phil and Bonnie now lived.

Now it was time to really go to work on our European trip itinerary. Millie and I had talked over such things as the ships on which we wanted to travel across the ocean, new places of interest that we wanted to visit, as well as cities that we had previously included in our European travels. I again used the Royal Oak Travel Service. Dorothy was still working there, and since she had done us a good job with the 1968 trip I asked her to do this one.

First I said, "What is the ship schedule leaving New York and returning from Europe?" To my surprise, North Atlantic steamship travel had diminished to the point that there were only about four ships making the North Atlantic run. Considering ship schedules, we decided to ride the *Nieuw Amsterdam* out of New York to Rotterdam, Holland, for the third time. The schedule called for it to leave New York on Tuesday, May 26, 1970, at twelve noon and to arrive at Rotterdam on June 3. Our return sailing was to be on the steamship *France*, the largest ship sailing on the high seas, leaving Southampton, England, on Friday July 10, 1970. By Christmas week Dorothy at the travel service had our itinerary and had already made some bookings. We had asked for either room 201 or 202 on the *Nieuw Amsterdam*, rooms that we had previously occupied, but they were already assigned so the steamship office gave us room 233 which was also an alternating room.

Dick and Carole invited us to spend New Year's with them, so we spent several days after Christmas getting packed and the house in order to leave from Kalamazoo for Florida on January 2, 1970. We bid Bonnie, Phil, and our sweet little granddaughter Stephanie goodbye on the morning of December 31, 1969.

Arriving at Dick and Carole's before dinner, we had a card-playing New Year's Eve and a very pleasant, happy New Year's Day watching bowl football games. Of course, Millie and Carole were not as jubilant about the tube's pictures as Dick and I were, but they tolerated it, planning dinner for the "between-games" period. During the day and night it was extremely cold.

When we got up for an early breakfast since Dick had to leave around 7:15 a.m. for his office, the temperature was around zero. I can still see Dick waving goodbye as his VW took off for the highway. When we left Kalamazoo about 8:30 a.m. the wind was blowing and there was a small amount of snow on the pavement. We were driving our Cadillac, and as we headed south the weather conditions didn't in any way discourage us because we knew from experience that every hour driving south took us that much closer to a land of sunshine and warm weather. As usual when we passed the big billboard on I-75 that read "Welcome to Florida," we yelled, "Hi, Florida, we're glad to be back."

We drove into the Nomad Motel Daytona Beach in the early afternoon of January 4, 1970. The managers, Arlene and Frank Ritchie, welcomed us with open arms, and it was only about three minutes before John Lenneys, Frank Shields, and others were helping us unload our car. Being from Montreal, they always came a month earlier.

As Millie and I stood at the sliding glass doors that led out to the ocean we both said, "It's a glorious feeling to again be back at the Nomad on the ocean in Florida." The three months of January, February, and March just went too fast. With the Thompsons living a short block from the Nomad at 111 Van Avenue and the many other friends and acquaintances we had made, we were busy almost day and night. It was walking on the beach, swimming, cards, shuffle, dancing, travelogue, basketball games at Stetson University, Deland only twenty-five miles away, and high school games. Some weeks we could hardly find a night to stay home and watch TV. So when April 1, 1970, came, although we had the ocean crossing ahead of us less than two months away, we nevertheless hated to leave for home. This was the first time in our married life that we didn't look forward to heading our car into the driveway at 250 West Maplehurst. Florida and Daytona Beach were getting their hold on us.

When I returned to the used-car office it was clear to me that things were happening in the Higgins Pontiac organization. Dick wanted me to get him a new car with air conditioning to drive to Houston. I talked with Mr. Higgins about the possibility of an official's car by May 15, and he thought he could get one. Dick came down around May 1, and he and I sat in Mr. Higgin's office discussing a car for him. "It's doubtful that at such an early time of year the type of car Dick wants will be available. Maybe we could find one on the used-car lot that he could have at a good deal," said George. Then George opened up his business heart and told me what he had to do. Mr. Nix, the used-car manager, was to be let go, and they had in mind a man to take his place just as soon as he could recover from a broken leg. I asked him if he thought I would still have a job when I got back from Europe, and George said he thought so.

I had learned enough about the car business to know that a new used-car manager would reorganize his sales force with the personnel he wanted. As I was getting ready to leave for Europe, Nix told me about his being let go and that he felt I should not come back in July feeling I had job security. I told Nix that I had enjoyed working with him and was sorry to see him leave. He had always treated me 100 percent square for four and a half years.

It was my last Saturday in the used-car office. Nix showed me a real nice-running 1969 Pontiac that in his opinion was the best car on the lot. It had air and everything Dick wanted. I put a "sold" sign on it even though I thought it had too many miles on it. The next Tuesday afternoon an elderly gentleman drove into the used-car lot with a 1968 Executive Pontiac sedan with air conditioning and only four thousand miles on it. I asked Nix, "Where did the car come from?" Nix said he was told by Mr. Higgins that it was a trade-in from a retired Pontiac executive and to sell it for what he could get.

Along with several others, I looked it over. It smelled new. I grabbed the phone and told the new-car manager to consider the car sold. "I want it," I said, "for my son." I asked Gary Duncan, President of Higgins Pontiac and George Higgins's son-in-law, "How much shall we offer the owner?" He said, "Let's try $2,295." My reply was, "Let's offer $2,195 and we can always come up." "Okay," said Gary, "I'll get in touch with him." Wednesday night Gary called the used-car office and told me it was a deal at $2,195. I was so tickled that I had gotten Dick a near-new car at the low price, I could hardly sleep that night. It was the best deal I ever made in the car business.

Chapter 14

Retirement Years—Back to Europe, 1970

Dick and Carole drove to Ferndale Friday night. Millie and I had our suitcases all packed because we were flying to Washington, D.C. the next day to stay the weekend with Whyle and Audrey. On Monday Whyle was going to drive us to New York from where we would sail on Tuesday at noon. We were up early that Saturday morning. We got over to the used-car lot by eight o'clock, and by nine o'clock the deal had been completed. Dick backed his car out of the garage where Jim, the porter, had cleaned it up like new. We drove home, and when I got in the house I breathed a great sigh of happiness. Phil and Bonnie with Stephanie came over to say goodbye and by 11:30 a.m. Dick and Carole were driving us in their new car to the airport. We ate lunch in the airport coffee shop, boarded our plane, and waved goodbye. To a degree it was a sad occasion because we knew when we returned home Dick and Carole would be residents of Houston, Texas, a long way from us.

Our flight was enjoyable. Whyle and Audrey met us at the airport. Sunday we all went to church. Audrey had to study so Millie took a rest while Whyle and I drove over to Baltimore to see a ballgame, which the Orioles won in extra innings when the great third baseman Brooks Robinson hit a home run to end the game.

Whyle had made reservations for two rooms at the same motel on the New Jersey Turnpike where we had stayed in 1965. Whyle said it was about four hours from Silver Springs, Maryland, where they lived, and if we left Monday about noon we would be there in plenty of time. So Monday night, May 25, found us at the motel thinking, "Tomorrow at noon we sail."

After eating an early breakfast at the restaurant next to the motel, 7:45 a.m. found us on the turnpike heading for the Holland Tunnel. We drove up in front of Pier 40, and seeing the *Nieuw Amsterdam* at the dock heightened my anxiety. The dock men took our suitcases out of the car trunk, stating they would be put in room 233 as the labels called for.

Whyle parked his car on the upper tier of the docks while I was in line to get our tickets and passports okayed. Whyle got a visitor's pass, and by the time I had the official okay to go aboard he and Millie were waiting for me on the gangplank with the ship's photographer ready to snap our pictures. It wasn't hard to find room 233, which was very conveniently located, since we had made that ship our hotel for sixteen days on previous trips. We walked the ship from top deck to bottom and from stern to bow. When the whistles gave three long blasts and two short ones at 11:30 a.m. announcing the sailing, Whyle said, "I guess I had better get off the ship." As the tugboats pushed the ship away from the dock into the river channel it gave me a thrill to be again sailing on our third trip to Europe in five years. I stayed on deck while passing the Statue of Liberty, Coney Island, and under the bridge into the open ocean. Then I joined Millie for lunch.

Wednesday morning it got noised among the passengers that we had a very sick man onboard and the doctor and captain were having a consultation on what procedure should be followed. As I was told by the ship's purser, the doctor said that the man would not live through the crossing although his doctor had assured the ship officers that he was okay to take aboard. On Wednesday afternoon the passenger's condition was announced over the P.A. system and that in order to save his life the ship was going off its course to hospitalize him at Halifax, and that we should reach Halifax about midnight. We wondered how they could take him off since the ship would just pull into the bay and anchor. Some thought it would be by helicopter and others thought a tender would come out and pick him up. After the ship had dropped anchor Millie and I stayed on deck until about midnight. The fog was so thick you could cut it with a knife. We couldn't hear or see what was going on, so I said to Millie, "Let's go to bed."

When we awakened in the morning the speculation was that the ship would make up part of the time lost by going to Halifax. However, two days later we were informed we would be twenty-four hours late arriving at Rotterdam and that the Holland American Line would do everything in their power to help passengers reschedule their commitments. We had met onboard a couple by the name of Cox who lived in the Palmer Woods section of Detroit located just south of 8 Mile Road west of Woodward Avenue, which is the south boundary of Ferndale. They too were scheduled to board the Rhine River steamship *Helvetia* at 8:00 p.m. for a five-day trip up the river on the day that the *Nieuw Amsterdam* had been scheduled to dock. Now that we would be twenty-four hours late, what were we to do about the Rhine River ship? After discussing various possibilities, we decided to have the Holland American Line get us railway tickets to a German city on the Rhine that would allow us to go aboard when the Rhine ship put in for a docking. The tickets were ordered and would be delivered to the purser's office at Southampton. However, the Coxes were on a tour, and as we got off the ship about 9:30 a.m. expecting to get a taxi to the Bahnhof Mr. and Mrs. Cox were met by a tourist representative. He explained that he had already sent a bus to the city of Emmerich, Germany. He wondered why we were not in the group that the ship had allowed to disembark at 7:30 a.m. The purser's office had failed to notify us of such arrangements when I called at the office in answer to their request. I told them I had my railway tickets, and nothing more was said. After about fifteen minutes of conversation the tourist representative told us he could get a taxi for fifteen dollars a couple to drive us to Emmerich, Germany, in time to go aboard the Rhine steamer. The four of us agreed to pay the fifteen dollars, so off we went to catch the ship.

By fast driving we got to Emmerich, Germany, at 11:40 a.m. and there was the bus with about fifteen people also waiting. All eyes were glued on the river to the north. It was exactly noon when we saw the ship coming around the bend in the river. Shortly after noon we were aboard, and I was the first to reach the desk to present my tickets and passports. "Before going to your room perhaps you would like to eat the dinner now being served," said the purser. So the Coxes and Wilcoxes became meal companions for the next five days aboard the Rhine steamer.

The trip up the Rhine was an enjoyable and educational one. It was easy to see the results of our Marshall Plan following the war, and also to understand why Germany is a great industrial nation. The cities of Koln and Dusseldorf told the story of U.S. aid in helping Germany rebuild. We have no cities in the United States that can compare to either or both of these German cities. They were almost totally destroyed during the war, and have now been rebuilt into model cities with the latest service improvements. We took a sightseeing bus tour around Dusseldorf, and I was amazed at its beauty. Parks, beautiful shopping center, no slums, etc., were to be observed. Slums do not exist within Europe's German-speaking nations. The five new bridges across the river were far superior to that which we see in our country. I had never seen such traffic as the Rhine has. Sometimes we wondered how they avoided traffic accidents. Later we were told that each ship and barge on the river had to observe the signals given by the boat's flags. We sailed during the day and tied up in some city for the night, enabling the passengers to have the daylight to enjoy the scenic views.

We arrived at Basel, Switzerland about 4:00 p.m., June 8 and boarded a big bus that carried passengers to their hotels. Our hotel, the Bristol, was right across from the Bahnhof, which made it very convenient. After getting located in our very nice, carpeted room with excellent beds, we walked across the street to the Bahnhof to purchase tickets for the train leaving in the morning at 10:13 a.m. for Vienna, Austria. Then we went to the hotel dining room for a nice dinner. Needing exercise, we walked and walked. We observed the attractive shopping center and the adult evening junior college with students hurrying to classes. Then we retired to our room and early to bed since we had a long train ride the next day.

After eating the continental breakfast in the morning, we got to the Bahnhof early in order to find the track on which our train departed. At 10:13 a.m. sharp Austria's best and fastest express train pulled out of the station, which would get to Vienna at 8:44 p.m. It was just getting dark as we saw the twinkle of lights that we knew was Vienna. Our taxi drove up to the Hotel Am Stephansplatz, which is located directly across the street from Vienna's famous St. Stephens Cathedral. We had a very nice room with all modern fixtures since it was a rather new hotel, as so many of the buildings were in these bombed-out cities. We compared prices and determined that while taxis, hotels, etc. were cheaper, food and clothing were about the price found in the States. Generally in most European cities if you eat what and where the natives eat it's cheaper. We walked, taxied, and bus toured the city for four days. The Blue Danube was muddy, and to me it was not as beautiful as the music of the Blue Danube waltz made you believe.

On Sunday, June 14, 1970, we were in for a new experience. We were going to the Communist country of Czechoslovakia. We were to arrive at 2:10 p.m. in Prague; however, we didn't get there. Our travel service had sent ninety-seven dollars and fifty cents for five nights and four days including meals to the Hotel Flora in Prague. This was twice the cost of our hotel. When we arrived at the Czechoslovakian border our train stopped at the station and officials came on to inspect our passports. As he thumbed through the passport I said to myself, "What is he looking for?" "No visa," he said in English. I told him I didn't know we had to have a visa. "Off train" he said, and the two of them grabbed our suitcases and we followed. We were taken into the office where a really nice, middle-aged lady explained to us that we would have to go back to Vienna and get a visa at the Czechoslovakia Embassy. There was a train in about one hour that would take us back to Vienna and she would put us on it. She marked our tickets so that we could use them when we had obtained our visa without additional railway fare.

Getting back to Vienna early in the evening, we were aware that we had no place to sleep. We took a taxi to the Hotel Am Stephanspltaz where we had had a room for five nights. On hearing our story, the desk clerk said, "I have no empty rooms, but I'll find you a hotel." He got on the phone, and after several calls he said he had a room just a short block away and asked one of his bellhops to carry our suitcases for us. The room was luxurious, costing us twenty-eight dollars, which was about twice the amount we generally paid. However, it was a place to sleep in style.

We had to get two photos for our visa so one of the hotel clerks who spoke good English took us about two blocks where there was one of those coin photo cameras. We got two photos of each of us. The next morning we took a taxi to the Embassy, where after about one hour we were able to get a visa. Going back to the hotel and knowing we would be taking the afternoon train to Prague that didn't get us there until midnight, I said to Millie, "We had better stop at the bank and buy some Czechoslovakia currency. We'll need some to pay the taxi, etc." The banker looked at me in a strange way and gave me Austrian currency. "No," I said, "I want some Czech money." He opened a drawer and counted out a lot of it for a twenty dollars traveler's check.

When we got on the train, an Austrian businessman was in the compartment with us. He spoke English, and when I told him I had already bought money he said, "That's bad. That is black market money, and it's against the law to take it into Czechoslovakia. Put it in your pocket and when we come to the border the girl comes through the train and will ask if you want to buy some money. Better buy some," he said. We did, and when we got to the Hotel Flora our hearts fell because it looked like an old, old hotel. The next morning in the daylight we could see that it wasn't as bad as our first impression. First we took a taxi to the American Embassy. When I explained our money situation to the lady at the desk her first words were, "That's bad!" "However," she said, "you can spend it, can't you?" The second day after a bus sightseeing tour Millie talked the hotel manager into giving us back part of our deposit, so we had plenty of Czech money with no place to spend it. We ate the best meals the hotel had on the menu.

We were so anxious to get out of this Communist country that we took a 10:05 p.m. train for Vienna, where upon arrival about 7:00 a.m. we took a train to Salzburg. From there we went by bus to Berchtesgaden and arrived at 2:30 p.m. We taxied to our Post Leithaus hotel where we had a nice room for four nights.

I was pooped, so I went to bed for a few hours' sleep. In the meantime Millie went exploring and found that Berchtesgaden had an American soldier's retreat as we had found in Garmisch. Among the several trips we took was up to Hitler's Crow's Nest, which cost many millions to build but was visited by Hitler only a few times. We ate all our meals there and had good American food at a cheap price.

Tuesday morning, June 23, 1970, found us at the Bahnhof to catch the train to Munich at 9:17 a.m. Arriving in that great big Munich station with its thirty-some tracks, our first interest was to find an "Information Man" to inform us of the time and the track number on which the train to Garmisch departed. Trains run on schedule to the second in Western Europe, and when 2:45 p.m. showed on my watch we were pulling into Garmisch.

We had previously spent several days in Garmisch, a city of twenty-seven thousand people. Being at the same hotel, the Markt Platz that we had enjoyed very much gave us a feeling of security. After our experience visiting Prague we sure needed it. Our room number 19 was a delightful one. We had given Phil, Dick, and our other relatives our itinerary, hoping that at each city we would receive mail. We were never disappointed. During the four days and nights we spent in Garmisch we went to the U.S. theater and ate our meals at the Green Arrow Inn, a U.S. military retreat where our dinners cost as little as one dollar and thirty cents. Millie and I played the slot machines and came away with dollars in our pocket since Millie won the jackpot. The Bavarian city located in the valley of the mountains was a picture of beauty. Free to tourists were band concerts given at 11:00 a.m. and 8:00 p.m. at the band shell located in the lovely park in the heart of the city's business section.

We had a very interesting and delightful breakfast our last day, which was Saturday. As we walked into the Green Arrow Inn dining room all the tables were filled. At one table a lady sat all by herself, and she invited us to join her. We did, and during our conversation she stated she had been a schoolteacher at the American military near Frankfurt, Germany for eleven years. She started her teaching in Mississippi, but took the opportunity to teach for the U.S. government. She liked Europe so much that she was going to continue for several more years. She was on vacation and enjoying herself driving around Europe.

The next morning, Sunday, June 28, 1970, we arose early. Our train to Munich departed at 7:41 a.m. We asked before retiring if we would be able to have the continental breakfast at 6:45 a.m. "Yes, we will serve you," was the reply of the young lady at the desk. By 7:15 a.m. we were in a taxi heading for the Bahnhof. It was only a ten-minute drive, so we arrived in plenty of time. To get to Interlaken, Switzerland, we had to make three changes, one at Munich where we got a train to Zurich, then a change of trains to Bern, and after an hour wait the train to Interlaken.

Interlaken is a small city that I first visited in 1924 and revisited in 1965 and 1968, sits in the valley between two Alp mountain ranges. It has just one long main street and just does not change very much from year to year. The winters are cold and the snow is deep. We arrived in my favorite European city at 8:30 p.m. A taxi took us to our Hotel Krebs, where we stayed five nights. During the four full days we were in Interlaken we took bus tours, went to concerts in the afternoon, and evening at the casinos, shopped, etc. We ate our meals at the hotel because we had found from experience that their prices were just as cheap as some of the restaurants we had eaten in.

One of our most pleasant experiences of our whole trip was dinner with Mr. and Mrs. Balmer and their daughter-in-law. Mrs. Balmer had a gift and souvenir shop right next door to her daughter-in-law, who had opened a small children's clothing shop. We had made purchases from both shops on our previous trips and Millie had mailed orders for Christmas presents the year before. We entered Mrs. Balmer's shop and she said, "Oh, I remember you, but I don't remember your husband." While she and Millie were visiting I went next door to the daughter-in-law's shop. As I introduced myself she said, "I remember you, but I don't remember your wife." Before we left the shop Mrs. Balmer invited us to have dinner with them on Tuesday evening. She and her daughter-in-law both spoke good English, and her husband spoke some. We had a delightful evening. The dinner lasted from 7:30 p.m. until about 10:00 p.m. When I said, "We must be going," he drove us back to our hotel. We stopped at the shops Friday morning, July 3, but neither was in, so we left a message of goodbye.

The hotel clerk had obtained our tickets to Reims, France, where we were to spend two nights and one full day. Our train schedule called for us to leave Interlaken at 11:50 a.m. and to arrive in Reims at 10:45 p.m. It was a long train ride, but interesting. We had to make one change at Basel, Switzerland, to a French train.

Our hotel in Reims was our poorest one, and we were glad that we had only two nights there. It was clean and cheap. This was the first time I had been in Reims since 1924. During World War I the Germans had leveled it to the ground; only the cathedral was left standing. But now it was a rebuilt city, having gone through World War II with little damage. It was a cool day. Aside from visiting the cathedral, walking around the city, getting our train tickets to London, England, there was little to see in Reims that interested us. We went to bed at 9:00 p.m. on this July 4 knowing that we would have to get up at 4:30 a.m. in order to get the 5:45 a.m. Channel train.

At 5:00 a.m. there was a knock on our door. The clerk had prepared the continental breakfast and was bringing it to our room. Since we were only one short block from the Bahnhof I carried our two suitcases. As time ticked away, more and more people arrived at the station. We realized we were not the only early risers. Our boat was waiting for the train crowd at the Channel. We asked a fellow on the train how to get to the boat, and he said just follow the crowd. He sure was right. It took just two hours to cross the Channel.

The train to London was waiting for its passengers. Our compartment was filled with one other man and five girls who were coming back to London after spending several days vacationing in southern France. Our train arrived at the Victoria Station in good time, and by 2:00 p.m. a taxi was driving us to the Strand Palace Hotel. The hotel had been remodeled since our 1965 visit to London. All rooms had baths and showers. We were given a front room right on the Strand, which is one of the busiest streets in London. Millie said, "I can't stand five nights of this," so she went downstairs to the desk and asked for a room change. She was told that there were no vacancies but to come down in the morning and there would be some vacancies. That she did, and it wasn't but a few minutes before a bellhop came up to move us down to the second floor, room number 290 inner court, where there was peace and quiet.

We did what all tourists do saw the Changing of the Guard that we had seen in 1965, along with other attractions. Tuesday we took a sightseeing bus that took us out to Windsor, where we toured the Queen's Windsor Castle. It was one of London's hottest days in history, a temperature of ninety degrees with no air conditioning in the bus. Millie felt it very much. When we got back to the Hotel Strand Palace she had had it. She stayed in bed most of the day. By Wednesday, though, it had cooled off.

It rained Thursday morning but cleared in the afternoon, and we went out and did some shopping. I got a good cheap haircut, and on our last full day in London we watched on TV the British golf tournament in which many Americans were playing. Then we went across the street from the hotel to Simpson's, the famous restaurant where men are men and women are second best, to eat a delicious beef dinner. We went to bed tired at about 9:30 p.m. I turned to Millie and said, "Tomorrow we sail." She said, "I'm ready to go home." We both agreed that with the exception of our visit to Prague, it had been a good, enjoyable tour. We had enjoyed our stay in the Strand Palace Hotel very much as well as being in London again, but after three tours of Europe in a span of five years I felt, as Millie did, that we had accomplished all that we had dreamed in European travel.

Friday, July 10, 1970, dawned a nice London day, cool, partly cloudy, but no rain. We ate our breakfast about 9:00 a.m. in the hotel dining room then leisurely packed our suitcases and tote bags. I put the "S.S. France Room V238" labels on all our baggage, and at noon, the checkout time, we had a bellhop take our bags down to the baggage room for safekeeping. During the week I had called the French Steam Ship Company office in London and was told the boat train would leave the Waterloo Station at 7:20 p.m. for Southampton, where the *France* would be docked. We walked the streets window-shopping, sat in the hotel lobby, had a good lunch at three o'clock, and waited for the afternoon to pass. When it was about 5:15 p.m., I said to Millie, "Let's get our baggage and take a taxi to the Waterloo Station."

As we left the taxi and with our bags at the depot, men with a truckload full of baggage for the *France* called out the track number on which our special boat train would depart. We found an empty bench and took turns sitting with our baggage. I enjoyed watching the passenger trains arriving and departing, some being pulled by an old steam locomotive. The many tracks provided constant railway action. I couldn't help but think of the days fifty years ago when the New York Central Station in Detroit had the same amount of passenger traffic, with trains going and coming every few minutes. As the hands of the clock reached 6:40 p.m., people started congregating near the gate of the track on which our train would load. I said to Millie, "Let's go and get a place near the track."

The French office had told me we would occupy "C 1," and the windows of the cars would have the numbers, so when the gates were opened at 7:00 p.m. Millie and I were among the first to file through. As we walked down the track platform, passing car after car looking for our number, we finally located it near the front of the train. Placing our suitcases in the racks, we sat and talked with a man and his wife who were sharing our compartment. They were Australians who were going to tour the United States. At 7:20 p.m. our train was on its way. Through the window I took one last look at Old Big Ben and said goodbye to London and England.

During our train ride to Southampton, which took about one hour and twenty minutes, officials came into our compartment to check our tickets and passports, after which we were given a blue embarkation ticket. I asked, "What do I do about our baggage in the rack?" The answer was just leave it on the train, "Our men will pick it up and see to it that it gets into your room."

As our train pulled around to get onto the tracks that went into the steamship passenger terminal I could see the *France* waiting for us to go aboard. Getting off the train, we went into the station where it was announced all passengers with blue tickets should take the escalator to the upper level. We knew then that our room was in the premiere class although we were considered tourist class. Coming onto the upstairs veranda of the docks, I stopped for a minute to see what the ship looked like. It was a big one, the longest ship now sailing the ocean.

"Let's hurry and get aboard," Millie said. We walked the enclosed gangplank and were met by a bellhop who took our ticket stub and showed us to our room. I put my arm around Millie and said, "We have made it; we're going home." Because we had not done any tipping during our tour since the Holland American Line advertises "no tipping," and hotels and restaurants in European countries add a 15 percent tip to your bill, I forgot to tip the bellhop. The result was our suitcases were left at our door instead of being put in our room. The ship sailed at 11:00 p.m., and after staying on deck until we were in the Channel we went to bed.

At our request we were given a table for two, first seating. We had a fine meal after we got aboard, so we didn't go to bed on an empty stomach. One novelty that we had not experienced on the Holland American ships was that for each meal there were always two bottles of wine on our table, one red and one white. We had a beautiful trip home, fine weather with sunshine. Because the ship was so large and we took only four days and five nights to make the crossing to New York, there was less organized activity than on the Dutch ships.

On Sunday, July 12, about 3:10 p.m. it was announced that in twenty minutes we would pass the *Queen Elizabeth II* on the starboard side. The two ships passed within a half mile of each other, both giving the salute of three long and two short blasts of their whistles. To me it was a thrill.

On Tuesday, July 14, 1970, it was announced that the following day the ship would enter the Hudson River at 6:00 a.m., that we would pass the Statue of Liberty at 6:30 a.m., and by 7:30 a.m. we would be docked. I was up on deck just after going by the Ambrose lighthouse, which terminates the ship's crossing. As we went under the bridge into the river, I looked at my watch and it was 6:00 a.m. sharp. We were right on time. Our baggage had been set out by our door at 6:00 p.m. the night before so that it could be ready to be taken off the ship right after docking. As the tugs guided the ship into its berth I said to Millie, "Let's go down and eat our last meal aboard." It was 9:30 a.m. when it was announced that passengers were able to leave the ship.

Before we left for Europe Whyle, who had driven us to New York for our sailing, agreed that he and Audrey would meet us and that we four would drive to Ferndale for a visit. So when we left the ship, got our baggage and went through customs without question, we started looking for Whyle and Audrey. There was a huge crowd of people waiting to see their relatives or friends disembark, so we took our baggage and went to the waiting room where Millie sat while I went out and combed the crowd of people, but no Whyle. Later he told us that he had called the French line the day before, asking for the docking time of the ship, and he understood that they expected the France in at noon. So we waited and waited, but as always good old faithful Whyle with Audrey got there shortly after noon. We loaded our baggage in the car trunk and took off by way of Canada for Ferndale. We arrived home Thursday late afternoon, July 16, 1970, fully satisfied that we would have no more thirst to travel Europe. We had many gratifications on our trip that we were truly thankful for. We both enjoyed good health on our tour. We also received mail from either Dick or Phil at every hotel except at Reims. One piece of mail I got at Berchtesgaden, Germany was greatly appreciated because it was on Father's Day. It contained a card with a sweet young lady's picture on its cover and stated, "From Your Girl, Grandpa." On the inside was a photo of Stephanie and "Happy Father's Day." Of course, it was from the three of them.

Chapter 15

Home From Europe and Moving to Daytona Beach, Florida

In early July Dick and Carole had moved to Houston, which left a lonesome spot in our hearts. Monroe and Ruth were again visiting Michigan, and we all were able to have a reunion in Kalamazoo with Lee and Al's families being the hospitality committee. It was a most enjoyable occasion.

In my two months' accumulation of mail I spied a letter from the Higgins Pontiac Company. It contained a check for the month of June. The letter stated it would be my last check from Higgins Pontiac. The reorganization program was necessary since automobiles were just not selling. I called George Higgins and expressed my great appreciation for keeping me on the Higgins Pontiac payroll for four and a half years, and that I understood the circumstances under which he was operating. He replied he was very sorry he had to lay me off, but it was absolutely necessary. I was not disappointed because I had planned to terminate my employment when we left for Florida the first of the year. I was seventy-one years old, and considered that long enough to be employed.

As September arrived we began to look for a phone call from Texas. Dick said his son would be born on September 16, 1970, the tenth anniversary of his and Carole's first meeting. However it was September 19, 1970, when the phone rang and the excited voice on the other end said, "Mother and Dad, you have a grandson." Of course, we were happy for them. A few days later the mailman brought a letter from Houston, and in it was a card: "Announcing the First Texan Wilcox. James Adrian, weight 8 lb., 4 ½ oz. and is 20 inches long born September 19, 1970."

The fall had its usual work, leaves, preparing the house for winter, etc. It was football every Friday night and Saturday. In October we went to the Kalamazoo College homecoming. There were a few returning "old-timers" whom I had known when we all were young college students.

We enjoyed both holidays, Thanksgiving with Phil's and Christmas week in Houston with Dick's.

New Year's Day 1971 found us packed and ready to leave Houston for Florida. Being "football" day, there was little activity. Dick and I were glued to the tube while Millie and Carole amused themselves.

We were up at 6:00 a.m., January 2, 1971, and by 7:15 a.m. we were on the pavement headed east. We always made the trip an enjoyable, one taking the greater part of three days to get to Daytona Beach. As we arrived at the Nomad Motel on January 4, we were joyful to be back to the ocean and southern climate. We renewed our friendship with the Ritchies, the Roys, the Lenneys, the Fields, and others at the Nomad. Of course, 111 Van Avenue where the Thompsons resided six months during the fall, winter, and spring received a lot of our attention. February 14, 1971, found Al, wife Recil, Whyle, wife Audrey, Debbie, Millie, and I celebrating together on the ocean beach of Daytona. It was another enjoyable occasion for all of us.

On April 1, 1971, Millie and I were on our way back to Michigan. For the first time we were sorry to leave Daytona Beach to return to Ferndale. Florida was getting us, slowly but surely. After several weeks I decided to go back to the Exchange Club. April 1971 marked my forty-fifth year in the Ferndale Exchange. I had held every office except treasurer and had made a good contribution to the club. I decided to resign, and on May 20, 1971, I presented my resignation to the president, Joe Barger, who was in my classes during my earlier years of teaching.

At the June 1, 1971, meeting President Joe announced that "Bud Brown has a presentation to make." After Bud had extolled all my virtues and achievements in education, sports, civic life, and Exchange, he presented a distinguished service plaque on behalf of Exchange. In my response I stated I had gotten a lot out of Exchange because I had put a lot into it and, addressing the younger members, I told them that they too would get out of it as much as they put in, not in dollars and cents, but in "unity for service." On August 6, 1971, I received a letter from the Exchange secretary, Ray Rowell, another one of my former students, stating that the club had made me an honorary member of Exchange with all the privileges that an honorary member is granted. I wrote Ray that I greatly appreciated the recognition that had been given to me by the Exchange Club of Ferndale.

The June 1971 "K" College Alumni Association honored the 1921, class fiftieth anniversary. Monroe and Ruth came since that was Monroe's class. During the weekend of commencement the fiftieth-anniversary class was entertained free by the college, and those class members present were taken into the Emeritus Club. Monroe wanted Millie and me to go for the weekend, and I arranged with the college to room (free) at the women's dormitory where all alumni were housed. We enjoyed the weekend activity very much. We also took time to spend a few hours with Leland and Allen's families.

The baseball All Star game was being played in Detroit on July 13, 1971. I called George Higgins, asking if he could get me a couple of tickets since they were hard to come by. He said he would if I would go down to the Tigers stadium to pick up some tickets for him. Believe you me, I said sure, and we got our tickets.

It was during the summer of 1971 that I received an outstanding service plaque from the Michigan Public Schools Adult Education Association for serving as state president from 1952 to '53. I also received a certificate of appreciation from the National Association in Washington, D.C. in recognition of dedicated leadership through membership on the board of directors. I served two terms on the national board, elected by the members of the National Association of Public School Adult Educators.

In July the library board sent me to Dallas, Texas, for the national conference. Millie accompanied me, and after the conference we took a bus to Houston to spend a week with Dick's family.

On July 12, 1971, I received a letter from Ferndale's mayor, Bruce Garbutt, stating, "The members of the Ferndale City commission cordially invite you and your wife as guest to be present at the dedication of the Commemorative Plaque, recognizing your past leadership and services as a city commissioner for the City of Ferndale." Of course we accepted and were present. We relived some of my eight years on the city commission with Arthur Bartlett and his wife Olive, George Higgins and wife, and others. The July 27, 1971, *Daily Tribune* had a picture of us seated in the chairs of the commissioners, with an article describing the dedication. It was an interesting and well-appreciated evening. The plaque with all our names and terms of office hangs on the wall of the commission chamber in the new city hall. There were a number of photos taken of us as individuals and as a group, and we all received full-sized copies.

On Thursday, August 19, 1971, the *Ferndale Gazette* reported that in 1944 Adult education was offered at the Ferndale High School during weekly evenings. The state of Michigan granted six thousand dollars to launch this program in Ferndale. Ferndale's Superintendent Paul Best was given this responsibility. I was appointed the Director of Adult Education and during the initial fall term we had four hundred adult students. The article mentioned that I served this capacity until 1965.

As my mother used to say, "I want my flowers while I am alive to enjoy them and not on my grave." I have greatly appreciated the honors bestowed on me in recognition of my fifty years of living and of serving the people of Ferndale. I have received my flowers while living and I sincerely hope that I have been deserving of all of them.

For four years Millie and I had been living at the motel Nomad, Daytona Beach, Florida during the winter months and greatly enjoying it. We had changed, our neighborhood had changed, and Ferndale had changed. We weighed all the pros and cons, the advantages and disadvantages, and after careful and prayerful thoughts came to the conclusion that we would rather spend the rest of our years in

Daytona Beach, Florida, than at 250 West Maplehurst, Ferndale. So when we left Ferndale the second week in November 1971, we departed with the intention that during the winter months we would look for and buy a house on the peninsula of Daytona Beach, Florida.

We looked and looked all winter long. Houses were selling like hotcakes. We would look at a house for sale one day with the idea of thinking it over, and the next day when we went back it would have been sold. Finally we went to Cardinal Realtors on the first Saturday of March. The agent said, "I have just one house that you might like." He drove us to 202 Venetian Way South. Millie said, "This is it. This is my dream house. Consider it sold." It had all wood-paneled rooms, central air and heat, and a stone yard. There was as little to do in the way of upkeep as you could find in any house. On March 30, 1972, we completed the deal and we were Floridians.

We had had some great winters at the Nomad. During the winter of 1970-1971 brother Al (Allen) and Recil arrived, as did Whyle's family, and we all stayed at the Nomad. We had a small Christmas tree in our unit 108, and on Christmas Day we celebrated by eating dinner out. During February 1971 Al and Recil had to leave the Nomad Motel for home due to Al's failing health. Christmas 1971 found Phil and Dick with their families at the Nomad Motel. It was a wonderful time with all of us being together during Christmas week.

During the winter months there was golf with my friends John Lenneys, Herb Manson, Alex Roy, and others. There was dancing, cards, shuffle, basketball games, etc. We had a great winter. Every Sunday night we were at the Thompson's at 111 Van Avenue to watch "The FBI," cards, plus many other activities.

The year 1972 brought sadness to the hearts of the Wilcoxes when brother Leland was taken away from us on March 12, and Allen departed from this life on October 6.

On April 1, 1972 we left the motel Nomad for the last time as residents. Already John and Theresa Lenneys had moved from Montreal to Daytona Beach, and at this writing they live in an apartment on North Halifax on the river. John and I have continued to play golf together now and then, and we four play bridge about twice a month.

Reaching home on April 3, 1972, there were the usual routine things to do. One of the first jobs was to contract a painter to redecorate our living and dining rooms and the hall. Then there was the usual spring yardwork to be done. After we had the house in what we considered selling condition, we began to ponder the question of what method should be used to sell. We could sell it ourselves and save the realtor fee, but this method could have many problems. We could put it in the hands of a realtor and relieve ourselves of all the details and responsibility. After careful consideration we chose the latter method. We called a friendly acquaintance, Forest A. Lindsey, a semi-retired man who was with The Home Company in Ferndale. Forest came to the house, and after surveying the property told us the amount of money he thought we should ask for it. We signed the contract and put the selling of the house in which we had lived over thirty-seven years in his hands. Over a period of two years we had done some real soul searching in order to make up our minds to move without a single reservation. Within three weeks the house was sold. It was a most attractive home that took the buyers' eyes just as quickly as it had taken ours over thirty-seven years before. Now there was the moving problem to be contracted for.

In the meantime, on Monday night, May 6, 1972, at 6:30 p.m. we had our Methodist men's bowling banquet. As president of the bowling league and having been gone all winter, I had delegated the responsibility of the organization to a committee chairman. They did a beautiful job. When I got home on April 4 and called a meeting of the banquet chairmen, I was pleasantly surprised to learn that the work was all done. The banquet was a very successful and well-planned affair. There was a lump in my throat when I thanked all of them, knowing I was meeting for the last time with as nice a group of men as I had ever had the privilege of knowing and bowling with.

In May 1972 I attended my last south Oakland County retired teachers luncheon. I had been president of this organization for two years and had gotten to know a goodly number of the one hundred, forty members, so when it was announced by the president that the Wilcoxes were moving to Florida I had a lot of handshaking and goodbyes.

June 1922 was a time I always remembered because it marked the finish to my Kalamazoo College days. I had run my last official race and had won and set a M.I.A.A. two-mile record that held up for over thirty-six years until it was broken by an Albion College boy. Now fifty years later, June 10, 1972, found Millie and me on the college campus for our fiftieth class anniversary. We left Ferndale Friday morning on June 9, 1972, stopped to visit with Hilda (brother Leland's wife) for a few minutes, called Recil asking about brother Al, who was in the hospital, and then proceeded to the Kalamazoo College campus. We were housed in the girl's dormitory as we had been the previous year, but this weekend belonged to the class of 1922 with no expenses to ourselves. There were twenty some of us back, a few that I had not seen for fifty years. As we gathered for our banquet Friday evening, it was, "Hello Charley – Louise – Harry – Dick – etc." It was just delightful to see and shake hands with those whom I had associated with fifty years before on the campus of Kalamazoo College for four long (to us then) years. There wasn't a single building left standing from our time, but we did walk the sidewalks, thinking that fifty years ago we might have walked on the same cement. The Emeritus Club breakfast was held Saturday, June 10, 1972. It was at this time that those of the class of 1922 who were present were cordially welcomed into its membership. Of our class about one-third were present, about one-third were unable to attend, and about one-third had passed on to another life. By Sunday afternoon, June 11, 1972, we were on our way back to Ferndale.

I stopped at the hospital to say my last goodbye to brother Al, for I knew I would never see him again. We drove Louise Every Crothers and Nellie Jacobs Thompson back to Ferndale with us. They were two of my classmates. Louise was living in Colorado and visiting Nellie, who lived in Ferndale.

Monroe and Ruth had intended to get back to the Kalamazoo College commencement weekend that included the Emeritus Club breakfast, but other activities delayed his arrival. He was honored with a citation by the Emeritus Club membership for his great work for forty-five years in the Montana Methodist Conference. Because of his absence, I was asked to receive it in his behalf and to respond in appreciation. That I did. A few days later Monroe and Ruth, and Whyle and Audrey arrived in Ferndale. Seeing our situation of packing etc., Audrey decided to spend her time in Flint with her sister. We had an enjoyable week with Monroe, Ruth, and Whyle at our house. Phil and Bonnie played their part in entertaining.

On June 12, 1972, we were informed the movers would be at our house in the forenoon of July 13. They were late getting there and didn't get our furniture loaded by nightfall. They said they would be back the first thing in the morning, so we stayed overnight at Phil's. We were back at the house at 7:30 a.m. We waited and waited, but no movers. About 9:30 a.m. the phone rang, and we were informed the men had overslept and would be out by eleven o'clock.

It was 2:30 p.m. when Millie and I said goodbye to the house we had lived in for over thirty-seven years. We turned the key in the front door, backed the Cadillac out of the drive, and headed for Phil's, where Bonnie had a nice lunch waiting for us. They wanted us to stay overnight, but Millie and I thought we had better start driving south, not knowing how long it would take the movers to get to Daytona Beach, Florida. I'll never forget the scene as we waved goodbye. There was Phil, Bonnie, and sweet little Stephanie standing on their front steps, all waving goodbye. It is a picture that will forever live in my mind.

We got to Daytona Beach in the afternoon of June 17, 1972. We stopped at Cardinal Realtor to pick up our key. Pulling into the drive at 202 Venetian Way South and opening the front door, we found the house like an oven. The air conditioning unit was dead. We called the York Air Condition Distributors and got little satisfaction because they could not correct the trouble for several days. For two nights we stayed at an ocean beach motel, and then we contacted Ruth and Howard Thompson who in the summertime live in Huntington Woods, Michigan, which is about three miles from our old home in Ferndale. They were glad for us to use their house at 111 Van Avenue. Their son Jack, who lives here in Daytona Beach, came over and opened it up for us. It was a lifesaver.

It took them seventeen days to finally get the air conditioner repaired. In the meantime, the movers came, and we did some shopping for new furniture. At the time it was a very disappointing nightmare. We had driven to our new home with the highest of expectations. To find it like an oven, a condition that continued for about two and a half weeks and made it necessary for us to eat and sleep elsewhere, really put a damper on our high regard for Daytona Beach. But gradually we got settled. We delayed the delivery of our new furniture until such time as we could use it. We spent a lot of time on the beach, enjoying the cool breeze after sundown that really cooled it off.

I went to several Daytona Beach Dodgers' ballgames. I generally obtained free tickets passed out by various businesses.

In September I started playing golf again, and as we got into October and November I could be found at Memorial Stadium on Friday nights, watching one of the two local high schools play football. In October we journeyed about one hundred and twenty-five miles to Gainesville to see the University of Florida get beaten by Auburn University in a really good game.

Then we were told by Dick that they were going to spend ten days with us Thanksgiving week. It was a grand ten days. Dick and I took in the city championship football game, and watched and heard the two large bands representing Seabreeze and Mainland High Schools compete with each other.

The Thompsons arrived for the winter and with native couples we danced, played cards and enjoyed the warm climate of Daytona Beach.

Phil, Bonnie, and Stephanie were planning on spending nine days with us over the Christmas holidays, and we lived in anticipation of their visit. Phil had just purchased a 1972 Pontiac station wagon and made the trip in two days. It was a big Christmas for all of us. Dick and Carole entertained her parents over the holidays in Houston.

The winter season was full of activity. My golf game greatly improved in respectability since I became a member of the Daytona Beach Golf and Country Club, and I now played about three times a week.

On December 3, 1972, Millie and I transferred our church membership to the "Westminster By the Sea Presbyterian Church" located on Peninsula Drive about a mile and a quarter from our house. It's a smaller church with about six hundred members, but very active. We both get a real spiritual lift out of our membership.

In the fall Millie became a member of the Peninsula Women's Club as well as the Newcomers Club, and with all her other social engagements these have kept her very busy doing "her thing."

We are planning a week's visit this month at Dick's in Houston, Texas, at which time we will see our second Texas grandson, John, who was born to Carole and Dick on March 14, 1972.

We had planned to drive to Michigan in August 1972 to visit Phil and see our other new grandson, Scott, who was born to Bonnie and Phil on February 20, 1973, but due to our Ford Torino being hit in the rear by a truck in Louisiana while driving to Houston we decided we should not go to Michigan. I was not injured, but Millie had to go to the hospital in Hammond, Louisiana, for x-rays, etc. where she remained overnight. The following day Dick drove over to Hammond and took us back to Houston. A week later on Monday we flew home to Daytona Beach.

Bub and my sister Donita drove in on Wednesday, and were we delighted to have them as our guests! Bub drove me over to the Olds used-car office, and we purchased a 1972 Olds Delta 88 with low mileage from our church friend. To date we are pleased with the car and enjoy driving it.

Christmas of 1973 we had both Phil's and Dick's families with us in Daytona Beach. Needless to say, we had a delightful time.

It is now May 1973. What is to be in the future will have to be written at a later date. It has taken me about three years of periodical writing to finish my memoirs. Dick was the one who first suggested that I do it. Without his inspiration and help I could never have finished it. Then too it was Millie's scrapbooks, my college "K" book and yearbooks, and Kalamazoo newspaper clippings, etc. that have made my memoirs complete.

* * *

Dad's story ended here. During the late 1970's Dad became a victim of Alzheimer's disease, which took his life on January 15, 1983. He was a wonderful father. He touched many lives. He was very supportive to me and also to my brother Phil.

After Dad's death Boris Sellers wrote to my brother. He stated he was a high school student of Harold. He said Harold was a dear friend during his early teens and provided a lot of counsel and inspiration toward him. Boris felt that Harold was a man of great integrity and was a good model for him. Harold went out of his way to do special things for him and took time to help solve a problem. He ended, saying, "I know you and your family will miss him but we are all so much the better for having known him."

Rick and Carole Wilcox at Adrian College.
July 2012

PART 2

The life of Rick A. Wilcox

Adrian College. Rick and Carole Wilcox seated on
their bench in front of the administration building.
Between Rick and Carole is a bench plate with the
following inscriptions:
Richard Wilcox 63,
Carole E. Taylor 64,
Met Sept. 16, 1960,
Married Dec. 21, 1963.
October 2014

Chapter 16

Gobleville, Where our Known Family Started

Gobleville (name changed to Gobles on April 10, 1922) is a small town just north of Kalamazoo, Michigan. The recorded population of Gobleville in 1890 was 595. I'm sure this number consisted of more children than adults. Gobles is not well known for anything, and most of Michigan's population has never heard of the small town of Gobles. Yet Gobles has been a mecca for my generation and the earlier generations of the Wilcox family. When anyone of the Wilcox family is in Western Michigan, they are pulled to visit Gobles to visit the barbershop of Allen Monroe Wilcox (205 S. State Street). Many of us have taken a picture of this shop from across the street to include the imprint on the top of the shop that reads "A. M. Wilcox, 1910." Then it is a walk down East Exchange Street, past the family's Methodist church, to the house number 410. It was in this house that my great-great-grandfather (Seth Wilcox) and his family lived. Later this house became the home of my grandparents and their family, consisting of my father Harold Brown Wilcox and Harold's five brothers and two sisters.

The family in Gobleville started with Seth (1814-1903) and Abigail (1811-1896) Wilcox moving to Gobleville from New York state in 1864. No one knows the reason Seth brought his family to Gobleville. Seth and Abigail had six children—Romaine, Thomas, Jannette, Sellie (male), Lorancy (female), and Nelson. Seth worked on building the Erie Canal in New York, and during this time lived in Clarkston, NY. It is said that he made his living making ax heads. Seth Wilcox either had the small house at 410 E. Exchange Street built, or it was purchased from a previous owner.

Seth's son Thomas Allen Wilcox went by "Al" and "Allen." He was born in January 1842. He was an excellent violin player. He joined the Union Army during the Civil War and was captured and put in the horrifying Confederates' Libby prison at Richmond, Virginia. He died in this prison, as did the majority of those placed there, in 1865.

Seth's oldest son Romaine (1839-1918) married Sabrina Bethia Standish (1843-1922). Sabrina is linked to Myles Standish (1584-1656), captain of the Mayflower. Romaine and Sabrina Wilcox had a house within a short walking distance of his parents' home. In the twentieth century the town authorized tearing down Romaine's house because it was abandoned and in poor condition.

Romaine and Sabrina Wilcox had four children—William James, Allen Monroe, Mildred Melvina, and Amber Sabrina. William, called "Will," was born in 1865, never married, and died during 1930. He was a gifted musician and could play most instruments by ear. He lived with his parents. In 1879 his father Romaine was blinded from a steam-boiler explosion at a lumber mill at Lake Mill, a part of Gobles. Son Will became the breadwinner for his parents from that time on. Will worked on the railroad, did a lot of fishing, and cut wood for heating and cooking for his parents. He also sold wood that he had cut.

Romaine and Sabrina's other son, Allen Monroe, is my grandfather. Allen Monroe Wilcox was born on July 4, 1871 and died on April 23, 1947. On May 6, 1896, Allen Monroe Wilcox married Susan Belle Brown (1871-1948). They met at Gobleville's Methodist church, which both families attended. Allen M. and Susan Belle Wilcox had nine children. Their first child, a boy, was born dead in 1897.

The baby was buried in the backyard of their house. The next six children were all sons: Monroe James (1898-1992), Harold Brown (1899-1983), Leland Dale (1901-1972), Allen Randell (1902-1972), Whyle Standish (1903-2002), and Paul Victor Homer (1906-1988). Yes, Paul had two middle names. Perhaps his mother wanted one of the names and his father the other so they gave Paul both middle names, and his parents were satisfied. Their two daughters were Abbie Irene (1907-1957) and Donita Belle (1913-2004).

My grandmother, Susan Belle Brown, came from a family of four children. She had two older sisters and one brother. Susan Belle Wilcox was born in 1871. She was five months older than her husband. Susan's father, George Nelson Brown, was born in 1817. He left New York for California in February 1849. A group of investors pooled their money together and hired George Brown to organize this exposition, and in return the investors received a percentage of the gold extracted from the goldfields. He kept one gold nugget, which was passed down to me. The last chapter of this book is about him.

Sometime after George N. Brown returned from California he settled in Joliet, Illinois, and worked as a schoolteacher. He also taught Sunday school, and may have preached for a time. In Joliet he met and married Lucy J. Rudd, who was eighteen years younger than her husband. She also was a schoolteacher. This Brown family moved to Gobleville, Michigan, as it was called then, sometime before their daughter Susan Belle was born in 1871. No one knows what attracted this family to Gobleville. George Brown taught at a small school north of Gobleville. The schoolhouse, Brown School, was named after him. I suspect that my grandmother Susan Belle had her father as a teacher. She left school before the ninth grade, and her husband left school after the fifth grade.

My grandfather Allen Monroe Wilcox was another family member who was a gifted musician. The same could be said for his sister Mildred M. Holland, and his daughter Abbie Irene Iles. Abbie was an excellent piano player. Allen Monroe Wilcox couldn't read music, but he could play the piano, violin, cornet, and trumpet by ear. He joined the circus band and traveled around the country playing the cornet or trumpet. His favorite was the violin; he could play it with the bow between his legs and moving the violin back and forth on the bow. When he asked Susan Belle Brown to marry him she said only if he gave up the circus life and settled down in Gobleville, which he did. They were married on May 6, 1896.

Romaine Wilcox's house was a short walk to 410 E. Exchange Street. My Uncle Whyle wrote that when he was a young kid growing up Romaine would walk almost every day to Allen and Susan's house and visit with their children while they were eating breakfast or lunch. He would tell stories of his life. The children's favorite story described a time he went into the forest to chop a tree for wood. While he was in the woods a big storm came and it started to rain heavily. He was near a huge tree that fell over and left a very large crater. It was so dark he couldn't even see his hands. While he was in this huge hole a creature also came into this hole opposite from him. He didn't dare move, and when daylight finally reappeared he was shocked to see a bear climbing out of this large crater. From this house Romaine would walk to the barbershop and spend a little time with his son Allen, and then go to the post office to pick up the mail and walk home. Remarkably, he did all this being blind and using a cane.

I'm told that during the time my father (Harold B. Wilcox) was growing up in Gobles there were only three churches: Catholic, Baptist, and Methodist. The Wilcox and Brown families were Methodist, but Seth Wilcox was a Baptist.

My grandparents and their children and their spouses are all gone, and the same for many of my generation of cousins. Not too long into the future memories of the Wilcox families of Goble will be gone. People come and go. What mark from their lives do they leave behind?

The Christmas season and comments

As a child, Christmas morning was always special. Living at home, we always went to the church's Christmas Eve candlelight services. There was one time during the early 1950's that a special Christmas *I Love Lucy* TV show was on. The *I Love Lucy* programs were my favorite. Before this special was over, it was time to leave for church. I asked Dad if I could skip the service to see the rest of this show. That was not an option. A few decades later, I have wonderful memories of Christmas Eve services, but can't remember much of the *I Love Lucy* shows. During current Christmas Eve services I remember the ones we went to as a family during the Ferndale era. So special! As married adults there have been Christmas Eves on which we have attended two different services. As a family, we have gone to church on every Christmas Eve. It's the highlight of the season. Christmas is all about Jesus Christ, and that is what makes it very special for me. For a long time and even now, Christmas for me is the church services, Sunday school class parties, time with friends, and Christmas music. When we get home from the Christmas Eve service or services, Christmas is over. Participating in the Christmas Eve worship service is "spiritual food" for me. I go to church to participate in worshiping and my soul is nourished.

When I was a youngster at home I asked Dad what Christmas was like when he was a child living at home in Gobleville, Michigan. He said that each child would have a Christmas stocking. The parents would put an orange or an apple in the sock plus some candy and perhaps some nuts. After the Christmas stockings were emptied of treats, the family would go to their church. The parents would buy each child one present and wrap it and take it to their church prior to Christmas morning. On Christmas morning the family would go to church and a church member dressed as Santa would pass out the presents to the kids. I forgot to ask if there was a short service at church on Christmas morning; anyway, I thought that was terrible to get only one present. A few years later I began to suspect that Dad (Harold B. Wilcox) and his brothers and sisters actually had a more enjoyable Christmas than we did.

The family didn't have very much money, which forced the family to seek ways to entertain themselves. Music was part of this family. Dad told me that many Sunday evenings the family would gather in the parlor around the piano and sing songs as their mother or sister Abbie played the piano. I'm sure it was special for the family. Dad said the last song they would sing was, "If you know Suzie." His mother's name was Susan, but she was called "Susie." This had to be special for their mother "Susie" Wilcox.

Chapter 17

My Grandparents

Allen (1871-1947) and Susan (1871-1948) Wilcox

My few memories of my grandparents

I don't remember very much of my grandparents, Allen Monroe and Susan Belle Wilcox. My memories of them probably all occurred when I was around four years old. Grandfather died in 1947 and grandmother in 1948. As I remember it, their house was old but well-kept. My memories of them are as follows:

- I remember being in their backyard, which included an outhouse. I must have been four years old. Unlike today, I could look out from their back yard and view the open fields for miles, with no structure blocking my view. What seemed to be very far away, I saw a train with many cars traveling across this open area. I was in awe to see so much of the train and watched it until it passed out of my view.
- Grandpa was on the front porch in a rocking chair, and I was jumping off the porch. I thought that was really "big stuff," and I was proud of myself. I told Grandpa that I could jump off of the porch. I don't remember if he responded. I'm sure I was more impressed with my jumping skill than he was.
- One time Grandpa asked me and my brother Phil if we wanted to ride on the running boards of his car as he drove to his barbershop, which was just down the street. Phil was on one side and I was on the other, and he drove slowly. That was a wonderful experience! I thought that was really fun.
- I can remember a lot about the inside of the house. Walking into the house, there was a small sitting area that continued to the kitchen. Before reaching the kitchen one encountered the large dining room table. On the left of the front entrance was my grandparent's bedroom and to the right was the parlor. Off the parlor was another bedroom. This bedroom was for their two girls, and the six boys slept in the attic.
- The time of crime that my brother Phil led me into probably occurred during the summer of 1944 when I was four years old. My grandmother and mother were getting dinner or lunch ready. We saw Grandmother come out of the kitchen with a platter of homemade cookies, then she went back into the kitchen. My dear brother, leading me astray, said, "Let's get a cookie!" So I followed him, and we both took a cookie and hustled back to the parlor. We were enjoying our cookie when we heard grandmother's announcement, "What are the boys doing? They are quiet!" We heard her coming, and Phil said to hide as he entered the bedroom off the parlor. He told me to find another place to hide. I got behind a chair. Well, I poked my head out to see where she was and of course she saw me. Since I had an unfinished cookie in my hand it was obvious to her that I had taken a cookie! She said, "That's your cookie

for the day." Of course, I could not be penalized and let Phil go free, so I told grandma that Phil took one too and that he was in the bedroom. After Grandma made the same statement to Phil she went back to the kitchen. Phil was mad at me for telling Grandma that he had a cookie, but he got over it!

- There was a wading pond in a park at the corner of E. Exchange Street and State Street. The water probably wasn't more than twelve inches deep. This was probably in the summer of 1944. Mother put my bathing suit on and walked me down to this pond. I loved it! I thought I was swimming as I used my hands to push the water down toward my legs. It was a fun time for me. Sometime after this event the park and pond were removed.

The Gobles, MI Wilcox family at family home, 410 E. Exchange St.
Left to Right, back row: Harold, Monroe, Leland and Whyle.
Front row: Allen, father Allen Monroe, Abbie, Susan Belle and Paul.
1912

Allen Monroe Wilcox outside his barber shop,
205 S. State St., Gobles, Michigan
August 1946

Allen Monroe Wilcox inside his barber shop,
205 S. State St., Gobles, Michigan
1928

Allen Monroe Wilcox within his Barber Shop.
1928

Allen Monroe and his wife Susan Belle Wilcox at their house. They were married during 1896.
August 1946

Kalamazoo College "K" Club.
Harold Wilcox front row, right end.
Early 1922

Cologne, Germany. Harold Wilcox back seat-driver side. Note Harold's cane as well as the two men standing left side. It was fashionable for men during this time in Germany to carry a cane. Harold' cane is saved within his family.
August 1, 1924

Mildred "Millie" Burrows. She will marry Harold Wilcox in 1933
1930

Mildred & Harold Wilcox married in chapel of
Kalamazoo College,1933. Behind Millie is her
sister Dorothy Burrows and behind Harold is his
brother Whyle.
August 1933

Mildred & Harold Wilcox married in
chapel of Kalamazoo College,1933.
August 1933

Picture of Harold Wilcox used for
running as Ferndale's commissioner.
1935

Millie Wilcox with sons
left to right: Rick & Phil
June 1944

Rick's boxer dog.
It was a hard night.

Jack Hinkins in front of Ferndale house.
Jack and I were like brothers during our high
school years.
July 1962

Carole Taylor-my future wife at
Adrian College. South Hall in background
and North Hall behind her.
Sept. 1962

American Commons Club Fraternity house (my home
for my last two and half years at Adrian College. What
appears to be a white shack on the roof is a small room I
used for college homework. It was the quietest room within
the house. This studying area was very beneficial for me.
May 1963

Carole Taylor who will be my wife by year-end is
seated at my desk in a room which from the outside
appear to be a shack on roof.
May 1963

Rick & Carole Wilcox wedding.
Niles, Michigan
December 21, 1963

Our wedding. Carole's grandmother
Vesta Taylor and Phil & Irene Rundell
with son Chris.
December 21, 1963

Carole Wilcox. Our first night
as husband and wife.
December 21, 1963

Carole Wilcox and our new 1964 VW
parked in our area behind our rented
3rd floor of house.
June 1964

Top Right window is our apartment in
Goppingen, Germany.
June 1964

At the Stein's house in Waldenbuch, Germany.
Left to Right Claus Lahmann, Hans Stein,
Babs Stein and Carole Wilcox. These were our
wonderful friends during our Germany tour.
June 1964

On our way to the Stein's home in
Waldenbuch, Germany. We are
heading to the Autobahn.
December 25, 1964

On our way to the Stein's home in
Waldenbuch, Germany. We are
heading to the Autobahn.
December 25, 1964

Waldenbuch, Germany
December 25, 1964

At Stein's house in Waldenbuch, Germany.
Couple is Babs Stein and her fiancé Claus
Lahmann. December 25, 1964

Rick & Carole Wilcox at Stein's house
in Waldenbuch, Germany.
Note: tree has real candles.
December 25, 1964

Carole Wilcox next to our 1965 VW near
Goppingen, Germany. The 1965 VW replaced
our 1964 white VW.
May 1965

Soviet Union WWII war memorial
located in East Berlin. East German
soldiers in distance.
May 1965

Brandenburg Gate from East Berlin.
No one was allowed to visit it. Berlin
wall is directly beyond this location.
May 1965

Rick & Carole Wilcox on ferry to
Germany from Denmark.
May 1965

Arc di Triomphe, Paris France
June 1965

Looking Down from Arc di triomphe.
June 1965

Rick & Carole Wilcox on the grounds
of Oberhofen castle on Lake Thin,
Switzerland. June 1965

Carole & Rick Wilcox in their second floor
house rental on Reed St., Kalamazoo,
Michigan. Note: the three Hummel figurines
on book case were purchased in Germany.
November 1965

Rick Wilcox's home of childhood
with many memories, 250 W.
Maplehurst, Ferndale, Michigan.
July 1962

Our Wilcox family home in Ferndale, Michigan.
Left to Right: Millie, Harold, Bonnie, Rick and Carole
December 1968

Easter Sunday. Harold & Millie Wilcox
April 14, 1968

Easter Sunday in front of home (250 W. Maplehurst, Ferndale, Mich.). Wilcox family left to right: Harold, Carole, Millie, Phil, Bonnie and Rick
April 14, 1968

Porch of Wilcox home, 250 W. Maplehurst,
Ferndale, Michigan. Left to right: Rick,
Carole, Millie and Harold. Carole is
pregnant with first son.
April 5, 1970

Taylor Family in back yard of Carole's parents located
in Niles, Michigan. Left to right: Chuck & Connie Tack,
Rick & Carole Wilcox, Candace Taylor, Bryce & Louise
Taylor and Kay Taylor.
June 1970

Rick & Carole first house located at
603 Velvet Ave., Portage, Michigan.
May 1969

Our last snow fall before our move to Houston.
April 2, 1970

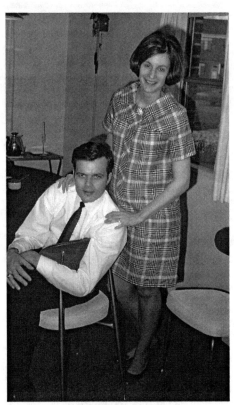

Hans and Davi Stein
November 1969

Rick and brother Phil in front yard
of our Portage house.
May 1970

Carole and Rick Wilcox in the back yard
of their Portage, MI house.
August 1969

Carole's grandparents Vesta and Rolfe Taylor
in our back yard of our Portage house.
August 1, 1969

Mammoth Cave, KY on the way to Rick & Carole's
new home in Houston, Texas. Carole's sister Candace
came with us to help get settled. Carole is pregnant with
son James. He was born during Sept.
July 3, 1970

Our son James Wilcox with Carole's
sister Candace Taylor.
August 1971

Hester family L to R:. Candace (Carole's sister), Melissa and Nash.
July 21, 2012

Carole Wilcox with son James at Nomad Motel in Daytona Beach Shores, FL
December 1971

Back yard of our Barwood St. house in
Houston. Rick & Carole with their sons
(baby) John and James.
June 1972

Carole and Rick Wilcox with their sons,
left to Right: John and James.
November 1974

Left to Right: Carole with her sister
Kay Taylor and sons James and John.
March 1975

Wilcox family in backyard of Harold & Millie Wilcox home
in Daytona Beach Shores, Florida. Wilcox family, left to right,
back row: Rick and Carole, Phil and Bonnie, Millie and Harold.
Front row: James, John, Scott, Stephanie. Harold has early stages
of Alzheimer at this time.
December 1978

Bonnie & Phil Wilcox in backyard of Mom and Dad's house located in Daytona Beach Shores, Florida.
December 1978

Ocean side of Nomad Motel located in Daytona Beach Shores, Florida. We stayed there many times over a period of twenty years.
August 1980

Cape Canaveral, Florida. Rick and
Carole Wilcox with son James.
June 1982

Harold & Millie Wilcox Grandchildren, Left to Right:
James, Stephanie, Scott and John.
August 1987

Rick & Carole Wilcox family, Left to right: Back row:
Rick and John. Front row: Carole, Ethan, Evan, Ellie,
Jody and James.
November 2008

John Wilcox and his family. Left to right:
Ethan, Jody, Ellie, John and Evan.
February 2010

A drive-in restaurant located in Delta Junction, Alaska.
Perhaps the only drive-in restaurant in Alaska. Phil Wilcox
looking out of van's window. We are on our way to Tok, Alaska.
June 2006

Adrian College chapel from
Madison Street. September 2013

Rick and Carole Wilcox's and their sons, Left to Right;
John Andrew and James Adrian.
December 25, 2013

Chapter 18

My Parents

I was blessed to have wonderful parents. My father, Harold Brown Wilcox (1899-1983), was born in Gobleville, Michigan. My mother, Iona Mildred Burrows, nicknamed "Millie" (1910-2002), was born in the area of Guelph, Ontario, Canada. She was the first of six children born to Norman Stanley (1881-1938) and Katrina Hulda (1886-1971) Burrows. It is interesting to note that Norman Burrows died on my mother's birthday (April 17) and Hulda Burrows died on my father's birthday (August 21).

Sometime within the years 1910-1915 mother's father took a job at the Henry Ford manufacturing plant in Detroit because he couldn't find employment in the Guelph area. Her dad moved the family to Highland Park within Detroit, Michigan. That is where Mother grew up and attended Highland Park schools. She graduated from Highland Park High School in 1928. During Mildred Wilcox's years at Highland Park High School she was on the girls' track team and girls' basketball team. Her specialty for track was the seventy-five-meter races. She was also involved in speed skating for the Trom Company in Detroit for five years, starting about the age of seventeen. She skated with Sonja Henie, the Norwegian figure skater, film star, and three-time Olympic champion (1928, 1932, and 1936). It should be noted that Mildred's mother, Hulda Burrows, was a figure skater in Canada when she was young. Mildred was a good skater, but according to her sister Flo Uhlig, her mother discouraged her from continuing her skating.

Mother was an excellent artist with silver, gold, and enamel dishes and trays. Her work also included making silver and gold jewelry. The basement of my childhood home served as her workshop. She had a huge market, but could never meet the demand for her products. Her items were sold in various shops, but later she agreed to sell to only one store in the area, which was in either Birmingham or Bloomfield Hills, both northern suburbs of Detroit. Later she agreed to sell her art items exclusively to the Detroit-area J. L. Hudson department stores. Her trademark on the bottom of enamel dishes and trays was "Iona." She made Lawrence Welk a pair of gold cufflinks.

Dad (Harold Brown Wilcox, 1899-1983) was apparently named after his mother's youngest brother, Harold Brown. From all indications, this brother died shortly after birth. This assumption is based on my dad's brother Whyle Wilcox's statement that he doesn't remember a cousin named Harold Brown. He said the Brown family also lived in Gobles, and the two families spent much time with each other.

Mom and Dad were married on August 27, 1933, at Kalamazoo College Chapel, Kalamazoo, Michigan. Dad's brother Whyle Wilcox was the best man and Mother's sister Dottie Pierce was the bridesmaid. Soon after marriage they purchased a house at 250 W. Maplehurst, Ferndale, Michigan just outside of Detroit. This was home for me and my brother, Philip Harold Wilcox. Phil was born on March 23, 1937. I (Richard Allen) was born on April 14, 1940. I think it is interesting that Carole and I were married thirty years after my parents were married, Mom was thirty years old when I was born, our oldest son, James, was born when I was thirty years old, and Carole was thirty years old when our son John was born.

Before I reached high school Dad left teaching to direct the evening adult education program at the same high school. He was very successful; enrollment reached a level of a few thousand adult students during evenings. Adults could finish their high school requirements for their diploma and/or take fun courses such as art classes. Dad hired Mother to teach art, using silver and gold but mainly enamel on copper disks. Mother's loving personality created a problem for Dad after a few years of her teaching: there was a waiting list for her class, but a large majority of her adult students continued to sign up for her class every school year. Dad wanted Mom to tell her students that they needed to sign up for another class in order to allow new adult students to attend her class. I don't believe she told this to the class; her students all enjoyed spending two evenings each week with her. When Christmas was approaching Mom's students would give her gifts. One of her students worked at Sanders Candy and Ice Cream shop. Apparently when a box of chocolate candy didn't sell by a certain date the employees could take it home. This lady gave Mom about twelve boxes of Sanders chocolate candy during the Christmas season. That was a big hit with the family.

Dad finally had to hire another teacher to teach the same art class that mother was teaching. Mother taught this class for around fifteen years. During the two nights Mom was teaching Phil and I were responsible for washing the dinner's dishes, pots, and pans. We also dried them and put them all away in the cupboards before our parents returned home. We were glad to help out. The pans were very hard to clean. Mother also had a talent for painting and ceramics. In 1972 when Mom and Dad moved to Daytona Beach, Florida, she ended her artwork activities.

Dad was a great organizer and was very efficient in his job. He was also well liked by his high school students. The senior class of 1929 asked him to be their counselor, which required him to chaperone the class for their senior field trip to Washington, D.C. The class gave him a gold ring with a gold "W" overlay on a flat black stone. Inside the ring was engraved "Class of 1929." Dad greatly appreciated this honor, and he wore this ring for the rest of his life. It was very special to him. Many years ago I gave this ring to Stephanie Wilcox, Phil and Bonnie's daughter. I wanted Stephanie to have this ring because she was Dad's favorite grandchild and they were very close. Stephanie always seemed to appreciate her Grandfather Wilcox and showed love toward him.

When I was in high school and taking a history course I would ask Dad a question in reference to history, expecting a short answer. Over time I realized that any history question directed to him would result in a very long answer, almost a lecture! Dad helped me to love American history, which is very true to this day.

I remember a few short things in reference to Mom and Dad. When Dad was a high school history teacher he enjoyed getting a cup of coffee across the street from the high school. It was a soda-fountain type small shop, a hangout for high school students after school. Dad enjoyed sipping coffee and visiting with the students. I remember one time when I was young Dad came home after this coffee event while Mom was in the kitchen. He was a little upset that the soda-fountain shop raised the price of a cup of coffee from five cents to ten cents. That was outrageous! Another time he came home announcing that he could no longer play tennis and that he was done with this activity. Another time in Florida when he was much older, the day came when he realized he had to give up golf. As we grow older we continue to relinquish activities that we can no longer do.

What Dad and I had in common was sports. He took me to many Detroit Tigers baseball games. We would watch football games together on TV.

Dad was also my private barber. A few times when Carole and I would visit Mom and Dad during our Kalamazoo years, Dad would cut my hair. He was a very good barber.

After Dad's death and years later when Mother could no longer drive safely and take care of the house, she agreed to sell the house and move into an assisted living complex nearby. Phil, Bonnie, Carole, and I agreed to help with her garage sale. Several years prior to the garage sale one of Mother's friends gave her a gift of a pewter teapot that had a cylinder on top for loading a tea bag. Mother couldn't unscrew this cylinder and had no use for this pitcher, so she put it away in one of the kitchen cabinets. This was one of the items in the garage sale marked twenty-five cents. The garage sale was on Saturday, and when we arrived late Friday afternoon Phil, Bonnie, and Mother had it all set up for early Saturday morning. Mother's car was parked in front of the house. During the evening Bonnie went out into the garage and spotted this teapot. She had an urge to remove the cylinder from this teapot. Phil, Carole, and I were visiting in the living room when we heard Bonnie scream. We all got up, rushing to the garage door, when Bonnie dashed in saying, "Look what is in the teapot!" We looked, and it was stuffed with paper money. What a pleasant shock! We pulled out the money and it was over five hundred dollars! In this pitcher was a note addressed to Mother from her good friend, which read, "Millie, I want you to have this." Unfortunately Mother never thanked her for this money while her friend was alive. The garage sale was a great success, and what made it even better, a man asked Phil if Mother's car was for sale. Phil said it certainly was, and the man offered to buy it. This is the first time I ever heard of selling a car at a garage sale.

When the house was sold and the time arrived for Mother to move to her assisted living complex I agreed to help her with this move. I didn't know how I could move the furniture by myself, but our son John offered to come with me. What a blessing for me! During a phone conversation with Mother before we left, I asked her how the packing was coming along. She said she was almost done. When the time arrived we drove to her sold house in Daytona Beach and discovered that the majority of her stuff was not packed! John and I had to drive to stores asking for boxes. Bonnie came down to help Mother pack, and was flying home the day we had planned to move Mother. We also made arrangements to rent a truck. We finished the packing on the last night before moving her. The next morning it was raining very hard and it never let up during this long day. We picked up the truck, backed it up to the garage, and loaded everything in the truck from the garage. The last thing we placed in the truck was a favorite tray stand, and we pushed it in and closed the truck's loading doors.

We left in this heavy constant rain, and I stayed in the right lane and drove slower than the speed limit. A car came up to our side and pointed to the back of our truck. I stopped and found one of the back doors was open and Mother's favorite tray stand was missing. It was behind us, flattened. When we got to the complex we found where to unload. There was no covering and we could not back the truck close to the door, so we had to unload everything in heavy rain from a distance. What a mess! Of course, John and I were soaking wet. It took us hours to unload and both John and I were really beat when we were finished. As I was carrying a box down the hallway to Mother's unit a resident lady said, "Oh it's good to have a man moving in." My thought was, do I look that old?

It was late in the evening when we drove to the Nomad Motel, where we had reserved an oceanfront room. I took a shower and was ready to go to bed when the wind got really loud and objects were flying in the air outside. I opened the back door as a man from one of the units opened his. He stuck his head out and asked, "What's going on?" I said, "Just a little storm," and he was satisfied and closed his door. I didn't know what to expect. In the morning we learned that there was some minor damage to a few of the homes' roof shingles. In the morning John and I drove home nonstop. I was so glad to have this experience behind us, and I was grateful that John came with me. I could not have moved Mother's stuff without John. It wasn't a vacation.

Chapter 19

My Early Years Growing Up in Ferndale, Michigan

I should note that my nickname during all of these years was "Dick." Sometime during the early 1980s I changed it to "Rick." I favored this name over Richard and Dick, and it was still similar.

I don't remember much of the 1940's. One event that really stands out was in September 1945. It was time for me to start kindergarten at Roosevelt Elementary School in Ferndale, Michigan. Mother walked me to school, and I cried all the way. I didn't want to go to school. I really cried when she pulled me into the school and took me to my classroom. She left, and I continued to cry. The teacher came to me as I was seated at a desk and asked me what was wrong. I told her that I didn't feel very well and I wanted to go home. She took me to the nurse, and she called mother to tell her that I was sick. Mother came and picked me up and we walked back to the house. I believe the next day or soon after I was taken to the doctor. The doctor discovered that I had rheumatic fever. I had it for two and a half years. I had to stay in bed for a year or more since I was supposed to continually rest. I remember that even on Christmas Day 1945 I was still not allowed to leave my bed. I pleaded with my mother, promising that I would lie still on the sofa during the opening of the presents. I was reminded that I still had to stay in bed. I remember crying as I heard the conversations and the enjoyment from the living room. I felt very sorry for myself. Eventually my presents were brought to my bed, and I could then open them.

The time came when I was allowed to spend some time in the living room sitting still, and then later sitting on the front porch during nice weather. The instructions were to stay put and sit still. I could not do anything. After perhaps a year and a half or two years I was allowed to move around. A schoolteacher would come to the house to work with me. I don't believe it was every day. I remember I was learning my coloring skills by coloring within the lines of an image. As all kids do at my age, I took a crayon and just moved the crayon back and forth on the paper. She showed me her example of coloring within the lines. Then she compared her artwork to mine, and asked me which one looked better. I said, "Mine!" I don't remember her reaction.

Finally September 1947 came and I was told I was healed. Age wise, I was supposed to be in the second grade and that was the grade I started school. Many years later I felt that I should have started school as a first grader. During summer 1948 after passing the second grade, the school contacted my parents and suggested that I repeat second grade. I cried. I felt that I had failed, even though I had passing grades. I was very embarrassed about this, and my self-confidence declined. I didn't want to continue my friendship with my best friends and any others advancing to the third grade. I kept these feelings to myself.

While walking home from school as a second grader the second time around, I came up with a brilliant idea. I thought that I already knew everything I needed to know in life, and therefore I no longer needed to go to school. Mom would surely love to have me home with her every day. I was so excited that my schooldays were behind me. I was so excited that I ran home from school, which was probably less than a mile. I enthusiastically told Mom my brilliant plan, but she didn't see it my way, which was a big disappointment and a surprise. She said, "Maybe so, but you still have to go to school." That proves that not all brilliant ideas will fly!

It took me several months to gain strength after not being active for two and a half years. I worked on running, but just a little running would cause me to breathe heavily with a sound from my throat. I worked at running, building up endurance, and eliminating this breathing sound.

I enjoyed reading books. I read several Hardy Boys books but also enjoyed books on known and little-known people. I enjoyed reading about how they lived and what they did. I also enjoyed stories related to American history. To this day I still enjoy these types of books.

Mother's brother, Lionel Burrows, was a carpenter and a housepainter. He was good in his work. He purchased some land up in northern Michigan on Bear Lake. He built log cabins on this land and rented these cabins on a weekly basis. We spent a week on the property for a few summers. It was fun being there and on the lake. During one of these times I would row the boat for Mother as she fished. I wasn't into fishing, but I had a fishing rod during this time. Mom would put a worm on the hook, and I would drop the line near the boat. The fish we caught were small. I let Mom remove the fish from my line. One time I just dropped the hook in the water without any bait. The water was so clear you could see the bottom, and thus the fish near the hook. I watched one of the fish bite the hook, and I had a fish without the use of bait. Another time I remember Dad and I were together on Bear Lake and I was doing the rowing. We were a distance from the cabins, and a storm came up very fast. The wind was blowing, and the waves were high. I rowed as fast as I could while going against the wind. I wasn't making any progress so finally Dad said to switch places and he would row. I was a little concerned, thinking the wind could push us further away from the cabins with the water getting rougher. Dad slowly made progress, and we got back safely. I was grateful for Dad because I realized if he hadn't been with me I would have ended up further away from the cabins, and who knows what would have happened to me in the storm.

This same brother of Mother's converted our Ferndale house attic into one very large room with windows on opposite sides. The window hinges were on the bottom, and thus we could open the window from the top and let it lay flat on the bottom wall. This room was like an apartment. It was enclosed with paneling, built-in shelves, and a built-in work desk. This room became the bedroom for Phil and me. When Phil moved out of the house to attend Adrian College the room was all mine! I loved it! I spent my evenings up there doing school homework, devotions, and listening to music. It was very special for me. I remember one Saturday morning lying in bed with the windows open and hearing the birds chirping and a neighbor speaking to someone. It gave me a warm and peaceful feeling. It was a wonderful situation for me during my high school years and the times I was home from college.

When I was very young Phil had a black cocker spaniel dog. This dog didn't like small children, and we had to keep her in the basement when there were small children in the house. When this dog died, I asked Dad if I could have a dog. During one of my birthday dinners, perhaps when I was thirteen, Dad and Phil excused themselves from the kitchen table and went outside. I didn't have a clue as to what was going on. Dad came back into the kitchen with Phil and a boxer on a leash. Dad said, "Here is your dog, Rick." I was surprised and excited. Dad had said he didn't want another dog! The dog was only about six months old and was very thin since it had been mistreated. In the beginning this dog was something else! Mother laid her new Easter hat on the bed, and Lady got hold of it and destroyed it. One time Mom cleaned the side of the stove with a chemical, and Lady licked it off. She was sick and threw up everything that was in her stomach. Another time I left small plastic tubes of paint used to paint a picture by the numbers on my bedroom floor. Lady came in while I wasn't in the room and ate all of these tubes, plastic and all! Again the dog was very sick, and what she threw up was in colors. Perhaps it was a miracle that she lived! Another time mother took a steak from the freezer and placed it on the kitchen table, and then went downstairs to her workshop. Later she came up to the kitchen and saw that the steak had disappeared! She walked out to the living room and here was Lady enjoying a raw steak meal.

The dog was becoming a real problem. When we left as a family we had to put her leash on her and tie the opposite end of the leash to the basement door handle. If we didn't, she would knock over the trash container and spread the trash throughout the dining room and living room, and chew on what she would find. When the dog was let out we couldn't get her back in unless one of us threw a stick or stone at her making a direct hit. To her, if the object didn't hit her it was a game. She would run around in circles until a thrown item hit her, then she would understand that it was time to go in the house. We were thinking of getting rid of this dog.

One time Phil was outside with the dog, and the dog took off running to the end of the street. Phil called and called for her, but the dog kept running. Phil went after her, and apparently Lady ran onto the heavy traffic of Woodward Ave. and was hit in the hip by a car, but nothing was broken. Her back left leg and hip were hurting, but she was able to get on the sidewalk and came to a car that had the back door opened. The lady was about to put her groceries in the back seat when Lady hopped onto the car's seat and urinated on the backseat. Phil finally caught up to this car and grabbed Lady's collar and dragged her out of the car. Poor Phil was very embarrassed and told the woman that he was sorry. Phil left the scene and took Lady home. This was bad, but it ended up being positive because we never had any more problems with this dog. She would always come when one of us called her, and she never ran away again. In addition, we could leave her loose in the house when we were gone and she didn't do any damage within the house. She was a wonderful, changed, calm, and lovable dog.

In early January 1957 Mother was in Los Angeles visiting some of her relatives. Dad was preparing our meals. On one particular evening he announced he was making pancakes for dinner, which we all liked. Phil and I took a bite, and we both thought it was terrible. Dad didn't really believe us, but when he took his first bite he agreed that the pancakes were terrible. He asked what we wanted to do. I said there was a coupon for White Castle hamburgers, twelve hamburgers for a dollar. These hamburgers were smaller than the regular restaurant hamburgers. Since I had my driver's license I could drive. So I volunteered to drive over there for these hamburgers. Dad put all of the pancakes in our boxer dog's food dish, and she rapidly ate them up. Dad made the comment, "Well somebody likes my pancakes!" I drove to White Castle and gave my order with the coupon to a girl at the counter. I was surprised when she said I couldn't eat twelve hamburgers. I had to tell her this was a takeout order. When I got home we sat down and started eating our meal when I noticed that the dog wasn't with us. This was very unusual, because Lady always kept us company when we were eating. I got up and went out to the dining and living rooms, and I was shocked to see piles of pancakes that dog had thrown up. The dog was miserable, lying on her side. The dog did survive!

As I mentioned, Lady became a very calm, easygoing dog. Most people could walk into the house and the person would not even be aware that there was a dog in the house. Kids could bounce on our dog, and she would recognize it as fun, but if a stranger came on the property and our dog sensed something negative about this person she would charge close to the person and growl with teeth showing and with glassy eyes and a strip of hair on her back standing up. In this situation Lady would look mean and aggressive and the unknown person would just freeze until one of us would pull the dog back. Once we came home on a Friday night from dinner and a show and my parents' bedroom screen was on the ground and the window was opened. Apparently someone knew we were gone and removed the screen and lifted the window. He was greeted at the window with a teeth-showing, growling dog. The person went to plan B, which was leaving the yard as fast as he could. This was the biggest plus Lady earned during her lifetime. Our front door was all paneled glass. The regular mailman could come up the stairs to our mailbox and the dog would ignore him. One day our dog was lying in the front room and a different mailman arrived. He was walking up the steps when Lady jumped to her feet growling, and charged the front door, knocking out a few of the glass panels. Then she backed away and just walked behind Dad's chair and sat down as though nothing had happed. The poor mailman probably came close to a heart attack.

The day came when we could leave her out on the porch or in the front yard and other dogs and people walking and on bikes would pass by the house and Lady would ignore them. I did train Lady to do her business behind the garage, and she was faithful in this even when she was in the front yard. She would travel to the backyard behind the garage on her own when she had to go.

Lady would follow me upstairs when I went to bed. In the wintertime she liked to get under the covers at my feet. Eventually she would get too warm and come out from under the sheet, panting, to sleep on top of the covers. Dad didn't like the idea of the dog under the sheets, but Mother didn't think it was any big deal.

Mother was a great cook and made wonderful bread. Bread is my favorite food. A peanut butter sandwich with thick-sliced homemade bread is one of my favorite meals. Lady would always be with us during a meal, hoping some food would fall to the floor or a little handout when Mother wasn't looking. One time Dad cut half of a toasted slice of Mother's bread, buttered it, and gave it to Lady. Mother protested, "Don't give my bread to the dog." Dad said, "Lady likes good bread!" Lady loved toast, but it had to be buttered before she would eat it.

There was one time that I really embarrassed Dad. I was probably sixteen years old. I had an interest in astronomy to some degree. I was mainly fascinated with planets and nebulas. Our front porch had outdoor chairs. One dark summer evening I took my binoculars and one of these chairs to the dark backyard to look at the sky with my binoculars. After I reached the backyard a car drove in our driveway to turn around. In the living room Dad got up to see who it could be. As the car left the driveway Dad noticed one chair was missing. He immediately called the police, reporting that someone had stolen a chair from his porch. As the policeman was writing up a theft report, here I came with the chair. I placed the chair where it had been and walked into the living room. Dad was so embarrassed when I asked why the policeman was here. I think the policeman took it all in good spirits. It was a good laugh!

Mother seemed to find a lot of money during her lifetime. When I was about four years old she took me to a 5 and 10 cent store, as I remember. While I was standing next to her, she bent down to pick up a dollar that was right next to my shoe. I remember being very disappointed that I didn't look down to get it. Years later when we were all in Switzerland, at Lucerne or Interlaken, the four of us were standing together outside of a building. Mom bent down and picked up a silver coin next to my foot. Another time when I was a teenager we were entering a grocery store. As we were walking past a swept pile of litter, she spotted a wadded twenty dollar note in the trash. That was a lot of money back then. She was always picking up money.

Mom enjoyed Hershey chocolate bars. She would buy the very large bars and stash them away in the cupboard and not tell anyone. One of her hiding places was the cupboard over the built-in desk in the kitchen. I looked there once and found one opened bar. She changed her hiding place. Sometime later we were in the kitchen and she was washing the dishes and I volunteered to dry them. When we were done, I said, "Why don't we have some Hershey chocolate candy?" With her unique giggling she said, "How did you know that I have Hershey chocolate?" as she pulled open the drawer of dishtowels, reached under the towels, and pulled out the large Hershey bar. I said, "I didn't know." We both laughed.

I remember another laugh sometime during my teenage years. Mom was in the back room of the house, and I walked in the kitchen for either a soda pop or an ice cream stick. As I opened the refrigerator door I heard her loud voice saying, "I'll take one too!" I was surprised she could hear the refrigerator door opening. She wanted whatever I was getting. Mom was always a lot of fun and she had a very outgoing personality. People couldn't help but like her. My brother Phil has her personality.

In 1952 we spent Thanksgiving at the home of one of my mother's sisters (Dottie Pierce) and her family in the Chicago area. They had two boys, David and Roger. David was one year older than Phil and Roger was two years older than me. We had a lot of fun hanging around together. Roger showed me his coin collection and gave me a lot of information on what he was doing with his collection. I was hooked! When we arrived home I started searching my parents' pennies and continued with the goal of completing the Lincoln cents set. Eventually I found enough coins to put sets together of the nickel through the silver dollar. In 1955 I started collecting silver dollars from 1878 to 1935. Just about every bank had silver dollars, and they were glad to get rid of them. It was possible to get brand-new silver dollars issued during the 1880s because the mint had many thousands of bags of new silver dollars that had never been released for circulation. Shortly after I started this new fun activity, Mother started to pursue the same goal of putting sets together. When summer came my most enjoyable activity was getting rolls and bags of coins and searching for specific dates and mint marks. Mother and I would do this together. We split the rolls and bags of coins equally and then searched the coins together. I have a lot of good memories of mother and me searching through volumes of coins. During these years there were coin shops in the area, and we could take the extra coins with values greater than face value and sell them to the coin dealer for a profit. I enjoyed making money from coins I had located from rolls and bags of coins. All of these coin sets were sold long ago.

I have always liked silver dollars. I remember when I was about four years old I had five or six silver dollars. Dad would keep them in his locked steel box in my bedroom closet. When I wanted to play with them he would retrieve them. I was fascinated by their size compared to my small hand. I don't know where these dollars came from, but this was all the money I had. One day Dad said something like, "Why don't we take these dollars to the bank and they will pay you money to keep them." It sounded good to me, so I said okay. Sometime after the savings account was created for me I asked Dad if we could go to the bank and look at my silver dollars. I envisioned that they had a lot of little wood shelf boxes and one had my name on it with my silver dollars. I was surprised to learn that this was not the case, and I was saddened that I no longer had these silver dollars. If I had understood that the bank wouldn't keep these silver dollars for me I would not have agreed to use this money for a savings account.

Silver dollars were very common but were rarely used for paying expenses. Most people were not aware that one could get nineteenth- and twentieth-century silver dollars dated 1878 to 1935 from the bank, many of which were never used for circulation. People requested them for gifts, especially for birthdays and Christmas. As a paper delivery boy I received silver dollars as tips during the Christmas season. I also enjoyed spending them. One could buy a lunch using a silver dollar and get a little change back. Most of the time when using a silver dollar or two to buy something the clerk would ask me if I really wanted to use these coins and express pleasure receiving them. It was fun.

Sometime during my freshman year at high school in Ferndale I started carrying a brand new but old silver dollar in my right pocket. These new coins were mostly dated during the 1880s. The luster would disappear after about four months, which meant I would spend it and get another new silver dollar from the bank. During my senior year in high school I decided to take the most common silver dollar, which was the Philadelphia Mint's 1921 Morgan dollar (silver dollars were minted at the Philadelphia, New Orleans, Carson City, and San Francisco mints), and have Mother engrave on the front "FHS class of 1959" (Ferndale High School). I believe she also engraved my initials, "RAW." I planned to carry this dollar in my right pocket for the rest of my life.

During this time I was a cashier at A & P grocery store. At the end of every business day we cashiers would balance the total money to the total purchases as shown on the cashier machine. One Friday night after I finished balancing, I went down the aisle and looked for any interesting coins in the trays of money the other cashiers had. This was a common procedure. One of the ladies had a silver dollar in her tray and I picked it up and got excited that it was dated 1895. All of the 1895 dated silver dollars from all of the mints were scarce, and each one was worth more than face value. The 1895 Philadelphia dollar was unknown, but the Philadelphia Mint showed minting twelve thousand for circulation and eight hundred and eighty proof surfaces for collectors. Only a few hundred of these proofs survived. It was during the 1980's that it was concluded that these twelve thousand coins had been melted down decades ago. Back to my story, as I turned the silver dollar to the back side it appeared to not have a mint mark, which means it would be from Philadelphia. I didn't have any money with me except for the silver dollar Mother had engraved for me. The cashier didn't care if I exchanged her silver dollar for mine. When I got home I discovered that this coin had a very faint "O," indicating that it was minted in New Orleans, and therefore was not from the Philadelphia Mint. Someone had tried to remove this "O" mintmark and was almost successful. I needed the "O" for my set, but the coin was damaged. I spent it. In the morning I was back at work (Saturday), but the lady who took care of the money each day didn't have my 1921 silver dollar with Mother's engraving.

At the end of August 1959 Mom and Dad came home from Montana. Mom had brand new silver dollars she got from a Montana bank, and I picked up an 1886 Philadelphia Mint, a very common date. I asked Mom if I could have this coin to keep in my right pocket during my four years of college. She agreed. I'm still carrying this coin in my right pocket, and it is very worn.

When Carole and I returned to Michigan from Germany in July 1965 silver dollars were no longer available. When the federal government announced that silver was going to be removed from our coins (late1963) and the value of silver was rising, there was a run by the public to hoard silver dollars. Thousands of people drained the U.S. Treasury of their one thousand silver-dollar bags. Banks no longer carried an inventory of silver dollars.

A short summary of my completing a silver dollar set (1878-1935) was published in the *Silver Dollars and Trade Dollars of The United States, a complete Encyclopedia, Volume II*, pages 2044-2045. I'm credited as the writer, but the author is Q. David Bowers. These two-volume books were published during 1993 and they are now out of print. This book is the bible for silver dollars. The last set I sold was my silver dollars set. It was my favorite set, and it took me eight years to complete it. I completed it during my last semester of college in 1963 when I came home during spring break. Mother got a thousand silver-dollar bag from a local bank that was sealed in 1911. Mom told me I could have any dollars that I needed to complete my set, which were about thirteen silver dollars. That bag had every silver dollar that I needed to complete the set. When Carole and I purchased our first house in Portage outside of Kalamazoo, I sold this set in 1969 so that we could pay cash to furnish our house. I later wished I hadn't sold it since it was a nice set and some of the dollars were very scarce, but we didn't have to get a loan and pay interest for furnishing the house. The days of searching through rolls and bags of coins are long over, but I have fond memories of those days.

I also enjoyed baseball. During these years at home Dad would take me to the Detroit Tigers games. He took me to the 1951 All Star game at Detroit's stadium. Dad enjoyed sports; that was his entertainment. He reminded me when I was older that the two of us went to a double header on a Memorial Day. He purchased tickets that didn't have seats assigned. There were no vacant seats, so we sat on the steps. Two men were sitting in two end seats on Dad's side who were getting drunk. They left during the first game and never came back, so we took their seats. Dad asked me if I wanted to go home, after the first game. I told him I didn't want to leave until the second game was over. He was pleased and probably a little surprised. A lot of my togetherness with Dad was sports, and with Mother coins.

I remember one Christmas in the early 1950's my brother Phil and I received a ping-pong rifle. This gun had two handles. When the barrel was expanded a ping-pong ball was pushed in the end of the barrel, which had a handle. Then your right hand would steady the gun and your left hand would quickly pull the extended barrel's handle toward yourself, and the ping-pong ball would really fly! We had a lot of fun running around the inside of the house firing ping pong balls at each other. I'm sure our parents regretted buying these toy guns for us for that Christmas. One Christmas we got an electric football game that we thought was really cool. The players had a magnet base and would move on the field's board when the power was turned on.

Dad put a basketball hoop on the top of the garage for us shoot basketballs. One summer we played baseball in our driveway using a ping-pong ball and a tennis racket for the bat. We played this a lot during that one summer. During the summers we played catch with a baseball. It was fun just throwing the ball back and forth. During the fall we also played touch football on our street with the other kids. When I was in high school the gym would be opened for kids wanting to play basketball on Saturdays. I walked to the high school a few times to join a group of kids to play basketball. We played a lot of cards and board games, especially during the winter. I also did jigsaw puzzles and even made up a baseball game with dice that I could play by myself.

Dad also gave us a ping-pong table, placed in the basement. We used this table a lot, and so did our friends. I could never beat brother Phil during the first several games. A day came when I could beat him in this game and did many times. I got good hitting the edge on his side of the table. We both enjoyed playing ping-pong very much. During my freshman year of college I lived on campus in one of the men's dormitories. In the basement were a couple of ping-pong tables, and there was one fellow student who could beat everyone. I was no exception. He was my favorite opponent because I loved the challenge, and the day finally came that I was able to beat him.

My brother Phil had a paper route on W. Lewiston Ave., which was the next street south of us and was two blocks long. Almost every house subscribed to the *Royal Oak Daily Tribune*. Royal Oak was a town next to Ferndale. I believe when I was eleven or twelve he wanted to give it up, and I wanted to take it. I started delivering newspapers after school, which I believe was only Monday through Friday. I had to collect the money weekly, and on Saturday Dad would take me to the newspaper office in Royal Oak to pay for the week's papers. My profit was what was left over, which was seven dollars and some cents.

When I was sixteen years old Dad got me a job at A & P grocery store on 9-Mile Road not very far from our house. I gave up my paper route and started work as a bagger. I also stocked shelves, and then I was promoted to cashier. I loved working at this grocery store. One could say I gave 100% to my job. I wanted to be busy all the time and always do what was right. As a bagger, when the customers were few, I would stock shelves, stock the paper bags at the end of the checkout aisles, or wherever I was needed. I always kept myself busy. I had a great learning experience during my employment with this A & P grocery store. The manager and assistant manager were very friendly and made it fun to work for them. The assistant manager joked a lot, and I never remember them being upset. They were always positive to everyone and made you feel that you were part of a team working together. This atmosphere made me enjoy working there and considered making a career in this business. During my senior year of high school the manager and the assistant manager were transferred to a new A & P store in Southfield, which were several miles from where I was. They wanted me to go with them, but I couldn't because I didn't have a car.

The new manager was very different, in fact just the opposite of the transferring managers. He turned me off from considering a career in a grocery store. He was very cold, quiet, and threatening. If you did something wrong his standard statement was, "If you do that again I will fire you." One time I was working as a cashier and few customers were ready to check out, so I went to the produce area to help with a customer returning soda pop bottles for a deposit refund. The procedure was to place the bottles on a specific counter at the back of the store to calculate the amount due the customer. As I gave her the credit slip for the refund, I left this area to help someone else with the intention of returning to remove the bottles to the storage area. Before I got back from this customer the manager approached me and asked why the bottles were there. I said I had delayed moving them to help someone else. He said that if I ever left bottles on the counter again he would fire me. Another time I was in an aisle stocking a shelf, and I felt that someone was watching me. I turned around and there he was at the end of the aisle just watching what I was doing. From this experience I learned, and never forgot, that you motivate people through love and encouragement and being positive toward them. Threatening people brings just the opposite response. I worked at this store up to the time I left home to go to college.

Summer trips

Dad enjoyed taking trips during the summer or renting a cabin on a lake. I remember when we were vacationing in New England in 1954. In Boston Mother wanted to visit a specific shop in Rhode Island in reference to her art business and Dad wanted to go to a baseball game. Dad asked Phil if he wanted to go with his mother or with him to a baseball game. He picked Mother, and when the same question was put to me I chose baseball. Dad asked me if I wanted to go to see the Boston Braves or the Boston Red Sox. I picked the Red Sox since I was an American League fan, and I wanted to see Ted Williams. To this day he is my favorite player. I only remember seeing Ted Williams; I don't know who Boston played or if they won.

Another trip that stands out was our 1950 western trip. At this time the movie theaters showed a lot of cowboy and Indian movies. They were my favorite movies. Dad mentioned this trip beforehand, and I asked him if we would see Indians. He said Indians live like we do, they have washing machines and stoves. I was excited that we would see real Indians. I went across the street and told my friend Bill Cowell, who was the same age as me, that we would see Indians that summer. Then I said, "Did you know that Indians have washing machines and stoves in their tepees!" He too was amazed.

We visited Aunt Winnie and Aunt Kittie in Southern California. Dad told me that these two women were his favorite aunts. They are from the Brown family, related to his mother Susan Belle Brown, who married Dad's father. From Southern California we drove to San Francisco and spent a day or two there. Dad wanted to go to a seafood restaurant on one of San Francisco's piers. I didn't want to eat there because at that time I only wanted hamburgers. Dad explained that this restaurant was owned by the New York Yankees star Joe DiMaggio and his brother Dom. I asked Dad if Joe DiMaggio would be there. Dad said perhaps. I didn't consider that this was baseball season and of course he would not be there. I was excited that we could meet Joe DiMaggio and his brother Dom. I wanted Joe's autograph. I was impressed with this restaurant because it had two continuous rolls of 8x10 baseball pictures around three walls. This was really a neat restaurant! While checking out after dinner, Dad asked the employee taking the money if Joe and Dom were available. He said no. Dad said his youngest son wanted their autograph. He said to give him his name and address and he would have them send him their autographs, which actually happened! I still have this small sheet of paper with their autographs.

As a kid I always wanted hamburgers when Dad would take us out for dinner. When we were on this western trip I wanted hamburgers for every meal. Finally Dad agreed that I could have two hamburgers for breakfast (apparently he was tired of saying no to me). He asked the waitresses if that was possible and the same for the next two mornings. For three straight days I had two hamburgers for breakfast, lunch, and dinner. The fourth morning I decided to have pancakes for breakfast, and Dad said, "Not ordering hamburgers?" I'm sure Dad figured I would eventually get sick of them. During this time Dad was calling me "Hamburger Dick."

As Dad was driving from California to Oregon we had a bad accident in the mountains of Oregon. The two curvy lanes were wet from rain and our car skidded on a curve off the road and fell down into trees. The trees saved us. Dad ducked as the top of the car on his side caved in, and we boys flew into Dad and Mother. My body going over the front seat onto Mother forced her head to crash against the dashboard, resulting in a fractured skull. At this time dashboards all metal. She was bleeding from her forehead. The driver of the car behind us stopped and helped us climb up to the street. He and his wife were pulling a boat. Phil and I sat in the boat, and Mom and Dad sat in the car. I guess Dad was able to take the suitcases out of the trunk. We were taken to the hospital where Mom spent a week. Mom's cousins came and picked up Phil and me and kept us for the week. We then took a train to the home of Dad's brother Monroe and his family and spent time there. Mother was inactive since she had a constant bad headache. Uncle Monroe took Dad, Phil, and me to Yellowstone. After a few days we all came home by train.

My parents' best friend picked (Howard Thompson) us up and drove us home in his 1949 Chevrolet. On the way home he offered to sell Dad his car and Dad accepted the offer, so Dad had a car before we arrived home. The Howard Thompson had purchased a 1950 Chevrolet. He would get a new Chevrolet every six months. Dad's Pontiac that crashed in Oregon was sold as junk. He didn't get very much for it. Right before this western trip Dad cancelled the car insurance to save money. After this trip and for a year or so we could not have ice cream on our strawberry shortcake. Dad said that was two desserts. Later in time we always had ice cream on our strawberry shortcakes, a very popular dessert during the strawberry season. Dad's statement of just one dessert is an indication that losing the car with no insurance created a financial hardship for the family.

The 1950's, my Favorite Decade!

I look back on the 1950's as my favorite decade. Life was so different compared to our current times. People were different, friendlier perhaps, but there was more respect for authority and for our teachers. Crime was nothing compared to today. During the 1940's and most of the 1950's one would not lock one's house doors, even leaving for vacation. Carole's parents still kept their windows and their back door open throughout the night during the 1960's. A very large percentage of mothers stayed home. There was no school bussing. Many times after elementary school we would play on the playgrounds and play kick ball, touch football, and baseball. No parent seemed to be concerned if their kids didn't come home right after school. We knew when dinner was, and when we had to be home. As a kid you felt good when you were away from home shopping, going to and from school, playing on the playground after school or at a friend's house. Children went by themselves to trick or treat on Halloween evening. Parents were not concerned when their children were on their own.

There was prayer in school and a few times reading from the Bible. We were a godly nation even though only half of the population attended church. Even though not all of the society was Christians, a large majority of people lived by what was right and wrong as recorded in the Bible. I heard a lot about the Golden Rule, "Do to others whatever you would like them do to you." People believed this rule. People knew what was right and wrong. Students read about the faith of the founding fathers of this country. Christmas was all about Jesus Christ, and that was accepted within our public schools. Some high school sports teams would pray together, and that wasn't a problem. Those who didn't want to pray just ignored it.

Some students did drink, but they were in the extreme minority. I never heard of anyone on drugs. There was shame if an unwed student girl was pregnant. It was rare when this happened, and the girl would drop out of school. Movie shows had no swearing, bad words or nudity. Another thing was that there were no credit cards. If you didn't have the money you didn't purchase it. It was just a wonderful time to be alive. Sometime during the 1960's our society started to change.

Chapter 20

Adrian College Years

All letters addressed to Mom, Dad, or both refer to my parents Harold and Mildred "Millie" Wilcox. The words "I" and "me" refer to Rick. I have identified myself as Rick during the rest of this book. I graduated from Ferndale High School in June 1959. The four years went fast; I enjoyed my high school years, especially my last two years. My class of '59 was the first graduating class of Ferndale's new high school. It was in November 1958 that our old Lincoln High School was closed and the students moved to the new high school. Lincoln High School was very crowded. The new school had considerably more space in the hallways, and the entrance had a large lounge area. I wished this school had been available three years prior.

During my junior year Dad asked me where I wanted to go to college. There was a time that I thought I wouldn't go to college. Dad said if I didn't go I would have to take a factory job, which didn't impress me. My friends were going to college, and it seemed like everyone I knew was planning to go to college, so I concluded that is what I needed to do. Dad suggested Adrian College, a small private college in southern Michigan. Dad knew that would be best for me. I believe he knew that I had always lacked confidence in myself. One Saturday he drove me to the University of Michigan at Ann Arbor. The campus was huge and overwhelmed me. Dad took me to the 1958 Adrian College graduation commencement and at that moment I wanted to graduate from this school. I told Dad I wanted to receive my diploma from Adrian. Dad was pleased, and I believe he was determined to do all that he could for my success at Adrian College.

I had never considered the career I would like to pursue, which meant I didn't know what my major of study would be. I was in line to register in September 1959 at Adrian College, and quickly learned that you had to identify your major during registration. I didn't have a clue what I was going to major in. The person in front of me said, "Business," and I decided that sounded good! So I said "Business" and that was it. That was my degree, but I also had a major in accounting when I graduated. My first year of college was by far the hardest. I spent a tremendous amount of time studying because I was determined I was going to graduate from Adrian College. The second year I started to take accounting and related courses and that is when I knew accounting was going to be my career. I enjoyed it. I graduated in May 1963.

September 17, 1959, letter to Dad and Mom:

Everything is fine here. It is 9:15 p.m. Thursday. I came in my room to write this letter. There isn't too much to do tonight. Tomorrow classes start.

When you two left Sunday night I went downstairs and then went out with some fellow students. Most of them live in Adrian. We all got in two cars and went out to a drive-in called "Bummies" but not as good as our own "Totem-Pole Drive-In" in Royal Oak, MI. Monday I took tests and went to camp. Camp was for the Freshman class. In the morning it got cold and it has been like that ever since. At camp we listened to speeches, danced, talked, laughed, ate and of course we slept.

Wednesday Phil came. Phil and I went over to the coffee shop in Rush Hall. We didn't do too much—sat mostly at one table and listened to the music.

My first day of classes I was amazed at the amount of the homework that was required for each class. I felt a little overwhelmed since I had never experienced large homework assignments at the beginning of a semester. I soon discovered that I had never learned how to really study for school homework. I also had term paper requirements for the majority of classes. I had to spend more time studying than the average student at Adrian College, but I was determined to graduate regardless of what it took.

September 27, 1959, letter to Dad and Mom:

I found out a week ago I could take a test in math, and with a B on the test and one dollar I could get credit for the three hours without taking the class. So last Tuesday I took the first part to see whether or not I could take the second part. I passed the first part and took the second part Thursday. I prayed to God if it was His will for me to pass it that I would, and if it wasn't His will to have me flunk it. Since I could gain three credits I could take one more subject and end up with sixteen hours. God must have been with me as I was the only one to pass the test with a B or higher. I thought I didn't make it. I was surprised when notified. I now have three hours of credit with a B grade behind me.

May 13, 1960, letter to Dad and Mom:

Dad, I guess by the time this letter reaches home you will be back from Lansing. How did it go? You probably did a good job as you always do.

My exam schedule has been changed. My night exams are to be taken during the Senior exam week. This is one week ahead of the exam schedule, so I will be through with my exams on Tuesday but Phil's last exam is Wednesday afternoon. Phil and I will be ready to leave here on Wednesday afternoon (June 1) or whenever it is convenient for you.

As the semester is coming to a close I have been thinking over the experiences I have had, especially the first semester. I believe my first semester was the best five months of my life and this second semester is second best. I just hope next year will be like last semester. I can try to make it the best. This semester things have slowed down and are quieter, while last semester things were happening every weekend. I like it here and have been enjoying myself. If I didn't benefit from the courses I took, I can say I have benefited in other areas of education. By the way, our baseball team (the one Phil and I are on) won our last game, making us the champs in our league. Each team plays three games, and we won all three. We play the champs in the other league, probably sometime next week.

I have been thinking on what I will be taking here in my next three years. I would like to major in business, and I have been thinking seriously about the field of accounting. I will then try to minor in history and my second minor will be in the religion group. I will pick something like philosophy. Next year I will take American Literature, Principles and Problems of Economics, U.S. History to 1865, Philosophy, and Physical Education.

During the summer after my freshman year, Dad was able to get me a job at Hodges for Dodge, a Dodge dealership in Ferndale. I worked five and a half days weekly and made seventy dollars a week, which was good income back then. My main job was picking up parts for repairing cars, either in downtown Detroit at Chrysler's parts warehouse or from other dealerships around the area. I also swept floors. I enjoyed this summer employment.

In my second year I was in a fraternity during the second semester. I found living in the fraternity house was much better than living in a school dormitory.

A dance in Ridge Gymnasium was held on the Friday of the first week of the college school year. It was called the "Getting to Know You Dance." I never got into rock and roll dancing, but I enjoyed the slow cheek-to-cheek dancing. This Friday fell on September 16, 1960. I went by myself. There were three freshman girls that I had seen on campus, and I wanted to meet them at this dance.

I walked in the gym and sitting on the lower bleachers on my left was a girl; I didn't recognize her but she appealed to me. I was still shy and it was hard for me to ask for one girl in a group. I walked up to her and asked her for a dance. She accepted. We danced, and after the music stopped I thanked her and she walked back to where she was seated. There was something about her that I really liked. One of the three girls I wanted to dance with was my next dance partner, but I kept thinking about the first girl. After the music stopped, I thanked her and looked to see if this first girl was alone and she was! I went back and asked her for another dance. This time I didn't let her go. After three or four dances I asked her if she would like to go for a walk. I wanted to get her away from this dance since I didn't want any competition from the other young men attending this event. I wasn't sure what her reaction would be, but to my delight she was agreeable. I was thrilled! While dancing I learned that her name was Carole Taylor, from Niles, Michigan. During our walk I also learned that our birthdays were just four days apart in April. We spent the rest of the evening walking and talking. The weather was great! When it was time for her to be back in her dormitory I asked her for a date to the movies the following day, Saturday evening. She accepted. Wow! I really had a strong "like" for her.

October 2, 1960, letter to Dad and Mom:

Well, it's Sunday and tomorrow will be Monday again. Next weekend will come, and that is the main reason I am writing. But first, did you ever get my last paycheck from Hodges? Next weekend is homecoming. It only comes once a year and is the biggest event of the year. If I could get home Friday night could I drive the car up here for the weekend? Carole and I could drive the car back home Sunday morning and go to our church. We could eat dinner there and then you folks could drive us back. What do you think of this idea? I think it's a fabulous idea myself. I just wonder how I ever thought of it! Please write soon and let me know.

Dad didn't agree that this was a good idea. Like the previous year, Mom and Dad drove to Adrian for homecoming. After the football game Dad and Mom took Carole and me out for dinner and then headed home. Carole and I went to the Homecoming Dance.

My ACC (American Common Club) pledge class consisted of Phil Rundell, Paul Dunlap, and myself. Phil was dating Carole's roommate, Irene Morse. The four of us formed a friendship that has lasted our entire lifetime. Carole and I were surprised when Irene wrote to Carole later in the summer of 1961 that they had been married during that summer. Irene did not come back for the 1961-62 school year at Adrian College but Phil did. The following school year he transferred to Lawrence Institute of Technology in Southfield, Michigan, which is now named Lawrence Technical University. We are still friends even though we left Michigan in 1970 and they remained in Michigan.

October 29, 1960, letter to Dad and Mom:

It is now Saturday here, but only by fifteen minutes. I went over to the ACC house for an hour and did some homework. Nelson came over for a while, and I understand Dick Kapnick is coming home this weekend.

I am now a fraternity man. I was accepted before dinner. Pledging starts Monday for eight or nine weeks. I am starting an experience that will never be forgotten. This day is one of the most important days of my life. I never dreamed I would be in a fraternity, but I consider it a starting point of a great experience of my life. I hope both of you are as happy as I am.

Dad, I have been thinking about an idea these last few days. Mid-semester will be over next week and then the weekend will be here again. There isn't a lot Carole and I can do around here due to the lack of transportation and places to go. I thought of an idea that could be fun for both of us. You probably know what I'm going to say, so please hold on and bear with me. If I come home Friday night, could I borrow the car and drive back to Adrian? Then Carole and I could leave early Sunday morning and go to church at Ferndale and eat dinner at home. Here you will have the opportunity of meeting Carole and to get to know her better. Believe me, she is wonderful. What do you think about the idea? I could come back up here on Friday night and study all day Saturday, and then Carole and I would go out Saturday night and then go to church at Ferndale. I will leave this decision to you since you know what is best.

Dad again didn't think it was a good idea, so I didn't get the car. Not having a car didn't stop Carole and me from spending time together on the weekends.

Carole and I spent a lot of our free time together. Soon we were eating our meals together, going to church together, and attending the many activities the college had available such as basketball games, football games, travelogues, plays, concerts, and walking downtown for a snack. Carole was accepted into the sorority Sigma-Sigma-Sigma. Her sorority was considered the sister to my fraternity due to some of my fraternity brothers dating girls from Carole's sorority, so we also had sorority and fraternity parties. After every home basketball and football game there was a dance in the student union. We were always there. We were recognized on campus as going steady. Eventually I gave her my fraternity pin, which indicated a higher level of going steady. I quickly took her out of circulation for dating! An older woman called "Mom Shipman," part of the college staff and well liked by students, referred to us as "The inseparable." Mom Shipman was a special woman. She had to be in her late seventies and was the librarian on campus. She enjoyed the students.

Carole made my college years really special and fun. We were in love. She lived in Niles near South Bend, Indiana, and I lived in the Detroit area on the other side of the state. During the summer we exchanged letters and a few times I drove over to Niles to spend the weekend with her and her family. She had three younger sisters, so it was hard to find time to be alone. During our college years Carole spent time with my family in Ferndale during the last three Christmas seasons. Her family was not pleased with this arrangement.

When mid-September came, we were back to seeing each other and back to our campus routine.

November 4, 1960, letter to Dad and Mom:

I won't have any free time this weekend. Saturday night I won't do any homework. There is an open house over at the fraternity house. I probably will be in early tomorrow night. Carole and I will probably go for a walk afterward so that we can both get a little more sleep and make it to church. Sunday night I 'm sure I will have to stay up late again due to a philosophy test on Monday. From now until Thanksgiving weekend I will have very little free time. I have a term paper to hand in two weeks from Tuesday. I have about two pages of information so far.

I will be through with school two weeks from Tuesday, at least for a half week. Even though I will try to do one term paper I am looking forward to coming home. I am really looking forward to Christmas vacation. I guess homework isn't that bad, but there are times I feel like I am knocking my brains out. I have never studied as hard as I am doing. There are the good times though, and I realize I will be rewarded in the future for what I am doing here on campus.

November 16, 1960, letter to Dad and Mom:

I received your check, Dad, in fact, the last two or three checks. Thank you. In fact, I should thank you for making this semester possible. I have never had a greater time. I think I am enjoying this semester more than my first semester. I'm sure this is due to Carole and ACC.

They are building the swimming pool next to the gym. They dedicated or broke ground for the new girls' dormitory a week ago. The business administration building is completed. We will also have a new men's dormitory by September.

See you Tuesday. Set the time for me, Dad, since I probably will have to work until 12:30 p.m. [in kitchen of dining hall] but could get excused if necessary. If you come late, I could get some more homework done and Carole isn't leaving early.

December 7, 1960, letter to Dad and Mom:

This week is going to be a lot of social life. I'm glad Christmas vacation is coming up next week.

Tonight I'm going to a party with Carole after dinner. Friday night there is the Christmas dance. Saturday night there is a basketball game plus dance. Also Sunday there is a band concert, but I probably will have to cut everything out on Sunday. I will try to make church. I may have to play in the ACC basketball game Saturday and I have to work over at the dining hall Saturday and Sunday of this week. Also, I will have an estimated seven-hour assignment for accounting to do on Sunday, which I probably will wait until Sunday evening to do. Monday night will be spent over at the fraternity house. We all get together and sing and exchange silly gifts. We may go out and sing around the town.

January 4, 1961, letter to Dad and Mom:

I want to thank both of you for making it possible to have Carole visit us [Carole spent a weekend at the Ferndale home during the New Year's weekend]. It was the greatest weekend of my life, as well as the most expensive. I had a fabulous time. I am sorry, Mother, for the extra dishes. I bet you are really tired by now.

January 6 1961, letter to Dad and Mom:

It looks like I will not be home between semesters. It's no sense going home on Friday when I will have to be back here on Sunday.

Tonight there is a big dance here which Carole and I will be attending. She really is a wonderful girl. I love her very much. Early next semester would it be possible to bring her home for a weekend?

It was early February 1961 that I moved from the men's dormitory to the ACC (American Common Club, not Greek) fraternity house. It was an improved environment for studying, and that was very beneficial for me. The study room I had was above the second floor, and there were only three of us in this small room. It was perfect!

March 12, 1961, letter to Dad and Mom:

I am here at my desk. The time reads 3:15 a.m. Sunday and everyone is in bed. I just finished my term paper for economics, and last Thursday night I typed my history paper. You would think I was tired, but believe me I am wide awake. It is funny, but I just can't go to sleep. I am not even having trouble keeping my eyes open.

Friday night I didn't go out but stayed in the house and studied. The house on Fridays is usually empty. It was like this last Friday, just right for studying.

Dad, I got a letter the other day referring to "un-atmosphere to study by" in the house. Also, I believe Mother mentioned it's harder to get sleep over here in the house. Well, first we have a house rule that sleeping rooms are only to be used for sleeping, so there is no talking in these rooms. The doors are always kept closed. I will confess that the beds are not as comfortable as in the dorm and there seem to be a lot of alarm clocks going off at 7:00 a.m., but I can sleep pretty well in the sleeping room. Studying conditions are much improved here in the house. We also have a study-room rule: the study rooms are be used to study only. Of course, if nobody is studying then they may be used by the fellows to talk. If one is studying he may mention that the noise is too loud and the person or persons will have to stop or lower their voice. It is better studying here than in the dorm. Last semester in the dorm it was very noisy, especially my neighbors. Many times I was forced to go next door and ask them to turn down the radio and their voices. They usually cooperated, but the whole floor was noisy. This is the reason Phil would like to get out of the dorm, it is too noisy! Also, I could always go to North Hall or the library for studying.

Saturday I worked all day rewriting my paper. I'm sure glad that it is finished. This past evening (Saturday night) was the big night for all the fraternities and sororities. It was the All-College sing. Each sorority and fraternity sings a required number and one other of their choice. Then each of these groups has a quartet singing two numbers. We lost in both. Many made comments at the dinner that they thought our quartet should have won. Even some of the other fraternity men thought our quartet should have won. It's now 4:00 a.m.

Carole worked for dinner so I ate with my fraternity brother, which was good. ACC sat in the front seats in the back and then Sigma-Sigma-Sigma sororities filed behind us, and guess who happened to sit right behind me? You're right, Carole. Her sorority did a lousy job in their competition.

After our performance I sat in a different spot and when the winners were announced we left without me saying goodbye to her. I doubt she would be upset about this, but I wasn't in the mood to hunt her up with all of the hundreds of people. She said earlier that she had to stay and clean up the tables, so she probably won't be upset. In fact, she never gets upset or mad. She is in the same mood every day.

Remember when I was home last and I mentioned I had lost my silver dollar? Well, when I got back we pledges went over to Jim King's room and turned everything upside down. Jim's room was the last room I was in before that vacation. My silver dollar was under his bed mattress, so I still have it. Another thing, I am in the student union committee here on campus.

I kind of hate to do this, Dad, but I wonder if it would be possible to send five dollars here to me immediately. You have been sending me ten dollars every other week and I appreciate this. As you know, I just got a check a week ago Friday. I took four dollars of it to pay up on the rest of what I owe for the spring formal (total of sixteen dollars). I also have six dollars in the bank, which I would like to keep there. So that is twenty dollars right there. I had a lot of expenses that week and still do. I had to get a haircut Friday, laundry soap, regular soap, toothpaste. I have two dollars and twenty-six cents on hand. Monday I probably will have to give up two dollars and twenty-five cents for an accounting book that is needed. I still need hair shampoo, a cheap towel rack, a new watchband (mine is now falling apart), stamps (completely out). I also need to have my pants cleaned and pressed from last night of the College Sing. I will also have to do a little washing next weekend. I promised Carole I would take her out and buy her a sundae to celebrate our anniversary (six months next week, how about that). So if you could possibly spare five dollars I sure could use it. I hate to ask you for money, but this time I honestly need money.

In four hours I will have to get up for breakfast and church. I promised Carole I would eat breakfast today since I didn't eat breakfast all this past week. I tried to get out of it, but she remembered the promise and insisted on me keeping it. I'm beginning to get a little tired now, but still wide awake. Funny, I have never been this wide awake at this time of day before. Ever since 9:30 a.m. Saturday I have been working. I didn't relax until dinner, and I was nervous the rest of the evening. I still have literature to do, so I guess I will work on that for a while.

Thank you for all of the letters. It is nice to hear from both of you. I will try and write more.

March 14, 1961, letter to Dad and Mom:

I got plastered with letters from home today. I really was surprised. Thank you for the money. I can sure use it.

About my sleep: Sunday morning I got up about 8:15 a.m. and was wide awake again. I went to bed at 5:00 a.m. and it took me a little while to fall asleep. I was going to stay up all night, but I thought when I was in church I would begin to be vulnerable to falling asleep. I decided the best thing to do was go to bed. I did get three hours of sleep and felt good all day. It is surprising I did not feel it Sunday. Since I got a lot of homework done Friday night, Saturday, and early Sunday morning, I just had my literature to do. Carole and I went to the student union, and I worked on the literature assignment for a little while. I spent just about the whole day with her. It is the longest time I spent with her in one day. I had a great time. Maybe that is why I did not get tired.

Last night we had our fraternity meeting until 10:30 p.m. (started at 7:30 p.m.). I then did my accounting assignment. I didn't get up until 8:30 a.m. and I was tired. I would have given just about anything to stay in bed, but I had class to attend. I feel okay now. I was awake by lunchtime.

ACC was robbed last Saturday night. It really meant a lot to me and the fraternity to win both of the cups, or one of them. We have been working on it for a month, and this one was the last year for our song director, Eric Sullivan. He wanted to win that cup for his last year since he is a senior. He is talented in music. Word got out today that it was discovered there was a mathematical mistake on the figuring that put ACC quartet on top, but it was too late since the cup had been presented to another fraternity.

April 12, 1961, letter to Dad and Mom:

Mom, thank you for all you did when I was at home [spring break]. It was nice being home. I'm glad I finished one term paper. I have just one more to do. [During spring break Dad allowed me to take the car to visit Carole and her family. April 10 was Carole's birthday.]

I got to Niles around 2:20 p.m. (20 minutes late); Carole was waiting there for me. I had a fairly good time. Thursday she showed me around the city. Friday we just drove around the area. Friday night Carole and I, her parents, and her three younger sisters [Kay, Connie, and Candace] went to an early show and then came back and played card games. Friday afternoon her Dad [Bryce Taylor] took us up for an airplane ride. Saturday we all went to Chicago for the day and came home in the nighttime and played cards.

Sunday we went to church with the family and ate dinner across the street at Carole's grandparents (Rolfe and Vesta Taylor). Then we came back to college. Adrian had two inches of wet snow. What a mess. In the evening Carole and I went to Big Boy and had some ice cream. By Monday evening the snow was gone. Thanks, Dad, for the car this weekend. I really appreciate it!

We might run into complications (future dance) because this is the second biggest school dance of the school year. The girls are allowed to stay out until 2:00 a.m. [Adrian College is a private school and back then there was a set time for the girls to be inside their dorm.] They did this because many of the girls take overnights each year and they don't want the girls to take overnights. Carole's housemother is going to take this matter up with the dean. Carole explained to her housemother why she is coming home with me; it isn't because of the dance. That is why the housemother is going to see the dean. If Carole doesn't get permission, then I will go to see the dean and explain the situation with her, then I will get permission for Carole. If not, then Carole will come home with me Friday and we will have to miss the ACC party, and maybe the dance also. It would cost one dollar and twenty-five cents more if we drove up Saturday night and back if we went to the dance. We would get your okay before we did this. If you feel that this would be too expensive then we won't do it, but I feel everything will come as planned. In other words, Carole will get permission [which she did] so everything will come off as planned. See both of you Friday between 5:30 p.m. and 6:00 p.m. [Dad did come to take us home in Ferndale]. Thank you all again. This weekend will be one of the best weekends of the school year.

May 16, 1961, letter to Mom:

You probably are not in too hot of a mood for anything [Mom was having a gall bladder operation]. I wish there was something I could do for you. I'm still not forgetting you in my prayers. I know God is with you. Just keep your faith and everything will turn out fine. Remember God is good and there are a lot of things we can't understand, but someday we will understand all. Don't forget that I love you. There may be times you feel like I don't appreciate all the things you have done for me, but believe me, I do. I couldn't have asked for a better mother than you. I have millions of memories of you, and I couldn't respect another mother as much as you. I feel very lucky to have a mother such as you. I'm proud to say Mrs. Harold Wilcox (or Slim, ha) ["Slim" was a nickname I used occasionally] is my mother.

As you probably know from yesterday's letter I mailed home, I am the vice president of ACC. This semester I am getting more and more responsibilities. I can already see that this fraternity is helping me. Maturity is based on responsibility I am beginning to enjoy it. Even though, Mother, the fraternity requires work and responsibility, it hasn't taken anything from my school work. It may take time away from Carole, but not from my schoolwork. Fraternity life can benefit a person and that's what it is doing for me, so try to explain this to Dad. I'm afraid he will feel that the fraternity is hindering my grades since my grades will be lower than last semester.

I sent a picture of Carole and me last night home for you. Remind Dad to bring it to the hospital

I felt that I had to sell Dad on the value I was receiving from ACC fraternity. It was a good group of young men, and I enjoyed being a part of this group. My years at Adrian College and this fraternity were an asset to me, and yes, there was a lot of fun with this group of men. I valued this. Dad was wondering if my grades would be better outside of a fraternity. I believe it actually helped me in terms of my grades due to a better environment for studying within the fraternity house. I'm very thankful that I had the experience of being a member of ACC and living in the fraternity house.

May 17, 1961, letter to Mom:

I received a telephone call from Dad a half hour ago. He said you pulled through this operation in good shape and will be there for about a week. Next week you will be glad that it is all over with. I will be home in two weeks.

With my term paper done, I am having a lot of free time, which I'm not used to. So this time I've been doing work for the fraternity. I also spent some time with Carole. We had at least two hundred and twenty-five people [open house] that came over to my fraternity house between 7:00 p.m. to 9:00 p.m. I'm glad it is all over.

This coming weekend Carole and I will go to the show Friday night. We will be back here on the campus about 9:30 p.m. and then we will go to a small dance at the student union. Saturday night Carole and I plus about five more couples will go out to our housemother's cottage on Devils Lake and spend the evening there. We should have a lot of fun. This will probably be our last weekend together until September. The next weekend we will have to study for our exams. Be good now, and I will see you in two weeks. I will try and write to you again soon.

May 23, 1961, letter to Dad and Mom:

Well, Mom as you read this you probably are home. I hope, Mother, you feel much better. I want you to take care of yourself.

Sunday night Carole and I went for a walk and I lost my fraternity pin. I felt bad about it. I took a flashlight out that night and tried to locate it, but no success. This afternoon a couple that Carole and I know found the pin on the sidewalk where we were walking. Somebody stepped on it though, and the lock is damaged a little. One of the little stones is missing. I will get it fixed in Ferndale next week.

November 26, 1961, letter to Dad and Mom:

Sunday night I gave Carole my fraternity pin to wear with her sorority pin. Carole and I didn't tell anybody that night. I did tell Elmer Schroeder. I went to breakfast (now part of each day) with Carole. They began to notice the pin by noon, and when I came to lunch many of our friends, sorority and fraternity members, were aware of our event.

Everybody congratulated us as we, in our separate ways, were met. Carole was taken to a shower two times that night and after I went to bed late again the pledges came over at 3:00 a.m. and caused a little trouble. They decided to take me to the shower.

January 21 1962, letter to Dad and Mom:

I have two exams behind me with four to go. Carole just has two to go, with one of these being a very easy one. She will be finished Tuesday while I will have a long way to go. By the way, don't come to pick me up. Dick and Nelson said they would drive me home.

I went to church this morning with Carole. It was a nice service. I left Carole at the dorm to let her study then I came back to the house.

February 28, 1962, letter to Dad and Mom:

Yes, I did see Glenn's flight into space [John Glenn, first American to orbit the earth, on February 20, 1962]. I only had one class that day, so I saw and heard about two-thirds of the adventure. It was quite exciting, and I enjoyed every moment of it. When the rocket went up I was a little nervous myself.

I am thankful for the complete success of his voyage. This flight of his was the most exciting TV and radio program seen or heard.

I have been thinking during the past year, and especially this semester, I would like to have a camera that takes 35mm slides as well as the regular snapshots. I would like to take pictures of the campus before I graduate from Adrian College (fall and spring time). Carole is going to have her roommate write to her dad (she is Japanese) in Japan and see if we can get such a camera at a cheap price. She is going to check it out and find one for a good price. She can have it shipped to the campus. Would that meet with your approval, Dad? [Mission was accomplished; I had a camera from Japan for the beginning of my senior year.]

March 11, 1962, letter to Dad and Mom:

We had the All College Sing again last night. We [fraternity] won the quartet trophy. It sure will look nice in the ACC library. We also won the scholastic trophy. Our point average was 1.71 (on a 3-point system. A=3, B=2, C=1, D=0 and F= -1), the highest average of any organization on campus. We even beat the girls on average!

May 7, 1962, letter to Dad and Mom:

We had our spring formal in Toledo Saturday night. It was held at the Toledo Club [Toledo, Ohio] and it was really nice, much better than last year. Sunday I spent the day with Carole. In the afternoon we studied together by ourselves in the basement of Estes Hall [Carole's dormitory]. During the nighttime we went downtown and continued our walk around the college. It was nice being able to be by ourselves. The wintertime killed that.

Dad, would it be possible to borrow your car for the weekend? I would really like to have one big weekend before I say goodbye to Carole for the summer. I would appreciate it if I could have the car for Friday night, Saturday, and Sunday. We would come home for dinner, if that's all right with you, Mother. Does this sound good with you two? I sure hope so because it would be great to have a car Friday night so that Carole and I could go somewhere together in a car without doubling with another couple. So if it is okay with you two, I will be home Friday between 4:00 p.m. and 6:30 p.m. [I don't remember if Dad was agreeable to this great plan and if so I don't remember how I got home].

My camera is now being ordered. I will have the camera in five or six weeks. It is just about completely automatic, so it is just about impossible to "goof" a picture. I am paying a lot more than was planned. I hope you folks don't mind, but this was a chance of a lifetime and this camera will last a lifetime. I could always sell it for what I paid for it. I already have the money for the camera saved, with the exception of the postage and maybe tariff. The Japanese girl said that she would have the camera shipped to her and maybe there won't be any duty on the camera. I have forty-four dollars in an envelope located in my locker for the camera. She told me to keep it and pay her when she gets the camera. She will be here at Adrian since she is going to summer school. As of now, the camera and case cost forty-four dollars. The postage and duty charge shouldn't cost more than eight dollars. This camera is really nice! Elmer Schroeder and I saw the same camera advertised for one hundred and three dollars.

The end of the school year came and Carole and I said our good-byes. The camera was ordered. I needed an advanced accounting course for a major in accounting, but Adrian College wasn't offering this course during my senior school year. I talked to the dean of men, John Van Valkenburg, asking if I could transfer a summer advanced accounting course from either the University of Detroit or Wayne State University. He assured me that Adrian College would accept this course for my major. I took this course at Wayne State University. Dad was agreeable to this. The last two summers I had summer jobs and made good money. After the class at Wayne State University was completed, I found a job at a small manufacturing shop making business signs. I worked there for the last few weeks of summer vacation. The day came when Carole and I were back on campus for my final college year.

I had never had a strong B grade average in a school year. I decided that since I was taking courses during my senior year, which I expected to enjoy, I was going to go for it. I talked to Carole about this and told her my plan. Friday night after dinner I would go back to the fraternity house and study as long as I could. This was the perfect evening for studying because the fraternity house was basically empty of my fraternity brothers. Then I would get up early Saturday and study as long as I needed to. Some Saturdays it was almost the complete day. When I was done, we would spend the rest of the weekend together. She accepted this. I would return to the house on Sunday night from spending the day with Carole, and while everyone in the house would be studying I would go to bed. My plans worked; my senior year's grade average was between a B and an A.

Carole was basically an A student, as she was in high school. Her point average for high school was around 3.97 on a four-point system. At Adrian College she did just as well. She only had to study a fraction of what was required for me, and she got better grades.

September 24, 1962 Now Dad, smile. I will state my financial situation---poor. I hope you are smiling. I don't have any money right now, but if you feel sorry for me I could accept a couple of dollars. Seriously though, I can live on two dollars this next week. I can get along with just a dollar or two, Dad. I know I have already drained out a good hunk from your income since my books were twenty-three dollars, and I gave the fraternity sixteen dollars, and I also spent a couple of dollars on Carole and Newsweek (annual subscription) three dollars. Those are the major expenses of this semester so far.

October 4, 1962, letter to Dad and Mom:

Don't forget that homecoming is two weeks from this coming weekend. I expect all of you to be here since I hope you can make it. It will be good to see you folks again. I will have to show you the fraternity house. The homecoming college dance is having a big-name orchestra with a cost of five dollars per couple. I can't see paying five dollars for a dance, so how does this sound to you: When it is time for you and Mom to leave for home, could Carole and I go home with you and spend the rest of the weekend at home? Dad, you could cut my hair for my senior pictures, which will be taken the following Monday. How does this sound to you two? Can this be arranged?

This plan was acceptable.

December 11, 1962, letter to Dad and Mom:

We had our fraternity party last night and had a good time. We sang to the orphan children, and they were cute. They had memorized every Christmas song you could think of. We also went to the old people's home and sang.

A week from last weekend I plus nine other brothers went to Cincinnati University's ACC and helped them rush. It was really an experience and enjoyable. We left Adrian at 4:30 p.m. and arrived at Cincinnati's ACC at 8:45 p.m. We left Cincinnati at 1:00 a.m. and arrived in Adrian College at 6:30 a.m. I drove back. Cincinnati is really a hilly city, and I guess its murder driving during the winter. We came home here, ate breakfast, and I studied until 10:00 a.m. and finally went to bed. I could only sleep for 2½ hours. I will see you Friday.

As mentioned, I drove back to Adrian from Cincinnati, starting the drive at 1:00 a.m. The other four fraternity brothers in the car fell asleep. I was driving down a road that ended at a traffic light. I fell asleep at the wheel approaching this intersection (the end of the road), and woke up just in time to see that I was going to crash into a tall brick wall at this intersection. I immediately turned the steering wheel to my left, applying the brakes, and as the car skidded I regained control of the car and kept it on the road. Of course, everyone was awakened, and they asked me if I was okay. I said in a calm voice, "I'm fine," and they immediately went back to sleep. Inside me my heart was still beating fast. I was not sleepy during the rest of the drive. I give credit to God that I was awakened at the very last second needed to avoid crashing into the brick wall and keeping control of the car. Since there were no seat belts during this era, we would have either been killed or in serious condition.

February 10, 1963, letter to Dad and Mom:

I have been sick again, and I still am. It was Thursday night that I came down with a sore throat. Friday morning when I got up, I felt so exhausted and tired with a sore throat. I went to the nurse, and she gave me some pills. Saturday morning I saw the doctor that came on the campus and he gave me some different pills. He looked into my mouth and said one of my tissues in the throat was swollen. He also said that if I continued to feel tired and exhausted all the time to come and see him Monday (tomorrow). I still have the sore throat, though better, but I don't seem to get as tired as I did.

I'm not going to do any homework this afternoon but just try to relax. I think that has been my problem this past week, I can't relax. I will write later. I'm going to see Carole. Thanks for the letters.

March 24, 1963, letter to Dad and Mom:

I think I can get a two point average [B grade] for this semester [which I did] but don't expect a two point for mid-semester though. Come to think of it, I put in more than thirty hours of studying last weekend. I was sick for three Sundays in a row. I figured homework is first, since God would want me to do the best I can in school. I feel guilty if I let my homework go and do something else besides studying when I have homework to do. I try to read at least the *Upper Room* [devotional] every day, and of course I pray every day. I feel God has been with me these past four years and it was He, you folks, and Carole that have gotten me through college. I don't see how I could have made it without you folks backing me up 100% and your encouragement and Carole. I will confess that I feel that God has been far away during this past year. I hope this will all change after school. Once in a while Carole and I will pray together, which brings a more-confident feeling. I don't seem to sweat school too much anymore, but now just finding a job. I hate this position of looking for a job without any experience in my field.

May 9, 1963, letter to Dad and Mom:

You realize that next week is my last week of classes plus I will have my final exam. It is just unbelievable that my college days are just about over. These past four years have been great, and I hate to see it end. I hate to close the friendships with some of my fellow students here. The college years have gone by fast, and now I'm almost out in the world without any idea as to what will happen.

May 1963 came, and I received my college diploma. My thoughts were, "I did it!" Graduation day was exciting! Of course, Mom and Dad came with my brother Phil. Our very good friends across from the Ferndale house, Larry and Faye Cowell, were also present. My best friend during my Ferndale era, Jack Hinkins, also came to my graduation. We were like brothers, but this relationship weakened and finally died due to Carole and me not living in the Detroit area.

At the end of the day everyone went home, but I stayed on the campus. I believe Carole went home on this day. I got all my stuff packed and waited in the morning for Dad to come and take me back to Ferndale. I remember as I waited there was a little sadness over leaving Adrian College. I learned a lot from this experience, had a lot of fun, and met the girl I hoped would be my wife. I realized that if I had to summarize what I had learned in one sentence it would be, "There is so much that I don't know." College opened my mind to realizing that one can't reach the goal of all knowledge; there is always more to learn. College opened the door for my employment world. The real textbook is what you learn during your employment. I was also very aware that now I had to find employment,which I realized wouldn't be as good as being a student on campus for another year.

I stayed in Adrian, got a job, and rented a room. I thought I would live a very special life for one more school year. Carole had one more year to go, and I planned to work and take in all of the school evening and weekend activities with Carole. This was perfect! I would get engaged on September 16 of 1963 and marry Carole when she was out of school, or perhaps during the school year. I had a very strong love for my Carole.

About a day or two after graduation I got a notice from the draft board to report for a physical, which I did. I asked an army personnel member what my chances of being drafted in the army would be, given my history of rheumatic fever and having a heart murmur. He said I wouldn't be drafted. The first question asked by a potential employer was, "What is your draft status?" No company would want to hire a person who would be drafted shortly. At Adrian a CPA firm that showed an interest in me asked me this question. My response was that I would be exempt. They hired me, and I found a room to rent at a house near the campus. Mother knew a friend that was selling an older Dodge car, and they sold the car to me. I found that the car burned a lot of oil. Now I was all set for another school year at Adrian College and I would marry Carole as soon as possible. I started my employment in Adrian on June 16, 1963.

June 16, 1963, letter to Dad and Mom:

I appreciate all your help and support in helping me get on my feet with my first job. It's nice to know that you have a family that really cares and is standing behind you. I'm grateful for all you folks have done, even though I may not show it at times.

It was nice of the Cowells to drop over when I left Ferndale. It was a nice feeling to know that they too care. They are really a great family

June 17, 1963, letter to Dad and Mom:

Here are a few lines about my first day at work. Everything went off very well. I got up this morning at 7:00 a.m. and walked to the office. We had our get together at 8:00 a.m., all six of us. Then I was assigned a desk, and I even got my own key to the office. I went over to a corporation here in town after I picked up my car. Say, it is a good thing that I have a car because I'm already using it. I won't go to the office tomorrow, but will go back to this same corporation. I am working with a senior accountant with inventory. I learned a lot today, and I also realize further that this won't be any easy job. There are some tough days ahead of me, but when the time comes I think I can handle everything. The men are just great. I couldn't have asked for a better group of men to work with.

The CPA company that hired me assigned me for training to a CPA who had been my instructor for my auditing class at Adrian College. Since he knew me, the employment was more enjoyable. I should have had an A grade in his course because all of the assigned written homework and the final exam had been graded A. He gave me a B for the final grade. The reason for this is that he said at the beginning of the class he said he would not take attendance, but he expected everyone to be present in his classes. He mentioned that there would be one surprise quiz during the semester. I attended every one of his classes except one. His class was early in the morning, and on one of these mornings I overslept. That was the day of his surprise written test. During that morning I learned about this test and went to him and explained that I overslept. He didn't believe me. He said that the test had little value in terms of the semester ending grade. When the semester was completed and I learned I had a B, he explained that I didn't deserve an A grade since I had one F grade. I didn't mention this issue during my time working with him.

July 8, 1963, letter to Dad and Mom:

Every time I drive home from Detroit to Adrian I always feel lonely. It has been like that for the last two to three years. I guess I still enjoy being home with you two and the friends back home. Once I get here the feeling wears off eventually, especially when I am with a friend. I also missed Carole a whole lot this summer. I wish I were going to Niles this weekend, but I guess I can hold out for one more week. I sure have fallen for her this past year. Every day I get more and more anxious to see her.

You know, after living here in Adrian these last three weeks I have decided that I don't like Adrian as much as I thought I would. I still enjoy seeing a lot of people and being in the midst of everything.

I received a letter from Carole today that was quite acceptable, and she mentioned a daughter and father talk. Her Dad is finally expressing his feelings and reaction about me. According to Carole, he likes me and is happy that I came from a good family background. He asked her how she felt about me and told her that it was up to her to decide as to the person she wants to go with and plan her future with. He always wanted her to finish schooling and has always felt that no one was good enough for his daughter. He was disappointed that I got a job in Adrian because he wanted her to really know that I'm the right man for her. He figured if I was separated from her for a year it would be a test of whether or not I was the right one. Carole mentioned we were very close, and I guess he doesn't completely realize our feelings toward each other. He mentioned one requirement of having her home for the recognition of students in his church next time [last Sunday in December]. You remember that day during Christmas vacation when Rev. Parrish asks all college students to stand up in the congregation and the after-service tea and coffee. Her church operates the same way, and Carole has been in Ferndale the last three Christmas vacations. He always wanted her to be there at his church during this event. I can't blame him, since she is the type of girl a father could be proud of. I can't really blame him for loving his daughter.

I went home to visit my parents on Saturday, July 13, 1963. Dad gave me an opened envelope from the draft board. He had never before opened someone else's mail. He apologized that he opened it, but he wanted to wait until the best time to give it to me. I was drafted! I think I lost a heartbeat! I couldn't believe it! I thought I was exempt. I thanked Dad and told him he made the right decision. My dream for the school year without classes was shattered!

On July 22 I wrote a letter to my parents when I was a little depressed. I was anxiously looking forward to another year at Adrian College with Carole and getting married. Dad told me that being a Christian is accepting what comes. I knew in the back of my mind that he was right, but my willpower was not strong enough to do what I needed to do. I responded to Dad at a bad time when I felt depressed and lonely. This was a big mistake, and I regretted it. My attitude reflected being immature, which is embarrassing for me. My faith and trust in Jesus Christ should have been strong during this time. With Jesus Christ as your Lord, He gives the strength to overcome every circumstance. I was wrong in not accepting His strength. I regret feeling this way. The outcome of this draft ended up being a blessing. Once I got settled in Fort Knox, I was back to myself and accepted life in the U.S. Army. Everything was then okay, and I knew it would work out. I was now ready to serve my country. I was very disappointed that I couldn't give Carole an engagement ring on September 16, 1963, as planned.

The next weekend I drove to Niles. Carole and I talked about this when we were alone in my car away from her parent's house. We both didn't like this new plan, but we both felt that there wasn't anything we could do about it, and we had to accept it. We felt that this was only a temporary separation. Carole easily accepted my draft, much better than I did. She could look beyond my two years in the service. She was very calm about it. I think her faith in Christ has always been stronger than mine. She knows that no matter what happens, God will take care of her.

I was so embarrassed and concerned that my boss would think I lied to him. On Monday, July 15, I explained what happened to my boss. He believed me and told me that I could work for him as long as I wanted to. I was relieved. The conversation went along these lines. I described the problem to him, and told him I was sorry. He stated that they believed I was acting in good faith, and that he wanted me to work right up to the last day. All five men of this organization were really friendly and understanding. They believed that I had the desire to learn and was trying, and showed an interest. He said they felt I would be an asset to the firm. They really made me feel good.

Chapter 21

My U.S. Army Era—Stateside

During the first part of summer 1963 I visited Carole in Niles a couple of times, and we would talk more about our situation. I knew she would wait for me.

Mom and Dad were on their way to Montana to spend the month of August with Dad's oldest brother, Monroe James Wilcox. He was a Methodist pastor. Dad, Monroe, and their brother Whyle were very close to each other. August 5, 1963, came, and my brother Phil drove me to the army deportation center in Detroit. We both got out of the car and said our goodbyes. Phil stayed at the car while I walked directly to the entrance doors and never turned around for a final goodbye wave. I was with hundreds of men, and we were here for our last physical for the army's acceptance or rejection. They knew of my rheumatic fever, and I was told that I should take two penicillin pills each day. They would get these pills for me once I was at my assignment. I did get the bottle of these pills, but I trashed them. I was told that penicillin saved my life, and once you have rheumatic fever the individual is more vulnerable to catch it again. It was also my understanding that the more penicillin is taken the less effective it becomes. For this reason I did not take these pills. After the physicals were completed they showed us where we would sleep—a very large room filled with bunk beds. Everyone picked their own bed; I picked a lower one. The lights were out at 10:00 p.m. and at 3:30 a.m. we were up. That day I found myself on a bus full of men heading to Ft. Knox, Kentucky, for our basic training. At this point I accepted reality, and I knew I had to accept this life and get the most out of it. It would all work out.

The few army recruits that arrived with me were too late to start a new basic group. We were told that we had to wait for additional men arriving toward the end of the week. That first week was called zero week. We still had to spend the regular eight weeks in basic training. I was very disappointed. I had a lot of KP (working in kitchen) work during this week.

On August 6, 1963, I mailed a short letter to my parents. I told them not to worry about me since everything would be okay. I mentioned it was really hot at Fort Knox and the army was keeping us busy continuously. I told them to have a nice vacation.

For the first five or six weeks of basic training we were not allowed to leave our area. As mentioned, I had planned to give Carole an engagement ring on September 16, 1963 when we would both be at Adrian. This was the third anniversary of meeting each other. I was saddened that I couldn't do that. Then an idea popped into my mind. Why not give her the rings with a letter and mark the outside of the package, "Do not open until Sept. 16th"?

August 24, 1963, letter to Dad and Mom:

Tomorrow I will go to the PX and try to pick up a ring for Carole. I will continue on with my plan of giving Carole a ring on September 16. If I can arrange it, I will send it to her and she will not open it until September 16th. I will also marry her when I come home in December [I was told that I should have a leave during Christmas time]. I will try to make it before Christmas, and I hope this will meet with your approval. If I get married before the end of this year I will get an extra one hundred dollars from federal income tax. Carole will also be receiving a monthly check (around fifty-eight dollars) from the government for being my wife. Other than being anxious to marry, these are additional reasons to be married during December.

Dad, thank you again for all you have done for me. I just can't find the words to express my gratefulness for your interest and love and you helping hand you have shown me over these past years. Both of you are parents any son could be proud of. I hope I will always be able to perform up to your expectations of me. We all have faults, but my memories of you two will always be of the good points and good characteristics as parents. I could never forget how wonderful you two have been to me, and I'm very proud to call you my mother and father. God bless both of you.

August 31, 1963, letter to Dad and Mom:

My face and hands are really brown from the sun.

You know, it would be nice if Carole, I, plus you two could make a trip together some future summer [this wish will become reality in June 1965].

I received today an eighty-five dollars bank order from closing my bank account in Adrian and my army check totaling fifty-two dollars, so I have a little money here.

Tomorrow I will go down to the main PX on base and buy a wedding ring set for Carole. I saw the one I wanted last Sunday for one hundred and twenty-two dollars. I asked my assigned sergeant of our unit if I could go to the PX to buy my girlfriend a ring. He said he would drive me over there. It was the most expensive one and has a list price of two hundred and forty dollars and it's the prettiest. I could buy a cheaper one, but Carole is very special. She deserves the best. She would never expect the best. She will appreciate this two ring set. I will send it to her next weekend with a request to open only on September 16th. The wedding will be in December for sure. No, Carole doesn't have anything to say about this. I know it will be favorable with her.

I miss you folks, Adrian, friends, and Carole. I'm looking forward to marriage even though it will be mainly by name only, but she will be completely mine.

We had some hand-to-hand combat; I wasn't really too impressed with it, and I could never see myself using it. The flipping is interesting, and I enjoy being able to do it. Not a whole lot of fun when you happen to be the guy flying around in the air! Ha!

September 7, 1963, letter to Dad and Mom:

This afternoon I took Carole's rings to the post office and she will get them on Wednesday or Thursday.

Five weeks from today I will be out of here. I can't wait. I sure miss Carole, but they do keep us busy and I don't think of her all of the time.

It's funny weather here in this state. It is real warm in the daytime and very cool during the night. This morning it was literally cold. The heat doesn't bother me, but the cold weather does.

Our barracks here are turning into a hospital: backs, ankles, feet, and sore throats. I had a bad sore throat a week or so ago and then a chest cold. I don't know how I got rid of it. In the past, sleep and rest were the cure for this sickness. It is just the opposite here. I took one day off and they gave me all kinds of pills and gave me work in the supply room. You have to be dead to get help here, and you can't get sick on a Sunday or holiday. A person could die waiting for a doctor at the sickroom, and if he didn't have the right channels and papers they would leave him there for a day or two. I can't figure out the medical system here. I'm fine now.

September 14, 1963, letter to Dad and Mom:

It's Saturday afternoon again at last, and we have the rest of the weekend off. I decided to spend the rest of the day writing letters and if any time is left before 9:00 p.m. I will read. Tomorrow I will go to church and try to see if Ken Wine [fraternity brother and also in my Adrian College graduation class] is in this area. I will also have to purchase some stuff at the PX tomorrow.

This morning we had a senseless inspection of our equipment and had to display it uniformly, thus getting the stuff in the right folds and position. It took several hours to set up and half an hour to clean up. The inspection lasted four hours this morning and didn't prove anything. We arranged the crazy stuff on our beds last night and this morning we made a change every ten minutes. Such things as soap dishes closed, and then the echo throughout the barracks of just the opposite. One set of stockings on a board starting on the right side, changing to the left side, and ending up in the center. We slept on the floor last night so that we wouldn't mess things up and by 2:30 a.m. I was ready to get up since it was cold and the floor was very hard.

I haven't heard from Carole whether or not she got the package. I sure hope there isn't any problem. She should have received it Thursday. I received a letter from her the other day dated last Monday and she was busy with a project helping out in the elementary school in Niles. This project is a requirement for those going into practice teaching at Adrian. Carole will teach some during her second semester. She will be successful at it and the little experience she will receive will be very enjoyable. Carole's dad took her back to Adrian Wednesday night and her first day of her final year was yesterday. When you folks get this letter Carole should be wearing my ring.

Today I received a long and interesting letter from Carole's grandparents [Vesta and Rolfe Taylor. Vesta is the writer]. They are really an interesting and young-looking couple. They are very active in the church and community work and enjoy life. They write once a week and I try to do the same.

September 16, 1963 became reality!

My letter to Carole Taylor dated Sept. 16, 1963, asking her to marry me.

U.S. Army-Ft Knox, Kentucky
September 16, 1963

Dear Carole,

Three years ago today I first saw you and asked you for a dance. Carole, I never recovered from that evening for I discovered a very unusual female that I know for sure is the sharpest woman God has created. I have told you before and I will tell you again no other woman could ever match you. Your inner self is so beautiful and perfect, more than any other female I have ever come across, and your physical beauty is way beyond the average female. That is why I want you for my complete self since you will make the perfect wife. You have everything I would want in a wife plus so much more. I will be proud to call you my wife because of what you are. You are the type that can make life so wonderful and fill the soul with happiness. You are the type that a male would come to for a problem or just to talk to. You can bring comfort to a person and just make him feel, "I never want to leave her," and boy, it sure is hard to leave her for she immediately puts you in heaven and that is why I could never let you go. Carole, I will be polite and ask you to marry me instead of telling you, for I will not accept a "No" answer. Carole, please marry me and make me the happiest person. Carole, you mean everything to me and without you I am nothing and life will never be with me again. Carole, whatever I do or wherever I go I want you at my side for I need you. You are everything to me, and it is a necessity to have you as my wife not only because I need you to continue my life but also I like the idea of having the sharpest female as my wife. So now, my little beauty queen, I'm asking you to wear this ring to symbolize our union of souls under God.

Love,
Rick

After Carole opened my package on September 16, 1963, she wrote the following letter and mailed it to me that same day.

Adrian College
September 16, 1963 Monday

Dear Rick,
    Yes, Yes, Yes, Yes, Yes, Yes, Yes: Of course I'll marry you. There is nothing in this whole wide world I want more than for you to be my husband and me your wife. You have been and you always will make me the happiest woman in the world. I'm so happy right now that I seem to be at a loss for words. My only wish is that you could have been here in person to ask me and give the ring. Rick, the ring is just beautiful!!! I just love it! Believe me, I wasted no time in getting it on. I can't wait to "show it off," but the very first thing I had to do was to write to you.
    I have locked the wedding band in my little cedar chest. We have been keeping our door locked all the time and I will be sure to now. I'm sure Jan will too. I won't breathe a word to anyone I have it either.
    Rick, thank you for such a beautiful ring set. I will wear it proudly not because it is so beautiful, but because it is a symbol of our union. Thank you, Rick, for being the way you are. I know very well there isn't another man anywhere that could top you. You are tops in character, understanding, goodness, religious convictions, interests, personality, love, and on and on. I love you for everything about you. There is nothing basically that I would want to change. I am so proud to belong to you and you alone. There is nothing in the whole world that could ever have made me any happier or done more for my life than you have. I love you, Rick. I love you very much and I need you very much. I promise you, and this is one promise I will keep if I never keep any other one, I promise you I'll be the best wife I can possibly be and I promise to try to always make you happy first. Because whenever I know that you are happy, then I am happy too. My whole life is wrapped around you. My future now really does lie in your future. It always did, but now it's "official."
    The sun is shining in the window now and it sure makes the ring sparkle. It's beautiful. I wish you were here to see it too. But come Dec., you will be and we can really celebrate then. Then I can also really begin to show you how I feel. I can't possibly in a letter, but I think, if I know you and I do! you feel the same way as I do.
    The way I feel now it's a very good thing I didn't have a 1:00 class. It's now 1:15. I opened your package after I got back from lunch. I honestly never ever thought that you would send an engagement ring so it was a complete surprise when I read the letter. I really thought it was some kind of joke that you wanted no one else to see.
    Once again, I'll say thank you for the loveliest ring a girl ever received from her husband-to-be and I will be most happy to be your wife!
    Take special care of yourself, lover! I will too. Had no dessert this noon!

Love from your wife-to-be,
Carole

P.S. Glad to hear it's paid for!

    I was counting the days when September 16 would arrive. The day came and I had her on my mind and hoping she didn't forget to open the box I mailed her. The end of the day came and the lights of the barracks went out. I lay in my bunk just thinking of her. I couldn't sleep. I was extremely anxious to know if she opened the package with my letter and rings. I got out of my bunk and got dressed. One of the men on my floor always had a lot of coins in his pocket. I woke up this person and said that I needed to call my girlfriend, would he please loan me a dollar or two worth of coins? I went outside to a phone booth near the barracks and was surprised there were about three men waiting to use the phone. When my turn came I asked the operator how much money was needed to call Adrian College. I think it was thirty-five cents for the first three minutes. I deposited the coins and dialed her dorm's floor. A woman said hello and I asked for Carole Taylor. She said she would go get her. Apparently she recognized my voice and told Carole that her boyfriend was on the phone. Several seconds went by, then I heard, "YES, YES, YES!" It was music to my ears! I told her that my sergeant believed that I would be home before Christmas. I told her I would like to get married at this time, which I didn't mention in my letter. I mentioned the benefit of her being my wife, which was she would be getting fifty some dollars monthly, which we could use. Then perhaps she could join me after she graduated from Adrian College. She was in favor of this. We agreed to a small family wedding including our college friends Phil and Irene Rundell. After our phone conversation Carole wrote another letter and mailed it to me the following day, Sept. 17, 1963:

Adrian College
September 17, 1963 Tuesday

Hi Lover!
How's my handsome husband-to-be?
I've been practically living on cloud nine these last two days, but I really won't be living high until I am with you again. I really do miss you now and I just can't wait until Dec. comes. You really do think we can be married for sure in Dec.? I guess that's really a silly question, but it just seems too wonderful to come true. There isn't a chance of your leave being cancelled, is there? I do definitely want to marry you then, even if it is in name only until June. Besides the reasons you gave which I agree with thoroughly, I want to be "Mrs. Wilcox" for my last semester. I really would. I want Wilcox to be on my diploma. I was really disappointed about that when you were drafted. I thought I'd have to end up with Taylor after all. Then, of course, the very most important reason of all is that I love you so very much. You say I will make an ideal wife, and I say you will make an ideal husband. Yes, I really mean that and don't you deny it!

I know very well there is no wife that will be loved and cared for as well as I know I will be with you. I know there is not a man anywhere, husband or not, that could make his woman feel any happier than you do me. There is no couple that could feel any closer or a part of each other than we do, so close and so free that we do not hesitate to confide in each other our problems and troubles.

Rick, you have no idea how much you have done for my life. Actually my life just began three years ago. You, yourself, have made me what I am today. You have put the sparkle in my life that did change me physically and spiritually. You have given me a purpose in life, someone to love and care for. You have made me the happiest person possible. Thank you, Rick, for all you've done. I do hope I can make you an ideal wife because I will be very disappointed in myself if I don't. You deserve to have the best of everything in life and I intend to see that you have it to the best of my ability.

You know, I still can't stop looking at the ring. It's so pretty. I never saw a fellow that had as good taste as you. I guess another reason I keep looking at it is that it's still hard to believe it's really there! I never expected to have one so soon. I'll admit I was kind of thinking you might give me one when you came home in Dec., but I think I feel as Peggy Richardson said, "It's the most romantic engagement I ever heard of!" Thank you, Rick. It was such a lovely thought to give it to me on that day and such a lovely ring. But of course, what it represents is the loveliest of all and it's what I think of every time I look at it—our future union, two lives made into one.

Everyone else thinks the rings are beautiful too and have been giving us "best wishes." Mrs. Shipman said to tell you that she "highly approves." Jan, my roommate, said to tell you you're a good boy, but you should have let her be with me when I opened it! Ha ha! She said she likes the ring. (Dick) Kapnick came in the library this morning and I showed him too. He seemed surprised and said, "I didn't think he'd do it."

I called my parents last night after supper to tell them. I talked to Dad first, since he answered. He was very nice about it. Mother didn't know quite what to say, I think. But I think I'll have to let them get over this blow before I hit them with our Dec. plans!

Rick that reminds me, how much have you told your parents? The only reason I'm wondering is that I have to write them a letter and I don't want to ignore it nor do I want to refer to something they don't know yet. Remember that green coat I left at your house last June? It's still there! I forgot all about it until I got ready for school.

It was so good to talk to you on the phone last night. It seemed so long since I had talked to you last. It was wonderful to hear your voice. How did you come out moneywise?

I got two letters from you today, one written the 12th and one the 14th. Both were postmarked 10:30 a.m., Monday the 16th. Did you realize this? They were such lovely letters. I don't know whether it was just me or what, but you know you sounded more like your old self in those letters than you have for several weeks. It really made me feel good and I promise to not "spout off" at the army and what they do anymore. I imagine things are different and if you say it isn't so bad, OK, I'll take your word.

By the way, I did get my shower last night. Right after the dorm meeting they came in after me. I think the whole floor was there! They put me in the shower and then a bathtub full of water! Cold, of course!

Well Rick, its 12 o'clock and I guess I should be saying good night. Take care of yourself. I love you very much.

With all my love,
Carole
(the future Mrs. Wilcox!)

P.S. I will write just as often as I can but I don't know, the way the work keeps coming in!

Carole's September 18, 1963, letter to me:

Just took a shower after finishing my studies and now I, of course, must write a few lines to that extra special person in my life. Before I forget again, sure, it's okay to pay just the twenty-five dollars next month. I told you before you didn't even have to pay any if you need the money yourself. I won't need it until January. I'll be getting over one hundred and fifty dollars at that time anyway with my checks from the [Indiana] toll road [summer job] and from the library [part-time job at the college]. So go ahead and keep it. [Carole had loaned me some money prior to my draft.]

I received your letter today, which you wrote after our phone call. I also got a very lovely letter from your mother. She's so sweet. I like her so very much. I'm so very happy to be getting such wonderful in-laws.

Still, when I think of our wedding being in December only three months away my head swims. As I said before, it still seems too wonderful to be true and to be so close at hand. But gradually, pretty quickly, my "noggin" is getting used to the idea. Don't misunderstand me, Rick, I'm not scared or it's not that I don't want to get married then, I do want to, very much so. I'll be extremely disappointed if something should come up to prevent it, but I can't think of a thing that could, thank goodness! As you said, we can keep it secret if we have to.

Yes, I'll see Dean Sanford as soon as possible. I knew when I first started thinking about the kind of wedding I'd like to have (and it was before you gave me the ring) that you would have Phil [my brother] be best man. I want him to be too. As to who should be our maid of honor, I have two girls in mind, but I think now I've decided on one. I would like to have either Irene [Rundell] or Margaret, she's the girl I was maid of honor for. However, I do think I would rather have Irene because you know her too and Phil and Irene have always been and always will be good friends of ours. What do you think?

Rick, I hope you agree with me on this and I think you will, but don't be afraid to disagree. I would like to have just a small family wedding in a church, of course. I would like just our immediate families and grandparents there and perhaps a few close friends, but I don't know where to draw the line on those few close friends so it may be better to stick to the families.

I have several reasons for wanting it this way. One of the most important ones is that to me a wedding ceremony is a close, intimate, personal thing and not a "public style show." Some people may think it's very nice to have all their relatives and friends there and it is nice to some extent, but to me it's not that important. The only important thing to me is that I will be marrying you and it doesn't take a church full of people to do that. If I did have a church full of people watching, I'd be nervous. I don't want that. I just want to concentrate my whole soul and body on uniting with you. I used to dream of a big church wedding until I was in Margaret's and then I could see what a physical and nervous strain it was. Ever since then I've dreamed of a small family wedding. Another reason is my practical mindedness.

I cannot see spending all that money, especially one hundred dollars or more on a traditional wedding gown. I could never see putting that much money into a dress you wear for a twenty-minute ceremony and then stick into a closet to yellow.

I would like to get a white wool sheath dress to wear for our wedding that you especially like and that I will be able to wear on other occasions, only with you, however. I will never wear it unless I am going with you. I think I'll use the rest of the money Grandma and Grandpa [Vesta and Rolfe Taylor] gave me to buy it. They've been so good to both of us. If you're wondering why I didn't choose one of my sisters for maid of honor, I feel it's impossible to choose just one because they are both so close in age. I'm sure the other one would feel hurt. I don't want that, and with a small wedding, one couple standing up for us is all I want.

Now as to place, in some ways it would be nice to have it in my home church, but I would rather have it held here in Adrian, because this is where we met, fell in love, and grew up together. I feel our lives are here and this is the place where we should be married. As chaplain of our college and because he is so nice, I'd like to have Dr. Emrick perform the ceremony. What do you say?

Would you like to have our wedding on a Saturday or Sunday? I think I've heard Grandma say that everyone (themselves, my folks, and Aunt Susie) in our family were married on a Sunday and she'd like to see the tradition kept. To me, it doesn't matter what day it is just so we are married some time. In some ways, I like Saturday better because then we could go to church the next day as Mr. and Mrs. and worship God to show our thanks.

Now one more thing, I believe I would like to have a double ring ceremony. I would like to give you a symbol of our union and never-ending love, also. Do you have any way of finding out your ring size for me? If not, maybe I can send you a ring size measurer out of some catalog.

I guess that's all about the wedding plans I've thought out so far. If I've forgotten anything, I'll let you know later. Let me know honestly what you think about them and suggest anything else if you want to.

I'm still staring at the ring. It is sure hard to study and pay attention in class, but I'll settle down after a while, maybe. Walt Radike heard the news elsewhere as he came up to me and said, "You have something I should see." He congratulated me and then said that he should congratulate me for finally bringing you around to doing it. Ha! Ha! John Sweet came up to me as I had just gone through the line tonight (dining hall) and asked if you had graduated. He had thought you had one more year, but he kept seeing me alone and wondered. I told him you had been drafted and then showed him the ring too! He gave us his congratulations also. Everyone has, in fact. Lee was cute. He said, "I knew but I didn't tell anyone." He was working in the library with me today. Did Don Turner know too? He has a class in N320 right after my accounting so I usually see him and today he asked to see it.

Guess I'd better be starting to taper off on this letter if I'm going to send you some blank sheets too!

Sigma-Sigma-Sigma is having a slumber party Friday night, but Jan and I have a notion not to go since you don't get much sleep and both of us have very much to do, so we probably won't.

I love you!

I gather you've written to my folks about December. In that case I should be hearing from them very soon! I'm sure they will go along with us.

I agreed fully with Carole regarding her wedding plans. I too wanted a small wedding and to be married in Adrian.

Carole's September 19, 1963, letter to my parents:

Thank you, Mrs. Wilcox, for your very lovely letter. It was good to hear from you folks again. I miss it this year since Rick is not here to tell me the news from Ferndale.

I was surprised, but of course extremely happy to receive the ring from Rick Monday. It is very beautiful and I do hope you will be here soon to see it. I may be prejudiced, but I think it's the most beautiful engagement ring a girl ever received. I still find it hard to concentrate on my studies without looking at it.

I consider myself a very lucky girl to be engaged to someone as wonderful as Rick. I know I could never find a better man than he. Thank you for raising such a fine son. I will always do my best to make him happy.

I also consider myself very lucky to be marrying into such a wonderful family. You have already made me feel like a member of the family and now I really will be. That makes me very happy. I couldn't ask for a nicer pair of in-laws.

And now, at long last, I will have a brother! You mentioned Phil's new job. Rick hasn't said anything about it in his letters. What kind of job is it? I'm glad he's in something he likes. Did you know that Rick called me Monday night? It was about 9:30 p.m. It was so good to hear his voice again and to talk to him. He said they were easing up some in the evenings so he could go to bed earlier, which I was glad to hear. We, of course, talked about our December plans. Tomorrow I have an appointment to see the dean of women about it. I hope it will not affect my loan or scholarship for next semester.

I can see this is going to be a very busy year for me. I will not be doing my student teaching until second semester, but I am anxious to begin. I observed and participated in the first week of school at home [Niles, MI] with a third-grade teacher and enjoyed it very much. I wish I could go back and do my teaching under her. This semester I am taking History, Problems of Education, Essentials of Art (for elementary teachers), Modern Grammar, American National Government, and Accounting. Guess who requested I take that last course! I do think I will enjoy it very much, at least so far. I am also working in the library again this year, eleven and a half hours a week. It is such a pleasure to work in such a lovely building.

Homecoming is October 12 this year. Will you be able to come down for it this year? I know you've always been here before for it and it would be all right too. I am anxious to see you again. [Mom and Dad did come for homecoming and took Carole out for dinner.] Oh, I almost forgot again. I think I left my green raincoat at your house last June. I forgot about it until I got ready for school. I think it was in the back bedroom closet. You can just bring it with you when you come. Hope to see you soon.

[As mentioned Carole's parents, Bryce B. and Lucille Louise Taylor were dissatisfied that she planned to marry me before she graduated from Adrian College. They wanted her to marry me when I was employed in the States. Carole told me what she said addressing this issue, but I can't remember her exact words. She made it clear that this was her decision and no one could change her mind. She would marry Rick that December. She was determined. She did explain the financial benefit and the fact that she wanted to live with me wherever I was stationed. Her parents did come to accept our decision. Carole and I communicated back and forth in reference to the wedding in December. She did pretty much all of the necessary tasks for our wedding. Eventually we decided that the wedding on Adrian College campus or at Adrian's Methodist church was not a good idea for family members.

I picked the date of December 22, 1963, since I thought this would be a date that I would definitely be home. Carole wrote that her parents wanted our wedding to be in the family church, First Methodist Church in Niles, Michigan, on December 21. The reason for this is that Carole's great-grandparents, Cora Edith Fellows and Artemus Daniel Bartholomew, were married there on December 21, 1892. Carole thought we needed to be agreeable on this issue.]

September I wrote to Dad, You mentioned in yesterday's letter that all of you would like to see me before leaving for Fort Polk. Well, I would like to see you two and Carole. Next weekend looks like the last opportunity to do this before Christmas. The following weekend I should be on my way to Fort Polk in Louisiana for eight to nine weeks. I'm in infantry, but that doesn't mean I will be just a soldier. I may have a desk job in the division of infantry, which I'm really hoping for. So if we plan anything it will have to be next weekend. What do you think? I'm almost positive I can get a pass, but I will check either tonight or tomorrow. I will call you two Tuesday night around 9:15 p.m. I hope you get this letter Tuesday. I sure would like to see Carole and you two before I'm shipped out. I know Carole would enjoy it too. I hope we can work something out!

It happened! I believe Carole, Mom, and Dad arrived late Saturday morning. We were together for close to twenty-four hours. We had dinner, and then Mom and Dad retired early to a nearby motel. Carole had a separate room, and I stayed with my parents. Carole and I spent a few hours together in her room. I talked about my military life, and she about Adrian College and our upcoming wedding. I was confident that I would be home in time for the wedding. When it was getting late I knew we needed to say goodbye for the night. We hugged and kissed and said to each other, "I love you and sleep well." Sunday morning came. We had breakfast, then the three of them took me back to Ft. Knox and went home. Carole was back at school Sunday evening, ready for Monday morning, and the same for Dad back to work. It was hard to see the three of them leaving me, but I knew I had to get back to my life in the U.S. Army. I knew the special day of our wedding would come.

Sunday, October 6, 1963, letter to Mom and Dad:

It's 3:00 p.m. and we are still here. I may be going out any time (to Ft. Polk). I have been thinking about the wonderful past twenty-four hours, and I sure had a good time. I hated to see all of you go, but I know we have to do this and soon we will be together again. I wish you didn't have the long drive ahead of you, but before you know it, all of you will be home. My prayer is for a safe arrival.

Mom and Dad, you don't realize how much of a "lift" I received these last twenty-four hours. I sure appreciate your long drive to come here to bring Carole and to see me. I know you sacrificed other activities for this and it was a tiring drive, but I appreciate it. I just can't express how grateful I am for your trip. It was so good to see you two again and Carole. It was also so nice being alone with Carole and talking with her with her head on my shoulder. Thank you for your understanding of our own personal desires to be alone. Carole and I think very highly of you two and we are very proud to call you parents and parents-in law. Carole certainly is thankful to you two for the opportunity to be together, even though it was short. It was so good just being a civilian once again and seeing all of you. Thanks again, Mom and Dad, for you two will never realize the wonderful effect it had on me seeing you three. I hope something can be worked out for Thanksgiving.

Shortly after this Sunday I was sent to Ft. Polk in Louisiana. My next training was in government administration. I was glad that I would have an administration job. Again, when I reached Ft. Polk I was too late to be a part of a group unit and therefore had another zero week. I was disappointed since that meant I had to be at the base for nine weeks instead of eight. Life was much better since almost all the training was inside. Near the end of the nine weeks we got our orders regarding our position and where we were going. I was to go to Germany. A lot of the other men had stateside assignments. I was disappointed because I didn't want to go overseas. However, when Carole and I were in Germany I was very thankful that it had worked out this way. This was a big benefit that I could not have foreseen. Sometimes when the situation doesn't look good, there is a rainbow waiting for you. We can't see God working in the background. That is why we need to praise God in all situations. He is awesome!

My activity during free time at Ft. Knox and Ft. Polk was reading books and writing letters. I would go to the library on base and read books that Mom would send me or books from this library. I enjoyed reading about other people and fiction stories tied to American history. The library had very few people, and I felt safe from being interrupted from a command for work duty such as in the yard or in the mess hall. I wrote many letters to Carole, Mom and Dad, and Carole's grandparents. When I visited Carole during the summers, I would always stay across the street from Carole's house at the Taylor grandparents. I would go to bed late and they would wake me up for an early breakfast by turning up their record player/radio very loud. I was amazed that they could bear the loud sound. When they heard me, they would turn the radio off. They wanted me to have breakfast early since they probably realized that once Carole was up they wouldn't see me until a mealtime with the others. Carole's grandparents were very special! They wanted time with just me and took an interest in me. We had good conversations. I got the impression they really liked me, and were interested in knowing more about me and my family. I enjoyed these mornings with them even though I was always very tired.

October 13, 1963, letter to Mom and Dad:

Well, your son is now going through another summer of July weather. It's hot outside, but I'm sitting on my bunk writing. I just completed writing to Carole and her grandparents." I went on to say that there were only thirteen of us not assigned to a company, and therefore we will have a zero week plus the regular eight weeks. Classes were only eight hours per day and most of the remainder of the time we would be free. I was told at that time that we would be released for the holidays on December 14. My thoughts were that life would be much better here, even though Ft. Polk base was not as nice as Ft. Knox. I ended my letter by saying, "I was thinking about you and Carole all day and daydreaming of the last two homecomings at Adrian College. I guess I really miss not being there yesterday [homecoming]. I can't wait for December."

October 20, 1963, letter to Dad and Mom:

There are thirty-two of us in the personnel clerk training. The majority of those here are from Louisiana, Texas, Alabama and Mississippi. We have had our bull sessions, and I talk with this particular one who graduated from Mississippi University in Oxford. We discuss a little of the race problem, which is a little touchy, and we realize that our feelings are different, but we both respect each other's belief. All of these guys, of course, are for state rights. They didn't approve of the tear gas at Oxford, and one who had graduated there said that he thought the tear gas set the stage for a riot."

Carole wrote that she had a good time with my parents the previous weekend. She enjoyed her fellowship with them.

A letter from Carole in early November said that her mother agreed to the wedding, and this is when Carole was told it would be on December 21 in Niles. Carole's sisters are delighted to have their oldest sister's wedding in December. Carole's grandparents sent me a letter stating they would do everything possible to make our wedding the most meaningful possible. They were always for us. Vesta Taylor said she was anxious to meet my parents

November 13, 1963, letter to Mother:

I received your long letter yesterday and it was such a nice and meaningful letter. I never doubt what you said and I think very highly of you and Dad. As a mother, I definitely believe that I could never find a mother that could match you. I'm very proud of you and thank you for your wonderful influence you have had on me. I too enjoyed our discussions and sharing our hobbies together. In the days at home, you helped to add the fullest enjoyment in my life and you were far from being selfish. That is one of your wonderful qualities of always wanting to help your sons and even desiring them to enjoy life at its fullest. Thanks again for such a warm letter. I will never be able to truly tell you how much I love you, for I just can't find the words to do so. We will always have our little "coin discussions," and I also wish we could see each other more often. I may never be active in coins again, but I still like to talk about them and see them.

November 18, 1963, letter to Dad and Mom:

The dinner bit is understood and I will see what can be worked out at Niles. The dinner would be Friday, December 20 and we all can be together, I mean go together. You can count on the Taylor family (5), the grandfolks (2), Phil (1), Phil and Irene Rundell (2), Carole and me (2), and you two (2). This I believe will be it. I realize we don't have too much influence in this, but I appreciate your desire to do all that you can. Carole has expressed to me your warm and helpful words. She thinks a lot of you two. The grandparents will pay for the reception. They are a family I really respect and love. I guess I'm really accepted by the grandparents, and they have opened their house to me. You will like them.

Although Carole's father was unhappy that we were getting married before Carole was out of school, I believe he understood our reasoning sometime after our wedding. I love Carole's family as they are a wonderful family.

My arrival in Michigan and Carole's start of the college winter break was on the same day. My departure for Germany and her departure back to Adrian College were also on the same day. I believe that this was God's plan because of a nine-week basic training instead of the normal eight weeks and advance training that was also supposed to be only eight weeks but lasted nine. Due to these two nine-week periods, I was sent home for the Christmas season. Prior to my leave day, everyone went straight to their reported assignment. If either the basic training or the advance training had lasted the normal eight weeks, I would have gone straight to Germany without getting married. Life for the two of us would have been completely different during the time I was in the army. I believe this was one of many blessings from God. Carole and I don't doubt that God made this happen!

November 23 1963, letter to Dad and Mom:

Still haven't completely recovered from the shock of yesterday. It is still hard to believe that John Kennedy is dead. Who ever thought he would be killed during his tour of Texas. We were in class Friday taking our weekly test. A few of us completed the test the same time, and we left the building to go outside. The time was 1:40 p.m. As we were visiting, a couple of other men came over to our small group and informed us, in a serious tone of voice that Kennedy was dead and Johnson seriously wounded. What! I didn't believe such nonsense. Then a few others came and verified the original statement. Then I believed it and felt sick. We found out that Kennedy was dead at 1:30 p.m. and Johnson was okay, but Texas governor John Connally was critically wounded.

Last evening (Friday) I felt really empty, and I also felt very sorry for Mrs. Kennedy. The poor woman, with pride for her husband and in the best years of her life with him, and to see him destroyed in a split second. I didn't realize how much I really respected and loved Kennedy. I truly respected him because he was a true and loyal American. He sacrificed his energy for his country with a true love for his country. He will go down in history with the greatest fame he could ever receive. His quick death added glory and fame to him, and his name is a boost for Bobby Kennedy.

Carole's November 30, 1963, letter to Dad and Mom:

I think winter has finally arrived. We awoke to see snow on the ground this morning and it has been snowing most of the day. It's melting fast, though.

Thank you for your letter, Mrs. Wilcox. I appreciate your taking time out of your busy schedule. I bet your trays are beautiful and I wish I could see them. As it turns out now, I didn't need part of the information I asked you.

As Mother, Grandma, and I were talking about the wedding and reception plans, we decided it would be best to keep the reception to just the wedding guests after all. With the wedding party, there should be about twenty to twenty-five, we figured. Mother did not think it was right to invite some people just to the reception, especially since it immediately follows the wedding ceremony. She had misunderstood me before and thought I planned on inviting these people to the wedding too. This is why she did not bring this up before. Because we are keeping the reception to the wedding party and guests we can hold it in our church parlor, which is the loveliest room in the church. It is small and "homey," with wood paneling on one wall.

I am very happy with this final arrangement because both Rick and I wanted to keep it as small and simple as possible. I was also concerned about the fact it would be practically one sided because so many of my relatives are around Niles. I'm sorry to keep changing things on you so much, but now I can safely say this is the way it will be. With the wedding only three weeks away, it better be all set and I'm sure it is. I hope it is satisfactory with you. Just to make sure you are clear on everything I'll go through the plans and also include what has been planned this vacation [from school].

The wedding is at 4:00 p.m., December 21. That I'm sure you know. From your side of the family we will be expecting you folks, of course your mother [Hulda Burrows], Phil [Rick's brother] and Bonnie [Phil's future wife] and the Cowells [they did not come]. On my side, there will just be my family [Carole's parents and her three sisters] and grandparents. There also might possibly be a couple of Rick's and my friends [only Phil and Irene Rundell]. The church will be decorated for Christmas so no worry about that [lots of poinsettias]. I am going to use roses and carnations for corsages and bouquets, I think. From the wedding, we will go right into the church parlor for the reception; cake, coffee and punch will be served. We will probably save some of the wedding gifts to unwrap then too.

Irene and Phil Rundell said they plan to get here about one o'clock Saturday, so they will not be here Friday night. Because of this and because it is such a small wedding, our minister said it was not necessary to have a rehearsal. It would be enough to see us in the morning and explain the procedure then. So I do not want you to feel you have to take us all out for a rehearsal dinner since there really won't be one, but if you would still like to do that, it would be perfectly all right. My folks will make the reservations for you as you requested, if you want.

The announcements are ordered and will be sent out after the wedding since they are announcements, I will write the Cowells, Bonnie, and your Mother personal notes inviting them to the wedding and reception in the next couple of days. I know you've talked to them, but I thought I should extend an invitation too.

I have also ordered thank-you notes with "Mr. and Mrs. Richard Wilcox" printed on them. Sure will be proud to use those. It won't be long until I can use them.

My wedding dress is all finished and ready to wear. I think I told you it is a white wool sheath dress with long sleeves. I imagine I will wear it as my "going away dress" too."

As to yours and my mother's dresses, go ahead and pick out whatever you want. Mother hasn't decided on hers, but she said it would probably be brown or green since she hasn't had a dress in those colors for a while. These are two of the colors you said you would not pick, so you're free to go ahead and pick whatever you would like.

I got home safe and sound about 8:00 p.m. Tuesday. My dad came and picked me up. Have been doing just about a little bit of everything since I've been home, planning the wedding, wrapping, and making Christmas gifts, writing letters, reading, and visiting.

We had a lovely Thanksgiving dinner at Grandma's [Vesta Taylor] with turkey and all the usual trimmings.

Doesn't really seem possible vacation is nearly over and tomorrow is December 1. Rick's coming home and our wedding is getting so close. I can't believe it, but I sure am glad. I miss him so much, as if you didn't know. It will be wonderful to spend Christmas together for the first time this year as wife and husband and to spend it with you two.

Well, I must write to Irene Rundell now. I hope I've made things clear for you; if not, just ask me.

P.S. Received our first wedding gift last night, but was told not to open it until the wedding. Feels like it might be sheets though.

P.S. My goodness, I don't even get your letter mailed and I already have to tell you of another change in plans. This is relatively minor, though. We've been over to Grandma's visiting tonight and she has offered the use of her home for the reception. She has everything we would need and it will be easier in many ways [the reception was held in the church parlor]. Boy, I'd sure hate to try and plan a big wedding if I have this much trouble with a small one.

I'll retract that statement I made about the snow melting fast. About 6:00 p.m. it really began to snow, nearly a blizzard, and it's been snowing like that ever since. It's now 10:30 p.m. We just came home from Grandma's [the grandparents lived across the street] and the snow was already above our boots. It's beautiful to look at though, so pure and white. It looks so pretty on the trees. Will be leaving for Adrian [College] tomorrow afternoon, so hope the roads aren't bad. We probably will run out of the snow soon after we get out of Niles, as usual.

I will continue to keep you posted on things. Write if you have a chance, I know you're awfully busy.

November 30, 1963, letter to Mom and Dad:

I received three letters from Carole today, and they recorded her activities of Thanksgiving.

If I'm in Asia, she won't be able to come over, except if it is in Japan. Carole makes all the difference, and I'm just hoping we will be able to be together. Carole and I always get along just great and the more we are together, the more fun we have. I always hate to leave her for she seems to be my happiness. You two probably went through all of this, centuries ago. We both are determined to be young for our first fifty years and after that we will fight it out. I know we will have a very successful and happy marriage. [Over fifty years now, and yes, we have had a wonderful marriage and we still are very close to each other. It couldn't have been better. We both are very healthy. We both feel very blessed.]

Carole's grandfolks are very anxious to see you two because they said that my folks "must really be the tops." You two will like them. The mother and sisters are also very easy to get to know and friendly and warm.

I got my sixty-five dollars today plus I have ten dollars and Mom sent me a check for five dollars, which I won't use, and Carole is sending me twenty dollars and I will receive a partial pay of twenty-five dollars or thirty dollars. In two weeks, and if I am stationed anywhere outside of Ft. Polk, I will get eight cents a mile from here to there in cash. So financially I'm all set.

The parents are taking care of the expenses, and the flowers are cheap. I have been reading a lot on Johnson in *U.S. News*, and I guess I understand his abilities and political experience. I think he will make a good president.

Carole's December 6, 1963, letter to Mom and Dad from Adrian College:

I just now got a letter from my mother and I hate to say it, but they've taken the reception back to the church parlor. Will things ever be set? I wonder. The reason they are putting it back in the church is that when Grandma called her Philathea class friends to tell them she would not need their services (they are the ones who always serve) they said four of them were already planning on doing it for us at no cost. They wanted to because Grandma has been with them for so many years and because my family and I have been so active in the church. Wasn't that nice of them? So it will be in the church parlor after all.

Mother has ordered the cake from a woman who teaches the cake-decorating course in adult education at Niles. She is only charging twelve dollars for a cake to serve 30-35 people. That sounds pretty good to me.

Mrs. Wilcox, Mother also has her dress picked out. She said it is navy blue and hopes that doesn't interfere with yours. I don't know what happened to her brown or green.

I also got my medical certificate for our marriage license in the mail today. I now need to get the marriage license. Sure hope Rick can get home by or on the fifteenth. We've been working on ceramics this week in art. I like it very much, but of course, I like to do anything with my hands. I have made a vase. This afternoon I'm going over to paint the glaze on.

I've gotten through this week okay, but still have another busy one ahead of me. I have a test on Tuesday and one on Thursday. Monday night is our hanging of the greens dinner and that's always nice. Tuesday at 4:00 p.m. is our first senior class meeting to discuss graduation. Boy! We go from one thing to another.

I imagine you're both busier than bees too. My roommate and I have bought some red net to make Christmas trees with. I can't wait to get started on it. She has gone home again for the weekend, but I have plenty to keep me busy. I hope I won't have to be writing you again about any changes.

Did I tell you we will have an organist for some pretty music a few minutes beforehand? She was the church organist for a number of years and is a friend of the family. Oh yes, Mother said again they would be very glad to make reservations for you for Friday if you still want to do it.

I think that's all for now. I hope I'll be seeing you in just another ten days.

December 7, 1963, letter to Mom and Dad:

I'm over here at the library now after doing a little shopping at the PX. I got Phil three t-shirts for only one dollar and twenty-three cents. This will be from Carole and me. I also got him something else. What I was looking for, I couldn't find.

Just two weeks from today and I will have a wife.

Let's have hamburgers and roast beef, okay? The food here is terrible. Remember, I can't eat as much as I used to.

The majority of my class is going to Germany. By the way, right now I don't know if I'm going to Germany. I'm going to be shipped to Europe, which most likely is Germany.

I hope you don't mind having Carole around all the time. I'm afraid we will be inseparable during my stay.

I will see you folks in nine or ten days. I can't wait. I have never been so excited in my life.

I have made some real close and loyal friendships here, and I kind of hate to say goodbye. The lawyer friend I sure hope to see again. We probably will write occasionally. There are some great guys here. Our barracks was the tops, especially my floor. I had the best thirty-five fellows in the company as floor mates.

It's almost time to take off for dinner. I'm not very hungry. The food is usually lousy. Every week the quality decreases as well as the quantity.

Tonight I and a friend will go and see Glenn Miller and his orchestra, a live stage program. This is the only good thing that comes out of Fort Polk.

December 11, 1963, letter to Mom and Dad:

This is final [this would not be true]. I'm afraid I have to bother you some more. I realize I'm making you folks run around, but if all of this can be done I certainly will appreciate it. Now I will give you all of the information. I will be arriving in Detroit by train (RR) at 8:25 p.m. Tuesday, December 17 [The Kansas City Southern Lines from Leesville, Louisiana through St. Louis to Detroit]. This cost is only twenty-six dollars.

Now, could you pick up Carole for me at Adrian College and bring her to the train station? I know it's a lot of driving I'm asking you to do, but I just can't find the words to express how grateful I would be for this. It means a lot to me.

So excited and anxious to see all of you and I'm afraid these remaining six days will drag.

See you two and Carole and who have you at 8:25 p.m. on Tuesday at the Detroit station. We can go home and have coffee, and I will tell you about everything. Got the best place in Germany and also a desk job!

I left Ft. Polk with two friends on December 14, 1963. The three of us were heading up north. The train finally left, and we were on our way. During that first night the train stopped for hours out in the country during the early morning hours. As the hours ticked away, the train was getting further and further behind schedule. When we reached Texarkana, we were many hours behind schedule. We had plenty of time to have dinner in Texarkana.

One of my two friends traveling with me was an African American. Ferndale High School had African American students, which was not a problem for me and probably not for the large majority of the other students. The first restaurant we came to had a sign "Whites only." This was all new for me, but I was aware that we might experience this situation in the South. I had told my two companions that we would eat together. We went into this restaurant and when we entered a man pointed his finger to my African American friend and said, "He can't eat here." He told us that the "blacks" ate at the bus station down the street. The three of us walked to this restaurant and it had a sign "Blacks only." We walked in and we were treated the same way. Only "blacks" (African Americans) could eat there. This was upsetting to me, that we couldn't have a nice meal together. We were Americans created by God. I told my companions that we needed to go back to the train station and buy food from the vending machines. I reminded my friends we were eating together. We didn't have much of a dinner, but we ate what we had together.

It was December 16, 1963 and we had only reached St. Louis! I thought at this rate I would be a day late reaching Detroit. I was scheduled for another train to Detroit, but that train had left several hours prior. The three of us were discussing what our options were. The African American friend said he was staying on the train. The other friend was familiar with St Louis and knew that the airport was not that far away. He was thinking of flying the rest of the way. I said, "I will go with you and we can split the cab fare," which we did. We said goodbye to our friend as we departed. On the way out I threw my train ticket in a trash can and we were soon in a cab for the airport.

When we were at the airport, we immediately searched for signs of flights leaving. I spotted Detroit, and he found his flight destination from another airline. Time was very limited for both of us, so we went our separate ways and I rushed to my airline desk. I was told there were vacant seats and the plane was leaving in about twenty minutes. I quickly paid, rushed to a phone, and called home. Dad answered and I told him my flight number and the time I would arrive at the airport, and that I would explain later since I had to go. I ran to the gate for my flight, and I made it on the plane. I was concerned that I would just miss it.

Dad was at the airport, but Carole was still at Adrian College. From the airport Dad and I drove to Adrian College and picked up Carole. What joy I had being with Carole again! She has always been a special woman and she would soon by my wife! We went home to Ferndale. The following day, December 17, Dad let us take the 1959 Plymouth and Carole and I drove to Niles. I stayed at Carole's grandparents' house, across the street from Carole's parent's house. The night of the 20th (Friday) I was in a hotel room and Mom and Dad in a different room at the same hotel. Dad and Mom came in their Pontiac. I can't remember very much of this week when we got married. I do remember it was very cold, with snow about fifteen inches high!

December 21, 1963, came. This was the day that I would finally be able to marry the woman whom I loved very much. We already were very close to each other. She was my best friend, and I enjoyed being with her since day one. Now in only a few hours I could call her my wife. We were married in First Methodist Church at Niles, Michigan. We came to the altar with our virgin status and with faith in Jesus Christ. In Ephesians chapter five, Apostle Paul wrote, "A man will leave his father and mother and be united to his wife, and the two will become one flesh." We understand this scripture because we feel this scripture has become reality in our life. The wedding was very small, but still I was very nervous. Perhaps I was uncomfortable with the awareness that everyone was watching Carole and me. Carole's hand sewn dress was attractive. She looked beautiful. I wore a regular suit.

Irene Rundell was the matron of honor. As mentioned, she and her husband, Phil Rundell, were our college friends with whom we have stayed in touch to this day. My brother Phil was the best man. We had a short and small reception after the ceremony. We were now married! Husband and wife!

I should add that I was the photographer of our wedding. I didn't take very many pictures. I gave Dad my camera and asked him to take a few pictures of Carole and me and our wedding group. I told Dad to make sure he got the feet and heads in the picture. He did get the feet in, but not all of the heads. We really don't have a good picture of our wedding group from my camera, but it really was not a big deal. I believe someone gave us a couple pictures of our wedding group.

That evening as everyone was leaving we headed toward Ferndale, but decided to spend two nights at a motel in Kalamazoo. I took a few pictures of Carole in our room. I wanted pictures of her the way she looked on the day we were married. In my eyes, she was very attractive. Her real beauty was her soul. She was special. Shortly after the pictures I became very sick, which was probably strep throat. My throat was really hurting and I just had to go to bed and rest, trying to prevent Carole from getting sick.

On this Christmas Eve all the family went to our Ferndale church. As we entered the entrance that leads to the sanctuary there was a friend, Doug Wells, from my high school Methodist Youth Fellowship days. As I greeted him, I introduced Carole as my wife. His surprise at me being married really showed on his face. I enjoyed it. Mother said there was a family reunion at Aunt Katie's house on Christmas Eve, so after church we drove to Aunt Katie's house for a short time. Her house was also in Ferndale. Aunt Katie's son, Dennis Gilbert Burrow, and his family were also there, as well as Mom's brother Lionel Burrows and his family. The relatives were all from mother's side of the family. Then we went to Dad and Mom's house, and that was our home base until Carole and I had to leave for school and military base.

The short time we were together really flew and it was now time for us to part. This was really hard for me, but I knew that I had to show strength to Carole, my parents, and our good friends the Rundells. After hugs and goodbyes, I walked to my plane that took me to Ft. Dix, New Jersey. Carole went back to Adrian College to finish her senior year.

I realize there are many thousands of Americans that were in the same situation as I was. We represented our country. I came back after my time of service. Many in my exact situation, leaving a wife and perhaps a small child, didn't come back or came back disabled. My heart goes out to those families who lost a husband or son. We must always honor those who give their life for America. They are all heroes!

Being married made it much easier for me to be separated from Carole. I knew she was mine and we would be together come June. This gave me greater peace than the months prior to marriage. I regretted some of the things I had said regarding being separated from Carole; they showed immaturity and lack of faith in Jesus Christ. I was different on my flight to Fort Dix and thereafter.

Carole's January 1964 letter to Dad and Mom from Adrian College:

It was so good to hear from Rick today. I imagine you did too because he said he would be writing letters. I sure hope he gets to Germany by flying. Right now I am at my roomie's house. She didn't want me to get lonely and I didn't want to be left alone either because when I am, I start thinking and missing Rick. This week has been really busy and so I've had little time to get lonely.

Finals begin in two weeks, but the schedule isn't out yet. Hope I'm through early.

The slides of the wedding came Tuesday. They turned out very good. There were only three blanks and the last picture was one of the best.

Yesterday I visited the room I'll be student teaching in. The teacher seems very nice, and one who will do anything to help you. This is the first time she has ever had a student teacher. There are twenty-eight second graders. They are a slow group. There are seven repeaters and two-thirds of the class are just finishing their first-grade readers. I'm really glad, though, because it will be a challenge and good experience. I'm really anxious to get started.

My darling husband left me his cold and sore throat, and I really made it a doozy. It started coming Tuesday and kept getting worse, so Thursday I went to the nurse. She gave me sulfa pills and cough medicine because I was coughing a lot. I seemed to feel better Friday, but got worse in the evening. My throat hurt even when I talked. I wasn't much better today, so Jan took me to her family doctor this afternoon. He gave me a shot and pills to take. Hope they do the trick. I'm getting tired of this and sure don't want to get worse. My voice is about shot, too.

I just finished all my thank-you notes, finally. Sure is a load off my mind.

Mother wrote there is a package at home for us, her guess was towels. The cookbook my roomy ordered for me just came. I've been looking it over and it really is nice. It tells you everything. I noticed a color picture of the lemon cake you make that Rick likes so well, I do too, of course.

Guess that's all for now. We're about ready to eat now. I'll try to write again soon and let you know how things are going.

P.S. I've been called Mrs. Wilcox more than Carole this week. Seems strange, but I like it.

January 8, 1964, letter to Dad and Mom from Fort Dix, New Jersey:

I'm here in New Jersey now, and after three moves, I'm at the shipment-out section of Fort Dix. I don't particularly like it here and from now on there will be lot of detail work. The last ship left today and the next one isn't until January 15. They are or were trying to get us on a boat. They say that our chances for a plane are fifty-fifty. There are so many here going overseas and the airport is flying a lot of navy and AF personnel. There are hundreds and maybe even thousands waiting to go overseas. So I may have to wait until January 15 to ship out of here. Sure hope not. This type of life is very undesirable. I will read a lot and try to get my mind off of it.

I arrived in Philadelphia at 9:40 p.m. Sunday and ran into some of the Fort Polk group. At 11:30 p.m. I left the airport and arrived here at 12:40 a.m. After a while, I was placed within a barracks for a few hours of sleep. I finished a book today.

I don't like it here at all, but there is a chance of a plane flight anytime. Because there are so many of us I kind of feel we will go by boat next week.

I am not going to Nuremberg after all. At Ft. Polk three different sergeants said that APO 326 was Nuremberg. How can these three men come up with the same wrong city? At the processing overseas place, the man who processed said that we were going to a small place called Goppingen.

Mom and Dad, I sure had a wonderful time when I was home. It felt very good being completely free and being with Carole. My thanks and appreciation for all you two have done for making those two and a half weeks the best in my life. Already I am very anxious for Carole to join me, but I realize I will have to wait.

Write any time after twelve days from when you receive this letter unless you hear differently. I don't know when I will get to Germany. I may have a weight problem of baggage if we fly. I will stuff my shirts and pockets if I have to. You know, maybe it is a good thing I didn't bring a radio. Besides size and weight, I couldn't lock it up unless I left something out of my duffel bag. I will get a good one though, Mother, in Germany, and the radio still will be from you and Dad. The radio will be the nicest gift Carole and I received.

I sure hate the thought of not being home for eighteen months. I'm very thankful, though, for Carole coming over in June. I just pray that the time will fly and I think it will once I get there.

Man, planes, planes all over the sky. They are coming and going all the time. The jets are interesting to watch. We are now close to the airfield and the passenger-type planes fly low.

I hope we didn't cause too much more work for you two. I appreciate your drive to Willow Run Airport and Adrian College on Sunday. Carole did also. Well, I'm going back to reading my *U.S. News* magazine. We have one and one half hours before lights are out.

Best of luck to you, Dad, in this new term and I hope it's a very successful one.

January 13, 1964, letter to Dad and Mom:

Its official, I'm leaving by boat next Wednesday. I will be in Germany at the end of this month.

So far today it has snowed about five inches. It's the first snow I have seen since I've been here. There is a cold strong wind also and this doesn't help outside activities. I just hate to go out in it but will have to for dinner and to the post office. They are not very far.

Hope things are just fine in Ferndale. I'm reading a good book called *Oliver Wiswell* by Kenneth Arnold. It's long, but I have plenty of time to read it.

This letter will be the last one for this month. I will write as soon as I can once in Germany.

I had KP Saturday and fire guard in my barracks this morning. I just have been doing a lot of reading these past hours. The men here just don't seem to impress me, and as a whole I just keep to myself. I'm just in the mood of getting out of here.

So far, I'm impressed by President Johnson and his aim to cut expenses, so unlike Kennedy. He could turn out to be a highly skilled president.

The food here still isn't too hot! I will be glad to get out of the service. I figure by August 1, 1965, I will be out. Twenty weeks to go from tomorrow and I should see Carole once again.

Visibility is terrible here and I don't hear any planes. The wind is strong too. The weather is really terrible.

Dad, about your visit, I think that you should think about mid-April to mid-May. There always is the chance I won't be able to take thirty straight days. I may have to take two weeks, work a week, and then take two weeks off again. There is that chance of leaving for home earlier too. We will be safe if we don't wait until the last forty days in Europe. We can wait and see. We should make definite plans during the start of next year. I sure will miss you folks and Phil and my friends. I think I would go insane if I couldn't see Carole for that length of time. The barracks here are better built than Polk and Knox.

This is it until I arrive in Germany. Take good care of yourselves and watch the waistlines. Mom, leave the candy alone!

Carole's January 18, 1964, letter to Dad and Mom:

This is a lazy weekend for me. I don't have much to do so I'm writing letters, listening to records, visiting, knitting, and so on. This afternoon one of the girls and I walked over to Shopper's Fair just to look around. It's a beautiful sunny day and we enjoyed the walk. I didn't have any money to buy so I couldn't be tempted to buy anything. Mother tells me there are six packages at her house!

The chances didn't look too good that Rick would get to fly over, did it? He was so anxious to get over there and get settled too. But I hope he doesn't have too rough a trip. It will seem strange not to get a letter from him until February.

I was very disappointed in my exam schedule. Exams start Saturday, January 25 and there are no classes the 24th. I was hoping I'd be through early, but my exams don't even start until Tuesday the 28th at 8:00 a.m. and then I have two scheduled for that same time. One will be changed, but I don't know when yet. My other two exams are 10:00 a.m. Wednesday and 1:00 p.m. Thursday, the last day of exams. Registration is the next Tuesday so I'll have just a long weekend. I'm really anxious to get this semester over and get home. I won't need all the time I have to study, so I'll work in the library all I can. I can use a little extra money.

About a couple of weeks ago a Mrs. Stepp called me (she's on the faculty and asked if I would be interested in a [graduate] University of Michigan scholarship. Of course, I wasn't and explained why. Well, just yesterday, she saw me and told me she had a note from the dean saying there is a Rotary Club foreign study scholarship for twenty-six hundred dollars and would I be interested in that. She said I am the only one who would possibly be interested in it. It does interest me, and Monday morning I'm going to find out more about it from the dean. In some ways I think I would rather teach than study, but I'll see what I can find out about this. It seems like twenty-six hundred dollars would be for traveling and living expenses. I found out from the travel agency here that it's three hundred, twenty-three dollars and fifty cents to fly from Detroit to Frankfurt. If the army wouldn't pay my way, it would be nice to have this.

My cold and sore throat is completely gone now. I started getting noticeably better on Monday. Thanks for the sympathy, but I really can't complain about this cold because if I had to do it over again, I would have done the same thing.

Was so sorry to hear you'd been sick too. I knew you both were busy this last week with classes beginning and I was thinking about you. Hope things will begin to settle down now for you.

Today I got a letter from Miss Spotts, the person I will be working under next semester. She gave me a list of science and language arts units she has in the second semester. She thought I might like to begin gathering materials and pictures. Some of the units were weather, birds, post office (we make a trip to the post office), telephone (maybe a trip to the telephone office), community helpers, plants and zoo (they visited the Toledo Zoo last year). It sounds like fun, and I am glad to have some idea ahead of time of what I'll have to do.

I'm moving again next semester, this time just down the hallway. It will be with another sorority sister. My roommate now graduates. Didn't particularly want to move, but couldn't find anyone I wanted who would move in with me. My new roommate is a senior too and engaged to be married in June. She's nice, has majored in French and did her student teaching this semester. Too bad it wasn't German. I'll write and let you know what I find out about that scholarship.

Carole's January 21, 1964, letter to Mom:

I don't think you intended this letter for me. So I am sending it back right away.

My dad just called me and wished me "happy anniversary." He really called to say he could pick me up on the 30th, but he said he had the anniversary in mind too since Rick couldn't call and say it. Wasn't that sweet? You sure would never know he was once opposed to a December wedding, but it sure makes me glad.

I haven't found out much more about the Rotary scholarship yet. The dean hasn't gotten all the information yet, but I do know it is for the Rotary Club district and not just Adrian College.

I must run to class now. Hope your letter wasn't anything urgent.

The Adrian chapter of the American Commons Club Fraternity, unique as an American-letter fraternity, is dedicated to these four principles: democracy, brotherhood, university first, and the open door policy. We depend on common loyalties to our group ideals to attract and retain our members.

Seated, L to R: Dr. Peelle, F. Fleetham, D. Wilcox. *Row 1:* L. Inouye, J. King, G. Montgomery, R. Varwig. *Row 2:* L. Krueger, J. Nixon, S. Copeland, D. Baur, J. Hollingsworth.

ACC Fraternity-1962
L to R, 1st row: Dr. Miles Peele, Floyd Fleetham, Dick Wilcox.
2nd row: Larry Inouye, Jim King, Gene Montgomery, Richard Varwig,
3rd row: Lothar Krueger, John Nixon, Stu Copeland, Doug Baur, Jim Hollingsworth.

American Commons Club

Seated, L to R: D. Krejci, W. Radike, K. Wine. *Row 1:* R. Huff, E. Potter, M. Faigle, S. Cagle, J. Dibley. *Row 2:* L. Stoddard, D. Sawyer, R. Felt, E. Schroeder.

Our distinguished alumni include John H. Dawson, president of Adrian College, Earl W. Kintner, chairman, Federal Trade Commission, and president, Federal Bar Association, and many others. We firmly believe that fraternity life has definite advantages and should bar no man on an undemocratic basis. Therefore in A.C.C. we practice Labor et Fraternitas.

Continued: ACC Fraternity-1962
L to R, 1st row: Dick Krejci, Walt Radike, Ken Wine.
2nd row: Ron Huff, Everett Potter, Mark Faigle, S. Cagle, Joseph Dibley.
3rd row: L. Stoddard, Doug Sawyer, Reginald Felt, E. Schroeder.

Adrian College-North Hall
1962

Adrian College-South Hall
1962

Chapter 22

My U.S. Army Era—Germany

I arrived in Ft. Dix and experienced cold weather and later lots of snow. I spent most of my time reading while waiting for our transportation to Germany. After four or five days, I boarded a troop ship that took us to Bremerhaven, Germany. It was very crowded. After two or three days in the Atlantic Ocean, we experienced a terrible storm. The ship was rocking, and we were confined within the ship as the waves were rolling over the ship. This storm lasted less than twenty-four hours. As I remember, it took us seven days to reach Bremerhaven, Germany. From the ship we boarded a train. It was evening when the train started taking us to Goppingen, Germany. I had a window seat, and I constantly looked out the window, trying to identify what life was like in Germany. I remember one peaceful scene that was a comfort to my soul. The train was in a populated area and there was an apartment that had a large window facing the train. In the window I could see parents and their two children at a table next to the window eating a meal. This view could have been in the States. I thought about this scene for a while.

When we arrived in Goppingen sometime in the morning of the following day, buses took us to Cooke Barracks. The base was a German Air Force base during World War II, and was never bombed. It was in a valley. Later in the day many were bussed to different areas of Germany. My name was never called for an assignment outside of Goppingen. After the majority of the group had left for their assigned locations, we were told that this was our base. Rooms were assigned in the barracks for the remaining men in uniform. I had three roommates. The four of us accepted each other, and thus no one in the group had a problem with another member of the group.

The Heinrich and Louise Stein family—Our German family

When I was settled in my barracks in Goppingen, I mentioned my location and address in a letter to my parents. One evening Dad and Mom were with another couple, Mr. and Mrs. Dave Wilson. Dad mentioned that I was in Germany and my location. The Wilson's daughter, Davi Wilson, was in my high school class of 1959. I knew her, but I can't remember ever visiting with her. I remember during our senior year in our morning unit room session, the tables were organized in a rectangle arrangement and she sat across from me.

The next school year when Davi Wilson and I were in college, her parents sponsored a German exchange student at our high school named Babs Stein. Davi got to know Babs when she was home from college. One summer, I believe it was after Davi had graduated from college, she flew over to Germany to spend some time with Babs in Waldenbuch, Germany. One of Babs's brothers, named Hans, was studying to be a medical doctor at the University of Tubingen in Tubingen, Germany. While Davi was visiting Babs, she met Hans. Hans had been an exchange student at an Ann Arbor, Michigan high school, I believe in 1958. Well, the "love bug" started to work on Hans and Davi.

The Wilson family contacted the Stein family who were living in Waldenbuch, Germany, and mentioned who and where I was. Dad immediately wrote a letter saying that I might receive German company shortly. This actually happened during April 1964!

These three persons were like a family for Carole and me during the months we were in Germany. Babs and Claus would visit us while we were in Goppingen, and Hans would come separately. We also spent time at the Stein house in Waldenbuch. We saw one or more of them many times while we lived in Germany. Sometimes Hans would want a hamburger on the base since hamburgers were nonexistent in Germany and he liked them during his school year in Ann Arbor, Michigan. On Sundays Hans would call for us to visit him in Tubingen. One Sunday evening while we were in Tubingen, I pointed out a little Fiat with a "Romney" bumper sticker! Romney was the governor of Michigan. Hans laughed! Hans knew the fellow student, who had also been a high school exchange student in Michigan. He had brought this sticker home and placed it on his Fiat bumper.

One weekend day before Carole came over, Hans, Christoph, brother of Babs and Hans, Babs, and Claus took me to a castle. It was a very enjoyable day with them. We spent time at the Stein's house visiting with Claus, Babs, and Hans. Hans would visit us in Goppingen and also Claus and Babs would have dinner with us in our small home. Carole and I spent Christmas with the Stein family in 1964. That too was special. The Stein family and Claus were just wonderful people, and we grew to love them dearly. They were wonderful to us and we always enjoyed their companionship.

Babs loved corn and we would bring cans of corn either to her home at Waldenbuch or when she was with us in Goppingen. Corn was unavailable in Germany because it was used only to feed pigs. She couldn't get American pizza in Germany and always wanted boxes of pizza mix. Hans and Davi were married on December 18, 1965, at a church near Ferndale; I was honored to be a part of their wedding. Currently Hans is retired from the medical profession; we still consider them to be our dear friends. On some of the weekends of our Kalamazoo era we enjoyed Saturday evenings with Hans and Davi during weekend visiting with Mom and Dad in Ferndale. We have also spent time with them while living in Houston.

Babs and Claus were married on December 29, 1965, in Germany. The newlyweds Hans and Davi Stein and Davi's parents, Mr. and Mrs. Dave Wilson, attended their wedding.

January 25, 1964, letter to Dad and Mom:

(Detroit time 12:40 a.m. Current time 6:40 a.m. Saturday): I'm still on the ship and will be glad to get off her. We are supposed to dock in about seven hours at Bremerhaven (Germany). Probably we will stay on the ship tonight and tomorrow will take a train to my permanent station. I will start this letter and finish it when I get there.

It has been a long time since I have heard from home. I hope everything is fine. It sure would be nice to be home again, but seeing Europe will be a great experience, especially with Carole.

Since I have had lots of time to think, I have been planning my leave time. I figure that when Carole flies to London, I will meet her there and we will tour Britain for a week and a half. I'm already anxious for that day. Then you folks will come over here and we expect you two to stay in Europe for about six weeks.

You two can see England before or after you visit Carole and me. I feel that we will be limited to only thirty days of leave time, so some things you will have to see for yourselves without me. I would like to visit the whole continent (west) if possible. We can spend two weeks in southern Europe (Switzerland, Austria, Italy, and maybe southern France). Our second two weeks would be in the north, probably a little more than two weeks: Sweden, Holland Belgium, Luxembourg, and Paris. I want to see the north more than any other section. They say that Holland is really beautiful in the spring and summer. We may be able to rent a car for the north. You folks and maybe even Carole could see Germany after that while I'm working. On weekends we could go to sections of Germany. We will make definite plans next year.

Well, as you two can see, I didn't take a plane. Since there were so many men, only about a fourth of us went over by plane. The last night they took a good percentage of the MPs and some infantry men to Panama instead of Germany. Someone mentioned that there were 200 that went over to Panama instead of Germany.

Wednesday we were supposed to leave, but it wasn't until Thursday that we left Fort Dix for Brooklyn for our ship ride across the ocean. The boat we sailed on is the USNS *Gieger*. I had doubts whether or not she would make it, but bless the navy she looks like she is going to make it!

The boat left New York at 9:00 p.m. [January 16] and today we will arrive at our destination. All I can say is thank God it will soon be over with. Tuesday I should be at my permanent station. You can imagine what I will do first. On that day, it will be exactly two weeks since I have had a shower, and a change of clothes. These last nine days have been the worst days of my army career, and I'm just dying to get on land and get settled with clean clothes. I will tell you more about this ride in the future. [All of the men's clothing was in the men's army-issued duffel bags. Near the bottom of the ship there was a very large open space, and every duffel bag was thrown into this center. There were many hundreds or perhaps a few thousand of these duffel bags piled up on each other. Finding your duffel bag involved a big search and moving duffel bags around. Only a handful of men retrieved their bags during this trip to Germany. The bunks for sleeping surrounded this area.]

Let me say that I pictured the worst living conditions imaginable before I got on this ship. Well, it was worse than what I could imagine! We had all of the comforts that cattle have on a cattle ship! The ride has been very smooth across the Atlantic. The ship rocked a little at the start and only a few got sick, but last Sunday we hit a storm and 95 percent of the fellows got sick, including me. Sunday night I was sicker than a dog! Monday it leveled off a little and then we hit a second storm. Water went right over the ship, and we not only rocked back and forth but would be lifted in midair and then crashed back into the sea and then repeat. This was the night we had to hold on in our beds or we would be on the floor. Monday I vomited a little, but ate lunch and dinner felt pretty good. Monday morning was the last time I vomited. Tuesday and Wednesday I spent a lot of my time in bed. From Thursday on, the sea has been very smooth. The English Channel was nice.

On about the 14th, at Fort Dix we had a really cold snowstorm. I believe it was the worst one I have ever seen. The last twenty-four hours there have been a lot of ships. Yesterday we saw land, England. It looked good.

A small World War II British plane flew down on us and circled our ship two or three times. It was only about 100 feet above the water.

A pigeon flew down on the ship, and it was very exhausted. We could handle him, and on his foot he had a tag stamped "Belgium 1963."

The excitement of Europe arose in me a few days ago when we started picking up radio stations. One thousand miles out we were listening to England and France. I was really fascinated by their music. Two-thirds of the music came from America. The English do a lot of talking on the air. An example is a ridiculous interview (long) with a female boat rower. Another was a talked about some small post office.

The meals here have been good, better than any of the other five months. February 4 I will have six months of the army behind me. Eighteen weeks from Tuesday, I will see Carole again. I have been married for five weeks.

If everything goes my way, it just could be that my draft into the army was beneficial. I still think about my period of time between Ft. Polk and Ft. Dix. I have to thank all of you again for making it so wonderful. Carole appreciated it too. She is very happy with her in-laws. She feels she couldn't find anybody better than you two. I have to agree with her.

January 28, 1964, letter to Dad and Mom:

I'm not permanently settled yet, but just about. I will send you a map and show you where I am. I'm on the edge of Goppingen [Germany] which is about thirty miles from Stuttgart. The base is very, very small. This is the record center for the Fourth Armored Division and is now turning into a replacement center. I will tell you about my job later after I'm assigned to one.

I have learned that there is an economy housing shortage. I have been told that the two worst places in Germany for finding housing for GIs are Nuremburg and Goppingen. I have talked to married men and those who seem to know, and they all said that trying to find housing for your wife is very hard to do. You have to find one where the couple is moving out. My hope is that everything will work out. Housing is very expensive and so are used cars, and I will have to buy one. I will have to pay around sixty-five dollars for two small rooms and no hot water. The Germans are aware of this situation and therefore will charge more for a room.

I will also have to work a half day on Saturday. I'm scheduled to leave here on July 15, 1965.

I saw a lot of Germany from our nice train ride. I had a seat next to the window. We left the ship at 7:00 p.m. (Sunday) and the train arrived in Goppingen, Monday morning at 9:20 a.m.

After I settled in on the post I wanted to discover what lay beyond it. I arrived in Goppingen during the night and thus couldn't see much from the train, and from the bus to the post. I took the first opportunity to leave the post to explore. Goppingen was a nice area in a small valley, and my guess of population was around forty-two thousands. There were parks with large flower beds loaded with flowers. The downtown had sidewalk flower pots loaded with flowers and hanging flower baskets from the light poles. There was never any trash in the streets, parks, yards, or sidewalks. This is typical in all of the German-speaking areas of Europe--very clean. Even the sidewalks and curbs in front of the shops were washed once a week. The flower pots on the sidewalks never had any trash in them. You wouldn't dare drop a candy wrapper and walk away.

On Sundays the walkers were always dressed up with the men in their suits and ties. When Carole was with me we also dressed up when we walked on Sundays. In London I wore a suit and tie every day. I remember the first time I walked from the post to downtown Goppingen. My route included residential streets. I admired the houses I was seeing; they could have been over 300 years old. Goppingen was not bombed during the war. The post I was assigned to in Goppingen was a German Air Force base during the war. It too was never bombed. As I walked, my thoughts drifted to the people who lived in these homes during the second half of the 1930's. I struggled with thoughts of getting a knock at the door late at night and finding a young Jewish woman and a child asking for protection and food. If this was my home and I had young children and a wonderful wife, what would I do? Would God not want us to protect this person and her child? But I'm responsible for my children and wife! If I were caught with this woman in my house, it would be death for me and my wife, and our children would be given to someone else. I gave this a lot of thought, and after a few minutes I pushed it out of my mind. I couldn't come to a conclusion of what I would have done, and I still don't know what I would do in this situation.

January 30, 1964, letter to Dad and Mom:

I'm going to bed fairly early after a shower. Yesterday and today I have been doing a lot of running around, by myself and with the guys from Fort Polk. We went to the show last night and saw a real good movie. The four of us from Fort Polk ate dinner at the snack bar earlier this week. I had two hamburgers, a half-liter of milk (larger than a half pint), bag of potato chips, two pieces of pie with ice cream on both, all for only Ninety cents.

I was quite fascinated by the Saturn rocket firing [January 24, 1964]. I'm impressed by its extreme power.

I'm in the records personnel section of the Personnel Services Division. I probably will be more involved tomorrow with assigned duties. The base is surrounded by forests and hills. It will be attractive during the summer.

February 6, 1964, letter to Dad and Mom:

It was one month ago yesterday that I said goodbye to my loved ones and my country. Even though I'm living in a U.S. military base, I can sense the difference and feel that we have the greatest country.

God gave us the men to form this country. Our country is the closest to being perfect.

Yesterday, I received my first mail. I got two letters from you two and two from Carole. It's certainly good hearing from home. Carole wrote four letters; her first two haven't arrived yet and I'm beginning to feel that I will never receive them. At least I got her last two. The only thing I know about Carole is about the last few days of her last semester and her short vacation. I hope the wedding pictures came out. Your letters were written January 29 and 30. Today I received one letter from you, Mother, and one from you, Dad. The money order came today and my thanks. I hope to get a good radio Saturday.

Dad, did you ever have the *U.S. News* magazine changed to my new address? If not, let me know and I will do it.

Most of the men in the office building where I work have to work tonight. I didn't ask questions and took off at 5:00 p.m. I came to the library after dinner so that just in case I have to work, they won't find me. I worked Tuesday night and I'm afraid there will be lots of nights I will have to work. This night work and the many detailed jobs and Friday night cleaning are an irritation.

Saturday afternoon, if nothing pops up, I will go to the PX in Stuttgart to buy a radio, trench coat, white shirt, and a pair of pants and a few more odds and ends.

The weather here has turned colder. It is snowing a little outside. The temperature since I have been here has been in the thirties and forties, very little wind also. So far, it has been a warm winter.

Dad, you didn't have any trouble taking Carole back to Adrian from the airport [she was part of the group that was with me for my flight to Fort Dix] did you? I bet she wasn't in the mood to go back to college.

German coins are small and simple designs and look like play money. Their largest coin is five marks (one dollar and twenty-five cents) and is smaller than our half-dollar.

February 9, 1964, letter to Dad and Mom:

I will immediately lead off with my best day in the army, which was yesterday. I had a fabulous time. I was out in the economy. I saw the people, I saw the drivers and I saw the city. I was in Stuttgart and Goppingen and I really had a wonderful time. F. Peggie [the army used the last name for communicating] and I left here at 1:00 p.m. with our passes. Now, Peggie is African American [I replaced the word "Negro," which was commonly used during this era], but he is one of the nicest and educated African Americans I have met. He is from Fort Polk, and his home is Little Rock, Arkansas. He graduated from college there. It's a little noticeable he is from the South in his manners. He is quiet among whites, and in most cases a white has to speak to him before he will speak. He more or less let me lead the way and do the planning. Well, I suggested things and he is okay lots of times. I don't like this because the African Americans' philosophy of "he should know his place" has reached him. He has principles and beliefs. He is of good quality. I like him.

Well, we took a cab to Goppingen and it took only a few minutes but cost one dollar and twenty-five cents. Cabs are very expensive. We got to the Bahnhof [train station], and we didn't know where to get our tickets in this small building. It is a very weird feeling when you are a little lost and can't communicate! In fact, it's terrible! Ha. Well, we asked a cab driver within the station and he figured out what we wanted and led the way. It was a little window in a corner. Eighty cents was the cost to Stuttgart (thirty miles). Trains are cheap. By the way, all trains run on the exact second and some places you have to walk fast or move fast. At one place the train never actually completely stopped, just rolled slightly for a half minute and then takes off. Trains come and leave right to the minute.

We were early for the train leaving to Stuttgart, so we did some window-shopping. The city is small and is like the old European style of narrow and pointed buildings. The land is hilly and the streets curve all over the place. At the movie theater for the coming week is *The Lone Ranger*, a Civil War picture starring Doris Day, and another American movie. Half of their record albums are American.

We found the train. We had to go underground to get to the trains. We followed a couple of Germans.

We didn't want to look too stupid! Ha. The ride lasted about thirty-five minutes and only cost eightly cents. Stuttgart is just great! The station is enormous, and we had trouble getting out of it. We made it. Going through the gate, we did something wrong, (probably the wrong gate), but we will never know. A man said something in German and we looked at him and walked away.

We took one more cab to Robinson Barracks [army post], costing One dollar twenty-five cents. He drove fast. We only had one hour before closing time at the PX so we hurried. I wanted a trench coat, but for three dollars more I purchased a German winter coat, and I can wear a suit under it. The cost was eighteen dollars, and it's fairly good looking. I purchased one white shirt three dollar and fifteen cents) and one pair of socks. I also got a record-stereo for two dollars and twenty-five cents (standard price). The best thing is with me now as I set here writing to you two at the library. I have the earplugs hooked up to it. It's really great, an AM/FM Japanese transistor radio. It's smaller than the first one you gave me [it was taken back to the store because it was too large for me to take to Germany] and the quality of the tone is excellent and it's powerful. It uses six penlight batteries and these are much cheaper. I consider this radio as a gift from you two and I appreciate it very much. I really like it. It cost thirty dollars. I'm sending back five dollars. I saved you a little money. In the States, the radio probably would have cost forty-five dollars or more. Merchandise like this radio is cheaper in the PX than in the German economy. It is nine transistors. Mother, ten transistors doesn't mean more power. The more transistors, the less electrical energy is needed. This is the main purpose of increasing transistors to save on batteries.

There is a U.S. Forces station on the radio for Europe. It's all American and most of the time it has good music. This station also includes lots of stories.

At 5:00 p.m. we went down to the snack bar for dinner and we came across two men with whom we started a conversation. One was a civilian living in Germany. His father works for Ex-Cello, a branch of this company is in Highland Park, Michigan [where I was born]. You could easily identify him as part of the U.S. Army. He is from Grosse Point [outside of Detroit]. I asked him how to get more German money because we greatly needed some to get back to our base. He hunted up a five-mark coin from someone for us. He said he would take us to the streetcar [to get to the Bahnhof instead of using a cab]. We had a good conversation going and he eventually decided to spend the evening with us. While we were walking away from the Robinson Barracks, the three of us, Ray, Peggie, and I, met a friend of Ray's. This fourth guy was playing in a band and he wanted us to come with him, but we explained our deep desire to see the city and time was short. We thanked him. We will see him again.

I'm listening to a German station right now, and they are playing "Exodus" and other American music. Pat Boone is singing.

Ray is pretty good in knowing the right German words in getting around. He helped us with the language. He was an asset for a fabulous time that night. I learned a lot that day, and it was a wonderful experience.

On the way to the streetcar, I was impressed to see in the immediate distance strings of lights winding into the "valley like appearance" and around up the hills in the background. A beautiful sight! In the distance was the appearance of a bridge outlined by lights. Really beautiful! A VW stopped and backed up to us. He said something like Bahnhof, and we said yes, and we hopped in. I learned that this isn't very common for a German. He was nice but couldn't speak English. Our army uniforms identified us as Americans.

He took us to the train station, and we thanked him. We crossed the street by going under it. What a sight! Under the street was a modern window display. Even saw a window of stamps from some country. Stepping out from under the street, it looked like a modern American city since there were lots of bright, colorful lights. All stores close at 2:00 p.m. on Saturdays, but Germans come out to window shop, eat dinner, and drink beer. The city was very attractive. This section is all new and modern. The Allies leveled the city during World War II, and now it is built up. We just shopped around and observed. It was interesting to see so many females wearing dark nylons due to hairy legs. Apparently they don't shave their legs but cover them up with dark nylons. This seems to be very common. In my short time in Germany, so far I find that the Germans as a whole are very friendly and will try to help you. Already I liked Germany.

Cigarettes are very expensive here, but at the PX the soldiers can get them for twelve cents a pack. Germany's pack consists of only ten cigarettes and cost either one or two marks (twenty-five to fifty cents) (I need to note that I was not a smoker, but on this day I was observing life in Germany). One German came up and wanted to buy a carton from us. Ray sold him his only pack for a mark (twenty-five cents). He wanted us to go with him to a place "with lots of females and beer." He was insisting that we should go, but we were against it. By the way, this selling is of course black marketing and if caught its four to twenty years in jail. This is what we were told when we first arrived in Goppingen. So it doesn't pay to make a quick profit.

Stuttgart is a nice place, and I want to go back there soon. While there, we also went into a restaurant. They had beer, and I tasted it, and it was terrible! The Germans drink beer like we drink milk. They look at it differently than the Americans. So many young Americans drink to get drunk, which is sad and wrong. It was only 7:30 p.m. when Peggie wanted to get back to Goppingen. We thanked Ray, and I think we will meet again.

I had a little trouble finding the ticket window for our train ride to Goppingen, but I was helped by a young couple. I said ticket [in English] to one person, but he didn't understand, and I tried this young couple and she told me to go downstairs to the left. I said thank you in German and she gave me a little chuckle since I apparently had an accent.

February 11, 1964, letter to Dad and Mom:

Dad, I received your first two letters from last month today. They and Carole's first two letters were lost in the mailroom. I was glad to get them plus three other letters. I am up to date now as to what has been happening back home since I left.

I'm now on a team at work. Each section is broken up into teams. My team is the best in the sense of working fewer nights.

The man who takes the orders for suits has been sick these last two days, so I can't order my suit. I have the material picked out.

February 13, 1964, letter to Dad and Mom:

This coming Saturday we will have to get up early and go out to the fields for the day. I'm glad we aren't staying overnight, for I'm not the outdoor type. They gave us about ninety lbs. of clothing and equipment.

During these past evenings, I have been at the library with my radio. I listen to music, read or write letters.

Carole's February 1964 letter to Mom:

Your plan for the weekend sounds great. I will be through at 4:00 p.m. Friday afternoon and will be ready then. I can't wait to see you again. I had the most wonderful surprise this afternoon. The librarians gave me some luggage for my flight to Europe. One is overnight size and the other is huge. I was so surprised, but thrilled to death. My luggage is much too heavy for flying and I was wondering what I was going to do. Now my problem is solved, beautifully.

Sounds like you had a houseful last weekend. I bet you all had a good time. I'm looking forward to that trip to Montana with you two. I haven't been any farther west than Oklahoma since I was eighteen months old. It'll be loads of fun. Sorry to hear you had the flu.

My second graders are so sweet. Today they started bringing in Valentines. It's been a long time since I'll have gotten so many valentines. I read part of a story to them today and I imagine I'll start teaching a class or two next week. I am getting rather anxious to start even though it is a little scary.

February 18, 1964, letter to Dad and Mom:

Today I came back from the hospital, don't panic. Just a little case of German measles paved the way for an enjoyable four day rest in Stuttgart. Friday morning I noticed the spots and I was so glad that I had to go to the hospital. Thus I read a lot, listened to the radio, played monopoly and cards and best of all, I didn't have to go out to the fields last Saturday [in my two years in the army I never spent a night outside of the base]. Heck, I was disappointed I had to come home today, but here I am. Friday is a free day because of George Washington's birthday on Saturday. Good old George!

I received a Christmas present today. It was postmarked December 13, 1963. It first went to Fort Knox and from there it went to Fort Polk and finally to here in Germany. The box consisted of stale cookies from our church [Ferndale Methodist]. It was nice of them to do this.

February 21, 1964, letter to Dad and Mom:

I think I know the general route or path of our vacation together in Europe. Thirty days is sufficient to get around since the area we will travel in is equal to only one-third of the United States.

Today we had off. I did work for two hours this morning. For lunch I ate at the snack bar. I had a real good meal for seventy-five cents, which consisted of two hamburgers, milk, French fries, and apple pie with ice cream. The four of us then left the post for Goppingen. We walked to town. On the one side in the distance, there was an enormous hill (or small mountain). We could see lots of buildings on the one side of it near the top. I'm really curious to see what's up there. A car would come in handy for this. This place is really going to be beautiful in the spring and summer. I'm anxious to take some pictures of the scenery. The huge hills or little mountains are very inviting.

We walked all over the city and went inside a few stores. A large percentage of the stores were closed. How they ever make money being closed is more than I can comprehend! [As I remember, during the week the stores were closed around 2:00 p.m., but I believe on Thursdays the stores would stay open until 5:00 p.m. The first Saturday of each month stores was open until 5:00 p.m.]

I would imagine you are just about on your way to Adrian, if not already on your way, to pick up my wife. She told me she was looking forward to seeing you two again. Tell me if she still looks the same. It has been a long time since I have seen her and you folks, but I think time is flying by faster than the Fort Polk and Fort Knox days. This Sunday it will be seven weeks since I left Detroit.

By the time Carole will have arrived, I will probably have a nervous breakdown from locating a good car and an apartment. Thanks Dad for your willingness for a loan. I appreciate it and will take you up on it.

Thanks for the letters. It's always good to hear from those whom I love.

February 23, 1964, letter to Dad and Mom:

Yesterday a friend and I went to Stuttgart for the day. I had another good time. The city is really modern and we got to see a lot of it during daylight. My friend took some slides while we were there. I will get copies of them. They also have a Space Needle just like the one in Seattle. A restaurant is also on top. We didn't get close to it. During the night, we saw the Baily Brothers Circus and it was pretty good. Two young men from India (students in Germany) sat next to us. They could speak really good English.

Here is my exciting account of my average weekday.

- 5:35 a.m. lights on.
- 5:45 a.m. I get up and wish it was 5:00 p.m.
- 5:55 a.m. formation outside.
- 6:00 a.m. eat breakfast.
- 6:20-7:55 a.m. shine shoes and may have detail work like cleaning hallways and bathrooms, etc.
- 8:00-11:45 a.m. on the job working.
- 11:45 a.m.-1:00 p.m. lunch and mail.
- 1:00-4:45 p.m. job working.
- 4:45-5:30 p.m. dinnertime.
- 5:30-10: 00 p.m. read, go to a show, or write letters
- Lights are out when all four of us so desire.

February 24, 1964, letter to Dad and Mom:

I am having Carole's checks from the government sent to the house. Please forward them to her. Next June 2 a check for one hundred and ten dollars should arrive for Carole, and she will be in London at that time. That money will be needed. Before Carole leaves for London, could you give her one hundred dollars and in return she will give you a check for one hundred dollars from her bank. When the government check arrives on June 2 would you send this check to Carole's checking account and then you can cash Carole's check. She will give you four dollars for lost interest if any.

I'm not going to be in any hurry to buy a car. I may just wait until May. We may have to borrow money from you two or have you take out a loan for us.

I did some "processing in" today. One army man who I completed forms on was married to a girl named Carole Ann Taylor.

Carole's February 27, 1964, letter to Dad and Mom:

Thanks for a very wonderful weekend. First time I've really enjoyed myself for quite a while and it was good. I have just one complaint, it went by too fast.

Guess who is coming this Saturday to take me out to dinner? It's Uncle Lee and Aunt Hilda [from Kalamazoo Michigan]. I got a note from them Monday saying they had the fever to go somewhere and wanted to come up Saturday to take me out for dinner if I wasn't busy. I was surprised but am very happy they thought of coming to see me. [Uncle Lee is Dad's brother. I don't believe Carole had ever met my Uncle Lee and his wife Aunt Hilda prior to this time.]

My passport came today. That really surprised me because it was only nine days ago that I applied for it. That is real service.

I had a nice long letter from Rick today too. He said it takes three days for my letters to get to him, sometimes two or four. That sure is a lot quicker than what I thought.

We have seven new pledges in our sorority now. One of them is Pam Meister from Ferndale. Another girl's parents are in Ireland now. He is in the navy. She went there for Christmas vacation and just last summer she was in Stuttgart (just to change trains, however). But still it makes it seem a small world.

Teaching has been going fine this week. There sure are a lot of things to think about or keep in mind though.

Tonight I've been working on a unit on wind for next week. In two more weeks I'll have one on birds. We'll be making a trip to the post office in another week also. Sounds like fun, huh?

March 1, 1964, letter to Dad and Mom:

Friday morning I rode on a truck as a helper to a driver. We drove some new men to their bases. The farthest one was Bamberg, Germany. I helped or tried to help keep the driver from getting lost and going to sleep. It was quite the experience. I saw some beautiful scenery. I am a little experienced with the highways, observed farmers and other outdoor workers, saw cities and trains. It was very interesting seeing more of Germany. The drivers are built of iron behind the wheel and they probably would get a ticket if driving in the U.S.

We got lost a few times, especially at the beginning. There were roads that didn't exist on the map. Very few signs at the beginning, but after an hour of driving the signs were good. In Nuremberg our route disappeared, but with the help of a gas station attendant we got on the right road.

We were forced three times to get help from a gas station. The two popular gasolines stations and about the only ones existing here are Shell and Esso.

Even though by a straight line our distance covered was about one hundred and forty miles, it took many hours of driving. The roads are very winding or curvy. We didn't drive on a straight path of road until we were out of Nuremberg. Just before it, it was good. In the cities and towns one just drives around in circles. The houses aren't built in straight lines.

Get your map out and I will tell you our trip. It is hilly also. We started in small mountains.

We left Goppingen and got on Highway 297 or 279 or something like that to Lorch (it's in a valley and you can look down and see the whole town, a beautiful sight). This town is ten miles from Goppingen and lots of pretty scenery in this area. At Lorch we turned right on I believe highway 19 to Schwab Gmund, to Aalen (nice city) to Wasseraffingen, Ellwangen to Crailsheim. We ate lunch at Crailsheim. It was the driver's permanent base also. It took us about three hours to get there. The truck had a heavy load. Lots of other trucks and the roads weren't very good, which caused us to average a speed of only about thirty mph. We were lost a few times also.

During the afternoon, we took off to Feuchtwangen and up to Ansbach. The highway from Ansbach to Nuremberg (N14) is what we came home on, but going we drove to Schwaback (to let three guys off) and then to Nuremberg. In Nuremburg we got on Highway N4 and we kept on that all the way to Bamberg. We arrived at the Bamberg military post about 5:50 p.m. It took an hour to get rid of our passengers and thus it wasn't until 7:00 p.m. when we left the post for home. It was dark and illegal for us to travel in the nighttime, but we did anyway. N14, the highway from Nuremberg to Ansbach, was foggy. We were aiming for Crailsheim. Ten miles from Ansbach the fog was too much, so we stopped and tried to sleep. It was too cold and too uncomfortable to sleep. At 1:00 a.m. we took off again. At 2:30 a.m. we arrived in Crailsheim. Well, I could only sleep two hours because I was doing a lot of thinking about what I saw. In Nuremberg I saw a huge castle and around the wall of the castle extending for a long distance from the castle was a stone wall. Probably the wall is of the original city. We drove near the heart of town. We saw some sections the Allies didn't level during WWII.

In the morning we waited for his pay and then we took off for Goppingen. We left at 9:00 a.m. and by 11:30 a.m. we were at my post.

The children under eight years old waved at us, but not the older females! Ha. The Germans, including older people, use their bicycles.

The young people seem to take pride in dressing up. I think they dress up more than we do. In Stuttgart just about everybody had suits on and neat looking.

My next weekend is a terrible one, KP and guard duty. I'm going to get ready to go to church now. Thanks for your letters. I always enjoy reading your letters and hearing about your activities and the news.

March 7, 1964, letter to Dad and Mom:

I'm reading a good book, *American Tragedy*, and it seems to be a little depressing. This is my first weekend I have stayed in since I have been assigned to this base. It would be nice to be out, but this month I'm going to take it easy and try to be a little more conservative with my money. Carole should have received another check by this time.

They made a mistake here, with the help of myself, in paying me two times this month. Carole received most of the second pay. I probably won't see much money from Uncle Sam until summer since I owe them more than one hundred dollars. No sweat, I don't care.

Thanks for the Stein address [Waldenbuch, Germany] and information. I think when April comes I will drop around to their place. I will either write or call beforehand. The first visit will be the hardest.

If we have a warm day next weekend I will do some exploring outside of the base, besides Goppingen. It would be nice to have a car. I was told you could rent a car in town for six dollars.

My next letter may have some good news pertaining to an apartment. I hope so!

You know, traveling to Bamberg I never saw a cow, except one or two pulling a wagon. Chicken and ducks are very common.

I received a very nice letter from Larry Cowell the other day and Mrs. Cowell last week, [The Cowell family lived across the street from Mom and Dad and they were good friends. Mrs. Faye Cowell grew up with Mom in Highland Park]. It was nice of them. I appreciated their letters.

Another excellent book is *Shade of Difference* by Allen Drury. This is one of the best books I have ever read. It centers on the UN and Washington, D.C. It's long, but worth it. I read this book at Fort Dix and one of my roommates borrowed it and also read it. He really enjoyed it. Another good book is *Oliver Wiswell* by Arnold Kenneth. It is a book that I didn't want to set down. This book is a historical novel on the Revolutionary War.

I received a nice letter from Uncle Lee and Aunt Hilda. They want me to write to their granddaughter Sue [Wilcox], which I have already done. There are so many on my writing list, and I'm behind in my letter writing.

Carole's March 8, 1964, letter to Dad and Mom:

I have been meaning to write for a while and finally found some time. I received the second check all right. It was for one hundred, ten dollars and twenty cents too. It was dated the 29th so this one must be my allotment for February, but what the one dated February 26 is for I don't know. Rick said that he received a voucher showing that they owe me seventy-three dollars and twenty cents (ten days of December and the month of January). I don't know if Rick would have told you two or not, but he got an extra pay too! They paid him seventy-three dollars and then he received his check in the mail for twenty-two dollars, my allotment having been taken out. He wasn't supposed to get the seventy-three dollars so they will be taking it out of his pay for the next few months. We'll see what happens to me!

He mentioned his German language school to me for the first time, but just to say that he had to pay four dollars for it and it started Monday. I've been forgetting to ask him about it since you told me.

I will be going over by Pan-Am jet for sure. Maybe Rick told you, but that other he heard about sounds no good. It only goes from New York to Frankfurt and leaves every Thursday. However, they can cancel the flight up to one week before. They have to have twenty-five on it. It's only a four-engine plane and takes eighteen hours to cross the ocean. Also, by the time I pay for Detroit to New York and Frankfurt to London, it would be about as much as this Pam-Am jet from Detroit to London. Rick said he read about their rates going down and that it will be forty dollars less, which makes it about two hundred and forty dollars.

Thanks, Dad, for the information about the Red Cross. I think I'll call them tomorrow and see if they can tell me about what immunizations I'm required to have. I have a publication from Washington that says there are certain requirements for military and their dependents, but it doesn't say what they are or where I can find out. I will get my shots here in Adrian since some may require a couple or three doses and also because the immunization certificate must be approved by the local or state health department where the physician practices and there is one right in downtown Adrian.

I am definitely planning on spending part of Easter vacation with you. I imagine I will go home first and then take the bus to Detroit about April 1 or 2. School begins April 6. I will have to get my

ID at Fort Wayne, and I would like to spend a day in the Detroit library getting notes for my term paper. They don't have much information here on what I'm writing on. I would also like to stop at Metro on the way back to get my ticket. I figure I should have the money by then with March's check, and this would be a convenient time.

Now, I haven't sprung this on my folks yet and I know they aren't going to be too happy about it, but these things have to be done. Reason I haven't said anything yet is that they weren't very happy about my leaving on June 1. I wrote back explaining everything, and I haven't gotten another letter from them since, which will be two weeks next Tuesday. They naturally want me to wait a few days so they can see me, and they didn't think I was giving myself time to get ready. But as I told them, I will have no lesson plans or homework that last week because it will all be done the week before. Packing is no problem because it would even be easier to pack for my trip and for storage at the same time I'm packing to leave the dorm. They didn't seem to think a week would make much difference to Rick and me, but I assured them it did. I expected this sort of reaction, but I thought they would also understand how anxious we are to be together. So I've been waiting to hear the second reaction before I tell them about spring vacation. I suggested my coming home for a weekend in May. I'll let you know how things come out, but plan on me for that first weekend in April, unless you have conflicting plans. Let me know if you do.

Last night I babysat for the first time in a long time. They called my roommate, but she was busy and asked if I was interested. I could use a little extra money and felt like a change of pace, so I went. It was a lovely home and a lovely family. The house was a new and modern split-level. The children were two, seven, ten, twelve, and fifteen. The fifteen-year-old had many activities outside of home, which is why they needed a sitter. The two-year-old was put in bed before they left, and the others went when they were supposed to. I had no trouble and didn't do a thing except watch color TV. I took my knitting along to do too.

It was a funny coincidence that this man's brother was stationed in Stuttgart and this man (not the brother) is an accountant, and he first started under the same firm Rick did. These people were very nice and I hope they call again. They asked if I was interested and I said I was.

The weeks are flying by now, which doesn't bother me one bit. School and lesson plans keep me hopping. This weekend I finished taking notes and wrote the rough draft of a term paper due mid-term vacation time. I have a couple more letters to write tonight so had better be getting to them.

Carole's March 8, 1964, letter to Mom:

It was so nice to get your letter yesterday. Rick didn't tell me about his trip because he'd already written about it twice and said I'd find out later on anyway, which is true.

I finally got a letter from my folks yesterday. Both Mother and Dad wrote, which is unusual for Dad, but they never said one more word about June 1, so I hope it's all "blown over." I'm not worried or upset about it because I know I will definitely leave June 1 no matter what. Mother has been sick and they have all been busy, which is why they didn't write, I guess.

I happened to think later that I can probably get my plane ticket right here at the travel center in Adrian so we wouldn't need to stop at Detroit's Metro. Would you mind if I waited until April or May to give you the money for my ticket? With this mix-up in pay, I don't know what I'll be getting for March.

Evidently your Red Cross knows a lot more than Adrian's. All she did was refer me to the County Clerk and the Health Department. All I've found out about inoculations are that smallpox is required, which I knew already. A doctor that I called said if there's something else, they can give it to me. No one seemed to know about any special requirements for Armed Forces and their departments. Maybe I can find out when I get my ID.

My spoons came today from Betty Crocker. I like them. I will bring one with me over vacation so you can see it too.

Carole's March 14, 1964, letter to Mom:

Enclosed is a check to pay for my suit [for Europe]. Thanks so much for letting me use your charge account. I found I didn't need to wait until next month. Rick wrote that I was supposed to get the two checks for one hundred, twenty dollars and twenty cents and will get one hundred, twenty dollars and twenty cents the end of this month so that will give me enough money to pay for my plane ticket. The other one hundred, twenty dollars and twenty cents was for January. They did take another fifty-five dollars out of Rick's pay. He has such a deficit balance he says if the government gives him nothing they will be even by June.

I suppose Rick has told you all about our apartment. Isn't it fabulous? I'm so excited about it. I can hardly believe we have had such good fortune. [This apartment fell through, and I had to continue looking for another place for us to live.]

I sure wish things would go better with his job though.

He said that I can get my smallpox vaccination at Fort Wayne free, so we will have to look into that while we are there.

Today I have been working on my bird unit and have it all planned, just have to make some things to carry it out. Tomorrow I have to, or I should say want to, type my term paper and type a couple of art lesson plans.

I had a nice surprise at school yesterday. I had just finished my unit on wind and Thursday afternoon the children asked Miss Spotts if they could write stories on wind for Mrs. Wilcox. She said, "Why, sure," and gave them paper for writing and drawing pictures. Some of them were very good, and all showed they had learned what I wanted them to learn. I was very pleased with all of them. Some of them were cute too. The slowest girl in the room even wrote a good story and she did not copy, which is quite unusual for her. Miss Spotts gave me her composite picture of the class so I'll be able to show you my little darlings.

I sure am enjoying Rick's records and his little radio. So much of the work I am doing this semester I can do with a background of music and I usually do!

I have just two midterms (since I have only two classes) and they are on March 23rd and 24th. One will require quite a bit of studying, but the other (house décor) will be no trouble at all

Well, it's getting late and I'd better get to bed if I'm going to get up for church tomorrow.

March 15, 1964, letter to Dad and Mom:

Thanks for your interesting letters and clippings. This week has been a rough one. Monday and Wednesday nights were German class time. Those two nights, I picked up a lot. It's still a start! The other nights we worked. Friday night we worked until 10:15 p.m. on some project. Saturday was work until 4:00 p.m. Next week will probably be the same story. We are having an inspection April 1st, so this requires more work. I was transferred at work with another team member. I expressed my dissatisfaction, which led to the transfer to my original battalion, but a different job. I will enjoy it more now and will learn fast. Everything is fine now, but lots of work now and night work ahead of us.

As for permission for Carole's arrival and what have you, don't worry. Everything is okay and all that has to be done on this side of the world; I will take care of it. Just eleven weeks from Tuesday. I'm sure getting anxious for that day!

Dad, could you loan me two hundred and seventy-five dollars in May? I want to pay interest on this and by the time you go to Montana, I will pay you one hundred and seventy-five dollars of it. How does all of this sound? I may not need all of this, but just want to be sure of having enough when I will need it.

Maybe you already know about this through Carole, we have a real nice apartment waiting for us in June. Our place is about one and a half to two miles from the post here. If it isn't the best in Goppingen, it is one of the best. I got it through my team chief leader. His name is Jim Connor, a real nice guy. I was talking with him, and he mentioned that he was moving out of his place around the first of June. I told him I needed a place around the first of June. He told me of the advantages of its location and its modernness. He said the average price is around seventy-two dollars per month. That includes hot water and electricity. This place really isn't an apartment, as it's really one-third of a house. It will be just the landlord and us (the landlord's husband was killed during the war and she has two children in college now, but home during the weekend). She (the landlord) has the first floor. The second floor has a large hall with cabinets and a bathroom with a shower. This is for the whole household. Our bedroom is on this floor, with a very large bed and plenty of closet and dresser space in this room. The third floor is completely ours. This is the top of the house. In the hallway to the right is a toilet in a small room and another small room with a toilet and sink. To the left of the hall is our front and living room. Of course, we have doors to all of this, except the hallways.

The living room is very small and next to it, through a doorway, is our small kitchen. The refrigerator is Jim's and I will have to buy it from him. The cost is sixty dollars and I will sell it for that when I leave. Also on the third floor there is an attic like room for storage or what have you. The place is new and attractive. We also have a large picture window. I like the place and I think Carole will also. There are very few places that offer oven, central heating, hot water, and shower.

Our rent may be a few dollars higher than the average rental, but we won't be paying eighteen dollars per month for coal during the winter. I really think we got a real break in finding this place. I ate lunch and dinner with them last Tuesday. I probably will buy their 1950 VW car for one hundred dollars. The body is in poor shape, but the brakes and engine are in good shape. The tires aren't very good. I'm hoping they will go out before June and he will have to buy new ones. Gasoline for the GIs is only seventeen cents per gallon. For our electrical appliances, he is selling a small and large transformer (Europe has 220 voltage for their electricity) for only ten dollars, and they are almost like new. He has been very truthful to me. The car is only a 22 horsepower car. The insurance rate is on horsepower, thus cheaper insurance.

March 29, 1964, letter to Dad and Mom:

Last Monday or Tuesday a fellow worker who I worked with crashed his car into a tree and killed himself, his wife, and their three-month-old baby. How terrible! He only had a few months left for his separation of his military obligation. We are still working nights.

Last week I was forced to miss both of my weekly German class sessions, one because of inspection and the other time I was sick. I'm going to drop the last two weeks. It's hard getting off from work. Friday I had KP [kitchen duty. Saturday I wrote a couple of letters and visited. I also spent a few hours of the evening at the library. I went to church this morning, wearing my new suit. I like it, but the pants are just a little too long. The cost was forty-nine dollars and it's all paid for. It was good wearing a suit again. I enjoy being dressed up at times. Probably, Dad, I can arrange for you to get a tailor-made suit from Alexandria when you are here if you want one.

I believe I know where the Stein family is living. Apparently they are about fifteen miles south of Stuttgart. I found this out last night. I'm thinking of writing Babs and Hans a letter really soon and ask if we could get together at a convenient time. I don't know if they are still living at home and also if their parents can speak English.

Oh yeah, Mother, before Carole leaves for Europe, tell her how to make good cookies, your lemon cakes, your lemon and apple pie and your special Jell-O.

In a week or so I will be PFC, making one hundred and three dollars per month.

A week from today, I will have completed eight months of my army career. I thank God for having those eight months behind me. That's one third behind me and two-thirds to go.

I almost bought a car yesterday. Yesterday morning I went over to the reenlistment center to talk with a man who was selling a 1957 Lloyd [English car] for one hundred and twenty-five dollars. He drove me to his home, about eight miles from the post. I drove the car and really liked it. It was in my price range and since I liked it I was agreeable to buying it. The transaction wouldn't take place for a few weeks. I didn't have any right to jump into such a transaction, but I was anxious to get a car other than an old VW and for one hundred and twenty-five dollars or less. I went back to his workplace and talked to another man who owns a Lloyd also. He told me the reason this car was so cheap is that this company went out of business in 1961 and parts were hard to get. I also learned that he has been trying to sell this car for a long time. I went back to the seller and told him I was no longer interested in buying his Lloyd. I probably will end up buying Jim Connor's car if he replaces the tires.

Within the next two weeks I will start doing the unfinished business needed for my and Carole's reunion here in Goppingen. I will be seeing Carole just nine weeks from today. I think I will go to the travel agency this morning and see what I can get on London and expenses.

April 4, 1964, letter to Dad and Mom:

Today I went downtown [Goppingen] and looked around for a little item for you, Mom her birthday was on the 17th]. I looked all over the town and came up with something I think you will like and need. I had our traveling in mind when I purchased it. I also purchased some apple turnovers and some German hard candy. I even had a German ask me for directions, and he was a little surprised to discover that I was an American.

I have already sent in my leave request. In another week, I will request the necessary paperwork for Carole's arrival. Lastly, I will request two hundred and fifty dollars or three hundred dollars, okay?

Carole really is looking forward in visiting with you two. More and more she is feeling at home in Ferndale. You two have made her feel she is part of our family.

One of my roommates is from Massachusetts and April 17th is a state holiday (Paul Revere Day).

April 7, 1964, letter to Dad and Mom:

Carole certainly had a good time at Ferndale and I would like to thank you two for being really nice to her and taking good care of her. She enjoys staying at your house. After dinner, a friend and I went over to get a Coke. The dinner was terrible except the dessert. I didn't eat very much, but there is German bread in our room and it filled me up.

Just eight weeks from today I will see Carole again. I'm very excited and anxious to see her again. Time is going by fast for me. Our trip is going to cost a little, but it will be a once-in-a-lifetime trip. I hope the sun will be out for pictures. I have sent in my request for leave. I have also started planning for the trip. I think I have the cities to visit already picked out. I have written for additional information to London and in a week I should hear from them. I will leave here by train Sunday night, May 31. The train leaves Stuttgart at 11:40 p.m. on that Sunday and arrives in London June 1 at 3:30 p.m. I will report back on June 14 (Saturday). I cross the Channel by boat, only twenty-three dollars one way. By plane it's seventy-seven dollars, so I'm going by train. Round way will be cheaper.

One week ago today I wrote a letter to Babs and Hans. They gave me one great surprise Sunday by coming down here and looking me up. It took them thirty minutes, but they found me and I had a really great time. There were three of them, the third one was Babs's fiancé, Claus Lahman. We went out to a real nice coffee shop and had coffee and cake and talked for about two hours. They have invited me over to their house and if it's convenient for them I will visit the family next Sunday. They are really good-looking young people and I like them very much. They are close to Carole and my ages.

I told Jim Connor that I would buy his old VW. He had new tires put on the car and now the cost is one hundred and twenty-five dollars.

April 14, 1964, letter to Dad and Mom:

I couldn't write Sunday because I spent the whole day with the Stein family (I took the train from Goppingen to their town, Waldenbuch). I had a fabulous time and saw a little more of Germany. Their house is really nice and I sure enjoyed this family and having dinner at their home. Everyone is so nice (family of eight) and very well mannered, intelligent, friendly, and warm. I sure enjoyed myself and just hated to come back to Goppingen.

Thanks for the three dollars and the ten dollars. I certainly can use it. Thanks also for the stamps.

April 18, 1964, letter to Dad and Mom:

It's almost time for bed, but I'm going to write a few lines. I was excited today because one of my roommates came back from a little trip to Berchtesgarden, one of the prettiest places in Europe. It is in the mountains and there are a lot of things to see. He said the scenery was out of this world. With the booklet he gave me, I have started to plan a three day weekend in July to that area. I'm really looking forward to it. I do a lot of thinking about traveling.

Mother, do not send my shoes! I will buy a pair here or in London. Thanks for selling my typewriter.

April 23, 1964, letter to Dad and Mom:

Carole will graduate five weeks from this coming Sunday. It will be a great day when we are together again.

Last night I went to the library since we had the night off. At 8:10 p.m. I was surprised to see Hans as he had come for a visit. We went to the snack bar after showing him my barracks, and I treated him to a couple of hamburgers and ice cream. He likes hamburgers and I guess it was a treat since they only sell them at one place in Tubingen, his college town. We never saw hamburgers in mainland Europe except at the U.S. Armed Forces snack bars. Hans claims that these hamburgers here are much better. He also enjoyed the ice cream since ours is much better than the Germans' ice cream (I agree with this). I enjoyed his visit. He had to leave at 10:00 p.m. He was working and had to drive up to this area for a delivery. Monday he will start school again. I sure like the entire Stein family. You will see Hans Stein when you are here in Germany. He wants to live in the U.S. (Hans's schooling is training him for the medical profession).

Mother, don't send Carole's iron. We will buy a German one. We need one with a 220 voltage instead of the U.S. regular 110 voltage.

April 26, 1964, letter to Dad and Mom:

I'm in the library now and the sun is getting low in the sky. It's a little cool outside.

I was amused over the Houston Astros' pitcher, Ken Johnson, pitching a no-hitter against Cincinnati and he lost the game 0-1 [April 23, 1964].

Yesterday afternoon Hans took me to Ulm, Germany (one-hour drive). We went up to a second-story café. We spent a lot of time there just visiting. We had the regular German cake and coffee. Our table was next to a window that faced the highest cathedral in Europe. It was huge! Hans told me that everything around this cathedral had been flattened during the war, but the cathedral did not suffer any damage. During this visit with Hans, he mentioned that he was flying to Detroit (the Wilsons also lived in Ferndale) to spend time with Davi. He wanted to make sure Davi was the right woman to be his wife. He was counting the days when he would see Davi again, and I was counting the days when I would see my own Carole. This session was the most special time I had with Hans. We each had coffee and a slice of cake. The bill was one dollar and seventy-five cents (7-marks). This appears to be expensive, but the prices are reality for these cafes. Coffee sells for twenty-five cents to thirty cents a cup. [Back in the States coffee was five cents to ten cents]. Hans didn't allow me to pay for it, which is typical of the Stein family. They tell me I need my money for our living in the economy. You folks will like Hans. Hans wants to finish his schooling in Michigan. Hans seems to have a love for Davilyn "Davi" Wilson.

May 2, 1964, letter to Dad and Mom:

One month from today Carole and I will be together.

Carole's plane will land in London around 7:15 a.m. I wonder if there is more than one airport in London. Your suggestion of The "Strand Palace" hotel sounds good and I will request reservations. Thank you for the information. Tomorrow I'm going over to the Stein's home.

I have some really bad news to tell Carole and it has made me sick. I'm worrying about it and trying to tell myself that things will work out. I no longer have that apartment mentioned earlier. Jim Connor, who was supposed to move out on June 1st, has extended his service time, and therefore he is not moving out. He told me this past Wednesday. Apartments are very hard to find. I have four weeks to get one, and I think in three and a half weeks if I don't have one I will have Carole stay in Michigan and I will cancel my leave. I will take anything, just so long as I have my own living room and bedroom.

The day I got this depressing news, I started immediately and I'm still asking around. I went to the subpost [German-run shops located on edge of our army post, such as dry cleaning, bank, post office and barber] and they couldn't help me, but I have an address and a few other people to see. I have an ad placed in the Goppingen newspaper, but I think it will be hard for them to reach me. I asked several people around the place. My only hope now is this one particular sergeant. He said that he knows of two places and he thinks he can help me and he is sincere. He is trying to get me to a town three miles from here. He has called several times, but can't reach the person. He said, "Don't be discouraged, Wilcox, I'll get you a place." He also told me there is another place in Goppingen he knows of. So out of his three places, I should get one. I went to this town today with a friend by bus and we looked up two places and couldn't get anything. I was kind of glad, though, because the places looked sickening and depressing. Something will just have to happen! Don't worry about me.

May 4 1964, letter to Dad:

I was beginning to think about buying a VW next year and taking it home with me. They are very dependable and require very little maintenance.

When I was talking with Hans [Stein] yesterday, he mentioned that he thinks I shouldn't buy that 1950 VW. He said it's too old and it won't be reliable. He recommends I buy a new one. He said I wouldn't have any expenses with it and if something did go wrong with it, it's guaranteed.

I have been thinking maybe there is something that could be done in getting a new one. I would have a reliable car and I could take it home with me. The cost is thirteen hundred dollars. What do you think about us having a new car here? Some of the men here have done this and that is what makes me think more of it. Insurance is just a little more. Hans is looking into car insurance for me.

Now, I can only get a new one if you help me borrow the money. I could only pay three hundred dollars this first year and the one thousand dollars plus interest the second year. I will also get better gas mileage with a new car, at least thirty mpg. Please let me know about you borrowing thirteen hundred dollars. I will pay it back, no sweat on that. I don't mind being in debt, for I know I can pay it back in one year of work in the States. Please let me know immediately. I am serious about this. The VW is very cheap to run.

May 5, 1964, letter to Dad:

Dad, I'm very serious now about buying a new VW. I would like to have you borrow twelve hundred dollars for me and send it to me the best method. Dad, I know you don't like to be in debt and I can't blame you, but this will be my debt and I'm positive that I can pay back five hundred dollars of it while I'm here. I will be receiving one hundred and eighty dollars per month and if rent is only fifty dollars, I will send home fifty dollars per month to apply against this debt. Dad, I want to buy this car because it's so reliable and inexpensive to operate. At the end, this will save me money. When you are here, we will have a good car. When in the States, I will have a good car. The cost to ship it to the States is one hundred and fifty dollars and that's it. This would mean a lot for both Carole and me. I will pay every penny of it. When I'm back in the States, I will pay up the balance in eight months. Write me immediately. Remember, in buying this car I'm not thinking about this year, but the next three or four years.

May 9 1964, letter to Dad and Mom:

Hey, Dad, I'm not going to say any more about the car. I probably will end up paying higher rent, but I should be able to pay three hundred dollars on it before coming home to Michigan. [I mentioned to Mom and Dad that I had looked at a couple more possibilities for renting, but no success.]

May 11, 1964, letter to Dad and Mom:

Even though we have started working nights, I feel good. Thanks, Dad, for the twelve hundred dollars. I really appreciate it. I insist on paying the first year's interest for this loan. I shouldn't have any car expenses while over here but the interest expense is worth it.

I have possibilities of three different apartments. It is beginning to look like I'm having a lucky streak in running into the right person at the right time. I will finish this after work tonight.

Hi again! As I said, in terms of housing, it's beginning to look good. I'm not going to say very much, but I know something will come out of these places. There is a good chance that a friend of mine and his wife will take over a nice house. We will definitely know for sure Saturday. It sounds like a real nice place and to have a whole house, the four of us—fabulous! Tomorrow night I should know the details on this place and Saturday we can make the transaction and it will be ours, if we go through with it. My friend John Jerca and his wife will be here July 2, but he wants to be sure of a place. I'm almost positive I will get a fairly good place.

I have started this evening inquiring about purchasing a car. I want to order it within two or three weeks so that I will have it when I return from London on June 15. Hans has offered to help me on this car transaction, but I wrote him a letter asking him if it would be better for me to see the dealer around here since he is so busy with his schooling. I don't want him to feel like he is indebted to help me. He would be glad to do so, but he is very busy. The Stein family told me if I couldn't find a place, they would help me. They are really great and have done a lot for me already. I could never repay them for all they have done for me. Carole will like the family.

Since I have been here, I have used up eight dollars worth of stamps [five-cent stamps for letters].

May 17, 1964, letter to Dad and Mom:

Today is another German holiday. The unions in the States want a shorter week. Germany has solved this with lots of holidays. May Day was a three-day holiday, the seventh was a holiday, today and tomorrow are holidays, and the 28th is a holiday.

It seems hard to believe that two weeks from this evening, I will be on my way for fifteen wonderful, glorious, free days. I hope the weather is nice. I'm very anxious for this time to come. The closer it comes, the more impatient I am.

I got a lot of literature on England and I looked up where Strand Palace was and it's in a beautiful location, as you said. It's definitely in the heart of the sights and according to the hotel information booklet the cost will be about seven dollars a day or a little cheaper. The cities I plan to visit are: London, Bath, Birmingham, Manchester, Windermere (lake area of England), Edinburgh, and Glasgow.

I may get down to Dover, I don't know yet. I will leave by train on Sunday, May 31, at 11:40 p.m. from Stuttgart. I will arrive in London on June 1 at 3:30 p.m. I will go to the hotel and then go to a bank or two and get some coins and English money. I may also buy a pair of shoes because my new military shoes are uncomfortable and irritate my little toes after walking a lot. I'm very anxious for the next Sunday, for it will only be one week to go—fabulous! Time is flying!

It appears that I'm going to have a nice place for Carole. Tuesday night, John Jerca and I will see a house near the post. We can rent the whole house for ourselves and there is a garden also. It's furnished and it won't be expensive, with the two of us sharing it. I will write Wednesday night and tell you all about it. It sounds good. We have a date with the owner at 7:00 p.m. Tuesday.

As for the car, Hans and I couldn't get together this weekend. I will see what can be done for this coming Saturday. I will let you know when to send the money. I'm looking forward to having a car.

My friend John Jerca and I were at Fort Polk together and we had CST schooling together. We came over to Goppingen together. He is from St. Louis and a very nice person. His wife is coming over here on July 2, but he wants a place for June to make sure he has one, so we have been helping each other to find housing for our spouses. He met a person who is a painter, and he told Jerca he has a house to rent. Jerca was told that the rent would be cheap. He agreed to show us the house this coming Tuesday. So I'm just about all set in housing. It will be fabulous having a whole house for ourselves, but we will have to see it before we make any more conclusions.

Mother, the English money will be fine because I can use it. Don't worry, Mother, about saving English money because it is always the same price, two dollars and eighty cents per pound, when you get here. Twenty shillings equals one pound.

May 21, 1964, letter to Dad and Mom:

I'm sorry that I haven't written sooner, but every night I have been out and tonight I probably will be out very late.

No good news yet for we are going around in a circle. This weekend, the German painter couldn't join us until last Tuesday night. We got together, and he said he would have to wait for the following night before he could show us the two places. He was also going to get the price knocked down for the house in Goppingen. Too expensive! Last night he didn't show up, but the German in the snack bar (a neighbor) said tonight he would arrange things. So far, I'm just running around trying to get housing for Carole. I just haven't had too much luck.

As for the VW, a German-speaking friend of mine and I were going to go down to the dealer this afternoon since they are open from 5:00 p.m. to 6:00 p.m., but they pulled an inspection from 5:00 p.m. to 6:00 p.m., the first time this has happened. Tomorrow after work I will try again to get to the VW dealership. I will write you a letter this weekend.

As for the VW, I will let you know. I want to pick up the car on June 15 (Monday) and pay for it then. Please mail the money order or cashier's check to me on or about June 7th. I will give you more details on this later.

As for England, I have a pile of material on it, but I haven't done too much planning. This housing and car has been on my mind. The weekend that I will leave, I will make an outline as to my fifteen-day vacation, but won't hold to it completely. It's up to Carole.

Tomorrow I will get the car, and it will cost about thirteen hundred and fifty dollars. The color will be white.

The Stein family has obtained an umbrella for me at a discount. It should cost me about eight dollars. It slides down to about seven inches long. It's neat and I don't believe they are in the States.

Thanks for the letters and stamps.

Doesn't seem possible I will soon see Carole again. I got so I can't do very much work because I get a little excited about the London trip, saying it mildly. I have a lot to say, but will have to save it for later.

I will leave Goppingen Sunday (May 31) to Stuttgart for London. I may spend some of the day at Waldenbuch, at the Steins.

June 1, at 3:30 p.m., I will arrive in London and I will go to the Strand Place Hotel. We will be in London June 1-3, then to Bath, England. No reservations yet; the cheap rooms are taken. I will hear from them any time now for ten dollars rooms with no baths. I have to go now.

May 22, 1964, letter to Dad and Mom:

It's Friday night and once again the weekend is approaching reality. I'm an owner of a VW and it's white. I have seen it already, but I haven't driven it. I have a lot to say, but I won't be able to cover everything. I have to write Hans a letter tonight also.

I'm going deeply in debt and I hate to, but I want to enjoy myself and see things over here. I want to travel and live in a house with a little comfort. Therefore, I'm borrowing a little for an experience in Europe. I just don't want to live in cheap housing and stay home for the weekends. With your help and your good credit, I can mortgage my good times for next year. I asked Dad if he could loan me two thousand dollars to buy a new Volkswagen and to have extra money for traveling in Europe. Our new VW had a stronger front window and the speedometer was in miles. I'm indebted to Dad for borrowing this money on our behalf because this allowed us to get the maximum out of our European experience. Dad made the monthly payments until I could pay him back with interest when we started our employment in Kalamazoo. Fortunately it took less than a year to pay off this debt once we were back in the States.

After work today a friend drove me down to the dealer, and I got the car. He had it waiting for me, but I will pick it up on June 15th.

Hi again,

It's very late and I have been exhausted since this afternoon, but tomorrow night I will go to bed early. I never ate dinner either, but I had an orange and I will have another one after this letter.

I'm getting very excited about seeing Carole again. More good news; starting Monday I will have a different job and it will be better, less work, especially nights. I probably hurt myself a little for a promotion in grade, but I had enough of what I was experiencing. A little storm, but the clouds will drift away and I can prove myself. I will write more about this later. I'm now the out-processing clerk in the pay section and I'm still on the same team only I work for a warrant officer. [My last day of this job the warrant officer told me that I was the best person he had ever had with my responsibilities. Working nights was eliminated with this job. I was not aware of any of my fellow workers complaining when I left at 5:00 p.m. and they were all still working into the evening. This schedule was just perfect for us since I was home and off the post in the evenings. Life was much better.

Today I picked up my round-trip ticket to London and Carole's ticket to Goppingen from London. Cost is seventy-two dollars. Cheap!

The best news! I have a beautiful apartment for Carole for only sixty-three dollars per month. It is better than the average German apartment. More on this later. John Jerca and I plus our wives will share it. Monday night we will pay the owner the rent. [I can't remember what happened, but the arrangement for our housing mentioned in the above letter fell through. Between May 22 and May 27 I found housing on the third floor of a fairly new house. I can't remember how this all came about. I remember thinking that I would prefer not to share a house or apartment with another couple. Apparently I found the house we would move into and made the required arrangements prior to May 27.]

It's sickening when our American men receive orders for Viet Nam. The U.S. should get out or win the war this year. U.S. is losing in Asia, our first major defeat.

May 27, 1964, letter to Dad and Mom:

I'm all set now because I got a fairly nice place here in Goppingen. The house is new and our two rooms are very nice and lack the "depressing look" of many of the places in the area. I like this place very much, except for one thing. The place is heated from a coal burner in the living room. We will manage it, though. The rent is forty-five dollars per month plus around seven dollars and fifty cents for electricity. The telephone is about one dollar and fifty cents to three dollars per month. I like the place in that the rooms are so nice and new and the house is in a beautiful location. Tell Carole that we will live in Goppingen and by ourselves. This summer I will send a few pictures of us, the car, and our place. [I found housing less than a week before I left for London. Our German home consisted of an attic of a fairly new house close to a major street in a nice neighborhood. The attic was converted to two nice rooms. One room was the bedroom, and the other room was the kitchen and everything else. The bathroom was very small, in a separate room outside our unit. It consisted of a very small sink and a toilet. There was no heat in this bathroom. There was a small room next to our unit in which an older man lived. We shared the bathroom with him. We rarely saw him. On each end of the floor in our unit there were large windows that could be opened. In the bedroom was a small pot stove. That was our heater. It could only hold two bricks of coal and took a long time to build up heat. During the winter we had to close the kitchen because the stove could only heat the bedroom. I left my plastic tube of shampoo one evening in the kitchen during one winter night and in the morning it was frozen solid.]

It just doesn't seem possible that there are only six days left until Carole's arrival. As you two can imagine, I'm very anxious for my departure. I'm the out-processing clerk for the pay department now. The job is less work and nights free. Just what I wanted, but the job will be very easy.

Yes, Dad, things are taken care of as to Carole's arrival. Thank you, though, for the information and your concern for a successful vacation. If you have a map handy, I will give you the route of my train and the general area of the train route Stuttgart, Koln, Aathen, Brussels, Oostende, Dover, and London. Saturday I will make a rough schedule to follow for our vacation.

We have a three-day Memorial Day weekend. Tomorrow is my last day of work until June 16, and you probably can imagine how I feel about this. It will be good to get away from this place. The morale here is low, and I can understand this.

Oh, yeah, it is a requirement for the GIs in the economy to have a telephone. This is for our monthly practice alerts and for the real thing [Soviet invasion] if it ever happens. Carole will have to go to school for a month. This class will consist of the necessary procedures if there is such an invasion.

May 28, 1964, letter to Dad and Mom:

No more work as we start the three-day weekend and of course, soon my fabulous vacation. I received two letters from you, Dad, and it was good hearing from you as usual. Right now I'm very excited about my trip and everything is all arranged over here. As for my apartment, it looks like I will only have to pay rent beginning from the day we move in. This is extra money for me. I like our place very much with the exception of the heating system, but we will manage it. [Babs Stein told us that we were living in an area in which the people were very frugal, and central heating was considered a waste of money.]

The house is in a nice neighborhood and in a good location. The house is new, clean, and attractive. The address is 3 Helferich Strasse, Goppingen 73033. Our landlords are Hans and Paula Hahnle.

Monday night I will write a letter [from the Strand Palace Hotel in London] to you two. Soon I will see Carole again. Life will be much better with her here.

I guess, Dad, your writing days to Adrian College are over with. These past five years sure went fast. In three days Carole will be an alumnus and I have to say her school year also went by fast. I just wish I could have seen a little of it.

I'm going to take a shower, get in bed, and work on my accounting lesson. [I took three correspondence courses through Louisiana State University when I got settled at the army post in Goppingen. I only took one course at a time, and when Carole arrived I was still working on my third course. I enjoyed studying and learning, but I ended it after I completed the third course.] Dad, I got car insurance. The cost is seventy dollars per year with a one hundred and twenty-five deductible. In 77 hours and 15 minutes, I will be on my way.

Memorial Day, May 31, 1964, finally arrived. Being a holiday weekend, most of the men were off base. I was to leave Stuttgart, Germany by train to London at 11:45 p.m. on the 31st and meet Carole in London at 7:15 a.m. local time at the London airport.

Dad and Mom attended Carole's graduation commencement at Adrian College on May 31, 1964. They took her home with them, and on June 1 they took her to the airport for her flight to Boston and another flight to London. Carole's family was also at the airport to send Carole off. I'm indebted to Dad and Mon for doing this for us, but I know they wanted to. They always supported our decisions.

Chapter 23

Carole's Arrival in London, England.

One of my most memorable moments was the day I left Goppingen, Germany to meet Carole in London, England. She was to arrive during the early morning of June 2, 1964. Her arrival and our reunion as wife and husband were on my mind each day during the first five months of 1964. As May 1964 approached, I started to get really excited. It was weeks, then a week, and then it was just hours away for our reunion. My last day in the barracks, which was Memorial Day, May 31, 1964, I just wasted the time away. I had several hours to go before my train departure from Stuttgart to London, but my decision was to wait in Stuttgart for the rest of the day, so I walked to Goppingen from the base and took the next train to Stuttgart.

The weather was perfect and so comfortable that evening, my last one in Germany without Carole. Near the Bahnhof in the heart of Stuttgart is a huge park stretching out on both sides of Koenig Strasse (King Street). I walked around and ended up in an area at the end of this park. This area has a huge water fountain with lights, surrounded by a ring of benches. Many delay their travel to rest on the bench, visit, and watch the water display. The sun went down, and I sat down on one of these benches and watched the young lovers strolling hand in hand, aware of only themselves. Many couples came and went. While observing these couples, my thoughts were of Carole, the good times we had during the three years we had known each other, and the things we would do together in the next thirteen months in Europe. I told myself that my turn for holding hands with the woman I loved was coming very soon. I was not counting days anymore, but just hours before I would at last be with Carole. It had been five months since we said goodbye, and we saw each other very little in the six months before that. I thought of the days when it seemed to be such a long time until June 2, 1964 and now it was so close!

Being excited and afraid of missing the train for one reason or the other, I walked to the Bahnhof about twenty minutes before the train was to arrive. When the train arrived around 11:30 p.m., I was one of the first ones to get on and finally, at 11:45 p.m., the train pulled out and I knew that this was it. I thanked God for this day and for this very moment. I didn't sleep too much due to not being very comfortable, and probably more because of my excitement. My seat was next to the window and I enjoyed seeing people, buildings, and scenery. My train compartment was filled with four or six people. When we reached Belgium we had daylight. Going across the Channel, I latched onto a GI with his wife and her parents. We had coffee together and visited. They were traveling around Europe and were on their way to England. I enjoyed this boat trip. I remember an English teenager and two really small girls singing one of the Beatles' songs. I enjoyed hearing their English accent.

When we got to England, I sat with a middle-aged Englishman on the train. I visited with him all the way to London, and he pointed out a few of the historical sites from the window. He was very enjoyable, which made the time fly. He didn't like England's weather, and for this reason he made his wife's country, France, his home. His job was selling Grundig (German) tape recorders and radios to U.S. military bases in Europe and Asia.

It was around 3:30 p.m. when the train arrived in London. I remember thinking how hard it was to believe that I was in London. I took a taxi from the Victoria train station directly to our hotel, Strand Palace, signed in, and went up to my room. I put my stuff there, washed, and went out to the street. I wandered down the street a little and looked in the window of a shoe store. It appeared that shoes were cheap in London. I needed a pair of shoes since I had only my military dress shoes, so I did purchase a pair. I also purchased a newspaper and then went back to my room. I looked around the lobby area since they had a travel agency and what seemed like a gift store. I then left the room again and went to the dining hall of the hotel and had a "minute steak" dinner. I remember a French woman was sitting at the table next to mine, about four feet from me. It was fascinating being there as I observed everything, thinking it all so very interesting.

I then went back to my room for the rest of the night. I told the desk clerk to wake me up at 2:30 a.m., June 2. I wrote a letter to my parents. I can also remember looking at the coins I received from paying for my dinner. I enjoyed them because England used large coins during this time. We never did master their shilling-pound system in regard to counting out the change from a paper note. I read just a little from the newspaper, then decided to go to bed early since I wanted to be refreshed the day Carole arrived. I had very little sleep the previous night and 2:30 a.m. would come fast. Well, I was awake a lot and only got a few hours of sleep that night.

June 1, 1964, letter to Dad and Mom from Strand Palace Hotel, London:

I'm in my Strand Palace Hotel room and as you may guess, I'm very excited about seeing Carole in ten hours. In four hours she will be stepping onto the plane and I'm very anxious for a safe landing early in the morning.

The weather so far is terrible, a little rain. The money is nice because their coins are large in size.

Sunday I waited impatiently for the hours to pass and while waiting, I read about England from a book from the library.

I left Goppingen around 6:00 p.m. and killed time shopping in Stuttgart's new section. It is the prettiest of any city I have seen. They also have a huge park of lights and water spiral pools. You folks will see it.

The time came for the train trip to London and I felt a little better. I feel good now, even though I got only one hour of sleep, if that much. Tonight I will try to get four hours of sleep because the airport is a long way from here. I will get up around 2:30 a.m. to make sure I make it to the airport before Carole arrives.

Belgium is a sickening-looking country from the train and I have no desire to see that country.

We reached Ostend, Belgium, around 9:30 a.m. (the German train was terrible) and the boat for Dover departed at 10:00 a.m. The Channel was a little rough and a few got sick. I ran into a GI and his wife's parents (from Toledo, Ohio) on the ship and visited with them. I also ran into four Air Force men and visited with them. When we reached Dover, England, most of the boat passengers loaded on the train for London. On the train I sat next to an Englishman, and we stayed together all the way to Victoria station in London. He is a salesman for Grundig Majestic radios and recorders. He sells to the U.S. Armed Forces and has been around the world selling. His wife lives in France. We talked about England, the U.S., and Germany.

He gave me a few tips on my traveling. London is really different, from the little I have seen of it. The travel bureau downstairs gave me some more stuff on London. I know London pretty well now, and I haven't even seen it yet. There are a lot of foreigners here, even from India.

It certainly would be nice if you two were with us. I think you would like this city. Their ice cream isn't as good either. Prices are better than Germany's. After I found out some more information on London, I went to my room and dumped my stuff and left. I purchased a pair of shoes for seven dollars and eighty cents. One can get really good shoes (Saxon) for twelve dollars to fifteen dollars. Even ten dollars will give you a real good pair of shoes, but I can't take advantage of it. I want to buy a trench coat since the weather is very cool and I'm afraid we will have some rain while in London.

This hotel is made up of French, Germans, Americans, and what have you. Some people are outside my room talking, but I don't recognize the language.

Tomorrow we won't see much, but probably will shop if a nice day. My latest vacation plans:

1. London June 2-5 (includes a boat trip down the Thames River to Windsor Castle an all day trip).
2. Bath June 6 (will arrive there on the night of 5th).
3. Stratford-upon-Avon June 7 and half of 8.
4. Maybe at Matlock Bath June 8.
5. Windermere June 9 and 10, Lake District.
6. Edinburgh June 11 and 12, and then back to London to Stuttgart.

Well, I'm going down to the main floor and see if I can get stamps to mail this. I'm very excited to see Carole. We will arrive back here [hotel] from the airport about 7:15 a.m. in time for breakfast.

Well, 2:00 a.m. did arrive and I was up. The desk clerk directed me to the street with the knowledge that taxicabs were plentiful twenty-four hours a day and I just needed to wait and flag one down when it approached. I was amazed to find this correct.

Off I went to the terminal. However, I was taken to the wrong terminal. There was more than one terminal! The taxicab driver was able to identify the right terminal by either knowing Carole's flight or he went inside to identify the correct terminal. Arriving at next terminal the cab driver asked that I go inside the terminal to confirm that it was the right one. I did as he asked and it was the right one and I thanked him. I realized that my arrival was way too early, but I really didn't care. Carole's plane arrived around 7:15 a.m. local time. I couldn't see the passengers leaving the plane until they went from a hallway to an open walkway that led to where I was standing. Many passengers came, and they walked to my right to be processed through customs. More and more passengers were walking toward me, but no Carole! I was really getting concerned and wondering what I needed to do if Carole didn't show up. Then there was a large gap behind the last passenger I could see, and then Carole appeared. What an exciting moment for me, seeing my wonderful wife. There was a rope separating the walkway from customs. We hugged and kissed, and Carole said, "I need to go through customs and it shouldn't take very long." I waited and in just a few minutes we were together, leaving the terminal hand and hand. That precious moment had arrived! Finally, we were together! My heart was filled with contentment and joy. She has always been very special to me.

Carole's June 2, 1964 journal entry:

Arrived in London 7:10 a.m., with Rick at the airport to greet me. After passport check and customs we were finally reunited! We went to our hotel, The Strand Palace, via bus and taxi. Weather was rainy and gloomy.

We had breakfast and spent the rest of the morning resting and catching up on things. About 12:30 p.m. we started out on foot, sightseeing. We saw St. Paul's Cathedral, The Royal Courts of Justice, The Bank of England, the Monument (fire of 1666), and many other buildings. Nearly all of these buildings were so dirty they seemed ugly to us. We ended our tour at the Tower Bridge and the Tower of London where we saw the crown jewels and old relics. We took a subway back to the vicinity of our hotel.

We found out that pedestrians have to fight for their lives and also that the only safe way is to look "all three ways" before crossing. Millions of black taxis and busses, all in fleets (traffic travels in the opposite direction compared to the U.S.).

Carole's June 3, 1964 journal entry:

We took another tour on foot today – from 9:30 -7:00 p.m.! Started out to see the Changing of the Guard at Buckingham Palace, which we thought was at 10:30 a.m. but was 11:30 a.m. We saw the foot guards, the horse guards, and band. We were very impressed with their precision and their colorful uniforms. We also walked awhile in St. James Park, watching the ducks.

Then we walked to Westminster Abbey and the House of Parliament. Visited the inside of Westminster Abby and were surprised by all this statuary, decorations, and graves—those of Kipling, Dickens, Chaucer, Tennyson, Browning, and others.

After the House of Parliament and Big Ben, we walked down to Scotland Yard and then over to Trafalgar Square where Lord Nelson's monument stands. Here are hundreds of tame pigeons residing. A man gave me some feed to feed the birds and immediately several pigeons flew up on my arm and one on my shoulder! The man explained that these pigeons are trained to do this. He gave us both more feed and took a picture. For 10 shillings he will send us four prints (two poses). We saw some of these birds on people's heads!

Then we walked to Piccadilly Circus which we found later on to be very colorful at night with all the neon ads. Then we walked onto Oxford Street to find Selfridges Department store. Didn't have much time to shop, but looked around a little bit and bought a record.

Ate a dinner and then walked to the New Theater on St. Martins Lane to see the play *Oliver*, which we enjoyed very much (Rick couldn't understand most of the words).

Weather was cloudy and late afternoon we were surprised to see the sun peep through occasionally.

Carole's June 4, 1964 journal entry:

We decided to take a boat trip down to Hampton Court and then a bus to Windsor Castle but found the boat took longer than we expected, 10:30 a.m. to 2:00 p.m.! The trip was interesting but it was very rainy and a little cool. However, we finally arrived at Windsor Castle but we didn't have too much time to look around because they were closing up parts. We did climb to the top of the tower and looked out over the countryside—a very beautiful sight.

We did some window-shopping and then took a bus to Hyde Park here in London. We went to see the Roosevelt Memorial and the U.S. Embassy.

Carole's June 5, 1964 journal entry:

After breakfast we walked to Piccadilly in the rain to buy a souvenir tablecloth of London that we had seen in the shop window the night before. We also saw a framed picture of Parliament Square on the Thames River that we bought for our home.

Returning to the hotel, we checked out and got a taxi to take us to the railroad station. We got to the wrong one but luckily our taxi driver asked us which train and soon told us we should be at Paddington, which we soon were.

We arrived in Bath about mid-afternoon, checked into our hotel, the Royal York, and took a short walk around town. We were surprised to find how fast we got around town and saw nearly all the sights in such a short amount of time. We saw the Abbey, the Roman Baths, and Poultney Bridge. There are shops around Poultney Bridge and it doesn't look like a bridge on the inside -- it just looked like any other street of shops. In one of the shops I've found some Hummel prints on P. C. and bought twelve at 9d each. We also visited a museum of sorts in which there was a "history of the bath." In it was a remote control bathtub!

We ate our best dinner at our hotel that night; luscious filet steak, french fries, and the tenderest peas we have ever eaten. Our meal was served on a cart and the peas heated on flame before our eyes.

June 5, 1964, letter to Dad and Mom:

We are at the train station in our train car preparing to leave London. After fighting the traffic and walking several miles, we are saying goodbye to London and here we come, Bath! We may stay only one day there and Friday night we may take off to Stratford upon Avon. We don't know yet.

The weather is very poor. Today and yesterday it has been raining, but our first few days here the sun was out for a couple of hours. Carole and I are really enjoying ourselves and our feet and legs are holding out in good shape. My new shoes are very good!

Dad, shoes and suits are very cheap here. A good suit costs forty dollars. I wish I could buy some clothing here. I did purchase a trench coat for nineteen dollars, which is a necessity for this weather.

Yesterday we closed out our London tour with a boat trip down the Thames River and then to Windsor Castle, which was very pretty.

Our hotel was centrally located, as you said, and the food there was the best with reasonable prices. As a whole, the food is very terrible and juices are very expensive.

So far this trip has been interesting and enjoyable for both of us, but the weather has been disappointing. We didn't do everything we wanted to do, such as seeing more of Windsor Castle and attending the British Museum. I guess you always can't do everything on a trip.

Here in England one has to be very careful in crossing streets because the traffic comes from the opposite side as in the States. In some intersections traffic seems to come from all directions and we had to be careful before crossing or just run across and hold our breath. We have learned the art of crossing streets with speed, though.

Mother, I called up the Bank of England and got the same answer as the other banks, "No crowns."

We have been spending very little money besides the necessities so far. We did get a little picture to hang for one dollar and forty cents and a record and some slides and postcards.

It is good being with Carole again. I met her at the airport Tuesday morning at 7:15 a.m. I got up at 2:00 a.m. that morning, but it wasn't necessary. The airport is very attractive and I was there for about three and a half hours, but I was there on time to meet her! Ha.

Carole's June 6, 1964 journal entry:

Even though it was raining and we were nearly soaked, we walked around some more and saw the Royal Crescent and the Circus.

We had lunch and got on the train for Stratford-upon-Avon. We arrived at 5:30 p.m. after changing trains; Bristol and Worcester.

We are delighted with our hotel, the Arden in Stratford. Our room is in a house next to the hotel itself, on the top floor toward the front. Our window overlooks the beautiful garden in our front lawn and the river and gardens across the road. Also across the road is the Shakespeare Theatre. The hotel also seemed to be centrally located for our walking tours.

Carole's June 7, 1964 journal entry:

Today we saw the sites of Stratford-upon-Avon (on foot again), which is Shakespeare's birthplace, Anne Hathaway's cottage, Halls Croft, the New Place, the Holy Trinity Church where Shakespeare is buried, and the gardens.

Carole's June 8-9, 1964 journal entry:

We decided to take the bus tour to Warwick Castle, which left at 10:00 a.m. Beforehand we walked around and watched the swans on the Avon River. There was a cute family of five baby swans.

Arriving at Warwick Castle, we first had to locate a bank to get enough money, then take a picture of the castle from the bridge, which didn't leave us much time inside the castle. However, we saw the grounds—the gardens and the peacocks. Two of them had their tails spread out for us. The entrance to the castle was very cool, dark, and damp—stone walls with trees and bushes and moss. There were also several beautiful rhododendrons on the castle grounds.

After returning to Stratford we had lunch and shopped, then went to the park to sit and watch the swans.

Our train left at 8:10 p.m. for Windermere with changes at Birmingham (waited 9:10 p.m. to 10:45 p.m.) and Crewe (waited 12:30 a.m. to 2:30 a.m.). We tried to sleep between Crewe and Windermere but with not too much success. The train pulled in about 5:30 a.m. and we found nothing open yet and a light drizzle outside. We left the luggage at the station and began to walk around. First we walked on a foot pass leading to a high peak, 783 feet. We were disappointed, however, that on getting there we couldn't see anything because of the rain and mist.

Then we walked around town until the bakeries opened. Bought our breakfast at a bakery and ate it by the lake. Walking back toward the station, we met a woman who had gotten off the train with us. She was an American from New York City and had spoken to us that morning. She was on her way to rent a car and asked us if we would like to drive around the area with her. She seemed so nice and was alone, so we told her we would and met her about an hour later at the train station. Her name was Jean Silver and she is a lawyer.

We first drove to Ambleside and then had lunch at a pub, the Drunken Duck, about three miles outside of town. The food was very good and not very expensive. We then drove back to Windermere via a different route. We were very impressed with the beautiful scenery but were disappointed that it was still raining and misty. This section of England is quite mountainous and the roads and fields are lined with stone fences.

At Grasmere we saw William Wordsworth's cottage and museum and grave. Jean drove us into Ambleside where we took a bus back to our hotel [Jean invited us to do more traveling with her, but we wanted to do our own thing].

Carole's June 10, 1964 journal entry:

Left Windermere 11:00 a.m. by train to Carlisle where we hoped to get to the Roman Wall. However, we found there was not much of it to see there and we did not have time to take a bus where you could see something, so we just looked around Carlisle for a while. At 3:35 p.m. we left by bus for Edinburgh, arriving there about 7:30 p.m.

We found another hotel with excellent location, the St. Andrew. We ate supper in the Milk Bar across the street from the hotel. The meal was very good. Walked around our area for a little bit before retiring to our room.

June 10, 1964, letter to Dad and Mom:

We are on our way to Carlisle to see the Roman Wall. After that, this afternoon we will travel up to Edinburgh, Scotland.

The weather is just terrible, rain all day yesterday, our only day here in beautiful Windermere. We are on the train, waiting to leave. We had a little rain this morning.

The scenery was very attractive, but no good pictures could be taken because of the rain. At Stratford-upon-Avon the sun was out most of the time. The best two days were in Stratford-upon-Avon. The previous night [when we left Stratford-upon-Avon] we stayed up all night. Of course, we slept well last night.

Mother, I'm greatly amazed over the old coins one can find at these small town banks. Farthings and silver three pence are no longer legal tender. A number of years ago the government authorized banks to transfer these coins to the treasury to melt them for their metal. A few of the small banks still have a small inventory of these farthings and silver three pence coins that were not transferred to the government. When we are in small towns we are asking the banks if they have any of these coins. A few of these coins have very little wear. A few banks will give us free coins, farthings, Irish pennies, and a Canadian dime. The clerks at these banks are very friendly. Today will be our last day for being in small towns.

Carole's June 11, 1964 journal entry:

In Edinburgh we spent all day sightseeing—on foot again!

First we walked across town and saw Robert L. Stevenson's birthplace and where he lived and where Sir Walter Scott lived and we went through the Botanic Garden—very pretty and there was a spot where you could overlook the whole city.

Then we walked back into town and visited the head bank (Royal Bank of Scotland) where Rick finally got a "Yes" answer to his question, "Do you have any crown coins?" [They had two new 1953 Queen Elizabeth II coronation crowns in the original hard-plastic case. Someone had turned them in. The timing was just perfect, being there at the right time. They are slightly larger than the U.S. silver dollar].

We walked to the top of the Sir Walter Scott Monument. It was very windy but we got wonderful views of the city and excellent pictures since the sun was out!

Walked through the gardens on Princes Street and saw the beautiful floral clock. Then we walked to the castle and toured that. The castle is high on a hill in the middle of the city. It was a very impressive sight in a very interesting place. In it were the crown jewels of Scotland, sealed there since 1777. The crown is the oldest of Europe, dating back as far as 1313.

We climbed up Calton Hill where we climbed the steps of the Nelson monument. Also on Calton Hill were the city observatory and the national monument, which consisted of only a row of columns because it was never finished.

Then we went over to the Palace of Holyrood, but we were not able to go inside because it was just closing.

When we were in Edinburgh, Carole and I were amazed that the sun was still up close to 11:00 p.m. and when we got up early the sun was out. We enjoyed having daylight during all of our touring hours.

June 12, 1964, letter to Dad and Mom:

The weather, very unusual, was nice at Edinburgh, and we took lots of pictures. I have had a fabulous time and hate to go back to Germany. We will have one and one third days in London again. I sure like this city. We will try to get back to the Strand Palace Hotel again. The food is really cheap.

We are now on the bus to London. Carole will write next week and tell you all about our trip. The weather was disappointing, but our spirits were high.

How we walked for ten straight hours is beyond my reasoning. It was much cheaper and we saw more. The best way for sightseeing is by foot. You two will love Shakespeare's town [Stratford-upon-Avon].

We are hoping to sleep on the bus tonight. Traveling by night eliminates hotel expense and saves the day for sightseeing. Northern England and southern Scotland are very beautiful. Here's for a good night sleep and take care of yourselves.

Carole's June 12, 1964 journal entry:

We arose very early this morning and got on the 6:53 a.m. train to Langholm. However, we didn't find much at Langholm, nor at Longtown where we went next. At Longtown we met a man who gave us a ride into Carlisle where we wanted to take a train or bus into London.

We decided to take a bus that left at 6:15 p.m., so until then we shopped and visited banks. One of the tellers we talked to is going to send us four crowns that he has at home—Victorian ones. [He told us to walk down the block to the post office and ask them what it would cost to send eight half-crowns to Germany, which we did. We gave him the amount, plus the face value of these Victoria crowns. [I did receive these crowns, and they dated from the late nineteenth century. I gave two of them to Mother and years later I sold the other two, which I now regret. I also regret selling all of the silver three pence coins; I believe I only kept one farthing coin, selling the rest of them during our

Kalamazoo era. I also sold the crowns during this time. A farthing is one-fourth of a penny and it's the size of a U.S. cent coin].

I bought a pastel checked tablecloth and napkins made in Ireland at one of the stores. Then we got on the bus for London. We had to change at Preston and moved into a double-decker bus. This bus stopped twice, once at 12:30 a.m. and another at 4:00 a.m. or 4:30 a.m. The first stop was at the Newcastle bus stop. This had a large cafeteria in which there was a "cinebox," a jukebox with color film for each record. The second stop was on a plaza on the expressway. This plaza had a large cafeteria too, restaurant, gas station, and several vending machines. You could also walk across the road by a bridge to the other plaza.

We arrived in London around 7:00 a.m., checked our luggage, and ate breakfast in the bus station. We waited in the BOAC terminal across the street until 9:00 a.m. or so to call a hotel. We were unable to get a room at the Strand Palace but got a room at the Imperial Hotel, which was near the British Museum. On the way to our hotel, our taxi driver mentioned that he was taking a roundabout way because of the Queens official birthday celebration. We asked him more about it and decided to go there. He told us that he could take us to the best area to view the parade after we dropped off our luggage and checked in at the hotel, which he did.

The taxi driver left us at Trafalgar Square and we hurried over to the Mall, but found hundreds of people waiting to see the Queen too. She had already left the guards in the ceremonial place, but we were early enough to see her leave on horseback. We got as close as we could, which wasn't much, and were packed in tight. Rick was able to get a good picture with the help of a man living in Scotland (who used to live in Montréal) who lifted Rick up when the Queen was in view. He told us he would lift Rick up when the Queen was in front of us if we would send him a copy of the picture, which we did. He sent us about four large slides, which were images of London. We then made our way down to Buckingham Palace where the Queen was to make an appearance on the balcony at 1:00 p.m. She was holding the baby Prince Andrew when she appeared. Prince Philip was also there.

We then walked to our hotel, stopping for lunch on the way. After settling in our room, we went to the British Museum but were disappointed to find out their coin collection was not on display at this time. We walked back to our hotel, bathed, and went to bed after a very long and tiring day.

Carole's June 14-15, 1964 journal entry:

After breakfast we checked out of the hotel and took our baggage to Victoria Station where we had to wait nearly an hour to get our luggage checked because they were full. It was 11:30 a.m., so we hurried over to Buckingham Palace to see the Changing of the Guard again. Then we strolled around St. James Park, watching the pelicans, ducks, and pigeons before train departure time, which was 3:00 p.m.. We arrived in Dover about 4:15 p.m. and went straight from the train to the boat. The boat left at 5:00 p.m. and arrived at Ostend, Belgium, about 8:20 p.m. The voyage across from Dover was very smooth, but a little chilly. Again we went straight from the boat to the train which left at 9:00 p.m. and arrived in Stuttgart, Germany at 6:35 a.m. We then got on the next train to Goppingen, Germany, 7:12 a.m. to 8:12 a.m. Took a taxi to our apartment where we left our luggage and then went on to the post. Then we spent all day trying to get our new Volkswagen and its license plates. It left no time for shopping except for juice and coffee cake for breakfast the next morning.

Carole and I could never count coin change with English coins. It took several weeks or months to be able to count coin change when dealing with purchases. The coins used when we were there were: penny (pence, slightly larger than a U.S. half-dollar coin); three pence (a much-smaller coin than their penny, but much thicker); sixpence; one-shilling; two-shilling (called a florin); half-crown (a little larger than a U.S. half-dollar coin).Their paper money notes were pounds (£). One pound note equaled four crowns, or eight half-crowns, twenty shillings, or 240 pennies. A half-crown equaled two shillings and one sixpence. A florin equaled two shillings. A shilling equaled twelve pence. Carole and I purchased a low-cost item in England and I gave the woman clerk a one-pound note. She gave me several coins for my change, counted one coin at a time. She then asked me if the change I received was correct. I said, "I don't know," as I put the coins in my pocket. I didn't have a clue if she was correct.

Another time in England after the cab driver took us to our destination, he told us what was due him using the nicknames of their coins. I remember one word was a "bob," which didn't mean anything to us. He knew from our accent that we were from America. He was having fun with us as he kept repeating the nicknames of the coins when I repeated my question. Not getting anywhere, I finally just held out my hand with coins and asked him to take the coins needed for his service. Again, I had no idea if he took only what was due to him or more.

Here is a quiz: You enter a store and you purchase an item that costs four shillings and seven pence. You give the clerk a one-pound note. What are the exact coins you would receive from the clerk? Don't ask me!

Chapter 24

My U.S. Army Era—Our First Home in Germany

Carole's June 16, 1964, journal entry:

I spent the morning unpacking and finding a place for our things. Rick picked me up at noon and we ate at the post's snack bar. I then spent the afternoon shopping. I spent twenty dollars at the PX and eleven dollars on groceries.

Carole's June 17, 1964, journal entry:

I stayed home all day getting more settled and writing letters.

Our landlords [Hans and Paula Hahnle] saw me at the window during the afternoon (it is a German holiday) and invited me to come outside and sit. I did about 4:15 p.m. They have a nice patio at the side of the house and have invited us to come and sit anytime. Then about 5:00 p.m. they invited me to come in for coffee and cake, and when Rick came home they called him in too. The cake was one layer with strawberries on top – very popular here.

Carole's June 17, 1964, letter to Dad and Mom from Goppingen, Germany:

Well, we're pretty well settled in our little place. It's pretty nice despite a little inconvenience or so. The house is new and our third floor apartment is quite cheery.

The rooms are quite large and roomy. We have sloping ceilings, as you can imagine being on the third floor. The place is very clean. Our landlord and his wife are extremely nice, very friendly. He speaks English pretty well and she only a little. He was in WWII and was an American prisoner of war. They are not trying to get all they can out of us either, only charged half a month's rent. Rick said any other German would have gotten a full month's rent. Surprising also because they think we have a lot of money, two weeks in England and a brand-new VW. It's hard to explain to them because they don't understand that well.

Speaking of our little VW, we really love it. As Rick wrote, it's white and has a white and beige interior, makes it light and cheery. We are to take it in every 300 miles for check over and oil change free, except we pay for the oil. We have a coupon book and I don't know for how many miles this applies, but there are quite a few coupons. The funny part is that we filled up on gas yesterday. Our tank holds 10.6 gallons; therefore we won't need gas until it's time for the oil change and checkup.

We spent all day Monday getting our car and arranging the license plates. It's too complicated to go into and you'll never understand the army anyway. (We get the plates through them).

So yesterday afternoon I went into the post with Rick and shopped. I spent only thirty dollars on groceries and kitchen supplies and such. Still need a few things, but am surprised it didn't take more money. However, everything in the PX and grocery isn't on discount; meats and eggs, for instance, are not cheaper. In fact, I think the meats are more expensive, sixty-one cents for one pound of ground beef.

By the way, we have received all of your letters. We also received the package of shirts and his jacket. And before I forget again, will you send his tripod. I almost got crowned for not having it. He has several pictures planned for using the tripod, I guess. Also, would you send two of our blankets for us? I think we will need them this winter. Rick brought two of his military blankets so with two more that should keep us warm. I guess it doesn't matter which ones. Most of them are in boxes, I think.

You should see my refrigerator. It's only about three feet high. But this is nothing unusual here because I haven't yet seen anything bigger in any of the stores we saw all over England. There is no freezer compartment to speak of, just space for an ice cube tray, little room above it.

Our stove is electric, not new though, but it will do nicely. The only running water is in the bathroom. This is a little inconvenient, but things could be worse. For hot water we have a nice set up in the bathroom over the sink. Over the sink is a little heater. You fill that with water (turn a knob) and turn it on (electric). It will shut off automatically or you can turn it off. It's really quite the thing.

Our bed is a sofa pulled out. We will probably keep it out rather then put it up and pull it out each day. It's quite large and fairly comfortable. I was surprised, really. We have a very pretty view outside our kitchen window. Looking to the right, we look out over the town and the hills beyond. We are on the side of a hill ourselves.

We took a bus overnight from Carlisle to London, arriving early Saturday morning. We got to Carlisle by train and a ride from a very nice gentleman (English). We stopped at a couple of small towns to visit the banks. In Carlisle one of the tellers said he had about six crowns, come to think of it, you already heard this. Anyway, as things turned out that Saturday was the Queen's official birthday. On this day she leads the guards down the Mall, and after a ceremony they marched back; she's riding a horse then. We didn't know all this until it was nearly time for it (our taxi driver told us). We managed, however, to squeeze in the crowd and were able to see her on her way back. Rick was able to get a picture with the help of a man who lifted him up above the heads. This man used to live in Montréal. Later on the Queen made an appearance on the balcony of Buckingham Palace. We saw her then too, although she was too far away to really see her. She was holding the baby Prince Andrew. We were really quite thrilled to be able to see the Queen. Guess what Rick said about her, "She looks like her image on" you know what [coins]. I'll write more about our trip later, am getting tired of writing. The trip across the Channel was very smooth.

After writing this, I went outside to enjoy the sunshine. Our landlord saw me at the window and invited me to come down and sit. (Today is a German holiday). They have a beautiful garden, even a little pool with big goldfish and water lilies. They have a lovely patio porch on the side of the house and said we were welcome to come down and sit anytime. The whole family was around. They have a boy about ten, and her parents live here too on the second floor of the house. They do not speak any English, but are very nice to us just the same. Just before 5:00 p.m. they invited me to come in for coffee, insisted I should stay because I couldn't get out of it. Coffee wasn't too bad, however. I took sugar and cream. They also had a delicious cake topped with strawberries, very popular here. Rick came home while we were eating so he was "corralled" in too. We had a real nice visit. They are so friendly and the Mr. [Hans] is always joking. Tonight he brought me a bouquet of roses from the garden. I had told him this afternoon that the garden was very pretty and he said then he would give me some roses. He said when these die he will bring me new ones.

Our German house was at 3 Helferich Strasse, Goppingen, Germany. Our landlords were a wonderful couple. They were very friendly and kind to us. Our rent for the third floor (a converted attic) was around sixty dollars a month. Their yard was very attractive due to their attractive flower gardens. Hans spoke some English and we spoke very little German, but we could communicate. Our living space was very limited, but we made it work for us and it was our home in Germany. The location was very good, not far from Cooke Barracks.

Carole's June 19, 1964, journal entry:

I stayed home today, writing letters, etc. After dinner we took our bath downstairs on the first floor and then did our laundry at the laundromat—expensive! Cost thirty-seven cents to wash and twelve and a half cents to dry (ten minutes). This was the sequence for our weekly, Friday bath. The wood-burning water heater was next to the bathtub. The house was not very old, probably less than ten years old. The house didn't have central heating. The landlord used their fire place in the living room for heat.

Carole's June 20, 1964, journal entry:

This afternoon we drove to Robinson's Barracks in Stuttgart. However, we got lost and only with the help of an MP at the U.S. hospital did we get straightened around.

Carole's June 24, 1964, letter to Dad and Mom:

Guess I'll finish this in the morning. Rick is getting ready for bed. There will probably be an alert tomorrow morning, which means they will call us sometime between 2:00 a.m. and 7:00 a. m. and Rick will have to go in. We've been expecting one since we got back. They have one once a month.

It's now Thursday morning 8:30 a.m. No alert this morning, don't know when they'll have it now, but sure wish they would hurry. This weekend on Sunday we are going to Tubingen to see Hans. This is where he is going to school (Tubingen University), south of Stuttgart. We hope we can see Babs too, but haven't heard from her yet.

Last weekend we drove to Robinson Barracks in Stuttgart, the big one. There are three or four in Stuttgart. Rick had never driven by car there before, but he had directions, so we "donned" our bravery and started out. We got lost just on the outskirts of Stuttgart. Somehow we got off our highway and couldn't find it again. Some of these intersections are really something, about five roads coming in and out and signs all over the place. You can stop and read them all; you almost have to know where you are going to turn before you get there. We had evidently turned where we weren't supposed to at one of these places. Anyway, we were totally lost and didn't know where to go but we were driving around. Then we saw a sign pointing the way to U. S. Hospital, so we followed the signs, but all of a sudden they stopped and we had no idea which way to turn and it sure wasn't in sight. This experience is not uncommon here, Rick says, so you can't depend on signs too much. Anyway, we drove around some more and came across some more U. S. Hospital signs. We followed them and wonder of wonders, we got there this time, although we almost went right by it! The MP at the gate gave us directions to Robinson Barracks. We really weren't very far from it. This time we made it.

The PX there is really quite a bit larger. We bought some things we needed that we couldn't get here. Didn't look at the pretty gifts and things too much because we didn't have a lot of time and were just plain too tired. We ate at the snack bar there before heading back. No problems getting back.

However, we didn't stop at Goppingen. We went on to this high peak next to the base. It was a beautiful drive through a tall pine forest and the views of the countryside were really pretty. Our little VW can really climb!

At Stuttgart's PX, we bought a small ironing board. It is a folding one with one side a sleeve board and the other a little larger. You set it on the table to use. Little slow, but works fine. Cost one dollar and sixty cents.

Well, wouldn't you know on Monday, my landlady (Paula Hahnle) brought up a regular ironing board for me. She said she had two of them. I will keep the other, though. The sleeve board is handy and the whole thing will be nice for sewing.

Rick can ship two hundred pounds free when he leaves, which reminds me. Don't count on me coming back to the states with you. Dependents can fly jet from Stuttgart to New York for only one hundred and ninety dollars. We'll no doubt take advantage of this.

Guess who is our assistant pastor in my Niles Methodist church? He is Bill Hertel, who is one of Rick's fraternity brothers. We double dated with him and his girl, who is now his wife, several times at Adrian College. It's strange how these things work out, isn't it? Rev. Paul is coming to your church in Ferndale and Bill to my church.

Yes, Mom, I did get things I wanted. You see, I knew what I was doing. I didn't say anything about visiting one bank after another (I really enjoyed the coin hunting myself, anyway). Then because I was so nice about letting him do what he wanted, he would declare a "Mrs. Wilcox Day," and I could do what I wanted and buy anything I wanted, especially when he got something good which was about every day! I bought a charm from London and one from Edinburgh. I want to make a bracelet of charms of places we visited here. Also bought two tablecloths, a souvenir one with London scenes and a large rayon pastel check with napkins made in Ireland. Also, from Stratford, I purchased an Irish linen tray cloth with an embroidered image of Anne Hathaway's Cottage, very rich looking.

To give you an idea of the expenses, we spent more than we expected we would. We brought just eighty dollars back with us, which means we spent three hundred dollars in England. This was just on hotels, meals, transportation, admission fees, slides and film, and souvenirs. We don't feel we wasted any; as you can see, we didn't spend much on souvenirs. We spent eight to ten dollars a night for hotels. We always followed those in a book Rick had of approved hotels. This always included breakfast. You probably will want to spend more on transportation and tours and other meals. We did a lot of walking and ate just a sandwich and/or soup for a cheap lunch sometimes. We also traveled a couple times during the night to save hotel bills.

Admission fees were never much, fourteen cents to thirty-five cents usually. Hope this gives you some ideas. The three hundred dollars does not include either of our transportation costs to and from England. If you have any questions please ask. You will like England. We would love to go back there. [Mom and Dad were thinking of traveling in Europe with us during the month of June 1965.]

Carole's June 26, 1964, journal entry:

Rick went to work as usual this morning but when he arrived at the post the alert was going on. He found out it had been called at 2:00 a.m., but we were not notified. Since it was not his fault he was not punished, although one sergeant would have liked to. [Someone from the base was supposed to have called me to report to post. An alert is a practice for getting ready on post for an attack from the Soviet Union. When the phone call was received I would drive to the base and get my rifle, then join the rest of the post's army men and wait for orders. This sergeant who was upset with me had the responsibility to make sure everyone was accountable. He reported that everyone was accountable. I showed up hours later and once I saw what was going on I went to the head office to notify them that I had not been called. The sergeant was mad at me because when he reported everyone was accountable, I made him a liar, according to him. This was soon forgotten and thereafter every month I received the monthly alert call.]

This afternoon Rick's unit was having a picnic, so there was no work. However, he had a few little things to take care of, so I went back with him to do some grocery shopping. Then we came back home.

About 4:30 we walked downtown and window shopped. I bought some more Hummel post cards and yarn to knit Rick's sweater.

Carole's June 27, 1964, journal entry:

Rick had KP today but surprised me by coming home about 2:00 p.m. He brought the mail with him, which included our slides of England. We looked at those and after he left at 3:30 p.m. (back to KP) I labeled them.

Rick said he wouldn't be home until 8:30 p.m. because they had to feed a baseball team at 7:00 p.m. However, the baseball team never showed up so he was home about 5:30 p.m.

Carole's June 28, 1964, journal entry:

We got up about 9:30 a.m. and had a soup and crackers lunch.

At 10:30 a.m. we left for Tubingen to see Hans. We got lost again in Stuttgart, but by accident found our way again. We stopped at Waldenbuch to see Babs, but she wasn't home. We arrived in Tubingen about 1:00 p.m. and again had difficulty finding our way, but it wasn't too bad. We found Hans in the hospital only because he heard us talking English in the hall.

We went to his room in town and visited awhile. Then we walked to a café near the river [Neckar River] and watched the boats while having a snack. For two dollars and fifty cents we had three strawberry cakes, two coffees, and one Coke [this was expensive compared to the States]!

Hans had to work 3:30 p.m. to 6:00 p.m. so we decided to wait for him and after 6:00 p.m. drive to his home to see the rest of the family. While Hans was working we walked around Tubingen --a park, the river, and around the town, trying to find the castle. We didn't ever get to the castle, but we did find the old town hall, which was a very unusual building.

At the Stein home we found Babs and Claus and his grandparents as well as Mr. and Mrs. Stein and Babs and Hans's youngest brother, Peter. We had a very nice visit there and a light supper.

Then we drove Hans back to Tubingen, and he gave us directions for a shorter way home. Wonder of wonders, we made it back without getting lost once! We were home about 11:00 p.m.

June 29, 1964, letter to Dad and Mom:

Just received your letter, Dad, and it was good hearing from you. We have been home for two weeks now and it's close to a "home." My new job and living off post greatly makes my life more enjoyable. I have waited a long time for this life, and it has finally arrived. We have had the VW for two weeks now, and it has 419 miles on it already. Tomorrow morning I will take it in for the suggested checkup. It sure is a fine car.

Yesterday we spent the day with the Steins, and they got us an excellent umbrella for only five dollars. They sell for ten dollars in town and probably fifteen dollars in the States. They can be reduced to fifteen inches long. Carole enjoyed them, and it was a fabulous day as they are so wonderful. Hans will be in Detroit in five weeks, August 6. He wants to see Davi Wilson.

Our slides came except the last roll. The last roll received appears that something went wrong with my camera because about twelve pictures are bad. I'm hoping that the roll not yet received will not be ruined. This last roll has slides of Queen Elizabeth. I should have one good picture of her.

Carole's July 3, 1964, journal entry:

We packed a picnic lunch of sandwiches, crackers, cookies, and lemonade and left for Nürnberg about 9:30 a.m. We went via Lorch, Schwabisse Gmund, Crailsheim, and Ansbach, taking pictures of the beautiful scenery along the way. We stopped along the way about 12:00 noon to eat our lunch.

We arrived in Nurnberg about 1:30 p.m. with amazingly little trouble—just a couple wrong turns where we quickly found our way again. In Nurnberg we eventually found the bahnhof. The U.S. Hotel was supposed to be right across from it, but we couldn't see it. However, we found an officer who pointed it out to us. The hotel was right across from the Bahnhof but didn't have much of a sign and was called the "U.S. Army Transient Billet." We walked over, checked in, and found we could park our car one block down. We did this and started touring the city on foot. We walked along the wall and then went inside. Just walking around, we found the St. Lawrence Church, the Church of Our Lady, Market Place, Gulden Fountain, the Holy Ghost Hospital over the river, and the castle, where we climbed to the top of the tower viewing the city. We also stopped in a couple of stores and bought a couple colorful hot pads for the table, some more silverware, and some postcards. There were also Hummels (which we didn't buy). Then we went back to the hotel where we ate more of our picnic lunch and then went walking some more.

Carole's July 4, 1964, journal entry:

We checked out about 10:00 a.m. and drove to Bamberg, getting to the base there about 11:00 a.m. We filled up on gas and ate lunch in the snack bar. Then we drove into the city, parked our car, and began walking. However, it took us quite a while to find anything of real interest. We found the old part of town in which there was a building with paintings covering both sides of it, the Dom, which is a big old church, and next to it the "Neue Residenz" in which there was a beautiful rose garden. On the way back, not far from here, we came across a coin shop, part of an antique shop. Naturally we went in—the proprietor was out but came back while we were there. Rick bought a 1914 five-mark silver-dollar-size coin for 12 marks (three dollars). Then later on we found a shop open that had Hummels. We bought the girl kissing her doll for 20.20 marks (a little over five dollars).

We got back to the car and drove back to the snack bar for a snack before heading home. We left there about 3:30 p.m. and arrived home about 8:00 p.m.

July 4, 1964, letter to Mom and Dad:

Happy Fourth of July! We just got back from Nurnberg and Bamberg. We have put eight hundred miles on the very nose of our VW. Not bad for nineteen days.

We arrived in Nurnberg yesterday afternoon and stayed overnight at the U.S. Hotel for four dollars and twenty cents. This morning we left Nurnberg to Bamberg and ate our meals at a U.S. Post. At 4:00 p.m. we headed back to Nurnberg, arriving at 5:30 p.m. We arrived at our home in Goppingen at 8:05 p.m. We had a picnic yesterday on the way. I took about fifty pictures because the scenery was just fabulous!

Carole's July 9, 1964, letter to Mom and Dad:

Right now I am in our car on the post. Had a little shopping to do so am using the rest of the afternoon for letters.

I still haven't gotten my license, but next Tuesday morning I will take the tests and if I pass it, I will have it then. Came to take it last Tuesday afternoon and found out they have moved it up to mornings.

The package with my clothes arrived this morning. Thanks a lot. We'll send you the money for postage for that and for the blankets. We had a really interesting time in Nurnberg and Bamberg last weekend. We really don't know too much about what we saw, can't read too much of this German. Ha. But we did manage to find out names by looking at postcards.

The scenery driving up there was beautiful, and we had a beautiful day. We stopped several times to take pictures. We had packed a picnic lunch to save money and stopped along a pretty parking spot beside the highway to eat it.

It took us four and a half hours to travel about one hundred and ten miles-one hundred and twenty miles, not counting those stops. You just can't make time driving over here as you can in the States for several reasons. Motorcyclists, bicyclists, hikers, oxcarts, and ancient tractors have as much right on the roads as cars do, and you run into them frequently. The roads in this area climb mountains and are full of curves, unmarked. They are no easy curves either that you can sail around at fifty or sixty mph. If curves are marked, there is no indication of their sharpness. We came across several hairpin turns going up and down the sides of these hills (almost mountains) with no warning whatsoever. Also on these hills, big trucks have a rough time making it up and you often get behind one; of course, even by yourself you don't go sailing up it. Then there are many small towns and villages that slow you up. So you can see you really have to be on "your toes" all of the time, plus keeping a lookout for signs.

We made it there without getting lost, although we made a couple of wrong turns but we found our way again quickly. Coming back we made a little better time; we're getting so we can drive these German roads pretty well!

On the way back we saw a stork in his nest on top of a chimney in a small village. First one we've seen. Then just the very next morning (Sunday) I heard our landlord, Hans, outside and looked out the window and there he was with a stork under his arm. I guess he lives in a swamp nearby and walked over here. He can't fly. Hans, our landlord, took him back home. So I guess you could say the stork paid us a visit! Ha ha.

I mentioned we took a picnic lunch to save money, also to save trying to read German menus. Saturday we ate at the post in Bamberg; filled up on gas there, too.

German food in restaurants and cafés is really expensive. At a recent date in Tubingen, we treated Hans to coffee and cake in a café. It cost two dollars and fifty cents for two coffees, one Coca-Cola soda pop, and three strawberry cakes.

Thanks very much for the ten dollars graduation gift. I decided I would like to put it toward an electric skillet. Sure would be nice for meats and other things. I think our stove has a mind of its own!

How would you like to go camping on our tour of Europe next year? We've just been talking with the fellow who had our apartment before us. He and his wife did it. A lot of the GIs do, I guess. He said they only spent two hundred dollars for their thirty-day tour, gas, food, and all. They had a 1964 Volkswagen too. There are many camping sites all over Europe and he said they are well equipped. They had a little camp stove that he has given us and they loaded up on groceries at army posts. Sounds great to us, saving money, how about you?

Another thing, Rick says they are shipping guys home thirty days before their ETS date which will mean if they continue it will be July 5 for Rick. I mention this because you said, Dad, you wanted to be here by June 15 (or something like that). It looks as though you'd better be here by June 1 or earlier depending on how much time you plan to spend. Guess I've run down for now. We plan to go to Ulm [Germany] and a castle this Saturday or Sunday.

July 10, 1964, letter to Mom and Dad:

I'm at work and waiting for lunchtime. I'm hungry, but I can wait. I finally got ahead with my work here, and for the rest of the month I will have lots of free time. The job that I now have is much better and less work. Everything is just fine now, except I'm ready to go back to the States with the army behind me.

We have seen a lot of Germany already since June 15th and have taken a lot of pictures. Tomorrow (Saturday), Carole and I will set out to Ulm and then further down south of Tubingen to the castle I was at last May with Hans Stein and his brother, Christoph, sister Babs, and her fiancé Claus Lahmann. I want Carole to see this castle also [we didn't drive to this castle for some reason].

Carole and I have enjoyed your letters, and we continue to look forward to receiving them.

Carole's Saturday July 11, 1964, journal entry:

After Rick came home at noon we drove to Robinson Barracks PX in Stuttgart for some shopping. Before we left for Ulm, we treated ourselves to a milkshake. This was the first time we didn't get lost in Stuttgart!

We arrived in Ulm about 3:00 p.m. after a detour taking us on the Autobahn! We easily found the cathedral and went straight to it. It's mammoth and beautiful. It was built over a period of five hundred and thirteen years, starting in 1377. It somehow escaped destruction during World War II. It had some damage though, but not much. We first climbed the 768 steps to the top of the steeple which is the tallest in the world—528 feet. The height you could actually climb to was 469 feet. Quite a climb! Of course, the stairs were circular, as all seem to be here in Europe! We could see quite a distance from the very top. After we descended the 768 steps we went inside the mammoth church and also bought slides, postcards, and a book.

We walked around Ulm a little after looking the cathedral over from the outside. We found a building with paintings all over its walls, a house that was about to fall into a canal it seemed and the Danube River. We ate our picnic lunch in the car before driving home. We arrived home about 8:00 p.m.

Just outside Ulm on the way there our VW reach one thousand miles!

Carole's July 15, 1964, letter to Mom and Dad:

Right now it's 7:30 a.m. and I'm on the post waiting until 10:00 a.m. so I can take my driver's test. I came yesterday morning to take it, only to find that it was postponed until this morning for some reason.

Rick is getting his three-day pass, so at 6:00 a.m. Friday morning we will be leaving for Berchtesgaden. It's in Germany but right on the Austrian border. It had an Armed Forces Recreation Center and Hitler's retreat is also located there. It's supposed to be beautiful scenery and no doubt, as it's situated in the Bavarian Alps, so we will be taking lots of pictures. There are several tours we plan to take advantage of, but we will tell you all about it afterward.

Don't remember if I have told you or not that I have started knitting Rick's sweater. Got the yarn a couple of weeks ago in Goppingen, but had to have my mother buy the right needles in the States and send it. It came last week and I have about six inches done so far. It's a cardigan with thin vertical stripes. Rick picked a dark green with red stripes.

I can't tell you much more about that church at Ulm. You have to see it to really know what I'm talking about and you will next year. It is huge and beautiful.

Sunday afternoon we drove to Heidenheim (approximately twenty-five miles from here) to see a castle. We were disappointed, however, because it wasn't much at all, mostly in ruins. Only thing we found really interesting were some reindeer in a huge pen.

Monday about 5:00 p.m. we saw something really interesting. Across from us to the left they are building a new house. That afternoon they got the roof up, the skeleton of it, I mean. While I was looking out our window for Rick, I heard some shouts from over there and looked to see a small tree or bush with gaily colored ribbons tied to it perched on top of that roof. There were three or four men up there too. One was pouring beer in another's glass and after he drank it, they gave three cheers. After the third time of this, he threw the glass into the house, smashing it. The tree is still up there and won't come down until the house is finished. Someone had told Rick about this custom before. Beginning this Friday, they're having a big clearance sale in all the PXs. Some of the prices are fantastic. Stereo record albums that we get for two dollars and thirty-five cents regularly are one dollars and twenty-five cents. Watches are one-third off. A Bulova men's watch regularly sixty-five dollars is twenty-nine dollars and ninety-five cents to begin with. There are many other good bargains too.

I wish we had the money to take advantage of some, but imagine there will be a similar sale in January. We won't be here Friday, but we may get to the one in Berchtesgaden.

Tonight Rick and I do our first entertaining. A couple of Rick's buddies are coming over for dinner. I was supposed to have it last night, but one of them had KP. I plan to have a roast beef dinner with apple pie for dessert. I was hoping it would be cooler today, but I can tell it's going to be another swelter. Yesterday the temperature was about 90 degrees and high humidity. Our little apartment doesn't get too bad though because we open both windows and get a breeze through the whole apartment. I think it's going to be even warmer today.

Carole's July 17, 1964, journal entry:

We got up about 5:00 a.m. to get an early start for Bertchesgaden, only to be held up at the post about an hour because Rick's pass was not there. We were finally on our way at 7:00 a.m. We stopped along the Alpine Highway to eat our lunch. About twelve o'clock noon we rolled into Bertchesgaden and found the accommodations office right away.

At 1:15 p.m. we left on the tour to Hitler's Eagles Nest. We were disappointed it was so misty but enjoyed it anyway.

After getting back from the tour we ate our supper in the car and then drove to our hotel (for U.S. Army and family) and walked around the shopping district.

Carole's July 18, 1964, postcard to Mom and Dad from Kehstein [mountain name] haus [house]:

This was our Friday afternoon tour. It's called Hitler's Eagles Nest. It was built as a birthday gift for him at the cost of ten million dollars (includes house, road, and elevator to get up there). Hitler was only up there five times. It was to be used as a retreat for diplomats and now it is a tea house or restaurant. The view shows you the building and the road up to it. The road only gets to four hundred and fifty feet of the summit; you go the rest of the way by elevator (two minutes!). The tunnel you see on the other side leads to this elevator. The elevator is a big one—room for sixteen people all sitting down on padded benches around the three sides.

Carole's July 18, 1964, journal entry:

We got up and went over to the accommodations office in time to get on the Jennerbaun tour. This took us to a cable car that carried us up on top of Jenner Mountain. The ride was thrilling, and we were glad the mistiness had cleared up a little bit.

This afternoon we took the cruise around Lake Konigsee. This was a beautiful cruise, the lake was very clear and green in color and mountains all around it. After the boat docked back at Konigsee, Rick thought we had time to look around. However, as we were we saw our busses pull out, but we ended up taking a train back for ten cents each!

Afterward we drove up to the General Walker Hotel to look around there. We saw some bombed-out barracks and the location of Hitler's house and the Gestapo headquarters.

Then we ate supper at our hotel—pizza for fifty cents!

Carole's July 19, 1964, postcard to Mom and Dad:

We rode the cable car that went up ten thousand and fifty feet to mountain peak.

Would you believe we rode up Jenner Mountain on this? Well, we did! Never thought I would ever get caught in one of those, but I really enjoyed it—we both did. This we took Saturday morning. The haze had cleared up a little more than Friday, and we had some tremendous views but could have been even more so. The top station was not on the highest point, so naturally we had to climb to the very top! There were several footpaths around this place. We did a little climbing on Kehlstein too, and of course took a lot of pictures! These trails don't have railings to keep you from falling down the side of the mountain, sometimes, though, there was a railing on the mountain side to hang onto, but I had no fears as I used to think I would.

Carole's July 19, 1964, journal entry:

We got up, ate our breakfast in the hotel and filled up on gas at the QM Station (for U.S. Army). We also took a few more pictures of mountain peaks we couldn't see before (due to the low cloud ceiling) and the Bavarian costumes of the people.

Then we drove to Bad Rechenhall to see a fairyland of wood carvings, but were unable to find them. So we drove on to Chiemsee. There we bought our lunch, looked around, and played a little miniature golf until it was time for the tour of Ludwig's Castle on Herren Island. The castle was gorgeous and unbelievable with all its gold and ornate details.

Then we left for home and stopped at a U.S. Army hotel for supper. As we were finishing, I thought I saw Jim Brazo walking in. He was a fellow student at my Niles, Michigan, high school. He saw me also and came over. I could hardly believe it was him. He is stationed in Munich, a truck driver for the U. S. Army. After talking with him for a while we headed for home arriving at 8:10 p.m.

Carole's July 20, 1964. postcards to Mom and Dad:

We stopped here at Chiemsee, another Armed Forces Recreation Center located there. We stopped on the way home to see one of King Ludwig II's castles. It was built on Herron Island in the middle of Lake Chiemsee, Germany's largest lake. However, he never finished it because of his death. Only twenty rooms were finished. It is a replica of the French's Versailles Palace. You just wouldn't believe how ornate and beautiful these rooms are. The view on the other side doesn't capture all the details and glitter of the gold. The chandelier on the left is of Meissen porcelain and is covered with delicately made flowers—just gorgeous. The middle is the hall of mirrors and the right the guest entrance. Every inch of space is used in these rooms—ceilings and walls are covered with paintings and the gold décor—drapes in the rooms were of heavy velvet with gold embroidery. The drapes for one window weighed two hundred pounds! It took two hundred women eight years to make theses drapes. You will have to see this place yourself to really know what I'm trying to describe.

July 20, 1964, letter to Mom:

Carole will write and tell you about the fabulous time we had. "Instead of climbing stairs, we climbed mountains," a quote from an American tourist named Carole Wilcox. You two just have to see Berchtesgaden and Ludwig's dream castle at Chiemese. The mountains are beautiful! Hotel cost for two nights (modern) four dollars and the food is very cheap. We saw car plates from all over Europe and even communist Czechoslovakia and Yugoslavia.

The oldest silver three pence I found in England's banks was 1874. The oldest penny was 1889 while the oldest farthing was 1860 (which had very little wear).

I would highly recommend flying over here for speed to start as soon as possible with us, close to June 1. I would also recommend taking a train to London, then a boat to New York.

Carole's July 21, 1964, letter to Mom and Dad:

Here it is our seven-month anniversary and Rick has KP all day long. Oh well!

Last evening we heard thunder and it looked like rain, but we never saw any. Supposed to have thundershowers tonight also, and I hope we do. We have a water shortage too, can't wash cars this week, a twenty-five mark fine if caught. We really had a wonderful time this last weekend. Berchtesgaden is a very pretty town. The Bavarian Alps are all around it, very pretty, and would have been even prettier for us if the air was clearer. Their houses in this Bavarian section are very pretty with their wood-carved decorations and always flowers. You have no doubt seen pictures of these typical houses.

The people were interesting here with their costumes. The men wore those leather shorts with knee socks or knee bands and hat. The women wore square-neck dresses with aprons. Some were plain, others fancy, and some in-between. We especially saw these costumes Sunday morning.

The Armed Forces Recreation Centers are really something. They have every kind of service imaginable, babysitting nurseries, every kind of sports facilities, tours, PX, QM [gas station], theater, everything we have on the post. All these things aren't right together, but scattered throughout the city or outside. There is an accommodations office that assigns you to a room in one of the hotels. Here also is a gift shop, snack bar, restrooms, and here the tours organize. They also have free bus-shuttle service to hotels, PX, and such for those without cars. The Germans gave these centers to the Armed Forces.

Berchtesgaden is a resort area for the Germans as well as the Americans, and I imagine this is true in the other places. The center at Chiemese is just a large hotel on the lake, but there are Germans everywhere else on the lake. Garmisch is the other center, and we plan to travel there sometime. They are all in the south here, only one to two hours from Munich.

We traveled the autobahn nearly all the way, but you know it's crazy. The autobahn ends just before Munich and picks up again outside the city. Meanwhile, you are given a nice "tour" of the city. Took us an hour or so to get through it, but we didn't get lost. We are catching onto their system over here.

The strangest thing happened to us while at Chiemsee. While we were eating in the hotel dining room, I saw three men walk in and one looked like Jim Brazo from my home church in Niles. I wasn't sure, mainly because I didn't think such a thing would be possible. But by golly, he saw me too and came over. He's stationed in Munich. He hopes to bring his girl over to marry her in November. Guess there's a lot of paperwork to it. He's going to try to get over to see us sometime. He's a real nice fellow, very active in our church. He is three years older than me. It's still hard to believe we met someone from my home church in Europe. You think of all the places you could have been at that time and you just happened to be in the same place at the same time. What a coincidence!

Our VW has sixteen hundred and forty miles on it now after putting on five hundred miles this weekend.

About the pigeons in Trafalgar Square (London), they are quite tame as you can tell. You had to be careful where you stepped. A man gave me some feed, and before I knew it I had pigeons on my arm and shoulders. He gave us both feed and took a couple pictures. This was his business and for a fee he sent us two copies each. These pigeons are trained to do this. Some we saw flew on children's heads!

Trafalgar Square had thousands of pigeons. As you walk through this area the pigeons clear your pathway. If you walk fast you probably would be kicking them.

July 25, 1964, letter to Mom and Dad:

I'm still at work and it looks like we are going to have a nice weekend. We won't do too much this time. Tomorrow we will go see the Steins and bring Claus, Hans, and Babs back for a hamburger dinner. Soon Hans will be in Michigan. He is looking forward to it. I'm also looking forward in seeing Michigan again.

It appears that my job won't require working during the nighttime. This is the best part of this job! My old section continues to get longer workdays.

Carole's July 26, 1964, journal entry:

We left about 9:30 a.m. for Waldenbuch (home of the Stein family) arriving there after 11:00 a.m. after being turned around a couple times in Stuttgart. Claus arrived the same time we did. Hans had worked during the night but came about 1:00 p.m. just as we were eating dinner with his family. After visiting a while, we brought Babs and Claus back to Goppingen with us. Hans had to sleep as he was working in the hospital that night too.

Carole's July 27, 1964, letter to Mom and Dad:

Right now I'm sitting in the car outside PSD (Rick's place of work) and it is 5:15 p.m. Rick has something they call CQ right now. He has to be on hand for phone calls and such between 12:00-1:00 p.m. and 5:00-6:00 p.m. Therefore, he has 11:00-12:00 noon and 4:00-5:00 p.m. off for meals. Between 4:00-5:00 p.m. we went to downtown Goppingen and bought your birthday gift, Dad, and a couple of Christmas gifts for Kay and Connie (Carole's sisters). There are sales going on all over downtown, just like home.

We have got our hot weather back with us again. Temperatures are in the nineties. Humidity was sixty-five percent at 8:00 a.m. this morning.

We had a real nice time yesterday (Sunday). We got to the Steins about 11:00 a.m. Everyone was there, but Hans came about 1:00 p.m. We had a very nice visit, and they had us eat dinner with them. It was very good, chicken, potatoes, noodles (homemade), gravy, cauliflower, and ice cream for dessert.

Hans needed to sleep that afternoon because he had worked the night shift and would again that night so we brought just Babs and Claus back to Goppingen with us.

Claus brought his slide projector so we could all see our slides. This is the first time we have seen any of our slides from a projector. We showed our England trip and Berchtesgaden and our wedding slides. It was really fun to see them.

They had supper here with us. I fixed hamburgers, potato salad, ice tea, and "snickerdoodles" (cookies) for dessert. Had everything prepared ahead of time, only had to fry the hamburger patties. They really enjoyed it, I think. It was the very first time Claus had hamburgers. He really liked them and he also really liked the "snickerdoodles." They are Rick's favorite too.

Next weekend is Hans's last one here [he was going to Michigan] so we will get together with him then. He is calling us Friday and we will make plans then.

Guess I forgot to mention how our other dinner party went. Well, things didn't go according to plans that day. I couldn't get the roast beef Wednesday morning because the store was closed, then I couldn't arrange to get it that afternoon, so we had macaroni and cheese in place of the beef. They seemed to enjoy the meal, I guess. They liked the apple pie. I know we had a good time visiting. Some day we will have them over again and maybe things will go according to plan.

Just been hearing on the radio about the World War II bomb they have uncovered in Victoria Street in London. Isn't that something? We were on Victoria Street several times and probably walked right by it! It's really different hearing about something like this when you have been to that particular spot. It means more to you or something. It's hard to explain what I mean.

Carole's July 31, 1964, journal entry:

I went back to work with Rick in the afternoon. On the way we had our first accident—a minor one. As we were turning onto Hohnestaufen Strasse [street], a woman on her bicycle was coming from the opposite direction in her lane on Rick's left. We were in our lane traveling the opposite of her and it appears that she intentionally turned her bicycle to cross the center and aimed it at our car. Rick couldn't speed up due to a beer truck parked in the lane in front of us and she didn't make any attempts to steer her bike back into her lane. She rode her bike directly into the back driver side of our car. She fell, and it appeared that she was OK. She was not hurt seriously, nor was her bicycle damaged. She had scratches on her glasses. We had two small dents in the driver's back side and the hubcap. It took us nearly the whole afternoon to get things settled with the army's MPs and German police. I told my story to a German interpreter to record what had happened for a German police report. I made it clear that the woman on the bicycle crossed the center line into our lane and didn't make any attempts to prevent driving her bicycle into our car. It should be noted that our license plate identified us as Americans. A few weeks later I was called in to the post's commanding officer. He read what the German police had recorded for my statement concerning this accident. I was shocked! The document stated that I crossed the street line and I thought I could pass her, but I didn't. They made it out to be my fault, and the woman claimed her bicycle, watch, and glasses were damaged, and that she had medical expenses. I told the officer that I didn't say what they wrote. I never heard any more about it. My car insurance company paid the claim.

When I arrived in Goppingen, it was mentioned during our briefing that if we drove in Europe, any accident we were involved in would always be our fault due to the fact that we were Americans in their country. If we ran over a chicken, the cost was not a replacement chicken but the value of all the estimated eggs this chicken would lay.

Carole's August 3, 1964, letter to Mom and Dad:

Several times in our travels, Rick and I have thought whoever would even dream last summer that one year from then we would be driving a VW around Germany. This certainly is a tremendous experience, and I am so thankful we have had the opportunity. Living here outside of your own country and living so near many other countries, you gain a completely different perspective of everything.

We had a really wonderful time yesterday with Hans, Babs, and Claus. Hans came to our place early Sunday afternoon and we spent the time "gabbing." I fixed him a hamburger dinner, and after more gabbing we took him home to Waldenbuch. Babs and Claus were there. We stayed a while and had fun joking around, watching TV, and listening to records. We hate to see Hans leave, but we will still have fun with Babs and Claus. The Stein home is really lovely.

Babs and Claus surprised us by giving us a gift. It is a tablecloth, very pale yellow with loose weave checked design. It's very pretty, and I really like it. They said they did it because we had done so much for them. Well, we feel it's just the opposite. All we have done is get them a few things on the post that they can't get or is much more expensive for them.

Carole's August 12, 1964, letter to Mom and Dad:

Well, Rick and I had quite a weekend this time. It was jam-packed with events, and even though the weather was miserable we had a good time. It rained off and on from Friday afternoon until Monday night. Instead of a Friday-Sunday weekend we took a Saturday-Monday pass. The thought of Monday and work was too depressing for Rick, and as it turned out, it was better for traveling. We missed the busy Sunday-night traffic.

We got up and left about 3:00 a.m. Saturday for Berchtesgaden, where we took the Salzburg tour. Then we left Berchtesgaden about 1:00 p.m. after eating lunch and drove to Garmisch via a route through Austria. What a trip that was. It was one hundred and thirty-five miles and it took us five and a half hours to drive it. That's an average of twenty-four and half mph. Great, huh? This road through Austria is marked on the maps as one of the best roads. It doesn't begin to compare with Germany's similarly marked roads, which don't begin to compare with our U.S. highways. It was a narrow, rough, barely two-lane road full of the curves you find everywhere. There's no such thing as a straight road over here. In some places in the towns the road was too narrow for two VWs to pass, and that's pretty narrow! You find things like this in Germany, but not like we did in Austria. You can't imagine what these roads are like, but you will find out for yourselves next year. [During our months in Germany we encountered situations in which there was only a one-and-a-half lane road for both directions of driving. These were in old, small towns. When an oncoming car was coming at you, one of the cars would have to use the sidewalk to avoid the other oncoming car. Other than the autobahn (freeway), Carole is correct that there were no straight roads.]

In one place there was an accident that tied up traffic, but it was nothing compared to what we ran into later on. Just outside of Innsbruck, Austria, we started up a mountain road and had to stop because cars ahead of us were all stopped. Well, we waited and waited, crept ahead a few feet and waited some more. We weren't moving for ten to fifteen minutes sometimes, and no shorter than five minutes. The road was full of curves so you couldn't see anything far ahead. Well, it took us one hour to go about four miles this way. We finally got to the cause of this pileup, and it was just a simple intersection and too many cars. No traffic lights, just a yield sign right of way for the other road. There were police directing traffic. Cars were lined up as far on this other road as we were. I bet there were five miles or more of cars bumper –to bumper on both roads. What a time!

We were going to Garmisch knowing that all the hotels were booked up, but we hoped to get a cancellation. Well, we were thirty-fifth on the waiting list and he only got about halfway through the list, so we spent the night in our VW. We had brought blankets and pillows in case this happened. We parked in one of the hotel lots so we could use their bathrooms and such. I had the back seat and Rick the front. Needless to say, there isn't much room to stretch out, but we were so exhausted from so much driving we slept very well. [We were so thankful that we had a blanket because it was cold during the night. Parked next to us were four American Armed Forces men in an American Chevrolet car. They sat up all night. I don't believe they had blankets.]

We got to the billeting office (where you get hotel assignments) by 8:00 a.m. so we could be first on the waiting list, but we were able to get a room right away for the night. We were relieved!

Church was at 9:00 a.m., so we walked around window-shopping a little before then. As we were walking back to the car, we saw a band and a few women dressed in their festive Bavarian costumes come from the bahnhof (railroad station).They got into formation and marched down the street playing. They no sooner left than another group came. Later on in the day we found out that this was the beginning of a festival week in Garmisch. They had a big parade at 1:30 p.m., but we were on the tour then. This is probably part of the reason there were so many cars heading toward Garmisch where we had that tie-up. However, I think the biggest reason is that this is vacation month here. Nearly all of France is on the roads and other countries as well. We saw cars from nearly every country, all those we saw last time plus a couple more, Turkey, and an "II" that may be Israel, I don't really know. In a parking lot in Salzburg we actually saw a Ford Falcon with an El Salvador license. By the way, what we thought was Czechoslovakia (CH code) was actually Switzerland. [The official name for Switzerland is Confoederatio Helvetica (CH is the European code for Switzerland). This name is shown on their stamps and money.]

The little chapel in Garmisch (for Americans) was really nice, and the service was inspiring.

Besides taking us to Linderhof Castle, the tour that afternoon took us to Oberammergau, which is famous for its Passion Play and woodcarvers. We were given a tour through the Passion Play theater, which was quite interesting. The story of the play is that in 1633 the village of six hundred was hit hard with the plague brought by Swedish troops. Two hundred died in two days. The villagers prayed to God and promised that from then on they would present the Passion and Death of Christ every ten years if they were spared. No one else did die, and they have kept their promise. Those participating in the play have to be born in Oberammergau or have lived there over twenty-five years. Also, all the costumes have to be woven and made by Oberammergau women. The next performance is in 1970.

There are now five thousand people in Oberammergau and nearly fifty percent of them are woodcarvers. Needless to say, there are numerous woodcarver shops in this town. We visited one and window shopped at several others. Most of their work is of a religious nature. We would love to get a statue of Christ but will have to save some money first. We did buy a wooden fork and spoon, though.

Then we also stopped at a monastery in Ettal. We only went inside the church, which was very interesting. There were magnificent paintings on the ceilings. There were also remains of early Christians brought there from catacombs in Rome.

Also in Oberammergau, we went by the Hansel and Gretel Orphanage and its little Red Riding Hood School. The two buildings had paintings of these stories on the outside. These paintings on the outside of buildings are nothing unusual in this area. You find them everywhere, as you will see. It's really an attraction.

Sunday evening we went to the Cosa Carioca. This is somewhat of a nightclub with an ice show. We had no advance reservations, but got one of the best tables in the house. We couldn't find our table by ourselves, and we were surprised when our guide took us across the floor to it. We had been told they have a floor for dancing that moves away, revealing the ice below it. Well, we wondered what would happen to us when this happened. Our guide told us, and sure enough we rolled all the way over to the other side with the floor! Intermission time included dancing, which gave us another ride back and forth. We have been on all kinds of transportation now! The ice show was really great. We were tired, but we really enjoyed it.

This is all part of the recreation center, because it was all in English but German too. In fact, we had a nice German couple sitting at our table with us. He could speak a little English and was a railroad stationmaster in Munich.

Monday's tour was a really long one. The bus picked us up at our hotel at 9:00 a.m. and dropped us off at 4:45 p.m.

Before the Neuschwanstein Castle we stopped at the Wies Church, which is quite famous and the most perfect edifice in rococo style in Germany. Rococo means excessively curved and very fancy or overly decorated. It really was something, a lot of white and gold and marble.

Then we went to the castle, and after that we drove through a bit of Austria, Austria's Alpine region of Tyrol. Rick and I drove through parts of these ourselves as well as on this tour. It's really gorgeous country, magnificent mountains and the most luscious velvety green grass you have ever seen, speckled with the dark forest green of trees and bushes and dark wooden storage huts of the farmers.

The highest mountain in Germany is right next to Garmisch. It's called the Zugspitz and during the night it snowed up there! It's over ten thousand feet. You can go up to the summit via cog train and cable car, but we didn't have the time nor the money to do it. But someday we would like to do it.

In coming back home we had to go through a little corner of Austria again, so we have been in and out of Austria four times already.

King Ludwig II (of Bavaria) built the three castles we have seen. He was a very romantic and eccentric king. He didn't build these castles to receive guests, but only for himself. He liked to be off in his own little dream world. He was the best-loved king of Bavaria.

Carole's four postcards to Mom and Dad:

Postcard number 1 (Salzburg, Austria): This was part of the tour we went on Saturday from Berchtesgaden. We were a little disappointed in it because we felt like we really didn't see too much and nothing was very pretty or outstanding. The most interesting place we saw was the catacombs where the early Christians worshiped in secret. They were hewn out of the side of the mountain. You see the medieval fortress on the other side. They date back to the third century. Another interesting place was Mozart's birthplace, which is now a museum. It is just a three room apartment on the third floor of a building. It had violins and pianos that he used as well as his personal objects, manuscripts, and letters of his.

We went up to the medieval fortress but didn't go in.

The left bottom picture (front of postcard) shows the cathedral, which has room for ten thousand people. It has one of the largest organs in Europe with seven thousand pipes. We heard it being played. Mozart was baptized here in 1756.

The right bottom corner picture shows the Neugebaude (New Palace), which was built about 1600 as a guesthouse for visiting sovereigns. We only saw it from the outside, but we heard the chimes in the belfry. They played some of Mozart's melodies.

Postcard number two (Konigssee, Germany's prettiest lake): This was a beautiful cruise we took Saturday afternoon. Konigssee Lake is seven miles long and one mile wide at the widest point. Mountains spring up nearly all the way around it, as you see here. The water did not look blue at all as it does on this card, but it was a very clear, cool green, very pretty and very tempting to jump in! The boat stopped about midway and the captain played his bugle so we could hear the echo, which was very clear.

Postcard number three (Linderhof Castle in Germany): This was our Sunday afternoon tour 1:00-6:00 p.m. The Linderhof Castle is one of King Ludwig II's (the same as Chiemese). He lived here for eight years, and it is the only one completely finished (he built three). It is small but beautiful. Again, there were lots of gold and paintings.

There were several beautiful gardens around it and from the statuary you see in the pond water sprays, shooting up one hundred and twenty-eight feet. They turn it on only at certain times.

On the castle grounds (eighty-six acres) he also built a grotto, which is an artificial cave. You can see the inside of it in the lower-left corner. He built it as a private concert hall to hear Wagner's music. The painting is a scene from one of his operas. Ludwig II would sit in the rowboat you see (a little fancy!) and row around this artificial lake. The peacocks you see are in a Moorish Kiosk (teahouse) which is also on the castle grounds. He purchased this at the Paris Exhibition of 1867 and transported it to his castle. It's a beautiful thing, as you can tell.

Postcard number four (Neuschwanstein Castle): This was Monday's tour 9:30 -4:00 p.m.

This Neuschwanstein Castle is the third one of King Ludwig II and is not completely finished because of his death. If this looks a little familiar to you it's because Walt Disney built a replica of it in Disneyland. The inside of this castle is completely different than the other two. It has more of an Oriental flavor to it. There was very little gold décor but lots of paintings and a lot of woodcarvings, woodwork, walls, ceilings, furniture, and statues. They were done by the woodcarvers of Oberammergau. His bed has a lot of intricate carvings on the top, which took fifteen woodcarvers five years to complete. There was a huge gilded brass chandelier in the throne room that weighed about one thousand pounds and had one hundred candles on it.

The surrounding countryside is really beautiful here. The castle is located on the side of a mountain and it's a twenty-minute walk to get up to it. We do more climbing!

Carole's August 15, 1964, journal entry:

Rick was off at 10:00 a.m. We stayed home the rest of the day except for shopping. However, in the early afternoon the driver's side window of our VW broke from heat and pressure. It took a while to clean that mess up.

Babs [Stein] came about 3:30 p.m. to get gas and coffee. She ended up buying a few more things at the commissary also. We had her stay for a hamburger, and then she had to leave.

August 22, 1964 Carole wrote to Mom and Dad:

If this letter is a little incoherent, don't worry, there's nothing wrong. I'm just baking cookies and writing this between putting them in and out of the oven.

Rick has KP today and also on Tuesday. They figure out weekdays and weekends separately, weekdays every two weeks and weekends about every two months. He was supposed to have it tomorrow, but since we wanted to go to Heidelberg he was able to switch with someone else.

I walked to the post and back this morning to get bread and luncheon meat for sandwiches to take tomorrow. It's about a five- to six-mile walk and I'm worn out! I don't know how we ever did it in England.

It's threatening to rain, has been cloudy all day. I hope it's not like this tomorrow. We probably won't go if it is. We have had rain every day this week, two days it rained the whole day long.

I will finish this after our trip.

It's now Tuesday and I'm on the patio enjoying the beautiful day we have. It's getting rather warm in this sun, though.

Rick was lucky today. He has KP as I said, and they also called the alert this morning. KPers don't participate and it means one less morning he doesn't have to get up early. Three out of the last four days he's gotten up about 4:00 or 5:00 a.m.

There isn't much more to tell about our trip to Heidelberg except there sure were a lot of people there. We also went to a nearby town and saw a beautiful palace garden. It was huge with a lot of flowers, trees, shrubs, paths, ponds, and stream with ducks and swans. There were lots of people there too.

This morning I scrubbed and waxed our floors, which is a job with those army boot scuffs.

Yesterday afternoon I did the laundry. After supper Rick and I both washed and polished the VW. It really was dirty. So I guess we are pretty well all cleaned up.

Carole's postcard from Heidelberg, Germany:

We had a beautiful sunny day Sunday and had a lovely trip here. This section [postcard picture] was all we saw of Heidelberg—the city is much larger. The bridge seems to be historic—originally built in 1799, we think. It includes the two-towered structure you see on the end of it. The castle on the hill is partially in ruins. It looked to us as if it would have been war damage rather than just time and deterioration. It was rather interesting to walk around it. We didn't go inside, didn't see a place where you could enter. The river is the Neckar River, which also flows through Stuttgart and Tubingen.

Carole's August 23, 1964, journal entry:

We drove the scenic route along the Neckar River to Heidelberg. We stopped at Eberback to take some pictures. At Heidelberg we just explored the bridge and castle and some of the old town. Then we went to see the "Schossgarten" at Schwetzingen. It was a huge area and we walked around most of it, taking pictures.
    We saved an hour and half by coming home via the autobahn (freeway).

Carole's August 30, 1964, journal entry:

After going to church and lunch we drove to Ludwigsburg to see the castle. We did not see the inside of the palace but walked around the beautiful gardens around it. We saw many different kinds of flowers and brightly colored arrangements, flamingoes, kangaroos, and other kinds of birds.

Carole's September 3, 1964, journal entry:

At 8:00 I went to the dentist to have my teeth checked and x-rayed; no cavities.
    At 10:00 a.m. I went to see about the job. Found out it was secretary to the field entertainment director, Claudia Horton--typing, filing, monthly reports, and even painting scenery and such. I have the job if okayed by headquarters in Stuttgart. [Carole did get a part-time job starting in September 1964 on the army base, working for Claudia Horton. The building she worked in was just a Quonset hut without any heat. Carole would have to wear sweaters, coat, and gloves during her winter job activities. During one occasion she had problems with her toes. She went to the doctor, and he said she had the next thing to frostbite.]

Carole's September 3, 1964, letter to Mom and Dad:

I started job hunting Tuesday without much success. There are only a few jobs open to dependents on post here, but luck was with me, and I have a job. I will be a part-time secretary to the field entertainment director, who is a woman. The job sounds very interesting, and she and the PFC who also works there seem very nice. I will work twenty hours a week (mornings) for two hundred and fifty-three DM a month (about sixty-three dollars). [Germany's official name is "Deutschland" and their currency is the "mark." DM stands for Deutschland mark. The English-language names of the countries in Europe are not their official names; for example, Austria's official name is Osterreich, Holland is the Netherlands, Spain is España, France is Republique Française.]
    I will type reports, file papers, and other office-type work, plus paint scenery props and other kinds of backstage work for plays. Everything seemed to work right in because I have had a little theatrical experience (college and high school) and I know a little about financial statements because of my semester of accounting and my accountant husband. She seemed very pleased about these things. I spent about an hour and a half filling out the necessary forms, and these will be sent to Stuttgart for approval. If they are approved then I will have the job and start next week. This is more of a formality than anything, so I should be all set. Oh yes, there are also chances for raises at the end of the first and second months. I will have a brand new typewriter and a new desk. It really sounds like a nice job.
    Rick and I were really relieved because we were quite discouraged in my earlier efforts. Every place was filled and had a waiting list. This was the last possibility we had. We will use the money I make for our European trip with you and start repaying you for the car.
    Monday, Labor Day, we are going to Stuttgart, the PX at Robinson Barracks and downtown Stuttgart. The fact that our PXs are open on American holidays shows you how many Germans are

involved. They close on German holidays. The PX in Stuttgart is even opening two hours earlier than usual on Monday!

We paid our electricity for the first time and it's only about eight dollars for the two months, July and August. They bill only every two months here.

I haven't had any signs of hay fever so far. It surprises me because it seems like they would have pollen as much as we. I must be allergic to just a certain kind that doesn't exist over here.

I got my hair cut the other day and they sure don't do a professional job like in the States. German girls run the post beauty shop. Rick has the same complaints about his German barbers

I now have four different kinds of money in my purse; German, American, English, and Swiss. I always have the first three since I saved an English penny to carry with me. Now I have the Swiss money for our trip in a couple of weeks.

Carole's September 9, 1964, letter to Mom and Dad:

I have my job for positive sure and I start tomorrow. I just got the call this afternoon.

Rick has KP tomorrow so that means I will have to get up with him at 4:00 a.m. to take him to work so I can have the car, ugh. Oh well, I shouldn't complain because I can come back to bed and Rick can't!

We had an enjoyable but not too eventful Labor Day weekend. Rick had to work Saturday morning, then all day Sunday and Monday it rained. We would have gone somewhere Sunday if it was nice. We just took it easy around here and played a game Rick invented for entertainment. Monday we went to Stuttgart in spite of the rain. We bought some things for ourselves and got some Christmas shopping done, won't say what or for whom!

At the PX we bought a Scrabble game, a record album, and a Swiss chalet music box. It's also typical of the Bavarian houses and very pretty. On the economy, we found a wooden slide container to put our slides in. It holds two hundred but we found we could easily get two in the slot for one, and got four hundred of our five hundred and fifty slides in it. We want to get a couple more of them for the rest of the slides we will be getting. Some sunny day we will go back and take pictures of the city. They have a beautiful park with gardens and fountains.

I really enjoyed my German class last night and am already looking forward to the next one. We meet Tuesday and Thursday, 6:30-8:30 p.m. for five weeks, twenty hours.

We played two games of Scrabble already and each of us has won one game.

We got a postcard from Babs and Claus in Yugoslavia and they are having a good time.

Also received a postcard from Hans at Beaver Island, Michigan (Davi Wilson's parents have a house on Beaver Island and they live there during most of the summer).

We have a beautiful day today, sunny but not too cool or too hot. Yesterday I really enjoyed myself at the PWOC Tea (Protestant Women of the Chapel). This PWOC meets once a month. It seems to be very similar to our Methodist WSCS. I think I will enjoy it very much. One young woman I met was a German girl who married an officer two months ago. She speaks English quite well, but sometimes I have a hard time understanding some words or a long speech. She was very nice and seemed a lot of fun. I met another young woman about my age that has a one-and-a-half-year-old daughter and does a lot of sewing.

Carole's September 9, 1964, letter to Mom and Dad:

While Rick is writing to Elmer Schroeder, I'll add my bit to his letter to you.

I have worked three mornings now and enjoy it. My main task now is setting up a filing system. It's not hard, just a lot of work, but I don't mind it. This week we will also start building scenery for some plays. I will be working pretty much on my own, at least I have been so far. Garry, the PFC who also works there, doesn't come until 11:00 a.m. Claudia, my boss, usually comes in at 9:00 a.m., but she is away from Goppingen a lot. She was at a conference in Frankfurt last Thursday and Friday and was in just for a couple minutes this morning on her way to a meeting. Tuesday and Wednesday she is taking off, so it will be Thursday before I see her again.

On Sunday Rick and I went to Stuttgart to take pictures. It was a beautiful, warm, sunny day. The city has quite a park there, unlike any I have ever seen. Lots of people were there too. [This park is very large and has greenery, gardens, and fountains of water. It's very interesting and I believe one of the few buildings is the opera house. There are a lot of benches, and it is separated by Koenigstrasse (King Street). The two sides are connected by a walk bridge over Koenigstrasse. The park is very close to Stuttgart's train station.] Then we went to the "Fernsehturm." Now I suppose you are wondering what that is! Well, it's Stuttgart's modern landmark, a huge TV tower. It's very similar to the Space Needle in Seattle. It has a restaurant and platform for viewing on top. We didn't go into the restaurant but did go up to the platform and took some pictures (cost us seventy-five cents for both of us). You could see for miles around at the top.

Saturday late afternoon we washed our VW. While doing so, Paula, the landlady, gave us a beautiful bouquet of flowers from their garden. They really love flowers over here and we do too, more than ever now. Everyone has a garden and you are always seeing people on the streets with a bouquet of flowers in their hand that they bought from someplace.

Saturday morning they delivered the winter supply of coal for our house, including us. You should have seen Paula. She was coal black from head to foot. It's hard to believe what she did because you would never see it in the States. The first half of the load was small chunks of coal that they put down a chute into the basement. She was black from that, but I don't know what she did. The last half of the coal was in the shape of bricks. The men carried these in their bags in the front door and down the stairs (next to the front door) and dumped them in the basement.

Paula stacked these bricks of coal neatly in their places. She also, of course, had to clean up all the mess. Our share of this coal is twenty bags of the brick coal. Don't know the cost yet. Shouldn't be much, from what our landlord said before. [Our pot stove for heat could only hold two bricks of coal.]

September 17, 1964, letter to Mom and Dad:

Decided I would write a few lines. We have enjoyed your letters, and I must confess I am always looking for a letter from home each noontime, so keep up your good writing habits.

I was disappointed to hear that for the third straight time my pass for Switzerland was revoked. Our company will go into a state of alertness next week, and they cancelled all leaves and passes for the next two weekends. I will try again on October 3rd.

A few weekends ago we went to Ludwigsburg [Germany] and on the edge of the city there was the typical detour. We followed the detour signs, and we ended up at the very starting point where we had started eight minutes prior. That was the extreme case of our driving.

I'm so glad you finally got to see Hans! [Hans was in the Ferndale area visiting Davi Wilson. He wanted to continue his schooling in the States and transfer as many credits as he could from Tubingen University.] We have only received one postcard from him so far. We certainly respect him and our hope is that he is successful in his ambitions and endeavors.

We just received a call from Babs. Babs and Claus are back from Yugoslavia and they had a really good time. They will be here this coming Saturday. It will be good seeing them again.

September 22, 1964, letter to Mom and Dad:

Dad, I was thinking about you in that you are in the last school year of your career. I bet it doesn't seem possible that you have reached that stepping stone [retirement]. You have seen a lot and learned a lot, and you can be proud of what you have done in Ferndale. Your successor to your job will find the shoes too big for him or her and will have a rough time keeping up with the superior standards you have set. You have also done a lot for me in improving my life and I will always be grateful for this. The same goes for you also, Mother. There are quite a number of youth who have not been very fortunate in having as fine parents as you two.

Carole's September 23, 1964, letter to Mom and Dad:

I will start a letter to you while Rick is figuring out his next Scrabble moves, so this will be sort of "hodgepodge" and hope I don't repeat anything Rick has already written or I have.

Still enjoy my job. Can't do any more work on the filing until I get more manila folders, but I have been doing quite a bit of typing, reports, and letters. This morning I helped Claudia tear off the upholstery of an old chair she is redoing for a play. I will probably be helping more on that.

We have just one problem at work, no heat. We call several times a day and they promise to turn on the heat, but we sure haven't felt any. Maybe someday!

Summer has left us. Temperatures this last week have been in the low forties at night and fifties or sixties during the day. Tonight it's supposed to be between thirty and forty, but every afternoon I make some excuse to turn the oven on. I close the door and it gets the kitchen nice and cozy. We don't want to use our coal until we have to, but if this keeps up we will reach that point soon. Our coal supply for the winter cost us only thirty-one dollars.

The other day I bought a pair of those big fluffy slippers like you have, Mom, the same color too, if I remember right—orchid. They were only two dollars and fifty cents. I sure do like them because they keep my feet warm.

Babs and Claus came over Saturday, and we had a good time. We got them gas and coffee, then talked them into staying for supper. I fixed wieners with cheese, Campbell's pork and beans, applesauce, and baked a lemon meringue pie. They seemed to really enjoy it. It was Claus's first for the wieners, beans, and pie. Even Rick said it was my best pie. It was the first time I made the pie crust from scratch (used mixes before). I used the Spry recipe and we like it much better.

Babs brought us some beautiful pale pink roses from their garden.

Rick slaughtered me [Scrabble game], so now we are going to bed.

It's Friday evening now and we have had our weekly bath.

On Sunday, October 4th, Babs and Claus have invited us over for dinner and to go with them to the "Folkfest" [English spelling] in Stuttgart. She said it is Germany's equivalent to our state fair. It should be fun.

Today and yesterday it has been a little warmer and this is good. Also good, we finally got some heat at work today. They found they had to turn on something outside the hut. I also got my manila folders yesterday so things are coming along. Working half days now really makes the weeks fly by. I didn't really realize how slow time was going by for me before this. I find it really keeps me busy with housework, my German class, letters and such, but I like it so much better this way.

Sunday, weather permitting, we may take a drive into the Black Forest. I hope we can.

We got a postcard from Hans today from Ann Arbor. He said he had a wonderful time with you two.

Carole's October 3, 1964, journal entry:

For some strange, unknown reason Rick had the whole day off. In the morning I made cookies only to discover the bottom part wasn't heating. I tried to bake them anyway even though it was awfully slow and they still weren't completely done.

About noon we left for Robinson Barracks and downtown Stuttgart before meeting Babs and Claus at the Stein's house in Waldenbuch at 3:00 p.m. Bought Christmas cards at Robinson Barracks although we went there to buy boots (they didn't have any size in the style I wanted). In Stuttgart we bought two more hankies and a pair of gloves for myself to wear with my winter coat.

We arrived at Waldenbuch just at 3:00. We visited with Babs and Claus and had "kuchen und kaffee" (cookies and coffee).

Then we left for the Volksfest in Stuttgart. After the fest we stopped in at Claus's house and tried a little Yugoslavian wine, which tasted perfectly terrible! We also saw a few slides of Babs and Claus.

Carole's October 5, 1964, letter to Mom and Dad:

We really had fun at the Folkfest Saturday night with Babs and Claus. There were all kinds of rides just like in the States, but we didn't go on any. There were many shooting galleries for prizes and lots of lotteries. We all tried just one and Rick pulled a good one although it was the smallest prize, a plastic funnel. There were many booths that offered something to eat, of course. We had French fries at one, a kind of candy-coated almonds, which was good, and bratwurst with Pepsi. Bratwurst (very popular in Germany) is quite good, about twenty-five to thirty cents. There were also many kinds of sideshows, but we didn't go into any. The "beer tents" were the biggest and about the only difference from our fairs. These were not actually tents, but permanent buildings, like a big tent. Each brewery had its own "tent" with its own band. We walked in one just to see what they were like. There wasn't an empty seat and the room was filled with smoke and noise, band playing and people talking and laughing. The only other thing we spent our money on was on silhouettes of ourselves.

There was a man who cut out your silhouette in just a couple minutes, and they are very good. It was amazing. Rick and I had ours done together, and Babs and Claus had theirs done together.

There were thousands and thousands of people there, so many you could hardly walk around but somehow everyone managed.

Sunday was overcast again so we didn't make it to the Black Forest again. The Switzerland trip still looks "go" for next weekend. I hope it's a good weekend.

We got a nice long letter from Hans last Friday.

This will be my last week of German classes. Hate to see it end, but in other ways it will be nice to be home those nights for knitting or writing letters or reading. I seem to be behind on all of them.

In the PX (ours) today, I saw boots just like those at Stuttgart and they had my size, so I got them.

October 9, 1964, letter to Mom and Dad:

Dad, I think we have to remember that there is a lot to see here, and we can see a lot of it. I don't want to spend all of the time out in the road either, but I don't want to spend a lot of time seeing the same thing over and over again. I want to see Europe, not concentrate on seeing every little thing in a few cities. There is a lot to see outside of the cities. This [European] circle I mentioned in a previous letter, we can do it without feeling rushed! It has been my experience that after I see something, I'm very restless to continue on in seeing something else. Remember, Dad, Western Europe is only two-thirds of the size of mainland United States. I hope it is understood that we are forced to start on June 2nd and because there is so much to see and probably the only opportunity we will ever have, we want to start immediately with our plans without any backtracking. Dad, I wish we could hold up until the middle of June for our leave, but I think you can see why this is impossible. According to U.S. Army regulations, I'm not allowed to take a leave thirty days prior to my rotation date [back to the States for separation], but so far they haven't paid any attention to it. You will have to give us more specific plans so that we can plan accordingly.

Dad was scheduled to retire from his education position in mid-June. The school district was scheduling a retirement ceremony to honor Dad. Dad's boss wanted him to complete the semester. Dad finally told his boss that this was a trip of a lifetime, and he was planning to take advantage of it. He reminded his boss that he had a large number of sick days that he had never taken. He would use some of these days. His boss finally gave Dad the okay, and his retirement party was then scheduled around May 18. Dad had already trained his replacement.

Driving in Germany

When we lived in Germany the autobahn (freeways) didn't have a speed limit. The best our little VW could travel was only around sixty-five mph. It seemed like all of the Mercedes cars on the autobahn would pass us at great speed. Our VW had a U.S. license plate. Once when we were on the autobahn a Mercedes with four men dressed in suits and ties came up fast and then slowed to our speed; for several seconds they were at our side, laughing and smiling at us, then the driver stepped on it and took off. We discovered early that cars would pass a car by driving between the oncoming car and the car being passed. This happened even on curves! After seeing this numerous times, we started doing it. The first time it was a little scary! The oncoming car would move to the right of their lane and the car being passed would move to their right and our car would pass between them.

During my youth I had two strong feelings that a specific thing was going to happen. I was at Ferndale's Roosevelt Park. I was running across the field, and to my left were the outfielders of a baseball game. I was a long distance from home plate. This feeling came over me that a baseball would hit me. As I was running I turned my head toward home plate and the batter wasn't swinging. I kept on running, and then a baseball slammed the top of my left shoulder after taking one or two bounces. It didn't hurt, but it surprised me. The other one was while I was watching a Detroit Tigers baseball game on TV. I had a strong feeling that the batter would hit a home run and at that moment, he did.

The worst incident we had in Germany was our accident with the white Volkswagen, which only had a little over 4,000 miles I had a three-day weekend pass. Carole and I decided to drive down to Switzerland and Liechtenstein for the duration of these days. It was Friday night, October 9, 1964. During the night it started raining and never let up. I couldn't sleep because I was hounded by a strong feeling that we would have a car accident if we left the house. I wrestled with this strong feeling throughout the night. I thought that the fact that it was raining the whole night might be causing this feeling. I decided to ask Carole if she still wanted to go, and she did. I thought all of this was just nonsense! We were going! As I remember, it was still raining when we left at 5:30 a.m.

I believe God's intervention saved us from a terrible experience. Driving slowly in Goppingen, we were approaching a ten- or eleven-year-old girl carrying an open bucket of milk that she had apparently just purchased. She was walking close to the curve. As I approached her, she dashed into my lane without looking, but saw the red bumper from the corner of her eye and jumped back just in time. She was only a couple feet away from the VW as I passed her. If I had been a couple of feet further back from her I would have run over this girl and our future would have been very different than what it was. This is one event I will never forget. To this very day I still shudder about what the consequences of killing this little girl would have been. I would have had to live the rest of my life aware that I killed her and perhaps spend the rest of my life in a German prison. In addition, Carole would have had to leave Germany, separated from her husband. This was and still is a horrible thought. I thanked God that He protected this little girl. I believe God prevented this accident, and I have thanked Him more than once.

October 12, 1964, letter to Mom and Dad:

The start of another week. Time is flying. In just about nine months from now, I should be on a ship heading home.

Well, Sunday was the nicest Sunday in two months, but we weren't in Switzerland. We have bad news to tell you. We had a major accident but were lucky we walked out of it unhurt. Things are already working out, so don't worry. We took care of everything this morning.

Saturday morning we got up and by 5:30 a.m. we were on the road, heading towards Lindau, Germany, on the border of Switzerland and Germany. At 8:30 a.m. we were only eighteen k's (eleven miles) from Lindau, and we could see the Alps in the distance covered with snow. Well, we had just completed one sharp curve and were headed towards another curve, not as sharp though (for mile after mile this road was just curves, and the road was a little narrower than our roads in Michigan). I made one bad mistake (speed 45-50 mph), I didn't stay to the edge of the road going into the curve, but in the middle of my lane. At the peak of the curve I went over the white line and a car was approaching with plenty of room. I turned the wheel right, but a little too much, so we were heading toward the guardrail. I turned the wheel to the left, and we started to skid as the oncoming car passed us. I turned the wheel to the right again and no luck as the car was skidding completely around sideways and hit a wire fence and flipped over on its top off the highway.

Some men quickly helped us out of the car and they tipped the car onto its wheels again. Someone called the German police, who in turn called the Ulm MPs because they were the closest. It took until after 2:00 p.m. in the afternoon to get everything settled. The MPs didn't get there until noon. The German police couldn't speak English. We finally went to a school where the English teacher served as interpreter.

Carole developed black and blue bruises on her legs and shoulders. She ended up in the back seat when the car flipped over on its top. Yesterday my shoulder was a little stiff, but besides that we are fine. The car has at least five hundred dollars of damage. The top and side are a mess, and the side and back windows were completely knocked out. My license will be lifted by the company commander for not more than sixty days, but he was in a good mood about it. The post is having an average of one accident per week since October 1 and there are not more than one hundred drivers, if that many. The accident rate is very high, but we will definitely be careful from now on. The car flipped over because it's so small and light. If I had been driving a large car nothing would have happened.

We drove the car back from the German police. It took us several hours to get these activities with the MP and German police completed. This morning we found out that the axle and one brake drum were damaged.

We had to pay a fine of 5DM (one dollar and twenty-five cents) and 23DM (five dollars and seventy-five cents) to the garage for oil and bringing our car to the police station, and 10DM two dollars and fifty cents) to the farmer for the fence, which the insurance company will pay.

The German police gave us written permission allowing us to drive the car home since they said only bodily damage was done.

We have a one hundred and twenty dollars insurance deductible and with this thought it looks like we will trade it in for a 1965 VW.

A friend will take us to work every day.

If we get a new car, then I think the dealer will let us pay for the difference in monthly installments (the insurance company will send the payment check to the dealer).

On Monday, October 12, 1964, we drove the car to the dealer GAG, and dealt with Mr. Vogel, the person who sold us our VW. After a few days we got a red 1965 Volkswagen. Mr. Vogel did all of the paperwork for us, contacting the insurance company and selling our white VW as is to three men. The bottom line is that we gave up a 1964 VW for a 1965 VW and the cost of this tradeoff was two hundred and fifteen dollars. We had a little trouble getting our new U.S. license plates, and on October 19 the MPs finally agreed to give us new plates. With the plates we were able to get our new red VW, which we did that afternoon. Carole did the driving during the suspension time period.

Carole's October 15, 1964, letter to Mom and Dad:

This has been quite a week for us with no car, especially for me. We have been packing our lunch to take with us and eat on the post, thus I have been staying on post all day long. Surprisingly, I have had little time to kill and haven't found time to do some things I like to do, such as spending a little time in the library.

We are really busy at work now, getting ready for the play *The Country Girl*, which is being performed on the 28th, 29th, and 31st of October. Next week I will be working extra in the afternoons because she wants me to upholster a chair by myself. I will enjoy it and will also enjoy the extra cash.

Monday October 26, I will go to Stuttgart to have my wisdom teeth taken out. Hope I don't have much trouble!

Carole's October 16, 1964, journal entry:

We thought we would get our car this afternoon, but the MPs didn't want to give Rick license plates because his driver's license was suspended. They told him to come back in the morning and if they gave them, it would have to be to me.

Carole's October 19, 1964, journal entry:

We got our license plate in the morning and went to pick up our car about 12:30 p.m. However, it was after 3:00 p.m. before we left with it. They hadn't installed the seat belts and they couldn't get any black tires to put on the car, which came with whitewalls. Finally, with Rick's persistence, they let us have the whitewalls at no extra cost to us!

October 22, 1964, letter to Mom and Dad:

Dad, we don't want to plan or make a daily schedule either in our traveling, but just want to travel along and once we see something of interest continue on to the next point of interest. There are so many things to see. Now, if we just make a seven-hour day, each day, then we will be quite limited. We can see a lot and do a lot in eleven to twelve hours. Carole and I have experienced this (longer days) since we have been here.

    If I leave for the States on July 10th, I can do everything in ten days that has to be done. By July 3rd, I have to ship my car home. Perhaps you would like to use it and take it home yourselves? This is something to think about. You would need an international driver's license.

    We live two and two thirds miles from the post. We can see that our place will be a little uncomfortable this coming winter. The problem is getting heat for the kitchen because we like to stay in this room during the evenings. Our little pot stove heater in the bedroom is too small to heat both rooms. Our neighbor's room is next to our bedroom and he listens to terrible German music that drives us nuts (not too much insulation between the walls), but we will make it.

    Financially we aren't in top shape, as we will pay off the two hundred and fifty dollars for the 1965 VW by November 1. We will have another month of beans, soup, and sandwiches, since these are acceptable for Carole and me [Carole had said in a letter "We aren't eating quite as bad as Rick made it out to be"].

    Just thirty-five minutes and I will be on my way home again! It's always my goal here to get home. I have two desires here in the army, 5:00 p.m. and the weekends.

    As for the military, I had it really easy compared to those going to Viet Nam and other areas of the world. I took advantage of being stationed in Europe and having Carole with me for the majority of my time in Germany. Others did this also. I'm very grateful for this opportunity that was given to me.

Carole's October 27, 1964, journal entry:

I had my two upper wisdom teeth removed at the army hospital center in Stuttgart. No trouble getting them out.

Carole's October 31, 1964, journal entry:

We went to Babs's parents' home for a slides and pizza party. Claus showed slides of his trip through Yugoslavia and Greece three years ago. Babs showed some of her 35mm slides that she took when she was a student at Ferndale High School during the school year of 1959-1960. We were greatly surprised that one of her slides showed Rick's best friend [Jack Hinkins] of his Ferndale years!

Carole's November 3, 1964, letter to Mom and Dad:

I'm at work, as you no doubt can tell. It's almost 11:00 a.m. and Claudia has gone home because she wasn't feeling too well. There is no work to do!

Rick did all right at KP Friday. As he was leaving, he asked the mess hall sergeant if he could take some potatoes home. The sergeant not only gave us some potatoes, but ten pounds of sugar, tomato juice, and some canned goods that the cans were too dented for sale. Apparently the commissary gives them to the mess hall.

Sunday was a Catholic holiday here where they decorate the graves of their families with flowers and evergreen wreaths. I was beginning to wonder Friday and Saturday when I saw many people carrying evergreen boughs and evergreen wreaths—looked like Christmas to me. Babs explained it to us when I asked about it.

Tomorrow afternoon I have the laundry to do and Thursday afternoon I have to take the car in for its three hundred-mile check-up. We reached three hundred miles Sunday.

I did all right driving to Waldenbuch and back, but I would just as soon let Rick do the driving and be glad when he can. These narrow curved roads are really something to drive. You don't really realize how bad it is until you are actually doing the driving!

Rick has applied for a three-day pass for November 21-23. We will just stay home and try to plan our European trip for June 1965.

What a coincidence that you saw the play *Everybody Loves Opal*! This is going to be our next production, and right now I'm in the midst of typing the script on dittoes to be run off. It is hilarious, isn't it? I can't wait to see it. This play should be put on about the last week of December.

Thursday night Rick and I went to see a couple that have been after us to come over. They have a real nice place (on the economy). It's quite modern looking (German standards). They have three rooms plus a small kitchen and bathroom. We had a nice time.

Tuesday afternoon after PWOC (Protestant Women of the Chapel) I went with one of the girls to her apartment in government housing. I have been curious to see what they were like inside. They are very nice, but Rick and I still wouldn't want to live there. They are too big (the buildings) and so many right together and too close to the army.

Yes, it sure will be strange not to be home for the holidays this year. We will miss helping you with your administrative education folders, Dad. What will you do without us? Ha!

Carole's November 8, 1964, journal entry:

We went to church in the morning and in the afternoon we drove to Waldenbuch to see Hans, who had returned from the States the previous Tuesday. It was so good to see him again. We visited and took a short drive with Hans driving. We, as usual, had cake and coffee and also a little supper before we took Hans back to Tubingen.

Carole's November 14, 1964, journal entry:

In the afternoon we received a surprise phone call from Hans asking if he could come over. We had no plans, so he did. We had a really nice visit, had him stay for supper, and in the evening before he left he took us to a nice café in downtown Goppingen. We had a "hot lemon" with him but it was too sour for our taste!

Carole's November 17, 1964, journal entry:

The dentist in Stuttgart took out Rick's two upper wisdom teeth. After the first day, he had no trouble with them whatsoever.

Carole's November 23, 1964, letter to Mom and Dad:

We have had a nice long weekend. We even went on an unexpected trip. Hans called us Friday and asked us to come down Saturday and he would take us to the Black Forest, so we did. He asked us to come at 2:00 p.m., so we didn't have time to go too far (it's dark here by 5:00 pm), but it was still nice. We drove to a town called Freudenstadt which is a lovely place. The shops looked very interesting. Even Rick said he would like to be there when they were open. Then we went to another place called Bad Wildbad. It was dark by the time we got there, but what we could see looked very nice. It's located in a valley and is a health resort, hot springs. No driving is allowed in the city after 10:00 p.m. It cost two dollars and twenty-five cents just for coffee and cake for the three of us! The café was very nice. I never saw a place so full of green plants in my life, except a greenhouse. It was quite attractive! Then we drove back to Waldenbuch. Oh yes, Hans did all this driving using our car. He knew the roads, and I had had enough driving by the time we got to Waldenbuch.

You wouldn't believe what we saw. An Austrian passed me with another car coming in plain sight and it was also plain to see he could never make it, but he did! I slammed on the brakes to slow down and I imagine the other driver did the same and the Austrian squeezed back into the right lane with hardly room to spare! I thought for sure he was a goner. I am glad he wasn't, though, because we would have probably been involved in the crash too. I could never have stopped in time. Then as if this wasn't bad enough, this same driver passed a long truck on a hill and curve. He made it! I wonder if he ever got where he was going!

Carole's November 26, 1964, journal entry:

Thanksgiving Day and Rick had KP all day. He brought home ham, nuts, oranges, and candy.

Carole's November 28, 1964, journal entry:

Babs and Claus came in the afternoon. They brought us a pretty evergreen candle centerpiece and a sack of Lebkuchen from Frau Stein. We went over our European trip plans for their criticisms and suggestions.

They brought word that it started snowing when they left Waldenbuch, and sure enough about an hour later it started snowing here, a very wet snow but our first.

November 28, 1964, letter to Mom and Dad:

We asked Claus and Babs for advice as we explained our trip. They gave us a few helpful tips, which we appreciated. Because of being in the U.S. Forces, I believe we can get Esso gas without taxes in all the countries in Western Europe. We will have to buy the coupons in Stuttgart, and they are redeemable when we return. Carole will send you our plans during the week coming up. The best part of our trip is the last week, slower pace in beautiful Tyrol (Austria) and Switzerland (one full week). The dates are 2-30 June. Tyrol, I believe, is the prettiest in Europe. After our trip, you will want to relax in Garmisch and Berchtesgaden in the Bavarian Alps. The cost per day will be the cheapest for you because the Armed Forces have their own hotels and restaurants. You will take a tour and see the castle that Walt Disney copied for Disneyland. You will love it there, with flowers all over the place and mountains around you. It is so beautiful down there! I believe you two will also enjoy visiting London, and make sure you get reservations at the Strand Palace Hotel. It's true that it is in a beautiful location and average prices. As for Switzerland and Austria, we want to spend a lot of time there. We still plan to drive to Berlin during early May.

Carole's November 30, 1964, letter to Mom and Dad:

About packing for the trip, you mentioned you would each have a suitcase. I hope you mean small ones. If at all possible try to arrange putting everything in one suitcase. Then you can have some kind of a bag (laundry, shopping, tote, etc.) for odds and ends, such as toothbrushes and such things. We have packing space behind the back seat and a little trunk space. We will have just one suitcase for the two of us. Plan to bring as few clothes with you as you can. It will save space for the things we accumulate along the way. All the time we were in England I wore only my suit, changing it once in a while with the blouse we bought for it. For this European trip I plan to take the same suit and blouse plus just one other outfit, light and cool for southern Europe, which will be quite warm probably. Northern Europe will be a little cool, fifties and sixties.

Yes, we have already sent the article on U.S. medicine on to Hans via Babs and Claus. I'm sure he will like to read it.

The reason Rick is having his lower wisdom teeth removed is because they are pushing against his other teeth and they will cause trouble in the future, so it is best to have them out now when it doesn't cost us anything and before they cause him trouble. He had no trouble with his upper ones removed and I don't think he will have a problem with the lower ones. The only reason I had mine removed was that they would push my other teeth out of line.

Carole's December 3, 1964, journal entry:

Thursday morning it started really snowing about 10:30 a.m. and gave us a couple inches by noon and very slippery roads! It took twice as long to get home. I decided to stay on post all afternoon so as to avoid driving home and back again. Rick went to see about getting his driver's license back and found out that he could have had it since November 19--it was only suspended for thirty days. At 3:00 p.m. they let all off post men leave so as to get home OK. It didn't stop snowing until 7:00 or 8:00 p.m.

It snowed some more during the night and started in again about midmorning. It quit for the afternoon (4th) but started in heavy again at 5:00 p.m.

The snow came heavy and fast, and the streets were like solid ice. With Carole driving carefully, it took us twice as long to get home for lunch. I drove home because they gave me my drivers' license after lunch. I was told I would permanently lose my license if I had another accident. At 3:00 p.m. they released all of the men living off-post. I drove slowly with a little nervousness due to the icy roads. Our parking area was on the side behind our house, and higher than the street. Carole stood on the street watching for oncoming cars as I tried to drive up fast to our parking area but couldn't do it. When I would get near to our parking area the car would slide down this miniature hill. After two or three failed attempts, Carole got back in and we drove around the long block and were able to park the car by driving in from the back street.

During the cold weather we had to spend our time in our bedroom since our little pot stove could not heat both the bedroom and the kitchen. There was no heat in our hallway bathroom. In the army I shaved using a razor blade. It was during this time that I felt like I was literally freezing when I was shaving. My breath steamed up the mirror and my body was shaking from the room's coldness. I had to buy an electric shaver and a separate mirror to shave in our bedroom. We lacked comfort, but we survived.

I also mentioned to my parents that we were now nearing our first anniversary, and that the time had flown. I mentioned that marriage is wonderful if you marry the right spouse. I was enjoying our relationship and we got along together very well. I also mentioned living here in Germany was a wonderful experience. We liked the German people and felt that overall they were nice people.

A sergeant by the name of Love came over to Finance while I was there. I asked him if he had any relatives in Michigan, and he said that the Love family that used to live a couple of houses from where I grew up is his relatives. He is a second cousin to them.

Carole's December 4, 1964, letter to Mom and Dad:

We have just been looking out the window at the blizzard we have had upon us for the last three and half hours (it's now 8:30 p.m.). It's really coming down and the roads are bad, terribly slippery. I dread the rest of this winter. All kinds of accidents are happening all around. There is one in view of our window right now, three cars involved. Not serious, evidently just bumped fenders from the slipperiness of the road. Our landlord just got back from Holland today and he reported there was ice on the autobahns and in one location there was a two hundred car pileup. You just can't imagine the situation. Roads are closed all around us because of hills impossible to get up or down safely, or because trucks or busses have slipped and gotten stuck so as to block the road. It's really something! All the roads are terribly slippery since the Germans do little to remove the snow or reduce slipperiness.

December 8, 1964, letter to Mom and Dad:

The weather is much warmer out now, and for the second straight day the snow is melting. It sure would be nice to see all the snow melted!

The other day I out-processed the records of an army man from Ferndale. His last name was Swanson.

Carole gave me my anniversary watch a little early because my old watch stem broke and the crystal was cracked and all of the chrome was off! The watch mechanism was excellent, but that was all. Remember when we got it, Dad? It was in May of 1959. It was a good watch and served its purpose.

Carole's December 9, 1964, letter to Mom and Dad:

December 1st we will be attending Claudia and Kent's wedding.

I have found a very good book to help us plan our European trip in June. It's titled *Europe on a Shoestring* (budget). It's really great, gives things to see, information on transportation, cafes, hotels and other tidbits you need to know. I am reading through it and taking notes.

Incidentally, we plan to park our car once we get into a big city and leave it until we wish to leave. We will see the sights of the city via foot, streetcar, or bus. Streetcars and busses are very cheap over here since they are used so much. Using them will save wear and tear on us and keep our sanity!

You know how driving is in downtown Detroit? Well, it's much worse over here!

Well, it's just about time I headed for the post to pick up Rick.

Carole's December 12, 1964, letter to Mom and Dad:

As you can see, I have enclosed a little ornament from Germany and from us to hang on your Christmas tree (or anywhere else, if you would rather).

We have a couple requests to ask of you again. Would you send Rick's birth certificate to us as soon as you can? He needs it to get a passport and an international driver's license that we would like to get over Christmas vacation. He will need the real thing. The international driver's license is a security measure, just in case we should have another accident, which we certainly don't plan on! Now another thing, and there's no rush on this at all. Rick's Michigan driver's license expires next April. If you are in or near the police station, would you ask and see what he is to do about getting it renewed or if he can wait until summer. Rick said he thinks there might be something about that if you are in the Armed Forces. [As a member of the Armed Forces in Germany, the U.S. state driver's license is valid for driving in Europe.]

Yes, we can send you all the information on visas, shots, and such that you will need. I'm almost positive you won't need any visas since they are only for over three-month stays for most countries.

About suitcases, two medium-sized suitcases should be all right. Buy lightweight. So we mean like my suitcases? They are really nice.

Carole's December 13, 1964, journal entry:

Rick had barracks orderly but was lucky and came home at 10:00 a.m. for the rest of the day. We then went to church.

In the evening we took our camera and tripod and went to downtown Goppingen to take pictures of the Christmas decorations on the stores. We were disappointed that there weren't more and that what lights there were all white. The city itself put up no decorations.

Friday was Claudia and Kent's wedding at 7:00 p.m. in the chapel and reception afterwards in Captain and Mrs. Walker's home in Eislingen—a very beautiful place!

December 15, 1964 I wrote to Mom and Dad: The snow is just about gone and the weather is a little warmer. Good, hey!

As for my driving, I have regained my confidence and I'm extra careful in driving. If I do have an accident, it won't be my fault.

If you want to buy us something and don't know what to get, may I suggest something? MONEY—ha, Carole and I would like to have a few things over here, and so far we are unable to get them. We only expect to have one or two dollars left over by the first of January (payday), so this month we are unable to get these items. Now, top on the want list is a foot trunk or I guess you call them just a trunk. They are on sale now until December 24 for seven dollars and twenty-five cents or seven dollars and fifty cents. We want this for storing our slides, records, tapes, film and clothing, etc. We will use this for storing our valuable stuff while on our trip next June and also for shipping our stuff home next July. I can ship two hundred pounds free through the army. So as you can see, this trunk for us will be a handy thing to have. We can use it in the future [we still have it, with a few items we used in Germany].

So if you still want to send something, a few dollars toward this trunk would make a welcome gift. But I know whatever you may do, we will appreciate it and I know we will be able to use it, whatever it may be. Remember, we are grateful just for having fine parents. We owe you two a lot!

Christmas Day it looks like we will be in Waldenbuch with the Steins. I will have to take a picture of their Christmas tree. We will see them this coming weekend. Babs was here last Saturday. We sure have been seeing a lot of them lately. They are fun to be with.

Carole's December 15, 1964, letter to Mom and Dad:

It's just a few lines from me. Rick pretty well covered things. Today I bought our first Christmas tree! It's a very small one, only about three feet tall, but has a beautiful shape and is not too thinly branched but just right with short needles. I got it for two DM (fifty cents), and I'm very pleased with it. I plan to make decorations for it, red pompoms from yarn I have and cardboard shapes covered with aluminum foil. Can't wait to put it up but will wait until Friday I think.

Work is still quite scarce on my job, but there has been a little here and there. Yes, it's a fine job except for getting my paycheck. In October and November it came about the 7th, 8th, or 9th. Well, this is the 15th and I still don't have it. I had to borrow from Claudia to get us by because we expected it to come about the same time and thus spent our other paychecks on the car and insurance and gifts for the Stein family and other things. It should come tomorrow though, because the library girls got theirs today and theirs come through the same channels mine does (Frankfurt to Stuttgart and then here).

Don't worry about visas; you won't need them. For your passport, you can save eleven dollars by getting one passport for the both of you. You will be traveling together all the time and thus really won't need separate ones and that saves money. To get your passport, take with you two duplicate photos, two and half inches by two and half inches (glossy). This would include both of you if you get your passport together, thus saving money here too. Tell the photographer it is for a passport and he will know what type of print to make. You will need birth certificates, driver's license, eleven dollars (nine dollars for passport and two dollars for clerk fee). I will be sending you more information later on.

Carole's December 18, 1964, letter to Mom and Dad:

Last night I got my hair cut. A couple of weeks ago I found out one of the GIs on Rick's team was a professional beautician in the States, so when we got some money we made arrangements to bring him to the apartment to cut my hair. The German girl in the beauty shop on post doesn't do a good job at all, but I really like Bob's work. His name is Bob Swirka. He cut my hair wet and with a razor, which is how I like it done. He then styled it a little bit for me, not much different, but a little. Rick likes it too! Bob wasn't going to charge me anything for it because he likes to do it just to keep in practice! But we gave him something anyway because I really appreciated it. It's so nice to have a professional job! We had him stay for coffee and cookies and then talked until 11:30 p.m.! Bob is a U.S. (draftee) and leaves in April. He is a real nice fellow.

This afternoon I will put up our tree and any other decorations I have time for.

This has been a busier morning than what I expected, calls for Santa Claus suits and people stopping by for this or that. Even my hubby has been by a couple times! He is running errands around the post.

Wonder if we will get any mail today. Ha! Yesterday Rick was harassed by the guys in the mail line (due to receiving a lot of mail).

December 18, 1964, letter to Mom and Dad:

We were surprised today in getting one magazine and thirteen letters and cards. We appreciate all you have sent us and we enjoyed all of it. We won't open the two letters or cards until the designated dates. It is very thoughtful of you two to send us packages. We must have at least six packages from you two already! The [Larry & Faye] Cowells gave us five dollars, which surprised us, and was very nice of them. They are very thoughtful, but we feel bad about not getting them anything. We can't afford it right now since Carole was paid less than anticipated.

We will have a nice Christmas. You two and Carole's folks will have made it possible.

December 21, 1964, letter to Mom and Dad:

It's snowing a little. Received your letters today and it was good hearing from the two of you, as usual. Thanks very much Dad and Mom for the anniversary card and ten dollars. We certainly appreciate your thoughtfulness and kindness. Money is always one thing we seem to need each month, especially this one. I just remembered you want "t-shirts." After payday (next week), I will send a dozen to you.

I wish Carole's ambulance would hurry up and get here! I'm waiting in the car for her and my feet are cold.

Probably Carole mentioned that this week and next I only have to work mornings, which is unusual for receiving time off. A few guys are not having any time off except a couple of days. I think I have the best job on the post. I won't be promoted to E-4, but I have a lot of fringe benefits.

Thanks, Dad, for the stamps. We must use about four dollars (one hundred stamps) of stamps each month.

You are right about the title of *Europe on Five Dollars A Day*, a very popular book, and there is a copy here at the post's library.

Dad, barrack orderly is supposedly cleaning up the hallways and keeping an eye on the place. Just about everybody in the barracks is in bed during this time.

I'm looking forward to our trip. Time sure is flying. Doesn't seem like I been married for one year.

Here it is 3:15 p.m. and still no sign of Carole. I sure wish they would hurry up. I'm anxious to get to our cold apartment. I will have to build a fire. What a life!

We had a good time at the Stein's yesterday. Hans is coming to our place tomorrow afternoon.

Mother, the silver-dollar necklace that Babs fixed up for us is very attractive. The coin is fitted into a small rim and it looks like part of the coin. The chain is pretty and eighty-three percent silver.

The total cost for everything was three dollars and seventy-five cents. The chain is two and one half feet long. Carole seems to be pleased with it. It is very attractive. [Many women in our area had necklaces of gold and silver coins. Babs had one with the American Peace silver dollar (issued from 1921 to 1935). I thought it would be neat for Carole to have one. Mom sent us a common new Peace dollar, worth only a dollar since the mint had one thousand dollar bags of them that were slowly being released, and we used it for Carole's necklace.]

Carole has promised me a beef dinner tonight, which will be a very rare treat. I think Carole is coming now. She still hasn't arrived. I expected Carole to be here at 2:30 p.m. and it's now 3:35 p.m. and I don't know when she will be here. This is part of the army though, waiting, waiting. I'm going inside and ask again when they are supposed to be here. My feet sure are cold!

I'm at the library now. I learned that the truck would be delayed because it had to wait for linens to bring back. So it's possible it won't be in until around 4:30 p.m. The afternoon is wasted! We won't have time for a roast beef dinner either since the oven takes a long time to warm up. Probably Carole has been bored to death. Just to see the doctor for ten minutes it takes a full day. Carole left at 9:00 a.m. and probably won't be here until 4:30 p.m.

Carole's December 21, 1964, journal entry:

Our first anniversary! I had an appointment with the dermatologist in Bad Cannstadt Hospital in Stuttgart at 11:15 a.m. I went by ambulance and didn't get back until 4:00 p.m., so there was no time to prepare a roast beef dinner as planned. Instead, we got two TV beef dinners and had those hot German rolls and apple pie I had baked Sunday evening. We ate by candlelight!

Carole's December 22, 1964, letter to Mom and Dad:

For our anniversary Rick gave me an electric shaver, so I didn't have to mess with the water and the cold bathroom and such. I knew about this before, but he also gave me a surprise gift, a beautiful cutting board. I had seen them in the PX and wanted one. Its Belgian made and has a trough all the way around to catch juices. The grains in the wood are really pretty. His card was cute, but he bought it before deciding on the surprise. It says, "I was going to give you an anniversary gift, but I read in a book that it wasn't the proper thing to do … (open card) our bank book! Happy Anniversary anyway!" His watch was my gift to him and I got him a card at the hospital PX.

Now about my feet—I have something milder than frostbite. I forgot what he called it, but it's just from my feet being cold so much of the time. So from now on I have to always make sure my feet are warm, especially on cold and damp days. This is fine for future prevention, but now the only time my toes ever bother me, itching, tingling or burning sensation, is when my feet get overly warm. So now I have to go about it moderately. However, he also gave me some cream to rub onto them and I think this helps to relieve the itching, etc., because my feet have been warm all night and this morning haven't bothered me. He also gave me some pills to take that have a dehydrating effect because in keeping my feet warm they are likely to sweat more. Such a time! These pills have a side effect of blurred vision for a few days but I haven't noticed any such effect as yet. He wants me to come back in four weeks, so I have another appointment for January 20th. I think we will try to get Rick's appointment with the oral surgeon for that same day.

I put our tree up Friday and got it decorated. I just made pompoms from the red yarn left over from Rick's sweater and then cut out cardboard shapes and wrapped them in aluminum foil. The Germans don't decorate their windows and outsides of their houses like the Americans do.

Babs and Hans took us to the Christmas market in Stuttgart. It wasn't really much, but was interesting to see. It was just a lot of outdoor booths selling everything from clothing and kitchen utensils to Christmas decorations and food. The smells were just delicious. We bought some of the candy-coated almonds that we have mentioned before. They make those on the spot and that really smells delicious! We also had some "pommes frites," or french fries as we know it. We were disappointed that Stuttgart didn't have more decorations than it did. Several of the big stores had beautiful decorations and lights up but that was just about it.

Claudia just called and said she was going back to sleep. Ha! Guess they got back rather late last night. So I don't have a thing to do this morning. Oh well, I will think of something. We have been getting some very nice Christmas cards from people back home. I have been putting them up on the kitchen wall in the form of a Christmas tree.

I sure wish I could see some of your things you made this year, Mother. You do such beautiful work.

We got an inch of snow last night, but this morning it wasn't bad driving.

Yes, Mother, we did get the paper you sent with the little gift inside. What in the world can you do with nine boxes of candy? [There was a woman student in Mother's evening art class that worked for Sanders' Chocolate and Ice Cream. When a box of candy reached its expiration date, the employees could take them. This woman gave Mother nine boxes of chocolate candy. She was an ongoing member of Mother's class, and one Christmas when I was living at home the same thing happened, to my delight!]

I wish too we could be home during Christmastime, but it will be almost as good a substitute being with the Stein family. They are so wonderful to us. They are our family here in Germany.

Carole's December 22, 1964, journal entry:

Hans came in the afternoon to go with us as interpreter to take our tape recorder in to have it fixed. He brought us seven lovely roses (pink) for our anniversary. We had him stay for a hamburger dinner.

Carole's December 24, 1964, journal entry:

In the morning Rick came over to the hut to get me for a coffee hour "pay" was having for the fellows and their wives. I was glad to go because we had no heat! (and temperature was twenty-seven degrees).

In the afternoon I baked another loaf of date nut bread to take to the Stein's and Christmas cupcakes for our landlord and his family.

They had us come down at 8:00 p.m. in the evening to see their gifts and tree and feed us Christmas cookies. They gave us a brush-scraper for our car and a plate of cookies.

They had electric candles on their tree with Christmas balls and other such decorations like we use.

They had lighted candles outside the windows for East Germans. Many other Germans do this also.

At 10:00 p.m. Rick and I were at the candlelight service at the post chapel. It was a very pretty service.

As we were coming home at 11:30 p.m., our landlord was just leaving for midnight mass, a widespread German custom. Even Protestants have midnight services. The Germans put up their tree and open their gifts on this day, so it is the main part of their Christmas. Then the following two days, the 25th and 26th, are Christmas. Then most factories close down or operate only on skeleton crews between Christmas and New Year.

Carole's December 25, 1964, journal entry:

Christmas! Rick and I had our breakfast in bed—coffee cake and then opened our gifts. We both got a Yahtzee game and airmail stamps and stationery from my folks. Rick got two pair of socks, the book *1984*, two Mexican coins, and a letter opener. I got a gold corduroy two piece dress, a flower-print blouse, nylons, Siamese bracelet, a ring, and gloves. All things we can use, needed, or wanted. We also received money, which helps us to get through the month! With part of it we bought a trunk to store our things.

At 11:30 a.m. we left for the Stein family home in Waldenbuch, Germany. Shortly after our arrival we ate a traditional goose dinner, which was very good. Then we opened our gifts from them and they opened theirs from us. We were thrilled when we opened our *Deutschland* book, Berlin kalendar, candle and candleholder, and "schokolade." They also gave us a plate full of candy, fruit, and cookies.

The rest of the day we visited, watched TV, had coffee and cake, etc.

Their tree was a beautiful, traditional "Tannenbaum." They used real candles (white), straw stars and angels that they made, and icicles.

It was 4:00 p.m. that afternoon and 10:00 a.m. in Michigan when our call to my house in Niles went through, which Dad had previously arranged with Rick. I figured it out ahead of time, but it was a complete surprise to my mother and my three sisters. We had a good connection, and it was really wonderful to hear their voices again. It was really something to talk with them across the ocean.

Herr (Mr.) Heinrich and Frau (Mrs.) Louise Stein have six children. Their names are from oldest to youngest: twin sisters, Gertraude and Hildegard, Hans, Babs, Christoph and Peter. They are a special and wonderful family.

As we started to go home, we found it was snowing. However, we took it very slowly all the way home and made it safely.

In regard to our drive from the Steins' house to our home, I had a problem driving on the autobahn. We thanked the Stein family, said goodbye, and drove away, heading home in the dark and snow. When we were on the autobahn for a little while, we experienced heavier snowfall and it looked like we were in a small blizzard as large snowflakes were flying parallel to the road, hitting the windshield. This situation was making it harder for me to keep alert and awake. As I was driving, I found myself dreaming that I was at a party and I was at a table that had a large punch bowl, visiting with a young woman. We were both standing near the punch bowl. I don't know how many seconds this took place, but standing there with her I realized that I wasn't really there, I was driving! I became alert again, but the snowflakes continued flying toward my face and once again I was back at the punch bowl with this woman. Again I realized that I wasn't there but on the autobahn. I can't remember if there was a conversation between the two of us. I finally told Carole that I couldn't stay awake, so she agreed to drive. I stopped our car, and we switched seats. I was wide awake for the rest of our driving time.

When we got to our apartment in Goppingen it was freezing! It was very late, and since it took a long time to get a fire going we decided to go without. We took the blankets we had and all of our clothing and towels and spread them out on the bed. We made it through the night. I got up in daylight, got the fire going, and jumped back in bed. About an hour later we had heat in our bedroom. I was so glad it was a weekend and I didn't have to drive to the army base

December 26, 1964, letter to Mom and Dad:

It's another Christmas behind us. We thank you two for the money and gifts. We were very surprised. You two are too kind, but we sure appreciate everything. Carole and I are so happy to know that at least we will have some money left over at the end of the month. We will have a few dollars left over each month from now on! It's a wonderful feeling. Two weeks ago I was beginning to panic that we would need just a few dollars to pull us through until payday, but now we are drinking an extra glass of milk! Ha!

We bought a small trunk at the PX for seven dollars and seventy-five cents, so we are all set. Thank you all again.

Everything we received was what we wanted and can use. We really came out well.

We did have a real nice Christmas in spite of not being in Michigan. We opened our gifts in bed and had breakfast in bed. We then went to the Steins for the day, and they certainly are spoiling us. They certainly are a wonderful family. They are really good to us and are concerned with our safety and our welfare, especially Hans.

We left their place quite late in the evening, and it was snowing really hard! Hans insisted on taking two snow tires off his Dad's car to put on ours, but I wasn't in favor of it. Well, we finally compromised to the plan of them following us in a second car to the autobahn. We got home before midnight and called them, notifying them of our safe trip. The top speed to the autobahn was 18 mph, on the autobahn was 25 mph, and the highways off the autobahn we averaged around 20 mph. We probably were the slowest, but we got home safe and sound.

If you get your car in a ditch over here you are really up a creek because there aren't too many gas stations and they are usually closed during holidays and the workers can't speak English. I hate driving in those conditions and will try to avoid such weather. They want us to come on New Year's, and we probably will be there during that time.

Carole wants to play a game now that we received from her folks, so I would like to thank you two again for your thoughtfulness.

I missed the bright colorful lights and the good Christmas music during this time of the year. It has been a meaningful Christmas, though. Carole and I have learned more about the interesting German customs. Many of the West Germany families have family members in East Germany. Placing a lighted candle on their windowsill during this time of the year honors their East Germany family members. My heart goes out to them. Communism is terrible, and I understand why they need a wall to keep them in East Germany. It's sad!

Christmas in Germany, by Carole Wilcox

The fourth Sunday before Christmas, the beginning of Advent, marks the beginning of Christmas celebrations. Every German family has their own Advent wreath. Each Sunday of Advent the family gathers together around the wreath, lighting the appropriate candle or candles for that Sunday, and hold a special family worship service.

Saint Nicholas comes early here – December 6, and he doesn't fill stockings, he fills the children's shoes, which they have carefully placed outside the door.

Christmas Eve is the main part of Christmas. Stores and factories close around noon or 1:00 o'clock so everyone is off work. That afternoon they put up and decorate their tree. Tradition says that the children are not to see the tree until it is completely decorated, so the parents may lock them out of the living room until they are through. We were surprised to learn that the Germans still used real candles to light their tree, although some families have modernized and use electric candles. Other decorations besides the real candles on the traditional German tree are straw stars and angels, which the family make themselves. This does not sound very colorful, but when the candles are glowing it is very beautiful in its own simple way. The Steins, our German friends, had this traditional tree with the addition of the icicles that we use on our trees. Other German families, whether they use real candles or electric ones, may use Christmas balls and similar decorations that we are familiar with.

Our landlord has such a tree with electric candles. Before or after dinner, they open their gifts. Our landlord had us come down about 8:00. They fed us Christmas cookies and showed us their gifts. They had lighted candles outside their window that, as they explained to us, were for the East Germans. We saw several other such candles on the way to our Christmas Eve candlelight service at the post chapel. At midnight you will find nearly every German family at church for a special Christmas service or mass.

Christmas Day is actually Christmas Days here since both December 25 and 26 are Christmas. These are just days of rest and relaxation and having friends and relatives in for dinner or just coffee and Christmas cookies or Christmas bread. We were very fortunate to be able to spend the 25th with a German family, the Steins. They are really wonderful people, always so good to us and looking out for our welfare; they have become "our family" over here. We had the traditional Christmas dinner, goose.

After dinner we exchanged our gifts. We were just thrilled when we opened up our book of *Deutschland*, which are about 240 full pages of Germany! They also gave us a "Berlin kalendar 1965," in which all the pictures are of Berlin, and candy, fruit, and Christmas cookies that we enjoyed! We spent the rest of the day in leisure, visiting, watching TV (we were surprised how much we could get from the actions and expressions and what few German words we know) and having coffee with breads and cookies. We also took pictures of their tree, which we sure hope turn out so you will be able to see it too.

We had a white Christmas but not much snow. It was quite cold and everything was covered with a very heavy frost, even at noon. It was beautiful while driving to Waldenbuch. The branches of the trees looked like they were covered with white fuzz.

The German towns and cities aren't decorated for Christmas nearly as much or as prettily as our American towns. The only decorations are what individual stores put up themselves. However, in places such as parks you will see evergreen trees strung with electric candles. We very, very rarely saw colored lights such as we use on our trees and outside decorations, and we really miss them. The downtown stores' decorations seemed to really lack something with only using white lights. I don't mean to imply that they didn't use anything but lights, because they use evergreens and other decorations with the lights.

The Germans do not decorate their windows and outside their homes like we Americans do. Occasionally you do see an outside evergreen tree strung with electric candles. though. Perhaps the reason for this is that most Germans live in apartments. However, have you ever thought of putting a Christmas tree in your car? Well, the Germans do, some of them anyway. They attach a small tree with tiny lights to their dashboard. It's really not so surprising when you know that most Germans have fresh or plastic flowers in that place at other times of the year. It's really something to see, however! Even truck drivers have them.

Have you ever seen a Volkswagen carry a large Christmas tree? It's quite a sight when you see it coming! It looks like a small tree on top of the car because they usually rest it on their back bumper and then tie it on in some way. Another comical sight was one VW that had put their tree in the trunk, which is in the front, you know, and closed it as much as possible. You could see branches sticking out all around and it looked like some huge mouth gobbling it up! A more common sight that looked a little strange to us was people walking home with a Christmas tree tucked under their arms!

The Germans really have it made this time of the year. Not only do they have two and a half legal holidays for Christmas, but most factories close down between Christmas and New Year's or at least operate on skeleton crews! How would you like that?

To sum it all up, it was very interesting and "ein sehr frohe Weihnachten" (a very Merry Christmas) for us.

Carole's December 28, 1964, letter to Mom and Dad:

I am having all kinds of fun this morning learning how to type with gloves on, so pardon my mistakes. There was no heat at all when I came in this morning, but we are getting some now; it will still take a while for it to really warm up in here. Our temperature is around twenty-five outside. The same thing happened last Thursday, but that day Rick came over to get me about 9:30 for a "coffee" they were having for the fellows and their wives in the pay branch. I escaped it then, but so far no one has come to get me so I just have to stick it out!

I hope you and my family had a nice time together yesterday, but I imagine you did. We were thinking of you. I no doubt imagine you have heard about the phone call Christmas Day, so I need not say much about it except it sure was nice to hear voices from home again. It's strange to think that you can talk like that to people across so many miles. We had a very good connection.

Rick has said the thank you, but I want to thank you again for all your gifts and thoughts. We really appreciate them. I have always wanted a bracelet like the one you gave me. We sold them (black and white ones) in the gift shop [Carole's summer job on the Indiana toll road], but I just never felt I could really afford to splurge on one. I really like the color of this one, too. Thank you so much. The ring fits perfectly and is also very pretty. I wore them both Christmas Days with my white wedding dress. The gloves are just exactly what I needed. I have some, but they aren't any good for driving because they are slippery. I sure will get a lot of use out of them.

We got to the Steins about 12:30 p.m. and had dinner about 1:00 p.m. We didn't have a turkey dinner, but a goose dinner which is more traditional at Christmas over here. We had never had goose before, but it was good, I thought. We also had potatoes, cooked cabbage (purple), and baked apples. For dessert we had a kind of lemon chiffon with whipped cream. The whole dinner was very good.

This afternoon we are going to take the car in for its checkup, and then while it's there we will walk downtown and shop. Rick has allowed me five dollars to spend any way I want. I forgot one gift I received, that was Arpege cologne from Claudia.

I didn't go shopping this afternoon after all. I was too cold and decided to stay home and get warm. I will do it another time.

I probably won't be writing until next year. We hope you will have a happy one!

December 31, 1964, letter to Mom and Dad:

Today is payday. At last the end of the year is near and it is hard for me to believe it! The weather today is amazing! It's around forty degrees right now and when the sun comes out maybe the snow will completely melt away!

Tonight will be a quiet one for us. This is okay with us. I wish we could see the football games tomorrow. But next year! Living in Germany has been quite the experience and I have learned a lot about these people and Europe that I would have never known.

Dad, we will get your T-shirts today and send them to you on Monday. You should get them first of February. Just deduct the total amount from what I owe you.

Carole and I had to get up this morning at 5:15 a.m. to get pay. They do this now so that we can get to work on time at 8:00 a.m. Payday used to be a holiday when I arrived a year ago!

Thanks for all of your letters! Happy New Year!

Carole's December 31, 1964, journal entry:

We worked in the morning, getting there for payday formation at 6:00 a.m.! It's now after work, shopping and lunch we took our bath and then read, wrote letters, etc.

In the evening we had pizza and Pepsi about 10:00 p.m. and played a Monopoly game we made. At midnight we went to the front window to see the fireworks we had heard would be there. They were there! The fireworks were all around the horizon, in town, in our front yard, and over our roof. We watched them for a half hour or so; the weather was very mild. Then our telephone rang and it was our landlord Hans wishing us a Happy New Year. Soon after that he came up to get us to come downstairs for coffee and cake. We couldn't refuse, so down we went. There was another German couple there and a real swinging party going on the TV. Something was going on all the time, singing, comedians, and clowns, and so on. Hans was feeling pretty "high" and clowning around himself. It was quite a time!

Hans was quite a comic too. We left at 2:30 a.m. when the TV party ended, but the rest were still going strong.

Carole's January 1, 1965, journal entry:

We drove to the Stein's early afternoon. Hans, Babs, and Claus and us two then went to Claus's home for tea and cookies and to see some very interesting slides on Vienna, Spain, and North Africa. Then we returned to the Stein's home for the rest of the evening. It was around this time that Carole and I started talking about where we should settle in Michigan. I told Carole that I didn't want to go back to Adrian, and I didn't want to live in the Detroit area nor in Niles. She said it didn't matter to her where we lived. Kalamazoo came to mind since we both had relatives there. Dad had always thought highly of Kalamazoo and I never heard a negative remark about it. It was a university town; both Western Michigan University and Kalamazoo College are located there. I asked Carole about moving to Kalamazoo and she thought that would be a nice place to make our home. It was decided that July would find us starting my career in Kalamazoo. Carole wrote to the school system in Kalamazoo and was given a teacher position in an elementary school there, so she had a job waiting for her starting in September 1965.

January 4, 1965, letter to Mom and Dad:

Yesterday I wrote a letter to the chamber of commerce in Kalamazoo requesting information. As of now, we are planning on moving there because we both like the city. I think Upjohn will be the first place I will write to. It sounds like a nice place to work. [Upjohn Company was a pharmaceutical manufacturing company founded in Kalamazoo in 1886. It was probably the largest employer in Kalamazoo. Dad knew one of the higher managers or officers in this company and arranged an interview for me, but that was as far as I got for consideration of employment. I was a little disappointed. Many years ago another company took over Upjohn and moved the business out of Kalamazoo.]

Carole's January 4, 1965, letter to Mom and Dad:

It's me, now at home, 3:00 p.m. We received your letter today saying you are sure you will be here June 1, which is just great! We are really looking forward to it.

I was able to pick up our slides today taken over Christmas. I'm very pleased with them, and I know Rick will be too. We really had no idea how they would be since nearly all were taken with the tripod and leaving the lens open a few seconds. I'm so happy they are okay, because this was our only Christmas here. Some of them are very beautiful.

Rick and I will go to the show tonight; it's a Jack Lemmon comedy, *Good Neighbor Sam*. The guys at work told Rick it was really funny.

We are still receiving Christmas cards, got five or six today. They were mailed boat mail about December 10.

We spent a quiet weekend at home except for Friday at the Steins. We played games, read, wrote letters, etc. I sure do have a lot of letters to write again. I have been sort of holding them back until Christmas was over. However, I won't have to write too much since I typed up a lot of copies describing Christmas over here so I don't have to rewrite it all the time. Did you know that Phil (my brother) sent us thirty dollars (Ten dollars of it for our anniversary)? We were really surprised. It's too generous of him. We will use most of it to extend our insurance one month, June 15-July 15. We found that it will cost us about twenty-seven dollars. I am going to write to him next.

Carole's January 7, 1965, letter to Mom and Dad:

We certainly will pick you up in Stuttgart, May 28. We are so glad you will be here a few days before we leave. There are some things we would like you to see around here.

My feet are much better now since they don't give me any trouble any more. We got a letter from my Aunt Susie (today, and they sure enjoyed your visit there. They think I have some pretty wonderful in-laws, but that is no news to me. I knew that a long time ago. [Aunt Susie is Susanna Borsos, the sister of Carole's father, Bryce Taylor. She lived in Dearborn in the Detroit area. I believe Carole's parents went to visit Susie and her husband Rick, and they all came to Ferndale to visit with Dad and Mom. Carole's grandparents, Rolfe and Vesta Taylor, also thought highly of Dad and Mom.]

Remember the fellow [Jim Brazo] from my home church we met at Chiemsee last summer? Well, he came by to see us Monday afternoon; he had to drive a truck here. He and his new wife (Ann) want to do something with us some weekend. We will make plans via mail. Sure was a nice surprise to see him again.

January 9, 1965, letter to Mom and Dad:

Dad, in a week I will send you a check for one hundred, ninety-five dollars and fifty cents. According to my books I will owe you fifteen hundred and twenty-five dollars on July 1, okay? We expect to have you paid off by the end of the year. I hope Carole can start teaching in Kalamazoo in September. We will use her wages to pay you off. So if this works out, we will have settled the debt by the first of January.

Carole's folks had a great time in Ferndale and Dearborn. They all like you, and Carole's grandmother (Vesta Taylor) mentioned that she was really impressed with all of your talents and interests, Mother.

Mother, you will leave Germany with the thought that they use more flowers than any other country. In Bavaria every window (just about) has flowers under it. The Germans love flowers and everywhere you go you will see them. They even put them in their cars. The car used for weddings has a row of flowers across the windshield.

January 17, 1965, letter to Mom and Dad:

Dad, I mentioned to you before about my writing to Kalamazoo. Well, the chamber of commerce turned my letter over to the employment bureau, and they in return sent me a letter and just mentioned for me to see them when I move to Kalamazoo. So I never received any information regarding companies and living facilities. Maybe they do plan to send something.

Carole's January 17, 1965, letter to Mom and Dad:

We are having a pretty quiet Sunday afternoon except for the howling wind outside.

I have another job now. Thursday afternoons I will be doing some housecleaning and ironing for Claudia. She will pay me four dollars for an afternoon and I start next Thursday. We will save a part of it for small emergencies, and I will spend the rest on things I want to buy here, which is why I want to earn this extra money.

I still haven't spent the five dollars free spending money yet, but I now know what and where I'm going to spend it. I just found out this week from a friend on post that the WMF factory not far from us has a "seconds shop" where they sell their rejects. WMF is the best silver and stainless factory in Germany. They make beautiful trays (my folks' tray is WMF), serving pieces and the like. In this seconds shop you can buy a six dollar tray for two dollars and pie servers fifty cents. She showed me some things she bought, and we can't see anything wrong with them. It's only open 2:00-5:00 p.m. Monday-Friday, so some time we will arrange to go together. I can't wait to go. We will have to go when you folks are here too.

January 20, 1965, letter to Mom and Dad:

I have decided to take one extra day. The maximum time I will have is now June 2- July. 1.

Carole's January 25, 1965, letter to Mom and Dad:

We had a nice visit with Babs during Saturday. Didn't see Hans, but we asked about him going to the States in March. I guess he is in quite a dilemma now. He doesn't know whether to finish school here or in the States. There are advantages and disadvantages to both and a lot of things to consider. Whatever he finally decides, we hope it works out for the best.

It's funny when you mentioned in your letter how crazy Davi is about Hans, and you wondered if Hans really loved her. Well, we have gotten the same impression over here only turned around. By that I mean that Hans is crazy about Davie (Wilson, in my high school class), but we have wondered if Davie really loves him. Let's hope they get together as soon as they can.

Last Friday Claudia went to Stuttgart to pick up some things for the office. We have a nice new executive chair, which is very comfortable. I get it in the mornings and she in the afternoons. We have a brand new ditto machine of our own. We have had to use the service club's before. Then she also brought back that you might call an "electronic drummer." You can set to any rhythm and add cymbals, cowbells, or what have you and it will make the sounds of a drummer in this rhythm. I haven't heard it play yet, but we probably will be fooling with it tomorrow. Today is her day off. There are a few other things that were there for us too, like a saber saw and electrical and paper supplies.

I rather enjoyed my afternoon of housekeeping for Claudia. They have a nice little apartment. I also did some ironing for her too, which she is paying me extra for. She has a conference in Frankfurt this Thursday through Saturday, so she probably won't want me to clean. She said I might as well take Thursday and Friday mornings off since I have been working some afternoons anyway.

Yes, Dad, I would appreciate it if you could get me the names and superintendents of the various school districts around Kalamazoo. I don't know anything about their districts or suburbs. Find out as many as you can, because by summer I will need as many chances for openings as I can get! I did plan on getting as much done as far as applications, transcripts, references and all that before coming home. We will have to wait until Rick gets his job before I can do anything final.

Thanks, Dad, for your advice on Upjohn's for Rick. It sounds good and we will follow it. However, let me clear up one minor thing. Rick will be released from the army right after arriving in the States, which will be near the end of July. They will not hold him until August 4th.

Carole's February 2, 1965, letter to Mom and Dad:

I'm not at work really, although I am at the office. It's 6:00 p.m. and I had to come back on post to buy some things I forgot earlier this afternoon. Rick is on KP but won't be ready to leave until seven, so I just came in here to spend the time typing a letter to you.

We had a real nice three-day weekend. Hans came over to see us Sunday afternoon and it was nice to visit with him again because it was New Year's since we saw him last. He is definitely coming back to Michigan in March. He leaves March 5th.

Carole's February 5, 1965, letter to Mom and Dad:

We can get you blankets and anything else ahead of time if you want. Did I ever tell you that from what I have read we will have to do a lot of hand laundry on our trip to get our clothes and underwear clean? This is what everyone does, from what they said, so those wash-and-wear shirts you got, Dad, are just the thing. Thus, as much as you can, bring nylon, Dacron, and other easy-dry fabrics

It's rather cold today, and it is snowing, We have about five or six inches of snow now. It's that very wet, heavy snow. Rick and those living off post were allowed to leave at 2:00 p.m. due to the weather.

Carole's February 10, 1965, letter to Mom and Dad:

This morning is our coldest so far, it was ten degrees at 8:00 a.m. I'm here in the hut almost sitting on top of the radiator with my coat and sweater on, trying to keep warm!

I got the 1964-65 book edition of *Europe on $5 a Day* from the library and I'm going through it too, marking and making notes on the hotel lists the travel offices sent to us. So between the two of us we ought to do all right.

PWOC meeting was yesterday and we went to an old folk's home here in Goppingen. We had a very interesting time. It was quite a large place. You could easily tell those old ladies and gentlemen were just more than pleased that we came and would think of them. They enjoyed it immensely and we did too. It was fun trying to communicate with them.

Saturday Rick and I went out to the woods beneath Hohenstaufen to take some pictures because there was still snow on the trees. It was beautiful there! There was even more snow on the trees there, and it was a really bright white winter wonderland. It was lighter there in the woods than in town. Never saw anything like it. While we were walking around we saw a deer. It's the first wild deer we have ever seen. Then as we were leaving to go home we got stuck in the snow, but with a few branches under the tires and the help of a German man we got out all right. There are always lots of Germans walking around out there.

Dad, you said you wanted to see Heidelberg and take a boat ride up the Rhine. The only way we could arrange that would be for Rick to take a pass right after you get here, but it is doubtful he could get it since our trip to Berlin is in May and we will be starting our big leave in just a few more days. You could do this on the way to England. We hate to take away time on our big trip because we are anxious to get to Switzerland and spend a lot of time there. We will, of course, cover Holland on our trip.

February 11, 1965, letter to Mom and Dad:

We both have February 22 off (Monday), and Carole and I will go down to the WMF factory for the buying of a few cheap "defective silver items." We only have 20DM (five dollars) to spend. We sure wish money grew on trees!

Five months from this coming Monday, I am scheduled to leave here. Tomorrow I will submit the paperwork for our Berlin trip. I just have to show Carole's passport for the forms to be completed.

Carole's February 15, 1965, letter to Mom and Dad:

We want to live right in Kalamazoo or on the outskirts, so we decided to just write to the school districts within ten miles. The thought of commuting twenty miles doesn't appeal to me at all unless that should be our only choice. I have taken the map the chamber of commerce sent us and located nearly all of the school districts you listed. As of now, I will write to Kalamazoo (of course), Comstock, Comstock Park (is that next to Comstock or an entirely different area?), Parchment, Richland, Gull Lake Community Schools, Galesburg, Augusta Public Schools and Vicksburg. Do you know where Mattawan Community Schools and Otsego Public Schools are? I couldn't locate them and am not familiar with them. Also, what about Portage? Do they have a separate school system? I appreciate you getting this information for me, Dad. Also, do you happen to know anything about any of these school systems, how good they are supposed to be, salaries or anything, because I know nothing at all. Don't go out of your way at all because in my letters I am asking some things of them. I just thought you might happen to know something that would shed a little light somewhere. You know, I may have an "in" at the Comstock School because I can say I have already taught there since I did my student teaching in Comstock School (that was the name of the school in Adrian). Ha!

One night when we were down at Hans's (our landlord) we told him about your coming here at the end of May. They seemed to get kind of excited about it! Anyway, a few days later when Hans was up here, he said that he has a room on the second floor that you two can stay in. Won't that be nice. "Hotels too expensive" he said. You probably will want to pay them something and they would be more than pleased if you paid in cigarettes (one dollar and fifty cents per carton) and coffee (one dollar and twenty-five cents)! But that is something we can think about after you are here. I know, though, the coffee and cigarettes would mean more to them than a little money because they are so expensive for them to buy. We buy them instant coffee, but we buy the Steins regular grind coffee. I can buy two pounds of Maxwell House regular coffee for one dollar and fifty cents and for them to buy just one pound of German coffee (which is not as good, they say) they pay two dollars. The same is true for instant coffee.

"Old Man Winter" has finally caught up with us here in Goppingen. Our snow from last weekend never melted away during the week. Thursday and Friday I think we got a few more inches. Then

Sunday it snowed heavily nearly all day long, giving us probably four more inches. And then again today it has been snowing heavily all day long, another three to four inches! I had planned to do the laundry this afternoon but have postponed it until tomorrow. The roads are pretty slippery. Rick was let off at three this afternoon and it took him thirty minutes to get up our little hill in front (only three houses long and not overly steep) and park! He tried three times to get up it and couldn't make it even with me and a couple or three neighbors pushing, and a VW just isn't that hard to push! But there was just no traction at all. So we finally had to back down the hill again and go around the block, which is really a long way around. And then when we got to our parking place someone else was taking it! But luckily one of the neighbors was waiting to see if we made it okay and he explained to this guy that it was our spot and he moved for us. Even then we still had to have help getting into the parking place because of all the snow, but we finally made it. It's a great life over here!

A couple of times this winter our gate out in front froze shut and we couldn't get it open. Every German house is well fenced in, and ours is no exception. There is no other way to get out or in except through that gate, so Rick lifted me over and then he hopped over the gate. [We were surprised to learn that the houses in our area, including the one we lived in, had only one door (in the front) for arriving and exiting.]

February 18, 1965, letter to Mom and Dad:

Boy, do we have snow! We have received more snow these last two weeks than the combined winter of 1963-64. Snow, snow, snow, piles of it! The roads are a mess but safe from sliding at 20-25 mph. I guess our winter is this month. We are hoping for an early spring because our coal is very limited, maybe just three weeks! We too are looking forward to the big trip. We received our clearance for Berlin this week and I believe our leave request for this trip will be approved.

Kalamazoo seems to offer a lot and I think this is why we are determined to live there, so we will and use every means to find a good job. We will need living quarters and where it will be, Kalamazoo or outside of the city, we don't know. We just take one thing at a time and continue our faith in God that he will get us through these tasks. Everything has turned out for the best in my past, and I have faith that it will continue in the same direction.

Carole has also been working with the 5 dollar a day book. She has made a lot of notes from this book and another one, plus the massive amount of literature we have received from each country. The big problem, seriously, is finding places to go to the bathroom. One officer told me they were desperate for one in Italy and they finally found a place in a train station. When nobody was looking they tore up a telephone book for toilet paper! A restroom can be hard to find. We have found that the German males relieve themselves off the road and behind a tree or in the open (one exception, we saw a man relieving himself on the road facing oncoming cars. From our distance it looked like he had a bent yellow-color cane in front of him, but as we drove by him it was obvious that it was not a cane). We are not sure with females, but we did see one woman squatting down behind a little short brush. We got used to it.

Carole's February 19, 1965, letter to Mom and Dad:

I'm at work, but by myself and no work except of my own. As Rick said, I'm also going thru the *5 dollar a Day* book. It's loaded with all kinds of helpful information. But you go ahead and read it too and jot down anything you want to because I may miss something for one reason or another. However, I would like to say a few things: for our budget, Rick and I will have fourteen-fifteen dollars a day. Of this we want to spend no more than five dollars lodging for both of us including taxes and service charges (watch this when you are jotting down prices; if he does not say its included, it isn't) Now I am pretty well through with the book, am just doing odds and ends now, and I know we can easily keep within this five dollars limit. In fact, as you get into it more you will see that we can get double rooms for two dollars and fifty cents to four dollars in what he says are clean, decent, comfortable, but plain places. Now this kind of thing really appeals to me, because the more we can save the better off we will be. You read this book and see what you think. Another thing to remember is that we will actually be spending very little time in the hotel room, just a place to rest and sleep. But as he suggested, we will always check the room first and if it isn't appropriate we don't have to take it.

For Copenhagen [Denmark] I have pretty well decided the Missionshotellet at 27 Longang Straede is where we will stay. Both the *5 dollar a Day* book and this other book I read said it was the best buy and it is centrally located also. I will let you look up the details on it. I will write ahead for reservations later on because this will be one of our first stops and there should be no delays. Is this one okay with you folks?

From your letter, Dad, I wasn't sure if you understood that only in England and Holland are huge breakfasts always included with the room. Elsewhere they do not necessarily offer breakfast with the room, but most offer it for an additional fee, of course, and these breakfasts are continental style, rolls and coffee or some other drink. I understand from Claudia that the croissants (breakfast rolls in France) are just delicious. I have gotten the impression from my reading that it is still cheaper to have your breakfast in a bakery or café bar than at your hotel or restaurant. Did you get that same impression? But sometimes we will have convenience to think of too. We will see as we go along. Another tip from another book was to buy oranges at fruit stands to get your orange juice because it is very expensive to buy. As far as the rest of our budget allotments go, Rick figures on two dollars and fifty cents for meals and I think this can be done also, although if it is three dollars or four dollars for the day that won't matter too awfully much. Breakfast is cheap and lunches we can get very cheaply by buying bread and sandwich makings from local markets and grocery stores. I don't imagine we will want to do this day after day, but lunches in most places (cafeterias especially) seem quite inexpensive too. The *5 dollar a Day* book seems to give quite a few restaurants everywhere where you get very-filling meals for one dollar to one dollar and fifty cents and sometimes less.

The rest of the fourteen dollars to fifteen dollars per day will go for souvenirs, booklets, postcards, slides that we want to buy, admission fees, and of course other things we want to buy. I think this is a very ample budget allowance because there will be days when we will be traveling and not spending much for these latter things. So this money can be added to other days! Have you noticed the section in the back on bargain shopping tips? Be sure and read it. I can't wait to get some of these things. By the way, what edition do you have? Mine is 1964-65. Doesn't really matter because I don't think there are a lot of changes, nothing drastic anyway.

I have and am copying the sections in the back, capsule vocabularies and menu translations, so you need not worry about those. We also have the money exchange rates.

Be sure and read the chapter on packing. It is a very good list and tips to go by. I have cut down their packing lists even further because we don't plan on going swimming (I don't have a suit in the first place) nor are we interested in any of the night spots where you would have to dress up, so for us, Mom, I don't think we will need dressy heels or evening wear. What do you folks say? I also don't think we will need slacks or shorts, Mother. In London, Mother, I wore my lavender three-piece suit and light raincoat. It was a little cool, but I was okay. It will probably be a little warmer for you in July. As of now, I plan to take my lavender three-piece suit, one cotton dress, one blouse, and maybe one other outfit. I will have to check my wardrobe to see if I have anything more that is wrinkle resistant and wash and wear! More later on all of this. We will be glad to have your comments, questions, or suggestions on anything.

February 20, 1965, letter to Mom and Dad:

We still have a lot of snow, but the sun is out. I am just waiting here at work to go home. Just about one and a half hours to go! We have been receiving a lot of mail from you two lately, and we hope this can continue.

Mother, thank you for the check. We may go to that factory this coming weekend. We will see if we can find something that we think you would like. Carole seems determined to get down there and since we are both off Monday I don't have too much choice, I guess, but to take her down there. I am hoping it will be worthwhile.

Carole's February 21, 1965, letter to Mom and Dad:

We just finished a light supper of sandwiches with German bread. This noon we had the bread with ham and cheese put in the oven a few minutes to melt the cheese, a favorite of ours now and a "trick" we learned from Frau Louise Stein recently.

Saturday morning I walked to a nearby German bakery to buy bread and on the way home I met an Indian (India). He stopped to ask me directions in German, and when I said I didn't understand (in German) and I was an American, he said "Oh, you speak English" and from then on spoke to me in English. He is working for a factory in Esslingen or Eislingen (both near here, and don't remember which he said) whose home plant is in Detroit, Michigan! It's a small world. The name of the plant is Excelsor or Excello or something along those lines.

We had a nice visit with Hans. Won't be long and he will be seeing you! Sure got cold last night, besides our five blankets we ended up putting all our coats over us too! However, part of the reason was that we didn't have a fire in our pot stove because we got home late and went right to bed. We are trying to conserve on our coal, which is getting low by heating just the one room. We are using the kitchen only for preparing meals and washing dishes. I wish the temperatures would get up out of the twenties.

Yes, Dad, you hit it right on the head when you asked, "Don't" the Germans believe in too much warmth?" Remember, they don't heat every room of their house and they are real "bugs" on fresh air. Lots of times, all through the winter, we see windows open on the way to work. Many just dress in heavy sweaters to walk outside while we shiver in our coats. Lots of times we see women or men outside shoveling snow in just an ordinary sweater, even on really cold days. But we also have a special problem with the heat in the hut [office] because we have so many flats, so much lumber, props, furniture, and such to store that we have to pile them in front of the radiators in the back, so those are turned off. It would help some if we could have those on, but that cold air still comes in the door pretty good, which is right by my desk.

It's Tuesday morning and I am at work, but not at the hut. Our temperature this morning is nine degrees, and when I found out there wasn't any heat at all in the hut it sure didn't take me long to decide to come over to the service club! We still don't have our phone service, so I know no one can try to call. I left a note on the door for Claudia and any visitors.

Carole's February 28, 1965, letter to Mom and Dad:

Mother, you spoke of a tote bag to bring with you, which you will certainly need! Do you know what you see everywhere here? Remember the black, plastic "fishnet"-type shopping bag you gave me for Christmas a year ago? That's the kind of thing they use over here exactly! I wish I had brought mine, because when you do go downtown they don't put things in bags, they wrap them for you and then the "natives" stick them in their "suitcase type purse" or in the bag I described, and that's how everyone does it. You even see the women carrying their own baskets to the market to put their parcels in. If you can easily find my shopping bag, bring it with you when you come; if you can't don't bother at all looking deeply for it. As far as I remember, it's still in the long, white box you put it in, but I am not sure where that is anymore!

Carole's March 2, 1965, letter to Mom and Dad:

Believe it or not, we finally made it to WMF today! I was a little disappointed because it wasn't quite the bargain place I was led to believe (maybe I just misunderstood). Prices seemed to range twenty to forty percent less than retail, which is still good, but not six dollar trays for two dollars; they were four dollars. But nevertheless, we are quite pleased with what we got and feel we got quite a lot for our money. Our "prize" is a rectangular tray that you hang on the wall. It has the swirls on it (similar to my folks' tray) with a plain border and a picture scene in black etching of a boat and what looks like a New York skyline. It is quite attractive and unique, we feel. Cost us 18DM or four dollar and fifty cents. A close second to this is a cake platter with ball feet. Again, it has the swirls with plain border and in the middle is a star-like decoration that is hard to describe, so I won't. You will see it later on. This was 26.50DM or six dollars and sixty cents. Then we also bought a pair of candleholders with candles for 18.50DM. These are of a modern styling and have the swirls too! Now, for your part, we bought a tray, a napkin holder and a small dish. These three items total nine dollars.

March 6, 1965, letter to Mom and Dad:

Dad, Carole will give you all of the information pertaining to trains over here. On the train to London I took the regular ticket, in which the seats weren't too good. The train is a little noisy also. I think I received one hour of sleep that night to London. If I am right, every night there is one train leaving Stuttgart for London. The train leaves Stuttgart 11:45 p.m. and it was in London by 3:30 p.m. the following day. Thus a fifteen-hour trip, but it is interesting seeing the countryside and the cities. You two will enjoy yourselves. We too are very anxious for our trip. I just wish we could take more days for this trip and also more money.

Dad, that's all right, we will share half of the gasoline expense. That is nice of you to offer us financial aid, but I expect to have enough when it's time to start the trip. We will have about three hundred and ninety dollars for our twenty-nine-day trip. I expect to average four dollars and fifty cents per night for the two of us (hotel) and food about three dollars and fifty cents. This is eight dollars a day for the two of us. In Germany gas will cost us twenty-five cents a gallon, and we will get thirty miles per gallon. France will be cheaper since we will have coupons. I think we can get everything in the car, but it will be stuffed!

After work and on the way home I will stop in at the bakery for some bread. There is a chance that they will be completely sold out of it when I get there. It is good for sandwiches!

If we continue to have over thirty-two-degree weather and no additional snow, it is possible we will have bare ground by the end of next week!

Carole's March 9, 1965, letter to Mom and Dad:

We had a very nice visit with Babs Saturday. We will probably be going down there next weekend.

I got my applications from Parchment and Vicksburg. Parchment sent a little booklet telling about their system and community. It seems to be an excellent system. They have an average financial support and nearly all buildings have been built within the last eight years.

Vicksburg must have a good system also since he said they have a very small yearly turnover. Salaries were five thousand dollars-four thousand, eight hundred respectively, so I imagine the others will be in that range also. I can't imagine myself making that much money!

Rick should be in the dentist's office right now having one of his wisdom teeth removed! Ha! Last time he did ask that dentist about the necessity of it. The dentist told him that the teeth are growing into the curvature of his back molars, and by the time he is thirty years old it will be giving him a lot of pain. Rick would probably have to be hospitalized for their removal because of the greater difficulty removing them from under this curvature. I'm sure that is a trouble and expense we can do without in another five years.

Now I will go through your letters: first, the most recent and in reference to your notes on Copenhagen and Amsterdam. I am almost sure I mentioned before that I thought the Mission Hotel Hebron was our best bet for Copenhagen. I even have it located on a map we have, so we shouldn't have too much difficulty finding it. However, the price is now more like two dollars a person, which is still all right.

Now on to Amsterdam: we have a leaflet on hotels in Amsterdam, and looking up the hotels you listed the prices are a little higher, Munttoren is 8.75 guilders, Buchof is 9.35 guilders, Fantasea is 9.20 to 11.50 guilders, Van Gilder is 9.80 guilders, Huize de Moor is 10.00 guilders. [The Holland exchange rate during this time was 3.6 guilders per U.S. dollar. On this trip we didn't make hotel reservations but used the hotel listings we had for possibilities of a room.] The others I couldn't find listed. We would still like to keep our hotel costs down as much as possible, three dollars to four dollars rather than five dollars, but also are trying to consider your wants. I'm no authority, of course, but I have gotten the impression that many of these lower-priced places are just as comfortable as the others, they just lack the "frills," but I could be wrong. Perhaps by June we will have a little more firsthand information after our trip to Berlin and Vienna. We have picked out a hotel in Berlin that seems to be nice for only three dollars for a double room. By the way, double room means room for two, not two rooms.

Hans left us the card from the hotel he stayed at in Barcelona named Central Residencia or something like that. Hotels are cheap in Spain, one dollar and twenty-five cents per person or thereabouts.

Rick just came in from the dentist. He didn't remove one of his wisdom teeth today because he was suffering from a hangover and couldn't completely see straight. He filled one of his cavities, though.

We don't know exactly what our plans are for after the trip. We will find a room somewhere, and I will probably leave as soon as possible, then Rick can stay in the barracks until "leave time" for him. I will be going to Niles since my family would want this and you probably wouldn't be home anyway. I will have to check soon with American Express about these dependent charter flights and find out when they are and how soon I should make my reservation.

March 14, 1965, letter to Mom and Dad:

Yesterday was our warmest day, and I think spring is coming! We still have snow here, but a few days of nice weather and we will lose it. We are so sick of winter!

We received our two additional bags of coal, and I think this will last us.

Yesterday I finally washed the car and the layers of dirt just rolled off. The winter was rough for the car and I hated to see it that way since it is a new car. A garage is needed to keep a new car in good shape. I found rust on the inside fenders but got most of it off. As for the body, I found three long scratches on one side of the car. I can't figure out how they got there! Also I found a few places where the paint has been chipped off.

Carole's March 17, 1965, letter to Mom and Dad:

Happy St. Patrick's Day!

I am in the laundromat right now and surprisingly it's not busy at all. Wouldn't have had any trouble except one of the washer's "spin dry" cycle didn't work properly and my clothes were wringing wet. Just will take more time in the dryers!

Guess where I went yesterday! Back to the WMF shop. The girl who first told me about it and I went together and I drove. I found another small dish similar to the one we thought we were buying for you last time, Mother. It is a little bigger and cost a little more than the other, but I bought it for you anyway. That extra dollar you sent me for postage will cover it (postage was only Ninety cents for something like that) so don't send any more money.

Now, tomorrow or Friday we will be sending you another package. This will include the new dish for you wrapped in the "dirty white" tissue again (no other way to describe it!) and a little package for Grandmother [Hulda Burrows, Mother's mother]. This is wrapped in blue tissue and I have a card taped on it with her name so that shouldn't be a problem. Would you please give it to her for us? It's just easier for us to send things together rather than separately. Hope you don't mind playing, "Santa." Ha! Don't say anything to her about this since I will write a little later and tell her we are sending her something.

Saturday I received a letter and application from Kalamazoo Public Schools, and surprisingly, Dad, they are not the leader in salaries for the area. I would start at four thousand, nine hundred dollars whereas in Parchment and Portage, I think it was, starting salary is five thousand dollars. Not much difference though. Anyway, he was the only one so far who was encouraging about offering a contract before a personal interview. They have done it on occasion in similar situations; it's on a tentative basis until a personal interview can be arranged, but that would be fine with me. Of course, they want as much information as possible now, and I think my lack of experience will probably hinder me, but we will just have to see how things work out. I really would rather teach in Portage or Parchment, not because of the salary alone but they seem to have excellent systems and excellent communities to back them up, but in my position I can't take a chance on them if Kalamazoo offers me a contract this spring!

Still haven't heard from three school systems: Comstock, Comstock Park, and Richland-Gull Lake.

We are having beautiful spring weather now, the snow is nearly all gone. Crocuses are blooming and I see the tulips and the daffodils are about three inches out of the ground in our front yard. We can't wait until they are in full bloom!

If it's still nice and sunny tomorrow afternoon, I think I will go downtown shopping. I have a couple Hummels to buy for my grandmother and Aunt Suzie [Carole father's sister]. They are paying for them. [Hummel figurines are made in West Germany; these cute figurines of children are based on the drawings of Sister Maria Innocentia Hummel.]

Carole's March 22, 1965, letter to Mom and Dad:

It's Monday morning and a rather gray, damp one. It rained nearly all day long yesterday and into the night. It's still spring like warmth so it's not too bad.

I don't have your Paris notes with me, but there were about three hotels whose prices were raised considerably, about a dollar. The others were the same or about so, anyway. I had concentrated on the same area you did. However, here is something else we have just learned about that could simplify things for us immensely in finding a hotel in Paris. On the Champs-Elysees (which would make it very easy to find) there is the Allied Armed Forces Personnel Service Center. We can go to them and tell them what we want in the way of a hotel, and they will get us rooms and tell us how to get there. The more I think about it, the more I think this is what we might do. I would write ahead for reservations, but there is always a possibility we may decide to spend a longer time in Amsterdam or take longer driving somewhere than we planned before Paris. But we aren't traveling in the peak season so we shouldn't have trouble getting the kind of place we want. This center is only for the military and their dependents, as you might guess, and they have all kinds of other services you can imagine, theater tickets, tours, even babysitting. So I think this would be a good place to begin our Paris stay; we can find out everything we want to know in one place and without language difficulties!

Yesterday I started putting all my notes that we will carry with us in their final form. I am even picking out and jotting down the routes to take, so should have everything down pat soon, although there is still room for changes as we go along. I have us to Luxemburg now.

Oh yes, I don't believe I have written since we finally found my paycheck. When my check still wasn't here Wednesday, I decided to call Claudia's boss in Stuttgart and find out about it (I had also found out that others had received theirs). He checked with his secretary the next morning and found that she had mailed it out early the previous week with another letter addressed in my name. I had received the letter that week just before Claudia left because she brought it to me, but I had certainly seen no check. Well, when talking with one of the service club girls she said that sometimes our mail comes to the subpost office, so we immediately checked over there and there it was, been there a week. I don't know why I have such troubles with my checks!

Rick has put in for a three-day pass for Easter weekend, April 16-18, to go to Vienna. Signs were encouraging that it would go through, and we hope so. Thus on your birthday Mother, we hope to be walking the streets of Vienna!

Thursday afternoon I walked downtown, mainly to look for a couple Hummels that my Grandma and Aunt Susie wanted me to get for them for gifts to others but also to do some looking around for myself. I only found one Hummel but still have time to get the other. For myself I found the cutest little bud vase and just couldn't believe the price when I looked at it. It only cost sixty-two cents. It's clear, crackled glass, about six to seven inches high and a very attractive shape. Rick likes it too. I saw lots of other things I would like, some way out of my price range and some other things I would like to pick up some other time. Bought a couple candy bars for Rick too.

I still haven't heard from three school systems I wrote to. I hope we will hear from them this week.

Carole's March 24, 1965, journal entry:

Rick had one of his lower wisdom teeth removed. (The post dentist never had done this before, and he had a hard time getting the tooth out. In fact, the tooth was broken into a few pieces during the process of removal. Rick suffered getting the tooth out and for the rest of week. The dentist did not want to attempt to take out the other lower wisdom tooth). Rick had the rest of the week off from work. The first day was miserable for him but better the next couple of days except for headaches and eye aches. Not much swelling.

Carole's March 26, 1965, letter to Mom and Dad:

You should see your son right now. He looks like a little chipmunk storing plenty of nuts in his right cheek! The dentist finally did take one of his lower wisdom teeth out Wednesday morning. But don't worry, he is coming through just fine and isn't having much trouble at all. The first day is always hard, but since then he hasn't had much pain and the swelling is enough but not too much. Don't feel sorry for him, because he is just as happy as can be getting three days off work and can't wait to have the other one out! April 7th is his next appointment. Today has been a very dark, gloomy day. We have had rain off and on with strong gusty winds, even had a little thunder and lightning this afternoon. But it is better than snow! I hope the weekend clears up, though! Claudia and Kent got back okay this week, but they didn't make it to Greece because they just missed the ferry. So they spent their time in Southern Italy and had a marvelous time. She said Pompeii was absolutely fascinating. Wish we had the time to go down there, but next time we will make it there!

Claudia has just had quite a blow; the doctor says that she is pregnant. They didn't want any children yet because Kent is planning on grad school next fall and they are saving all their money for that. Plus I know Claudia would like to pursue her acting career. She has been taking birth control pills, but guess it is true that they are only 98 percent effective. Too bad she had to fall in the other 2 percent, though. Pregnancy will be hard on her too, because she had a back injury followed by surgery a couple of years ago. The doctor said she would have to spend the last two months in bed or sitting in chairs unless she wanted more back surgery.

I told you about talking to Jackie about Copenhagen. Well, while doing Claudia's laundry for her on Thursday afternoon I got to talking with a woman who has been all over Europe, but we talked mainly about Italy. She said of all the places in Europe she would choose Florence to live in (outside of the U.S., of course). So many people rave about Florence that we may want to spend more than one day there. Florence has good leather goods (*5 dollars a Day* says this too). She said you can get a good-quality calf leather men's wallet, the real flexible kind, for two dollars and fifty cents. You can buy many straw items there plus beautiful lace, tablecloths, and marble statues. It is the place to buy gold jewelry, she said, because they go more by weight than craftsmanship.

She said not to spend much time in Venice because there isn't a lot to see, a day as we have planned will be fine. Also we seemed to have provided ample time traveling from Barcelona (Spain) to Florence. The roads from Barcelona into France are good, but once you get around Monaco and the rest of the way into Italy it is slow going because there are so many curves and ups and downs. This is where the road follows the coastline, so it should be beautiful scenery anyway!

Rick is overjoyed that he can sleep in tomorrow and Sunday too. He has really had the "life of Riley" the last couple days, lying in bed all morning while I was at work!

Did we tell you we finally got a letter from Jack Hinkins last week or so? He had written a thank you letter earlier, he said, but it may not have gotten mailed.

During my high school years Jack Hinkins and I were like brothers. He was Ferndale High School class of 1960 while I was 1959. We sent him an attractive blanket, the reason for the thank you letter.

Carole's March 27, 1965, journal entry:

In the afternoon we went to Claus's house to visit with him and Babs. We played the Parcheesi game Rick made, and saw more of Claus's slides of Berlin and Italy.

Carole's March 30, 1965, letter to Mom and Dad:

I am alone this evening. Rick has his CQ tonight instead of tomorrow night. It's just as well. They have three of them on duty tonight instead of the usual two because they are sitting on quite a pot of money. Tomorrow morning is payday and so all that money (cash) is there for that.

We had a nice time with Babs and Claus on Saturday. We stayed at Claus's "haus" (house), had tea and cake as usual, played a Parcheesi game that Rick and I made up. That was fun. We also saw some slides of Berlin, Genoa, Rome, and a few others. There is a very interesting cemetery in Genoa that we will stop and visit while going through Italy.

Yes, we still will include Austria on our trip with you, that is, the western part Tyrol and the Alps. Vienna is too far to the east to try and include on our trip; not enough time.

Next Saturday we are going shopping and antique hunting in Stuttgart, and then in the evening we will see *My Fair Lady* in a downtown Stuttgart theater. They are having an English showing at 8:00 p.m. I'm so anxious to see it. Babs and Claus have seen it and like it too. They are making reservations for us and said we can get good seats for 6DM (one dollar and fifty cents). Rick isn't as enthused about it, but I really want to go now and said this could be my birthday treat, and so he agreed.

We were thinking yesterday that it would be just two months from then that we will be picking you folks up in Stuttgart. That reminds me, later this week I must go to the travel office to check on the trains and my plane for flying home.

Rick is no longer an out-processing clerk in PSD. While he was gone last week they eliminated all pay branches' out-processing clerks because they are getting short of men. Each clerk will do the out process for their own men now. Rick has been made a pay clerk and will work with another man on a battalion. He likes his team and fortunately the team leader wanted to keep him on his team, so he is. This new job will make him more subject to night work and TDY (Temporary Duty, such as going to Bamberg with a truck driver to deliver or pick up items or troops), but we are almost sure he will get out of any TDY because it will probably fall during our Berlin leave. Night work, though, will remain to be seen.

Rick is coming along, but not as well as we would like (wisdom teeth). It is healing up fine and the swelling is nearly all gone, but he is still bothered with headaches and bad eye aches and jaw aches. Anytime he uses his eyes at all he gets these eye aches. I don't understand why the tooth extraction could cause such eye aches, especially this long after the extraction, but it must be. However, he seemed to feel much better this afternoon, so maybe he is all right now. I sure hope so.

Just a note this morning from work (31st). Rick got home all right this morning from all night CQ. His aches are easing up some, but he still has them. He got the word that our June leave is all set! We are having another beautiful day today! I will run my errands and do my shopping before going home this noon. I imagine we will go downtown or somewhere this afternoon.

Carole's April 3, 1965, journal entry:

After work we went shopping at Robinson Barracks and downtown Stuttgart—bought my Aunt Suzie's things and another mug for Phil [Rick's brother]. Had sandwiches for supper and in the evening we went to see *My Fair Lady* at the Atrium Theatre in downtown Stuttgart and enjoyed it immensely.

Carole's April 5, 1965, letter to Mom and Dad:

We really liked the movie *My Fair Lady*. It was just beautiful, music and all. In fact, we loved it so much we are going back again to see it tonight. And mind you, this second trip is on Rick's initiative, not mine! He was really impressed with everything about it and believes it's the best movie he has ever seen! I imagine if we have a chance to see it in the States again when we get back we probably will! We both really thoroughly enjoyed everything about it. You have got to go see it! During intermission we got to talking with an Australian woman in front of us. She had seen it in German and said she thinks she is going to have to come back again to see it a third time this week. Maybe we will see her again tonight! She was really nice, and is in Germany for two years. We got to talking with her because Rick was wondering out loud to me how they could translate this into German because of the different English accents or dialects, whatever you would call it. She turned around and explained to us the different dialects or slang in Germany, and said that for the movie they used the Berlin German, which is comparable to the English Eliza started out with. She said there are separate dialects in Bavaria, Wurzburg, and the Swabians. In our area here they have their own too. She said it's very hard to understand someone from another of these regions because they are so different. I guess this is so because I had an American here on post tell me her husband learned German while in Bavaria and could get along well speaking with the natives of the area, but when he came here he couldn't understand these Swabians at all. [Before this movie started they showed scenes of a John Wayne cowboy movie with the cast, including John Wayne, speaking German. We enjoyed this also.]

We left here Saturday after lunch and went to Claus's house first to pick up the [movie] tickets then we went to Robinson Barracks and then downtown Stuttgart. We did the shopping for Aunt Susie, but all we got for ourselves were a pair of sunglasses for me and Anacin for Rick! But while looking for a Hummel for Aunt Susie, I got Rick interested in getting another Hummel for ourselves. I didn't even say anything; he just asked if I planned to get another one before we left because he would kind of like to have another. He saw a big one of three boys he especially liked, so we will see if we can get that one.

Boy! We never saw so many people in a downtown area as we did in Stuttgart. The sidewalks were packed and you could hardly get through some of the stores because of all the people. Reason? This was the first Saturday of the month, the only Saturday that the stores are open after 2:00 p.m. Plus the really big department stores were having a special sale on American-made goods. At least, this is what we could figure out from the displays and the signs "Aus Amerika." They flew big American flags outside with a huge skyline of New York. These were the stores you could hardly get through. We are going to ask Babs and Claus more about it when we see them.

We have a serious shortage of Campbell soups in our commissaries over here. About two weeks ago our commissary ran out of the popular vegetable and tomato. Last week the noodle soups and the other common ones disappeared. The shelves are literally bare! So while we were at Robinson Barracks we figured we would stock up on soups there. Well, they weren't really much better off. All they had were potato, minestrone, bean with bacon, cheese, clam chowder, and maybe a couple others. We hope they get some in soon!

We still have our beautiful, sunny, warm spring weather, have had it for a solid week now. Temperatures get up in the sixties. I just wore my gold corduroy outfit around Stuttgart, no coat during the afternoon. The leaves on the bushes are coming out, daffodils are blooming, and even the buds on fruit trees are just starting to blossom forth, we noticed on a short walk yesterday afternoon.

We have a circus in the next block to us now. It is just a big tent with all the trailers around it with a few booths selling foodstuffs.

Wednesday is the big day in our household. That's the day Rick hits ninety-nine days until his rotation date, and that really classifies a fellow as "short"!

Rick's headaches and eye aches are finally going away. He still gets them occasionally, but not as bad nor constantly.

I found out they haven't changed the one hundred, ninety dollars fare for a dependent's jet flight to New York. They won't have the July schedule until the end of this month, so after our Berlin trip we will start making arrangements for that.

I also found out about trains for you. There is train number D164 leaving Rotterdam (Holland) 7:58 a.m., arriving in Stuttgart 4:33 p.m., which will be just perfect if you can make that 7:58 a.m. You make no changes either, which helps. Just guess how much the fare is for that? It's only about sixteen dollars per person! The boat train to London leaves Stuttgart at 11:43 p.m. and arrives in London at 3:42 p.m. the following day. This fare is about twenty-five dollars per person.

This afternoon I will be sending you another package. This one contains a beer stein that we bought in an antique shop and would like you to try and sell for a profit at an antique shop around you. We paid two dollars and fifty cents for it. Also in this package is another Stuttgart mug for Phil [Rick's brother] like the one we gave him before. He said he wanted another to make a pair and they had them at Robinson Barracks Saturday, so we got one for him. We will write him about it too.

Carole's April 6, 1965, letter to Mom and Dad:

We enjoyed *My Fair Lady* just as much last night if not more than we did Saturday night. It is really a tremendous movie. I just heard on the radio that it won the Oscar for the best movie and I am not at all surprised. I am glad Rex Harrison got his Oscar too, but Rick and I can't understand why Audrey Hepburn didn't get even nominated for best actress. She was just as wonderful as Rex Harrison.

You said in your letter that your boat will be docking between 8:00 and 9:00 a.m. That eliminates that 7:58 a.m. train and it is too bad because the only other train leaves in the evening, 7:41 p.m. It arrives in Stuttgart 4:11 a.m. So we would suggest that after docking you check your baggage in the train station and then tour Rotterdam for the day. We won't be stopping there on our trip. After you get here you will no doubt want to rest up because we know how that overnight train ride is. Then in the afternoon (this will be Sunday) we can go visit the Steins. The next day Monday (May 31—Memorial Day) we can show you around the sights a bit, will take you to see the Ulm Cathedral and don't know what else yet.

Claudia has the sewing machine she has on rent here in the hut now, and said I am welcome to use it anytime I want to. Wish I had the money to get material and pattern for a dress to sew, but there are other things I would rather buy while here that I can't in the States, and I can always sew. However, I do have those placemats and apron that require some machine stitching and so will do that this week. Then too, I have offered to help Claudia sew her maternity wardrobe and she said she just might take me up on it.

I believe I told you about Rick losing his out-processing job, didn't I? Well, he has it back again, only it is more of an "undercover" job. The other clerks got together with the team leader and want him to do it for them since they don't know what they are doing and things are all messed up. Officially to everyone he is a clerk for 3/35th BN., but he will actually be doing the out-processing for the team. They claim that another team is doing this. Rick agreed to do it, but he is not really too happy to get it back since he was getting quite bored with the job, but yet he didn't like being a pay clerk either, so? He is just fed up with the army as a whole and is getting "too short" to care about any job he would have with them!

I asked someone who works at the commissary why they are so low on so many things, especially soup. She kind of shrugged her shoulders and said one reason may be because the central supply store is moving to another location, but other than that they don't know. They are getting a truckload during Wednesday but don't know what will be in it!

Carole's April 12, 1965, letter to Mom and Dad:

Well, here it is Monday again. The weeks are sure flying by. However, no one is complaining on this side of the ocean, and I'm sure you aren't either.

I really had a nice birthday on Saturday (April 10th). I want to thank you so much for your pretty card and five dollars. How did you know I would best like cards too, and more of that "extra green stuff"! Rick has already received a couple too. My family sent him a cute one. The outside says "Didn't know whether to get you Rolls Royce, T-bird, or Cadillac…" then on the inside "so here is a shiny new Lincoln" and there was a shiny Lincoln penny (1962)! We have already got just about all our birthday money spent, in the planning stage anyway.

I may buy a set of stainless silverware from WMF. There is a certain WMF tray we would like to get and thought we would at Robinson Barracks Saturday, but they had sold both since we were there just a week ago. Their prices are roughly the same as the reject store; some are higher. However, Rick did buy himself a big beer stein there that he wanted. Our PX here in Goppingen sells some very high-quality knives at reasonable prices. We have already bought some previously and with our birthday money we will complete our set. We also plan to get Rick a dozen T-shirts and some more underwear and me some nylons. That is all I can think of right now.

Incidentally, we are going to buy Phil and Bonnie a set of these knives I spoke of above for their wedding. Don't tell them, I just thought I would let you know so if people ask you what they need. These knives are German made. We may throw in a Belgian cutting board too. I have one and like it really well. Don't know if our PX still has them, though.

Saturday afternoon we went to Waldenbuch, stopping at Robinson Barracks on the way. We had a real nice time with Babs and Claus. We visited and went for a walk around their beautiful neighborhood. Played our "Parcheesi" game and watched an Italian international circus on TV. It was quite entertaining. Next weekend while we are in Vienna, they will be traveling in southwestern France with another couple.

You asked about the boat train to London and crossing the Channel. You thought right; at Ostend, Belgium, you change to a boat and then at Dover you get off the boat and onto the train to London. You will have no problem finding the boat at Ostend or the train at Dover because they take you right to it, just a short walk from one to the other.

In reference to the suit, Rick said it probably will be better to buy a ready-made suit and have it altered than to have one tailor made. You probably be sure of a good fit that way, contrary to what you may think. Alexandre's, who has a representative here in our PX, seems to make them a little tighter than what Americans prefer. Rick's trousers are quite snug on him, and he says it is quite a widespread complaint.

We asked Babs and Claus about your train from Rotterdam to Stuttgart. Babs said trains like to leave either in the morning or in the evening. It seems strange to us, but that's the way it is here in Europe.

This week is going to be quite busy for me. Wednesday we want to go to Munich for the day, and of course, we take off for Vienna, so I have to get ready for that. This afternoon I have to bake the last half of the cinnamon buns since I can't keep the dough in the refrigerator any longer. I stirred up the dough Friday afternoon and baked the first half Saturday morning. We are eating those now and this week, and then the ones I bake today are to take with us on our trip. Also this afternoon I want to make some cookies to also take with us for Munich and Vienna. Tomorrow afternoon is our monthly PWOC meeting, and then I have to do our wash at the laundromat and iron then.

Either tonight or Tuesday night I hope Bob can cut my hair because he leaves next Saturday. He was to tell Rick today whether he can or not. In a way I hope he can't because I can use the time for other things, yet I hate to go to the post beauty shop to have it cut. I had wanted to bake an apple pie for Rick's birthday, but I don't think I will really have the time so will do it next week. But I hope to have time to stir up a small "jiffy" box cake tomorrow. I made one for mine Friday and we had ice cream with it. I wouldn't be surprised if Claudia asks me to do her laundry Thursday afternoon, but that will be all right since there really isn't much to getting our things together for Vienna. But if I can just make it through till then, getting everything done I want to!

Last week I received a letter from Miss Spotts, the teacher I did my student teaching with. She wrote of some very tragic news from Adrian College. Helen Davidson, a senior at the college, died suddenly. The news clipping said she was taken to the hospital the day before and Miss Spotts wrote a note that it was pernicious anemia or some form of it. I knew her fairly well since we were in a couple of organizations together. She was a very nice girl, very talented at the piano and organ. She played for many, many campus activities, and the paper said she played organ for a church every Sunday. She was very intelligent, well mannered, neat and clean, etc. It is such a shame she had to lose her life. It really shocked me. She was engaged to be married, the paper said, and just that next Saturday she was to direct a group in the All College Sing. Then this wasn't all. Within the next week, Dr. Horn, head of the education department of the college, was found dead in his office of a heart attack. The paper said he was under treatment for a heart ailment. What a tragic week.

Miss Spotts also has been keeping me informed of Adrian School System's financial mess. It's too complicated to go into details, so I won't, but the extra millage rate to give teachers a raise has been voted down twice. The starting salary is now four thousand five hundred dollars. The board of education has voted to give the teachers a five hundred dollars raise anyway and cut back in other areas of the budget, which they are having a hard time doing. But the way they went about this and ignored the teacher's request for a meeting with them angered many of the teachers and they are leaving the system. All through this there have been hard feelings and emotions running high and the community is quite split. MEA (Michigan Education Association) is investigating or studying them and University of Michigan, Michigan State University, and Eastern Michigan University are all telling their prospective teachers to avoid Adrian. Needless to say, I am glad we are not going back to Adrian.

Claudia has come in and really put a kink in my plans. We have to get some letters out today, and so she asked me to come and work this afternoon. I said I would, but how I am going to get everything done? I don't know! Guess I will just have to eliminate the cookies for today.

I'm home now and it is about 8:15 p.m. I'm waiting a few more minutes for my cinnamon buns to rise so I can pop them in the oven. I just finished with the dishes. I will bake cookies tomorrow evening. I decided to eliminate the haircut, and put up with a post cut for a couple months.

Didn't get all the letters finished, so will do so tomorrow morning at work.

Carole's April 14, 1965, journal entry:

Rick got his birthday off work and we drove to Munich for the day. The weather was cloudy and rain—not at all good for pictures. We first saw the Rathaus (Munich's town hall: interesting building), Frauenkirche (cathedral), and a couple other buildings, and then went to the Deutsches Museum for the rest of the afternoon. Then we came home.

Carole's April 16-18, 1965. "Our trip to Vienna, Austria" journal entry:

We left about 6:00 a.m. Friday morning in heavy rain, which lasted all through the day and into the night. (It had started the night before with just a once-in-a-while letup, but never completely quit.) I started out driving and drove until Augsburg (Germany). Then Rick took over and I drove once again for a stretch in the middle of Austria. It turned out we picked a very bad time to go to Vienna, but we didn't realize that Good Friday was a legal German holiday and that everyone would be taking off that day for a long weekend.

The whole trip to Vienna was an ordeal we hope never to go through again. The traffic on the autobahn was just unbelievably heavy—almost bumper to bumper, you would call it. The ways these Germans and Austrians drive make conditions dangerous. You think you are doing well driving between forty-fifty mph, sometimes sixty mph with the rain and all, and then they zoom by you at speeds that seem to be twice yours! You really had to be alert to what was going on behind you and what was going on in front of you, trying to see further ahead all the time than you really could—all in all, it was quite a strain and we were both glad that we could take turns driving as we did.

We saw about four or five accidents along the way, and just think how many we didn't see! We saw three accidents in just one spot alone. It was where they are doing some construction on the road and we had to go across the median into the left lane of the other side. With the heavy traffic you can imagine the cars piled up considerably and we came to complete stops, inching the rest of the way. As we approached, two accidents had already happened, and as we were in the line of cars waiting I happened to glance in my rearview mirror and saw a car bang into the back of the car ahead of him, causing him to hit the back of the next car in front of him. We think part of the cause for these accidents at this spot is that previously there were several danger signs and signs indicating men working and one-lane traffic that were meaningless because the men were not working then and had opened the lane they were working on for traffic. So it could be that the drivers just got used to not believing those signs and didn't pay much attention to the signs for this particular spot, which were valid. Anyway, we made it through safely (this was when I was driving).

Another accident we saw was along the Austrian autobahn. We passed a car that was parked along the parking strip on the right side of our two lanes that had branches on its front and underneath it and the side of the car was all dirty. Puzzling over this, it suddenly dawned on us that he was facing in the opposite direction of traffic. We soon came upon branches and dirt on the road and a spot on the median where part of the hedge was broken down as if a car had crossed through there, which was evidently what happened. We had no idea what made them cross over the road, but they certainly were very lucky people that no cars were in their path on the other side with traffic as heavy as it was, although it wasn't quite as heavy in Austria as in Germany.

Then besides the rain and heavy traffic to slow us up, it took us an hour to get through customs at the border—not because of difficulty with the guards or officials, but because of the line of cars, busses, and trucks ahead of us two miles long and two lanes wide! This was around noon, so we ate our lunch while creeping along those two miles.

We thought we had the autobahn all the way from here to Vienna. On our map it showed three different sections of the Austrian autobahn in red and white stripes, which according to the legend meant "pass road in bad condition." The first section appeared to be brand-new road, so we figured maybe they were all fixed now. Well, they weren't—in fact, the other two sections were under initial construction! Bad condition, ha! The longest section about in the middle was about twenty to thirty miles long, which we traveled on regular highways all in one single-file parade of vehicles with the buses and the trucks setting pace up hills and down. It seemed an almost hopeless case to try to pass if you had the chance because there were just so many cars ahead, but of course, some did. One thing we will give credit to the Austrians for is that on most of the hills they made the roads three lanes so that those ascending could pass the trucks and busses, which really have a hard time making it up. For those descending they have no passing signs. By the way, this happened to occur when I was driving again! The last strip of an unconstructed autobahn was a short one just before getting to "Wien" (that's German for Vienna).

On the outskirts of Vienna we stopped at an information place and got a good map of Vienna and could also get room reservations there, but we decided to go on and try to get one ourselves. The more we got into the big city with heavy traffic and growing darkness and rain, the more discouraged we got about finding a room ourselves, so we turned back and went to the information place again. We told her we wanted a room for about four dollars, and she said for that price we'd have to go outside of Vienna—about eight miles from the center of Vienna. We said okay, and she called this place. They had an offer of two hundred shillings, which is eight dollars and was too high for us, so she talked to them again and they offered one for one hundred and sixty shillings, which we decided to take because she said everything was booked up because of the holiday weekend and we were so tired and anxious to get a room that we took it. She gave us the directions, and we finally made it with the help of a couple more people along the way. One kind man showed us the way by having us follow him, and we probably would never have found the tiny little street our hotel was on if it wasn't for him because you had to make a U-turn to find it and the girl had just told us to turn right. Anyway, it was about 7:00 or 7:30 p.m. when we got to the hotel. Its name was "Schlosshotel, Martin Schloss," and it turned out to be one of the many castles or palaces turned into hotels in Austria. ("*schloss*" means palace or castle). This was nothing fancy at all, but clean and fairly comfortable except it was cold! Then because of some trouble with our key fitting it was 8:00 p.m. or so before we could really relax. We had our supper and then went to bed so we could get an early start in the morning.

We got up at 7:00 a.m., dressed, ate our own breakfast of cinnamon buns that I had baked, and then went down to the lobby and had a hotel breakfast that was included with the room. This consisted of two rolls (not sweet rolls, but they were good) and coffee, tea, or milk. I made the mistake of ordering coffee the first morning—it was absolutely horrible and I couldn't drink it. The next morning I ordered tea and that tasted like tea, thank goodness. Rick stuck to the coffee.

Then we left the hotel and drove down to the center of town, found an unmetered parking place right away, and left the car there until we were ready to go back to the hotel about 7:00 p.m. or 7:30 p.m. that evening. Nearly all the rest of the time we were on our feet. We took our umbrella with us as an assurance against it raining, and it worked! It was really a pretty nice day—a little cool and partly cloudy, so we had the sun for some of our pictures and some not. It was quite windy too, and so one of our first stops was in a store to buy a scarf for me. It just so happened we picked one that had souvenir scarves, so I got a small one with pictures from Wien, color is brown. The stores were only open until 1:00 p.m., and we really didn't have time to shop so this turned out to be our souvenir of Vienna—that is, besides postcards and slides (35mm) that we bought.

We had our map showing the different monuments, churches, and buildings to see and we walked around and saw them all—at least all the well-known ones. They were all beautiful or interesting buildings and churches. Vienna is a pretty city itself because of its numerous parks, trees, and shrubbery. The "Ring" is divided by a median with trees and shrubbery, and a walk with benches. It was nice to walk down it. Near St. Stephens Cathedral, which was our first stop, we saw several horse-drawn carriages and from then on all through the day we saw them taking people around the city. We got several pictures of them, so you will be able to see them, too.

Speaking of the cathedral, we went inside a couple other churches also. They were all Catholic and each of them had a special altar on the side with a life-size image of the body of Christ as he would have been between the crucifixion and the resurrection, lighted candles, and potted white hydrangea blossoms. Each one of them was completely in gold and white—very beautiful.

Another interesting thing in Vienna was their underground passages for pedestrians under the big intersections. They have these in Stuttgart with windows of displays from different stores, but we were really surprised in Vienna to find complete shops down there. The biggest one outside the opera house even had a café in the center!

We ended our day by taking the streetcar out to the cemetery where we saw the graves of Beethoven, Johann Strauss, Brahms, a couple other composers I can't think of right now, and the memorial to Mozart. These were all in a circle together. We almost didn't find them even with directions. This cemetery is huge—miles long and miles wide.

Sunday morning we awoke to rain and overcast skies again. After our two breakfasts again, we walked around the town. We were in a little hurry to see their cathedral—didn't go inside, though, because they were starting services at the time. Then we drove to Shonbrunn Castle to see that before leaving. We took a tour of the inside (had an English-speaking guide), but it didn't even begin to compare with the castles of King Ludwig II. It was interesting, though. We could tell the gardens would be very beautiful with the flowers out and in bloom. There were some tulips planted, but it was too cold for them to bloom! The only color was some pansies. The gardens were vast and there was even a zoo, but we didn't have the time or desire to walk around them since the weather was bad.

I forgot to mention that on the way to Shonbrunn the driver's side windshield wiper broke! We could tell that it only needed tightening, though. We were lucky the rain stopped just then, but we had it fixed before starting on our way home. We started for home about noon. Along the Austrian autobahn Rick had a strong gusty wind to fight to keep the car on the road, and then it rained occasionally. Had no trouble getting through customs fast this time, but into Germany we missed our turn to get gas where we had gotten it on the way to Vienna and so took next exit, but it was a very small village and we had a lot of trouble finding a station open. To make a long story short, a young girl finally came along and helped us find one. We had stopped at the one she took us to but didn't know there was a button to press to bring the person from his apartment above the station. We ate at Chiemsee [Germany] and there got directions to the next Esso station that was open. We get Esso gas coupons minus the taxes of sixty cents to twenty- five cents a gallon! Then it soon got dark and started raining steadily. I took over driving after we got through Munich and drove the rest of the way home. We got home about 11:00 p.m.

[I was very much concerned that we would run out of gas on the autobahn. This was a holiday in Germany and Austria and everything was closed. The gas tank had been showing empty for many miles, yet we kept on driving for many more miles. It was a long ways to the next exit, and our VW was still running. We drove to what appeared to be just a village and there was one gas station. We drove in for gas and there was no one around. We noticed that there was a little tobacco shop that was open that we passed to reach the gas station. I drove back to this shop and there was a man behind the counter who couldn't speak any English. I can't remember the German word for gas [it may have been petro or benzene], but I mentioned this word and somehow I got across that no person was at the gas station. He called the station to let him know I was coming. I thanked him in German and drove the short distance to the station. Still no one was there. The tobacco man somehow identified a bell to ring for service. I didn't see a bell or doorbell button. What to do? I drove away, down a residential street, and there was a family walking. I drove to them and got out of the car and asked if anyone could speak English. A teenage girl said she could, in perfect English. I explained what happened and that there was no person to pump gas. She said, "Do you mind if I go with you?" Of course we didn't. She got into the back seat and I drove back to the gas station. She walked behind a pole and there was a doorbell. She pushed the button and a man from the second-story small apartment came down. He told her to tell me he was waiting for me to ring the bell. We thanked this teenage girl probably more than once as I drove her back to her family. I thank God and just wondered if He expanded the gas for us to make it to this little village. I think He did!]

April 19, 1965, letter to Mom and Dad:

Here I am with only eighty-seven days to go! It gives a guy a good feeling to know he is getting short! I read that you two are getting anxious to see Europe. Our trip to Vienna was helpful or beneficial for our trip. We discovered that gasoline stations are spread far apart and thus we will have to plan better. Needing a bathroom is also a problem, but we will arrange everything and things will turn out okay.

Dad, I don't think designating a city or place for a mailing address is very practical. I would like to have a worry-free trip! What we don't know won't hurt us! If there is a death, the person will still be dead after we get back and we will have enjoyed our European trip. If there was an emergency, our trip would terminate right then and there. So let's say that our mailing address is Strand Palace Hotel July 1. I'm sure nothing will happen in our twenty-eight days that we are traveling.

Stuttgart's train station is only forty-five minutes from where we live. We are quite familiar with the train station and there are people who can speak English. There is a U.S. Army information office that is open every day except Sundays. Of course, you can always call us. Carole and I will send you two mark coins in case you want to use the telephone. Maybe I'm very confident about not having any problems for our reunion in Stuttgart because this area to us is like Detroit to you. We are getting to know the area around here.

The biggest problem is the VW. It is not built for long-distance traveling. In other words, it is very uncomfortable to sit in it, but we will make it. Carole and I drove to Vienna (twelve hours in the car) then walked all over Vienna the next day and then drove another eleven hours the next day and we were just a little stiff! We will make it.

Thank you very much for Lincoln's portrait [five dollar-note]! The money sure came in handy. For some reason, we never seem to have enough of that green stuff! It was very thoughtful of you two to remember our birthdays. Mother, I hope you had a nice birthday [Carole is the 10th, mine is the 14th, and Mother's is the 17th]!

Hans is a wonderful young man and his family is also wonderful. The parents have learned some more English from Babs since we started to visit them. They know more English than we know German! You will also like Claus! They are all wonderful people!

It is the young German people who are the friendliest. Many of the old people will stare at you and will say nothing and show no facial expression.

Carole's April 26, 1965, letter to Mom and Dad:

It's fairly warm here this morning, surprisingly. All last week it was rather cool in the early morning and so I would go to the service club for the morning. It was also not so lonely over there and we still don't have a phone hooked up [in the hut], so there was no need to stay here to answer phone calls. Claudia should be in today. I can tell that she has been here to look at her mail, so I know she is home. We will probably be busy writing letters again to company commanders, the general, etc. I may be working this afternoon to do it, which is all right since I have last Friday morning to make up plus the coming four days we will be on our Berlin trip.

Last week and this weekend I have finished putting my travel notes in their permanent form and have things pretty well set. I ran across a couple things I want to tell you. Someone suggested putting your ID on the inside of your suitcases as well as on the outside, which is a good idea. You mentioned you had your vaccines and I am sorry Mother was so sick with it, but I want to be sure you have your health certificates stamped by the local or state health official. The clinic probably told you this, but I just wanted to make sure because it is not valid if it isn't. Do you know that you won't need it until you go back to the States? They don't ask to see it over here; it is so you can get back into the States.

This month we will buy our French Esso (gas) coupons over at Robinson Barracks and we will buy one more German Esso book (we have one now) and these should take us all the way into Italy, I have figured, with the exception of buying some gas in Holland, and by some I mean not a full tank. The cost is fourteen dollars and thirty cents for two German Esso books, which is about fifty-two gallons (two hundred liters), and for two hundred liters of French gas will be a little less. These prices are less than half of what we would have to pay buying it directly in the economy. Pretty good, hey? At the border in Italy we can buy tourist coupons for Italian gas, which cuts down the price; we don't know how much the discount will be, but I think we get a twenty-five percent discount. Austria and Switzerland have no such plan that we know of. Just outside Vienna gas was about fifty-eight cents a gallon. [During this time in the States gas was around twenty-six cents to thirty-one cents. Gas was seventeen cents on our post].

Sometime during this week I will try to figure out about how much money of each different country we will need. We won't exchange all of our money at American Express here on post before we leave, but we will at least get about five dollars of each currency unless my plans indicate we would need more in case we get into a country after banks and businesses close. You can do the same when you get here.

We have also got to start thinking seriously what and how we are going to send home and when we can. I did a little thinking on it this weekend but have to start getting it down on paper. What a job that is going to be, getting all that stuff ready. Doesn't seem possible though that the time for our trip is coming up fast. This next week will be the last time we will pay our rent in German marks!

This weekend we stayed at home. Babs and Claus were busy and the weather was lousy so we didn't go anywhere. I sewed, worked on the trip, we played some games together, wrote a few letters and worked out our budget for next month. It was really quite a relaxing and enjoyable weekend although we are getting so tired of cloudy skies and rainy day after day. It ought to be clear next week though while we are in Berlin. I don't see how this can go on much longer.

Last night just as we were going to bed Hans, our landlord, came up to use the telephone and brought us a plate full of pieces of cake, about five or six different kinds. (We were going to bed early because of KP today). I can't wait to try the cakes, they really look good! Saturday was Reina's [his son] birthday and Sunday his first communion (Catholic).

I am enclosing another picture of Vienna that shows the city from the Rathaus Tower [city hall]. The building you see in the foreground is Burg Theatre, a famous one, as we understand it. The tallest steeple in the background about in the middle is St. Stephan's Cathedral, which we visited. This was taken from a booklet on Austria that we wanted to keep some pictures from, and since we had a postcard of this same scene I thought I would send this to you. I am sending one to my family too since we had two of these booklets.

I have also enclosed a small leaflet I found in the service club, which shows you the traffic signs. It would probably help you to familiarize yourself with them. You could do that on the boat on your way over here. They are not at all hard to remember.

Last week I visited my friend Sonja. She and her husband made a four-day trip through Amsterdam, Brussels, and Luxembourg. She gave me a few helpful hints, the most important of which is to drive as little as possible in Amsterdam because she said the bicyclists are really terrible. There are a lot of them, and they swarm the cars at stoplights and cut in and out in front of you while driving. Sometimes they made it impossible to turn where you want to or even see where you want to turn! [We were amazed to see so many bicyclists in Amsterdam. There were considerably more bikes than cars on the road. During this time bikes were the main vehicle for transportation within Amsterdam.]

This week I would like to make a trip over to the WMF place to see if I can get that certain tray that Rick and I want, and also to check on the stainless ware.

Won't be long now and you will be boarding that boat [to Rotterdam, Holland]! Almost forgot to ask you, Mother, if you could buy a small clothesline with small clothespins for traveling. They have them specially for traveling, I think. It was suggested in my reading somewhere. They don't seem to have them in our PX, at least I haven't seen them yet. I think it would be handy.

Carole's April 30, 1965, letter to Mom and Dad:

It's 6:50 a.m. and I have been here in the hut since the ridiculous hour of 6:00 a.m.! It's payday; we have already got our money and Rick is here now until time to go to work. We got up with just enough time to get dressed and brought our breakfast here to eat. We are both sitting practically on top of the radiator; the heat just started coming in at 6:00 a.m. and it takes a while to feel it away from the radiator.

I'm enclosing a more detailed daily account of our trip. I made a carbon copy for my family too, so they can somewhat keep track of us. Now, about the weather around Europe for June. From what we have read and heard and surmise ourselves, it will be cool in Copenhagen and Amsterdam (high fifties maybe or sixties) and hot in Barcelona and maybe the Riviera and Italy, but not as hot as Spain. I heard someone say a friend was in Barcelona in June and it was hot. I would imagine that means in the eighties, maybe nineties. Don't think it would be hotter than that in June in that area. The other places will range between the sixties and seventies. This is just my feeling, so I may be wrong. We would suggest that you wear the "little heavier" (than summer suit) suit. I think the only time we will be going around in our shirtsleeves is in Spain, the Riviera, and Italy. After Italy we will be in the mountains all the time so would imagine it will be cool, sixty to seventy. You have been in mountains more than we, so you should know about that.

Dad, one suit, extra pair of trousers, a sweater, and an all-purpose coat sound ideal. That's what Rick will be taking minus the sweater though. You may want to keep the sweater with you in the VW's back seat.

I heard about France's new "smile" policy on the radio one day. We will see if it is working!

I got a letter from Miss Spotts about the same time you sent the articles on Adrian High School. They have also eliminated dramatics and extras such as that and half days for junior high. That system sure is in a mess. Grades 7-12 are worse off than elementary grades, though. She also said Adrian College's tragedies did not end with Dr. Horn. Dr. Cruisinberry (Rick's and my astronomy professor) died very suddenly about a week later of a heart attack. Then a student of Adrian College teaching around Detroit was killed when a truck ran into his auto driving home from Ypsilanti. His name was Harmes. We are not sure that we remember the name.

I am hoping that I will have a teaching contract coming in the mail soon from Kalamazoo Public Schools. I got a letter this week saying my credentials and application were on file and that as soon as my husband located a position and we were sure of being in Kalamazoo to let him know "so that further arrangements" for a teaching position could be made. He then mentioned again it was possible to offer a contract delaying the interview. I wrote right away that it was very definite that we would settle in Kalamazoo and that I would appreciate consideration for a contract before an interview. We will see what happens!

Did you know that cute girl Jack Hinkins was with in church is his fiancée? At least we would assume so since he wrote to us he was engaged. She is in nurse's training, I think it was.

We will be going to visit Babs and Claus Saturday about 6:00 p.m. after Rick is through with KP. Sunday we will go to Rothenburg come rain or shine! Then, of course, Monday is our trip to Berlin!

Carole's May 1, 1965, journal entry:

Because Rick had KP scheduled (but then cancelled) I agreed to work for Claudia typing a script, and then at 5:00 p.m. we were going to see Babs and Claus, but it turned out I didn't have to work either because no script! We showed Babs and Claus our Vienna slides, listened to the *My Fair Lady* album, and had a really nice time.

Carole's May 2, 1965, journal entry:

We drove to Rothenburg about 10:00 a.m. and found it to be a very interesting place to walk around. (The town and its wall around the old town looks just like it was several centuries ago. It was never bombed during World War II). We came back early because we wanted to get an early start to Berlin in the morning.

Carole's May 3-6, 1965, "Our trip to Berlin, Germany" journal entry:

We left home at 5:00 a.m. Monday morning (May 3rd), had beautiful weather all the way, and no trouble at all. At the East German border all Allied personnel must check with the border Allied checkpoint first as they explain just exactly what to do and not to do through the rest of the checkpoints and on the East German autobahn. We had nothing at all to do with the East German officials, and were not to have anything to do with them; we only dealt with the Americans and Soviets. It was really a strange feeling to be dealing with Soviet soldiers! At the checkpoint outside of Berlin, the Soviet enlisted men seemed quite friendly and smiled at us, but the others we met had just cold, blank expressions. Even though we had no holdups at the checkpoints it still took about an hour's time to go through normal procedures, and then U.S. Forces personnel are limited to fifty mph on the East German autobahn, which slowed us up some more. We arrived in Berlin 4:30-5:00 p.m., a long trip, but not nearly as tiring as Vienna. Berlin is about five hundred and forty miles from our house, autobahns all the way. We stayed in a U.S. Army hotel that was brand new and only a couple of blocks from the QM gas station, PX, snack bar, and shopping center.

Tuesday morning we decided we would try to drive our own way around Berlin instead of taking the streetcar, and we always made it where we wanted to go although we usually didn't arrive there the way we planned! Our map did not give all the names of the streets and was hard to follow. We first drove near the airport to see the airlift of 1948–49 memorial and a nearby national monument situated on a natural hill.

Then we made our way to the downtown area and Tiergarten (large park). Here we parked our car and walked the rest of the day. But before we got there we accidentally stumbled onto Potsdamer Platz, which used to be the center of town (before WWII), a busy shopping and business district, now it is dead with the wall going right through the middle of it and empty, war-damaged buildings and empty spaces where buildings once stood. The only life there now is tourists coming to look over the wall on this wooden platform they've erected and the souvenir shops open there for those tourists. We learned that on one air attack from the Allies over one hundred thousand people lost their lives. This was the heart of Berlin. It is impossible to put into words the feeling we got as we looked over that wall and saw the barbed wire, iron blockade, the guards, and the "deadness" of the place. We sure have gained a deep appreciation of being Americans and being free.

Then, as I said, we walked around to see the places of interest around the Tiergarten (former hunting grounds and a major battlefield during the war), Congress Hall, quite an unusual building, German Parliament building, Brandenburg Gate, a Russian war memorial (two Russian soldiers are on guard there and the British have enclosed the small park with barbed wire and have British soldiers on guard outside it to prevent political incidents.), and the Victory Column, where we climbed the two hundred and eighty-five steps to the top to look out over Berlin.

After lunch we went into the zoo until it was time for our East German tour. It was a very attractive, clean zoo, and we wished we had more time to explore it, but we didn't, and we wanted to see the Kaiser Wilhelm Memorial Church before getting on the bus at 4:00 p.m. The church was really interesting, very different and modern.

The East German tour lasted three hours, but at least an hour of that was spent in getting ready to leave and at Checkpoint Charlie and, of course, we saw some of West Berlin while on our way to and back. The tour of East Berlin was very interesting; a number of things impressed us. One was the lack of color, which made a very depressing atmosphere. Adding to this atmosphere was the number of war ruins still around; we were really surprised to see so many. We saw some apartment buildings partially damaged in the war, but people living in the parts that were livable! The new apartment buildings they have put up are huge, very plain, all-alike buildings. They are prefab, the exteriors put up in forty-two days! All over East Berlin we saw the Red Communist flags and East German flags big and small all over the buildings and everywhere, as well as propaganda banners from the May Day parade. That was some color at least!

The only place that we stopped to get off the bus was at a Russian war memorial (not the one I mentioned before). This is a very beautiful and impressive place.

After we got back from East Berlin we ate and then walked to the Ernst Reuter Platz but were disappointed the fountains were not on, and so then walked to the car and drove back to our hotel, about five miles.

The next morning we planned to walk into East Berlin on our own to take some pictures and walk around it some, but when we got to Checkpoint Charlie the MPs said we could not go because Rick didn't have "East" Berlin typed on his pass, he had only "Berlin." Rick was the one who typed his pass and he didn't realize he had to include the words "East Berlin." We were quite disappointed because we were really looking forward to it. We were glad then we had taken pictures from the bus the day before, and just hope the window reflection isn't too great. So then we drove around to some of the West German war ruins still standing that the bus drove by. One of them was the fourth-largest railroad station in Europe; the only thing left now is the front entrance! We were surprised to see so many war ruins left in West Berlin too, but these were mostly along the wall where I suppose they don't want to rebuild.

After getting the pictures we wanted, we drove back to the hotel so Rick could get out of his uniform. All Armed Forces personnel have to wear their class A uniform going into East Berlin and East Germany.

Then we drove to Charlottenburg Castle, where we walked around the gardens but didn't go inside. In the gardens we saw a peacock with his tail spread and putting on quite a show for the females, who completely ignored him!

Then we drove along the wall for a while on our way downtown. We saw buildings that they made part of the wall by bricking in every one of the windows and doorways and usually barbed wire along the rooftops. Another thing I forgot to mention about East Berlin was that we saw quite a few buildings that either had no or very few windows on one or two walls; some of these were along the wall but we saw some inside East Berlin as well. This wall is really a horrible, ugly thing; everyone ought to see it to get an appreciation of what we have.

Then we went downtown to walk around some more, window shop, and see some of the big department stores. One very interesting place that they are still completing is the "Haus des Nationen." This is a complex of small shops and restaurants of different world nations and includes an ice skating rink! It's really an interesting place. Its two stories now and they are working on the third. Then we went back to our hotel and ate supper in the snack bar.

Thursday morning we left about 8:00 a.m. and got home about 8:30 p.m. We lost about a half hour going by Frankfurt at the 5:00 p.m. rush hour and some time at one of the checkpoints because of a long line of cars.

All in all, we had a wonderful time and quite an experience!

Carole mentioned the bus tour we took of East Berlin. We got on this bus at Checkpoint Charlie. Carole mentioned bombed buildings standing exactly as they were after the war. We were told on this bus tour that the churches and museums were never restored. One small Catholic church was pointed out that had been built during the Communist era. I took a few pictures through the bus window. My pictures taken in Europe were all 35mm slides that I loaded onto my computer during my early retirement years. I found that two pictures from the East Berlin group had lost their images over the years. One of these two slides was one of my favorite pictures, taken when the bus stopped at a light. Right in front of me was the remains of a small apartment building; I believe it was a two-story building at one time. The remaining section of the front of this building was a small area on the right, the size of a small apartment, extending to the roof from the second floor. The rest of the front was completely open, lacking a wall. The inside was only a floor with external wooden stairs leading to the top floor. There was no roof to protect the wooden stairs. There in the top right apartment was a window with a lace curtain and between the curtain and the window was a small thin vase with one red rose in it. I took a picture of this structure and it turned out very well.

Carole mentioned the large Russian (Soviet) war memorial in East Germany. It was indeed impressive! There was a small building on the left of the open grounds. We were told that the names of the Soviet officers who lost their lives in "liberating Berlin," as we were told, are recorded on the inside walls of this building. We did not walk to this building but stayed only on the wide plaza overlooking the burial grounds. On each side of the open plaza was a huge statue on a tall pedestal of a Soviet soldier holding a machine gun. In the center grounds extending past this plaza over five thousand Soviet soldiers are buried. I'm not sure if they know the names of these soldiers killed in action. The field was not large enough to give each soldier an equal amount of space to be buried separately.

A special event took place at this memorial while we were there. There is a requirement that an American in the armed forces has to wear their uniform when in a Communist country, therefore I had to wear my army uniform when we were in East Germany and East Berlin. This made me very uncomfortable since everyone would look at us. As Carole and I were walking on this plaza toward the Soviet statues, three young boys in East German army uniforms came toward us in shoulder-to-shoulder formation. They looked about eighteen years old. They were approaching us our right, staring at us. When we got close to them I smiled at them and said "good day" in German. They each gave us a sincere smile and repeated my words as they passed us. Their smiles and words gave me a feeling that we were not enemies but were all in the same situation that was not our choice, that is, having been drafted into our respective country's army. I believe this was their feeling as well. This was the only positive moment we had in East Berlin. The atmosphere there was so depressing, and we were glad to get back to West Berlin.

When we started our trip through East Germany we had to stop at the West German border. We got a briefing from the U.S. personnel. We were told that we could only travel on a specific route to West Berlin, which were all autobahn highways. They took my mileage and calculated our two or three turns necessary to reach Berlin on the authorized route. If we missed any of these turns, we would be arrested by the Soviets or East Germans. They listed the signs we would see for our turnoffs and what our mileage would read. In addition, we were told that we had a certain window of time to reach the border of East Germany and West Berlin; we couldn't arrive before a certain time and we couldn't arrive after a certain time. They suggested the speed that we should keep. They documented all of this for us. I was glad Carole was my codriver. We were told that once our car crossed the border there was no turning back or backing the car to the border. We were also told that if an East German soldier stopped us, we were to demand to speak to a Soviet officer since the U.S. didn't recognize East Germany. They gave me paperwork to show the Soviets for the pass to give to the East Germans.

We both felt uneasy driving this route to Berlin through East Germany. What really helped me was having the mileage we would be at for each of these turns and a picture of the sign or the printed words on the sign in front of us. This was a blessing.

Our VW left the border and entered through the first wall manned by East German soldiers. They let us pass. We had to turn partially to the right for the opening of the second wall, manned by the Soviet Union soldiers. As we had been told, there was a small building (a shack) that I parked in front of. There was a Soviet private standing on the porch directly in front of us. When I turned to look at his face he would quickly turn his head to the side. From the corner of my eye I watched him as I turned my head and then his face turned toward me. I repeated this and the same reaction took place. He would not look at me when I was facing him. I had to get out of our VW, walk up two or three steps to the door, and enter this very small wooden building. There was one very low window painted to block the view of the other side. It opened about two inches, and I slid my papers through the open space. The window was then slammed close. I looked around and there was a picture of Lenin and Stalin. I really didn't feel welcome. After a few minutes I began to think what would happen if they didn't give me my papers back. I didn't know what to do. Shortly after this the window opened slightly and the papers were pushed out. What I needed was a pass from the Soviets to allow me to get through the third wall and to be on our way to Berlin. The pass was with my papers. I left the shack and the soldier in front of our car was still there. We drove through the second wall to the third wall. I gave the Soviet pass to the East German soldier and the final gate was opened. We didn't have a problem as we drove to Berlin.

We certainly stood out driving on the East German autobahn in a red VW (these cars were not sold in East Germany) and a red U.S. license plate with the driver in a U.S. Army uniform. There was almost no traffic and we couldn't see any towns from our route. We saw lots of large plots of farmland. One time on this drive we were surprised to see a car come up fast behind us. When this car got close it slowed to our speed and passed us, but lowered their speed so that we were right behind them. It was a family of four with two kids in the back seat. The kids turned around and stared at us, and I'm sure the driver was looking at us in his rearview mirror. They stayed this way for about two to three minutes, then the car took off and they were in the distance within a very short time.

Carole's May 8, 1965, letter to Mom and Dad:

Enclosed is an account of our Berlin trip. I cheated again and killed three birds with one stone, to both our folks and one for our diary account (using carbon paper)! Time is really getting short for you folks, and we don't have much time we can write to you! It sounds like you have already got a good "sendoff" at your dinner club. [Dad and Mom were scheduled to leave New York City on May 21, 1965, on the *Nieuw Amsterdam* ship for Rotterdam, Holland.]

A couple of things we want to remind you of or tell you before you leave. Don't forget to bring an umbrella. You will need it in England, if nowhere else, or you can buy one here, and there are plenty to choose from. The popular ones can be "folded down" into compact size and slip into a case. We got one for five dollars.

Here are some words you might need to know: W. C. is toilet or toiletten and Herren, Manner (or Mannen) is men. Damen, Frauen is woman, Eingang is entrance, and Ausgang is exit.

We are still having rainy weather, though something happened last Saturday, Sunday, and Monday and they were beautiful sunny days. That Friday before, though, was the twenty-sixth consecutive day it rained here! We hope it is nice tomorrow though, because we would like to drive down to the Black Forest.

Last Sunday we drove to Rothenburg, a well-preserved medieval town. It was really interesting, and we wished we could have more time to explore it. The wall around the city is still intact, and we walked around it quite a ways (not on top but on a platform about level with the rooftops).

We got the information on the ninety nine dollars charter flights and I have decided to take it. I sent in a deposit for the July 2nd flight, don't know what time yet and probably won't until we get back from our trip because they said the planes are usually chartered about ten days prior to the departing date.

We were quite surprised about your statement that it would take a Philadelphia lawyer to figure out the European road signs. They are really quite simple to learn, I tried to generalize for you. You will catch on fast once you get here.

May 9, 1965, letter to Mom and Dad:

We are getting a lot of rain again.

Carole and I drove over to the Black Forest today and saw Germany's highest waterfall, Triberg Falls. The small city of Triberg is known for their many (hundreds) kinds of cuckoo clocks. There are many stores selling these clocks, and we wished we could have purchased one. The falls and this area were very beautiful, even though it rained all the time.

Just three weeks from today you folks will be over here. Time is flying! We are looking forward to our trip.

We sure had a good time in Berlin, quite the experience. It was a worthwhile trip. It was quite the experience just driving through East Germany and viewing a lot of barbed wire. We had priority crossing the border, which was good. They could not inspect our car. The other cars going from East to West Berlin were inspected inside and outside for hidden people. They even had a mirror on wheels to roll under cars for inspection under it!

The most impressive site was around the Potsdamer Square and area. Prior to World War II this was the center of Berlin, the busiest square of any other intersection in Europe. A 1943 WWII bombing raid over this area completely destroyed this center, and sadly over one hundred thousand people lost their lives! Now the wall that separates East and West Berlin passes through the middle of this huge square. As I remember, this site also had a large hotel across the street from a very large train station. The train station was the fourth largest in Europe. Only a small part of the front doorframe and a little part of the wall around it is still standing. The large hotel is gone. There are only a few bombed-out buildings and an ugly wall! The other side is East Berlin, and not very far from the wall in this east section are Brandenburg Gate and the German Parliament Building.

We lived cheaply while we were in West Berlin due to the U.S. Army hotel and restaurant located there. Of course, it is always good having a hamburger and milkshake, which are not available anywhere else!

Bring a deck of cards for those evenings we just want to relax.

We would like to enclose a one German mark for the telephone, but we don't have one at the moment. I don't think you will really need one. We will be at the Stuttgart train station at 4:00 a.m. Sunday morning. I wish it was a little later, but Carole and I are used to getting up early. It won't be the first time. You two probably would like to have some comfort after the train ride, but don't expect too much comfort in our apartment. Unfortunately we have very little.

May 13, 1965, letter to Mom and Dad:

Well your time is coming and I bet you two are getting excited! Time is going by fast and soon we will be on our way! We still have a lot to do yet before I leave here in July. When the time comes, I will be ready to leave!

I took my separation physical today and they discovered that I am a little color blind!

We will meet you at the train station in Stuttgart since we will be there at 4:00 a.m. We will find you, so don't panic if you don't find us immediately. Just stand in the open and we will find you two. I would imagine you two will look like typical tourists, American tourists that is!

Don't forget that "WC" (Water Closet) is restrooms for both sexes! Just one person at a time is allowed in them, of course!

This weekend we will see about my car shipment at Stuttgart and will try to get the French gasoline coupons. We already have the German gas coupons. We will also enjoy the fine weather this weekend with the camera. The flowers are just beautiful in Goppingen. Probably Goppingen has more flowers than all of Southern Michigan.

My alert orders are now being generated and I will use it to ship some of our stuff home next week.

Take care and we will see you May 30, at some ridiculous hour!

Carole's May 15, 1965, journal entry:

This day was Armed Forces Day, a holiday for us, but we still got up early and washed and polished the car. Then we drove to Robinson Barracks in Stuttgart to get information on shipping our car (to the States) and French gas coupons. We accomplished both. In the afternoon we climbed the hill to investigate the Rechburg ruins.

Carole's May 16, 1965, journal entry:

We went to church and found it packed mostly with Germans! It was German-American week. Then after lunch we drove to the Stein's house for a get-together with Babs and Claus. The four of us went to Hohenzollern Castle (at Hechingen, thirty-one miles south of Stuttgart). The weather was beautiful and the castle interesting.

Carole's May 21, 1965, letter to Rick's brother Phil and Grandmother Hulda Burrows, Mother's mother (the "leftovers" at 250 W. Maplehurst):

Well, the folks will be sailing just one hour from now. Doesn't seem possible they are on their way and will be here in just a matter of nine days. It sure will be good to see them.

The other day I got a letter from Kalamazoo Public Schools offering me a position teaching on a part-time basis until a full-time opening occurs; at such time I will get top consideration. I accepted but will still try to find a full-time position in the suburbs if one hasn't opened there by July. Their openings were already filled by the time we got things settled or I might have had a contract. It's better than nothing.

This morning Rick had his last wisdom tooth extracted by the oral surgeon in Stuttgart. He took it out in ten minutes whereas the dentist on post took an hour to get the other lower one out. The numbness hadn't started wearing off when I left for work, but he shouldn't have near the trouble that he did with the last one.

Carole's May 24-28, 1965, journal entry:

This is my last week of work which is making up for three mornings taken for Berlin. The other two afternoons I spent cleaning the apartment and getting ready for Rick's parents, [Harold and Millie Wilcox] arrival and our big trip.

Thursday evening we had John Roethe over and Friday John Sferra took us out for a steak dinner. These are friends of Rick.

Carole's May 29, 1965, journal entry:

Rick got off training early Saturday and we went to Robinson Barracks in Stuttgart and made arrangements for our car to be shipped home and bought a raincoat for me. We also shopped downtown for a Hummel (figurine) for us, and one for Kay (Carole's sister)—successfully.

My post's commanding officer was a kind and understanding officer whom I have high respect for. He allowed me to take the month of June off since my parents would be here for their trip. He said it wasn't the policy to allow more than two weeks, but he would make an exception. I'm indebted to him. I wish I remembered his name. I was scheduled to leave Germany during the first two weeks of the following month for separation from the army. Carole planned this trip on a daily basis, where we would be every day, and the activities for each day. I sent this itinerary to Dad, and he said it couldn't be done in thirty days. I wrote back to him and told him that Western Europe is smaller than mainland United States, but I would change it to have one free day in case we needed it. This day wasn't needed. The original itinerary was perfect without the extra day.

We got up on May 30, 1965 at 2:45 a.m., dressed and drove to Stuttgart's bahnhof. We were at the Bahnhof by 4:00 a.m. Mom and Dad were one of the last to reach the front gates, but we saw them and I said, "There they are!" Dad heard me and there were happy faces! What a reunion at the bahnhof that early morning!

We walked around Stuttgart a little and then we drove back to Goppingen. We had breakfast at our apartment and gabbed. Eventually Dad took a nap and Mother and Carole and I visited. After a roast beef dinner we drove them around Goppingen and up to Hohenstaufen. Then at 5:30 p.m. we went to visit the Steins. Babs and Claus were late, but we were amazed how well we conversed with Herr and Frau Stein before they arrived. We had a nice visit and supper with them. After we left the Stein's house both Mother and Dad agreed that they were great people!

That weekend I got an infected big toe. I received a shot on Memorial Day, soaked it in hot water and salt. Then before we started our trip my camera was knocked off the shelf to the floor. I wondered if there was damage. It was only slightly damaged, we discovered at our first stop at Lubeck, Germany, but some of our slides from the trip were a little blurry in the bottom-right corner.

Our landlord Hans generously offered a bedroom to Mom and Dad on the second floor of their house. We all greatly appreciated this. Hans and Paula showed true friendship toward us during the time we lived there.

It was a great thirty-day European trip, an experience that very few people experience. We were very fortunate. It was our greatest trip!

Chapter 25

Our June 1965 European Tour

Carole's May 31, 1965, journal entry:

We all slept in and then ran errands on post and took the folks to Ulm, Germany.

Carole's June 1, 1965, journal entry:

We made final preparation for our trip and packed.

Carole's June 2, 1965, journal entry:

We left bright and early 5:00 a.m., all packed and ready to go! Beautiful weather all the way, and made very good time arriving at Lubeck [northern Germany] at 2:45 p.m., found a hotel right away with rooms available. After unloading our things, we walked to the center of town to shop, sightsee, and eat supper.

Carole's June 3, 1965, journal entry:

We left Lubeck at 8:00 a.m., arriving at the "ferry" (Puttgarden) about 9:30 a.m. We were quite surprised to learn the ferry was a large ship and that total cost for all was 94DM twenty-three dollars and fifty cents)! We got to drive on the boat right away; it left at 10:25 a.m., arriving at Rodbyhavn, Denmark, in less than an hour.

The drive around this area was beautiful because of the bright yellow fields of mustard and the thatched-roof houses and barns.

Arrived in Copenhagen about 1:30 p.m. and went to the railroad station to get a room reservation. We got two rooms for the Mission Hotel Hebron (one I had written to, getting a negative answer!). Took our things to the hotel and then set out to see things. Were quite disappointed in the Den Permanante (well known for Danish crafts) but saw the Radhaus (beautiful city hall located in City Hall Square in central Copenhagen), walked down the famous shopping street where I bought a charm and later the next morning a stainless steel pan and teak wood hot pads, saw Christiansborg Palace (the seat of the Danish Parliament, the prime minister's office, and the Supreme Court located in central Copenhagen), and then walked around Tivoli (consisting of flower gardens, restaurants and amusement park, and is well known worldwide), which we really liked. Later in the evening after dinner we went back so we could see it with the lights on and it was even more beautiful and fascinating than in the daytime. It was one time we went out of a place with more money than when we went in! Mom was lucky at the slot machines (Mom would restrict herself to putting in a few coins in a slot machine and then walk away from it, regardless of winning or losing)!

Carole's June 4, 1965, journal entry:

After breakfast in our room Dad went with us to see the mermaid [statue] while Mother went shopping and to visit the jewelry makers. After seeing the mermaid and the harbor, we went to the grounds of Rosenborg Castle (Rosenborg Castle has some of Denmark's greatest cultural treasures. Christian IV had this castle built for his own pleasure. Within this castle are the Danish crown jewels and regalia). Then we took Dad to the hotel and we went to get the things I wanted to buy. On the way we went up to the Panorama Lounge of the Royal Hotel to get the best view of the city.

Then about 11:30 a.m., after paying the hotel bill with the help of a Kennedy silver half-dollar, we went on our way to Amsterdam, Holland. We arrived at Rodbyhawn just in time to see the boat pulling out and so had to wait about forty-five minutes for the next boat. Ate lunch on the boat and watched the seagulls following the boat.

Starting from Puttgarden at 4:00 p.m., we drove past Lubeck and Hamburg, where we got into a terrible traffic jam to Rotenburg off the autobahn, and stayed overnight at the Bahnhof (train station) Hotel. Also ate a good beefsteak dinner there.

Carole's June 5, 1965, journal entry:

After breakfast in the hotel we left about 8:30 a.m. to continue to Amsterdam. We were still seeing thatched roofs, but lots of beautiful rhododendrons (flowers) took the place of the mustard fields.

Just after crossing the border, we stopped at a tourist information place and made reservations for two rooms in a private home in Alkmaar. The man told us hotels were all filled up around Amsterdam because of the holiday, but we are glad that happened because they were beautiful rooms in a lovely spot—a windmill and canal right in front of us! The couple that owned this home is really nice people. Showers were fourteen cents per person!

In Holland we stopped at Groningen to do a little shopping since the stores would be closed Sunday and Monday while we were here. I bought a pewter pitcher and a pair of glass candleholders.

Carole's June 6, 1965, journal entry:

After a delicious breakfast which was included with our room (four dollars), we drove to The Hague, hoping the rain would let up by the time we got to Amsterdam. It did soon after. We merely drove around The Hague (Holland's government).

In Amsterdam we parked our car in the center of town and "forgot it." First we walked over and saw the Royal Palace (this is one of three palaces in Holland, used by the royal family) and the post office (which looked more like the palace!), and then found where to get the water canal tour. The one-and-a-quarter-hour trip took us all over the canals and out into the harbor for only fifty-six cents for each person. It was very interesting--an average of one car per week falls into the canals, whereas before some small railings were put in it was five to six cars per week. During one year one hundred and eighty people fell into the canal; thirty of them drowned. We saw the smallest house and smallest warehouse and many other interesting things as well while walking around. Saw many houses that were sagging quite badly, some having to be propped up.

After the canal tour we walked over to visit Rembrandt's House and then the house Anne Frank and her family were hidden in during World War II, but the house was closed. Then we walked to the Rijksmuseum (Holland's national museum) to see Rembrandt's paintings and bought a couple reproductions for ourselves. By this time it was five o'clock and we were all pretty hungry as we hadn't eaten lunch, so we headed back toward the car, finding a restaurant on the way.

Carole's June 7, 1965, journal entry:

After breakfast (it was an excellent breakfast) we left Alkmaar for the miniature village of Madurodam. We stayed there about an hour, walking around and taking pictures, very interesting and cute place. Then we started on our way to Luxembourg via Belgium.

Belgium seemed quite a bit poorer and very dirty, and yet we saw quite a few "rich" homes and again a lot of rhododendron. The roads were quite poor also. We were glad we were not going north towards Brussels (capital of Belgium) because as we were going south we passed a line of cars that must have been five miles long! Because of it we missed a turn and had to take a little-longer route to Luxembourg. Due to this and poor roads and rain, it was about 6:30-7:00 p.m. before we got into Luxembourg. There we found the railroad station and hotel rooms right across from it with shower and bath for approximately five dollars for each room. After settling in, we found a restaurant and had dinner.

Carole's June 8, 1965, journal entry:

After a breakfast of oranges in our rooms Mother went with us to see the sights in the drizzling rain while Dad stayed in. We first crossed the Pont Adolphe (an interesting bridge in Luxembourg City) and then walked down in the valley, "discovering" the old catacombs and fortresses in the walls. Then we stopped at a bakery for a snack and to buy something for later on.

After checking out of the hotel we started on our way to Paris (about 11:00 a.m.). The French countryside is pretty, we found, but the towns are very ugly, dirty, and poor! We stopped along the way at the Verdun U.S. Army post snack bar for lunch and at the PX found a camera like ours for Mother to buy for Phil.

We arrived at the outskirts of Paris about 5:00 p.m. in rush-hour traffic, but somehow miraculously found our way safely to the Avenue of Champs-Elysees (one of the world's most famous streets, the highest-priced real estate in Paris with cafes, luxury specialty shops, cinemas, and restaurants; both sides of the street are lined with chestnut trees) where we walked into the U.S. Armed Forces room service office just as they were about to close (6:00 p.m.)! Paris was full up, they said, but they managed to find us a couple of clean rooms in a hotel near the Moulin Rouge (a cabaret in Paris). [The rooms were old in appearance and the only light was a cord from the ceiling with a light bulb without a shade.] We again fought our way through traffic and found our hotel, got settled, and had our pastries for a light supper.

Carole's June 9, 1965, journal entry:

We had our breakfast downstairs in the hotel since it was included with the rooms. Afterward we walked over to the church, "Sacre-Coeur" (Basilica of the Sacred Heart. This beautiful large church is on the highest hill in Paris. The hill is called Montmartre. One can see this church from a long distance away). From this church we took the Metro to the (fascinating and beautiful) Arc de Triomphe (the most famous triumphal arch located on the Avenue of Champs-Elysees), where we went up to the top for a view around. [From the top it was very interesting to watch the cars coming into the circle that surrounds the Arc de Triomphe. I took a couple of pictures looking down at the traffic from the top.]

We walked down to the Avenue of Champs-Elysees and stopped at an outdoor café and rested, with each of us having a forty cents Coke! [This was the most expensive Coke we had ever had up to this time, but the avenue was attractive and it was fun watching all of the people walking by.]

We saw the Place de la Concorde (one of the major public squares in Paris) and then crossed over the Seine (River) to the Dome des Invalides, where we saw Napoleon's Tomb. After this we took a taxi to the American snack bar for lunch, after which we walked down to the Seine River and took an hour and a half boat ride. Then we walked over to the Eiffel Tower and took the lift up to the very top for a stupendous view of Paris.

Then we went back to the snack bar for our dinner and on to our hotel via the Metro.

Carole's June 10, 1965, journal entry:

After breakfast we found an Esso garage to have our oil changed and a grease job. About 10:30-11:00 a.m. when it was ready, we drove back to the hotel to park the car. Then we took the Metro down to the Arc de Triomphe and walked to the American snack bar for lunch. [The American snack bar was mainly for the U.S. Armed Forces and their families. We had American food, and it was considerably cheaper compared to the Paris restaurants.]

After lunch we started our sightseeing, and amazingly the cloudy skies started clearing up. We saw the place of the Bastille (it was originally called Bastille Saint-Antoine. During the French Revolution this Bastille was a prison and it was destroyed); Notre Dame Cathedral, where we climbed to the top of the tower; The Pantheon (a beautiful, large building that used to be a church and now holds art); visited Luxembourg Gardens; saw the Mona Lisa painting at the Louvre; the Opera; Church of Madeleine; and President de Gaulle's official palace, where the guards were all fancied up and lined up to greet chauffeured guests.

On the way to Madeleine we saw a group of students demonstrating in the streets, shouting and mobbing cars. A newsboy told us he guessed they were celebrating the end of their exams.

After dinner at the snack bar and a brief period of relaxation in our rooms, we went for a short walk around our hotel area. Paris is a very attractive city.

Carole's June 11, 1965, journal entry:

We left our hotel about 8:30 a.m. for Versailles. Somewhat miraculously, we made our way through and out of Paris, but still found no signs to Versailles. We had to ask the way. Got there about 10:15 a.m. and took the English-speaking tour at 10:45 a.m. The tour ended about 12:30 p.m., and we were surprised how late it was. Then we had lunch in the palace café, after which we walked around the gardens. We left Versailles about 2:30 p.m. and started on our way to Barcelona, (Spain), and stopped at Vierzon (France) for the night.

Carole's June 12, 1965, journal entry:

After breakfast of oranges and cookies in our rooms, we left about 7:45 a.m. and arrived in Torrelles de Folx to stay overnight about 5:00 or 5:30 p.m. The only stops were to buy bread and to take a couple of pictures. We had dinner in our hotel after waiting until 7:30 p.m. for the dining room to open.

Carole's June 13, 1965, journal entry:

After breakfast in our rooms, we left Foix for Barcelona about 8:30 a.m. It was a beautiful day for a beautiful though tiring trip through the Pyrenees mountains. We took a side trip through Andorra [a very small country in the Pyrenees Mountains but nice scenery. This country's population when we were there was probably no more than sixty-five thousand. Andorra is between France and Spain].

After making a wrong turn, we arrived in Barcelona about 5:30 p.m. and found that hotels were filled up because of a fair and bullfight, but thanks to the help of a Spanish man we got nice, modern hotel rooms with a private bathroom with shower for four dollars.

I had parked the car in front of a large hotel and walked to the front desk. I was told that I wouldn't find rooms in Barcelona due to special bullfights in the city. As I walked away from the counter toward the exit doors, a young man approached me and asked me if I needed a room. I told him I needed two rooms. He said there was a brand-new hotel a short distance away, close to the Mediterranean Sea, and the owner could speak English well because he had lived in Boston for a while. He was talking as we walked down to the parking area. He had a small moped and told me to follow him and he would take me to this hotel. I got into our VW and told the family that this man would take us to a brand-new hotel. Dad wasn't too sure about this, but I told Dad we had nothing to lose since we were not obligated to accept an offer and there weren't any vacant rooms in Barcelona. Sure enough, what this man said was true. He went into the lobby with us and we made reservations for four dollars per room. I gave the man with the moped a tip; he seemed glad that he could help us and appreciated being rewarded financially. Everything in our rooms was new, and each room had a private balcony facing the Mediterranean Sea. They were the best rooms we had on this trip since we also had our own bath and shower! It was the only room with such perks during our era in Europe.

Carole's June 14, 1965, journal entry:

We started our sightseeing tour about 8:30 a.m., first walking to the Columbus Monument and the replica of his *Santa Maria*. Then we walked down Ramblas Street window-shopping and looking at the flowers and bird markets [Barcelona's most famous street, extending from the main city square, Placa Catalunya, to Columbus Monument]. Then we took a taxi to the Sagrada Família church. [The taxi cost was only around thirty cents. I gave the driver a tip of around thirty cents and you would think I had given him five dollars. He offered to be our taxi driver to wherever we wanted to go.]

Sagrada Familia church was a really interesting and unique structure. Basically all that was standing was the outside wall, and it was roofless. The construction of this church started in 1882 and the construction ended many years ago. There were no blueprints for finishing the construction of this huge church. The outside walls have hundreds of humanlike figures and animals, and Bible stories shown with humanlike figures that included the Apostles and Christ and many more. The church has several very tall steeples with these figures. Very impressive! [Many years after we visited this church structure construction started again with a new architectural plan for merging with the current structure. It will take many years to finish the construction of this church.]

From Sagrada Familia church we traveled to the Spanish Village, where we watched the craftsmen working and bought a "few" things!

Then we taxied back to Ramblas and found a nice restaurant where we had a delicious roast chicken dinner.

Afterward we walked to the cable car that goes over the harbor and got a ride on that—full round trip. At the Montjuic Park end (the top overlooks the harbor) we walked around to see the different cacti that we had seen before on a taxi ride. As we went back to our starting point we could see a ship getting ready to leave, so we stayed on the tower and watched it.

Then it was back to Ramblas again for more window-shopping, and finally to our hotel where we showered (public shower and bathroom for that hotel's floor) before suppertime, which was 8:30 p.m. Then we played some gin rummy before retiring.

Carole's June 15, 1965, journal entry:

We left Barcelona on our way to Italy about 8:30 a.m. It took a while to get out of the city, but we finally made it. We followed the Mediterranean Sea's coastline pretty much up into France, stopping for a lunch-dinner and arriving near the Pont du Gard (known for their Roman Aqueduct) about 6:00 p.m. for the night. We found a hotel and got a snack.

Carole's June 16, 1965, journal entry:

First thing (after breakfast) we went to see this Pont du Gard and then started on our way to Italy along the French Riviera, stopping at Nice about 3:00 a.m., found a hotel and then found a small naval base near Nice where we were disappointed to learn there was no snack bar, but we bought bread and peanut butter plus other things for a picnic lunch that night and the next day.

Then we drove on to see Monaco, saw the Prince's Palace and the Casino.

Carole's June 17, 1965, journal entry:

Got up at 6:00 a.m. so we could drive along the Mediterranean Sea and through the French Rivera (which was very beautiful) to reach Pisa (Italy) during daylight. Stopped only at the border to exchange money and for gas coupons, for a few pictures and dinner, and we arrived in Pisa about 6:30-7:00 p.m., a distance of about two hundred and thirty miles! Found a nice motel room with one dollar discount for military men.

Carole's June 18, 1965, journal entry:

First thing in the morning we drove to see Pisa's Leaning Tower, which we found very interesting and worthwhile. Rick and I climbed to the top of the leaning tower and had fun trying to keep our balance! We then had our first breakfast of donuts [during our time in Europe] in a little place nearby before going on our way to Florence. [The two other buildings on the grounds of the Leaning Tower were also very attractive. One of the buildings is a church. The Leaning Tower is the church's bell tower. I'm sure the third building has a connection to the church.]

    We arrived in Florence about noon and first found a place to stay and put the car into a garage. Then we started our sightseeing by walking to the Palazzo Pitti (Pitti Palace, a very beautiful Renaissance palace) then over the Vecchio Bridge (an attractive bridge with little shops on one side of the bridge. It is only a walking bridge) and to the Ufizzi Galleries, which is one of the major museums in Florence. It is one of Europe's most famous art museums. During this walk to Efizzi Museum we came across leather and jewelry stalls where Rick bought his two wallets. After we toured the inside of the galleries we bought a string of crystal beads and a wallet for me.

    Then we saw the Palazzo Vecchio Palace (which is a very impressive town hall of Florence) and came upon the Straw Market on our way to our hotel.

Carole's June 19, 1965, journal entry:

We started out sightseeing about 8:30-9:00 a.m. and got back to our hotel about 5:30 p.m. We saw most of the rest of the sights in Florence including Michelangelo's David.

    Florence is very impressive and beautiful. There is much artwork from earlier centuries. After we left this city I thought it would be nice to visit it again and perhaps spend more time there. It was one of my favorite cities that we visited.

Carole's June 20, 1965, journal entry:

We left our hotel about 9:15 a.m. We were on our way to Venice, where we arrived about 1:00 p.m. We found a place to stay in Mestre (most populated urban area of Venice), and then went on to Venice where we spent the rest of the afternoon. We visited Piazza San Marco and St. Mark's Square which is a very huge square with a very large church on one end and the water canal on the opposite end, and both sides with buildings. This area is very interesting and very attractive. It's the most popular tourist site in Venice. The church had a marvelous gold and jeweled altar. The church was very attractive, and on the outside of the church there is a tall bell tower. Rick and I went up to the top of the belfry and nearly deafened ourselves when the bells started ringing. We walked around and window shopped, and saw the Rialto Bridge. This bridge is the oldest of four bridges spanning Venice's Grand Canal. The bridge is short in length and is a walking bridge only and very attractive. I'm sure every tourist takes a picture of this bridge. After viewing and taking pictures of the Rialto Bridge, we took a water taxi along the Grand Canal, which was fun and very enjoyable. We bought some Murano glassware for ourselves (fancy glassware made on Venice's island of Murano. This company has been a glassware maker for centuries).

Carole's June 21, 1965, journal entry:

We drove to Verona in the morning and happened to come upon an army post right away, so we stopped there first and had our lunch, shopped at the PX and commissary. Dad and Rick got haircuts.

Then we drove further into Verona to see the old Roman Coliseum. [This coliseum was built during the first century AD.] We sat in it and wondered what it was like nineteen hundred years ago. It was very interesting. We took pictures of some of us seated in this coliseum.

When we left this site we drove to Lake Garda (northern Italy). There we found a hotel right on the waterfront for four dollars per room. After unloading we took our groceries we had bought for a picnic lunch and drove further along the lakefront, where we happened to come upon the enlisted men's picnic grounds. We stopped and it was very pleasant, so we spent the rest of the afternoon and evening there.

Our day at Lake Garda was the extra day in which Carole didn't plan any activity. We could have used this day if we wanted to stay longer than what Carole had scheduled. Not needing it, we spent this day resting. Lake Garda is Italy's largest lake and is in the lower Alps mountain range. One event that I never forgot was when we were in our room on the first floor. There were two women who had walked down the two or three steps to Lake Garda's water and were washing clothes in this lake. This is the only time I have seen someone washing clothes in a lake. I was fascinated by it.

Carole's June 22, 1965, journal entry:

We left about 8:30 a.m. for Innsbruck, Austria arriving there about 3:30 p.m. with a stop for dinner in Brenner on the border. We decided to drive on and stay overnight in Landeck. Innsbruck is located in western Austria. This area is beautiful, and is my favorite area of Europe. Innsbruck is in the Alps. Landeck is a small city in western Austria, and the population was probably around fifty-five hundred when we were there. At the back of our hotel was a small river, perhaps only twenty-five feet across, but this rapid water was very loud and the water was high almost as high as the base of the hotel. Apparently this water was from the melting snow higher up in the mountains. I thought this was really neat. I enjoyed watching it for a few minutes.

Carole's June 23, 1965, journal entry:

We left our hotel about 8:30 a.m. and first went to the bank to get some fifty and twenty-five silver shilling coins, and we were quite successful (can't remember how many different ones the bank had but it was exciting for Rick and Mother). Every year Austria would issue for circulation commemorative silver 50 and 25 shilling coins. Each coin would commemorate a different historical event in reference to Austria. I was hoping to get some of these coins. Then we drove as far as St. Anton, a village in Western Austria, where we left Mom and Dad. They wanted to wander around St. Anton while we drove up to a high mountain via the "Flexenpass." [St. Anton is a village and popular ski resort in the Austrian Alps. The area is very beautiful.] This was a beautiful drive within the Austrian Alps (5,817 feet) outside of St. Anton. Rick took lots of pictures during this minitrip. After we picked up the folks we went on our way to Vaduz, Liechtenstein, where we had a delicious roast beef dinner. Vaduz is the capital of Liechtenstein, and the city is very small. Rick took a picture of the Vaduz Castle, which could be seen on a hill from the main street. Vaduz is a very interesting town.

We then went on into Switzerland and found a hotel along Waldensee. Waldensee is one of the largest lakes in Switzerland.

Carole's June 24, 1965, journal entry:

We left about 8:30 a.m., eating our breakfast in a café along the way. We took the route through Klausenpass and arrived in Lucerne (north-central Switzerland) about 1:00 p.m. First we found a hotel, which took some time because they were all out of our budget. We still ended up outside our budget (just outside of Lucerne), but got more for our money such as showers and new rooms. Then we snacked and took in some sights, checked on a boat excursion schedule, and went to Birnbaums and bought our watches. Then we ate dinner and came back to the hotel.

Switzerland is a small country with three languages. One section, which includes Lucerne, is a German-speaking area. There is an area that speaks French and another area that combines these two languages. A lot of the stores in Lucerne had their prices in U.S. dollars. Rick asked a clerk why U.S. dollars? She said the locals stay home during the summer and the majority of their business is from American tourists. She also said the requirement for a clerk positon in a store is to fluently speak French, German, and English. Rick was amazed because he thought this employment probably paid only minimum wage! Switzerland was the most expensive country and Spain the cheapest of our trip.

Carole's June 25, 1965, journal entry:

After breakfast in our hotel we went back to Lucerne for the day. We took a boat excursion on the lake, shopped, bought a clock and Dad bought Rick a watch, and we just sat on a bench near the lake, taking it easy on a hot day. After dinner we had to wait until after a rain shower to get to our car. Later in the evening there was quite a wind and thunderstorm, and the lights were out for a half hour or so.

[During this time Switzerland was the watchmakers' capital of the world. Their industry was destroyed when the country's watchmakers refused to accept the battery powered quartz watch invention demonstrated at a worldwide watch fair. At this convention a Japanese company purchased the rights from the inventor, and the rest is history.]

Carole's June 26, 1965, journal entry:

We left Lucerne for Interlaken about 8:30 a.m. and arrived there in about two hours. We first located a place to stay, got settled, and then started our sightseeing. First we went to the cable car at Heimwehfluh but found it closed for lunch, so we had our dinner and came back for the first afternoon trip. We were quite disappointed with what was up there—not much of a view and the model railroad was anything spectacular. Then we drove down through the "Valley of Waterfalls" (we all enjoyed the waterfalls that we saw; there are supposed to be seventy-two waterfalls on this route) and the other valley to Grindelwald (an attractive village in the Alps). We came back to Interlaken to see the Casino Kursaal and hearing the last part of the afternoon concert (a complex for conventions, park, gardens, and an area used for concerts and other events; the grounds were very attractive). After lunch we walked around the town window-shopping.

Carole's June 27, 1965, journal entry:

After breakfast or about 9:15 a.m. we left for a drive around Lake Thun. We stopped at Oberhofen to see the (Oberhofen) castle with its beautiful gardens, and drove on to the city of Thun to walk around and have a little lunch. The air was very hazy, which spoiled the scenery, and it even rained the last half of the drive. We got back to Interlaken about 2:30 p.m. and planned to walk around town until the 4:00 p.m. free concert at the Casino Kursaal, but it rained so we stayed in our hotel reading and playing cards until 3:30 p.m., and then went to the concert despite the rain still pouring down. The concert was very nice and after it was over at 6:00 p.m. we found a place to eat our dinner (the rain had stopped by then).

Carole's June 28, 1965, journal entry:

We left Interlaken about 9:00 a.m. for Zurich (a very large city, largest in Switzerland, and on Lake Zurich), driving through Bern on the way. Arriving in Zurich about 1:30 or 2:00 p.m., we found hotels too expensive and so decided to spend a couple hours there and then continue on our way to find a hotel outside of Zurich, which we did. While in Zurich we walked around and took a boat trip on the Zurichsee (Lake Zurich).

Carole's June 29, 1965, journal entry:

We continued on to Schaffhausen (northern Switzerland) and the Rhine Falls (outside of Schaffhausen), getting our breakfast in Schaffhausen where we also climbed up to the "Munot" or casements (sixteenth-century fortification overlooking the town of Schaffhausen). The rest of the morning was spent at the Rhine Falls. One of the viewing areas that extended out toward the falls was actually a part of the Rhine Falls. A few inches of water were speeding across over this viewing area. This was due to the high water level. Then about noon we continued on to Konstance (Switzerland) where we took the ferry across the Bodensee to Meersburg (Germany). We drove along the lake to Friedrichshafen (Germany), where we got a hotel and had our dinner.

Bodensee is also called Lake Constance. This lake, near the Alps, is situated in Switzerland, Germany and Austria.

Carole did not record the journal entry for June 30, our last day of our trip. We had our breakfast at the hotel in Friedrichshafen, Germany, and drove to Goppingen, Germany. We found a small hotel and rented just one room. I told the woman at the desk we only wanted one room, just for Carole and me. We didn't go to bed since the four of us visited or played cards until around 9:00 p.m., then we took Mom and Dad to the bahnhof in Stuttgart for their train to London, England, which was the same train schedule (11:45 p.m.) as my trip to London to meet Carole. We knew in a few weeks I would be back in Michigan. Then Carole and I went back to this same hotel and went to bed. When we got up early to check out the woman billed us for four people. I can't remember if she couldn't speak much English, but I got nowhere explaining that Dad and Mom had not used a bed. We paid the bill, and we drove to our home in Goppingen.

We packed our things for shipment to my parents' house in Ferndale. I only needed my army clothing. We went to our German home on July 1, 1965. In the early morning of July 2 I drove Carole to Frankfurt for her flight home and continued to Bremerhaven to leave the car for shipment to New Jersey. I was able to locate an armed-service man to drive me to our German home.

On this same day our landlord, Hans Hahnle, drove me to the post. I had a little sadness as I knew this great experience was ending. As I was about to step out at the entrance of Cooke Barracks, Hans reached over and gave me a big hug. He said that we were the best renters he had ever had. He also told me that if we ever came back to Germany he would have a room for us. I thought we would, but it didn't happen. Hans and Paula Hahnle was a wonderful couple!

For many years we mailed a letter and card to Hans and Paula at Christmastime. Their second son, Bernd, born after we left Germany, would interpret the letter. Hans's letters were always in German. They were interpreted by a member of Chapelwood Methodist Church. Later Bernd Hahnle would write the Christmas letters to us in English. Bernd and a friend visited us in 1991.We were never were able to travel back to Europe. Hans died in 2013 and his wife Paula died several years prior. When Bernd Hahnle notified us of Hans's death I felt sadness, wishing I could have seen him one more time. Hans was in the German army during World War II. He was on the Eastern front and was wounded. I wished I had taken a picture of Hans and Paula during the period that we lived in their house.

We had already said goodbye to Claus and Babs, but they came to the post right before I left for the States. They wanted to say their last goodbye, and expressed sadness that we would be gone. They would get married on December 29, 1965.

I could have extended my time in Goppingen by a couple of months to enjoy more trips, coming home in September, but I was anxious to start my working career and make new friends and be near families. When the time came to leave Goppingen I was put on the train traveling to the port city of Bremerhaven, Germany. Sometime between July 10 and 12, 1965, my ship left Germany for New York City. We had smooth sailing all the way. We landed in the New York City area, and I was discharged from active duty at Fort Hamilton, New York, on July 19, 1965. When I was discharged I got the address where our VW car would be unloaded from a ship. I was on Wall Street in New York, and I didn't know which subway to take to the port where our car would be. I approached a policeman and he told me which underground subway to board. His directions were perfect. Apparently I wasn't the first one to ask for the subway to the unloading dock.

When I arrived at the port the sun was very low in the sky. I planned to drive nonstop to Ferndale, Michigan, to the home where I grew up. When I got to the unloading dock I was surprised that my car was not waiting for me. They were still unloading cars from Bremerhaven. I told the man in charge that I was driving that night to Detroit, and if there was any way he could locate it soon I would greatly appreciate it. He said he would do his best as he left for this search. In about twenty minutes here he came, driving my car.

The previous night on ship I had only had four hours of sleep, and here I was attempting to drive all night to reach home. I was excited that I would soon see Dad, Mom, and my brother, and start a life with Carole in Kalamazoo, Michigan. Carole already had a public school teaching job, but I would have to search for employment. It was on the Pennsylvania Turnpike that I started to feel the lack of sleep. I opened the fly window at an angle to have the air blowing toward my face. I even slapped my face a few times in my effort to keep my eyes open. Our VW didn't have a radio, and for the first time I wished it did. I finally pulled off at a rest area hoping to get a little sleep, but after being parked between five to ten minutes I realized this wouldn't work. I decided to continue my driving but stop for coffee at the next rest area with a restaurant. As I was drinking my coffee at the counter, a man around my age sat down next to me. He was very friendly, and we visited for a period of time while we both enjoyed our coffee. I learned he was hitchhiking to Harrisburg, Pennsylvania. He said he lived close to the Turnpike. I offered to take him home, and he accepted my offer. I was so glad to have company as I headed back on the Turnpike. As I remember, the time flew until I reached his exit due to our continuous, enjoyable conversation. I drove a few blocks from the exit, and when I reached a particular street he told me to stop. He said there was no need for me to drive him to his house since he lived close to this intersection and all I had to do was make a U-turn and I would be back on the Turnpike. I really appreciated this man since our conversations and coffee refreshed me, and I was awake all the way to Ferndale.

I was so glad that the sun was coming up and I knew I was getting close to the house that was home before I was drafted into the U.S. Army. It would no longer be my home since Carole and I would soon have our own home in Kalamazoo, Michigan. Around 8:00 a.m. on July 20, 1965, I arrived at Mom and Dad's house in Ferndale. I felt such excitement that I cannot put it into words. I rang the doorbell and in a few seconds the hallway door opened slowly and I saw through the glass door that it was Dad in his pajamas. He shouted, "Rick is home!" I was at the home of my parents and the home of my younger years! I was filled with joy! I was wide awake as Mom and Dad quickly got dressed. We had breakfast and had long conversations throughout the day. It was so good being at my parents' home. Phil came over during the evening, and it was also so good to see him.

I was wide awake and tempted to spend only a few hours with my parents then drive to Niles, Michigan, where Carole was staying with her parents. As I remember, it was about four and a half hours to her parent's house. Shortly after thinking of this option, I realized that in the last forty-eight hours I had only had four hours of sleep. Driving to Niles at this time might not be a good idea. Another thought was that Mom and Dad would enjoy a day with me, so during that morning I called Carole and told her I was spending the day with my parents and I would leave in the morning for her parents' house. I didn't take a nap, and I didn't go to bed until late that night because I was too excited being home with Mom and Dad.

Many years after this thirty-day European trip that Carole and I took with Dad and Mom, Dad said this trip was the best trip he had ever had. There was no planning he had to do; he and Mom just sat in the back seat and enjoyed each day. The companionship was also very good, in fact it was special! I'm thankful to God that we were allowed to make this wonderful trip. We also realized the Stein family and our landlords Hans and Paula Hahnle had made positive contributions to making our life in Germany very special. Babs told us that we had seen more of Germany than the average German. The past two years had flown by, and I realized that Carole and I had a wonderful experience during my overseas military career. In fact, it was a great blessing for us! I was very fortunate to have had this experience. It was all wonderful!

Chapter 26

Kalamazoo, Michigan

On July 21, 1965, I left Ferndale and drove to Niles to reunite with Carole. We were now together, ready to start our lives in Kalamazoo, Michigan. We expected Kalamazoo, Michigan to be our home for the rest of our lives. We loved this area of Michigan, and had families and wonderful friends nearby. The only negative aspect was the snow, ice, and cold weather. I had always hated the winter weather, even as a child. I didn't like wearing heavy coats and boots. Kalamazoo was in the snowbelt from Lake Michigan, and we got a lot of snow during the winters.

    My brother Phil and his wife-to-be Bonnie waited until Carole and I were back in the States for their wedding. I was honored and appreciative that Phil and Bonnie scheduled their wedding when I would be home because they wanted me to be their best man. Their wedding was at our family's church, Ferndale's Methodist Church on Woodward Avenue.. The wedding took place on July 30, 1965. I was to give an envelope with money to their pastor. Phil had given me the envelope earlier, which I put in my suit's inside pocket. After the ceremony I gave the pastor the envelope and thanked him. Later Phil approached me with cash and told me to put it in the envelope I had given to the pastor. I sure was embarrassed when I had to go back to the pastor and give him the money he didn't receive in the envelope!

    Carole had a job teaching at one of the elementary schools in Kalamazoo. I didn't have a job. I think it took me close to two weeks to find a job. We rented the second story of a house in Kalamazoo, close to Portage Avenue on Reed Street. It was nothing special, but it worked for us. I did find employment with a paper company, but it would close their doors about nine months after I was hired. They let me go after about five months, telling me they were doing me a favor. Then I was hired with a company called Westab, a paper company of Mead Corp. I spent three years working for this company. I loved working there, but eventually I left because I felt my salary was too low and I was confident that I would shortly find a job with a higher salary. I did find such a job that included more accounting.

    When I started work at Westab the office men told me I had to play golf with them every Monday evening after work. I told them I had never played before, but they said that didn't matter because they would teach me. I purchased a golf set and bag and included some practicing and found myself on the golf course with the men. We played nine holes and I would play on about fourteen fairways because I had a problem hitting the ball straight. It was a great group of men and I enjoyed the fellowship with them, but I was terrible at this game.

    We loved living in Kalamazoo. We had family and very close friends from our church, First United Methodist Church in downtown Kalamazoo. Eight of us started a new Sunday school class; we agreed to name this class the "Lamplighters." We were even Methodist Youth Fellowship counselors with two other couples, the Kings and Southerlands. The children of my cousin Marcia and her husband Dick Husted (Nancy, Rick, and Launa) participated in our MYF. We enjoyed being with this young group. After Sunday evening's MYF we would either go to the Kings' house (Woody and Ann) or the Southerlands' house (Ted and Nancy) to watch *Mission Impossible* and then play canasta for the rest of the evening. We spent a lot of time with these two couples, including camping. It was a wonderful time.

During my life in Michigan I was a big Detroit Tigers Fan. I wanted to experience Detroit in a World Series. Detroit was in first place most of the 1950 season, but lost this position to the New York Yankees during the last two weeks of the season. This was a disappointment. The 1967 season looked very promising, but when the last weekend of the season came they had a double header with the California Angels on both Saturday and Sunday, due to two rained-out games during the season. If Detroit won all four games they would be in the World Series. If they won three of the games they would be tied for first place with Boston. If they won only two games Detroit would end up in second place, one game out. Carole and I were in Niles visiting her parents and grandparents. I brought my radio to listen to these games. On Saturday Detroit won the first game but lost the second one; on Sunday Detroit won the first game and again lost the second game. Boston was in the World Series. Another disappointment!

The next season, 1968, Detroit did it! They were in the World Series against St. Louis. Unlike baseball today, many of the season baseball games were played during daytime, so it wasn't unusual that the 1968 World Series games were day games. During this time I was employed by Westab in Kalamazoo. I just had to watch these games on TV. Right before the first game was to start I left work without telling anybody. Next morning my boss asked me where I was yesterday afternoon. I told him I went home to watch the baseball game. He was a little disappointed that I did this, but I explained I had been waiting all my life for Detroit to get into the World Series and I had to watch these games. It meant a lot to me. I did not tell him I was determined to watch all of these games even if I got fired from my job. My boss realized my seriousness and my determination, so he told me that I could go home for each game but I could not leave before a certain time, which would cause me to miss one or two innings of the game. I worked less than ten minutes from home. I agreed and I thanked him. It was a very exciting series. Detroit was behind three games to one but won the last three games for the World Series championship.

Carole taught at public elementary schools in the area in the five years we lived in Kalamazoo. In 1967 we wanted to buy a house, but a bank told us that we had to be able to make a down payment of 25 percent of the selling price. We couldn't do that during this time. We had been saving most of Carole's salary, and by the end of 1968 we had enough money for a down payment on a house. In January 1969 we purchased a house outside Kalamazoo in Portage (603 Velvet). We loved this house, and it would be our home forever. Several people mentioned our house was attractive. We expected our children would grow up in this house. Wrong! We lived in this house for only eighteen months.

January 13, 1969 I wrote to Mom and Dad. Well, we are in our house, broke and in debt, but we have a roof over our heads. This is the first letter we have written from our house. Sorry for being so late in writing, but we spent all of last week packing our stuff. This past weekend and today we have been unpacking. It's 9:30 p.m. and I'm very tired. Almost everything is put away and our furniture arrived today. I didn't go to work today, but Carole did. Carole will take tomorrow afternoon off since the gasman will come to hook up the dryer. The Sears man will also come to hook up the washer. Our refrigerator is still in Grand Rapids on a freight car. Because of the snow they can't get it off the freight car, so they brought us one until we receive our copper-colored one.

It has really been winter here, and I think you picked the right time to go down to Florida. Right now we have about 22" of snow on the ground, and for a time we were also having severe cold weather. For two days it was below zero all day!

It's good to have our house, and I will appreciate it more once everything is in its place. We hope to be completely settled by this weekend. Two more nights and everything will be put away, but there is a lot of cleaning to do.

We moved late Saturday afternoon. There were eleven of us, and it didn't take very long. We piled the stuff in the kitchen, ate sandwiches, donuts, coffee, and pop and played cards (spoons) until 11:15 p.m. We had a real good time, and I believe everyone else did also.

We appreciate your warm letters and are very anxious to have you over for a weekend. There is plenty of room now! Just our kitchen alone is almost as large as our living room and bedroom combined in the old apartment.

January 21, 1969, letter to Mom and Dad:

Our chair [Mom and Dad's gift] arrived in Kalamazoo last Thursday, but we didn't pick it up until today, with the help of a friend. We really like it and it looks nice in our room. We would like to thank you two again for such a nice [La-Z-Boy] chair.

We are looking forward to your visit next March. We will have a deck of cards ready for the action. If Phil and Bonnie come, we will have room for them also.

I still have more boxes to burn in the fireplace and a couple of odds and ends to do in the house. The house also needs a thorough cleaning, and we will do it little by little. Carole is doing report cards this week, and we had her folks over last Sunday. They seem to like the house, but it doesn't matter since we like it.

Babs and Claus are coming to the States on July 27! We are excited about this!

This house was fairly new when we moved into it. The Lamplighter Sunday school class helped us move to this house. We didn't have much furniture, but we did have a card table. After we all had dinner we played the card and spoons game on the floor in the living room. It was just a fun evening and we greatly appreciated all who helped us move into our house. We had a lot of social events with these Sunday school class members, including fun weekend camping.

The previous owner had designed the house to their specifications, and we just loved the layout of the rooms, especially the kitchen. Looking out the second-floor window, you could see the nearby lake when the trees were without leaves. The front of the house had a couple of trees, and we had a cobblestone walkway from the driveway to the front door. On the outside of this walkway was a two-foot-high picket fence. Between this walkway and the fence we planted tulips, my favorite flowers. The front of the house was attractive. In summer 2012 Carole and I with our son James visited this house. James wanted to see the house we lived in before we moved to Houston. The family allowed us to visit their back yard. The small hill in the back yard was removed so that the yard was an even level. In the front yard the picket fence was gone as well as the trees, and the grass had grown over the cobblestone walkway. There was no greenery along the front of the house. It just didn't look the same as it did when we called it home.

Ever since I can remember I had been very interested in the moon and planets of our solar system. I wanted to see pictures of the moon surface. Another desire was to learn what the surface of Mars looked like. Today we have tens of thousands of pictures of Mars's surface to my delight. I have three different books of photos of Mars's surface. I find these images very interesting. There are events that our nation remembers, such as Pearl Harbor and John F. Kennedy's assassination. Apollo 11's launch to the moon was an event that was a thrill for me and that I will never forget. The Apollo spaceship was launched to the moon on July 16, 1969. The three-man crew was Neil Armstrong, Buzz Aldrin, and Michael Collins. Sunday evening July 20, 1969, found Carole and me in front of our TV watching and hearing updates from Houston's Mission Control Center. Late in the evening was the time for the launch. This was a very exciting time as the small lander left the spaceship that was orbiting the moon. I was also a little nervous during these moments. We listened to every word spoken and all the updates from Houston's Mission Control Center. It was mentioned seconds before the moon landing that the lander had only a few seconds left of fuel, and we immediately became concerned. They landed, and we could hear the first words from Neil Armstrong from the moon, "Houston, Tranquility Base here, the Eagle has landed." This was so exciting for us. A few minutes later we saw Neil Armstrong climbing down the lander's ladder, and when he was standing on the surface of the moon we heard his words, "One small step for man one giant leap for mankind." We saw the surface of the moon, and we couldn't take our eyes off the TV screen! We watched their activity on the moon and were in awe that we could see the surface of the moon from our living room in Portage.

This event was broadcast live to TV viewers worldwide. The Soviet Union blocked this transmission from their citizens. Soviet Union citizens eventually learned that Americans landed on the moon. The TV broadcast ended at either 11:00 p.m. or midnight. I didn't want to see it end. It was announced that a few companies, including my employer and the schools, would be closed on Monday to allow their employees to watch the continuation of the moon's mission. I can't remember when this broadcast started on Monday morning, but we were in front of our TV when that time came. The total broadcast from the moon was around twenty-one hours. When the time came to leave the moon, the planted camera broadcast the capsule with the two men separating from the lander. The capsule took the two men to the spaceship that was in orbit of the moon. Michael Collins manned the spaceship. It took three days to reach earth. I was glad that I could watch one of the greatest events of my life.

When we were in our Portage house Babs and Claus Lahmann from Germany and their son Jens flew to Michigan. They spent two to three days with us in August 1969. One day we took them to Chicago. Claus had never seen slums, and back in Germany there was a TV program on the topic of U.S. slums. Claus wanted to see them for himself. I remember driving through a slum area of blocks of buildings with broken windows. He asked me, "Why do the people in this area break windows?" I really couldn't answer this question, but said, "They just enjoy breaking windows."

Then the five of us drove to Charlevoix, Michigan, and took a boat to Beaver Island. Davi and Hans Stein and Davi's parents were on the Island. We all had a very enjoyable time. Here we were with Claus, Babs, and Hans again, not in Germany but on Beaver Island! It was so good to see Babs and Claus during this time. I assumed we would see them again at a later time, but it never happened. Carole and I didn't realize then that we would never see Claus and Babs again.

September 15, 1969, letter to my parents in Ferndale:

We had a good weekend. We went camping Friday night to late Saturday night with two other couples. We were joined by two other couples on Saturday and the game of baseball really made me stiff and sore yesterday and today, but I'm making a fast recovery and should be just about normal tomorrow. Sunday after class and church we spent the balance of the day with the Southerlands except for MYF. We have our best group of kids this year and we are actually enjoying all of them. It's good that the last year will be the best.

Next Saturday I will take out two peach trees and two small treelike bushes from the back yard and trim and prune the area a little. I will have to buy a saw this week.

Dad, I have been thinking that we would appreciate it if you (and mother also) would write a book, a detailed history of your life. I know all of us would appreciate such a document. I will type it and treasure it. You two may think this is crazy, but it would be nice. You could write it like you are talking to someone. It may be published, who knows? [It took more than this statement to persuade Dad to write his story. I encouraged him a few more times. Finally, soon after they moved to Florida during 1972, Dad developed a strong desire to do this.]

Next Saturday night we may have three couples over for dinner and cards. I haven't called the third couple yet. It's a good method for cleaning the house.

Living in Kalamazoo and Portage was a period in which we saw a lot of the family on my side and also Carole's family. We rotated Thanksgiving and Christmas with the parents of the two families. On our last Christmas, 1969, we had both families at our house. We all knew this would be our last one in Michigan. In addition, my parents would visit us and during the fall we would go to a football game, either at Western Michigan University or Kalamazoo College. We four would be dressed up, Dad and I with suits and ties. After the game we would go out for dinner. It was so special! Most of the months we spent one weekend visiting my parents in Ferndale and also brother Phil and his wife Bonnie.

Another tradition that ended when we moved to Houston was our birthdays. Carole's birthday is April 10, mine on April 14, and Mom on April 17. One Saturday night during April we would be at my parents' house celebrating our birthdays. This was a lot of fun. Phil and Bonnie would also be there.

We had a loving friendship with my Uncle Lee and Aunt Hilda Wilcox. Lee is my Dad's brother. They lived in northeast Kalamazoo, not very far from us. We would have them over for dinner at our Portage home, and they in turn would have us over for dinner at their house. Kalamazoo Central High School would show five or six travelogue films each year. We would buy season tickets, and all loved the travel films and the narrators. At the first one Uncle Lee and Aunt Hilda picked us up at our house. Uncle Lee wasn't wearing a suit, but I was. I took the tie off. For the next show Carole and I drove to their house to pick them up. I didn't have a suit on, but Uncle Lee did. We all laughed!

We often had Aunt Hilda's wonderful pancakes. Several times when my parents drove to Kalamazoo, the four of us would have pancakes at Aunt Hilda's house. These are all wonderful memories of long ago! How I wish we could go back and relive these wonderful moments! Uncle Lee and Aunt Hilda is a very special couple. We loved them!

Our Lamplighter class grew to around ten or eleven couples, as I remember. This was a fun group. We spent some weekends camping, had social parties together at different members' homes, and of course meeting Sunday morning at church. Sometimes when we were in Ferndale we would visit our wonderful friends Hans and Davi Stein, or Phil and Irene Rundell.

In 1966 we decided to go to Niagara Falls, Ontario, during the weekend. I also wanted to get one roll of Canadian silver fifty cent coins. I felt this would be the last year of silver coins for Canada. The last year for silver coins for the States was 1964. In my opinion the design of the fifty cent coins is the best of any coin Canada has ever issued for circulation. I believe it was in St. Thomas, Ontario, that I walked into a bank while Carole stayed in the car. I asked the teller for a roll of new 1966 fifty cent coins. To my surprise she said, "I don't have any, but in the vault we have some. The unmarked door over there will take you to the basement. At the end of the hall is the bank's vault, walk into it and there will be someone that can get you a roll." I couldn't believe this! I was very uncomfortable opening this unmarked door, going down the hallway, and walking toward the vault with its opened door. I thought I was going to be in trouble and perhaps a siren would go off. I stood at the open vault and there was no one to be seen. There was a counter island with bags of money and on the counter against the wall I could see piles and piles of strapped paper money. I didn't think I should be there but the teller had told me to enter the vault, so I walked in the vault, not knowing what would happen. To my left at the end of the vault was a man in a security uniform who said, "Hi, how can I help you." I made it clear that a teller had told me to come here to get a new roll of 1966 fifty cent coins. He said, "How many rolls do you want?" I said "Just one." We visited for a few minutes, and I found that he was born, as I was, in Highland Park within Detroit. He was very friendly, and I enjoyed this experience.

In July 1967 Carole and I visited Expo67 in Montreal, Quebec. This exposition was very impressive and so large we couldn't see every pavilion during our three very-long days there. We would be at the gate when it opened and stayed late for the daily fireworks. The third day our feet and legs were starting to revolt, and I remember telling Carole that my feet were so sensitive that I thought I could stand on a coin with my bare feet and identify its date. We took a lot of seated breaks and went back to our rented room early evening.

In all of our travels in Canada we found the people to be friendly. Canada is a great place to live if you enjoy cold weather.

After I left Westab in 1969 for a higher salary I took a job in Battle Creek, an accountant position with a higher salary. The company was linked to a family of mutual funds and was called Channing Inc. After one month on the new job I learned that the company had been sold to American General and the company was moving to Houston! The move was scheduled for July 1, 1970. I couldn't believe it! They didn't tell me this when I was hired! My mind was made up that I would not leave Kalamazoo!

During my early Channing Inc. employment, I got to know two other fellow workers in the same department, Bob Daniels and Dave Parsons. We became friends and started playing pinochle card games with our wives outside of work. This friendship with them and their wives continued during our years in Houston since both of them agreed to stay with the company.

When I started employment with this company I was assigned a very large bank account that no one could reconcile. Many hundreds of checks were issued daily from this account, and the large majority of the check amounts were even amounts such as one hundred dollars or two hundred dollars. The current person reconciling it would take the discrepancy for the month and add it to the running total. The account was out of balance by a large five-digit amount, something like thirty thousand dollars plus. They had others trying to reconcile it without success. It took me two or three months to reconcile the account to the cent, going back over two and a half years. I documented the procedures for reconciling this account. Management was very pleased that I accomplished this assignment successfully.

There was a clerk that had a huge ledger, and she took the large daily volume of checks and posted them by hand. Every entry posted had to be in balance (debit-credit). I don't think there was a day that she was in balance after posting the many check entries to this ledger. She spent hours each day balancing it. I had an older woman supervisor, and I approached her and told her that I could put this function on the computer and the printed entries ledger from the computer would be balanced. Each check had to have a code (account number) and the computer would print total so-called ledgers that would be in balance. That would probably save her four hours a day to work on something else. This woman said, "It can't be done, and this is the way we have always done it." I went to her boss and reported all of this, and he said, "Do it, but don't let her know you are doing it." I designed the input document, the output ledger, and the new job procedure, and outlined what the programmer had to do. When it was done I sat down with this employee and showed her the procedure, and she loved it. Every day the printout ledger was in balance. My female boss was really angry at me for going over her head. I don't think she ever got over it while I was in her department. Her boss told me to just ignore her. Management was again very pleased with this accomplishment.

I believe these two accomplishments led to management wanting me to take over the accounting department in Houston. There were about fifteen of us in the company that they wanted in Houston. My problem was I didn't want to move to Houston. We had too many friends and family members in Michigan, and we loved where we were living. As I remember, I told them a couple times I didn't want to move.

One night during the winter of 1969-70 I thought I had a good chance of freezing to death. I worked really late one night, and I was the only one left at work. Outside the weather was a low freezing temperature, and I only had a thin jacket. I walked outside to my car, the only car in the parking lot. I was instantly cold as I walked to the car. I quickly got in and closed the door, turned the key, and nothing happened. I tried to start it, but the battery was dead. I ran back to the building but the door was locked. Apparently one could leave but couldn't re-enter. There was no one around, and I wasn't familiar with this area beyond that street. I started walking down a street, not knowing if I could find someone to help me. The cold was painful, and I knew my body was literally starting to freeze. I kept walking as fast as I could and in the distance I spotted a gas station. When I approached this station I was surprised that it was still open because it was close to 10:00 p.m. There was one man in this station, and I told him my story. My body was shaking as he said he could help me as he had a tow truck. The heat in the cab felt so good. When we got to my car I told him I would help him as I opened my door. He told me to stay in the cab to get warm and he could charge my battery without me. I realized that I chose the right street to walk for help and how close I came to freezing to death. I was thankful. I learned to always have a winter coat in the car during wintertime.

It was also during this winter that I was at work during a bad snowstorm. This was a Friday night, and two representatives from American General would soon be leaving for Houston. I overheard one of the representatives asking the other, "What are you going to do this weekend?" The reply was, "I think I will go down to the beach and look at bikinis." I thought, "Can you go swimming during the winter down at Galveston?" I realized I never liked cold weather and ice and snow. All at once it sounded good. I thought I would make my final decision and stick to it. I would leave it up to Carole. That Friday evening when I arrived home I asked Carole, "What do you think about moving to Houston?" She shocked me! She said, "I think it would be interesting to live in a different part of the country." I couldn't believe she said that. Looking back, we both believe God wanted us in Houston.. We loved Kalamazoo and had never considered leaving this city. We had many friends and family members there that were all special to us. We didn't know anyone in Texas! Leaving Kalamazoo and Michigan was very hard to accept, but God had blessings for us waiting in Houston.

Everyone was shocked when we told them we were moving to Houston. We were slow to make the announcement. We waited until Dad and Mom were visiting us at our home in Portage, Michigan. When I mentioned it they were surprised, but Dad's comment was, "You have to do what is best for you and Carole." Many years after Dad had passed away, Mom disclosed that she cried on the way home from that weekend.

During May 1970 the company flew Carole and me down to Houston to find housing. Prior to this flight I asked an American General representative if Houston had trees. He said the city had lots of trees, which was hard for me to believe. I asked him where there were a lot of trees and a good school district. His response was Spring Branch. We didn't know where Spring Branch was, but we knew that is where we wanted to live. When our plane landed at Houston's airport, we rented a car and drove down to I-10 and saw a sign for assistance in locating an apartment. We stopped, went inside, and said we needed an apartment in Spring Branch. In just a matter of minutes we knew where Spring Branch was, and the woman in the office knew the "perfect" apartment for us, an older, small, brick complex with four-unit buildings and lots of trees. She said the walls were built to block out sound from the other units. It sounded good to us, and sure enough we loved it. . Everything she said about this complex was true. It was a small complex but really nice. The lady manager of this complex was very nice. She noticed Carole was pregnant and mentioned that children were not allowed, but we could stay until the child was two years old. We didn't care because we expected to move to a house in six months. The company paid the down payment for this apartment.

We drove downtown and were amazed at how clean it was; most of the buildings didn't look very old. We drove over to the American General complex where I would be working in July. We also made reservations for our one night at a motel close to the American General building. The moving van would deliver our furniture and belongings to our rented apartment. A lot of our furniture was going into storage until we had a house. The company paid for all of these expenses.

In May 1970 our out-of-town family members and our friends the Rundells came to visit us for the final time at our house. Our friendship with the Rundells started when we were at Adrian College. Our hearts ached when the Rundells left for home.

Carole's June 22, 1970, letter to Mom and Dad in Europe:

We have enjoyed your letters so much. Glad you are having a great time and both feeling well. I was amazed to find out in looking over your (Europe) itinerary this morning how near the end of your trip you are. Doesn't seem possible! Sorry we haven't written more often, but I'm sure you understand that things have been pretty hectic and confused for us.

We just had a very nice family weekend in Niles. Connie [Carole's sister] and Chuck had gotten back from California Tuesday noon. It was so nice to see them again and to see their dog Pepper. He sure is a playful one.

Candace [Carole's youngest sister] is going with us to Houston. We will leave here Thursday evening, spend the night in Niles, and then leave from there early Friday morning. Doesn't seem possible that's just a little over a week away. Rick got the S and H stamps for a crib as a Father's Day gift! Connie and Chuck also gave us fifteen dollars for something for the nursery. Don't know yet what that will be.

I have my last doctor's appointment here this afternoon. I also want to get material to make a bathing suit. The mother of one of my third graders gave me a pattern. I'm going to make use of that swimming pool! My third graders were so sweet at the end. Several of them brought me gifts; some were for the baby, some for me. One of the mothers made some darling ceramic dishes for Baby Wilcox. I also got a nice blanket, a couple of outfits, bibs, booties, soap, and Q-tips. For myself I got some pillowcases, powder, and a couple of glass things, and a darling arrangement of tiny roses. The whole room gave me a ten dollars gift certificate, which I used to get a baby outfit plus a pretty nightgown and hose for myself. The teachers gave us a crib sheet plus white Dacron comforter for baby. I think our little one is getting well supplied! Oh, I was going to tell you the letter you wrote in Vienna and mailed on the 10th, we received it on the 13th. Pretty fast service, I think!

It seems strange to be out of our house. Rick probably told you about the water pump [well water] trouble we had in the last two days, but it could have been worse than the forty dollars to fix it. The other couple who purchased the house had to put in a new hot water heater, so we didn't fare too badly.

We are enjoying being with the Southerlands. It's a little different though with two little girls (three years and nine months) and two dogs!

Rick has been working overtime every day. Because he had to work during Friday, we didn't get to go out to the Lamplighters (our Sunday school group) retreat, but only three couples were there (one of them Southerlands) so we really didn't miss much. We were just going to stay out there Friday evening.

We are anxious to hear more about your trip. Still seems strange we won't see you to talk about it though until Christmas.

We moved out of our house near the end of June 1970. The house sold quickly. Ted and Nancy Southerland graciously opened their house to us and the movers cleared out our Portage house and moved our items to Houston.

June 28, 1970, letter to Mom and Dad in Europe:

We hope all is well in your traveling. Doesn't seem possible you are almost to London and this coming Friday we will be on our way. I will start work in Houston on Monday, July 6th. You will be in London at that time.

On our way south we will drive through Kentucky and Tennessee. The first night we will stay at Decatur, Alabama. Then during the afternoon of the next day we will stop at New Orleans. Sunday morning, the third day, we will drive to Houston from New Orleans.

The weather here has been on the cool side. Today is really nice, in the seventies. We have been having a lot of fun staying with the Southerlands. We told Uncle Al [Dad's brother] and Aunt Recil we would drop over to their house on Tuesday evening. I don't see how we will be able to see everyone before leaving. Time sure is going by fast!

Ted [Southerland] and I will be leaving shortly for a game of golf. May be the last game in Kalamazoo.

Carole's June 30, 1970, letter to Mom and Dad in Europe:

Yesterday and today are hot and humid. It's only 9:00 a.m. and it's already 86 degrees. Supposed to be around 100! I think they are preparing us for Houston!

Ted and Rick never did get to golf Sunday. Ted's parents came right after dinner, and just as they were leaving my sister Connie and her husband Chuck dropped by on their way from Niles to Delton. Sister Kay also came over. Then it rained!

Rick doesn't think he will be at work much, if at all, because they are loading up Thursday morning.

We had a nice hamburger cookout with the Kings (Woody and Ann) last night. Wednesday (July 1) night almost all the Lamplighters will be here for a picnic in the back yard. It will be nice to get to see everyone before leaving.

It's really been fun staying here with the Southerlands. I enjoy helping with Kelly and Kristy. It sure hasn't been boring! They also have two dogs.

While here I have made a swimsuit, an apron, and a purse. The last two were kits. I have also started a baby sweater. I plan to work on that while traveling too. Won't be long and we will be on our way. It's hard to believe!

I have been feeling fine. Doctor put me on water pills, which helped more than I thought I needed.

A little later this morning a couple Lamplighter friends are coming over to visit and let their little girl play with Kelly in the pool. Saturday we did some shopping and errands. Rick got the car all set for the trip. We also made our reservations for our trip to Houston, all at Ramada Inns.

Hope you are still having a great time.

We miss hearing from you. Should be able to catch up on your doings when in Houston though.

Our last day at the Southerlands' house, July 1, 1970, the Lamplighter class gave us a party. This was so special to us! After the party we left our wonderful friends, and with much sadness and a few tears we drove our car out of the Southerlands' driveway in silence. We drove to Niles to Carole's parents and grandparents, arriving in the late evening. Leaving our relatives, family and several wonderful good friends was very, very hard. Our hearts ached as we left Niles for Houston. A new chapter in our life was about to begin, leaving the past behind us.

When we were settled in our apartment in Houston we got Mom and Dad a leather three-picture frame. We inserted three pictures, all taken during May 1970 in front of our Portage house. One picture was just Carole and me, one of Mom and Dad, and lastly one of Phil and Bonnie with their baby daughter Stephanie. We mailed it to Dad for his birthday with this note: "Here we are near the end of our lives in Kalamazoo. This was another great chapter in our lifetime. Carole and I loved our five years there, and it was fun when all of you visited us in our Portage home. Well, it's behind us now and we hope you enjoy the pictures of all of us in front of our Portage house. Guess we will always have fond memories of this house back in good old Kalamazoo. Dad, we hope you have a nice birthday and many more to come. Speaking from all of us in the pictures, we really think the world of you and Mom. We can honestly say we sure miss you and Mom an awful lot! I guess all we can say is that the old deck of cards are getting dusty! Love, Rick and Carole, Houston, Texas.

Our favorite pastime for Dad, Mom, Carole and I was playing cards. We would play hearts and I believe near the end of our Kalamazoo era we started playing pinochle. We played the card games Hearts with the Rundells and Canasta with the Kings and Southerlands, and later Pinochle with the Daniels and Parsons. Pinochle became our favorite card game which has continued to play throughout our lives.

We settled in Kalamazoo during the second half of July 1965, and we left Kalamazoo on July 1, 1970. After about two years of living in Houston, we felt that this move had actually been a blessing for us.

Chapter 27

Houston, Texas

The company had a great package for our transfer to Houston. They would reimburse us if there was a loss selling our house; reimburse us for the realtor fee, all closing costs, and movers for packing and moving house items, driving expenses, plus five hundred dollars for anything they left out. Salaries were also increased, and in Texas there was no income tax! The company paid for the deposit needed for an apartment, and they also agreed to pay all moving costs from the apartment to a purchased house.

Carole's youngest sister Candace (age seventeen) came with us to help us move into our apartment in Houston. She was an asset for us, and it was comforting to have a family member with us. In later years she would work for Campus Crusade for Christ and marry Nash Hester Jr. in North Carolina. Early on Friday, July 3, 1970, the three of us left Niles for Houston. On the way to Houston we took a tour of Mammoth Cave in Kentucky, which we all enjoyed. We arrived in New Orleans on July 4 in the late afternoon and spent the night there. We got our first taste of a hurricane in New Orleans. While driving to the French Quarter from our hotel, it got really dark and the wind began to blow. We could really feel it in the big Pontiac. It was blowing papers, smoke, and sand every which way. We found out the next day on the radio that there had been hurricane-force winds of 86 mph. Several people drowned who were caught out in their boats. The temperature dropped eighteen degrees.

We arrived in Houston on Sunday July 5, 1970. We stayed at a motel just down the street from the American General Insurance Co. on Allen Parkway. Carole and Candace dropped me off for my first day at work on the 6th (Monday) and then went directly to our apartment. Our apartment was a block south from I-10 Freeway and off Campbell Road. The apartments were in a small complex of two-story buildings with two units on each floor. The living quarters were very small, but we enjoyed living there. We could have used more space, but it worked out for the six months we were there.

I was told that I would not have to do any hiring because the insurance company would hire the employees needed. When I arrived I was shocked that all my employees were recent high-school-graduate girls that didn't know the difference between a debit and a credit. I talked to the group and let them take any desk that they wanted. For six months I went from desk to desk, training them to do the required accounting functions including paying bills. This was done every day during the eight-hour workday. Several times a girl complained that I wasn't spending enough time with her. After everyone went home for the day, I worked at my desk. During these six months dinnertime at home was about 9:00 p.m. or later.

Candace stayed with us and helped us get settled in our apartment, then flew home on August 1st. We are indebted to Candace; I don't know how we would have gotten organized in our apartment during July with Carole being seven months pregnant. While she was with us we spent a Saturday on Galveston Island and later another trip to the San Jacinto Battlegrounds on the east side of Houston. The last battle for Texas's independence on April 21, 1836, was fought on these grounds. Texas became a Republic, but Texas hero Sam Houston wanted Texas to join the United States, which took place on December 29, 1845. After Texas became a state, some of our government members in Washington

D.C. started to have a desire to expand the southern part of the country beyond Texas to the Pacific Ocean. This became reality when the additional land west of Texas—New Mexico, Arizona, Nevada, and California became part of the United States. The impressive San Jacinto Monument and museum stands on the battlegrounds. This monument is taller than the Washington Monument in Washington D.C. It is lighted up at night and can be seen from a far distance. Another weekend in July we drove to Laredo, Texas, and crossed the border to Nuevo Laredo, Mexico. I believe we were only in Nuevo Laredo for about one hour. On the way back to Houston we spent some time in San Antonio and toured the Alamo. That was neat.

I told many people that our expected baby was a boy and named James and that he would be born on September 16, 1970, because that was the tenth anniversary of our meeting each other at Adrian College. September 16th came, and no James. I came home on Friday the 18th, and Carole was getting the meal on the table. I said, "Don't wreck the weekend by having the baby during the weekend, but wait until Monday. I won't have to work that day." About an hour later Carole lost her water, and we were on our way to the hospital. James Adrian Wilcox was born early in the morning of the 19th. Our special friends Bob and Verdie Daniels came to the hospital and spent the evening and early hours of the following day with me. We played cards on the floor to pass the hours away. James was all red when the nurse lifted him up for my view of him. I asked the nurse what was wrong with him but the nurse said all babies were like this. I was very joyful and thankful that we had a healthy son. I thought it was a miracle. How can anyone look at a newborn baby and think there is no God? Bob and Verdie stayed after the birth and then we all went home. The 19th was their wedding anniversary. They wanted to spend this time with me, which was a big blessing for me! I was back at the hospital early Saturday morning. This was a wonderful experience. James takes pride that he was born in Texas. He only made it by a little more than two months! We might not have been forgiven if he had been born in Michigan.

It was in our Sunday school class during the early 1970's that we met D.C. and Linda Weiss. We became good friends, and I'm sure we have spent more times together than any other couple during our Houston era. We had outside activities as well as playing card and board games in our homes. It was always fun when we were together. We also went to events together in Houston. D.C. is talented with his hands. He enjoys working with cars and repairing and building houses. His garage is a workshop. He has done a lot for us over the years. I can remember in the early 1970's one Sunday morning that D.C. told me they were going to be parents. Brandy was born, and married Keith Texter after she graduated from college—another wonderful couple.

Our good friends Ted and Nancy Southerland from Kalamazoo decided to move to Houston in 1971 and got an apartment not far from our Barwood Street house. We were delighted that they made this decision. At this time they had two daughters, Kelly and Kristy. We spent a lot of enjoyable time with them. The last Easter weekend that we were living in Kalamazoo the four of us went to Washington, D.C. to tour the city and on the way home we spent a few hours in Philadelphia. It was a fun trip. Now we could, and did, spend a lot of time together. Ted and I purchased a beach house in Crystal Beach on Bolivar Peninsula. At this time Ted was in house construction and a lot of good wood was trashed. With permission he took a lot of this wood, and we used it during our Saturday trips to our beach house, which we named "Wil-Land's Sunny." A lot of work was needed, but we got the house livable. Sometime during 1975 Ted and family had the opportunity to run a catalog store in Santa Rosa, New Mexico, owned by a family member. As I remember, Ted was not satisfied with his employment in Houston, and that encouraged him to accept this job offer. Eventually he and his family moved back to Michigan. We hated to see them leave Houston. It was also about this time we sold the beach house.

In May 1972 our friends from Kalamazoo Woody and Ann King came to visit us and the Southerlands. These friends were like family to us. This unity of the six of us was very special during the few days the Kings were with us.

During summer 1976 we traveled to Michigan and our Kalamazoo Sunday school class organized a party for us. This special gathering meant a lot to us, and it reminded us of the good days we had when we lived in Kalamazoo. This was the last time we spent with our Kalamazoo group.

In January 1971, after six months and two weeks, we moved into our first house in Spring Branch, directly west from downtown Houston at 10302 Barwood Street. The company again paid for the move and the packing. We enjoyed this house and lived there until the boys were in college. The day the movers came Baby James slept soundly in his bucket seat on the floor of the living room.

July 2, 1972, letter to Dad and Mom:

This is the last time I will address my letters to 250 W. Maplehurst. It seems odd that you two will no longer be at that address. I know I'm not alone with many memories of old "250." It was a very good house for you two, as well as for Phil and me. I will take to my grave many good, happy memories of my life there with you two and Phil. I feel life is just a series of stages and you don't know where you will be in the future.

This is just a note in wishing you all good packing and that we are still glad you two are moving to the sunny south, Florida.

Don't leave an old coin behind that may have been left in the dining room or upstairs a long time ago. Just say goodbye for us and close the last door. Remember, there is a new door awaiting you that will bring continued happiness. We are thinking of you two, and miss y 'all!

In another letter to my parents I wrote: I will always be grateful to you two for all you have done for us. If it wasn't for you two, I wouldn't have what I have and it would have been a completely different life for me. I will always be indebted to you two and unfortunately I will never be able to repay you.

I was always grateful to my parents for all the support and love they gave me, as well as to Carole. What came to mind as I wrote this is that we can't repay Christ for what He did for us.

I loved my job and liked most of the people at the company very much. However, sometime in 1973 I started thinking that I needed to leave this company because the salary and salary raises weren't what I expected. I really didn't want to leave, but I knew I had to. My problem was, I didn't know the other companies within the Houston area. A few months later a life insurance agent called and wanted to talk with me during the day. I agreed; he came and we visited for a while. He asked me if I liked my job, and I said, "Very much so, but I'm planning to leave." He offered a job to do what he was doing, visiting people during the day. It would be a commission job only. I didn't think of myself as a salesman, but I would learn about companies in Houston. I said I would like to know more about it. I met with him and his boss, and agreed to take on this insurance job.

After I gave my two-week notice at the company, I met with my group. When I mentioned that I was leaving one of the young ladies started crying. She was born in Germany and married an American in the army. She came from another department because I was going to have a vacant desk. When she arrived I told her I had heard good things about her and I was so glad she would be working for me. When I released the group I asked the woman why she was crying. She told me that she didn't want me to leave because I was the only boss that had ever told her that he was glad to have her in his department. During my career I have learned that the best way to motivate people is encouragement and making them feel they are wanted and important to the company. I left the company on August 1 for this new employment. I was told that during 1972 there was a seventy percent turnover within the company. I was losing employees due to low salaries. In addition, salaries were frozen. Still, I enjoyed my job, and I didn't want to leave.

I didn't make enough money to live on working for the insurance company, but what this job did for me was identify a very large heavy construction and engineering company called Brown & Root, Inc. After visiting an employee of this company on the east-side campus, I felt this was the company I wanted to work for. In March 1974 I felt that the time had arrived for me to find a job in the accounting field, and my first choice was Brown & Root, Inc. At that time the company had over ninety thousand employees worldwide. I went to the employment office there early one morning and asked for an accounting position. I was told there were no openings, but I could talk to someone if I liked. I said I would appreciate talking to someone. I spent a long time talking with a person in the employment office. He said that he wanted me to talk to the manager of the Internal Audit Dept. He led me to this manager's office. I had another long interview, and I thought he was going to offer me a position but that didn't happen. Instead, he told me that he wanted me to talk to the manager of the corporate payroll department, Phil Elting, since there might be a position opening soon. I again had another long interview. At the end of this interview Phil said that there was a position opening up soon, and I would be considered.

I had also planned to drive over to Texas Instruments on the southwest side of Houston, but it was lunchtime so I went directly home. When I walked in the house the phone rang and it was Phil Elting; he said, "When can you come to work?" Looking back, I believe God guided me and made all of this happen. The timing for being hired was perfect. I started employment with Brown & Root Inc. on April 1, 1974. My new responsibilities included being involved with a lot of our field sites throughout the United States by phone.

At that time the company was a heavy construction company building roads, factories, bridges, dams, and later maintenance at chemical plants and also engineering. I was able to streamline a major computer report that I used, and this new report saved me a lot of time each month. I was also able to get another function on the computer. My boss told me that I was the first college-degree person he had hired, and from then on any new hires would have to be college graduates. I was in the payroll accounting section, which included the major responsibilities of all payrolls, and payroll tax payments consisting of federal, state, and local. It also included tax levies and garnishments, payroll accounting functions, and other responsibilities. We were also involved with the other companies of Brown & Root, which were located in over half the states and overseas. Working with field offices throughout the country enabled me to learn other jobs within this department. This helped me learn most of the functions within the department. This job was very enjoyable and beneficial.

I learned a big, big lesson early in my employment with this company. One summer we came back from visiting my parents in Florida. My first day back I learned the payroll accounting supervisor was gone and had been replaced by Jim Rogers, who had been in the department for less than a year. I couldn't believe it! I should have been the one to have this job! The thought came to mind that I should leave the company, but I couldn't because I had a wife and two small kids. I admit that he was smart, had a college degree, great personality, and very good communicating skills, which was my one weakness. I believe my poor communicating skills hurt my career, but I did okay. I went home feeling hurt. I considered what Jesus would do in this situation. I'm sure I prayed about it. I quickly concluded that I should be happy for Jim and help him succeed. There was so much he needed to know. In addition to my job, I would work with him with the thought of making him successful.

In the morning I went in his office, told him I was glad that he got this promotion, and that I wanted to help him. We spent a lot of time together. There were many annual procedures needed to close the year, including making sure all of the W-2 forms (over one hundred thousand of them) were correct by making the necessary adjustments to this file. I was the only one in the department that knew all the necessary procedures needed. The final night for printing W-2 forms we worked together and finished correcting and balancing the forms W-2 file around 1:00 a.m. As I remember, it was less than a year later that another department in the overseas area wanted Jim. Our department manager, Jerry Young, asked him who should be the next payroll (accounting) supervisor. As told to me by our secretary, Trudy Lloyd, Jim Rogers said, "If you put Rick Wilcox in that position, everything that needs to be done will get done," Finally, I was the payroll accounting supervisor. Jim Rogers and his wife (Waej) became our good friends. We rotated houses for dinner and playing pinochle card games throughout the years. We played tennis together. This move for Jim Rogers worked out well for him, and I was glad for him. This was the lesson that greatly benefited me for many years. We are still friends even though he and his wife now live far away. God helped me to make the right decision.

Brown & Root, Inc. was my best employer, and I'm very fortunate to have had the opportunity to work for this great company. I took a lot of pride in working for Brown & Root, Inc., and the company was good to me. I worked for them for twenty-seven and a half years, and I enjoyed my work throughout those years. There were some bad times that all companies, I'm sure, experience. The early 1980's saw massive layoffs, which are always very sad. I had to lay people off, and I felt their hurt. I hated doing this. It's terrible when this happens.

Carole was a stay-at-home mother, caring for James and John. John was eighteen months younger than James. When the boys were much older Carole was asked to come and work with the preschool kids at our Chapelwood United Methodist Church. She was always home when the boys were home because her hours were 9:00-12:30 p.m., and one day each week there was an extra hour. The salary wasn't much, but it did help. Most importantly, she loved the position, and she had an opportunity to have a function outside of home. She did this for about fourteen years. I always thought that my job was easier than Carole's job of caring for the children and preparing meals.

During April 1976 in a letter to my parents I included the following:

You two have been wonderful parents, and we miss you two. Guess I will always have wonderful memories of my home life in Ferndale. I notice, Mother, in a few letters we talked a lot about coins. It was a real part of our lives during the 1950's and early 1960's. Between the two of us we probably have looked through bags of coins equaling a million coins. There are times I wish I had not sold my silver dollar set. It took eight years to complete it, and it was only through your connection at the Detroit Bank that I was able to get the last thirteen or so, mostly "CC" mint mark dollars during the spring of 1963.

It was a lot of fun looking through all of those silver dollars during that time. We both had beautiful sets. I remember about one-third or more of the dollar coins in my set had mint luster.

During the 1950's I thought about 1976, the country's 200th birthday. Congress authorized commemorative silver halves and gold coins during the years of 1892-1952. The U.S. Mint was opposed to this continuation, which resulted in the end of commemorative coins. I like a lot of these previously issued special coins, and I was positive come 1976 we would have a bicentennial commemorative coin. Congress wanted special coins, but the Mint was still opposed to this idea. The members of the committee in Congress responsible for coins had a strong desire to change all of our circulating coins to commemorate the Bicentennial. The Mint agreed to change the reverse designs only for the quarter, half-dollar, and dollar coins. The new one-year reverse designs would not include any year dates. The obverse (front) date of these three coins would be dated 1776-1976 and they would be issued during 1975 and 1976. During the early 1980s the Mint accepted the concept of issuing commemorative coins for collectors for a premium. This practice has been continued every year since 1982, except 1983.

July 4, 1976 fell on a Sunday. I had been looking forward to this day for many, many years. Monday was a holiday, so we had a three-day weekend. I recorded how we spent this weekend for my parents in Florida:

The Great Nation is now 200 years old, and I'm glad that we all lived to see it. We had one great fabulous time, and I hope James and John will remember this weekend. Time will tell. I can remember thinking about this 4th of July 1976 way back during my youth in Ferndale. I was so positive that the United States would issue a commemorative coin, and naturally I'm disappointed that this didn't happen. It seemed back then that this day was so far away. I probably would be married and in my thirties. Well, it came, and so fast!

Houston has a very attractive commemorative medal for the Bicentennial. A bank downtown is selling these medals. I thought by giving these medals to the boys on the 4th this might help them to remember this "special" birthday party (James is five and a half and John is four years old).

Friday after work I went into the bank to purchase three of these medals for three dollars and fifteen cents each. The third one I kept for myself.

Saturday morning we all got up. Prior to this day and also during the weekend I explained to the boys that this was a real special weekend and it was the 200th birthday of the United States, the country that we are living in. Thursday night I told this to the boys and John asked, "What is the United States?" I told him it was the country we live in, the land that includes Houston, and Houston is in Texas, and Texas is part of the United States. I didn't ask him if he understood what I said. I didn't know any other way to explain this to a four-year-old child. Friday morning before I left for work, I showed James and John a map of the United States. James immediately recognized Texas, and I pointed out Florida and Michigan and California (their Aunt Candace lives in California). Interesting that James likes the song "This Land is my Land." I don't know if John understood any of this.

After our Saturday donuts we headed toward downtown and were there around 9:15 a.m. The 10:00 a.m. parade was okay, but nothing really special for a city of this size! It was enjoyable and the boys liked it. The Goodyear blimp was overhead. A two-and-a-half-year-old girl and her parents were next to us. She was so cute and attractive with a bonnet on her head. I took three pictures of her and the grandfather asked me to call him if they came out. The pictures were just her head and I was quite sure the last one would be an excellent and attractive picture. After the parade and going through what I thought was a roll of film I discovered that the film never advanced after each picture was taken because the film was cracked at the beginning of the film, preventing the film from advancing. Thus I don't have any pictures during the time of the parade. Needless to say, it was disappointing.

We then walked over to the Sam Houston Park and at that time there wasn't too much going on. We then walked over to a craft and art display nearby. That is when the boys started to get a little tired. Right after the parade we stopped into a Roy Rogers restaurant for some soda pop, which helped their spirits. After the craft and arts we walked over to the reflection pond between city hall and One Shell Plaza. It has water, flowers, grass, trees, and benches. We sat down on the ground and the boys lay down. We listened to a fantastic concert by the Bayou Banjos. There were about fifteen banjo players, and they were very good! You could listen to their music for hours! After about an hour or so we left this concert because the boys were hungry, and so were we. They were still playing their banjos when we left to get hamburgers at the Roy Rodgers Restaurant. Once again the boys were revived! It was at this time that the dark clouds were rolling in and we lost our blue sky. It looked really bad in the west! During this day the boys took a "car ride" at a small carnival, which they enjoyed. We walked down to "Allen's Landing" on the Buffalo Bayou (a river part of the ship channel). There were decorated yachts, concerts, arts and crafts, and lots of people. After an hour it looked like we were going to get a storm. It was about 4:00 p.m. and the boys were very tired and wanted to go home. On the way to the car a few raindrops were falling, but just as we got into the car it really broke loose! Boy, did it rain! By the time we got home it was over with.

The boys went to bed and both went to sleep immediately. They got up at 6:30 p.m., and off we went to dinner. Shortly after we arrived home our good friends Bob and Verdie Daniels came over. We all went over to Westbury Square for the 10:00 p.m. fireworks. This is a very attractive shopping center with a very large courtyard. We were there around 9:30 p.m., and there were literally thousands of people there. The fireworks lasted about forty-five minutes and were excellent. The boys enjoyed them. We stayed in the area for ice cream cones and then went home. We all had a lot of fun.

Sunday morning it was church time and the service was excellent. I taped a good share of it. After the service we (the church members) had a picnic in our courtyard area, and with all of the music and food it was a wonderful time. This area had a temporary stage next to the waterfall close to the gym area. The music entertainment was very good. James and John were with us during the church service, and they did well.

About 2:15 p.m. we left for home, got reorganized, and then back to downtown Houston. We went back to Sam Houston Park and were delighted to see the Bayou Banjos playing in the band shell. We sat on the grass under a tree and listened to them. I took some photographs while they were playing. They played for over two hours, and we loved it and so did the other hundreds of people who were there. The boys were thirsty and what saved them was a family next to us who had a picnic and offered cans of soda pop to the boys, and they gratefully accepted. Their spirits were again revived! I thought that this was really nice of them, and they refused to take any money. I would say that there was an atmosphere of friendliness at this park, and everyone was having a lot of fun. This Sam Houston Park is the area right on the edge of downtown's tall buildings. It includes a pond with an old country church and old houses from Houston's past. It also has a large open area in the center of the park. It's a very attractive area and one of my favorite areas of Houston. We did tour a few of these old houses after the banjo concert. We listened to a Girl Scout concert for about twenty minutes, then went over to a puppet show for the boys, then it was home. We got home at 6:00 p.m. and the boys were tired. They went to bed after a bath and milkshakes. They were asleep instantly! Carole and I then watched TV for the rest of the evening. We saw what was happening or had happened in the rest of the country and also the Bob Hope Special.

On Monday morning the 4th was behind us, and we started our third century. It has and continues to be the greatest country! We have been so blessed and should praise the Lord for this land of ours.

After a quick simple breakfast we found ourselves headed toward Galveston. We drove through rain to and from Galveston, but it was nice when we were there. The boys had a great time, and of course we enjoyed it also. There were very few people down there at that time. Around noon we headed back home, and after a quick shower we rushed over to the Daniels' house for the rest of the day. Bob grilled hamburgers outside. Dave and Connie Parsons joined us. After we ate we played pinochle. It was a fun evening.

Carole, the boys, and I had a fun time during several Friday or Saturdays during 1979. The value of silver was rising and there were a few shops paying six times the face value of U.S. silver coins, then it was seven times face value, and this number kept growing. Half-dollars were no longer circulating and banks had rolls of half-dollars. Banks were open to 6:00 p.m. on Fridays and Saturday mornings. Many rolls had silver half-dollars. Some Fridays after work Carole and I plus the boys would go visiting banks and asking for half-dollar rolls. I would have several hundred dollars with me. We would go to bank after bank, buying all of their half-dollar rolls until the banks were closed. I would share the rolls with the boys, and they could keep any silver halves they found. We would always get at least a few silver coins; sometimes we would get a lot. When I had a large number of silver halves, I would sell them at a shop which generated a profit. John wanted to sell his when I took them, but James wanted to save his.

Mother and Dad visited us from Florida during this time, and on Friday Mother, Dad, and I drove down to the end of Long Point Road to a bank that had several hundred dollars of half-dollar rolls. At the bank's drive-in window I asked for rolls and they asked me the number of rolls I wanted. They had more half-dollar rolls than the cash I had in my pocket. She asked if I was a customer, and I had to say no. She said I could only have so many rolls. I took what she gave me. When we got home, we found that these rolls were loaded with silver. On Saturday morning Mother and I went back to the bank's drive-in window armed with more money. They would not sell us any more rolls because we were not customers. I went inside and opened a savings account, depositing one hundred dollars. Then I went back to the drive-in window and told her I had an account with the bank and I wanted to buy all of their rolls. She gave them to me, and what a jackpot! Mother got half of the silver so we both did well. I made hundreds of dollars during this short period of time. It was fun!

When our sons were in college we moved to a larger house at 3023 Kevin Lane, about two miles north of our Barwood Street house. This house allowed Carole to have her own quilt room because she needed the space. Carole was a big quilter and even taught classes in quilting. This move took place on December 18, 1990. Since the distance between the two houses was very short, I decided to move everything myself, except for the heavy items. I hired Two Men and a Truck to move the heavier items. We had a deadline to be out of the house that night. We had a very early breakfast and I started loading the pick-up, and perhaps the car too with Carole driving it. As the hours passed, I felt I wasn't making a lot of progress because we sure had a lot of stuff! In the late afternoon John's friend Ralph Hendrick showed up with a trailer hitched to his pick-up. He asked if we could use help moving. What a lifesaver he was. Later John showed up from college and we continued to move our items from the old house to the new house. Finally James was home from college and all of us were moving our items. Ralph was a fast worker. In the evening I was dragging; the young men were moving faster than I was. When we thought we were done I found a closet loaded with stuff we had forgotten in our packing. It was late evening when we finally had everything out of the house and garage, and Carole and I hadn't eaten anything since breakfast. I was so exhausted, weak, and hungry that I felt I couldn't do anymore and the group finished the move for us. Without Ralph I would never have been able to complete our moving out on time. It was very late in the evening and I had promised the group a good dinner, but all of the restaurants were closed. We finally found a pizza restaurant that was open, so I treated the group to a pizza dinner and felt relieved.

Our water heater died on our first morning in the new house . We were able to get a new water heater installed before Christmas. Within two days after moving into our home Carole's sister Kay came for a visit, as did my mother from Florida the following day. Kay helped me paint one of the bedrooms, which was greatly appreciated. It took us several weeks to unpack, but it was a special time that Christmas with our boys, Mother, and Kay. The unopened boxes everywhere didn't hinder our Christmas season.

I enjoyed going to baseball games at Houston's Astrodome stadium and later at Minute Maid Park. Mark McGwire and Sammy Sosa made the 1998 season very exciting for me. It was the most exciting baseball season I had experienced; except when Detroit won the 1968 World Series in seven games against the St Louis Cardinals. When St. Louis was in town, we were at games when McGwire hit home runs on his way to a record total of seventy for the season. I would write the updated total number of the home runs on my ticket stub. There were one or two times I left work in time to be at St. Louis batting practice in the Astrodome. Along with several thousand others, I was also there to see McGwire consistently hitting balls during batting practice at distances that I have never seen before. I believe one ball he hit to the outfield would have left the stadium if there hadn't been a dome on the stadium. It was just incredible! This was real entertainment for the thousands watching.

When Mother and Dad visited us during the baseball season we would go to a game if the Houston Astros were in town. Dad told me that the Astrodome was his favorite baseball stadium. In 1979 Mother and Dad were in town for our birthdays, and the Astros were playing at home. We went to the April 9 game against the Atlanta Braves. Astros pitcher Ken Forsch pitched a no-hitter, and that was exciting. The last three innings were a little tense, hoping we wouldn't see a hit from the Braves. Dad said that was the only no-hitter he had ever witnessed, which was the same for me. Houston won six to nothing. Ken Forsch only had two walks, and he retired twenty consecutive batters. At that time this was the earliest no-hitter in the majors. It is interesting to know that Ken's brother Bob also pitched a no-hitter in his career. This was a better game than the one on April 23, 1964, when Houston's Ken Johnson pitched a no-hitter against the Cincinnati Reds, losing the game zero to one. Two Astros errors in the ninth inning allowed the run for Cincinnati.

One of my great baseball memories was when the Houston Astros started the 2000 season in their new stadium, currently called Minute Maid Park but on opening day it was Enron Field. A lot of the stadium was built by Brown & Root, Inc. The new stadium was built attached to the old Union (train) Station in downtown Houston. This train station served downtown Houston for many years during the twentieth century. It ceased to be a train station in 1974. The stadium construction restored this building very nicely, and it provides the major entrance to the stadium. It is very attractive. The Astros administrative staff use the upper floors.

I wanted to be at the first game played in the new stadium. This game was not the opener of the season, but it was an exhibition game against the New York Yankees. The same teams played in the first game in Houston's Astrodome stadium on April 9, 1965. The Astros beat the Yankees two to one in that game in twelve innings. Mickey Mantle got the first hit, single, and the first home run. I couldn't get a ticket at a reasonable price. A large number of tickets ended up in the hands of third-party ticket agents, but apparently a lot of these tickets were not sold because there were a lot of empty seats during the game. Some of these tickets were auctioned off on Ebay. Many were offered here in Houston at unrealistic prices. The day of the first game, March 30, 2000, I called four different ticket agents from my Brown & Root, Inc. office. The cheapest price was one hundred and twenty-five dollars per ticket. I wanted to be at the first game, but not badly enough to pay twenty-five dollars. During the afternoon at work I decided that I would not pay more than fifty dollars for a ticket. I even prayed prior to driving downtown that if it was His will that I get a ticket, let it be. The Lord knew I really wanted to be there at the opening pitch. I thanked Him.

After work I drove to the new stadium, which is only about two miles from where I worked. I parked a block and a half from the stadium, paying a premium parking fee of ten dollars. Closer to the stadium on the other side of the street it was twenty dollars. A few blocks away the parking cost was five to six dollars. I had a small sign with me reading "Need Ticket." I read in the paper that they expected sixty percent of the crowd to enter through Union Station. I also read or heard that it was illegal to sell tickets on the stadium grounds, so I crossed the street from the Union Station entrance and found that there were several persons wanting to buy tickets. I went to the opposite end of this block in front of the stadium, and there too were five or six people wanting tickets. I walked across the street away from the stadium and took charge of this corner. I noticed that across the street on the stadium block there were a few individuals with signs wanting tickets. Some wanted as many as three tickets.

After standing there for about fifteen minutes, a man came up to me and asked if I only wanted one ticket. I said, "Yes, I need only one ticket." He gave me a story that he had an extra ticket that belonged to his girlfriend, and she wanted fifty dollars. It was a ten dollar upper-deck seat and he wouldn't budge from this price. I said, "That is high!" He insisted on fifty dollars for his ticket, so I quickly said, "OK" even though I was hoping he would reduce his price. I realized that he could easily sell this ticket and it was probably the cheapest ticket available. This all worked out because I wanted to be in the stadium early. Having a ticket would also get me the special baseball hat commemorating the first game in the new stadium that was free to each ticket holder. The starting pitcher for the Yankees was Roger Clemens. I'm a fan of his and at that time I had never seen him pitch. Roger Clemens is also a graduate of Spring Woods High School, the same as our sons. Also in the game was Chuck Knoblauch, a Houston boy, and I also wanted to see another favorite player Derek Jeter, a Kalamazoo boy. It all worked out, and I was as excited as a little kid going to his first professional game.

Once inside I walked around the stadium on the field level. I fell in love with this stadium. Enron Field is much closer to our home than the Astrodome and the fans can exit the parking lots much more quickly than the Astrodome. I'm glad we have a new stadium and that it's located in downtown Houston. It's smaller than the Astrodome; the seating capacity is only forty-two thousands. Most of the field can be seen from the walkway around the seating area of the stadium. This makes it possible to watch the game from behind the seats. This walkway also includes the stores and food vendors. I enjoyed walking around the seating areas and looking out at the field from the different areas. I like the left-field area walkway in the outfield area. It's the shortest distance from home plate, measuring only 317 feet. A lot of practice balls land in this area.

My seat was in the third-base area, a fairly good area. I enjoyed seeing Nolan Ryan, one of my all-time favorite players, throw out the first pitch. My favorite Astros player is Jeff Bagwell. I had hoped he would hit the first home run in the stadium, but that was not to be. It was a Yankee player, lesser-known Ricky Ledee, who would go down in the record books as the first player to hit a home run at Enron Field (later Minute Maid Park). In the same inning Yankee Paul O'Neill hit the second home run. All of the Yankees runs were scored in the sixth inning. Astros player Daryl Ward hit the only Astros home run in the bottom of the eighth inning to put the Astros in front for good, 6-5. Jeff Bagwell will go down in the record book as getting the stadium's first hit, the first stolen base, and the first Astros run batted in at Enron Field. Jeff Bagwell had one single and two doubles in this first game. It was a great game. I enjoyed the open air, even though around the eighth inning it started to get a little cool. I was glad that I was wearing a long-sleeved shirt. It was pure enjoyment being at the first game in Enron Field. It was fun having the Astros beat the world champion New York Yankees. After three innings I left my upper-deck seat and walked down the aisle stairs to an open level area like an open platform where I stood to watch the game until the top of the ninth inning. I then left this level and went down to the field level to watch our star relief pitcher Billy Wagner get three easy outs for the Astros victory. A man next to me and I traded high fives. This occasion was a joyful one among the fans, and I was one of them!

The third and last preseason game at Enron Field was with the Texas Rangers. There were four of us at this game—Carole and I, our son John, and his wife Jody. The Astros lost this game. Carole and I were at the first opening season game at Enron Field on April 7, 2000. The Astros won against the Philadelphia Phillies by the score of 4-1.

Dad would take me to Detroit Tigers games and I always enjoyed being there. I always wanted to get a major league ball while at a game. I came close to getting a ball a few times. On May 29, 2004, we were not in our regular seats at Minute Maid Park, but Carole and I were together in section 323, row 3. I was in seat number 2. The seats were between home plate and first base but much closer to home plate. Astro Jeff Kent was at bat. The people around me were not paying attention when Jeff Kent hit a foul ball looping down right to me. I stood up and caught the ball, but I had to use my left arm to block the arm of the man behind me as he was trying to steal the ball from me. I dropped it between my legs but immediately picked it up. I showed it to Carole and it was pure joy for me. She said something like, "Very good!" When we left the game I called a family member and announced that I finally got a baseball. On the ball I wrote the section number, row number, seat number, date, and "Jeff Kent's foul ball."

Very few people have been hit by a baseball during a game. I'm one of the few. It was September 3, 2005. Carole and I decided to go see the St. Louis-Houston game during the evening. St. Louis's star pitcher Chris Carpenter and Houston's star pitcher Roger Clemens were pitching in this game. The game was a sellout. Total attendance was 42,817, including tickets for standing only. I told Carole that probably one of these pitchers would be awarded the Cy Young award for this season. Chris Carpenter had nineteen victories going into this game, the most in the majors. Roger Clemens had an ERA of only 1.56 going into this game. After this season it was Chris Carpenter who was awarded the 2005 Cy Young Award.

We drove over to the stadium a little early, knowing that we would have to find two tickets for the game. There were a couple of ticket "buy-sell" vendors that we visited. I wanted seats in the terrace section, which were normally nineteen dollars tickets. We could get upper-deck tickets for forty dollars, but the terrace tickets were one hundred dollars for two. I wanted to pay no more than fifty dollars for two tickets. There was another individual on the way to the stadium that was also offering two terrace tickets for one hundred dollars. Neither of these people would come down from these prices.

We walked one block away from the stadium, and at the intersection I saw a young man talking with a young couple. Apparently they couldn't agree on a price. They just stood there as we approached this person. I asked him if he had tickets. He had several upper-deck tickets and two club-section tickets, which were great seats, but more expensive. The regular ticket price for club tickets was thirty-eight dollars. I told him that I wouldn't pay his price. He asked what I wanted to pay and I said fifty dollars. He wanted to deal, and so we went back and forth. He even indicated that we shouldn't have a problem paying sixty dollars from seeing my camera. I told him that wasn't the issue. He would give me the tickets, and I would give them back. I said, "Okay, I'll give you fifty-five dollars," but that didn't work. After more haggling I got them for fifty-eight dollars, and they were great seats in the club area past first base. I apologized to this couple still standing next to the seller, thinking I might have interrupted their attempt to negotiate a purchase price for two tickets. He said they had really enjoyed listening to the haggling.

During the game I had to get up several times from my seat to allow individuals in and out of the row. I normally keep my eyes on the batters all the time, watching where each ball is hit. The other side of the aisle was filled with a large group from St. Louis. Once as someone left the row I delayed sitting down because I was distracted by this St. Louis group. As I stood in the aisle, I heard Carole say, "Look!" I looked at the field while still standing and couldn't see anything unusual. Immediately an unseen baseball hit my left arm and then apparently hit the back of my seat and shot over to the other side of the aisle. When the ball hit me I immediately looked down and around me for the ball. I never saw it. The man across from me mentioned someone got the ball in his area. I was disappointed that I didn't see this foul ball because I believe if I had seen it I could have caught it. There were women to the left of Carole and apparently they didn't try to catch it. So close for getting another ball! It just missed Carole. I told Carole to yell "Ball coming" next time, if there is a next time. Someone was excited to go home with a game ball. I know the feeling of getting a ball, and I'm glad for that person. Houston lost this game by a score of four to two. The pitching was great!

Sunday, April 10, 2005, was Carole's sixty-third birthday. Part of our celebration was going to an Astros game at Minute Maid Park in downtown Houston. I called ahead of time to pay for an announcement on the stadium's large screen. I was told which inning the message would appear. My message was, "Happy Birthday, Carole Wilcox, you're special! Love, Rick!" When the time came for these announcements on the big screen I told Carole that I knew someone who would be recognized and I had my camera ready to take a picture of that announcement. It came, and it was a big surprise for Carole. I'm sure Barbara and George Bush in attendance were pleased that Carole had a birthday while they were at this game. With my long lens I took a picture of them looking down from the terrace section. They had season tickets, and I knew where their seats were, in the first row behind home plate. Later in the game they were shown on the screen, and I took a picture of their images shown on the screen. It was a fun day, with the Houston Astros beating Cincinnati five to two.

Our favorite Astros attendant in all the years we lived in Houston is Hazel Gilchriest, She really made attending Astros games a lot of fun. She was a die-hard Astros fan and her favorite player, as well as mine during this era, was Lance Berkman. She could get the fans in her section cheering and when the Astros scored it was high-five time. We loved it. She would help families with kids by carrying their food to their row. We saw her once bending down on the steps at a row seat where a little girl was crying. She tried to comfort this little girl. She was smiling all the time and welcomed everyone coming into her section. I wrote a letter to the owner of the Astros Drayton McLane, Jr., addressed to his office in Temple, Texas, telling him of his exceptional employee and how she made every game enjoyable. He in turn wrote a nice letter to Hazel. We had weekend season tickets and a few weeks later we walked into our section and there was Hazel. She came up to us and said, "I know who you are! You are Rick Wilcox!" and gave us big hugs. I asked her how she knew my name. Her response was that Drayton McLane Jr. wrote her a letter and she had it framed and hanging on a wall in her house. That letter was a treasure for her and really made her day. I still don't know how she connected who I was from Drayton McLane's letter.

Hazel took pictures of us a few times with my camera when we were at a game. She took two good pictures of Carole and me when we were at the April 10, 2005 game. One time during our conversation during the game she told us that she had tickets for the Rangers –Astros game coming up in Arlington. I told her that we had Saturday tickets for that same weekend series. I mentioned we would be there with our son James. She asked where we would be sitting, but I couldn't give her the location of our seats. When that weekend came we were in our seats. During the early part of the game I told Carole, "I think I hear Hazel's voice" as I looked up to the next level. There was a woman with her back facing the field, trying to lead a cheer for the Astros. There was also an Astros sign on the railing. It sure looked like Hazel. I yelled up to her, but I was drowned out from the noise generated from the fans. So I kept looking up and there she was facing the field. I yelled again and waved my arms and she spotted us. She pointed to the empty seat next to Carole and somehow I related with my hands that no one had that seat. She came down and sat with us for a few innings until she felt that she needed to get back to her girlfriend. She complimented us to James as she left. Hazel was a fun person to be with.

I admired the past Astros owner Drayton McLane, Jr. He would attend Fan Fest and would give you his autograph on the asking. He made himself available to the fans. Once he came up to me and asked what I thought of the new Astros uniforms, and I commented positively. Later I wrote a letter to him making suggestions for the annual Fan Fest. He surprised me with a nice letter and a Craig Biggio autographed baseball. He made my day! Of course, I wrote a letter thanking him. Craig Biggio is the only Astros player inducted into baseball's Hall of Fame. On one season's opening day there was a celebration outside of Union Station (the stadium). I approached Mr. McLane and thanked him again for this autographed baseball. He said, "Why not, you're an Astros fan." He allowed me to have my picture taken with him using my camera. It is an excellent picture of him and me.

Our lives were changed by becoming parents. Our activity centered on our boys. When they were young kids I looked forward to what their adult future would be, the professions they would be involved with. I prayed hundreds of times, asking for the blessing that both boys would commit their lives to Christ and live a life based on the life of Jesus Christ. My second request to God was that they would both graduate from college. My prayers were answered. In my life I have found that through this commitment to Jesus Christ we will have an abundant life (not in terms of wealth), forgiveness of our sins (if we repent and turn away from sins), a wonderful peace not from this world, and joy in our heart knowing where our eternal home will be. Having this is worth more than the wealth of the world. During this time I mentioned in a letter to my parents, now living in Florida that I could clearly see that the two most important things for life are confidence in oneself and believing with faith that Jesus is with you wherever you are in life. God will help us, whatever situation or circumstances we may encounter. No one will ever walk a path of roses and die without encountering a bed of pain or tragedies. Knowing that God/Jesus is real will make the road of life easier and at the end, a road of light and love.

Carole was a very loving, patient mother and was always there when the boys needed her. We had so much fun with them. During April 1976 James, age five and a half, wanted to buy me a tie. Carole took him to a store and James picked out a green tie with the Liberty Bell included in the design. James insisted that was the tie for me because it was green, my favorite color. It was my belief that it was the bell on the tie that attracted him since he had seen this bell on the Eisenhower dollar coins. That evening he asked me a few times if I really liked the tie he had picked out. I told him I really, really liked the tie and I would have picked that same tie if I was buying a tie, and I assured him he had done a good job selecting this tie. That satisfied him, and he didn't ask me again. The boys were a lot of fun, and I felt blessed to have them as our sons. When they were very young they would really give me a big welcome when I came home from work. It was all special for me.

James enjoyed working with his hands. In junior high or earlier he wanted to be a carpenter. Sometime after that he started to enjoy working with cars. Both boys always enjoyed small Matchbox cars and larger toy cars. It was during early high school that James became more involved with cars. He gave up Spring Woods High School track to take an elective automotive class. James was gifted in the knowledge of the operation of cars (this probably came from his great-grandfather Allen Monroe Wilcox). He wanted to build a car during his last two years of high school. He loves Camaros, and purchased two, a 1971 and 1972. I believe only one was running, but they both needed a lot of work. He picked the 1972 to be his running car. He removed everything from the frame of this car, painted the frame with some kind of black sealer, and then started to put it all together. He took the best parts between the 1971 and 1972 cars, and from car junkyards he removed parts from abandoned Camaros from the series he had. Of course, he took over our garage. James gained tremendous knowledge from this project. We lost the use of the garage, but it was worth it.

I was amazed that one Saturday James came home from a junkyard dragging a wire harness into the garage. I saw all of these wires and I asked James, "Where do you hook up all of these wires?" His response was, "I don't know, but I will figure it out." He did, to my amazement! This was James' God-given gift. Carole and I were also amazed that when we went to Spring Branch Career Center where James took the automotive course his teacher, Craig Clark, told us that James was exceptional. The shop had cars donated from dealers. James' teacher said he would explain to the class what they would do during the class time and how it was to be done, then he split the class into two groups and James would take one group and the teacher the other. James understood immediately what was needed, and he worked with his group to complete the assignment.

James didn't finish building his car before graduating from high school. He was accepted at Texas Tech University in Lubbock, Texas. He stated that after he got his degree from Texas Tech he wanted to attend Texas State Technical Institution (now called Texas State Technical College) in Waco, Texas. He wanted to get a two-year associate's degree in automotive work. Carole talked him into attending there first, then getting his degree at Texas Tech. He agreed. Instead of Texas Tech after Texas State Technical, he got his degree from Tarleton State University in Stephenville, Texas. When James was studying at Waco Carole would pick him up on Friday nights, and I would drive him back to school late Sunday nights. This arrangement allowed James to finish his car and have a working car. James graduated from college in June 1994. He did not have the desire to come back to Houston after he graduated from Tarleton State University. He settled in Burleson right outside of Fort Worth, Texas. His Christian ethics had been a problem at a couple of his jobs in the automotive field that eventually led him to open his own automotive repair shop in Burleson.

Like James, John played the trombone in the high school marching band, and due to this we went to all of his home high school football games to see the band during halftime. John marching in the band made halftime our favorite time at the games, which we wouldn't have attended otherwise. John was a very good student. He always did what was required in his classes. John earned his degree in computer science from Texas Tech University and graduated in December 1994. He graduated within the top ten percent of his class, which we thought was outstanding. Shortly after John graduated from Texas Tech he started employment with a small company in Houston that has grown considerably. John does the programming for this company, creating and revising programs. He is my computer man and a good one.

In high school John and Jody Wagner dated and fell in love. We got to know Jody from the time she spent at our house, which included meals. They both graduated from Spring Woods High School. Jody got her degree from the University of Texas Nursing School. Her career was a nurse at Woman's Hospital of Texas here in Houston. We were delighted when she committed her life to Jesus Christ, got baptized at our church, and also joined our church, Chapelwood United Methodist Church. It was amazing to witness her changed life. She was a different person, filled with love and a passion to know Jesus Christ through reading and studying the Bible. She treats us like her parents, and we love her as our own daughter. She is part of our family. Carole and I felt that now we had a daughter. John and Jody were married in January 1998. We are very close to them, and they invite us to many of their activities. It is wonderful having this relationship with John and Jody. We share many meals together.

In fall 2003 Jody told us she was pregnant. We were very pleased to hear this. Later we were told she was pregnant with twins. That was really neat! A month later we were told that now it was triplets! They were due to arrive during June. During early April this pregnancy became hard for her and she was admitted to the hospital for the safety of the babies. One evening we visited her, and she was hurting. Carole, Jody, and I held hands and I prayed for her and the babies. As I ended the prayer I felt warmth passing through me, and I was almost in tears because I knew this was the Holy Spirit. Jody said, "Did you feel that? That was the Holy Spirit!" We both had a comforting experience. Later in April it was necessary to take the babies by C-section; they were named Ellie, Ethan, and Evan. The two boys were identical twins. For six months Carole spent weekdays with Jody, helping her with the babies. What a job! Of course, we babysat when needed. We fell in love with Ellie, Ethan, and Evan. Jody is a wonderful mother, which really impressed me. She is very loving and has a tremendous amount of patience. It is hard raising three babies all the same age.

An event that many Houstonians remember was Christmas Eve 2004 because it snowed! The agreement with John and Jody was that Carole and I would attend the 9:00 p.m. Christmas Eve service at Chapelwood United Methodist Church, and then we would drive to their house so that they could attend the 11:00 p.m. service. When we left church it was snowing! Snow on Christmas Eve had never been recorded in Houston. Jody was very excited, and when they returned Jody made a little snowman. Christmas morning the remaining snow was mostly on the roofs of houses.

It took me a couple of years to adjust to life in Houston. We had trees, but Houston was so flat! I loved my job at American General and our house on Barwood Street. We were still aware of the life, the wonderful friends, and our Wilcox and Taylor families that we had left in Kalamazoo. I missed Kalamazoo, a smaller city of forests and lakes, but gradually we enjoyed what Houston had to offer. Houston and Texas eventually became our home. I remember several years after living in Houston my brother Phil on the phone asked if we would consider moving back to Michigan when retired. I told him Houston and Texas was our home, we would not move back. Years later we were thankful that we were living in the Houston area. It's one of the best large cities one could live in. It is also an international city consisting of people from all over the world.

Chapter 28

Vacations, Including our Alaska Cruise

As a family we made a lot of trips within the States and Canada. The boys had seen a lot of the United States and Canada prior to graduating from high school. They can say that during their youth with us they visited the majority of the States. Our trips were always a lot of fun. Mountains have always been our favorite areas to spend time. When I'm in mountains I'm constantly aware of God. Every summer we would go outside of Texas. We found early that places like Savannah, Georgia, with its history didn't appeal to our boys. They did enjoy Washington, D.C. and our tour through the White House, and Washington's and Jefferson's homes, but the greatest times were when we were in the mountains, so most of our family trips were centered in mountain areas of the States, Ontario, and western Canada.

Carole and I enjoyed the Alps when we were living in Europe. Our favorite area in Europe is western Austria, the second is Switzerland. Our favorite national park in the States is Yosemite. Our top favorite national park is in Canada, Banff National Park in Alberta. Further north of Banff is Jasper National Park, also a favorite national park. I have thought how wonderful it would be to spend a July in Banff and Jasper National Parks. We have been to these national parks of Canada three times, and I still want to return to them.

Carole and I attended Expo67 in Montreal when we lived in Kalamazoo. We found Expo67 to be very entertaining and interesting. New Orleans had Expo 84 and Mother flew to Houston to join us and our sons for a trip to this Expo. There was no comparison to Montreal's Expo67; it was very small. We still had a good time during the one day we were there. Harry Jerolleman, a fellow worker and friend in our department, said he and his wife Lois would meet us at the Expo84. He is originally from New Orleans. It was special spending a little time with him and his wife. When I was a kid I read Mark Twain's books *Tom Sawyer* and *Huckleberry Finn*. I enjoyed these stories and they gave me a strong desire to travel on a paddlewheel boat on the Mississippi River. This desire never left me. When we were at Expo84 in New Orleans we accepted the opportunity to travel a short distance on the Mississippi River on a paddlewheel boat. It was very special to finally make my childhood dream a reality!

In summer 1986 our family visited Expo86 in the beautiful city of Vancouver, British Columbia. Vancouver has the Pacific Ocean on one side and the mountains on the other side. It can only grow north and south. There are some houses on the lower part of the mountains. We have been in this city three times, and each time the city is larger in terms of more tall buildings. The last time we were there in 2008 we saw more buildings under construction. This Expo86 was huge and very impressive. We found it to be interesting and fun. We spent three days at Expo86 without seeing it all, and a separate day touring Vancouver. I remember thinking that I thought Expo67 was a little better.

We left Vancouver and drove through the beautiful Canadian Rockies, and as I remember over 500 miles of mountains. It was an all-day drive, but the scenery was outstanding. We settled that evening in the tourist town of Banff located in Banff National Park, Alberta. We spent part of a day at Johnston Canyon along the water from the waterfalls. This is a very attractive place where chipmunks have no fear of humans and will take peanuts out of your hand and climb on your lap. A chipmunk saw that James had peanuts in his pants pocket and couldn't wait for a handout and ran up his leg toward the pocket.

At Jasper, in Jasper National Park, we took a scenic boat ride on Maligne Lake. The trip took us to Spirit Island, which is probably the most photographed scene in Canada. The lake is surrounded by mountains, and on a clear day it's a wonderful trip.

We saw several beautiful waterfalls and other lakes. At Lake Louise we did a couple trail hikes; one was up to Lake Agnes. Our favorite trail hike is at Moraine Lake, just three or four miles from Lake Moraine. Moraine Lake's elevation is higher than Lake Louise. Moraine Lake is really beautiful, and at the end of the lake is a little waterfall. Moraine Lake is shown on the back of Canada's twenty dollars note of the 1979 series. Our favorite walking/hiking trail, Eiffel Trail, is located at Moraine Lake. This trail goes along one side of the mountains with snowy mountains on the other side of this deep valley. The scenery is so beautiful. The lake also has a nice lodge and cabins with a small restaurant. Everyone always goes to Lake Louise, which is very understandable. Beautiful Lake Louise Chateau faces the lake, and on the other side of the lake is Victoria Glacier. About two hundred yards from Lake Louise Chateau is Deer Lodge, which we like very much. One great advantage of this lodge is having a room on a higher floor facing the small river rapids flowing on the other side of the entrance road. The sound of this river is loud; you can roll your window open and have a wonderful sleep to the sound of the rapids.

A few years ago Carole and I drove from Windsor, Ontario, all across eastern Canada to Nova Scotia and Prince Edward Island. We thought Halifax, Nova Scotia, would be a nice place to live, and we loved Prince Edward Island.

We made it a point to visit my parents in Florida each year. If Phil and his family were down at the same time we would stay at the Nomad Hotel on the beach because our parents had a small house. We would use the motel's pool for all of us as Mother and Dad enjoyed this pool also. Mother and Dad's house was only two short blocks from the ocean. I have many memories of getting up early before the sunrise to take a long walk on the beach and seeing seagulls, sandpipers, and pelicans. It was wonderful. Many times I would take my camera to photograph for attractive sunrises and birds. I would be alone and I would talk to God as I did my walking on the beach. It was special for me. We made over twenty trips to Daytona Beach Shores. When we were in Florida in June 1982 we went to Titusville, Florida, on the 27th to witness the fourth launch of the Columbia spacecraft. That was neat. The ground shook when the rocket was launched. We also visited Disney World a couple of times, and Sea World in Orlando. The kids, our James and John and Phil and Bonnie's Stephanie and Scott, loved being on the beach, in the ocean and in the pool. It was so special, and we all have memories of it.

I will never forget two events associated with the beach. One late afternoon I was sitting alone outside of our room at the Nomad Motel, facing the ocean. There was a nice breeze from the ocean, and the ocean was as calm as it could be. The sun was behind me, somewhere at the four o'clock position. The ocean had multiple but similar colors from the soft light from the sun. The view was peaceful and my eyes were just glued to this water scene. I couldn't get enough of it! I felt captivated by it! It was so peaceful. After several minutes of soaking this in, I heard my mother's voice coming from the side of the building. "I'm hungry, let's go eat!" I didn't want to leave. I didn't care about food; I just wanted to be left alone to continue soaking in this scene. My request to my mother to wait a while wasn't accepted as she made it clear that she was hungry. I waited a few more minutes and then joined the family for an early dinner. We have stayed at the Nomad many times, but this was the only time I had this experience.

The second event was on early Christmas morning in 1975. I had left Carole, James, and John in the room sleeping, and started my early walk on the beach. For a while I had the beach to myself, but eventually I reached a woman walking ahead of me. We started visiting while walking together. She was probably twenty-five years older than me. I can't remember all of our conversation, but we walked a long distance and turned around and walked back toward the Nomad Motel. She told me she had one living daughter who was married and lived with her family in Chicago. The woman I was walking with lived alone here in the area. Her daughter had not invited her mother to visit them in Chicago for the holidays. This woman, my beach companion for this Christmas morning, was very lonely and sad. When we reached the Nomad Motel I was debating whether or not to invite her to stay with us, but I didn't. I pointed out where we were staying, but I had planned to walk some more with her. The sun was up and she said, "You need to go as you need to be with your family. I will be all right." We separated and I hoped she was able to have peace for the rest of this Christmas day.

On one vacation to the Grand Tetons National Park, I did a dumb thing. In a large open field there was a small herd of large elks. I love photographing scenery, birds, and large animals. I parked, and we walked toward these large animals. The boys and Carole stayed behind as I started walking toward these elks, each one weighing more than fifteen hundred pounds. One of these elks with large antlers started to walk toward me. I stopped walking and realized then that I should not have gotten this close to these animals. I knew I couldn't outrun this animal. He finally stopped and we just stared at each other. My mouth was closed so that I wasn't showing my teeth, thus being a harmless creature. A few seconds elapsed and this animal made a ninety-degree turn, and then I started taking pictures. I learned right then not to get so close to these large animals.

I had planned a cruise to Alaska from Vancouver, British Columbia, in summer 2006. The trip would also include three weeks traveling around Alaska and Dawson City, Yukon. My brother Phil and his wife Bonnie thought this was a great idea, and they decided to join us! Phil selected an AAA travel agent to arrange accommodations on the cruise ship for the four of us and their flight to Seattle. Each couple had a great room with a private balcony. The two units were next to each other. When the time came for this adventure we met in Seattle, rented a car, and drove to Vancouver and spent a couple of days in that beautiful city. Our hotel rooms were close to the ocean. I believe Vancouver is the prettiest city in North America, although the cost of living is high. I could spend a summer month in this city.

On Monday, June 12 we were ready to board the *Princess Island*. It was necessary to go through lines for customs, the ship's paperwork, and their handouts. We also had our ID cards issued and our pictures taken for their computer system. Their computer has a person's image linked to their ID. The ID card didn't show the person's image, but it could be seen on their computer screen. It took a little while to get to our cabin rooms, but when we did we were very pleased. The private balcony made our room even more special. Later during our own tour of the ship we found it all very attractive. At a later time we learned that this ship was built in 2003. Our luggage was to be delivered later in the day when we were out at sea. After viewing our room and some of the documents given to us, we went to the buffet dining room. We had our lunch while seated next to a glass wall facing downtown Vancouver. It was a nice view.

The four of us went on deck to wait for departure. I took pictures of the city and across the inlet from the ship. At 5:05 p.m. the ship started to move forward, and we were on our way! Heading toward Lions Gate Bridge, passing Stanley Park, and seeing Prospect Point, where we had been the day before, from the water was fun and exciting. I thought about the fact that I had wanted to do this for many, many years. I thought about Mom and Dad and how they loved their cruises to Europe. This moment was very special for me as I thought about these things. It would have been nice to know how Mom and Dad felt when they started their first cruise. I thought too that I would finally be in Dawson City, Yukon Territory. Dawson City witnessed the last major gold rush in North America, which started in 1896. In the mid-1950's a specific box of cereal included a certificate for one square inch of land in the Yukon Territory. I didn't like the cereal that much, but I wanted to be a landowner in the Yukon. I had to eat the cereal before I could get another box. I went through four boxes for four certificates of land. I couldn't stand to eat any more of that cereal. It was at that time I wanted to see Dawson City and the Yukon. That desire never left me. I left these land certificates at home and eventually Mom threw them away. I sure wish I had them.

It was a thrill being on deck and seeing Stanley Park and Lions Gate Bridge fade into the distance as the ship moved near land outside of Vancouver. Being on the top deck gave us great views. We stayed on the top deck for a lengthy time before gathering in our private cabin balcony. I enjoyed seeing snow on the mountain peaks and was amazed to see houses in some areas along the shore of the water. The mountains sloped to the water and the area is all wooded. We spotted at least one small town tucked away in a wooded area. I wondered how those living along the ocean could make a living. There had to be a road to some town, although we couldn't see one. The ship passed a very small island with houses on it, and I took a couple of pictures.

The ship took us to Ketchikan first. It was interesting, and we did some shopping. Our next stop was the capital of Alaska, Juneau. Juneau is on the water in an inlet. The city lies on both sides of the inlet; a bridge connects the two sides of the inlet. The mountains come right up to the city. Houses are located at the foot of the mountains. The city is very narrow due to the mountains, but very long in terms of distance along the inlet water. I would like to live here during their short summer; the city and area are very attractive. We really enjoyed our time in Juneau.

As we walked off the ship Phil walked directly to a yellow minivan taxi. Phil called me over. The driver of the taxi, Bob Harris, told us he could take us to an area of eagles, show us St. Nicholas Orthodox Church, tour Juneau, and finally take us to Mendenhall Glacier. He further explained that he could take up to six people and his charge was fifty-five dollars per hour, regardless of the number of people in his taxi. Phil immediately recruited another couple (Joel and Ginny from Indiana) standing a short distance from the taxi. We found them to be a nice couple. Bob Harris said the passengers decide how long to stay in each area. This was just perfect! Bob Harris drove us to St. Nicholas Orthodox Church and allowed us to get out of the minivan to take pictures. This very small, wood-frame building is the oldest original Russian church in Alaska. He then drove us around the city, explaining things and answering questions. From there he drove us to a waste dump area and what appeared to be a small manufacturing company with a hundred plus eagles in trees. We all got out seeing them in the trees and in flight to and from these trees, listening to their sounds. This was the first time I had ever heard the sound of an eagle. One even flew directly above me and landed in one of these trees. I took several pictures of these wonderful birds with my film camera (long lens: 80-300mm). This was a real thrill for me. I could have spent a lot of time there just watching these eagles. We saw more eagles during our drive to Mendenhall Glacier, which wasn't very far from Juneau.

Mendenhall Glacier was really neat. The water in front of this glacier had a few small icebergs. I discovered that there was a trail that took us right down to the beach in front of the glacier. The rest of the group went the opposite way to a higher level near the glacier. The view we had was very impressive. I took several pictures of the area, including some of these icebergs. I believe Carole and I spent thirty plus minutes there. We walked back to the minivan and the other four people were ready to get in the van. I wanted to spend more time there and walk over to the area where the rest of the group viewed this glacier. I thought we had the best view of the two viewing locations, and I mentioned to the group that the walk down to the beach in front of the glacier was fantastic, but the group was ready to go so Carole and I joined them. Bob Harris drove us back to downtown Juneau near our ship and to the tram station. Our cost for this over-two-hour tour was only forty-two dollars. This was one of the best bargains of our trip.

The city tram took people up to a high peak above Juneau named Mount Roberts. I learned that it was possible to walk up to the top, which really appealed to us. Bob Harris suggested that we ride up and then walk down. Once in the station we learned that the cost per person for this ride up to Mount Roberts was around twenty-eight dollars per person. While we were in the ticket line I mentioned to the person behind me that we wanted to walk down. This person said it's easier on the legs if we walk up. At the ticket window we were told that the ride down was free if we spent five dollars for food or in the gift shop. She too said it was better to walk up versus walking down, so no tickets were needed. We thought this was great news!

The walk to Mount Roberts started at the end of 6th Avenue. On the way over there we stopped at a café and asked them if they could prepare a couple of sandwiches for our hike. They seemed pleased to do this. They also packed two cups of fruit. They didn't have bottled water, but they did pack two Styrofoam glasses of water with a good sealing top on them. Carole carried our lunch sack and I carried my two camera bags. We enjoyed our walk through the residential area to the end of

6th Avenue. This day was also the warmest day we had experienced so far on our trip. The sun came out a few times during the afternoon. We also had a short light rain during our walk. At the start of the hike to Mount Roberts were wooden stairs leading up to a wooden balcony, next to and higher than a house. This balcony had a wooden bench. The view was very attractive; we could look over the houses and down at the house next to us. The actual start of the trail to Mount Roberts begins at this deck. We sat down on the bench and ate our lunch, enjoying the great view. I could have stayed longer because it was very peaceful.

Our hike was accomplished in a little less than two hours. We stopped at a few places for pictures. Our hike went through beautiful areas of greenery. This hike was a treat to our souls! While on our hike I picked up a little stone that was attractive. Carole found a small slab of a stone that came from a larger stone, commonly seen during our hike. I would have liked to bring one of these large stones home with me, but of course this couldn't be done. Once at the top, we purchased a few things from the gift/souvenir shop and took the tram down to the tram station in the heart of the business center of Juneau.

We immediately spotted Phil sitting across the street. Bonnie was shopping and Phil had decided to sit down on a bench in front of a store. We visited briefly, and then separated again. Phil and Bonnie went back to the ship, and we did a little shopping and I took more pictures. Our purchases for the day were a book for our grandkids, a duplicate Alaska gold rush license plate with "Juneau" as the number on the plate, three flowery pins made in Russia, a wooden Easter egg made in Ukraine, an Alaska sweatshirt for Carole, postcards, two decks of Alaska cards, and an Alaska pin for my backpack. After our shopping we went back to the ship and went directly to the buffet dining room where we had a little snack of a piece of cake, tea for Carole, and coffee for me. While we were enjoying our snack we watched a cruise ship leaving Juneau. Later we joined Phil and Bonnie for dinner at our assigned dinner table in the dining room. The dinner lasted two hours, but it was very enjoyable. It was a great day for Carole and me.

The next morning, June 16, we were in Skagway (population only around eight hundred). This day had the most sunshine since the first full day of our cruise. We walked the short distance from the ship to downtown Skagway. We purchased our train tickets for the trip to White Summit, British Columbia, on the narrow-gauge White Pass & Yukon Route. This train was built in 1898 to transport those going to the Dawson City, Yukon, goldfields. The train ended at Whitehorse, Yukon, south of Dawson City. Skagway was the leading route to the goldfields around Dawson City. The narrow-gauge train tracks followed parts of the walking trail. This train made trips to Whitehorse, Yukon, but our trip was only to White Summit and back. This three-hour, round-trip train ride cost one hundred and ninety dollars for the two of us. It was really worth it!

We walked around this small town and shopped a little. The four of us got to the train station several minutes early and visited until the train arrived. Once the train was out of town those passengers wanting to stand on the outside platforms of the train cars could do so. This arrangement was just perfect for picture taking. I wasn't alone on our train outside platform. Everyone on the platform was agreeable to sharing the sides of the platform when others wanted to take pictures of a particular scene. The mountain scenery was just wonderful. We saw snow and ice on the way, especially when we got fairly close to White Summit. A section of the actual 1896 trail to the goldfields around Dawson City was still visible from the train at one point of our train journey. The trail we saw seemed to be only two feet wide! I took pictures of this trail from the train using both cameras.

People on the train were offered a special baseball hat for this train line for fifteen dollars. Phil and I each purchased one. It is a nice looking hat with "2006" included in the design, as well as the date when the train line was started, 1898. Skagway, Alaska, is shown on the back of this cap. We were told that only the train riders were eligible to purchase this hat. The train also gave us neat plastic bottles of water from Canada with a special label designed for this train. I brought three unopened bottles of water home. The train dropped some of the riders at the train depot and the rest of us at our ship.

We took our purchases to our rooms, and then went to the buffet dining room for a snack since we hadn't had lunch. On the ship we went to the dining room for dinner. This room was very large. We were promised our own turkey dinner that evening. You could ask for certain food for the following evening, and they would accommodate you. I had a dish of strawberries included for each of my dinners while on the ship.

The next day we entered Glacier Bay National Park. Two park rangers from the park entrance were boated to our ship, I believe around 6:00 a.m. One of these rangers was a woman, and she was in the buffet dining room while we had our light breakfast. During the time we were cruising Glacier Bay she identified each glacier (only three of them, Reid, Lampuch, and Margerie) and gave us information on the bay and its glaciers. She made it more interesting. This was all done through the ship's PA system. The ship stopped at Margerie Glacier for quite a while so that all interested could view this glacier and perhaps witness some calving (ice separating from the glacier). There were only a couple really small calvings. On the way out of Glacier Bay the ship stopped to view Lampuch Glacier. There was a lot of snow on and around the mountain peaks and the cloud ceiling was very low. We had very little sun on this cruise. During this time in Glacier Bay it was very cold. I had five layers of clothing on and I still never got warm. In addition to the cold we had a lot of light rain off and on for most of the day. Even though the weather was bad the scenery was very attractive. In some places the clouds would open up temporarily and you could see more of the mountains. I also enjoyed seeing small icebergs and pieces of ice in the water.

I used the treadmill before dinner and I thought I was having a problem. I was losing my balance slightly, and wondered if I should stop. After a few minutes I noticed that a cord to the window blinds at my side was moving back and forth. That was it! The boat was rolling slightly for the first time. I realized I was not experiencing a problem and was relieved! On June 18 the ship was rolling slightly during the night, but by morning the ship had only a slight roll. The ship cruised into the Gulf of Alaska and in the morning all we could see from the ship was water. I missed not seeing land.

At lunch we sat down at a table for six people. A couple was facing each other at the end against the glass wall overlooking the water. I sat next to the wife. I asked her where they were from and she said, "Houston." I said we were also from Houston. I said "where in Houston?" I asked, She said "Spring Branch." I responded that we too lived in Spring Branch. They only lived a few miles from us. We were surprised that we were almost neighbors. The husband's name was Wayne and he too had two cameras with him. He was a serious photographer of birds and big animals. He told me that he had a Web site of his nature pictures (http//birdshooter.smugmug.com). They were members of Houston's Second Baptist Church. After we arrived home I did look at his Web site and it was very impressive! You could spend all day looking at his nature pictures. The rest of the day I read a lot and had a session on the treadmill.

The last night's dinner was special since it would be our final one of this cruise. There were balloons, and after the lights were turned off all of the waiters came marching out holding the famous flaming Alaskan mousse. This was after the dishes were cleared from the tables. This flaming Alaskan mousse has three kinds of ice cream with an outside covering of cake in the shape of half a basketball. It was very good.

After dinner we told our waiter, Ronnie from the Philippines, how much we appreciated him. He was a Christian. After he saw us giving grace before our first meal he asked me what church we belonged to and if we were active in our church. He said he was a Baptist. He mentioned we were brothers in Christ. Both Phil and I gave him a nice tip. His wife was still back in the Philippines, but he was working on the papers for her to enter the States legally. Before saying goodbye for the final time we included him in a picture. He was a wonderful person. May God bless him for the rest of his earthly life. Perhaps we will find him in our eternal home.

The morning of departure came with some sadness because our wonderful time on our cruise was ending. The ship docked at Whittier during the night. We were told that this village was established during World War II. The military built a facility at this location for storing fuel for the Pacific Fleet. With the mountains surrounding the area and low cloud ceilings most of the year this site was ideal for hiding a large inventory of fuel. During the war there were two buildings with an underground tunnel connecting them.

The cruise ship's bus took us to the airport. We saw mountain goats (Dall sheep) from the bus at one location. There are mountains all the way to Anchorage; the scenery was beautiful. At the airport Phil and I dealt with the rental car companies. Phil had a reservation with one company for a four-passenger van, but Phil thought they were asking too much for it. We went to another car rental and they too were too high, but the rental company's representative said she knew of a company that would give us the requested van much cheaper than they could, and they would come pick us up. The driver drove us to a vacant lot with a trailer parked on it. There was one van, the only vehicle, and we got a great deal on it, but it was an older van. The tires had wear and it was dirty inside and out. The man told us to get it washed down the street, and he would reimburse us, so we got it cleaned and started our trip. Anchorage was our base for our Alaskan journey and our hotel was Hawthorn Suites. We graded this hotel highly.

Our plan was to drive to Dawson City, Yukon, spending a day at Denali National Park on the way. When we reached Denali we learned that only the first thirteen miles into the park are open without a permit. This park is huge, consisting of over six million acres. The park is also known for having the tallest mountain in North America, Mount Denali. This mountain is 20,320 feet high. We couldn't see the mountain because of the clouds hiding it. This was the only disappointment. It was a twenty-seven-mile drive from our Anchorage hotel to Denali's Wilderness Access Center. We arrived around 8:40 a.m. At 9:00 a.m. our shuttle bus ride started its fifty-three-mile trip. We had some sunshine that day, but it was mostly overcast. At the end of our shuttle bus ride it started raining lightly. We had a fun and very knowledgeable driver/guide. He would stop every time an animal was spotted by one of us passengers, which was several times. We could open the top window by sliding it down, which was what I did every time an animal was spotted on our side. We also had a few shuttle stops during the trip to the park for pictures of the scenery and restroom needs. I also had my backpack loaded with food, which was needed.

The scenery was fantastic, and we saw many animals. According to our driver, Nick Weaver, we had an above-average number of animal sightings. In addition to beautiful scenery we saw a couple of snowshoe hares (rabbit family), brown bears, multiple caribou, and many Dall lambs (mountain goats). A black wolf was spotted; he crossed the highway and went up the mountain to where there was a small herd of Dall lambs. We all watched as the Dall lambs gathered together and kept moving higher. The wolf kept climbing, but when he was about hundred yards from these Dall lambs he just stared at them for a few moments and then turned around and came back down to the highway. The driver drove up the highway about two hundred yards and stopped the bus and turned off the motor. He said the wolf would come out at a little patch between some small bushes and a small stream of water parallel to the road. Sure enough, that was exactly where he came out, which was on our side of the bus. We got a good look at him, but I wasn't fast enough to get a picture of him. I guess I really didn't believe the driver could pinpoint where he would come out to the highway. I was impressed! The wolf walked to the back of the bus, then came forward on the other side of the bus. Since he was on the opposite side and walking fast, I couldn't get a good picture of him. Once he passed our bus he stopped and went to the bathroom right in the middle of the road. Then he left the road and disappeared into the bushes. We thought all of this was really neat. The boy on the opposite side of me had his window open and got an excellent digital picture of him. The wolf completely filled up the picture's frame. Nick said the black wolf was only the third one he had seen in over two years. According to Nick, bear sightings on these tours were rare, but we saw six bears. We didn't see a moose on this tour, to my disappointment. Due to all of these stops, our tour was over two hours longer than the scheduled six hours. No one complained. Everyone thought this was a great tour for viewing animals, and we all clapped for Nick. Nick made this trip very special with his information and his enthusiasm about seeing the animals. Several times he would turn off the bus motor, and seemed to enjoy viewing the animals as much as everyone else did. It really was a special tour.

As we departed the shuttle bus at Wilderness Center and drove our van out of the parking lot there was a large moose across the street. She went deeper into the woods before I could photograph her. Then we drove a little further, made a turn, and there was a mother moose and her baby at the edge of the road. Cars had stopped, and I got out of the van and started taking some great pictures with my film camera of mom moose and her baby. There was only about fifteen feet between us. Carole took some digital pictures with my other camera from inside the van. This was very exciting for me and I got some great pictures. The two of them started walking down the street and I followed them, taking more pictures.

Before we started the tour I asked God for a blessing of seeing a bear, caribou, and a moose. I asked for this blessing but also asked that His will be done. With all of these animal sightings, and the driver/guide amazed with so many sightings, I believe God was giving Carole and me a blessing and answering my prayer. When we were near the end of our tour I kept looking for a moose, but without success. I thought it was not the will of God for us to see a moose, but we did once in the van! I believe God was involved with this. Of course, I thanked God for this very special day.

We then drove to Healy, eleven miles north of Denali toward Fairbanks. We found the Rose Café for our dinner. After our meal there we were convinced that this was the restaurant for all our meals while visiting Denali. It added around twenty-one miles to our driving, but it was worth it. Cantwell doesn't have much, nor does the area around the entrance to Denali Park. Rose is the owner of this restaurant, and she is a very likeable person and is interested in her customers. She was born in the Philippines but married an American GI. He got up very early in the morning to make the pies and other desserts. I asked Rose where they got their food and supplies, and she said from Anchorage. Each week she called in her order and the company's truck made a circle around Alaska and delivered the food. This restaurant and the one in Homer were the best on our trip. The prices were very reasonable. During our meal we talked about the day and how exciting it was. The animal viewing really made our Denali bus tour very special. We kidded the driver that we needed to see a moose, but we didn't see one until we pulled out of the parking lot.

After our very long day visiting Denali Park and a good night's sleep, we headed toward Fairbanks. We had a lot of rain, and when we passed Denali Park it was raining and we were thankful that we had toured the park the previous day. I was driving, and it wasn't long before we were hearing a loud continuous "thump" from the top of the van. I stopped and immediately we saw the problem. The top of the windshield rubber molding was coming loose and the wind created by the speed of the van was making it pound the top of the van.

We drove into Fairbanks and came to an auto shop close to the University of Alaska-Fairbanks campus. We purchased rubber glue and blue tape, got that windshield's rubber glued and taped, and didn't have any more problems. As Phil and I were working on this problem we all were joking about it and laughing. Before we left Fairbanks we stopped at a Buick dealer and asked if they could identify the reason the passenger sliding door would not open using the automatic switch. The problem was easily identified. There was a button on the front overhead that was pushed to deactivate this function. Pushing it again activated this function.

We got on Richardson Highway (Highway number 2) on our way to Tok. Soon we came to North Pole, Alaska. Their post office was identified by a large sign "North Pole, Alaska Post Office." We took pictures of this sign with each couple in the picture. On Richardson Highway we also saw mountains in the distance with a lot of snow on them. Very beautiful!

When we drove into Delta Junction we were surprised to see the Buffalo Center Drive-in just like in the Detroit area in the 1950's. Most likely this was the only drive-in restaurant in Alaska. Phil said, "Let's eat here." This restaurant was a small log-cabin building. I think Phil was more excited than the rest of us to find a drive-in restaurant in Alaska. A young lady brought our hamburgers on a tray that she hung on our van's door window. That was our lunch. Carole and I had a buffalo burger, and we shared a small soft ice cream cone. It was all good. Per Phil's request, I took a picture of the drive-in that also included our van. As of 2012 the population of Delta Junction was nine hundred and seventy-four people; the majority is males.

As we continued our drive to Tok the temperature was falling and reached a low of fifty degrees. We also noticed that the mountains had more snow on them. By the time we got to Tok it was a steady light rain. The cloud ceiling was very dark. We had sunshine only on our route to Fairbanks and a short distance after that. We stayed at the Westmark Inn-Tok. They gave us a big discount, a rate of only eighty nine dollars. My reservation was for one room on the first floor with a king-sized bed, but they had us set up for two rooms on the second floor, with a lot of stairs to the second floor. Fortunately they had one room left on the first floor with a queen-sized bed. Phil talked them into giving us another ten dollars discount for our rooms, which was by far our cheapest room rate in all of Alaska. Our room was excellent and very clean. Westmark Inn-Tok is a good place to stay when in Tok.

Carole and I got up at 6:45 a.m. and Carole had tea and I had coffee. We had our devotions and prayed together. Our joy and peace comes from our Lord and Savior. We hold on to His promises. We got a late start from Tok. The weather was cold and overcast. We had breakfast at Fast Eddy's; it was a very nice restaurant, the best so far on our trip. Their pancakes were also the best. A man at Delta Junction told us that it was the best restaurant in the area from Delta Junction to beyond Tok. The Mile Post and AAA recommended this restaurant.

The only direct route to Dawson City, Yukon (Canada) from Alaska is "Top of The World Highway," a road of gravel, small craters, and dirt. What an experience we had on this small road high up in the mountains. We could only go thirty-thirty-five mph, which included trying to avoid the craters that were everywhere. We were shocked to find a community high up in these mountains! The road sign stated "Chicken, Alaska." We wanted to see this community! We turned onto the short dirt and gravel road leading to this community. There were a couple of small buildings on the right side and a few yards further to the left were a small gift shop. All the buildings were log cabins. The center of this community included three outhouses that were located a short walking distance from the gift shop. These were the community restrooms. Down a little way was an abandoned dredge machine used many years ago for mining gold. There was also a trough where a man and woman were panning for gold flakes. There was a small rock and dirt pile close to the trough. This was the source for their panning gold since parts of this pile was transferred to the trough when needed. Each time they panned from this dirt in the trough, they would get a few little specks of gold. One of them told us that they were going to work this dirt pile throughout the weekend. It was hard for me to understand how any person would do this for more than one hour.

The gift shop had sandwiches, candy, ice cream, soda pop, some souvenirs, and gold nuggets that her father had found. The family owned this small store and their daughter helped run it. The girl got her education in Homer, which was over six hundred miles south. The father had been mining gold in this area for a long time. His nuggets were the cheapest price that we had seen on this trip. Driving to this community, we drove through a burned forest for around one hundred miles. In 2004 there was a massive forest fire in this area of Alaska, burning over five million acres of forest. This family and the community escaped this fire, although it came very close. The daughter thought they were going to lose everything. The community of Chicken had a population of fifteen people year round, but in the summer the population rapidly increased to as many as thirty-two. They come to search for gold. I also asked this teenager, "Why did they name this community 'Chicken'?" She said that they needed a name and they agreed to name it after Alaska's state bird, the white and black ptarmigan, but no one knew how to spell this bird's name. Someone in this group said, "Let's just name it 'Chicken,'" and they all agreed. We took some pictures outside of the gift shop and then got back on this terrible gravel/dirt road heading for Dawson City, Yukon. We can now say that we have been to Chicken, Alaska.

We continued our journey to Dawson City and it wasn't long before it happened! A flat tire! We found the tire changing equipment, but couldn't get the bolts off the tire. This road, if you want to call it as such, had almost no traffic, but during our unsuccessful attempts to loosen the bolts, a car approached us from the opposite direction. The license plate showed he was from British Columbia. He stopped and helped us remove the flat tire, and soon we were on our way again. Our British Columbia helper was a great blessing to us! The timing of his appearance was perfect. We finally got the spare tire on and found that it was slightly under deflated. I continued driving and tried to avoid all of the potholes, but I didn't have a hundred percent success rate. When I planned this trip, I didn't realize that we would be driving on hundred plus miles of dirt/gravel road to reach Yukon. The positive thing about this road is that the scenery is very pretty as well as the view of the mountains.

Before reaching the border we were surprised to find four log-cabin buildings close together on our right. We pulled off the road and drove up to the little closet like building that had a sign for repairing tires. One cabin was abandoned with the center had caved in; we soon learned that this building was one hundred, twenty-five years old. The owner, Tony, lived in one log cabin with his wife, three daughters, and one son. The fourth building was a very small cabin used to serve sandwiches, beer, and snacks. This building also had some souvenirs, old stuff, and license plates. There was a wooden fence behind the store and the house, and on the other side of the fence was a huge drop-off since we were in the mountains. There were many license plates, including from Germany and Holland, all over the fence and on the outside of his store as well as on the store's door.

This family was isolated from the world. Dawson City, Yukon, is their closest town. The elevation of this area was around thirty-seven hundred feet. There was no pavement, and the back of their house was near the edge of a cliff. The children's play area was the small front area of the building and the narrow road. The children were home schooled. The house was very small, and I'm sure during the winter they were snowed in. Perhaps they had another house somewhere in Alaska for the winter. I didn't think to ask Tony. Tony's teenage son stood around in front of the store and house. The four children had no other children to associate with. The winters were very long, and they had no TV and probably no radio. Their shopping would have to be at Dawson City. I felt sorry for these kids. They had to be bored living on land that was probably less than an acre and half in size, and all dirt.

Tony fixed our tire and put air in the spare. His charge was very reasonable. In his store I found an Alaska plate with a bear in the center. I later found out that this plate was the state's 1976 bicentennial plate. He wanted fifty-five dollars for it but came down to thirty-five dollars which I accepted. A car junkyard owner in Cantwell told me he had these bear plates and sold them for one hundred dollars. He said, "The bear plate is one that everyone wants." I found this to be true. All of the plates Tony had were in excellent condition. I also purchased a bumper sticker that read "I survived the Top of The World Highway." Before we left I took pictures of his buildings. Standing near the border of Alaska and Yukon, it does look like you are on top of the world. There are treeless rolling hills for many miles in the distance and some small, short greenery at a very far distance. We had been in many mountains here in the lower States, Canada, and Europe, and we have never seen anything like this view. It was very interesting.

We were finally on our way, and in less than ten minutes we were at the Yukon border. From this location it was only sixty-five miles to Dawson City. At the border I took some pictures. This area of high, rounded hills without trees is very attractive. We continued in the mountains all the way to Dawson City. We noticed that the trees we saw were very small, probably due to the severe cold and long winters. There were also some areas along the road with snow. To the north were distant peaks with some snow on them. The closer peaks were very attractive. About half of the road from the border to Dawson City was paved and the scenery was outstanding.

At this time Phil was driving, and he made a few stops allowing me to take pictures of Dawson City located below. The city is on the opposite side of the Yukon River, with mountains all around. It was neat seeing the complete city from a higher elevation. We learned that the current population was around fifteen hundred. During the gold rush days it peaked to around forty thousand in 1900.

We went down to the Yukon River at the ferry dock. We had no wait to drive our van onto the ferry for taking us across the river to Dawson City. Now we could say that we were on the Yukon River! It didn't take very long to reach the other side. We drove off the ferry and drove around the town, and then went to the Bonanza Gold Motel. Our first impression of the town was positive and I was looking forward to our scheduled time in this town. There were a few old-looking buildings boarded up, but for the most part the town buildings were clean looking and in good shape. This town was the center for the 1896 gold rush, the last major gold rush in North America.

We unloaded the van at Bonanza Gold and then drove down the street to the motel's recommended restaurant. Prior to leaving for dinner, one of the ladies at the motel's desk looked through their twenty-five cents coins and found me a 2005 Alberta's centennial commemorative twenty-five cents coin. Alberta is my favorite province of Canada. I thought it would be neat to carry this coin in my pocket once we were home in Houston. It's one of Canada's best-designed coins. I also got some dollar coins at the desk for using their manual car wash behind the motel. The van had mud on the bottom of the van and also had a coat of dirt one-third up, and the back window was completely covered.

We went to the recommended restaurant, but they were closed due to running out of food. We went to another restaurant, and we were told they were closed. The time was between 8:00-8:30 p.m. local time. Another restaurant had a closed sign at their door. We finally found an open restaurant and had dinner, then went back to our own motel room. It was after 11:00 p.m. when we went to bed and the sun was still high in the sky. The drapes did a good job keeping most of the light out. So far we hadn't seen darkness in Alaska and Yukon.

On Sunday morning I told Carole that I wished we were at our church in Houston, Chapelwood United Methodist. We had our devotion together. We prayed for James, Jody, and John and also we wouldn't have any more problems on our trip back to Anchorage the next day. Carole and I read a while, and then Phil and Bonnie came to our room around 10:10 a.m. We had all had a hard day yesterday. We stayed in bed until 6:45 a.m., the latest for us during this vacation. We were glad that Phil and Bonnie got a good rest. Our motel was about a mile out of town, which was not convenient for short walks to town or down to the Yukon river. We had our breakfast at Bonanza Gold, and then walked around the town buying some coffee mugs and some older used Yukon license plates. I also purchased books relating to Dawson City. I read all of them at home and the best one, which was very enjoyable, was *I Married The Klondike* by Laura Beatrice Berton. She wrote about life in Dawson City at the turn of the twentieth century. I learned a lot about Dawson City and the gold rush experience there. The large majority that came to the gold rush were unsuccessful. Many of those seeking wealth on their journey to and around Dawson City died. It should be noted that the winters were long and extremely cold with lots of snow. All of the big animals would migrate at the start of cooler weather. There was very little food during these winters.

The four of us took a walking tour of the town. Our tour guide was a young lady named Anna. She made the tour very interesting and enjoyable, and she knew a lot of historical knowledge about Dawson. The old post office, built in 1901, was very attractive inside. It was no longer in use. The bank building we toured was also no longer being used, and it too was very attractive and interesting. We also visited a saloon that had been restored. Early in the century the customer base for this saloon was mainly the more well-to-do people in Dawson. "Mde. Tremblay" opened a women's clothing store during the early days of Dawson. The building was closed, but the large front window displayed clothing from early in the century. Anna had a verbal presentation for each building we visited. During the tour we had light rain off and on; in fact, it rained most of the day.

Anna said that her mother was a goldsmith and had a store, the Fortymile Gold work Shop. After the tour we walked over to her attractive but small shop. It was a two-story building; it appeared that the second floor was the mother's living area. This building was located at the corner of Third Ave. and York Street. The mother's name was Leslie Chapman. I had to tell her that Phil's and my mother was also a goldsmith as well as a silversmith and enamelsmith. I purchased a gold nugget from her. The weight was 2.1 grams and it cost me one hundred Canadian dollars (US: eighty-nine dollars and fifty cents). This nugget came from Gold Run Creek, a tributary of the Indian River in the Dawson area. One gram equals $1/28^{th}$ of an ounce. If this nugget is one hundred percent gold, then it would have forty-five dollars of gold based on six hundred dollars per ounce. As I remember Leslie said this nugget was ninety-two percent gold. Phil and Bonnie also purchased a nugget from her. Many people collect gold nuggets; there were a lot of stores in Alaska selling gold nuggets.

Wooly mammoths were in the Dawson area fifteen thousand years ago. Leslie Chapman's shop had a large tusk from one of these mammoths that she found in the area while searching for gold. It was buried two to five feet below the ground surface. It was displayed nicely on one of her shop's walls. I took a picture of it. She searched for the mammoth's other tusk but couldn't locate it. Before we left, Phil took a picture of her with Carole and me. I did the same for a picture of her with Bonnie and Phil. She also autographed her business card for me, and on the other side she wrote the location where my purchased nugget had been found. She was an enjoyable person. We had lunch at Westmark's Restaurant in their very nice dining room.

At the visitor center we saw a very interesting short movie called *City of Gold*. The film was produced in 1957. We all enjoyed it very much. We wandered around some more, stopped for ice cream, and then went back to our rooms. The rain discouraged Carole and me from taking a walk along the Yukon River. It was also getting colder. At the motel room we watched the rest of the Houston Astros vs. Chicago White Sox baseball game. It was the bottom of the ninth inning. We later learned that Roy Oswald pitched seven innings with a nine to two lead. Houston's relief pitching was a total disaster! Chicago scored three runs in the eighth inning (a three run home run by Tadahito Iquchi). We saw Brad Lidge come in to pitch the ninth inning with a four-run lead. Brad Lidge loaded the bases and then served a home-run pitch, a grand slam (again, Tadahito Iquchi) to tie the game. The TV announcer mentioned that this was the third straight game, all against Houston, that a Chicago player had hit a grand-slam home run. Houston won this game in the thirteenth inning.

On Monday morning Phil and I went to a tire shop to have the bad tire replaced. After this business was completed we went back to the motel, loaded up, checked out, and then went to the Eldorado Hotel's restaurant for breakfast. The man replacing our tire had recommended this place. We visited the Dawson museum, which was very interesting. They had a separate building for the original train engines; there were four train engines at this museum. I took pictures of a couple of these engines.

Dawson City is a neat town. We all liked it and wished we could have stayed longer. We heard stories of people coming here for a short stay but never leaving. Our weather was terrible, but it was fun being there. What stands out at Dawson is that there are no concrete roads or driveways. In addition, there is very little grass in this town. Rain makes the roads and parking areas muddy!

We then drove to the ferry to transport our van to the other side of the Yukon River. I was going to take pictures of the mountains during our drive to the ferry, but the low clouds and rain prevented this. We got to the border and noticed a log cabin house on the Alaska side. It had been there the previous week when we crossed over into Yukon, but this time it caught our attention. The house had a sign on its front, "Poker Point, population 2. Most northern town in U.S." We stopped at Tony's place and told him that the bad tire got us to Dawson City and we had replaced it.

The drive from Dawson City to Anchorage was a little over 500 miles. We had to contend with terrible roads, light rain throughout the day, no sunshine, thick clouds, and in some cases very low clouds. We actually drove through clouds. Alaska has only eleven major roads, and all are two-lane roads. On our way back to Anchorage from Dawson City on Alaska's Highway number1 we had to stop for five minutes. This part of Alaska is a permafrost area. All concrete roads in the permafrost area need to be repaired each summer, and our road was being repaired. There was only one lane open for both directions of traffic. Ahead was a young woman holding a pole with a sign on top with the word "stop" on one side and "go" on the other side. A couple of miles or so ahead was another woman with the same sign. One would tell the other pole holder by cell phone that cars from their end were coming on the open lane, and the last car coming would be identified. This process would last all day from both ends. I was driving, and the car in front of me was the last car allowed to continue on their journey. There was no sign of life anywhere in this area of Alaska. You might see a moose, but that was about it. I rolled down the window and asked the young woman where her home was. She named one of the western lower States. I learned that she was a college student in the lower forty-eight states. I asked her why she was working here in Alaska, and her short answer was, "Thirty-five dollars an hour." That made sense to me! It would be a rough life for the duration of a summer. Using the word "summer" in Alaska probably isn't accurate. Alaska really doesn't have summers as we know them. Then it was our turn to go, and I wondered if these workers spent their nonworking hours in a wooden building or in a tent. As I recall, this situation of just one lane lasted around one hundred miles.

It was fortunate that we had purchased a new tire in Dawson City because on our way to Anchorage we had our second flat tire. This flat tire occurred on Highway number 1 in Alaska's permafrost area. We would laugh about this experience. We pulled off the road onto a private road that included a large gravel area, which was very helpful for changing the flat tire. At a restaurant we asked for the closest service station. We were told that the nearest service station was at Glenallen, around eighty miles ahead. When we were in Glenallen we stopped again and asked for directions to a service station. We were told that there was a Chevron station two and a half miles up the road; the station was open until 10:00 p.m. It was currently 9:15 p.m. We drove to the station and there was just one person, a very young man, seated. He wouldn't come out, so we went to him. The immediate impression I got from him was that we were imposing on him. When I mentioned the tire needing fixing he showed a little irritation. We had to bring him the tire. Three young girls that knew him came in the station. At that time he looked at the tire and then told us he couldn't fix it. He said he didn't have patches. We asked where we could get it fixed and he said everyone was closed and we would have to wait until tomorrow. Phil wanted to buy window-washing fluid for the windshield, and he just pointed to where it was, remaining seated. It was obvious we were not welcome. After the windshield-washer tank was filled the automatic washer didn't work.

The little spare tire and the other three regular tires held together during the rest of our drive on Alaska Highway number1 to Anchorage. I have no desire to ever drive from Tok to Dawson City again; that is, I would not want to drive the long road of just dirt and gravel to reach Dawson City. I have never driven on such roads. The area from Dawson City to Anchorage has very little population, and little car traffic. The mountains are always in the distance. As we got near Anchorage through the lower parts of mountains the view was fantastic! There was snow on these peaks. We stopped around 10:00 p.m. to take pictures of a peak valley with a glacier. The sun found a hole in the clouds right above the head of this glacier.

The balance of our trip to the Hawthorn Suites in Anchorage was without any problems. It took us around fifteen hours for this trip from Dawson City (five hundred and five miles). We arrived at the, Hawthorn Hotel at 1:15 a.m. and it was dusk outside. It was overcast, as it was all day, but I could still read the map without any lighting. I saw a couple riding their horses after midnight. There was a woman out walking at this time. There were others outside during this time. Very interesting!

The next morning Carole and I got up before 8:00 a.m. and went down to have our free continental breakfast at Hawthorn Suites-Anchorage. The day was sunny with a slightly cool temperature. After breakfast we walked to Resolution Point, which has a monument of Captain James Cook. Apparently he landed in the area. It was a short walk. Phil and I took the car to a service center to get the tire fixed and have the van washed at a coin car wash. Then we drove over to the rental place where the van had been rented. The owner agreed to reimburse us for our total van expenses plus hundred dollars for inconvenience. Before driving to the rental place Phil wanted to stop at an A&W Root Beer shop for root beer and a hamburger. I had just one small hamburger. Bonnie and Carole did some laundry while we were gone.

When we got back we agreed that Carole and I would drive over to the start of the Flat Top walking trail. This trail is located at Chugach State Park, a little northeast of Anchorage. This park has lots of trails. Phil and Bonnie were very generous to allow us to take the van. We dropped them off at the post office where they mailed a package as well as our package. We decided to mail the purchased books because of the weight. The Hawthorn's desk clerk gave us incorrect directions to the Flat Top trail. The map showed the route starting from Huffman Rd, but she said O'Malley would take us to it. We ended up at the start of another trail. Fortunately there was a man waiting in his truck. I drove over to him and asked him for directions. He said you have to get on Huffman road to Upper Huffman. We went down Huffman Rd, but this road changed to Birch St. There was a man on the road that appeared to be measuring the intersection. I asked him for directions, and he said we had to go back to O'Malley Road. He also told us to turn right on a street that would lead us to Upper Huffman. Upper Huffman would take us to this trail. His directions worked!

Our walk included some steep hills. The walk was wide open, allowing us to look down at Anchorage and the surrounding area. We could also see the mountains across from us, and in addition see the top of Flat Top and a lot of the trail ahead of us. As we got much closer to the actual Flat Top the trail became very narrow, with stones. When we reached an area that appeared to be less than one-third of the trail to the actual Flat Top we found that section of the trail was jagged with rocks and stones. At this point we would have to climb over these large jagged stones at a very steep incline. We decided not to go any further. We were concerned about keeping our balance if we went any higher. I took several pictures with both cameras while walking on this trail. We enjoyed the great view of the mountains, Anchorage, and the Gulf of Alaska.

We came back to Anchorage and found a restaurant, and had turkey dinners. The turkey was warmed up deli meat. The dinner was very disappointing. There seemed to be very few restaurants within the city limits of Anchorage. After dinner we came back to our hotel and spent some time with Phil and Bonnie before retiring to our rooms.

The following morning, Wednesday, we had the warmest weather of our trip. The temperature might have reached the low seventies. We went down to the breakfast room around 8:10 a.m., and to our surprise found Phil and Bonnie waiting for us in the lobby area. They were reading the newspaper and had already had their breakfast. We could have been down earlier because we normally spent some time reading. After breakfast we went downtown to the Ulu factory. This company makes Eskimo knives and cutting boards. The blade of these knives is hundred and eigthty degrees. Cutting takes place when you roll the blade back and forth over the object to be cut. We purchased two of these sets, one for us and the other for Jody and John. We had "Carole" and "Jody" engraved on their respective blades.

The next activity was getting on the free trolley bus and riding it on a complete loop. We stayed on it for the next loop but got off at the visitor center. We then started visiting a few souvenir shops. I asked one of these shops where license plates could be purchased. He said, "Go to Alaska General Store down a few blocks." We walked there and found they had several gold rush centennial plates in excellent condition. They had a few older plates, including the bear plates. We found out from this store that the bear plates were issued for the 1976 bicentennial and the gold rush plates were issued in two years, 1996 and 1997. I purchased two bear license places in excellent condition for thirty dollars each, and one brand-new bear license plate in the original issued envelope for only thirty dollars. Other purchases were an Alaska plate with a flag in the center in excellent condition for five dollars, eight gold rush license plates in almost new condition for five dollars each, and an almost new 1960 Alaska plate for thirty-five dollars with the 1961 medal tag that could be removed. I felt that I got these plates for a bargain price. Phil also purchased two bear plates from this store. Carole purchased a button cut from an antler for only one dollar. In addition we purchased an Eskimo nativity set for only twenty-five dollars from this same store. The nativity set was well done. Phil and I agreed that this was the neatest store we had visited. Phil also looked at an older pocket watch and a gold nugget. The owner had a few large gold nuggets. I would have enjoyed looking through many hundreds of old postcards at this store, but everyone else was ready to leave the store.

We had lunch at Humpy's outside courtyard, the same place we had lunch on June 19th. Then we drove to a quilt store where Carole purchased some fabric. After that stop we came back to the hotel and we each went to our rooms. We all wanted to start organizing our stuff for leaving the next day. I put all of the license plates together in our tote bag, which I carried on the airplane.

It was interesting that during our breakfast at Hawthorn Suites I spotted a woman with a sweatshirt with "Katy" printed on it. I asked her if she was from Katy, Texas, and her response was yes. Katy is near us, further west on the Katy Freeway. She said she and her family were moving to Anchorage. They really liked Anchorage and Houston summers were too hot for her, although she added that perhaps in January they might feel differently about living in Anchorage.

I had been wearing a Houston Astros baseball hat during this vacation. While we were seated on the trolley bus in Anchorage an older couple got on and he was wearing the same Astros hat. When they were seated I walked up to him, bent down slightly, and told him I liked his hat. He just said "Thank you" without looking up. The wife saw my hat and started laughing. At that time he looked at my hat and he too laughed. They too were from Katy, two blocks from Mason Road. I'm sure there were a lot of people from Houston and its suburbs traveling in Alaska during our time in the state.

On Thursday, June 29, we were headed south on our way to Seward, Alaska, located on Kenai Peninsula. What a beautiful scenic trip it was from Anchorage to Seward. It was the best yet. I took pictures on the way using the digital camera with a new memory card. When we reached Portage we drove over to Portage Glacier Lodge. They had a gift shop and a cafeteria with homemade pies. We found that you could not drive or walk to Portage Glacier, which has retreated considerably over the years. It was reachable only by boat. We drove the short distance to the dock and purchased our tickets for a cruise on the *Ptarmigan* to Portage Glacier. The one-hour boat ride was just wonderful. The sun was blocked by the thick clouds, which really contributed to the beauty of this area. There were small icebergs in the water and snow on the mountain peaks surrounding us. The boat drifted close to this glacier, much closer than the *Princess-Island* came to the glaciers we visited while on our cruise. Some of Portage Glacier's ice was blue. This was my favorite glacier. The boat had a heated lower deck enclosed with big viewing windows, but I spent most of the hour on the top open deck taking pictures. This picture activity helped me to forget how cold I was. The view was fantastic and I enjoyed watching the icebergs. A crewmember scooped up a small iceberg and broke a large piece from it so that anyone could touch it. The remaining iceberg was put in a fish tank filled with water to show that ninety percent of the iceberg was under water.

After this wonderful cruise we went back to Portage Glacier Lodge and ate lunch. We then continued our trip to Seward. This drive to Seward included a tremendous amount of beauty along the road. The center of Kenai Peninsula and most of this peninsula is solid ice, so to get to the other side of the peninsula one must travel to the top of the peninsula and then back down on the opposite side. We soon arrived at Seward and checked in to Murphy's Motel, and then we went to Crab Pot Restaurant and had the best dinner since leaving the *Princess-Island*. After dinner we went down to the waterfront docks and signed up for a four-and-a-half-hour cruise from Major Marine. The two hundred passenger *Star of The Northwest* ship traveled up and down Resurrection Bay. It was our understanding that we might see sea otters, bald eagles, puffins, whales, porpoises, stellar sea lions, seals, and mountain goats. They would also serve a salmon or prime-rib lunch. The weather for the next day was supposed to be what we had this day, cold and overcast. Phil and Bonnie wanted ice cream, so after getting our cruise tickets we went across the street to Seward's ice cream shop. Next door to the ice cream shop was a bakery that served breakfast, so we decided to have our breakfast there. We came back to the motel and went to our respective rooms for the rest of the evening.

It rained during the night, and we had a very low cloud ceiling. This cloud covering was consistent everywhere we went in Alaska and Yukon except for Anchorage. We had breakfast this morning at the bakery. After this meal we went over to the Alaska Sea Life Center and saw puffins, whales, and a sea lion. Of course, I took pictures of these creatures. We also saw a wonderful film on Alaska's animals. Because we wanted to see it again and perhaps our grand triplets would enjoy seeing it when they were older, we purchased a copy of it.

We came back to the motel for about thirty minutes, and then drove over to the dock to board the *Star of the Northwest*. The sky was overcast. We did see one otter, a few puffins, and several sea lions on a very large boulder. That was neat. The boat got fairly close to this boulder. This boat also went by a glacier, but I can't remember its name. We did see whales, but we didn't see one jumping out of the water. We had a steak lunch, which was a good meal. The weather got worse after lunch. The cloud ceiling got lower, and the weather turned very cold with continuous light rain. We all enjoyed this cruise.

The following day the sun was out with blue sky! Other than in Anchorage, this was the first morning during this vacation that we had sun and blue sky. How nice! We could see the tops of the mountains surrounding Seward. We went back to the bakery for breakfast. After breakfast I took pictures of the mountains then we went back to the motel and checked out.

On the way to Exit Glacier the police stopped us because our headlights were not on. It's a state law to drive with lights on, and I had a hard time remembering to turn on the lights when I was driving. The policeman asked me to turn on the headlights, and we were told that one headlight was out. There was also a problem with the backlights. In addition, the policeman found that the van's license plates didn't match our van. The police would contact the rental company to address these issues. We were allowed to continue our drive without receiving a ticket. We found this very interesting. Carole and I walked to the side of Exit Glacier, and then we walked to the front area of the glacier. I took pictures, as expected. After this we headed to Soldotna, also on Kenai Peninsula.

On the way to Soldotna we stopped outside of Sterling at Suzie's Café for a late lunch. Their specialty was sandwiches and soup with good pies. Carole and I each had a turkey sandwich, which we believed was real turkey, not deli turkey. Carole and I shared a piece of apple pie with ice cream. The sandwich had a lot of meat and the pie had two scoops of ice cream. This was a very good lunch! We were continuing our drive to Soldotna with Phil driving when he spotted a moose. He turned around and went back, and I got two great pictures of this moose from the window. This moose was very close to the road.

Our accommodations at Soldotna Bed and Breakfast Lodge were beautiful and very expensive. It was on the Kenai River; this lodge was very attractive both inside and on the outside grounds. There were twelve rooms to this lodge. The lodge had two or three really nice reading rooms and a nice deck in the backyard. The breakfast room had a lot of glass facing the back yard. We read a little on the back-yard deck, and then went down the street to "Sal" for ice cream. When we got back to the lodge we went to our own room. Carole and I read a little then went to bed early. We stayed at this lodge for two nights.

On Sunday we had sunshine all day! Carole and I had breakfast with the remaining residents at the lodge. Their breakfast consisted of whatever they had prepared, which could be an egg dish or French toast. The other option was cold cereal. Their breakfast on the two mornings we were there were not to my liking since I don't eat eggs. I did enjoy the coffee and juice that they had. Carole and I enjoyed looking at the backyard while in the breakfast room.

Phil and Bonnie didn't get up before the 9:00 a.m. closing time for breakfast. When they were up all four of us went to a bakery called The Moose is Loose. They had a small souvenir area, and one item was a T-shirt of several moose. The shop owners asked us to send them a picture of us wearing it when home. Some pictures of people wearing this shirt were on display, and one of them showed a couple with the woman wearing this shirt and the man wearing a Houston Astros T-shirt taken at Houston's Minute Maid Park.

We drove to Kenai National Wildlife Refuge Visitor Center. We toured the center and then took a short walk to a deck on a lake. Bonnie didn't come due to her physical situation with her hips. It was so peaceful and quiet except for bird sounds off and on. We each mediated and took in the peacefulness and beautiful scenery. Our next stop was the small town of Kenai on Cook Inlet. I was driving at this time and had the experience of a moose walking across the road in front of us. I didn't have a chance to photograph this moose. At Kenai we saw the remains of an old fort and two small Russian churches, more like chapels in terms of size. We went inside one of these very small churches and noticed pictures of men in front of the church, which I assumed were Russians of long ago. There were no chairs in this small chapel-sized church. Twenty people would make this church very crowded. We went up to a hill where we could see the Kenai River flowing into Cook Inlet. On the way back to Soldotna and outside of Kenai, we stopped at Chiles Buffet Restaurant for an early dinner.

Back at Soldotna Bed and Breakfast Lodge Carole and I did some reading. Around 7:45 p.m. Carole and I drove back to the Wildlife Refuge Visitor Center for a walk on a trail of less than two miles. The center was closed, but the gate was open. There was a sign at the gate stating that this gate would be closed at 6:00 p.m. Since it was after 6:00 p.m. we were concerned that we would be locked in for the night, so we came back to the lodge and read for the rest of the evening.

On Monday morning we again enjoyed breakfast in the sunroom. The backyard view was so peaceful and attractive. I went outside and took pictures of the lodge from the front yard as well as from the back yard. Carole and I really enjoyed staying at this lodge; it was one of the most enjoyable and attractive places we have experienced. The owners, Steve and Monika, were very nice and friendly. They had owned this lodge for eight years. She was German and could speak four languages. We then finished our packing, loaded up the van, checked out, filled the gas tank, and then started our trip to Homer, Alaska, at the bottom of the Kenai Peninsula.

During our drive to Homer we enjoyed the view of mountains and the water of Cook Inlet. Right before entering Homer from Highway number 1 there is a great view of Kachemak Bay. Before entering the Homer Spit Road where our motel was located, we drove up East End Road where we found houses and businesses. The road has great views, including a chain of mountains with snow and glaciers. A lot of the houses have a great view of these mountains, making it an attractive area for living. We stopped for lunch; Carole and I had a buffalo burger on the outside deck of a small sandwich type restaurant. The good weather with sunny days continued. There were only a few clouds during the day.

We came back to Highway 1, a short distance from Homer's Spit Road (three and a half miles of a very thin peninsula that is a part of Homer). Phil spotted a quilt shop, so he drove in and he and Bonnie stayed in the van while Carole and I visited the shop. Carole purchased fabric and a kit for making a wall quilt with a moose theme. I visited with the lady in charge. She said the winters are mild in comparison to the rest of Alaska. The temperature rarely gets below zero.

After the quilt shop we drove down Spit Road. There is water on each side—Kachemak Bay and Cook Inlet—and I believe the widest distant of land between these two bodies of water is only one-third of a mile. Some areas seem to be only the distance of a couple of football fields. There are businesses, restaurants, and souvenir shops along Spit Road. In addition, there is a boat graveyard and RV parks, which had many hundreds of parked RVs. The fishing industry is big in Homer, and it's base is on this road.

Our motel at the end of Spit Road was very disappointing, but there wasn't much we could do. The one positive thing was that the narrow beach, water, and the mountains on the other side made the view very attractive. We saw otters in the water and eagles flying near our motel from the other side of Kachemak Bay. These events were very enjoyable. One otter was trying to eat food found under water, but four seagulls wanted it also. They would float on the water close to this otter while the otter was floating on its back. One time a seagull tried to land on the otter. Otters live completely on the water all of their lives. Their babies are born in the water and grow up on the mother otter's stomach. A large majority of their life is spent floating on their backs. We found that Spit Road is truly the best place to observe eagles. They were everywhere! I loved it. Seeing and taking pictures of the eagles made Homer a wonderful place to visit. We went to the visitor center and found it to be very interesting. They had a very interesting film on wildlife and the ocean area of Homer. Carole and I really enjoyed the time spent at this center.

When we left for dinner Phil was driving. There was an eagle flying parallel to the road just a little higher than the van, and not that far from the road. Phil caught up to the eagle and then tried to drive at the same speed of the eagle. I opened the sliding door and with my 300mm lens attached to the film camera I took three pictures of this eagle. It was very exciting to be that close to a flying eagle.

We found a great restaurant on East End Road, Destiny's Gallery Family Restaurant. The servings were large portions of good food—more than we could eat—at a very reasonable price. Carole and I had roast beef, baked potato, and string beans. It was the best baked potato since leaving home. The string beans were also good as well as the meat. I felt that this was the best restaurant in Alaska/Yukon. It's a small family-owned restaurant. Our waitress Shannon said the next day's lunch would include hamburgers for fifty cents and free homemade ice cream. Hot dogs would also be free. This was for their 4th of July celebration. In addition, Homer's 4th of July parade would pass by the restaurant at 6:00 p.m.

After leaving this restaurant we drove to the end of the airport road. I was told that was one of the best places to see moose. We stayed there for forty minutes and then gave up and left. After driving several blocks we saw an eagle on top of a utility pole. I got out of the van with my camera, hoping to catch him in flight. After five minutes and the eagle still on the pole, I got back in the van and we left. Phil got back on East End Road and that was where we spotted a moose near the road. I got a good picture of her around 10:00 p.m. We came back to our motel and I stepped out on the balcony, and there was an eagle on the beach sitting on driftwood and eating something. The eagle was about one hundred and twenty yards from us. I took some pictures of this eagle. By this time it was a little after 11:00 p.m. I was told that sunset would be around 11:30 p.m. While we were watching this one eagle on the beach another one joined it. There were a few people on the beach who were also watching and photographing these two eagles.

On July 4, 2006, we left late for breakfast/brunch. There were two eagles visible when we walked out to the parking lot, one on a tower and the other on a utility pole. We drove back to Destiny's Gallery Family Restaurant. I had pancakes and Carole had scrambled eggs and a pancake. They were the best pancakes we'd had since we left home. The cost for the two of us with coffee, hot tea, and orange juice was less than ten dollars and fifty cents, unbelievable for Alaska. In fact, this restaurant was cheaper than in Houston.

We came back to Homer's Spit Road and stopped at some small shops. I purchased a coffee mug that was a little larger than the standard mug, and with a moose on each side. It was made in the United States, very rare since all of the other mugs we purchased were made in China. Carole purchased an ornament for the Christmas tree. Prior to the shopping we stopped at a spot where men were cleaning huge fish. At that location I photographed many seagulls and a couple of eagles in the air. These pictures were taken with my digital camera using the 70-300mm lens from my film camera.

We left the motel for our dinner back at Destiny's Gallery Family Restaurant. While in Homer we ate all of our meals at this restaurant, except for the first meal down the street from Destiny's Gallery. That morning they told us they would reserve one of the few tables for us on the front deck. That way we could eat our dinner and have a great view of the 4th of July parade. We also received free homemade ice cream with strawberries, which was very good. There was also free cake and that too was very good. The restaurant also had free hot dogs, but we didn't take any of them. Carole and I ordered the same dinner as the day before. Instead of string beans we got corn, which was also very good. We enjoyed the parade, and I took a few pictures including a few older cars and pick-ups. Marlene, the owner, joined us during this parade time. She seemed to enjoy being with us. It was a very short parade and not much to it, no bands, but still enjoyable.

Marlene was also the cook and her daughter-in-law, Shannon, was the waitress. Shannon's 16 year old daughter also was employed part time at this restaurant. Marlene and Shannon made us feel like we were good friends, which made our meals at their restaurant more enjoyable. During this time on the deck Marlene revealed some of her past history. It was easy to conclude that she had a hard life, which included a bout with cancer. Her parents had started the restaurant. The restaurant was very small but very clean and attractive. Unfortunately this restaurant was permanently closed sometime after we flew back home.

We went back to Homer's Spit Road and stopped at the store where I got my moose image mug earlier. Bonnie wanted three more of them, and I purchased another one. We went back to the motel. I watched an otter and photographed an eagle flying over our motel. We also saw a moose and her calf after dinner, but they were too far away to photograph.

Early on the 5th of July, while Carole and I were waiting for Phil and Bonnie to get up, I watched for eagles and otters from our room's balcony. The top of the mountains across the bay was buried in low clouds. There was no sun during this morning, nor for the rest of the day. The fishing boats were taking fishermen a distance that I couldn't see from the balcony. These boats started their course between 5:00-5:30 a.m. Within two hours they were on their way somewhere in Kachemak Bay or out into the Gulf of Alaska. This bay is attractive. I saw three eagles from the balcony that morning and another otter. The eagles are my favorite. The view made me aware of God. God is awesome!

On the way to our morning breakfast we saw eagles while driving on Homer's Spit Road. There was an eagle on a short post near the road. Phil stopped and I got out and took pictures of this eagle. This is the closest I had been to an eagle; I was only about ten feet away and the background sky was perfect as it was an even white. White backgrounds are always perfect for portrait pictures, and this is what I had for this eagle's portrait pictures. I took several pictures that ended up being my best eagle pictures. On this same drive we saw two eagles together on the beach to our left side on Cook Inlet. I also photographed these two eagles.

At the restaurant I had my pancakes and Carole also ordered them. They were so good! Our pancakes included a topping of homemade ice cream left over from the day before and strawberries. Marlene appeared glad to see us again. We also met a couple of Shannon's children. She and her husband had four children ranging in age from two to sixteen years. We learned that her sixteen-year-old daughter also worked there part time. We told Marlene that we considered her restaurant our favorite and best during our two weeks plus of traveling in Alaska/Yukon. When breakfast was over we expressed our appreciation and said goodbye to Shannon and wished her the best. She told us to go in the kitchen and give Marlene our goodbyes, which we did. She gave Phil and me a big hug and said, "Don't wait five years before coming back. I may not be here in five years." She also asked us to send her pictures of the parade, which I did with a letter of appreciation. I also included pictures of the outside of her restaurant.

What a great experience we had, not only at Marlene's restaurant, but also Homer's three-and-a-half-mile peninsular called Spit Road. I was thrilled to see eagles every day and watch otters from our room or from the balcony. Eagles could be seen every day on light poles, utility poles, and in the air. Some were crossing the bay and flying near our front window or balcony. I also enjoyed seeing moose every day in Homer. These sightings were off Spit Road. We also enjoyed seeing the mountains and their peaks. My favorite areas were Juneau, Homer, and Dawson City. We need to come back!

We went back to our rooms, loaded the car, and drove back to Anchorage. The scenery was very attractive from Homer to Anchorage (around two hundred and twenty miles), but on the drive from Portage to Anchorage, probably the last twenty miles to Anchorage, the scenery was outstanding. On this trip we saw one moose and her calf, and I saw two eagles in a tree.

We checked into our rooms at Hawthorne, and then went to 4th Avenue for souvenir shopping. Carole purchased a jade bear pin at this shop. We never took time for lunch, so when we were finished shopping we searched for a restaurant. We found Boston Restaurant for our lunch/dinner. Carole and I ordered lasagna, and it was filling and good. We then went back to our rooms for the rest of the evening. All four of us were thinking, "This is it, the end of this wonderful vacation." That evening I thought over what we had done and what we had seen, and some of the people we had met. I had a strong desire to come back some day. We needed to spend more time hiking, perhaps a little gold panning, and take the train to White Horse, Yukon. At White Horse I wanted to make a round trip to Dawson City by rental car, boat (Yukon River), or bus.

The van rental company came to Hawthorne and picked up the leased van. Very convenient! In the morning we had our last free continental breakfast at Hawthorne. I had my waffle loaded with mashed strawberries, a treat for me. Phil and Bonnie joined us. They were shuttled at 11:15 a.m. to the airport for their home journey to Chelsea, Michigan. We seated ourselves in Hawthorne's lobby, spending the time reading. At 2:10 p.m. we too were shuttled to the airport. Our plane was scheduled to leave at 8:50 p.m. local time and arrive at Houston at 6:30 a.m. on July 7. We were looking forward to being home and seeing James, John, Jody, and the triplets, Ellie, Ethan, and Evan. We missed them all! What a wonderful trip! Our cruise and driving around Alaska was a wonderful experience! The fellowship with Phil and Bonnie made this trip very special. This was the only trip the four of us took together. We will never forget it!

When we were home I sent the following two letters:

July 24, 2006
Fortymile Gold Workshop/Studio, Attn: Ms. Leslie Chapman, Dawson City, Yukon

Dear Leslie,
    Carole and I were at your attractive workshop last month while we were in Dawson City. My brother and his wife were also with us. We all love Dawson City. I'm very much interested in the 1896 Gold Rush. We saw part of the trail during our train ride from Skagway to White Summit, B.C. That was neat! I'm almost done reading I Married The Klondike by Laura

Berton. What a great book! When I finish this book I will read <u>Klondike Fever</u> by Pierre Berton. I have a couple more books relating to Dawson City that I will also read.

It was a thrill for me to be in Dawson City as I thought about this area during my younger years. Your daughter, Anna, gave us a wonderful and very educational walking tour. We enjoyed your shop very much and having an opportunity to meet you (which we also enjoyed) and buying a gold nugget that was mined nearby. This nugget is a little treasure linked to Dawson City. All of this made our stay at Dawson City more special, and we want to thank you and your daughter for this. It was a wonderful part of our trip to Alaska/Yukon.

I have enclosed a couple of pictures that we hope you will enjoy. Again, our thanks to you and Anna for making our Dawson visit more special.

July 14, 2006
Destiny's Galley Family Restaurant,
Attn: Marlene Thibert, 378 E. Pioneer Ave., Homer, AK 99603

Dear Marlene,

Carole and I and my brother and his wife want to let you know how much we enjoyed eating at your wonderful restaurant. I like pancakes for breakfast, and your pancakes were the best I had in Alaska/Yukon. Unfortunately, our first meal in Homer was up the street from your restaurant. Fortunately our search for the next meal brought us to Destiny's Galley Family Restaurant. We continued eating at your restaurant during our remaining time in Homer. The food was all excellent and the price was also excellent! We rated Destiny's Galley Family Restaurant the number one restaurant we ate at during our two and a half weeks in Alaska and Yukon. We also appreciate you treating us as locals and making our meals special with you and Shannon. You and Shannon made our stay in Homer very special, which is greatly appreciated

I took pictures of the 4th of July parade, and I have enclosed copies of them. I hope you will enjoy them. While Carole and I were waiting at Anchorage's airport I visited with a woman from the town of Kenai. She is familiar with Homer and knows where your restaurant is. I strongly recommended your restaurant to her and the reasons for it. She said she would have to eat there the next time she is in Homer. I'm hoping she will.

Thanks again for everything, Marlene. The homemade ice cream was fantastic! We want to come back to Homer, but it probably won't be any earlier than 2008. When we come back we will let you know so that you can save a table for us. We hope only for the best for you and your family.

Note: We were unable to return to Alaska and Dawson City.

Chapter 29

Kingwood, Texas

When John and Jody's triplets were around three years old, we were told that when the children got close to school age they would move to Kingwood because they wanted their children's schooling to be in that school district. Kingwood is a little over fifty miles northeast from their house in Houston. We told them that we liked Kingwood and just loved all of the trees. The nickname for Kingwood is "The Livable Forest." We told them that our friends Jim and Waej Rogers used to live in Kingwood. We rotated homes for dinner and pinochle. We thought Kingwood would be a great place to live. We liked the format of the first floor of the Rogers' house.

We had spent a large amount of money remodeling our house in Spring Branch. We had the two bathrooms and the kitchen remodeled, plus all of the windows were replaced, the floors were replaced, and we had a new roof. We planned to live there for the rest of our lives. Sometime in early 2008 John and Jody said the time had come for them to move to Kingwood. They wanted us to move also. We have been close to John and his family and we spent a lot of time together. We had meals together and were included in many of their activities. I told Jody we could always drive to Kingwood when needed. Jody didn't accept this. She pressured us, but she always told us she wasn't putting pressure on us. She told us if we would move, they would get a SUV so that we could all travel in one vehicle (they had planned to buy one regardless). She also said she would cook our favorite meal each week. Not too long after this, they put a contract on a house in Kingwood.

After church we drove to their house to spend the rest of the afternoon with them. When we came over to their house, Jody was waiting for us with the computer on. She said she wanted to show us something, so we followed her. On the computer screen was a house in Kingwood. She said, "Look at this house!" We looked at the rooms and outside, and the house appeared to be very attractive. She said, "I'm not putting any pressure on you, but they are having an open house this coming Sunday, and this house is just down the street from the house we put a contract on. After church, drive to Kingwood and look at this house, and then you can see the house we placed a contract on." I felt pressured, but I said, "OK, we will do this." She was pleased. I'm sure she was praying that if it was God's will we would move to Kingwood.

Sunday found us at this house in Kingwood. We were impressed with it. The house was much larger than our Spring Branch house. The master bedroom and the master bathroom were very large. The kitchen and the living room were large. As we walked into this house, I was surprised that it had a similar format to the Rogers' house. Even the office with French doors was the same. This house was really nice, and the house was all brick! Many years ago doing my walking for exercise, I would talk a lot to God. One time I mentioned that if He wanted us to move, I would like to have an all brick house with lots of trees in the area.

Carole and I talked about it on the way home. Of course, Jody called later to ask us what we thought of the house. We told her we liked it and added that it must be God's will. I told her we would pray about it. We prayed, and after a few days we felt that God was telling us to move. Sometimes

God will speak in voice, but most of the time the Holy Spirit will respond like a strong feeling that this is what we need to do.

Jody and John's house sold in eleven days. We hadn't told John and Jody that God gave us the green light to move. I called a realtor who dealt with homes in our area and left a message on her phone then we drove over to John and Jody's house and told them that we would move and that we really liked the house Jody had picked out for us. She asked me if we had talked to a realtor, and I mentioned that I left a phone message. She told us that we needed to use the realtor they used then she picked up the phone and told the realtor, Christine Duncan, that we were using her.

Jody came over to our house and staged it for us; she did a good job. Our house sold in three days to the very first couple that looked at it. The first realtor that I had called returned my call and was disappointed that she didn't get our business. She told me what she would have listed the house for. The realtor who sold our house listed it for fifteen thousand dollars more than that amount, and the buyer accepted the listing price. We are so thankful to be in Kingwood, and we believe this is where God wanted us to be, close to John and Jody.

We have enjoyed our grandkids and seeing them grow up. They each have their own personality. A few years ago they would comment to us that we were old. We enjoyed these comments because we realized we do look old from their perspective. I will never forget one event with Ellie. Jody was taking the boys somewhere and wanted to drop off Ellie at our house. I told Jody that would be fine because I was almost finished planting flowers. When Ellie arrived I was in the back yard. I told Ellie I had just a few flowers to plant. After a couple of minutes had passed, Ellie said, "Grandpa, if we had a race, do you think I would win?" I said, "Oh no, Ellie, I would win." Ellie then said, "But grandpa, old people have a hard time running, and your face looks very old." I laughed to myself and enjoyed the honesty of a child. The parents soon convinced the triplets not to call Grandma and Grandpa old. Now they have gone to the other extreme and tell us we are young. We sure love them.

I had a one humorous phone conversation. I answered the phone and the lady on the other end told me she could save me money by bundling Internet, phone, and TV. She mentioned that I hadn't connected our TV with our phone and Internet. I said, "The deal sounds good, but we don't have a TV." After about two seconds of silence she said, "What do you do with your time?" I said, "We read books." She said, "Oh, I suggest you keep doing this." That was the end of the phone conversation.

Jody wanted the four of us to have a Bible study on the Gospel of Mark during summer 2010. This study involved homework. We would read a chapter, then we would write what the author was saying, what the Scripture meant, and how we could apply it to our lives. We met in the evening each week. During one of these weekly sessions Jody made a statement that meant a lot to me and that I will never forget. She said, "Dad, you told me once that a long time ago you would get up early before work and have a quiet time reading Scripture and praying. You said this has changed your life. I didn't believe you. Earlier this year I started getting up early in the morning reading Scripture and praying, and Dad, this has changed my life." I found that you can't have a relationship with God if you completely ignore Him.

When I was in my teens I started reading Scripture and praying before I went to bed. I did this consistently except when I was in the army and in college. I never stopped praying. Sometime many years ago, I switched to getting up before I went to work to read Scripture and have prayer. This changed my life and gave me a real and loving relationship with God, which I realize is made possible only through Jesus Christ.

On Sunday morning, January 4, 2009, I got up early as usual. I had been growing concerned about our 401K investment. This and our Social Security benefits were all that we had to support us for the rest of our lives. As 2008 closed out, my 401K had declined by slightly over 27 percent. On paper, we had lost a very large sum of money. I was doing my own Bible study using the *Life Application Bible Commentary—Book of Luke*. I started this particular morning by reading the twelfth chapter of Luke, with the issue of reduced wealth on my mind. The verses that stood out were the following. In verse 15 Jesus says, "Be on your guard against all kinds of greed: a man's life does not consist in the abundance of his possessions." A little further Jesus says "I tell you, do not worry about your life, what you will eat; or about your body, what you will wear. Life is more than food, and the body more than clothes" (verse 22-23). In verse 25 Jesus says, "Who of you by worrying can add a single hour to his life?" In verse 34 Jesus says, "For where your treasure is, there your heart will be also." I had read these verses before, but that morning these verses seemed to come alive in my mind as I opened the Life Application and read what they had to say in regard to these verses. I got to the words, "Never put your hope and pride in real estate, insurance or mutual funds. God should be your security and joy." I knew that, but this time I felt like God was speaking to me! Finally, I got it! How slow I am to apply God's truth and promises to my life. I prayed for forgiveness for not putting His truth to my life and accepting His promise. I told Him that all that I have was His. I mentioned the decline of my investment was His problem, not mine. I told Him our beautiful house and everything that I had is His. Peace flowed into my heart, and I have had this peace ever since. From that day on my trust was in God for our future here on earth. My real home is with Him, which is for eternity. God has given us many blessings. The fruit of the Spirit of God is listed in Galatians 5:22-23: "But the fruit of the Spirit is love, joy, peace, patience, kindness, goodness, faithfulness, gentleness and self-control." Peace, joy, and love come from God. All priceless!

I was excited about this peace that I received, and I shared my story with my Sunday school classmates that morning. I was surprised that our senior pastor, Dr. Jim Jackson, preached on the same Scripture and mentioned some of the things I told my Sunday school Class. This was unbelievable! I got the message, God! I sent an email to this pastor about my experience. He asked permission to use my statement and I agreed. Later it was published in a Sunday morning bulletin. After that morning service, a member that we know came up to tell me that my printed message had helped him, and he thanked me for it. Glory to God!

Both Carole and I feel very blessed, and we realize that we don't have a lot of years left here on earth. We also feel like we have had a wonderful life with many blessings from God. As for our future, it's unknown, but we do know we have an eternal home and Jesus Christ will be with us until the end of our earthly journey.

Chapter 30

My Faith Journey and Other Writings.

Introduction to My Life Journey of Faith in Jesus Christ

Sometime in 2009 I was visiting with our daughter-in-law, Jody Wilcox, in her kitchen. I told her that I was thinking of writing about my early years and good memories. Jody said, "Don't do this, Dad, but write about your faith journey. This would be a legacy for the children." I replied, "That is an option to think about." Shortly after this conversation during one of my early morning sessions of devotion, Scripture reading, and praying, this idea came to mind. Then I heard a voice, "Do it now!" My immediate thought was that I didn't have long to live and for that reason God was telling me to do it now. I told God I would do it and, within a couple of days I started it. I prayed a lot while doing this, asking God about the structure, what to include, and the wording. Every time I stopped and asked God for help, the words came to me. I believe the Holy Spirit assisted me in writing this faith journey document. I'm thankful that I did it. Looking back at when I completed this document, I feel that the timing of the writing was good because currently my memory is not as good.

I'm thankful to God who demanded that I write it, and for Jody planting this seed in my mind. Jody read it and said it was very good. She also said that even if no one reads it, God was glorified! So far, I'm alive and alive in Christ. God has given us many blessings.

My Life Journey of Faith in Jesus Christ, Experiencing God, and my Beliefs

I was raised by parents who believed in Jesus Christ and attended church each Sunday. My family attended First Methodist Church of Ferndale on Woodward Ave. I grew up in this church and I was expected to be there with the family every Sunday without exception. There were times that I would have preferred to stay home, but I knew it was not an option. I can't remember my Sunday schoolteachers except for one, Mr. Black, who told our class that someday we would have to choose to make a commitment to accept Jesus Christ as our Lord and Savior. That comment stayed with me all my life. In the fifth or sixth grade I attended a class required for joining the church. I learned about the Bible and listened to sermons. I learned about Jesus Christ and His love, but it really didn't take hold of me in my heart and soul. I remember when the sessions were finished, each of us got on our knees and asked Jesus Christ to come into our hearts. There was no effect on my life from this prayer, but I did believe Jesus Christ was the Son of God.

The Billy Graham Crusade came to Detroit in November 1953. My brother, Phil, said to me, "Let's go and see Billy Graham." I had not planned to attend, but since he wanted to go I decided to go with him. Phil is three years older than me and he had his driver's license, so transportation was not a problem. We attended the crusade, and near the end of the presentation Rev. Graham invited all who would publicly accept Jesus Christ to walk to the front. Moved by the Holy Spirit, Phil and I were among the many who accepted Jesus as our Lord and Savior through faith and to pray for forgiveness of our sins. I felt no extraordinary emotion from this commitment. However, the next day I realized something in me was different—I now had a hunger to read Scripture. I got into the routine of reading Scripture and praying before going to bed. I also looked at people differently.

There was a young boy named Harvey in my grade at school. His mother rented a house a few houses down from my parents' home. He lived in this house for only one school year. His classmates constantly made fun of him. His mother couldn't afford to buy him a belt and his pair of jeans was too large for him, so he used a rope for his belt and rolled up the pant legs. He didn't have much clothing. After asking Christ to live within me, I realized that this teasing of Harvey was wrong, and I immediately became his friend. One day walking home from school together he asked me why I was so nice to him. I can't remember exactly what I said, but I think it was something like, "I love Jesus." Another kid was being picked on by a bully, and I probably took the incorrect approach as a Christian, but I went up to this bully and started pushing him backward. I told him the boy he was picking on was my friend and to leave him alone. It worked. Since November 1953, my faith that Jesus Christ was alive and with me began to grow.

During the rest of my school years I continued to grow spiritually, attending the Voice of Christian Youth club in high school but not consistently, and still keeping my Bible reading and prayer time. At my church I made a commitment to read the Bible from cover to cover. It was a two-and-a-half-year program, a book or multiple books per month with questions to answer (homework) in reference to the reading assignment. I finished this course during the first semester at college.

I didn't read the Bible every day during my years in the army and college, but I never stopped praying. Carole and I believe it was God that brought us together. Carole and I attended church together during our college years as well as when we lived in Germany. We didn't go all of the time, but as I remember it was the majority of the time. We both kept our faith in Jesus Christ. We also believe that it was God's will for us to move to Houston. It was in Houston that my spiritual life started another round of growth. During these years in Houston I would have spiritual growth spurts, not continuous growth. During these same years God touched me a few times and answered prayers. I have experienced God and miracles. The first time I felt God touching me was when I was a teenager, alone in our Ferndale house. One evening I was reading the Bible and praying when I felt touched, which I can't explain. It gave me a wonderful joy. I soaked it in as long as it lasted. This same thing happened to me a few times during my life in Houston. When our Jody was in the hospital shortly before the triplets were born, Carole and I visited her. Before we left the three of us held hands and I prayed. When I ended my prayer "in the name of Jesus," a warm comforting feeling shot through my body. Jody then said, "Did you feel that? That was the Holy Spirit!" Praying for Jody, the Spirt touched both of us.

During the twenty-seven and a half years I worked at Brown & Root, Inc. I had moments of experiencing God. I believe God was behind a few management decisions that tremendously benefited me financially. When our boys were in middle school I realized we didn't have any money to send them to college. I gave this problem to God, telling him I didn't understand how we could get our boys through college and I told God it was now His problem. Shortly after this prayer, a few events materialized that led to large monthly salary increases. The story is incredible, but I won't describe it in detail. I have thanked God several times for answering this prayer. In addition, after the boys graduated from high school they both got good salary jobs at Brown & Root Inc. for the summer. I give God the credit for this. The boys graduated from universities without Carole and me having to borrow money until their senior years. When they were small, I prayed hundreds of times that they would place their faith and trust in Jesus Christ and graduate from college. James graduated in May 1994 and John in December 1994. They are both faithful to Jesus Christ. This is another prayer that was answered. God is awesome!

During fall 2001 God responded directly to me during a meeting that I needed to accept an employment offer from a fairly new company, Exult, Inc., which I did. Later this company merged with Hewitt.

My Major Instant Miracles

I believe in miracles (direct intervention from God/Jesus Christ); they occur every day around the world. Many Christians, if not the majority, believe that the miracles that Jesus and the Apostles performed were just for that period of time. This is not true. If I did not believe that miracles could happen, I would not have experienced them. There is an unseen power out there and only faith in Jesus Christ and the will of our heavenly Father can activate this power.

The first miracle that I experienced was when I was around seventeen years old. I had a date with a Christian girl who had a strong faith in Christ. Her name was Barbara Kusner, and I liked her very much. She was miles ahead of me spiritually. It was Saturday night and I had borrowed Phil's car. We drove to somewhere in downtown Detroit for a night of gospel singing by many groups. We loved it! We were told that there would be groups singing until the last person left. I believe we left around 11:00 p.m. while the concert was still going on. I had parked Phil's car on the street. When we were in the car, I turned the key but nothing happened. There was no phone booth around, and it was just the two of us, and I was responsible for getting her home. I was almost in a state of panic! She immediately said, "When I have a problem I give it to God. Let us pray." We held hands, and she prayed that the car would start when I turned the key. She ended this prayer "in Jesus' name." Immediately after the prayer she said in a confident voice, "Now turn the key." When I turned the key the car started immediately and I got her home without any problems.

I want to share what I refer to as my major and direct miracles. There are others, but these are the ones that God responded to instantly. The first took place in 1989. Our son James was attending Texas State Technical Institute's automotive school (now called Texas State Technical College) in Waco, Texas. I took James to TSTI at the beginning of his first semester. I noticed there were many characters that appeared rough natured. Yes, I know this is judging, and later God showed me this. I got James settled in and then drove home, concerned about James keeping his faith and being faithful to our heavenly Father. On the way home I prayed strongly that James would not lose his faith. Then I had a strong feeling that God was telling me I no longer had to pray about this this because James would keep his faith. What joy I experienced during the rest of the way home. I praised Him many times that night and this joy lasted all the way home.

Another miracle was again driving James to TSTC with in Waco (Texas State Technical College), Texas on a Sunday night. We owned a 1968 Executive Pontiac for a long time, with over 100,000 miles on the odometer. The dashboard was very wide and originally had several lights across the dashboard. All of the lights were out, except one at the far right. This one light was not enough to see the speedometer. I only used this car to travel to and from work, but for some reason I used this car to drive James to Waco on a Sunday night. I was traveling on Highway 6 and didn't have a problem getting James back to his room. I left James and drove home on Highway 6. At that time Highway 6 was mainly a two-lane country road. There was no moon and it was pitch black. There was no other traffic, but I couldn't identify my speed since there was no light on the speedometer. I couldn't identify if I was going thirty-five mph or eigthty-five mph! I was growing fearful and I called out to God, "Help me, Lord! I can't see the speedometer." I heard a very loud voice saying, "Hit right here," as my arm automatically hit a spot on the dashboard. Then wow! All of the lights for the dashboard came on! It had been years since the lighting on the dashboard had been complete! I was high all the way home, constantly thanking God and praising Him. I seemed to reach home very quickly. The next morning the dashboard lights were off again. I hit the dashboard in the same area, but the lights did not come on.

Another miracle occurred in my office at Brown & Root Inc. Winnie Tejada, a friend who was strong in his faith, had spent some time in Saudi Arabia working with the underground church. The Saudi religious police were always searching for people with a connection to Christianity. If a Saudi was found with anything relating to Christianity, it was a death sentence. He told me some of his experiences with these Christians and the danger, as well as he, was in. When a church home reached more than eight people it was time to split the church. His stories were spiritually uplifting and some were sad, such as Christians arrested. I felt I couldn't do what he was doing in regard to mission work. After he left my office, I felt a little low and starting questioning if I was really doing the will of God. I was disturbed and wanted to know. I had a Gospel of John in my briefcase. I took it out and told God, "I want to know right now if I'm doing your will in my life! I'm going to open this Gospel and lay my finger on the page and right above it I want you to tell me whether or not I'm doing your will!" I opened the Gospel of John and placed one of my fingers on a page with my eyes closed. I opened my eyes and I read, "You are doing the will of God." There was a verbal "Wow!" from me while I was closing the book. Then I wished I hadn't closed the book because I wanted to know what chapter and verse I had read. I then realized I couldn't duplicate another person's talents, but I could still serve God with the talents He gave me. I thanked the Lord for responding and the lesson I learned. I had a deeper joy that I can't explain. Shortly after this experience I read the Gospel of John and my intention was to find this verse. When I completed reading it, I got so involved with it that I forgot I was searching for this verse. I realized that there is no such verse and that God planted these words right above my finger. He is awesome!

Another major miracle that God responded to instantly happened in late September or early October 2001, again in my office. I thought I might have to work a little overtime that evening, so I had a slice of homemade bread in my briefcase. Late in the afternoon of Friday my boss came in and told me he wanted specific general ledger accounts reconciled and on his desk no later than 8:00 a.m. Monday morning. He said he didn't care how long I had to work this weekend to accomplish his request. This request was a surprise because I had already worked a lot of overtime during the week. I was physically tired, mentally exhausted, and hungry. I started with the hardest general ledger account. I downloaded the monthly debits and credits (many hundreds of large numbers) from our accounting system to an Excel spreadsheet. I had to identify those debits and credits that would wash (total zero). I went through my normal procedure with a block of numbers that I thought should zero out. As stated above, I was very tired, had difficulty thinking, and was very hungry. I spent a lot of time without success. I excluded one particular invoice that I thought was an open item. I had three two-digit dollar amounts. This was unusual because the dollar amounts in this account generally consisted of five to seven digit dollar amounts. I played with the numbers and couldn't come up with a group of debits and credits that totaled zero. Finally I stood up, closed my door, and took the slice of bread from my briefcase. I looked out of my window, down at the rows of streetlights and the blackness, and I thought of the people in that area. Then I said, "Lord, I need your help. When I get done eating this bread, I believe you will give me the wisdom to identify the dollar amounts that will zero out." Then I heard a voice that said that the three small numbers had their sign in reverse (debits instead of credits). The excluded billing invoice amount needed to be included with the numbers selected for zeroing out. (There may have been one other dollar amount that needed to be included that was told to me, but I can't remember). The voice continued: "Add these numbers and they will total zero." The word "Wow!" left my lips! I immediately did what the voice said, and indeed these dollar amounts (debits and credits) totaled zero! I thanked the Lord for what He had just done. After thanking Him, my mental exhaustion, tiredness, and hunger left me. I was now refreshed. I thanked Him again for restoring me. God is awesome!

I believe God enjoys answering prayers that are of very little significance but bring joy to the requestor. This is what happened to me on March 17, 2013. I have been carrying two silver half-dollars in my left pocket (Walking Liberty and Franklin) and a Native American golden dollar. In addition, I also include in this same pocket my jackknife and cell phone. Memories of silver coins, of which the half-dollars were my favorite of the circulating silver coins, drove me to do this. I also confess that I like the sound of silver coins.

On the morning of March 16, 2013, I got up before 6:00 a.m. to do my morning routine of shaving, dressing, placing my coins and knife in my left pocket and my silver dollar in my right pocket (I have carried the same 1886 dated silver dollar in my right pocket since August 30 or 31, 1959). Then I entered my office room for my morning devotions. I have a sofa in this room with two cushions. I sit on the cushion closest to my desk. This morning I noticed that my Walking Liberty half-dollar was missing. I couldn't image how it could have fallen out of my pocket the previous day. When I retire for the night, I always grab the coins and my knife and drop these items in my stone bowl on my dresser.

I wasn't aware that one coin was missing. During the day I searched the office room, removing the two cushions of the sofa and looking under these cushions. I also checked all of the chairs in the living room without finding my coin. During my devotions, I asked God for a blessing that He would lead me to this coin if it was His will because this coin was special for me.

Carole and I went to our church's Sunday school class party that Saturday evening. When we came back I wanted to read a few emails together. We entered the office room, and Carole sat in the desk chair. I pulled up a folding chair next to the front of the sofa cushion that I sat on during my devotions. The front of the cushions ended on my right side. The lamp lit these cushions and there was no coin laying on it. After this session, we turned off the light and went to bed.

The next morning, March 17, I shaved, dressed, and then entered my office for my early morning devotions. On the middle of the sofa's cushion was my half-dollar that was lost. My spirit soared! I spent a large part of my devotion thanking God and felt in awe of what he had done. God took the lost coin during the night and moved it to the sofa's cushion where I had my devotions.

Thoughts

I have wondered why God has given Carole and me so many blessings, some of which are listed above. I have pondered this thought for years. I really haven't come up with an answer, but perhaps John's Gospel 15:7 may be part of the reason for these blessings. This verse is Jesus speaking: "If you abide in me, and my words abide in you, ask whatever you wish, and it will be given you." If I live within the spirit of Jesus Christ, striving to do so, and his words are applied to my life, I will only ask for things in accordance to His will. I believe those prayers will be answered currently or in the future. The answer will be in accordance with His will and His response may be better than what I requested.

Activities that helped the growth of my faith

The following really helped me with my growth of faith. First, many years ago I wanted to have a close relationship with God. I started getting up early in the morning and spending thirty to forty-five minutes on Scripture reading, a devotion lesson, and talking to God through prayer. Doing this for many years has brought me to a closer relationship with God. It changed my life! Second, several years ago I took a course at our church taught by Rev. Wick Stuckey. This course was based on the workbook *Experiencing God*, by Henry T. Blackaby. This book included actual examples of Henry Blackaby's experiences with the work of the Holy Spirit. I wanted to experience God at a higher level, and this course helped me to accomplish this goal. Third, I was involved with multiple Bible studies during my Houston years. The one that affected me the most was an organized study at a church member's home. Each week we had questions to answer, and then we would discuss our answers at the next meeting. The last part of this gathering was the group leader lecturing on what we had read and studied that evening. This Bible study format lasted two years and helped me with my personal relationship with God and my faith more than any other Bible study.

My beliefs

I believe that when a person goes from a religion (of the head) to a relationship with Jesus Christ (of the heart), then that person can experience inner joy and the assurance of spending eternity in His kingdom. Christianity was never meant to be a religion, but a way of life based on the example of Jesus Christ. We Christians strive to live a lifestyle that is not based on the world's lifestyle. I fail many times, but that is my desire.

Jesus Christ is my Savior and He has all authority over heaven and earth (Matthew 28:18). It is through his death and resurrection that I, through faith and trust in Christ, have access to God and eternal life in His Kingdom. My approach to God is through Jesus Christ. That is why I end my prayers to God with the words "in Jesus' name" (John 14:14). It is through Jesus Christ that we have the Holy Spirit and the opportunity to have a real and personal relationship with God, which is not possible with any other religion. The eternal things I have are from Jesus Christ. He is my Lord.

I believe what the Scripture states in reference to eternal life, that it is only through Jesus Christ that we experience eternal life. Jesus told his disciples, "I am the way and the truth and the life, no one comes to the Father except through me."(John 14:6). The Apostle John wrote, "For God so loved the world that he gave his one and only Son, that whoever believes in Him shall not perish but have eternal life. For God did not send his Son into the world to condemn the world, but to save the world through Him. Whoever believes in Him is not condemned, but whoever does not believe stands condemned already because he has not believed in the name of God's one and only Son" (John 3:16-18). The Apostle John, who spent three years with Jesus, wrote in 1 John 5:11-12: "God has given us eternal life, and this life is in His Son. He who has the Son has life; He who does not have the Son of God does not have life." Acts 4:12 states, "Salvation is found in no one else [Jesus], for there is no other name under heaven given to men by which we must be saved." Jesus said, "My sheep listen to my voice; I know them and they follow me. I give them eternal life, and they shall never perish" (John 10:27). You can't earn your way to Heaven. The Apostle Paul wrote, "For it is by grace you have been saved, through faith—and this is not from yourselves, it is the gift of God—not by works, so that no one can boast"(Ephesians 2:8-10). The Apostle Paul also wrote: "The righteous will live by faith" (Romans 1:17). We can do a lot for the church; we can help others outside of the church. We can be kind, but that will not earn us a place in heaven; it's only by faith in Jesus Christ. This is what I believe in reference to living eternally with Christ.

I also believe there is a hell because Jesus believed there is such a place. Jesus said hell was an "eternal fire" (Matthew 25:41), an "eternal punishment" (Matthew 25: 46). Jesus refers to hell in Matthew 5:29. Jesus said we should "not be afraid of those who kill the body ... rather, be afraid of the one who can destroy both soul and body in hell" (Matthew 10:28). Jesus told the Pharisees, a group that were very knowledgeable about the Bible and were respected leaders, that their religion was wrong and they were going to hell (Matthew 23:33). Jesus said, "Everyone who looks to the Son and believes in Him shall have eternal Life" (John 6:40). The opposite is eternal separation from God. Jesus said, "If anyone does not abide in me, he is like a branch that is thrown away and withers; such branches are picked up, thrown into the fire and burned" (John 15:6). I read that there are more Scriptures relating to hell than to heaven. If Jesus said it, I believe it. There is one fact that I think is ignored, that is, God is holy and hates sin. There is a consequence for every sin committed. The consequence takes place on earth, and unless there is a repenting spirit there could be eternal separation from God. Sin separates us from God, but through Jesus Christ we can be forgiven regardless of our sin. Just being a good person and doing good works will not earn you this gift. It is only through belief and faith in Jesus Christ and repentance of sin that we have this gift of living with Him for eternity. I know a belief is growing in our society that it doesn't matter what you believe because all roads lead to Heaven. The Christian Bible doesn't support this, but just the opposite. Jesus said, I believe the Bible is the word of God. In our striving to grow in our faith in Christ, Carole and I have received many blessings during our life together, and we have had prayers answered. We are thankful and have praised God for our blessings.

My favorite verses

I love Jesus Christ for what He has done for me and knowing that He first loved me at the cross. This verse says it well: "I have been crucified with Christ and I no longer live, but Christ lives in me. The life I live in the body, I live by faith in the Son of God, who loved me and gave himself for me" (Galatians 2:20). This is my belief! I praise Jesus for this!

Another verse I like to quote first thing in the morning is, "Be joyful always; pray continually; give thanks in all circumstances, for this is God's will for you in Christ Jesus" (1 Thessalonians 5:16-18). I think of Paul, in chains in a dungeon and in pain from a beating, praising and thanking God. I know where I'm going after this life, which is joy by itself. I realize from studying the Bible that God wants us to be in touch with Him throughout the day. We should be joyful. He wants us to talk with Him even though He knows our needs. Praising God is also uplifting for me.

The fruit of the Spirit is mentioned in several passages, but I like the Apostle Paul's statement recorded in Galatians 5:22: "The fruit of the Spirit is love, joy, peace, patience, kindness, goodness, faithfulness, gentleness and self-control. Against such things there is no law." Quoting this verse helps me to live by these traits, but I fail every day. My heavenly Father knows this, and I have asked Him to help me live a life filled with the fruit of the Spirit. I find it very hard to consistently display all of these traits. I need a lot of help. Actually, I need a Savior!

After I wrote my Faith Journey,, I started writing more articles on Scripture, which I have enjoyed doing. The Bible is truth, inspired by God. His hand is on every page. The Bible tells us how to live an abundant life, how to have a real and loving relationship with the living Jesus Christ, how to have His inner joy that stays with us, and most of all, His requirements for eternal life with Him. The Bible is my favorite book. Writing in reference to Scripture is a very enjoyable activity for me.

Answered prayers must be in Jesus Name

A couple of years ago while doing errands in Kingwood I turned on the Christian radio station. A man from Tibet was being interviewed on this station. He was a Muslim when the Chinese put him in prison because he had been identified as a terrorist. He said that while in prison he prayed to Allah, requesting something that I can't remember. He kept repeating this prayer request, but nothing ever happened. As he was praying for this same request, he heard a voice saying, "Pray in the name of Jesus." He did, and his prayer was answered. He became a Christian from this experience. I didn't hear the beginning of this interview, and I also missed the ending. What I heard gave me a desire to write a document in reference to praying to God in the name of Jesus.

When we pray, we should always be aware that due to Jesus' death on the cross and His resurrection He made it possible to become children of God. The writer of the Gospel of John wrote, "Yet to all who received Him, to those who believed in His name, He gave the right to become children of God, children born not of natural descent, nor of human decision or a husband's will, but born of God" (John 1: 12-13). Jesus also said, "I am the way and the truth and the life. No one comes to the Father except through me" (John 14: 6). Jesus is truth, the only way to His eternal kingdom. Acts 4:12 states, "Salvation is found in no one else [Jesus], for there is no other name under heaven given to men by which we must be saved. Jesus is the model for our life. His examples are recorded in the New Testament. We learn from Scripture that He was a person of prayer. The disciple John gives the reason for writing his Gospel: "These are written that you may believe that Jesus is the Christ, the Son of God, and that by believing you may have life in His name" (John 20: 31). Note the words "in his name." It's through Jesus Christ, our Lord and Savior.

Jesus died for us. He has all authority in heaven and on earth (Matthew 28: 18). He knows our needs and He knows all of our thoughts and spoken words. All of our prayers need to be in His name. The Apostle Paul wrote in I Timothy 1: 5, "For there is one God and one mediator between God and men, the man Christ Jesus." Paul also wrote: "Who is he that condemns? Christ Jesus, who died, more than that, who was raised to life, is at the right hand of God and is also interceding for us" (Romans 8:34). It is through Jesus Christ that we are linked to heaven. He represents us to God. He is our spokesman to God. No other person can represent us to God. It is only and strictly Jesus, the one who died for us. Thus it is important that every prayer to God be in Jesus' name. If we want a response to our prayers, we must make our requests in the name of Jesus. He is the one who died for us and is our representative to God as stated above.

I have had prayers answered when I prayed in Jesus name. Below are Scriptures supporting praying in Jesus' name.

Colossians 3: 17: "And whatever you do, whether in word or deed, do it all in the name of the Lord Jesus, giving thanks to God the Father through Him [Jesus]."

John 14: 12-13: "I tell you the truth, anyone who has faith in me [Jesus] will do what I have been doing. He will do even greater things than these, because I am going to the Father. And I will do whatever you ask in my name, so that the Son may bring glory to the Father."

John 14:14: "You may ask me for anything in my name, and I will do it." I'm adding another verse from John 15: 7: "If you remain in me and my words remain in you, ask whatever you wish, and it will be given you." It is assumed that when we ask in Jesus' name, we have to put our faith in Him and will only ask what is in accordance to His will. If we don't receive a response to our request, the response may be delayed or it's not in accordance to Jesus' will. Jesus hears all of our prayers to God prayed in His name.

John 15: 16: Jesus said, "You did not choose me, but I chose you and appointed you to go and bear fruit, fruit that will last. Then the Father will give you whatever you ask in my name."

John 16: 23-24: Jesus said, "I tell you the truth, my Father will give you whatever you ask in my name. Until now you have not asked for anything in my name. Ask and you will receive and your joy will be complete."

Ephesians 5: 20 "Always giving thanks to God the Father for everything in the name of our Lord Jesus Christ."

I Thessalonians 5: 16-18 "Be joyful always; pray continually; give thanks in all circumstances, for this is God's will for you in Christ Jesus."

God has one standard. To be His child, to gain eternal life, to have a loving and real relationship with God, and to have prayers answered, we must follow the requirements established by God. God hasn't changed. God is the same yesterday, today, and into the future. Reading New Testament Scripture reveals God's standard and requirements for that special relationship with God.

How to Pray and Prayers

As followers of Jesus Christ (Christians), we need to live by Jesus' examples as taught to his first generation of followers. The followers of Jesus noted that He prayed to His Heavenly Father on a regular basis. The twelve disciples asked Jesus to teach them to pray. Jesus said that our prayers should include that God be glorified. Second, that God's will be accomplished in our lives. Third, we should ask for our needs, even though God is aware of them, God wants us to ask for our necessities. Fourth, we need to repent of our sins to God. This request is throughout both the Old and New Testaments. This is significant to God. Repentance includes avoiding sin. Lastly, we need to ask God to help us to avoid situations that will tempt us to sin. That is the model of prayer given to us from Jesus Christ.

Being followers of Jesus Christ, I believe we all need to have a daily routine of praying and learning what God wants our life to be through studying Scripture, attending a church where the Gospel of Jesus Christ is preached, and associating with people having the same faith in Jesus Christ as we do. It is God's desire for us to strive to be more and more like Jesus. Am I like Jesus? Absolutely NOT! I'm trying and stumbling, but I have made a little progress during my many years here on earth. It's impossible to duplicate Jesus' life, but still I believe that striving for it is what God wants us to do. You can summarize Jesus Christ's life in one word: LOVE! Love needs to be our life's standard of living. This includes loving Jesus with all of our heart, soul, mind, and strength. God knows what is needed to have a satisfactory and abundant life and to have a soul of joy and peace in Him, which the world can't give to us. The guide for this life is called the Bible. I believe a follower of Jesus Christ can overcome the bad things that happen in our lives, including persecution due to our faith. I also believe that prayer is power! Praying in the name of Jesus Christ is the connection to God through Jesus Christ.

I like what Dr. Jim Jackson, senior pastor of Chapelwood Methodist Church in Spring Branch, Texas said in reference to prayer. "Prayer is how we get the strength to do what we must do." He also said, "Prayer enables things to happen on earth that would not have happened if we had not prayed." This is truth! As stated before, prayer through Jesus Christ is power!

One example of prayer power in my life took place at the airport in Anchorage, Alaska. Carole and I were waiting to fly home. A young mother with two small girls, one about eight years old and the other four or five years old, sat down in the seats directly across from us. The mother, dressed in business attire, was holding a cell phone to her left ear and had a legal pad binder on her lap with a pen in her right hand. She was trying to listen and at the same time was writing on her legal pad. The oldest girl sat on the floor playing, but the younger girl stood next to her mother crying and wanting to be picked up. The mother was holding out her left elbow, apparently hoping the little girl could hold on to it and be satisfied while she was doing her business. The little girl kept on crying and crying. I felt sorry for both the mother trying to attend to business and the little girl needing to be loved. I closed my eyes and asked God to have this little girl feel loved and for her to have contentment. After I said "in the name of Jesus Christ, Amen," the girl immediately stopped crying and then sat down with her sister and seemed content. She did not cry anymore while they were there. Of course, after this answered prayer, I thanked God. It is very, very important that we always thank God for every answered prayer and for every blessing received.

In his first letter to the church at Thessalonica, Greece, the Apostle Paul said, "Be joyful always; pray continually; give thanks for all circumstances for this is God's will for you through Christ Jesus" (I Thessalonians 5: 16-18). Note that we should have joy in our heart for what Jesus has done for us and for being our Savior. Paul is saying that it is God's will, through Jesus Christ, that we should be in prayer mode throughout the day and thus talk to God anytime during our waking hours. We should be in a prayer mode whenever a situation of need arises. Being in this mode is to have an awareness that Jesus Christ is in us by faith and with us. I believe reading and studying New Testament Scripture and prayer can eventually put us in this mode. It's a wonderful mode to be in. This mode can help us to pray for people we know and don't know. Sometimes you may want to pray for someone you don't know, such as people you see in the newspaper or TV.

Prayer is centering on God/Jesus and being aware of God. Being in a room of silence will help you reach this awareness. Prayer is talking to our Heavenly Father just like you would talk to your earthly father. God knows your situation, but He wants you to tell Him about the situation. Prayer and faith in Jesus Christ build a relationship with Him. This real relationship with God through Jesus Christ can be a reality for every one of us. Without prayer and faith in Jesus Christ we can't please God, and thus there is no relationship with God.

It should be noted that all prayers need to be in Jesus' name if we want our prayer to be answered by God. I refuse to be politically correct about being a follower of Jesus Christ and wanting my prayers to go to God through Jesus Christ, the only one who intercedes for us (I Timothy 2:5, Ephesians 2: 16 and 18, Hebrews 7:25 and 8:6, Romans 8:34). Jesus is our Lord and Savior and this role as mediator comes from Jesus' death on the cross and His resurrection! He is our high Priest! He loves us! He is with us! This is Wow! Awesome! How can we not thank Jesus many times for what He did for us? What a gift from Jesus! How do you measure the value of this gift?

Billy Graham once said: "The Scripture says that the only mediator between God and man is Jesus Christ. You must know Him, and you must pray in His name. Your prayers must be directed according to the will of God" (*Decision Magazine*, January 2011). This statement has been proven in my prayer life. Prayer through Jesus Christ has power and can have results that we cannot accomplish ourselves. Does that mean all prayers will be answered? No! The timing may not be right, our request is not in accordance to God's plan, or He has something better for us to be given at a later time. God's plan may not be our plan because his plan stretches out to the end of life here on earth.

As followers of Jesus Christ, it's important to pray for God's responses for needed major decisions such as switching jobs, moving, or marriage to a particular person. Prayers are also welcome for answers to solutions and decisions relating to our employment. I found that God's responses may be through the Holy Spirit or a direct response verbally.

Some prayers

Heavenly Father, help me to have the fellowship with you that you desire. Speak to me as I read and study your words and to be a person of prayer. Let your words come alive within my heart. Let me be aware of your love for me throughout the day and may this love flow to others who I will meet today. May my relationship with you grow and may joy from Jesus Christ fill my heart. In Jesus' name, Amen.

A prayer based on Apostle Paul's prayer to the church at Colosse, Turkey: "Heavenly Father, help me to understand your will for my life and to gain spiritual wisdom. May my life be one pleasing to you and bearing good fruit through good works and growing in the knowledge of you. May I be filled with your strength and have great endurance and patience and be filled with the joy of Jesus Christ and keep me always on the right path that leads to life eternal with Jesus Christ. In Jesus name, Amen" (Colossians 1: 9-12). This is a great prayer from the greatest evangelist! Many scholars believe that Paul died during April 68, AD. He would have been over seventy years old, which was a very old man at this time.

Parts of this prayer may be used to pray for others. These parts are: understand God's will, gain spiritual wisdom, please and honor God, bear good fruit (see Galatians 5: 22, "The fruit of the Spirit is love, joy, peace [comes from God], patience, kindness, goodness, faithfulness, gentleness and self-control"), grow in the knowledge of God, be filled with God's strength, have great endurance and patience, stay full of Christ's joy.

The author of this prayer is unknown: "Lord, I hunger for your Word. Teach me in the way that I should go and help me to walk in your truth each day. May your praise always be on my lips, and may you fill my heart with the joy of your love and blessing. You are a gracious and loving God whose mercy is new every morning. In Jesus name, Amen."

A prayer for forgiveness and glorifying: "Lord Jesus, I'm a sinner, but you are perfect and sinless. Because of my sins, you were tortured on a cross. Be merciful to me and forgive me my sins and help me to make my life a model of you as recorded in the New Testament. Help me to have a life consisting of love and kindness. Fill me with your spirit and never leave me, for you are my Savior and I want my life to be filled with your spirit. Your name will be glorified for eternity. May it be so in my life. In your name I ask this. Amen."

A prayer by Ann Spangler: "Father; it's your love that heals us, body and soul. Thank you for the way you reveal this tremendous love through other people. Help me to realize that persistent prayer is nothing other than persistent love. May I remember this when I am tempted to quit praying. As I persist, reveal your love through me. In Jesus name, Amen."

Dr. Paul Cedar's prayer for our national leaders: "I pray for the president of the United States and for those leaders who serve with him. I pray that you will be with him and that he will have success in all that he does. I pray that you would give him discretion and understanding and that he would be strong and courageous. May he not be afraid or become discouraged. Instead, may he trust in you with all of his heart! I pray this in the wonderful name of Jesus. Amen."

Lastly, commit to Christ, commit to praying daily, strive to establish a life based on Jesus' example, and commit to growing in your faith and trust in Jesus Christ. To end this document, I have included a quote from the Life Application Bible Commentary-Romans: "God is at the center of a Christian's life. God supplies the power for the Christian's daily living. Believers find that their whole way of looking at the world changes when they belong to Christ." Amen!

Identifying The Upper Room House

For many years I wondered where the house was where Jesus and his disciples held the Last Supper in the upper room. One morning in 2013 when I was reading Acts 12: 2-17, the information I wrote below flooded my mind and I was convinced that the upper room was in the home of John Mark's mother. Here is how I came to this conclusion.

Jesus asked Peter and John to go prepare the Passover supper. Jesus told them when they enter the walled city of Jerusalem; they would see a man carrying water. They were to follow him to the house he entered. At that time they were to ask for the owner of that house and tell this person, "The Teacher asks: 'Where is the guest room, where I may eat the Passover with my disciples?' He will show you a large upper room, all furnished. Make preparations there" (Luke 22: 7-13 and Mark 14: 12-16).

The Last Supper was held in a two-story house, and apparently the person bringing water to this house was a servant of the owner. Such a house reveals that the owner was wealthy. Jesus received an offer from this wealthy homeowner to use a large furnished upper room for his last meal with his disciples. In my opinion, this reflects that the house owner was a believer in Jesus. Jesus knew when the servant or perhaps a slave would be bringing water for the household. This function of a man getting water for the house was unusual since this was usually a woman's job. It's interesting to note that Jesus didn't say ask for the "man" of the house, but instead the owner of the house. I believe this could be interpreted as Jesus knowing that the owner was a woman.

John Mark is the author of the Gospel of Mark. At the end of the story of Jesus' arrest, he writes, "A young man, wearing nothing but a linen garment, was following Jesus. When they seized him, he fled naked, leaving his garment behind" (Mark 14: 51-52). This event would have been sometime around 1:00 to 2:00 a.m. Friday morning. The person with the linen garment has to be John Mark. The linen garment indicates a person with wealth. Apparently John Mark wanted to be added to his story in the Gospel. The community would have been asleep at this time, and no one would have been aware of Jesus' arrest unless they were in the same house. When Jesus left the house with his disciples, John Mark put on his garment and followed Jesus and the disciples. He was somewhat close to the room where Jesus had the supper with his disciples. John Mark probably heard the conversations and apparently followed Jesus and the disciples when they walked to the Mount of Olives at Gethsemane.

Now we go forward to Jesus departing to heaven after the forty-day period of appearing many times to his followers. On his final appearance He ascended to heaven. Right after this event Luke records that after Jesus was lifted up to heaven, these followers of Jesus walked back to Jerusalem and went upstairs to the room where they were staying (Acts 1:12-14). This has to be the same two-story house where Jesus had the Last Supper. This group consisted of Peter, John, James, Andrew, Philip, Thomas, Bartholomew, Matthew, James son of Alphaeus, Simon the Zealot, Judas, son of James, women not named, Mary the mother of Jesus, and Mary's other sons (Jesus' stepbrothers). Remember that the disciples didn't have homes in Jerusalem, nor did the women and others in the group. Most of these people were from Galilee. I believe one of the women not named is Mary, the owner of the house and mother of John Mark. Acts 1:15 Shortly after this ("in those days") the group of 120 believers were together, which would have to be in a building with a large room. I believe they were still meeting at the house of John Mark's mother.

On Pentecost Day, we read in Acts 2: 1, "They were all together in one place. Suddenly a sound like the blowing of a violent wind came from heaven and filled the whole house where they were sitting." "All" has to refer to all of the believers, which would have been a large group. I'm assuming this "all" is the same 120 people mentioned above. This scripture also states it was in a house, which has to be the same house as the Passover meal Jesus had with his disciples.

In Acts 12:2-17 we read that Peter was led out of prison by an angel and walked to the house of John Mark's mother. Luke states that the house owner was Mary (Acts 12: 12), the mother of John Mark. This Scripture states that many believers were praying for Peter in this house. To me this indicates that the house was a meeting place for believers since Peter knew believers would be at this house. We also learn that Mary had a servant girl named Rhoda, and that this house had an outer door and an inner door to the house. Does this confirm that all of the above events were in this house? I believe so. Mary and son John Mark were believers, and this was a large home. Second, the house was used for believers to meet, and it was used for Jesus and his disciples' Last Supper. Since Luke refers to the owner as Mary, this is a clue that her husband wasn't alive. The large house, servant girl, and probably a manservant or slaves that fetched water every day all indicate that Mary was wealthy.

We know that the Jews didn't recognize women as being important and any contribution they made would most likely not be publicly recorded. The Gospels of Matthew, Mark, and John rarely mention women in their writings. On the other hand, Luke, a doctor and a Gentile, recognized women's contribution to Jesus' ministry. Luke provides the majority of the information that we have regarding Jesus' mother Mary and the birth of Jesus Christ. Luke also states that it was women who financed Jesus' ministry. In his Gospel, chapter 8, verses 1-3, he wrote, "After this, Jesus traveled about from one town and village to another, proclaiming the good news of the kingdom of God. The twelve were with him and also some women who had been cured of evil spirits and diseases; Mary (called Magdalene) from whom seven demons had come out; Joanna the wife of Cuza, the manager of Herod's household; Susanna; and many others. These women were helping to support Jesus out of their own means." I'm sure one of these nameless financial supporters was John Mark's mother, Mary.

Did Jesus Christ Rise From The Dead?

It's my understanding the Jews believe Jesus' body was stolen and Islam believes that Jesus was only a great prophet and never went to the cross. They believe He eventually went off somewhere and had a quiet life and died a natural death. The four Gospels of Mark, Matthew, Luke, and John in the New Testament record the resurrection. Mark (John Mark) knew Jesus but was not one of the twelve disciples. Tradition states that John Mark recorded his Gospel after interviewing the disciple Peter. Matthew and John walked with Jesus, and Luke interviewed those who knew Jesus before and after the resurrection, and from his notes he wrote his Gospel and also the book of Acts.

Crucifixion was a horrifying death because it was an extremely painful experience that could last up to three days. It was also humiliating since the victim was nude, nailed to the cross. When Jesus experienced this death, his followers, except John, went into hiding because there was fear among them that they too would be arrested and experience this death. Jesus' disciples, the women, and other believers were locked in the upper room, probably in the home of John Mark's parents. Other believers of Jesus were scattered in hiding.

The Gospel writers recorded Jesus' appearances to His followers after his death. It is also recorded that he appeared to a group of 500 men. It is recorded that Jesus appeared to his eleven disciples (and probably a few more) several times during the forty days after his resurrection.

This resurrection of Jesus Christ is truth because:

- His followers became fearless because they knew that Jesus was the Son of God that Jesus was alive and His message was truth. No matter what happened to them, they had a place in heaven with Jesus.
- Jesus' followers became fearless and turned the world upside down. This would not have happened if there was no resurrection.
- There would be no Christianity if the resurrection didn't take place. Jesus would have been considered a prophet and very little would be known of Him.
- The eleven original disciples and other believers, except John, were all tortured to death. No one would accept being tortured to death if they knew their message was a complete lie.
- If there was no resurrection, the followers of Jesus would have gone back to their previous lives and Jesus' message would have been forgotten.
- To this day, Jesus continues to change lives for those coming to Him in faith and repentance.

Other Writings

National league championship: St. Louis vs. Houston
Game five, Monday evening, October 17, 2005

On Monday, October 17, I was thinking how great it would be to attend the evening game which was game five of the series. I was confident that Houston would beat St. Louis that evening to win Houston's first National League Pennant. Houston was up three games to one in the best of seven series. During the afternoon I received a call from a fellow worker, Candace. She was a big Houston Astros fan and loved baseball. She was calling from Las Vegas, Nevada. She and her husband were on vacation there. That day he had flown to Japan for business and she was on the plane to Houston. She said she had an extra ticket, standing room only, and wanted to know if I wanted it. I was the first person she contacted because she knew I too was a big fan of the Astros and baseball. I immediately told her that I would take it and asked her what she wanted for it. She just wanted to give it to me. I did reimburse her the original cost of twenty-six dollars plus I purchased a game program for her when I was in the stadium. She said she would drive from the airport and should arrive at the stadium around 6:00 p.m. I was told to meet her at the will-call window. At 6:00 p.m. I arrived at the will-call window area, but it took me a couple of minutes to locate her.

The ground floor was just packed with people, so I suggested we go up to the top level to section 425/325 since we had to stand. The large majority of the standing ticket holders would pick the first level. Section 425/325 was between home plate and first plate and we would have a good view of the playing field. After getting some food, we walked to this section. I told Candace, "Let's sit in the terrace section, section 325." There are only around eight rows in this section, and I picked the fourth and fifth seat, the third row from the back. I told her these were great seats, but when the ticket holders came to claim these seats we would just stand on the deck, the entrance area to this level.

Thousands of ticket holders kept coming in and the seats around us were filling up. We both thought we would have to give up our seats shortly. Shortly after the game started, it appeared that all of the seats around us were taken except the first six seats in the row where we were seated. We made it through an inning, and we were both surprised that no one had claimed our seats. Three other people filled the first three seats, but they were not the ticket holders for these seats. I told Candace that if we made it through the first four innings, these seats should be ours, which was the case. Deep into the game it appeared that there were no vacant seats in the stadium. I had never seen this before in sold-out games.

Houston took their lead into the ninth inning. The crowd was loud throughout this game, more than I have ever experienced at any previous baseball game. It got louder at the top of the ninth inning. Everyone thought Houston had the pennant, and everyone was ready to celebrate. A machine for shooting confetti into the air was placed near our row in the entrance area. Everyone was excited that Houston would win their first pennant in just a few minutes. When Brad Lidge came in, I began to have a sick feeling. I was surprised that he was called to pitch the ninth since he had almost lost the last two games.

When he struck out the first two batters in the ninth inning, I started to think he would succeed this time. Then with two strikes, David Eckstein singled. I was concerned! Then Lidge walked Jim Edmonds, with Albert Pujols the next batter. At this time I had a strong feeling that Pujols was going to hit a home run to win the game. I didn't want to look anymore, but I didn't sit down. I was hoping that the manager Phil Gardner would take Lidge out, but that wasn't the case and Pujols did hit the home run. The crowd was really into this game and they were loud, but it ended with the home run. I was disappointed that I wasn't going to experience being at the Houston Astros game that won the pennant. I also believed that they couldn't win one of two games in St. Louis, but they did!

Due to the fact that everyone left the game at the same time, I had to wait a while in my car before I could get out to the street. I thought a lot about this game and my feelings of disappointment. My thoughts were centered on the eternal value of this game. The answer was none. There was no eternal value from this evening's experience. What provides true eternal value is our relationship with Jesus Christ and living a life by His standard, not the standard of the world. It is His will that we stay connected to Jesus Christ on a daily basis. God has blessed my life tremendously. Life with Him is eternal. The peace and joy from Him is lasting value. It's priceless.

Rick's journal entry from June 20, 2006, from Anchorage, Alaska

We had a long phone conversation with Jody this morning. She and John are a blessing to us. She may have a medical problem, but she is determined that this problem will not decrease her faithfulness to Christ. She wants God's will in her life even if she has to deal with a major medical problem. She wants His name to be glorified in her life even while dealing with a medical problem. It was very uplifting to our souls this morning. A true relationship with Christ brings God's love into our lives. Christ has made Jody a beautiful (spiritual) person. John is also a Christ-loving person. Their love for Christ will strengthen their love for each other, and then they will understand the passage from God that the two will become one. This has happened to Carole and me. Our love for each other is stronger than ever. God has also given us many blessings and we also know where our future eternal home will be. That new life and home will be better than any home on earth. Only through Christ will we have this eternal home. Thank you, Jesus! You are the Lord of our lives and we will praise you!

Email message sent to family and friends in reference to Hurricane Rita

It appears that the worst of Rita is over for all of us on the west side of Houston. We still have gusts of wind that make the tree branches roll back and forth and will probably have rain showers off and on this weekend. We really do need the rain since we have only received an inch of rain from this storm; so far we are very grateful and thankful that our area was spared from Rita's wrath. We feel badly for those east of us that have suffered extensive damage to their homes and businesses, and those who tried to get out but ran out of gas on the highways. This proves that you cannot evacuate the majority of Houston's population during a seventy-two-hour timeframe. In addition, there is not enough gasoline to do this.

We didn't sleep much last night because the wind was very loud off and on. A few times we got up to check out what was happening outside. We also got very little sleep Wednesday night. I was very much concerned in regard to this storm. We heard that this would be the strongest hurricane to hit Texas. We could have had winds up to one hundred miles an hour in our area. Houses here are built to withstand winds up to seventy-five mph. I was not very comfortable about all of this. Late Wednesday afternoon at work we were told to clean up our area, secure all confidential papers, and remove all loose important documents near the windows. The building I work in is constructed with all-glass walls with a lot of trees around it. Apparently Mayor White of Houston had asked all employers to close their offices Wednesday, which was a good thing due to the evacuation of two to two and a half million people.

Yesterday, Wednesday, while talking to some of the neighbors we learned that some of the families in our subdivision attempted to get out, but after burning up most of their gas within a short distance they turned around and came home. We thought about leaving for Fort Worth where our son lives, but we realized we could not get there due to the gas shortage and the hundreds of thousands of cars trying to get out. Our good neighbor next to us told us Wednesday night they were leaving for Dallas but were going to take a longer western route. They left between 9:30-10:00 p.m. Wednesday evening. We learned that they arrived near College Station at 7:00 a.m. and that was not even close to being halfway to Dallas. The normal time from here to College Station is only one and a half hours. By Wednesday morning there was no gas in our area. Most of the businesses were closed, and the traffic in our area was horrifying with long lines of cars going north. Cars were lined up at gas stations, hoping that a gas tanker would arrive. Carole and I have never seen anything like this.

We packed almost all of our family things along with a few other things. We also taped the windows, rearranged some things in the house, and moved the pots from the patio to the garage. I found one plywood sheet in the garage that I used to cover up our dining room window. We spent hours packing and rearranging things in the house. Now we have to undo all of this, but it's worth it. I'm sure the people east of us would all be glad to have a trade-off. Our loss is only a yard full of debris from trees, but no trees are down on our street. In addition, we lost our chimney covering. We found it in the yard this morning.

Carole and I prayed a lot during these past two days. We believed that no matter what happened to everything we own, God would be with us and would help us to get back on our feet. I wanted to save all of our pictures (thousands) documenting our lives from the 1960's and older pictures of our families, but even these are not that important in terms of eternity. We have learned that there are only two things that really matter in life. That is our relationship to God/ Christ, and our family and friends. Nothing else has eternal value. If we lost everything I'm sure we would be grateful for these things. We are thankful for all of you who told us you would be praying for us during this time. We were very conscious of this fact during these past two days. Carole and I greatly appreciate your prayers. It meant a lot to us. Now we will start to reverse what we did yesterday and Wednesday. We are thankful for this blessing of life and having a home intact. We are very thankful through Christ that we can have a real and loving relationship with God. Carole and I have been truly blessed and our family and friends are a part of this blessing.
Rick and Carole Wilcox
September 24, 2005

Letter to my brother shortly after I heard of his diagnosis of cancer, December 4, 2007

Dear Phil,

Every day I have been thinking about you and praying for you, Phil, ever since we got word of your illness. You are dear to me and not only do I love you, I really appreciate you being my brother. I have also admired you for your generosity and your warm, friendly personality. These are the characteristics that Mother had, a personality that is warm and friendly and very outgoing. That's a wonderful asset to have. Even though we don't see each other very often, we have a special relationship between us.

These are thoughts I have had, and I wanted to put them in writing. We all have memories that perhaps at times we would love to relive. Of course, this is impossible. I have wonderful memories from our Ferndale days, my Adrian College days with Carole, and wonderful memories of when Carole and I lived in Germany, our Kalamazoo years, and our home in Houston where our sons James and John grew up. There are also great memories of the many times we all spent with Mom and Dad at Daytona Beach Shores, Florida. Even James and John remember some of these wonderful times. I'm sure Stephanie and Scott also have great memories of these days. Sometimes I wish we could go back in time and enjoy them again with you, Bonnie, Mom, Dad, Stephanie, Scott, James, and John. As you know, we can't go back. Life is multiple chapters. Once we have lived out a chapter in our life, it's closed, finished! A new chapter opens up; the scene may be different and some of the characters involved in this chapter are new and some are excluded in this new chapter. One day the book will be closed! It will be finished! The End! But is it? Those who have their faith in Christ will receive His promise. That promise is life with Him, forever and ever! A life that is grander than anything we can imagine. Once we are in His Kingdom, we will never want to go back to our earthly life because death is actually a beginning for those who have placed their faith in Christ.

Phil, Carole and I are praying and pulling for you. We know you have had some hard times and there will be more ahead of you, but we will pray that in the future your body will not react to the treatments as severely as perhaps other people have. When I phoned Dad while he was in the hospital, I believe in 1979, he said, "Christ really suffered, didn't He?" I said, "Yes, Dad, He really did suffer for us." You can make this journey these next few months, Phil. I'm confident that these treatments will be successful. Remember that Christ is with you and He has a great love for you. He suffered for all of us because of His great love for us. I wish I could do something to heal you, Phil, but all I can do is pray for you. You are a great brother and I'm proud to be your brother!

Here are two verses that I like. Galatians 2: 20, "I have been crucified with Christ and I no longer live, but Christ lives in me. The life I live in the body, I live by faith in the Son of God, who loved me and gave himself for me." The second one I try to repeat when I first get up. I Thessalonians 5:16 "Be joyful always; pray continually; give thanks in all circumstances, for this is God's will for you in Christ Jesus." I think of Saint Paul in prison, chained and in pain from his severe beating, and he is praising the Lord. These verses have much meaning for me. Here is another verse that I like, from I Peter 5:7: "Cast all your anxiety on Him because he cares for you."

Phil, you are on our minds and we love you! There is light at the end of the tunnel! Hold on!

Love, your brother Rick
Note: On October 30, 2014, Phil, moved to his eternal home.

Chapter 31

Our Fiftieth Anniversary
1963   December 21   2013

My letter to Carole

Dear Carole,

    Our fiftieth wedding anniversary came so fast! What a marriage we have had! It's been just wonderful! God has showered us with many blessings! The years flew!

    Do you remember? It started on September 16, 1960, the Friday of our first week of the new school year at Adrian College. I spotted three girls during that first week and hoped to meet them at the Friday evening dance. You were a freshman and I a sophomore. The dance was called "Getting to know you" and held in Ridge Gymnasium. When this Friday evening came, I walked to the gym and as I entered I spotted you sitting by yourself, wearing a black skirt and a white blouse. I immediately wanted to dance with you and you accepted my invitation. After our first dance I thanked you and you went back to your seat. I spotted one of the three girls I wanted to meet, but you were on my mind while I was dancing with this other girl. There was something about you that I really liked. When this dance ended, I thanked the other girl and walked toward your direction, thankful that you were still seated there. I was never into rock and roll, but the slow cheek-to-cheek music was my style. I asked you for another dance and you accepted. We visited while we danced, and I kept you for a few dances then I asked if we could go for a walk, and you accepted. We spent the rest of the evening walking and talking. I had a strong feeling of liking you. Before the evening was over, I asked for a movie date for the following evening and you accepted. I walked back to my dorm with a happy, warm heart. It was only a short time before I developed a very strong love for you.

    Eventually we spent more time together on the campus, eating meals, church attendance, and campus activities such as travelogues, football games, and basketball games. There was always a dance after every home football and basketball game and we were at every one of them. During the summer I would visit you in Niles, and you even spent part of three Christmas school breaks with my family and me at my parents' house. My parents loved you and were happy that we were married.

    During your first semester of your senior year at Adrian College I was in basic training at Ft. Knox, Kentucky, for nine weeks and advance training at Ft Polk, Louisiana, for another nine weeks. I was drafted in early August 1963. How I missed you during my army life. I proposed to you by letter from Ft. Knox. My letter and the rings were mailed to you and on the box I wrote, "Do not open until Sept. 16th", our third anniversary of meeting each other. My late phone call on the 16th to you confirmed that you wanted to be my wife (I really didn't doubt that you wanted to marry me, but I wanted to hear, "YES!"). My final completion date at Ft. Polk, Louisiana (December 14, 1963) was also the date when the army stopped transferring men to their new assigned locations, so I was able to come home to marry my

Adrian College sweetheart. We believe God made all of this possible. We are thankful for this wonderful blessing from the King of Kings.

After you graduated from Adrian College (May 31, 1964) you went home to my parent's house. Dad and Mom drove you to the airport the following morning and put you on the plane for London, England. We met at the airport terminal on June 2, 1964, around 7:15 a.m. local time. We were finally together as husband and wife. What a joy this was! It was basically our honeymoon, and what a great time we had! Every day was wonderful as we traveled around England and Scotland. Then the time came to travel to our home waiting for us in Goppingen, Germany.

While in Germany we were able to have many three and four day passes, and also the month of June 1965 off duty that allowed us to travel all around Europe with my parents. The Stein family that befriended us made our stay in Germany more special. What a wonderful era we had during our life in Germany. We are thankful to God for the wonderful opportunity we had in Europe.

We made our home in Kalamazoo, Michigan after I was discharged from the U.S. Army. We had friends and families in southern Michigan. Then we moved to Houston in July 1970 and our family came to be, two wonderful sons, James and John. Our relationship with Jesus Christ continued to grow; we felt that Christ was the head of our family and we became one under Christ. Our marriage and love for each other has always been strong. You were the perfect mother, always there when James or John needed you. You always supported me and showed a great love and respect for me. Our marriage, even after fifty years, consists of a strong love for each other. You have been the perfect wife! In all of our many trips we took as a family, and just the two of us, it was always a fun time. You have always been my best friend. Now, my Adrian College sweetheart, happy fiftieth anniversary! What a ride it has been. God made it possible! He brought us together and we are His adopted children, made possible through Jesus Christ. Our life together may end briefly on earth, but continues when we are in Christ's kingdom. Listen! Can you still hear Ma Shipman on the campus saying, "There are the inseparables!"

Our prayer: Thank you, Heavenly Father, for our very special marriage and the great experiences we have had and what Jesus Christ has done for our lives. Father, we love you dearly! Guide us for the rest of our lives here on earth, when death becomes victory!

Your husband of fifty years. You are special and I love you.
Rick Wilcox

My Journal

Our fiftieth wedding anniversary came so fast! What a marriage we have had! It's been just wonderful! God has showered us with many blessings! The years flew, the blessings grew!

Carole and I first met at a dance on September 16, 1960, at Adrian College, Adrian, Michigan. We became engaged on September 16, 1963, and married on December 21, 1963. Carole was in her senior year at Adrian College and I was on short leave between Ft. Polk, Louisiana, and Germany when we were married at First Methodist Church, Niles, Michigan. It's interesting that Carole's great-grandparents, Artemus Daniel and Cora Edith Bartholomew, were married at this same church on December 21, 1892.

When the year 2013 became a reality we became more focused on December 21, 2013. The last couple of months before this date I thought about our fiftieth every day. Like any other day, it came and it went. Carole and I had a fun time on the 20th and 21st of December. We referred to Dec. 21st as "The Big Day." Earlier in the month of December Carole had her hair cut very similar to the way it was on December 21, 1963. She thought it was too short on the back of her neck, and she was right. She received many compliments on her hairstyle from our pinochle group, Sunday school class, and other church members. She also received compliments when we attended a Christmas party with our former Sunday school class at Chapelwood United Methodist Church in Spring Branch, and also from neighbors here in Kingwood. She has never received as many compliments as she did from this hairstyle. She does look younger with this shorter hairstyle. I got a haircut about two weeks prior to our Big Day and no one said anything! Prior to December, I purchased two red dresses and two skirts that I liked for Carole. She wore these outfits off and on during these two days, mainly to be photographed by her favorite photographer, ME!

On Friday the 20th we had breakfast at home, and then we got dressed up and headed to a photographer's shop for our official fiftieth pictures. Carole wore one of her new dresses and brought the other one to change into. She looked great in both outfits. The session lasted about two hours. They took over one hundred pictures, and we had to pick the best of thirty-seven different settings. It was actually fun. After the photographing session we went to the mall and did a little shopping. We knew what we wanted, and it didn't take long to find the items, but were unsuccessful in finding red flat shoes for Carole.

After shopping we went to our area's favorite restaurant in our large area, Italiano's, for our lunch/dinner meal. We love their hot rolls made onsite. We always order lasagna. I try to restrict myself to only four rolls. I stuff the lasagna in the rolls; what a tasty excellent meal. The few times we've had pizza at this restaurant I do the same, stuffing the pizza into the rolls. So good! One waitress remembers me based on that fact. It's a mystery why more people haven't discovered the best way to eat pizza and lasagna.

The following day, The Big Day, came. I was in awe of it, recalling memories of Adrian College and our honeymoon in the United Kingdom. I took a train from Stuttgart, Germany, to London, England, to meet Carole in London. My parents attended Carole's Adrian College graduation on May 31, 1964, and took her home to Ferndale, Michigan. In the morning they put Carole on an airplane and she landed in London on June 2, 1964, at 7:15 a.m. local time. I will never forget that moment of meeting Carole at the London airport terminal. It was the beginning of a life of husband and wife living together in our own home. It was a great honeymoon in England and Scotland.

We took John and the grandkids Ellie, Evan, and Ethan to IHOP. We told the waitress that this was our fiftieth. I believe we told just about everyone we met that this was our fiftieth! I asked her if she would take a picture of all of us. She wanted to do this, but couldn't get us all in due to the table next to ours. A lady at this table said she would take the picture. She took a couple of pictures from her table, with my camera, and they turned out very well.

John and the triplets gave us a very special present. It was a statue of a couple dancing cheek-to-cheek. We opened the box at IHOP and we were told that Ellie selected our special gift. When John mentioned that Ellie selected this present for us, I immediately knew why. On the previous Wednesday Ellie had told John her stomach was hurting so she stayed at our house for the day. While Carole was at Bible Study Fellowship, I told Ellie I was just finishing a letter to Grandma, a present for her for our fiftieth anniversary. I was making a few changes to complete this letter. Ellie asked me to read it to her. I told her that my document for [Grandma]Carole included things she would not understand, but I would read it to her. I read it to her, and she said, "I don't understand it all, but that is very good, Grandpa!" Ellie remembered from this letter that we met at a dance. When Ellie, her brothers, and John spotted this figurine, she knew this was the perfect gift for our fiftieth anniversary.

After IHOP we came home and I took a lot of pictures of Carole dressed up. I love seeing her in dresses and skirts. I must add that my love for her is just as strong as the day we were married if not stronger. We have grown very close to each other. I feel like we have become one. We are the best of friends. Carole is very loving and a very supportive wife. She is the perfect wife, and I'm blessed to have her for my wife.

On our first night together as wife and husband, we stayed at a Kalamazoo motel. I wanted a good picture of her in her wedding dress, which she had made. She sat on the end of the bed and supported herself with her right arm and her left arm was on her lap. I wanted to duplicate this picture, using our guestroom bed. I could not find a white dress that looked close to this original dress, so I had her wear one of the new red dresses. The picture turned out very similar to the 1963 picture, only she looked a little older on the current one.

Our plans for the day of December 21, 2013 were to attend the Taste of Texas, one of the best (or the best) steakhouses in Houston. It's a huge restaurant and is very attractive inside and out and includes many artifacts from Texas history. During this time of year this huge restaurant is heavily decorated for the Christmas season inside and out. It is about forty miles from our house here in Kingwood. Since the meals at this restaurant are heavy dinners, one needs to have an empty stomach. For that reason, we decided to go to our local donut shop for coffee and a treat for lunch. Carole wore one of her new skirts. There was a man that appeared to be in his forties with his three sons seated at a table. Carole and I took the other available table. I asked the woman behind the counter if she would take our picture. She wasn't too sure of herself doing this, but the man with the kids said he would. He was impressed that we were celebrating fifty years. He was interested in knowing more about us, and I told him that we were probably the only couple that got engaged by letters. I mentioned that Carole was a senior in college and I was in the army, knowing that I would be home before Christmas. I proposed to her by letter and she responded positively. I can't remember all that we told him. When he got up to leave he congratulated us again and said that it had been such a blessing for him to hear our story, and he appreciated this moment at the donut shop.

The Taste of Texas Restaurant does not take reservations. Every December we keep moving our leaving time a little earlier. This December I decided that we should leave at 3:30 p.m., which should reduce the waiting time by an hour. We arrived around 4:40 p.m. and the place was packed! I dropped Carole off and parked the car while she got a number. Our estimated wait time was one hour and forty-five minutes. It was close to two hours before we had a table. We walked next door to Bed and Bath to purchase picture frames. After making our purchase we wandered around the restaurant, looking at decorations and artifacts. One of the open rooms for waiting had televised high school football games, which I watched for a few minutes. There were three screens in this room with different football games. I also had a staff member take some pictures of us during our waiting time and at our table. During this waiting time we also went outside to their covered roof area. They had an old original horse-drawn four-seat sleigh. Carole and I sat in the front of this sleigh and a person took a good picture of us. I asked him to make sure the head and legs were in the picture. He did a great job centering the picture. I improved it by cropping the image.

Finally, we had our table for two, which was one of our favorite table locations, up against a short partition wall. We always order a ten-ounce filet and split it (cooked perfectly), a baked potato (cooked perfectly). Carole makes her salad at the salad bar. They make their own rolls, which is a miniature loaf of bread. I get the bread from a bun warmer next to the salad bar. There are also two huge blocks of cheese to cut from, and you take all of the hot rolls you want. Of course, you stuff a piece of the filet streak in the rolls. I restrict myself to eating only three rolls because that is what it takes for a five-ounce filet. There have been times I have eaten four of them because they are sooooo good! You may have guessed that good bread is my favorite food. I judge restaurants by their bread.

After our steak and potato, it was time for our complimentary dessert; as usual, we picked cheesecake with strawberries. So good! We also had their complimentary cinnamon coffee, which is also very good. They took our picture when the dessert was brought to the table. It was a fun evening. Shortly after we got home, we went to bed. It was a wonderful Saturday, and Friday was also a fun day.

Sunday morning was also special for us. The church bulletin announced our fiftieth at our current church, Kingwood United Methodist Church, as well as our previous church of over forty years, Chapelwood United Methodist Church. After the 8:30 p.m. church service we started receiving congratulations. We brought three-dozen donuts to our church class. The class was told that this was our fiftieth. I mentioned to the class that the number was high, but we were still young.

All of this was a very special time for Carole and me. It will be remembered.

Carole and I [Rick] are thankful to our Heavenly Father that we could experience our fiftieth wedding anniversary in very good health.

Rick & Carole Wilcox with their son John
and his children.
December 21, 1963

Carole and Rick Wilcox on their
50th anniversary at their favorite
restaurant, Taste of Texas, west
side of Houston.
December 21, 2013

Chapter 32

George N. Brown's 1849 Exposition to the Gold Fields of California.

His background and his letters.

George Nelson Brown
Image of him around 1849

My dad's mother, Susan Belle Wilcox, (1871-1948) is the daughter of George Nelson Brown. George Brown was born during 1817 and died during 1891. It is not known when he married Lucy J. Rudd. Lucy was born during 1835, but I speculate that it was when he returned from the gold fields of California they were married. My grandmother Susan Belle Wilcox was George and Lucy Brown's third child, born during 1871.

George Brown's birthplace is unknown as well as his earlier life. We know he went to the California gold fields during 1849. It is also unknown how successful he was in his gold mission, but he kept a gold nugget which was given to his daughter, my grandmother, Susan B. Wilcox. Eventually I became the owner of it. Sometime after his return from California, he settled in Joliet, Illinois with his employment being a school teacher. During his time in Joliet, he married Lucy J. Rudd, also a school teacher. I assume they taught at the same school. George and Lucy moved, probably during the late 1850's to Gobles, Michigan and lived there for the rest of their lives. They had four surviving children. He continued to be a school teacher in a small school house which was named after him. He also taught Sunday school, and he also did some preaching at a church.

James Marshall discovered gold at Coloma, California on January 24, 1848, at the American River, and the news of this discovery spread quickly across the United States and the world. Thousands saw California Gold fields as a ticket to wealth, and they made their way to California, seeking their dreams of wealth. This great historical event speeded California's increasing population resulting in a quick entry as a new state in 1850. I found it interesting that when this gold rush started, San Francisco was a small town and its population grew to over twenty-five thousand in one year.

Whyle S. Wilcox (brother to my father) in reference to this event wrote, "Like bees to honey the "forty-niners" swarmed into California, lured by visions of untold wealth. Farmers mortgaged their farms, clerks left desks, ministers their pulpits, and workmen their tools to seek that gold. Tens of thousands came by wagon across the plains and mountains suffering hardships (many didn't make it). Those who could afford to pay for a six months ocean trip made the trip around Cape Horn. Six month! Large numbers crossed the Isthmus of Panama; Mexicans, South Americans and Chinese joined the Americans in the struggle for gold. The 49ers drank, gambled and fought in a land that was without law. And so it was."

There were individuals within the eastern section of the United States that had money to invest and chose not to participate in this great migration to the gold fields. Instead, their money was pooled together to form a company with the intent of financing a gold mining exposition. This company would have an overseer (manager) who would do the actual organizing and the hiring of miners. The company's investors expected their company to be successful towards making profits from the gold fields. My great grandfather, George Nelson Brown, was the manager of such a company. He wrote a letter on February 4, 1849, summarizing the organization of equipment and giving an account of the company's expenses to a W. P. Collins. This letter is copied below. I'm assuming that Mr. Collins is George N. Brown's contact with the investor's group. If a word of his letter is not identified, I replaced this word with a ? (question mark).

1849 dated Letters from George Nelson Brown

letter number 1

"On Board Ship-Robert Bowne   New York, Feb. 4, 1849
Sunday Afternoon, 2 o'clock

Mr. W. P. Collins

Dear Sir,
   In the few lines which I sent you I told you I would write again before we left this port. I now sit down to do so.

We received your letter dated the 23rd of January and were happy to hear from the harbor once more, before we left York State. We were particularly pleased to hear that our friends were all well. That word friends means a great deal and we hope in this case not only our own family connections; but all of our acquaintances without exception. But I am speculating.

Then to our business. The tenth, you know, we left the harbor. That was Wednesday; and Friday evening, ten o'clock, we arrived in this city (New York). We put up at the Western Hotel, Cortlandt St. On Saturday, Sandford found his uncle and has stayed there most of the time. Since Cyrus and myself stayed there until the fifteenth. On the fifteenth we engaged our passage. We then bought our mattresses and have lodged on board since that time and have boarded at these eating houses here. We stayed at this hotel about three days. It cost us about $15. We have lived much cheaper since. Three dollars is as cheap as board can be got by the week; I mean anything about half way decent.

Sandford (as you know) bought his pistol at the harbor for ten dollars. Cyrus and myself bought ours in Rochester. We had to pay $11.50. We concluded that the demand for such things here would enhance the price. And we found on inquiring when we got here that our conjectures were right. The same articles are now selling here for twenty dollars. And in fact, everything which we have to buy is in about the same ratio above what it should be.

These shop keepers here have learned the routine of fixtures that people going to California require, and they spread it on thick and no mistake. All the people from the country come here without any preparation thinking that they can get these things very cheap in New York. But we all get badly taken in and no help for it either.

And now with reference to some of the suggestions contained in your letter of the 23rd. The first is how many owners in this ship. The bill which I sent you, (the reception of which you acknowledged in your letter), I think states that the ship and cargo is divided into 200 shares of $250 each. Whether the bill makes that statement or not, that is the fact. The next is; does the company pay the captain and hands. Doctor Townsend, the Sarsaparilla man, is the getter-up of the company. He owned the vessel and puts cargo on board. More than is advertised in the bill, sets up the vessel in good style with staterooms for four. He furnishes the vessel with a new suit of sails throughout (they came on board yesterday), and extra set of spars, also. Pays the Captain, officers, crew, stewards, cook and to San Francisco. The captain is a first rate man and understands his business. He is quite an elderly man, I should think more than 50. His head is almost white. And a man of sobriety and worth, highly spoken of by everyone who knows him as a seaman and a gentleman. The first-mate, Captain Bailey of New London, Connecticut, has been Master of a ship, even voyages around Cape Horn, one voyage in this vessel.

There is a Certificate of the vessel inspectors now hanging up before me. They pronounce her seaworthy and they are obliged to make oath that they have examined her thoroughly and state or set forth the particulars of their examinations. Her bottom is newly coppered and copper fastened. That means that the bolts that she is put together with are copper.

Doct. Townsend is a responsible man, good for $500,000. And judging from what information we can get he is a man that does as he agrees. I think there is a little gas about him, probably no more than in most of us. He likes to make money and I would like to know where the man is that does not. If a little gas or soft soap is necessary, most men use it, and some freely. Everything in regard to the ship cargo, Captain Doct. Townsend the getting-up of the whole matter. We made diligent and thorough inquiries before we engaged in this ship. I will state here before I forget that we have entered into no company or association any farther than the ship and cargo is concerned.

If we ever get to California we cannot tell what we shall do with the vessel, but most think it advisable to keep her there. There is one man on board who has or says he has been in San Francisco, and that we can get the vessel up the Sacramento as far as Sutter's Fort. If we can, I think it will be an advantage to keep her there. The Apollo which we had so much talk about had not sailed when we got here. But on inquiring, we found that she was nearly or quite thirty years old and was not safe. There are plenty of these vessels, some for one price and some another. We could have got a passage out and bound for $135 and bound but must go ashore when we get there. On the whole we thought and still think that the engagements we have made is the best one offered. The above is necessary I think and all of any consequences in regard to the fact of our engagement on investment in this ship.

We have entered into an association with nine others in a tent and camp hampers or cooking tools. The tent cost $30 and the hamper $25. We bought a second-hand tent and got it for about half the first cost. We cannot buy anything in the shape of a tent for less than thirty dollars. As I told you before we have entered into no engagement with anyone in the digging business.

The insurance comes next or the enquiry in regards to it. With an earnest request to which seems to be attached as much or more importance than all the other part of the matter; "don't fail to do this and send on the papers as per contract." I will here state to you that we have effected none insurance nor shall we. And for the good reason that we have not got money enough to do it. We in the first place had seven hundred and fifty dollars for our passage. You may think that is enough to buy a pile of stuff, but we have been as economical as we could well be, and live decent. And further, we have not got now some things that are actually necessary to enable us to get along as we shall require. We ought to have a wagon or cart. How are we to get from San Francisco 150 miles back into the country? A cart and harness will cost $75. And we ought to have a set of instruments for testing or trying gold, which will cost another hundred. But words are useless. We have got but about $60 left. Our insurance will cost $102. That is the long and short of the whole matter.

I will state that we feel a little green over our engagement with the company. A Company at Albany have agents going out in this vessel. They find there everything necessary for the voyage and for working when they get there. And pay them $300 per year whether they get any gold or not. And if they do get anything they have half they get together with the $300. Rather different from ours.

It seems to me that what I have written is all that is necessary. We leave this harbor tomorrow at twelve o'clock. A steamboat will tow us down to Sandy Hook **(a)**. I will drop you a line from Sandy Hook if I can get an opportunity to write. The vessel will be crowded full of people down to there.

All (is) well.

Our best respects to all,

George N. (Nelson) Brown

End of 1st letter.

George Brown is addressing W. P. Collins' question, "how many owners in this ship." Brown response was that there are two hundred stock shares worth two hundred and fifty dollars each share. This fifty thousand dollars total stock worth represents not only the ship, but also all of the cargo. I like to think that most of the cargo was food. Was a passage on this ship worth one share of stock, and therefore, there were a total of two hundred passengers? I suspect this was the case as near the end of Brown's first letter, he mentioned the cost of their passage was seven hundred and fifty dollars (3 shares at two hundred and fifty dollars per share), which would be for the three of them (Brown, Sandford and Cyrus). Therefore, the cost per person was two hundred and fifty dollars and most likely there were two hundred passengers.

Further down the letter, Brown mentioned their conversation as to what is to become of the ship when they reach San Francisco. Many of the ships sailing to San Francisco ended up stranded in the San Francisco Bay, due to the crew members abandoning them for the gold fields. The Bay was loaded with abandoned ships. In addition, the retail business in San Francisco also had a serious problem of keeping clerks as they too left in droves to the minefields. I think that this issue of the ship's fate mentioned in Brown's letter is most interesting. Even though this abandoned ship problem was known, the original planned voyage did not include a return trip from San Francisco.

It is very interesting to read in this letter that a Dr. Townsend is the owner of the ship. Brown referred to Dr. Townsend as, the "sarsaparilla man." This Dr. Townsend is Samuel P. Townsend **(b)**, who was an apothecary and physician. He made a fortune selling his Sarsaparilla bottle drink during the 19th century. By the mid-19th century, his Sarsaparilla drink had nationwide sales. Today, his bottles are collectables. Dr. S. P. Townsend moved to New York City in 1846 and he made this city his base. He sold his Sarsaparilla business in 1855 and his death was sometime during the 1880's. George Brown apparently met this person and got to know him on a personal basis. So it appears that this Dr.

Townsend invested in at least one ship for a voyage to San Francisco. According to George Brown, Dr. Samuel P Townsend was already a wealthy man when Brown wrote his letter.

George Brown mentioned the vessel's Inspectors Certificate. The certificate confirms that the ship has copper bottom flooring. This was not the case of all of the ships during this era. Copper flooring would be considered a safer ship and would have a higher rating compared to a wooden bottom. Of course, the passenger would pay more for a voyage on a safer ship.

George Brown referred to a conversation of getting the ship up the Sacramento River, to Sacramento. If this happened, the crew would have reduced their land distance to the gold fields considerably. Further down into the letter Brown mentioned that their funds were low and they didn't have enough money to buy a wagon for getting them and their supplies to the gold fields. This was a big issue as by land it was about one hundred and fifty miles to Coloma from San Francisco as Brown mentioned in his letter. Somehow, they reached the gold fields where they found their gold.

We know from Brown's first letter that there was representation of at least one other organized company on board the ship. This company had a better salary plan for their miners compared to Brown's company. Their income for each miner consisted of a three hundred annual salary plus fifty percent of the gold mined. I suspect that a salary of twenty five dollars per month would not be enough for food. I believe Brown's company found enough gold above the amount needed to survive during their time of mining gold.

The actual physical letters labeled as number 2 and number 3 of this document are in the possession of the Bancroft Library located on the campus of the University of California, Berkeley, California. The Bancroft Library has given written permission to include the letters below in this book.

Letter numbers two and three were owned by my Dad's brother, Whyle S. Wilcox. He sold these two letters to Barry Smedley and he in turn sold them to Bancroft Library.

Letter number 2

Latitude 8 Degrees & 8' minutes South
March 26, 1849

At Sea. Lat 8" 8' yesterday South Long. 33

Dear Sir,
We have just hailed a ship bound for New London, Conn. I cannot write much but you'll know that we are all well. We expect to be in Rio de Janeiro on Saturday next and then I will write you again. Say to our own families we shall all write to them from that port.

Our Best Regards to All,
G. N. (George Nelson) Brown

We are out 48 days.
The name of the ship is Columbus of New London.

Letter number 3

At Sea
South of the Equator
(not dated)

(This third letter was written while he was at sea, between February 6-April 6, 1849)

Dear Brothers and Sisters and all, I now take my pen in hand, to write you a few lines.

When I wrote to Mr. Collins, I stated to him that I should write again from Sandy Hook, but we did not sail until the sixth (Tuesday, Feb 6, 1849). We expected to have sailed Monday, the fifth, but were detained. Wind being contrary, until sixth, then when we got down to Sandy Hook, spread our sails and away we went. The steamer Hurculese towed us out into the stream. We had a north west wind and we headed our course southeast. The wind blew quite hard when we first got out to sea. We left the pier at 2 o'clock in the afternoon and before the next day at 2 o'clock there was but few on board but were sick and a great many very sick too. The wind continued to blow harder and more hard for five or six days. The deep blue sea rolled mountains high and no mistake. I was very sick but no worse than I expected to be. I was on deck most of the time except two days I layed in my birth (berth) the most of the time. Sandford was sick but little. Cyrus not much. I did not get well until we got into the trade wind, that was about 24 degrees north lat. We did not get the trade winds as far north as they generally do. Sometimes as far north as 28 and 32 deg. (degrees) then they do not extend so far south. They carried us down to the Equator.

I did not sleep much the first week we were out, nor eat either (as) there was not much cooked to eat for anybody. The table was set a number of times but generally the dishes, meat and everything else was piled off on to the floor and smashed up into a heap. Three or four nights I did not sleep scarcely one wink, no light was allowed between decks, people sick. Some going on deck and others coming below. Some cursing and swearing some vomiting and laughing, some sliding heels over head across the cabin floor, and maybe a half a dozen trunks and chests at the same time. Shins badly bruised and knocked end way. A pretty tolerable crazy time I thought, but I stayed on deck most of the time. Almost every passenger stuck to their staterooms but me. I could not stay in my room anyway; I was on deck two nights, all night holding on to the blay (belay) pins and ropes. It was the only way anyone could keep themselves right end up, for the deck of the ship was as steep as the roof of a house first one way and then the other and then about the same endways.

The next Friday night after we left New York the wind blew the hardest, sails all furled, except main gallant **(c)**, foresail **(d)** and fore gallant sail **(e)** and those close seam. I was on deck all night, it rained and the wind blew a perfect gale, it blew the foresail to shreds (?) in just no time. I thought if Luceretia and Johnson had been here they never would say again that they had a rough time crossing Lake Ontario. When the ship rolled the main yard **(f)** would dip into the water, and that is what I called crazy times, but the old ship rolled it out like a duck and on the 14th the wind changed and blew from the south, and not hard.

Our Latitude at this date, 34" 4' and our longitude 49" 10' so you can see that we went a head from N.Y. which is longitude 14' and lat. 42' 20'. The wind continued to blow from the south most of the time until we got to the trade winds. We had to beat all the time down to about 25" deg. Lat. and then the wind began to have sound into the east until we got into the regular South East Trade Winds. They then blew very steady just a good stiff breeze. Sometimes we sailed eight miles an hour and not a very heavy sea, in fact some days the sea is as smooth as any lake except a steady roll of the sea.

On the eighteenth we spoke to an Austrian merchantman bound for New York. She was the first ship we spoke (to) after we left the Yankee Shore. We crossed the equator on the 17th of March, we were 4 miles north at noon when the Captain took his observations. He always takes the Lat. at noon. The same day in the forenoon we saw a ship direct ahead coming towards us. We watched her closely with our glasses, we could see her colors, she held down for us until she could see us plainly and then she hauled down her colors and opened her port holes and ran out her guns, and steered off; when she got up broad side. We were satisfied that she was a British East India man on her return home and thought strange to see a ship in that latitude with so many men on board and had heard nothing of the Gold Fever. We concluded that a shipload of Yankees was enough to make John Bull (g) run, and had some fun over it. These East India (men) always go armed, so our sailors say.

On Tuesday, 20th of March, we came in sight of an island in latitude 2' 51" south long. 32"degrees west. We were not near enough to it to see anything but rocks and mountains. The sketches which I send give a tolerable correct appearance of the island. It is used as a convict island by the Brazilian government where they banish criminals. We did not pass this Island until 22nd. There is a strange current on the east and head winds so that we could not get by it. Tack ship three times and finally passed it about fifteen miles on the east.

We see a great many fish in the latitude of the equator. The porpoises, <u>s?p</u> sharks, black fish and the diamond fish, and various other kinds. The diamond fish is a triangular shaped animal. We only saw one that was close to the stern of the ship. It looks in the water as if it had wings and of three cornered shape. Its mouth seemed to be large enough to take in a man, there are small fish that always go with it called Pilot fish. They are about two feet long and almost white and they lay on his back and swim along his head and appear very affectionate.

We cannot see the North Star south of the equator. The moon dips to the north instead of the south and we see the evening star when the sun is two hours high. I have not seen the sun rise nor set clear since I left N.Y. Always some clouds hanging around the horizon.

(This letter was written sometime shortly after April 7, 1849)

The above <u>I wrote while at sea</u>. We are now in the harbor of Rio de Janeiro. April 7th we dropped anchor at five o'clock this afternoon, making sixty days from New York. We crossed the equator 17th of March. So we have made a long passage from there. The southeast wind or trades have been very light but at the same time we have had very fine weather. Yesterday morning we came in sight of Cape Rio.

About sixty five miles nearly east from here, we came into the Bay last night and laid to, about noon we got the sea breeze and run up into the harbor. The officers soon came on board to examine the ship to see if any sickness and if any goods to go on shore and etc. The coast from Cape Rio down to here is very rocky and bold shore. It is entirely useless for me to undertake to describe this place, as viewed from the deck of the ship, for it is beyond the power of any human mind to describe the appearance of the place and surrounding country. We read of the Bay of Naples as one of the most sublime scenes in the world but that Niagara Falls and associated together it seems to me cannot compare with what our eyes behold here. The most I can say is that when we go into the harbor we pass through a narrow passage two miles wide on each sides is a fort and on the left hand is a rock 77 feet high looks as much like a sugar loaf as one thing can look like another, and all around the rocks are very high from one to five hundred feet high. There has been a dozen boats around the ship to take passengers on shore all rowed by Negroes, some of them with nothing on but a pair of pants. More when I go on shore.

Sunday: Went on shore about 8 o'clock this morning. It cost us ten cents to go on shore and five to come on board again at night. The laws are very strict in regard to foreigners. We are not allowed to go on board of any other vessel (five or six here bound for California). When we go on shore we are obliged to go to government vessel and when we come on board and if anyone is caught on the water after nine o'clock they are liable to be fined five dollars or imprisoned until it is paid. The streets of the city are very narrow, many of them are not more than twenty feet wide and four feet of sidewalk on each side. Two wagons cannot pass each other, mostly very straight and regular paved and very clean, no docks here consequently vessels are obliged to anchor off in the harbor..............."

Apparently, the rest of this letter is lost. In addition, the letter is not dated, but the writing time frame can be identified from using the above letters.

Notes:
(a) Sandy Hook is a sandy and narrow peninsula in east New Jersey. The exact location is the south entrance to lower New York Bay.
(b) The information in reference to Samuel P. Townsend is from Dave Cheadle of Colorado.
(c) Furled meant sails rolled up. In this case, all of the sails were rolled up, except for the main gallant sail, foresail and fore gallant sail. The gallant sail is the small sail above the foresail.
(d) The foresail is the lower front sail.
(e) The fore gallant is the front sail near the top of the ship on foremast.
(f) The main yard is the rod or spar which support sails.
(g) "John Bull" is a personification of England.

* * *

George and Lucy Brown and their three children,
1878. Children left to right: Grant, Abbie
and Susan Belle. Susan married
Allen Monroe Wilcox

Chapter 33

Son James' Story

James Adrian Wilcox

Memories of my life

Some of my absolute favorite things in life are the outdoors, cars, and bicycling. I was five or six when I got my first bike for Christmas. My Dad tells me I would have nothing to do with training wheels; I quickly learned to ride without them! I do remember all through my school years hopping on the bike and going for a ride whenever I was bored. When I was a little older I would take the bike apart and grease all the bearings. When I was a teenager I saved up my money to buy a twelve-speed Huffy! I was so proud of it and tried to keep it in mint condition while still riding it all the time!

I am forty-five years old now and I don't think I have ever told my parents I did this back when I was in high school. So here goes the cat out of the bag. I grew up in Spring Branch, west of downtown Houston, Texas, about four to five miles north of Interstate 10. This was one of my boundaries in high school; I was not supposed to bike beyond it when I started wanting to venture out more. I was too bored with all the neighborhoods I had biked through growing up and there was an exotic Italian car dealership ten plus miles from the house that I loved to dream and drool over. I discovered a nice easy back way that was safe to ride my bike on, so I biked under the I-10 freeway and rode down Memorial Drive. It was a very enjoyable route! That afternoon I was enjoying my ride while looking for the turn, but didn't see it and started approaching a bunch of businesses and leaving the residential area. I kept thinking this isn't right, where am I? As I entered into the business area I realized where I was! Oh my! I had ridden my bike to The Galleria mall! I wasn't sure how far I was from the house, but it could have been up to twenty miles away! On the way back, I realized where I had missed my turn. I never told my parents how far I rode that day, but it was an awesome bike ride! Obviously I didn't forget it! I was shocked and impressed that I was able to ride my bike that far, regardless of how exhausting the ride back was!

I ran cross-country and track in high school but focused more time and effort on cars in my senior year and through tech school and college. After college I started riding mountain bikes primarily, and enjoyed the peace and challenges of trails, mountains, or just Texas hills. When I was forty I got a really nice road bike and started riding long distances with groups. At the age of forty-three I completed a seventy-two-mile ride and intend to break that record someday.

My college experience

After I graduated from high school [Spring Wood] in 1989, I went to Texas State Technical Institute, (later changed to Texas State Technical College), in Waco, Texas, to complete an associate's degree in automotive repair. During my second year at TSTI, I accepted an invitation to attend a Choice Bible study led by Louis Giglio. It was an experience like no other I have witnessed. The worship was so moving and heart touching. I had never experienced anything like that before even though I had attended church and some youth groups my whole life. I deeply wished I could have attended the year before if I had only known!

After Waco I transferred to Tarleton State University at Stephenville, Texas. While making new friends there, I quickly noticed something different in many of my new Christian friends who I greatly respected. That's when I realized what I had been missing. Being a Christian is about a relationship with Christ, not simply obeying commandments and attending a church service once or twice a week! Those things are secondary. It was then that I accepted Christ into my life and started seeking a relationship with Christ for the first time in my life. I soon learned that when you accept God into your life and give Him control, you never know what he has in store for you until you allow God into your life. I was constantly amazed at how God would work and care for me in my life. It was new; it was a rush! One Monday evening on campus I heard a classmate's moving testimony at the Baptist Student Union Center. I felt totally convicted to completely give my life and desires to Christ and give God total control! It sounded so scary! I wanted to work on cars, not go to Africa and be a missionary! I realized that the time before I had not released everything to God when I said, "Take all, Lord." This time I had to give all. I went home to my rented house, closed myself in my quiet room, and gave all to God in the most sincere prayer I had ever prayed. Letting go of everything was hard! After ending the prayer, it was time to listen for God. It wasn't easy either. Nothing spectacular happened that night, but that week I was so busy working on friends' cars I hardly had time to do homework. I typically worked on friends' cars and made some side money, but never like this week. It wasn't until that Saturday in the calm of a shower, after helping yet another friend with their car situation, that I realized it wasn't just coincidence that I had so much side work. I remembered that I had made a serious prayer. All this extra work on cars was God moving in my life. It's difficult to explain, but if you've ever experienced that, you know. The busy week of doing what I love was God's answer, God's direction. God works in many ways; when we are still and give time to Him we can "hear" His voice and sense direction and wisdom. I was so relieved I could still use my tools and knowledge and didn't have to relocate to a foreign land!! God wanted to use me in the automotive business! God gave me tools to use. I love cars and fixing them when they are old or broken. That's my ministry field. We all have a ministry field, not just those who go overseas.

I also fell in love with the small-town Texas country life right away while at Tarleton in Stephenville, back roads and all, even to the point of feeling like I grew up in the wrong place! I made lots of new friends, many from the Fort Worth area. Several were from the Burleson-Crowley area. While I was in college and considering where I wanted to live after graduation, I liked how these towns sounded and wanted to visit them. I really didn't feel living in Houston was for me after graduating. I couldn't have asked for better parents, so I didn't want to be too far from home. Fort Worth was as big a city as I wanted to be close too! The first time I visited the Crowley and Fort Worth area, I knew that was the area I wanted to live in. The country started and ended at the city limits! I heard a lot about Burleson next to Crowley, and thought it sounded like the place for me. It wasn't until my last semester that I made time to take a trip to Burleson. I prayed before I left. I wanted God to show me if this is where He wanted me and to line up a job for me at the Chevy dealership. Upon exiting I-35 onto Renfro Street leading into downtown Burleson, a feeling of being home immediately overcame me even though I had never set foot or even seen a picture of the town! There wasn't any Google yet! For that reason I knew this was the place for me. I went ahead and got a job application from the Chevy dealership in town and only that dealership because that was my goal, to work at a Chevy dealer in the same town where I lived. I turned in the application and had the job lined up before graduation. I started a week after graduation.

My passion for cars

I've always thought it was very interesting how God guided me into my own business since I had never planned to open my own repair facility. I had thoughts of retiring early and restoring cars as a hobby and extra money, but not a full business. I have always loved cars and almost anything with wheels, and I think I was born with a Hot Wheels car in my hand! Sometimes I am asked what made me want to work on cars. Other than my strong passion for cars and tinkering in general, I would have to say my first memory of wanting to work on them was partially curiosity. I like to know how things work. I can remember at age fifteen Dad started letting my brother and me wash the car. He actually let us drive the car from the driveway to the yard so the runoff water would go into the yard instead of down the driveway. I remember I would wipe down the interior with the damp drying towel after drying the body. I noticed all the trim screws holding the interior together and wondered what was behind all these parts I could see. I wanted to take a car apart and see what it was like and how everything worked. My first car was a project; I wanted to build a car. I basically took a '71 Camaro and a '72 Camaro, stripping them and rebuilding every component onto the '72 to learn and have the thrill of building my first car. It's a car I could never sell. It's time to restore it again with the 93,000 miles I put on it driving all over Texas. It was my learning curve and only fueled my passion for cars.

Starting my business

From May 1994 through 1998 I worked at the Chevy dealership in Burleson, Texas. It wasn't until 2002 that I opened my own automotive shop. I worked for a couple of dealerships during summers in Houston between college semesters, then a couple more after college, mostly Lynn Smith Chevy in Burleson, and then a local tire and auto care shop prior to opening my own shop. In every place I worked, my Christian ethics seemed to get me into trouble or just made it miserable at times, until the last independent shop I worked at. I was so relieved to work alongside a fellow Christian and for a Christian shop owner in 2001. However, 9/11 hit, ending the growth spurt for businesses. The owner was forced to let me go after only a few months of employment. For months I was unable to find work or a place that met my work ethics and integrity level. A few attempts to find employment outside the field were met with closed doors. It was a trying and disappointing time. Even the usual side work that had taken place for years was not available. Then that spring, even though I had never considered it before, I felt God leading me to open my own shop. Ever since college I have done side work for friends and neighbors who would come to the house for minor repairs. I soon realized how much knowledge of running a business I had gained from my last employer, even though it was only for a few months. It was clearly God's plan. I could see that God had been preparing me, I just didn't realize it. Immediately the side work started coming in. I felt the need to have one hundred customer names before starting the business in a proper facility. Until then I needed to continue working out of the house, do the necessary legal things, and look for a potential shop to move into. As the weeks passed, the business grew and it didn't take long to have more cars than driveway and curb space! Fortunately my neighbors were patient with me, probably because I worked on their cars too!

With few options for an available existing building and no capital to work with, my frustration started to grow. I wanted to keep the shop in the town of Burleson. my customer list was nearing 100, and I felt the time of working out of the house was probably about to expire. One Sunday afternoon in September, with my desperation level high and prayers seemingly unanswered, I felt led to plea to God and drive around one more time, taking roads less traveled to find an undiscovered potential shop building. I hopped in my old tried-and-true Camaro and said a deep and sincere prayer pleading to God to reveal this shop location. Only then did I start the engine and drive off. When I had almost finished cruising around and feeling more peace than frustration, I passed a shop building out on a country road that seemed to be never open or in business. I noticed one of the three shop doors was actually open and could see furniture and junk cluttering one side. It didn't look like a running business. At the point of passing the shop, it dawned on me—this is what I just prayed for! This is why I took the drive! Quickly making a U-turn and pulling into the parking lot, I was able to speak to owner of the land and shop. Three months later I had a signed contract to rent half the building with no down payment because the current owner was planning to soon retire. Wilcox's Automotive of Burleson, Texas, was now in business! Later I found out that at the same time that I was negotiating the contract to rent the shop building, someone else had been desperately trying to buy the building from the landowner. However, the landowner was not only hesitant to give up the place, but was also concerned about not letting someone else use the building for automotive repairs unless their level of integrity was at least as ethical and high as his.

Through all these times and launching a business, I learned a whole new meaning of trusting God to provide. At one point, during the time I was preparing the shop building, I told God that I needed him to provide an extra five hundred dollars for a lawyer to write up the contract for renting the automotive repair shop. The phone rang and a friend of mine was on the other end of the line, saying he and his wife had decided to sell her car. She asked if I would sell it for them while they were out of town. Of course, I accepted. I fixed it up, and it sold immediately. The buyer and the owner met that upcoming Saturday at my house. The buyer paid cash, and after the transaction my friend shook my hand to thank me. I felt paper in my hand. As my friend left, I looked at what was in my hand—it was five one-hundred-dollar notes, just in time for the lawyer. It should be noted that in praying, the prayer must end with "in Jesus' name" because Jesus said this was necessary for answered prayers.

In writing this and reflecting on the highlights of my life, I want to share one final thought; The more I grow as a Christian and understand God's word as I get older and live in this world, I really understand the difference in wisdom and knowledge as explained in the Bible. I can't imagine having to go through this life without the knowledge of truth that the Bible gives us when we learn and use it in our daily lives.

James Adrian Wilcox

Comments from James' father, Rick Wilcox

We have been blessed with both of our sons, James and John. They never gave us any problems. I'm surprised to learn that James rode his bike to The Galleria! I'm glad we didn't know about this adventure of his!

Acknowledgements

There are several people to whom I am indebted for their assistance and advice: David Cherry helped me with tech support, Candace Hester typed the first part of this book, and Jim Seitz gave valuable assistance to this project. I'm grateful to Irene Rundell and Cyndy Brown, who read my book and made helpful recommendations. I'm also grateful to Steve Khalaf, owner of Kingwood Photo Lab, Kingwood, Texas, because he continually processes high-quality photos. I'm also indebted to Michael Hyatt for his online courses relating to book publishing and his book *Platform: Get Noticed in a Noisy World*. Michael Hyatt's resources opened the door to understanding the requirements for getting a book published. Without his online course and book, my book probably would not have been published.

I would welcome comments in reference to this book. In addition, I would be delighted if you would share memories that you have in regard to your life or family. If you send me your story, please consider giving me your name and written permission to include your story in a future book.
My email address is: rick.wilcox.author@gmail.com

Rick Wilcox